Recent Advances in Theory and Application of Dynamical Systems

Recent Advances in Theory and Application of Dynamical Systems

Editor

Chunrui Zhang

MDPI • Basel • Beijing • Wuhan • Barcelona • Belgrade • Manchester • Tokyo • Cluj • Tianjin

Editor
Chunrui Zhang
Northeast Forestry University
China

Editorial Office
MDPI
St. Alban-Anlage 66
4052 Basel, Switzerland

This is a reprint of articles from the Special Issue published online in the open access journal *Mathematics* (ISSN 2227-7390) (available at: https://www.mdpi.com/si/mathematics/Theory_Application_Dynamical_Systems).

For citation purposes, cite each article independently as indicated on the article page online and as indicated below:

LastName, A.A.; LastName, B.B.; LastName, C.C. Article Title. *Journal Name* **Year**, *Volume Number*, Page Range.

ISBN 978-3-0365-7884-2 (Hbk)
ISBN 978-3-0365-7885-9 (PDF)

Contents

About the Editor

Chunrui Zhang

Dr. Zhang Chunrui is a professor and doctoral supervisor at Northeast Forestry University. Her research field is functional differential equation theory and its application in life science and control theory. Her research results have won the second prize of science and technology achievements in Heilongjiang Province.

Preface to "Recent Advances in Theory and Application of Dynamical Systems"

Modeling using dynamic systems has been widely used to describe dynamical behaviors in almost all areas of science and engineering. This book focuses on the most pressing issues in the field of dynamical systems. When studying dynamical systems, researchers are not only concerned with the qualitative problem of a solution, but also with whether the topological properties of the solution change under small perturbations, that is, the problem of structural stability. Bifurcation and chaos appear when the stability of a structure is destroyed, which is the main problem of bifurcation theory. Hopf bifurcation and Turing bifurcation are important research issues in the field of bifurcation. This book collects 11 papers. The research content of the papers includes Turing bifurcations, the pattern dynamics of reaction–diffusion equations, the delay of differential equations in Hopf bifurcation, the stability of biomathematical and ecology models and other research fields. These 11 papers have been widely received since their publication.

Chunrui Zhang
Editor

mathematics

MDPI

Article

Dynamical Analysis of a Delayed Diffusive Predator–Prey Model with Additional Food Provided and Anti-Predator Behavior

Ruizhi Yang, Xiao Zhao and Yong An *

Department of Mathematics, Northeast Forestry University, Harbin 150040, China; yangrz@nefu.edu.cn (R.Y.); zhaoxiao@nefu.edu.cn (X.Z.)
* Correspondence: anyong@nefu.edu.cn

Abstract: We studied a delayed predator–prey model with diffusion and anti-predator behavior. Assume that additional food is provided for predator population. Then the stability of the positive equilibrium is considered. The existence of Hopf bifurcation is also discussed based on the Hopf bifurcation theory. The property of Hopf bifurcation is derived through the theory of center manifold and normal form method. Finally, we analyze the effect of time delay on the model through numerical simulations.

Keywords: delay; diffusion; predator–prey; Hopf bifurcation

Citation: Yang, R.; Zhao, X.; An, Y. Dynamical Analysis of a Delayed Diffusive Predator–Prey Model with Additional Food Provided and Anti-Predator Behavior. *Mathematics* **2022**, *10*, 469. https://doi.org/10.3390/math10030469

Academic Editors: Mustafa R.S. Kulenovic, M. Victoria Otero-Espinar and Ioannis G. Stratis

Received: 9 December 2021
Accepted: 29 January 2022
Published: 31 January 2022

1. Introduction

The interaction between predator and prey is ordinary and widespread in nature, it could affect the ecological balance. There exists an interesting phenomena in prey called anti-predator behavior, that is, adult prey kills young predators in order to overcome the predation pressure and improve their population density in the future [1–5]. Sometimes, this behavior may lead to species outbreak and do harm to the stability of the ecosystem. Hence, providing additional food for predator is a manner to avoid it [6]. Complex dynamics would be shown if anti-predator behavior happens.

The following predator–prey model (1) was proposed in [7]. In the absence of predators, the growth of the prey population follows the logistic equation. Assume Holling IV functional response exists in this system.

$$\begin{cases} \frac{dN}{dT} = rN(1-\frac{N}{K}) - \frac{cNP}{(qN^2+1)(a+\alpha\eta_1 A)} \\ \frac{dP}{dT} = \frac{b\left(N+(qN^2+1)\eta_1 A\right)P}{(qN^2+1)(a+\alpha\eta_1 A)} - mP - \tilde{\eta}NP \end{cases} \quad (1)$$

All parameters are positive and their biological description could be found from [7] as Table 1. In addition to the main food prey u, the predator has additional food sources A in the model (1). An the term $\tilde{\eta}NP$ represents the anti-predator behavior in prey. K. D. Prasad et al. [7] investigated various bifurcations of the system (1), including Bogdanov–Takens bifurcation, Saddle-node bifurcation, and Hopf bifurcation. They also considered the global dynamics of this system.

The predator–prey model has important research value in biomathematics; therefore, many experts have investigated it and obtained plenty of valuable results [8–12]. For example, time delay is an element that cannot be ignored in population dynamics. In nature, the development of population is not only related to the current state, but also related to the past time state, which is often called time delay. Generally, time delay often causes instability and periodic oscillation. In this paper, we are going to study the effect of time delay on the model (1), and intend to observe whether some new dynamic phenomenon happens.

Table 1. Biological description of parameters in model (1).

Parameter	Definition	Parameter	Definition
T	Time	r	Prey intrinsic growth rate
N	Prey population	P	Predator population
K	Carrying capacity of prey	c	Maximum rate of predation
b	Maximum growth rate of predator	m	Predator mortality rate
q	Group defense in prey	$\bar{\eta}$	Rate of anti-predator behavior
$\bar{\eta}_1$	Effectual ability of the predators to detect additional food relative to the prey	A	Quantity of additional food provided to the predators
a	Normalization coefficient relating the densities of prey and predator to the environment in which they interact	α	Ratio between the handling times towards the additional food and the prey

Further, the distribution of prey and predator are usually nonhomogeneous and different concentration levels of them would cause different population movements [13]; then, the diffusion phenomenon occurs. Some scholars provide different approaches of mathematical modeling of some ecological interaction in the presence of spatial diffusion [14–17]. In [15], the authors considered a predator–prey model with herd behavior and the cross-diffusion and fear effect, they mainly studied the Turing patterns and Turing–Hopf bifurcation induced by cross-diffusion. In [17], S. Djilali and S. Bentout studied a diffusive predator–prey model in the presence of predator rivalry and prey social behavior. They mainly studied the stability and Hopf bifurcation, and they show the nonhomogeneous periodic solution induced by diffusion. These works show that the diffusion term often causes the Turing pattern, spatial non-uniform periodic oscillation and so on.

Inspired by the above works, we incorporate the diffusion term and time delay to the model (1) and investigate the following model (2). We mainly study the Hopf bifurcation by the theory of center manifold and normal form method by using time delay as the bifurcation parameter.

$$\begin{cases} \frac{\partial N(x,t)}{\partial t} = D_1\Delta N + rN(1 - \frac{N(T-T_1)}{K}) - \frac{cNP}{(qN^2+1)(a+\alpha\eta_1 A)} \\ \frac{\partial P(x,t)}{\partial t} = D_2\Delta P + \frac{b(N+(qN^2+1)\eta_1 A)P}{(qN^2+1)(a+\alpha\eta_1 A)} - mP - \bar{\eta}NP \end{cases} \quad (2)$$

where D_1 and D_2 represents the diffusion coefficients of prey and predator, respectively. Suppose there exists a time delay T_1, which denotes the resource limitation of the prey logistic equation. It is convenient to non-dimensionalize the model with the transformations as $u = \frac{N}{a}, v = \frac{CP}{ar}$, and $t = rT$. Then, the following model is obtained.

$$\begin{cases} \frac{\partial u(x,t)}{\partial t} = d_1\Delta u + u(1 - \frac{u(t-\tau)}{\gamma}) - \frac{uv}{(wu^2+1)(1+\alpha\epsilon)}, & x \in (0, l\pi),\ t > 0, \\ \frac{\partial v(x,t)}{\partial t} = d_2\Delta v + \frac{\beta(u+(wu^2+1)\epsilon)v}{(wu^2+1)(1+\alpha\epsilon)} - \delta v - suv, & x \in (0, l\pi),\ t > 0, \\ u_x(0,t) = v_x(0,t) = 0, u_x(l\pi,t) = v_x(l\pi,t) = 0, & t > 0, \\ u(x,\theta) = u_0(x,\theta) \geq 0, v(x,\theta) = v_0(x,\theta) \geq 0, & x \in [0, l\pi], \theta \in [-\tau, 0]. \end{cases} \quad (3)$$

where

$$\gamma = \frac{K}{a},\ w = qa^2,\ \epsilon = \frac{\eta_1 A}{a},\ \beta = \frac{b}{r},\ \delta = \frac{m}{r},\ s = \frac{\bar{\eta}a}{r},\ d_1 = \frac{D_1}{r},\ d_2 = \frac{D_2}{r}.$$

All parameters in the model (3) are non-negative. $\frac{\partial u(x,t)}{\partial t}$ and $\frac{\partial v(x,t)}{\partial t}$ denote the gradient of prey and predator densities, respectively. The boundary condition is Neumann boundary condition, based on the hypothesis that the region where prey and predators live is closed and no prey and predator entering or leaving the region.

In this paper, we mainly study the effect of time delay and diffusion term on the model (3), such as delay inducing instability, homogeneous or inhomogeneous bifurcating periodic solutions. The rest of our paper is divided as follows. In Section 2, the local stability of the equilibrium is studied, some conditions under which Hopf bifurcation occurs are also derived. The property of Hopf bifurcation is investigated in Section 3 and numerical simulations are presented in Section 4. At last, we give a short conclusion.

2. Analysis of the Characteristic Equations

The equilibria of system (3) are the roots of the following equations

$$\begin{cases} u(1-\frac{u}{\gamma}) - \frac{uv}{(wu^2+1)(1+\alpha\epsilon)} = 0, \\ \frac{\beta(u+(wu^2+1)\epsilon)v}{(wu^2+1)(1+\alpha\epsilon)} - \delta v - suv = 0. \end{cases} \tag{4}$$

The existence of positive equilibrium is exactly investigated in [7]. The results are as follows.

Lemma 1. Ref. [7] *For the model (3), the following conclusions about the existence of positive equilibrium are true.*

1. *$(0,0)$ and $(\gamma,0)$ are two boundary equilibria.*
2. *There exists a unique interior equilibrium $E_1(u_1,v_1)$, when $\beta - s(1+\alpha\epsilon) > 0, \beta\epsilon - \delta(1+\alpha\epsilon) \le 0$ and $f(u_c) < 0$, $u_1 < \gamma < u_2$.*
3. *There exists two interior equilibria $E_1(u_1,v_1)$ and $E_2(u_2,v_2)$, when $\beta - s(1+\alpha\epsilon) > 0, \beta\epsilon - \delta(1+\alpha\epsilon) \le 0$ and $f(u_c) < 0$, $u_1 < u_2 < \gamma$.*
4. *There exists an instantaneous equilibrium $E_c(u_c,v_c)$, when $\beta - s(1+\alpha\epsilon) > 0, \beta\epsilon - \delta(1+\alpha\epsilon) \le 0$ and $f(u_c) = 0$, $u_c < \gamma$.*
5. *There exists one equilibrium $E_2(u_2,v_2)$ if $\beta\epsilon - \delta(1+\alpha\epsilon) > 0$ and $u_2 < \gamma$.*

where

$$\begin{aligned} f(u) =& sw(1+\alpha\epsilon)u^3 - [\beta\epsilon - \delta(1+\alpha\epsilon)]wu^2 \\ &- [\beta - s(1+\alpha\epsilon)]u - [\beta\epsilon - \delta(1+\alpha\epsilon)], \\ f'(u) =& 3sw(1+\alpha\epsilon)u^2 - 2w[\beta\epsilon - \delta(1+\alpha\epsilon)]u \\ &- [\beta - s(1+\alpha\epsilon)], \\ f''(u) =& 6sw(1+\alpha\epsilon)u - 2w[\beta\epsilon - \delta(1+\alpha\epsilon)]. \end{aligned} \tag{5}$$

Proof of Lemma 1. Case 1. For $u > 0$, suppose $\beta\epsilon - \delta(1+\alpha\epsilon) \le 0$, then $f''(u) > 0$ and $f(0) \ge 0$. If $\beta - s(1+\alpha\epsilon) > 0$, $f(u) = 0$ has a local minimum value at $u_c(u_c > 0)$. Because by analyzing $f'(u)$, we know $f(u)$ is decreasing in $(0, u_c)$ and increasing in $(u_c, +\infty)$. When $f(u_c) < 0$, $f(u)$ has two positive equilibrium written as $E_1(u_1,v_1)$ and $E_2(u_2,v_2)$ with $0 < u_1 < u_2$; when $f(u_c) = 0$, $f(u)$ has only one positive root $E_c(u_c,v_c)$. If $\beta - s(1+\alpha\epsilon) \le 0$, then $f'(u) \ge 0$ for all u. Thus, $f(u)$ has no positive root in $(0,+\infty)$.

Case 2. Suppose $\beta\epsilon - \delta(1+\alpha\epsilon) > 0$, then $f(0) < 0$ and $f''(u) = 0$ admits a positive real root u_{cc}. We know $f'(u)$ is decreasing in $(0, u_{cc})$ and increasing in $(u_{cc}, +\infty)$. If $\beta - s(1+\alpha\epsilon) > 0$, easily know $f'(0) < 0$. The equation $f(u) = 0$ has one positive real root u_2 because its discriminant is either positive or negative. If $\beta - s(1+\alpha\epsilon) \le 0$, then $f'(0) > 0$. The equation $f(u) = 0$ has one positive real root u_2 and a pair of complex conjugate roots because its discriminant is always negative. To know the detailed discussion, one can refer to the literature [7]. □

Next, suppose the model (3) has a positive equilibrium $P = (u_0, v_0)$, then analyze its stability.

Denote

$$u_1(t) = u(\cdot, t),\ \ u_2(t) = v(\cdot, t),\ \ U = (u_1, u_2)^T,$$
$$X = \{u, v^{2,2}(0, l\pi) : (u_x, v_x)|_{x=0,l\pi} = 0\},\ \text{ and } \mathscr{C}_\tau := C([-\tau, 0], X).$$

Linearizing the model (3) at $P = (u_0, v_0)$, it becomes

$$\dot{U} = \mathbb{D}\Delta U(t) + L(U_t), \tag{6}$$

where

$$\mathbb{D} = \begin{pmatrix} d_1 & 0 \\ 0 & d_2 \end{pmatrix},\ \ \mathrm{dom}(\mathbb{D}\Delta) = \{(u, v)^T : u, v \in C^2([0, l\pi], \mathbb{R}^2), u_x, v_x = 0, x = 0, l\pi\},$$

while $L : \mathscr{C}_\tau \mapsto X$ is represented as

$$L(\phi_t) = L_1\phi(0) + L_2\phi(-\tau),$$

and $\phi = (\phi_1, \phi_2)^T \in \mathscr{C}_\tau$ with

$$L_1 = \begin{pmatrix} a_1 & a_2 \\ b_1 & 0 \end{pmatrix},\qquad L_2 = \begin{pmatrix} -\frac{u_0}{\gamma} & 0 \\ 0 & 0 \end{pmatrix},$$

$$\phi(t) = (\phi_1(t), \phi_2(t))^T,\qquad \phi(t)(\cdot) = (\phi_1(t + \cdot), \phi_2(t + \cdot))^T.$$

$$a_1 := \frac{2u_0^2 w(\gamma - u_0)}{\gamma + u_0^2 w\gamma},\ \ a_2 := \frac{u_0(u_0 - \gamma)}{v_0\gamma},\ \ b_1 := -sv_0 + \frac{\beta(u_0^2 w - 1)(u_0 - \gamma)}{\gamma + u_0^2 w\gamma} \tag{7}$$

The characteristic equation of model (6) can be known through [18], that is

$$\lambda y - d\Delta y - L(e^{\lambda} y) = 0,\ \ y \in \mathrm{dom}(d\Delta),\ \ y \neq 0. \tag{8}$$

Then, $\mu_n = n^2/l^2$ $(n = 0, 1, \cdots)$ are the eigenvalues of

$$-\varphi'' = \mu\varphi,\ \ x \in (0, l\pi);\ \ \varphi'(0) = \varphi'(l\pi) = 0.$$

and the corresponding eigenfunctions are

$$\varphi_n(x) = \cos\frac{n\pi}{l},\ \ n = 0, 1, \cdots.$$

Substituting

$$y = \sum_{n=0}^{\infty} \begin{pmatrix} y_{1n} \\ y_{2n} \end{pmatrix} \cos\frac{n\pi}{l}$$

into the Equation (8), we have

$$\begin{pmatrix} a_1 - \frac{d_1 n^2}{l^2} - \frac{u_0}{\gamma} e^{-\lambda\tau} & a_2 \\ b_1 & -\frac{d_2 n^2}{l^2} \end{pmatrix} \begin{pmatrix} y_{1n} \\ y_{2n} \end{pmatrix} = \lambda \begin{pmatrix} y_{1n} \\ y_{2n} \end{pmatrix},\ n = 0, 1, \cdots.$$

Hence, the characteristic Equation (8) is the same as

$$\Delta_n(\lambda, \tau) = \lambda^2 + \lambda A_n + B_n + (C_n + \frac{\lambda u_0}{\gamma})e^{-\lambda\tau} = 0, \tag{9}$$

where

$$A_n = (d_1 + d_2)\frac{n^2}{l^2} - a_1, \quad B_n = d_1 d_2 \frac{n^4}{l^4} - a_1 d_2 \frac{n^2}{l^2} - a_2 b_1, \quad C_n = \frac{d_2 u_0 n^2}{\gamma l^2}$$

Make the following hypothesis,

$$(\mathbf{H}) \quad a_1 - \frac{u_0}{\gamma} < 0, \qquad a_2 b_1 < 0. \tag{10}$$

Then we obtain the following lemma.

Lemma 2. *Suppose* $(\mathbf{H})$ *and* $\tau = 0$ *hold, then* $P(u_0, v_0)$ *is locally asymptotically stable.*

Proof of Lemma 2. If $\tau = 0$, Equation (9) turns into

$$\lambda^2 + (A_n + \frac{u_0}{\gamma})\lambda + B_n + C_n = 0, \quad n \in \mathcal{N}_0. \tag{11}$$

By direct calculation, we have $A_n + \frac{u_0}{\gamma} > A_0 + \frac{u_0}{\gamma} > 0$ and $B_n + C_n > B_0 + C_0 > 0$. That is to say all eigenvalues have negative real parts. Thus, $P(u_0, v_0)$ is locally asymptotically stable. □

Based on $(\mathbf{H})$, easily to obtain $\Delta_n(0, \tau) = B_n + C_n > 0$. Then the following conclusion could be established.

Lemma 3. *Suppose* $(\mathbf{H})$ *holds, when* $n \in \mathbb{N}_0$, *we know* $\lambda = 0$ *is not a root of Equation* (9).

To find the critical values of τ. Suppose $i\omega(\omega > 0)$ is a solution of (9), next

$$-\omega^2 + i\omega A_n + B_n + (C_n + \frac{i\omega u_0}{\gamma})(\cos\omega\tau - i\sin\omega\tau) = 0.$$

We obtain

$$\begin{cases} -\omega^2 + B_n + C_n \cos\omega\tau + \frac{u_0 \omega \sin\omega\tau}{\gamma} = 0, \\ A_n \omega - C_n \sin\omega\tau + \frac{u_0 \omega \cos\omega\tau}{\gamma} = 0, \end{cases}$$

which leads to

$$\omega^4 + (A_n^2 - 2B_n - \frac{u_0^2}{\gamma^2})\omega^2 + B_n^2 - C_n^2 = 0. \tag{12}$$

Denote $z = \omega^2$, then (12) becomes

$$z^2 + (A_n^2 - 2B_n - \frac{u_0^2}{\gamma^2})z + B_n^2 - C_n^2 = 0, \tag{13}$$

and its roots are

$$z_\pm = \frac{1}{2}[-(A_n^2 - 2B_n - \frac{u_0^2}{\gamma^2}) \pm \sqrt{(A_n^2 - 2B_n - \frac{u_0^2}{\gamma^2})^2 - 4(B_n^2 - C_n^2)}].$$

If $(\mathbf{H})$ holds

$$A_n^2 - 2B_n - \frac{u_0^2}{\gamma^2} = (d_1 \frac{n^2}{l^2} - a_1)^2 + d_2^2 \frac{n^4}{l^4} + 2a_2 b_1 - \frac{u_0^2}{\gamma^2},$$

$$B_n + C_n = d_1 d_2 \frac{n^4}{l^4} - (a_1 d_2 - d_2 \frac{u_0}{\gamma})\frac{n^2}{l^2} - a_2 b_1 > 0,$$

$$B_n - C_n = d_1 d_2 \frac{n^4}{l^4} - (a_1 d_2 + d_2 \frac{u_0}{\gamma}) \frac{n^2}{l^2} - a_2 b_1.$$

Define

$$\mathbb{G} = \{n \in \mathbb{N}_0 | Equation\ (13)\ has\ positive\ roots\}. \tag{14}$$

Then the following lemma holds.

Lemma 4. *Suppose* $(\mathbf{H})$ *and* $\mathbb{G} \neq \emptyset$ *hold, then Equation (9) has a pair of purely imaginary roots* $\pm i\omega_n^+$ *or* $\pm i\omega_n^-$ $(n \in \mathbb{G})$ *at*

$$\tau_n^{j,\pm} = \tau_n^{0,\pm} + \frac{2j\pi}{\omega_n},\ j \in \mathbb{N}_0, \tag{15}$$

where

$$\tau_n^{0,\pm} = \begin{cases} \frac{1}{\omega_n^{\pm}} \arccos(V_{\cos}^{\pm}), & V_{\sin}^{\pm} \geq 0; \\ \frac{1}{\omega_n^{\pm}} [2\pi - \arccos(V_{\cos}^{\pm})], & V_{\sin}^{\pm} < 0. \end{cases} \tag{16}$$

and

$$\begin{aligned} V_{\cos}^{\pm} &= \frac{\gamma(-B_n C_n \gamma - A_n u_0 (\omega_n^{\pm})^2 + C_n \gamma (\omega_n^{\pm})^2)}{C_n^2 \gamma^2 + u_0^2 (\omega_n^{\pm})^2}, \\ V_{\sin}^{\pm} &= \frac{\omega_n^{\pm} \gamma (-B_n u_0 + A_n C_n \gamma + u_0 (\omega_n^{\pm})^2)}{C_n^2 \gamma^2 + u_0^2 (\omega_n^{\pm})^2}, \\ \omega_n^{\pm} &= \sqrt{z_{\pm}}. \end{aligned} \tag{17}$$

Assume $\lambda_n(\tau) = \alpha_n(\tau) + i\omega_n(\tau)$ is the root of (9), which satisfies $\alpha_n(\tau_n^j) = 0$ and $\omega_n(\tau_n^j) = \omega_n$ if τ is close to τ_n^j. Calculate the transversality condition.

Lemma 5. *If* $(\mathbf{H})$ *holds, we have*

$$\alpha_n'(\tau_n^j) = \frac{d\lambda}{d\tau}|_{\tau=\tau_n^{j,+}} > 0,\ \alpha_n'(\tau_n^j) = \frac{d\lambda}{d\tau}|_{\tau=\tau_n^{j,-}} < 0,\ \ with\ n \in \mathbb{G},\ \ j \in \mathbb{N}_0.$$

Proof of Lemma 5. Differentiate both sides of the Equation (9) with respect to τ, that is

$$(\frac{d\lambda}{d\tau})^{-1} = \frac{2\lambda + A_n + \frac{u_0}{\gamma} e^{-\lambda\tau}}{(\lambda C_n + u_0 \frac{\lambda^2}{\gamma}) e^{-\lambda\tau}} - \frac{\tau}{\lambda}.$$

By calculation,

$$Re(\frac{d\lambda}{d\tau})^{-1}_{\tau=\tau_n^{j,\pm}} = \frac{A_n^2 - 2B_n + 2\omega_n^2 - \frac{u_0^2}{\gamma^2}}{C_n^2 + \frac{u_0^2 \omega_n^2}{\gamma^2}}\Bigg|_{\tau=\tau_n^{j,\pm}} = \frac{\pm\sqrt{(A_n^2 - 2B_n - \frac{u_0^2}{\gamma^2})^2 - 4(B_n^2 - C_n^2)}}{C_n^2 + \frac{u_0^2 \omega_n^2}{\gamma^2}}.$$

Thus $\alpha_n'(\tau_n^{j,+}) > 0$, and $\alpha_n'(\tau_n^{j,-}) < 0$. □

Assume $m \neq n$, then $\tau_m^j = \tau_n^k$ could happen sometimes; however, we ignore that and only think about

$$\tau \in \mathcal{D} := \{\tau_n^j :\ \tau_m^j \neq \tau_n^k,\ m \neq n,\ m, n \in \mathbb{G},\ j, k \in \mathbb{N}_0\}.$$

Let $\tau_* = \min\{\tau \in \mathcal{D}\}$. In conclusion, the following theorem is given.

Theorem 1. *In the model (3), if* $(\mathbf{H})$ *holds, the following statements are true.*

1. *Suppose* $\mathbb{G} = \emptyset, \tau \geq 0$, *then* $P(u_0, v_0)$ *is locally asymptotically stable.*

2. *Suppose* $\mathbb{G} \neq \emptyset$, *when* $\tau \in [0, \tau_*)$, $P(u_0, v_0)$ *is locally asymptotically stable, and it is unstable when* $\tau_* < \tau < \tau_* + \epsilon$ *for some* $\epsilon > 0$.
3. *When* $\tau = \tau_n^j$ $(j \in \mathbb{N}_0)$, *the system* (3) *undergoes a Hopf bifurcation. There exists inhomogeneous bifurcating periodic solutions for* $\tau \in \mathcal{D}/\{\tau_0^k : k \in \mathbb{N}_0\}$.

3. Stability and Direction of Hopf Bifurcation

In this section, we obtain some formulas for determining the property of Hopf bifurcation through the method in [18], the following are detail computation. Fix $j \in \mathbb{N}_0$, $n \in \mathbb{G}$, make $\tilde{\tau} = \tau_n^j$. Assume $\tilde{u}(x,t) = u(x, \tau t) - u_0$, $\tilde{v}(x,t) = v(x, \tau t) - v_0$. Then drop the tilde for the sake of simplicity. The model (3) becomes

$$\begin{cases} \frac{\partial u}{\partial t} = \tau[d_1 \Delta u + (u+u_0)\left(1 - \frac{u(t-1)+u_0}{\gamma} - \frac{v+v_0}{(w(u+u_0)^2+1)(1+\alpha\epsilon)}\right)], \\ \frac{\partial v}{\partial t} = \tau[d_2 \Delta v + (v+v_0)\left(\frac{\beta(u+u_0+(w(u+u_0)^2+1)\epsilon)}{(w(u+u_0)^2+1)(1+\alpha\epsilon)} - \delta - s(u+u_0)\right)], \end{cases} \tag{18}$$

with $x \in (0, l\pi)$, $t > 0$. Suppose

$$\tau = \tilde{\tau} + \mu, \ u_1(t) = u(\cdot, t), \ u_2(t) = v(\cdot, t) \text{ and } U(x,t) = (u_1(x,t), u_2(x,t))^T.$$

For convenience, we denote $U_t(\theta) = U(x, t+\theta)$. Under the phase space $\mathscr{C}_1 := C([-1,0], X)$, (18) could be denoted by

$$\frac{dU(t)}{dt} = \tilde{\tau} D \Delta U(t) + L_{\tilde{\tau}}(U_t) + F(U_t, \mu), \tag{19}$$

where

$$L_\mu(\phi) = \mu \begin{pmatrix} a_1\phi_1(0) + a_2\phi_2(0) - \frac{u_0}{\gamma}\phi_1(-1) \\ b_1\phi_1(0) \end{pmatrix} \tag{20}$$

$$F(\phi, \mu) = \mu D \Delta \phi + L_\mu(\phi) + f(\phi, \mu), \tag{21}$$

and

$$\begin{aligned} f(\phi,\mu) &= (\tilde{\tau}+\mu)(F_1(\phi,\mu), F_2(\phi,\mu))^T, \\ F_1(\phi,\mu) &= (\phi_1(0)+u_0)\left(1 - \frac{\phi_1(-1)+u_0}{\gamma} - \frac{\phi_2(0)+v_0}{(w(\phi_1(0)+u_0)^2+1)(1+\alpha\epsilon)}\right) \\ &\quad - a_1\phi_1(0) - a_2\phi_2(0) + \frac{u_0}{\gamma}\phi_1(-1), \\ F_2(\phi,\mu) &= (\phi_2(0)+v_0)\left(\frac{\beta(\phi_1(0)+u_0+(w(\phi_1(0)+u_0)^2+1)\epsilon)}{(w(\phi_1(0)+u_0)^2+1)(1+\alpha\epsilon)} - \delta - s(\phi_1(0)+u_0)\right) \\ &\quad - b_1\phi_1(0), \end{aligned}$$

with $\phi(\theta) = (\phi_1(\theta), \phi_2(\theta))^T \in \mathscr{C}_1$.

Consider the linear equation

$$\frac{dU(t)}{dt} = \tilde{\tau} D \Delta U(t) + L_{\tilde{\tau}}(U_t). \tag{22}$$

By the previous analysis, we know the origin $(0,0)$ is an equilibrium of (18), and for $\tau = \tilde{\tau}$, $\Lambda_n := \{i\omega_n\tilde{\tau}, -i\omega_n\tilde{\tau}\}$ are eigenvalues of system (22) and the liner functional differential equation

$$\frac{dz(t)}{dt} = -\tilde{\tau} D \frac{n^2}{l^2} z(t) + L_{\tilde{\tau}}(z_t). \tag{23}$$

From Riesz representation theorem [19], a 2×2 matrix function $\eta^n(\sigma, \tilde{\tau})$ $-1 \leq \sigma \leq 0$ exists, whose entries are of bounded variation such that, then

$$-\tilde{\tau} D \frac{n^2}{l^2} \phi(0) + L_{\tilde{\tau}}(\phi) = \int_{-1}^{0} d\eta^n(\sigma, \tau)\phi(\sigma),$$

with $\phi(\theta) \in C([-1,0], \mathbb{R}^2)$.

In fact, we can choose

$$\eta^n(\sigma, \tau) = \begin{cases} \tau E & \sigma = 0, \\ 0 & \sigma \in (-1,0), \\ -\tau F & \sigma = -1, \end{cases} \tag{24}$$

where

$$E = \begin{pmatrix} a_1 - d_1 \frac{n^2}{l^2} & a_2 \\ b_1 & -d_2 \frac{n^2}{l^2} \end{pmatrix}, \qquad F = \begin{pmatrix} -\frac{u_0}{\gamma} & 0 \\ 0 & 0 \end{pmatrix}. \tag{25}$$

Let $A(\tilde{\tau})$ denote the infinitesimal generators of semigroup included by the solutions of Equation (23) and A^* be the formal adjoint of $A(\tilde{\tau})$ under the bilinear paring

$$\begin{aligned} (\psi, \phi) &= \psi(0)\phi(0) - \int_{-1}^{0} \int_{\xi=0}^{\sigma} \psi(\xi - \sigma) d\eta^n(\sigma, \tilde{\tau})\phi(\xi) d\xi \\ &= \psi(0)\phi(0) + \tilde{\tau} \int_{-1}^{0} \psi(\xi + 1) F \phi(\xi) d\xi. \end{aligned} \tag{26}$$

with $\phi(\theta) \in C([-1,0], \mathbb{R}^2)$, $\psi(r) \in C([0,1], \mathbb{R}^2)$. Then $A(\tilde{\tau})$ and A^* are a pair of adjoint operators, see [20]. From the discussion in Section 2, we know $\pm i\omega_n \tilde{\tau}$ are two simple purely imaginary characteristic values of $A(\tilde{\tau})$ as well as A^*. Suppose P and P^* are the center subspace, that is, the generalized eigenspace of $A(\tilde{\tau})$ and A^* associated with Λ_n, respectively. Then P^* is the adjoint space of P and $\dim P = \dim P^* = 2$, see [18].

We can obtain $p_1(\theta) = (1, \xi)^T e^{i\omega_n \tilde{\tau}\theta}$, $p_2(\theta) = \overline{p_1(\theta)}$ $(\theta \in [-1,0])$ is a basis of $A(\tilde{\tau})$ associated with Λ_n and $q_1(r) = (1, \eta) e^{-i\omega_n \tilde{\tau} r}$, $q_2(r) = \overline{q_1(r)}$ $(r \in [0,1])$ is a basis of A^* with Λ_n, where

$$\xi = \frac{b_1}{d_2 \frac{n^2}{l^2} + i\omega_n}, \qquad \eta = \frac{a_2}{d_2 \frac{n^2}{l^2} - i\omega_n}.$$

Let $\Phi = (\Phi_1, \Phi_2)$, $\Psi^* = (\Psi_1^*, \Psi_2^*)^T$, with

$$\Phi_1(\theta) = \frac{p_1(\theta) + p_2(\theta)}{2} = \begin{pmatrix} \mathrm{Re}\left(e^{i\omega_n \tilde{\tau}\theta}\right) \\ \mathrm{Re}\left(\xi e^{i\omega_n \tilde{\tau}\theta}\right) \end{pmatrix}, \Phi_2(\theta) = \frac{p_1(\theta) - p_2(\theta)}{2i} = \begin{pmatrix} \mathrm{Im}\left(e^{i\omega_n \tilde{\tau}\theta}\right) \\ \mathrm{Im}\left(\xi e^{i\omega_n \tilde{\tau}\theta}\right) \end{pmatrix}$$

for $\theta \in [-1,0]$,

$$\Psi_1^*(r) = \frac{q_1(r) + q_2(r)}{2} = \begin{pmatrix} \mathrm{Re}\left(e^{-i\omega_n \tilde{\tau} r}\right) \\ \mathrm{Re}\left(\eta e^{-i\omega_n \tilde{\tau} r}\right) \end{pmatrix}, \Psi_2^*(r) = \frac{q_1(r) - q_2(r)}{2i} = \begin{pmatrix} \mathrm{Im}\left(e^{-i\omega_n \tilde{\tau} r}\right) \\ \mathrm{Im}\left(\eta e^{-i\omega_n \tilde{\tau} r}\right) \end{pmatrix}$$

for $r \in [0,1]$. Then we can compute by (26),

$$D_1^* := (\Psi_1^*, \Phi_1), \; D_2^* := (\Psi_1^*, \Phi_2), \; D_3^* := (\Psi_2^*, \Phi_1), \; D_4^* := (\Psi_2^*, \Phi_2).$$

Let $(\Psi^*, \Phi) = (\Psi_j^*, \Phi_k) = \begin{pmatrix} D_1^* & D_2^* \\ D_3^* & D_4^* \end{pmatrix}$ and construct a new basis Ψ for P^* by $\Psi = (\Psi_1, \Psi_2)^T = (\Psi^*, \Phi)^{-1}\Psi^*$. Then $(\Psi, \Phi) = I_2$. Furthermore, define $f_n := (\beta_n^1, \beta_n^2)$ and $c \cdot f_n = c_1\beta_n^1 + c_2\beta_n^2$, for $c = (c_1, c_2)^T \in \mathscr{C}_1$, where

$$\beta_n^1 = \begin{pmatrix} \cos\frac{n}{l}x \\ 0 \end{pmatrix}, \quad \beta_n^2 = \begin{pmatrix} 0 \\ \cos\frac{n}{l}x \end{pmatrix}.$$

Therefore, the center subspace of linear Equation (22) is given by $P_{CN}\mathscr{C}_1 \oplus P_S\mathscr{C}_1$ and $P_S\mathscr{C}_1$ represents the complement subspace of $P_{CN}\mathscr{C}_1$ in $\mathscr{C}_1$,

$$< u, v >:= \frac{1}{l\pi}\int_0^{l\pi} u_1\overline{v_1}dx + \frac{1}{l\pi}\int_0^{l\pi} u_2\overline{v_2}dx,$$

where $u = (u_1, u_2), v = (v_1, v_2), u, v \in X, < \phi, f_0 >= (< \phi, f_0^1 >, < \phi, f_0^2 >)^T$.

Let $A_{\tilde{\tau}}$ be the infinitesimal generator of an analytic semigroup induced by the solution of linear system (22), then Equation (18) becomes

$$\frac{dU(t)}{dt} = A_{\tilde{\tau}}U_t + R(U_t, \mu), \tag{27}$$

with

$$R(U_t, \mu) = \begin{cases} 0, & \theta \in [-1, 0); \\ F(U_t, \mu), & \theta = 0. \end{cases} \tag{28}$$

Through the decomposition of $\mathscr{C}_1$, the solution of (19) can be written as

$$U_t = \Phi\begin{pmatrix} x_1 \\ x_2 \end{pmatrix} f_n + h(x_1, x_2, \mu), \tag{29}$$

where

$$\begin{pmatrix} x_1 \\ x_2 \end{pmatrix} = (\Psi, < U_t, f_n >),$$

moreover,

$$h(x_1, x_2, \mu) \in P_S\mathscr{C}_1, \;\; h(0,0,0) = 0, \;\; Dh(0,0,0) = 0.$$

In particular, the solution of (19) on the center manifold is given by

$$U_t = \Phi\begin{pmatrix} x_1(t) \\ x_2(t) \end{pmatrix} f_n + h(x_1, x_2, 0). \tag{30}$$

Suppose $z = x_1 - ix_2$ and $\Psi(0) = (\Psi_1(0), \Psi_2(0))^T$, find that $p_1 = \Phi_1 + i\Phi_2$, then we have

$$\Phi\begin{pmatrix} x_1 \\ x_2 \end{pmatrix} f_n = (\Phi_1, \Phi_2)\begin{pmatrix} \frac{z+\overline{z}}{2} \\ \frac{i(z-\overline{z})}{2} \end{pmatrix} f_n = \frac{1}{2}(p_1 z + \overline{p_1 z}) f_n,$$

and

$$h(x_1, x_2, 0) = h(\frac{z+\overline{z}}{2}, \frac{i(z-\overline{z})}{2}, 0).$$

Thus, (30) becomes

$$\begin{aligned} U_t &= \frac{1}{2}(p_1 z + \overline{p_1 z}) f_n + h(\frac{z+\overline{z}}{2}, \frac{i(z-\overline{z})}{2}, 0) \\ &= \frac{1}{2}(p_1 z + \overline{p_1 z}) f_n + W(z, \overline{z}), \end{aligned} \tag{31}$$

and

$$W(z,\overline{z}) = h(\frac{z+\overline{z}}{2}, \frac{i(z-\overline{z})}{2}, 0).$$

Based on [18], z satisfies

$$\dot{z} = i\omega_n \tilde{\tau} z + g(z,\overline{z}), \tag{32}$$

with

$$g(z,\overline{z}) = (\Psi_1(0) - i\Psi_2(0)) < F(U_t,0), f_n > . \tag{33}$$

Assume

$$W(z,\overline{z}) = W_{20}\frac{z^2}{2} + W_{11}z\overline{z} + W_{02}\frac{\overline{z}^2}{2} + \cdots, \tag{34}$$

$$g(z,\overline{z}) = g_{20}\frac{z^2}{2} + g_{11}z\overline{z} + g_{02}\frac{\overline{z}^2}{2} + \cdots, \tag{35}$$

by Equations (31) and (34), we obtain

$$u_t(0) = \frac{1}{2}(z+\overline{z})\cos\Big(\frac{nx}{l}\Big) + W_{20}^{(1)}(0)\frac{z^2}{2} + W_{11}^{(1)}(0)z\overline{z} + W_{02}^{(1)}(0)\frac{\overline{z}^2}{2} + \cdots,$$

$$v_t(0) = \frac{1}{2}(\xi z + \overline{\xi}\overline{z})\cos\Big(\frac{nx}{l}\Big) + W_{20}^{(2)}(0)\frac{z^2}{2} + W_{11}^{(2)}(0)z\overline{z} + W_{02}^{(2)}(0)\frac{\overline{z}^2}{2} + \cdots,$$

$$u_t(-1) = \frac{1}{2}(ze^{-i\omega_n\tilde{\tau}} + \overline{z}e^{i\omega_n\tilde{\tau}})\cos(\frac{nx}{l}) + W_{20}^{(1)}(-1)\frac{z^2}{2} + W_{11}^{(1)}(-1)z\overline{z} + W_{02}^{(1)}(-1)\frac{\overline{z}^2}{2} + \cdots,$$

then

$$\begin{aligned}\overline{F}_1(U_t,0) = \frac{1}{\tilde{\tau}}F_1 =& \alpha_1 u_t^2(0) + \alpha_2 u_t(0)v_t(0) + \alpha_3 u_t(0)u_t(-1) + \alpha_4 u_t^3(0) \\ &+ \alpha_5 u_t^2(0)v_t(0) + O(4),\end{aligned} \tag{36}$$

$$\overline{F}_2(U_t,0) = \frac{1}{\tilde{\tau}}F_2 = \beta_1 u_t^2(0) + \beta_2 u_t(0)v_t(0) + \beta_3 u_t^3(0) + \beta_4 u_t^2(0)v_t(0) + O(4), \tag{37}$$

with

$$\begin{aligned}
&\alpha_1 = \frac{wu_0v_0(3-wu_0^2)}{(1+wu_0^2)^3(1+\alpha\epsilon)}, \quad \alpha_2 = \frac{wu_0^2-1}{(1+wu_0^2)^2(1+\alpha\epsilon)}, \quad \alpha_3 = -\frac{1}{\gamma}, \\
&\alpha_4 = \frac{wv_0(1-6wu_0^2+w^2u_0^4)}{(1+wu_0^2)^4(1+\alpha\epsilon)}, \quad \alpha_5 = \frac{wu_0(3-wu_0^2)}{(1+wu_0^2)^3(1+\alpha\epsilon)}, \quad \beta_1 = \frac{wu_0v_0(wu_0^2-3)\beta}{(1+wu_0^2)^3(1+\alpha\epsilon)}, \\
&\beta_2 = \frac{\beta(1-wu_0^2) - s(1+wu_0^2)^2(1+\alpha\epsilon)}{(1+wu_0^2)^2(1+\alpha\epsilon)}, \quad \beta_3 = \frac{wv_0\beta(6wu_0^2-w^2u_0^4-1)}{(1+wu_0^2)^4(1+\alpha\epsilon)}, \\
&\beta_4 = \frac{wu_0\beta(wu_0^2-3)}{(1+wu_0^2)^3(1+\alpha\epsilon)}.
\end{aligned}$$

Hence,

$$\overline{F}_1(U_t,0) = \cos^2(\frac{nx}{l})(\frac{z^2}{2}\chi_{20} + z\overline{z}\chi_{11} + \frac{\overline{z}^2}{2}\overline{\chi}_{20}) + \frac{z^2\overline{z}}{2}\chi_1\cos\frac{nx}{l} + \frac{z^2\overline{z}}{2}\chi_2\cos^3\frac{nx}{l} + \cdots, \tag{38}$$

$$\overline{F}_2(U_t,0) = \cos^2(\frac{nx}{l})(\frac{z^2}{2}\varsigma_{20} + z\overline{z}\varsigma_{11} + \frac{\overline{z}^2}{2}\overline{\varsigma}_{20}) + \frac{z^2\overline{z}}{2}\varsigma_1\cos\frac{nx}{l} + \frac{z^2\overline{z}}{2}\varsigma_2\cos^3\frac{nx}{l} + \cdots, \tag{39}$$

$$
\begin{aligned}
< F(U_t,0), f_n > &= \tilde{\tau}(\overline{F}_1(U_t,0)f_n^1 + \overline{F}_2(U_t,0)f_n^2) \\
&= \frac{z^2}{2}\tilde{\tau}\begin{pmatrix} \chi_{20} \\ \varsigma_{20} \end{pmatrix}\Gamma + z\overline{z}\tilde{\tau}\begin{pmatrix} \chi_{11} \\ \varsigma_{11} \end{pmatrix}\Gamma + \frac{\overline{z}^2}{2}\tilde{\tau}\begin{pmatrix} \overline{\chi}_{20} \\ \overline{\varsigma}_{20} \end{pmatrix}\Gamma + \frac{z^2\overline{z}}{2}\tilde{\tau}\begin{pmatrix} \kappa_1 \\ \kappa_2 \end{pmatrix} + \cdots.
\end{aligned} \tag{40}
$$

with

$$
\begin{aligned}
\Gamma &= \frac{1}{l\pi}\int_0^{l\pi} \cos^3(\frac{nx}{l})dx, \\
\chi_{20} &= \frac{1}{2}(\alpha_1 + \alpha_2\xi + \alpha_3 e^{-i\tilde{\tau}\omega_n}), \\
\chi_{11} &= \frac{1}{4}\Big(2\alpha_1 + \alpha_2(\xi + \overline{\xi}) + \alpha_3(e^{-i\tilde{\tau}\omega_n} + e^{i\tilde{\tau}\omega_n})\Big), \\
\chi_1 &= W_{11}^1(0)(2\alpha_1 + \alpha_2\xi + \alpha_3 e^{-i\tilde{\tau}\omega_n}) + \frac{1}{2}W_{20}^1(0)(2\alpha_1 + \alpha_2\overline{\xi} + \alpha_3 e^{i\tilde{\tau}\omega_n}) \\
&\quad + W_{11}^2(0)\alpha_2 + \frac{1}{2}W_{20}^2(0)\alpha_2 + W_{11}^1(-1)\alpha_3 + \frac{1}{2}W_{20}^1(-1)\alpha_3, \\
\chi_2 &= \frac{1}{4}(3\alpha_4 + \alpha_5(2\xi + \overline{\xi})), \\
\varsigma_{20} &= \frac{1}{2}(\beta_1 + \beta_2\xi), \\
\varsigma_{11} &= \frac{1}{4}(2\beta_1 + \beta_2(\xi + \overline{\xi})), \\
\varsigma_1 &= W_{11}^1(0)(2\beta_1 + \beta_2\xi) + W_{11}^2(0)\beta_2 + W_{20}^1(0)(\beta_1 + \frac{\beta_2\overline{\xi}}{2}) + W_{20}^2(0)\frac{\beta_2}{2}, \\
\varsigma_2 &= \frac{1}{4}(3\beta_3 + \beta_4(2\xi + \overline{\xi})), \\
\kappa_1 &= \chi_1\frac{1}{l\pi}\int_0^{l\pi} \cos^2(\frac{nx}{l})dx + \chi_2\frac{1}{l\pi}\int_0^{l\pi} \cos^4(\frac{nx}{l})dx, \\
\kappa_2 &= \varsigma_1\frac{1}{l\pi}\int_0^{l\pi} \cos^2(\frac{nx}{l})dx + \varsigma_2\frac{1}{l\pi}\int_0^{l\pi} \cos^4(\frac{nx}{l})dx.
\end{aligned} \tag{41}
$$

Denote

$$\Psi_1(0) - i\Psi_2(0) := (\gamma_1 \ \ \gamma_2).$$

Notice that

$$\frac{1}{l\pi}\int_0^{l\pi} \cos^3(\frac{nx}{l})dx = 0, \ \ n = 1,2,3,\cdots,$$

then

$$
\begin{aligned}
&(\Psi_1(0) - i\Psi_2(0)) < F(U_t,0), f_n >= \\
&\frac{z^2}{2}(\gamma_1\chi_{20} + \gamma_2\varsigma_{20})\Gamma\tilde{\tau} + z\overline{z}(\gamma_1\chi_{11} + \gamma_2\varsigma_{11})\Gamma\tilde{\tau} + \frac{\overline{z}^2}{2}(\gamma_1\overline{\chi}_{20} + \gamma_2\overline{\varsigma}_{20})\Gamma\tilde{\tau} \\
&+ \frac{z^2\overline{z}}{2}\tilde{\tau}[\gamma_1\kappa_1 + \gamma_2\kappa_2] + \cdots,
\end{aligned} \tag{42}
$$

$g_{20} = g_{11} = g_{02} = 0$ can be derived from (33), (35), and (42), with $n = 1,2,3,\cdots$. If $n = 0$, we have

$$g_{20} = \gamma_1\tilde{\tau}\chi_{20} + \gamma_2\tilde{\tau}\varsigma_{20}, \quad g_{11} = \gamma_1\tilde{\tau}\chi_{11} + \gamma_2\tilde{\tau}\varsigma_{11}, \quad g_{02} = \gamma_1\tilde{\tau}\overline{\chi}_{20} + \gamma_2\tilde{\tau}\overline{\varsigma}_{20}. \tag{43}$$

and for $n \in \mathbb{N}_0$, $g_{21} = \tilde{\tau}(\gamma_1\kappa_1 + \gamma_2\kappa_2)$.

Now, a complete description for g_{20} is derived. Next, we need to calculate $W_{20}(\theta)$ and $W_{11}(\theta)$ for $\theta \in [-1,0]$ because they appear in g_{21}. It follows from (34) that

$$\dot{W}(z,\overline{z}) = W_{20}z\dot{z} + W_{11}\dot{z}\overline{z} + W_{11}z\dot{\overline{z}} + W_{02}\overline{z}\dot{\overline{z}} + \cdots,$$

$$A_{\tilde{\tau}}W(z,\bar{z}) = A_{\tilde{\tau}}W_{20}\frac{z^2}{2} + A_{\tilde{\tau}}W_{11}z\bar{z} + A_{\tilde{\tau}}W_{02}\frac{\bar{z}^2}{2} + \cdots.$$

Furthermore, by [18], $W(z,\bar{z})$ should satisfy

$$\dot{W}(z,\bar{z}) = A_{\tilde{\tau}}W + H(z,\bar{z}),$$

where

$$\begin{aligned} H(z,\bar{z}) &= H_{20}\frac{z^2}{2} + W_{11}z\bar{z} + H_{02}\frac{\bar{z}^2}{2} + \cdots \\ &= X_0F(U_t,0) - \Phi(\Psi, < X_0F(U_t,0), f_n > \cdot f_n). \end{aligned} \tag{44}$$

Thus, we have

$$(2i\omega_n\tilde{\tau} - A_{\tilde{\tau}})W_{20} = H_{20}, \quad -A_{\tilde{\tau}}W_{11} = H_{11}, \quad (-2i\omega_n\tilde{\tau} - A_{\tilde{\tau}})W_{02} = H_{02}, \tag{45}$$

Noticing that $A_{\tilde{\tau}}$ has only two eigenvalues $\pm i\omega_n\tilde{\tau}$; therefore, (45) has unique solution W_{ij} in P^* given by

$$W_{20} = (2i\omega_n\tilde{\tau} - A_{\tilde{\tau}})^{-1}H_{20}, \quad W_{11} = -A_{\tilde{\tau}}^{-1}H_{11}, \quad W_{02} = (-2i\omega_n\tilde{\tau} - A_{\tilde{\tau}})^{-1}H_{02}. \tag{46}$$

From (42), we know that for $\theta \in [-1,0)$,

$$\begin{aligned} H(z,\bar{z}) &= -\Phi(0)\Psi(0) < F(U_t,0), f_n > \cdot f_n \\ &= -\left(\frac{p_1(\theta)+p_2(\theta)}{2}, \frac{p_1(\theta)-p_2(\theta)}{2i}\right)\begin{pmatrix} \Phi_1(0) \\ \Phi_2(0) \end{pmatrix} < F(U_t,0), f_n > \cdot f_n \\ &= -\frac{1}{2}[p_1(\theta)(\Phi_1(0) - i\Phi_2(0)) + p_2(\theta)(\Phi_1(0) + i\Phi_2(0))] < F(U_t,0), f_n > \cdot f_n \\ &= -\frac{1}{2}[(p_1(\theta)g_{20} + p_2(\theta)\bar{g}_{02})\frac{z^2}{2} + (p_1(\theta)g_{11} + p_2(\theta)\bar{g}_{11})z\bar{z} + (p_1(\theta)g_{02} + p_2(\theta)\bar{g}_{20})\frac{\bar{z}^2}{2}] + \cdots. \end{aligned}$$

Therefore, by (44), for $\theta \in [-1,0)$,

$$H_{20}(\theta) = \begin{cases} 0 & n \in \mathbb{N}, \\ -\frac{1}{2}(p_1(\theta)g_{20} + p_2(\theta)\bar{g}_{02}) \cdot f_0 & n = 0, \end{cases}$$

$$H_{11}(\theta) = \begin{cases} 0 & n \in \mathbb{N}, \\ -\frac{1}{2}(p_1(\theta)g_{11} + p_2(\theta)\bar{g}_{11}) \cdot f_0 & n = 0, \end{cases}$$

$$H_{02}(\theta) = \begin{cases} 0 & n \in \mathbb{N}, \\ -\frac{1}{2}(p_1(\theta)g_{02} + p_2(\theta)\bar{g}_{20}) \cdot f_0 & n = 0, \end{cases}$$

and

$$H(z,\bar{z})(0) = F(U_t,0) - \Phi(\Psi, < F(U_t,0), f_n >) \cdot f_n,$$

$$H_{20}(0) = \begin{cases} \tilde{\tau}\begin{pmatrix} \chi_{20} \\ \varsigma_{20} \end{pmatrix}\cos^2(\frac{nx}{l}), & n \in \mathbb{N}, \\ \tilde{\tau}\begin{pmatrix} \chi_{20} \\ \varsigma_{20} \end{pmatrix} - \frac{1}{2}(p_1(0)g_{20} + p_2(0)\bar{g}_{02}) \cdot f_0, & n = 0. \end{cases} \tag{47}$$

$$H_{11}(0) = \begin{cases} \tilde{\tau}\begin{pmatrix} \chi_{11} \\ \varsigma_{11} \end{pmatrix}\cos^2(\frac{nx}{l}), & n \in \mathbb{N}, \\ \tilde{\tau}\begin{pmatrix} \chi_{11} \\ \varsigma_{11} \end{pmatrix} - \frac{1}{2}(p_1(0)g_{11} + p_2(0)\bar{g}_{11}) \cdot f_0, & n = 0. \end{cases} \tag{48}$$

By the definition of $A_{\tilde{\tau}}$, and from (45), the following equation holds.

$$\dot{W}_{20} = A_{\tilde{\tau}}W_{20} = 2i\omega_n\tilde{\tau}W_{20} + \frac{1}{2}(p_1(\theta)g_{20} + p_2(\theta)\bar{g}_{02}) \cdot f_n, \quad -1 \le \theta < 0.$$

Note that $p_1(\theta) = p_1(0)e^{i\omega_n\tilde{\tau}\theta}, \quad -1 \le \theta \le 0$. Hence

$$W_{20}(\theta) = \frac{i}{2i\omega_n\tilde{\tau}}(g_{20}p_1(\theta) + \frac{\overline{g}_{02}}{3}p_2(\theta)) \cdot f_n + E_1 e^{2i\omega_n\tilde{\tau}\theta}, \tag{49}$$

where

$$E_1 = \begin{cases} W_{20}(0) & n = 1, 2, 3, \cdots, \\ W_{20}(0) - \frac{i}{2i\omega_n\tilde{\tau}}(g_{20}p_1(\theta) + \frac{\overline{g}_{02}}{3}p_2(\theta)) \cdot f_0 & n = 0. \end{cases}$$

Using the definition of $A_{\tilde{\tau}}$ by (45) and (49), we have that

$$\begin{aligned} &-(g_{20}p_1(0) + \frac{\overline{g}_{02}}{3}p_2(0)) \cdot f_0 + 2i\omega_n\tilde{\tau}E_1 - A_{\tilde{\tau}}(\frac{i}{2\omega_n\tilde{\tau}}(g_{20}p_1(0) + \frac{\overline{g}_{02}}{3}p_2(0)) \cdot f_0) \\ &- A_{\tilde{\tau}}E_1 - L_{\tilde{\tau}}(\frac{i}{2\omega_n\tilde{\tau}}(g_{20}p_1(0) + \frac{\overline{g}_{02}}{3}p_2(0)) \cdot f_n + E_1 e^{2i\omega_n\tilde{\tau}\theta}) \\ &= \tilde{\tau}\begin{pmatrix} \chi_{20} \\ \varsigma_{20} \end{pmatrix} - \frac{1}{2}(p_1(0)g_{20} + p_2(0)\overline{g}_{02}) \cdot f_0. \end{aligned}$$

Notice that

$$A_{\tilde{\tau}}p_1(0) + L_{\tilde{\tau}}(p_1 \cdot f_0) = i\omega_0 p_1(0) \cdot f_0,$$

and

$$A_{\tilde{\tau}}p_2(0) + L_{\tilde{\tau}}(p_2 \cdot f_0) = -i\omega_0 p_2(0) \cdot f_0,$$

Then for $n \in \mathbb{N}_0$, we know

$$2i\omega_n E_1 - A_{\tilde{\tau}}E_1 - L_{\tilde{\tau}}E_1 e^{2i\omega_n} = \tilde{\tau}\begin{pmatrix} \chi_{20} \\ \varsigma_{20} \end{pmatrix}\cos^2(\frac{nx}{l}), \quad n = 0, 1, 2, \cdots.$$

From the above expression, we can obtain that

$$E_1 = \tilde{\tau}E\begin{pmatrix} \chi_{20} \\ \varsigma_{20} \end{pmatrix}\cos^2(\frac{nx}{l}),$$

where

$$E = \begin{pmatrix} 2i\omega_n\tilde{\tau} + d_1\frac{n^2}{l^2} - a_1 + \frac{u_0}{\gamma}e^{-2i\omega_n\tilde{\tau}} & -a_2 \\ -b_1 & 2i\omega_n\tilde{\tau} + d_2\frac{n^2}{l^2} \end{pmatrix}^{-1}.$$

By the same way, from (46), we have

$$-\dot{W}_{11} = \frac{i}{2\omega_n\tilde{\tau}}(p_1(\theta)g_{11} + p_2(\theta)\overline{g}_{11}) \cdot f_n, \quad -1 \le \theta < 0.$$

That is

$$W_{11}(\theta) = \frac{i}{2i\omega_n\tilde{\tau}}(p_1(\theta)\overline{g}_{11} - p_1(\theta)g_{11}) + E_2.$$

Similar to the above procedure, we can obtain

$$E_2 = \tilde{\tau}E^*\begin{pmatrix} \chi_{11} \\ \varsigma_{11} \end{pmatrix}\cos^2(\frac{nx}{l}),$$

where

$$E^* = \begin{pmatrix} d_1\frac{n^2}{l^2} - a_1 + \frac{u_0}{\gamma} & -a_2 \\ -b_1 & d_2\frac{n^2}{l^2} \end{pmatrix}^{-1}.$$

So far, $W_{20}(\theta)$ and $W_{11}(\theta)$ have been expressed by the parameters of the system (3). Hence, g_{21} can also be expressed. Then, we can calculate the following quantities:

$$\begin{cases} c_1(0) = \frac{i}{2\omega_n\tilde{\tau}}(g_{20}g_{11} - 2|g_{11}|^2 - \frac{|g_{02}|^2}{3}) + \frac{1}{2}g_{21}, & \mu_2 = -\frac{Re(c_1(0))}{Re(\lambda'(\tau_n^j))}, \\ T_2 = -\frac{1}{\omega_n\tilde{\tau}}[Im(c_1(0)) + \mu_2 Im(\lambda'(\tau_n^j))], & \beta_2 = 2Re(c_1(0)), \\ \epsilon^2 = \frac{\tau-\tilde{\tau}}{\mu_2} + o(\tau - \tilde{\tau}^2). \end{cases} \tag{50}$$

From [18], we can obtain the system (3) has a family of bifurcating periodic solutions when μ is near 0 (that is τ near $\tilde{\tau}$) with the following representations

$$U_t(\mu, \theta) = \epsilon Re(p_1(\theta))e^{i\omega_n\tilde{\tau}t} \cdot f_n + O(\epsilon^2),$$

where $\mu(\epsilon)$, the period $T(\epsilon)$, and the nontrivial Floquet exponent of the periodic solutions are given by

$$\mu(\epsilon) = \mu_2\epsilon^2 + O(\epsilon^3),\ \ T(\epsilon) = \frac{2\pi}{\omega_n}(1 + T_2\epsilon^2) + O(\epsilon^3),\ \ \hat{\beta}(\epsilon) = \hat{\beta}_2\epsilon^2 + O(\epsilon^3).$$

In particular, we have the following conclusion.

- μ_2 determines the directions of the Hopf bifurcation: if $\mu_2 > 0$ (respectively, < 0), then the Hopf bifurcation is forward (respectively, backward), that is, the bifurcating periodic solutions exists for $\tau > \tau_n^j$ (respectively, $\tau < \tau_n^j$).
- $\hat{\beta}_2$ determines the stability of the bifurcating periodic solutions on the center manifold: if $\hat{\beta}_2 < 0$ (respectively, $\hat{\beta}_2 > 0$), then the bifurcating periodic solutions are orbitally asymptotically stable (respectively, unstable).
- T_2 determines the period of bifurcating periodic solutions: if $T_2 > 0$ (respectively, $T_2 < 0$), then the period increases (respectively, decreases).

4. Numerical Simulations

Here, in order to prove the above theoretical results, some numerical simulations are shown by using Matlab. For the system (3), fix parameters:

$$\begin{aligned} &d_1 = 2,\ d_2 = 2,\ \alpha = 0.5,\ \beta = 0.5,\ \gamma = 4, \\ &\delta = 0.4,\ w = 0.3,\ \epsilon = 0.6,\ s = 0.01,\ l = 5. \end{aligned} \tag{51}$$

Then, we know $u_0 \approx 0.4845$, $v_0 \approx 1.2230$, and

$$a_1 - \frac{u_0}{\gamma} \approx -0.0055 < 0,\ \ a_2b_1 \approx -0.1286 < 0.$$

Hence, $(\mathbf{H})$ holds. $\mathbb{G} = \{0, 1\} \neq \emptyset$. Let $n = 0$, then $\tau_* = \tau_0^0 \approx 0.8015$ and $\omega_0 \approx 0.3771$ are obtained through calculation. From Theorem 1, $P(u_0, v_0)$ is stable for $\tau \in [0, \tau_*)$. It is shown in Figure 1, here $\tau = 0.5$. In Figure 1, we can see that the predator and prey coexist, and as time goes on, they tend to the positive equilibrium (u_0, v_0). $P(u_0, v_0)$ is unstable and Hopf bifurcation occurs when $\tau = \tau_*$. From last section, we have $\xi \approx -0.9796i$, $\eta \approx -0.9232i$. Next,

$$\Phi_1(0) = \begin{pmatrix} 1 \\ 0 \end{pmatrix},\ \Phi_2(0) \approx \begin{pmatrix} 0 \\ -0.9796 \end{pmatrix},$$

$$\Psi_1^*(0) = \begin{pmatrix} 1 \\ 0 \end{pmatrix},\ \Psi_2^*(0) \approx \begin{pmatrix} 0 \\ -0.9232 \end{pmatrix}.$$

$n = 0$, through (43), easily know

$$g_{20} \approx 0.1632 + 0.2342i, \;\; g_{11} \approx 0.0378 - 0.0672i,$$

$$g_{02} \approx -0.0876 - 0.3686i, \;\; g_{21} \approx -0.0341 + 0.1860i.$$

By Lemma 4 and its proof, we obtain

$$\frac{d\lambda}{d\tau} \approx 0.0079 + 0.0239i.$$

Finally, we can calculate the following parameters

$$\mu_2 \approx 1.7199 > 0, \;\; \hat{\beta}_2 \approx -0.0271 < 0, \;\; \text{and} \;\; T_2 \approx -0.2369 < 0.$$

Thus, the direction of Hopf bifurcation is forward because $\mu_2 > 0$. There exists the locally asymptotically stable bifurcating periodic solutions whose period is decreasing (see Figure 2). At this moment, $\tau = 1.3$, prey and predator will coexist in the form of periodic oscillation.

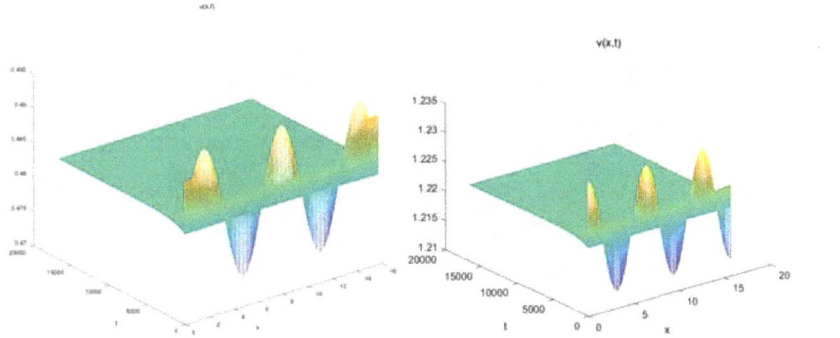

Figure 1. The numerical simulations of system (3) with $\tau = 0.5$ and other parameters is given by (51). **Left**: component u . **Right**: component v.

If we choose other parameters, Hopf bifurcation with period-2 can also occur. For the system (3), fix parameters

$$\begin{aligned} &d_1 = 2, \; d_2 = 2, \; \alpha = 0.5, \; \beta = 0.5, \; \gamma = 4.1, \\ &\delta = 0.4, \; w = 0.3, \; \epsilon = 0.7, \; s = 0.01, \; l = 5. \end{aligned} \tag{52}$$

Then, we know $u_0 \approx 0.4109, v_0 \approx 1.2762$, and

$$a_1 - \frac{u_0}{\gamma} \approx -0.0135 < 0, \;\; a_2 b_1 \approx -0.1141 < 0.$$

Hence, (**H**) holds. $\mathbb{G} = \{0,1\} \neq \emptyset$. Let $n = 0$, $\tau_* = \tau_0^0 \approx 1.4414$ and $\omega_0 \approx 0.3638$ are obtained through calculation. From Theorem 1, $P(u_0, v_0)$ is stable for $\tau \in [0, \tau_*)$. It is shown in Figure 3, here $\tau = 1$. In Figure 3, we can see that the predator and prey coexist, and as time goes on, they tend to the positive equilibrium (u_0, v_0). $P(u_0, v_0)$ is unstable and Hopf bifurcation occurs when $\tau = \tau_*$. From last section, we have $\xi \approx -1.0825i, \;\; \eta \approx -0.7964i$. Next,

$$\Phi_1(0) = \begin{pmatrix} 1 \\ 0 \end{pmatrix}, \;\; \Phi_2(0) = \begin{pmatrix} 0 \\ -1.0825 \end{pmatrix},$$

$$\Psi_1^*(0) = \begin{pmatrix} 1 \\ 0 \end{pmatrix}, \Psi_2^*(0) = \begin{pmatrix} 0 \\ -0.7964 \end{pmatrix}.$$

$n = 0$, through (43), we easily know that

$$g_{20} \approx 0.3125 + 0.5641i, \quad g_{11} \approx 0.0668 - 0.0999i,$$

$$g_{02} \approx -0.1789 - 0.7639i, \quad g_{21} \approx -0.3361 - 1.4048i.$$

By Lemma 4 and its proof, we obtain

$$\frac{d\lambda}{d\tau} \approx 0.0112 + 0.0177i.$$

Finally, we can calculate the following parameters:

$$\mu_2 \approx 15.4938 > 0, \ \hat{\beta}_2 \approx -0.3484 < 0, \ \text{and} \ T_2 \approx 1.1019 > 0.$$

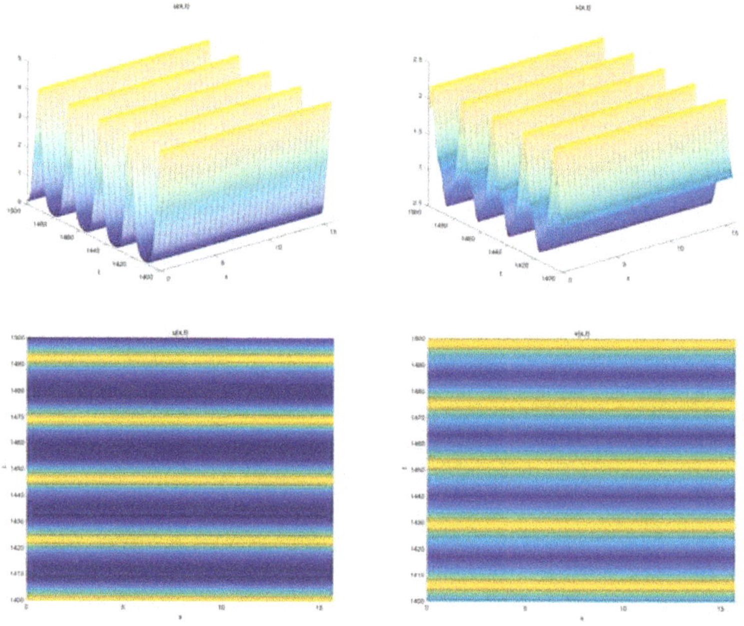

Prey u Predator v

Figure 2. The numerical simulations of system (3) with $\tau = 1.3$ and other parameters is given by (51).

Thus, the direction of Hopf bifurcation is forward because $\mu_2 > 0$. There exists the locally asymptotically stable bifurcating periodic solutions whose period is increasing (see Figure 4). At this moment, $\tau = 1.5$, bifurcating periodic solutions with period-2 appears.

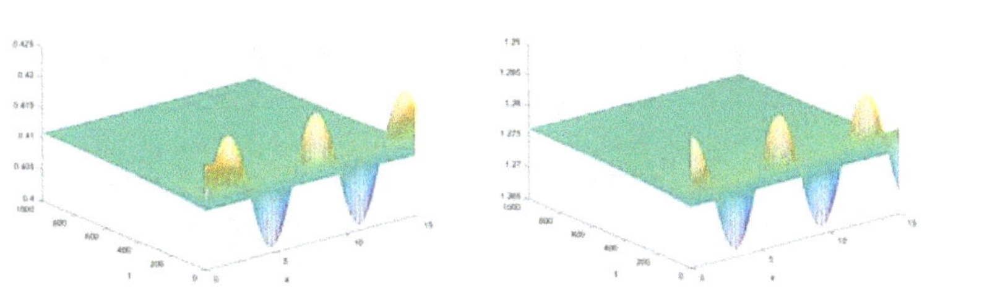

Figure 3. The numerical simulations of system (3) with $\tau = 1$ and other parameters is given by (52). **Left**: component u. **Right**: component v.

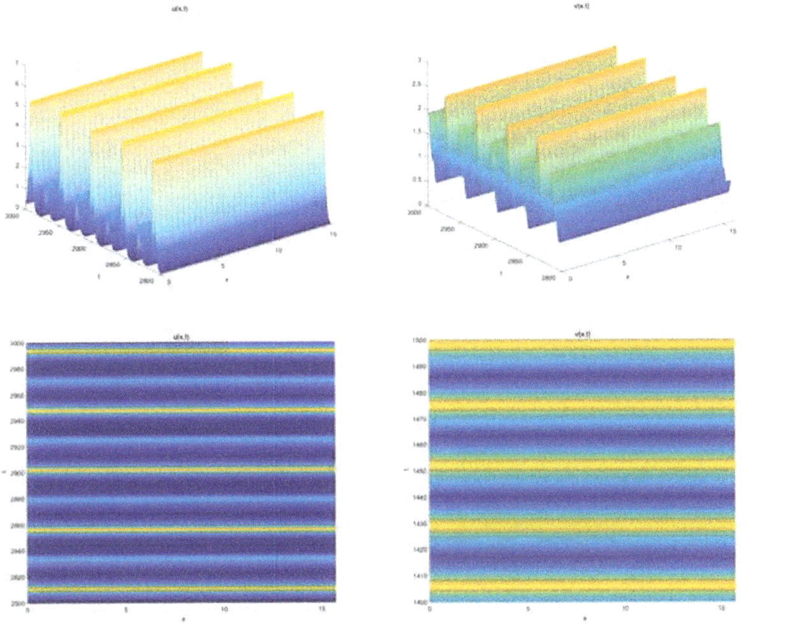

Prey u Predator v

Figure 4. The numerical simulations of system (3) with $\tau = 1.5$ and other parameters is given by (52).

5. Conclusions

In this paper, we incorporated time delay and diffusion on the model (1), and studied the dynamics in a delayed diffusive system with anti-predator and additional food provided for a predator. By using time delay as a parameter, we mainly studied the local stability of coexisting equilibrium, the existence of Hopf bifurcation induced by delay, and the property of Hopf bifurcation by the theory of the center manifold and normal form method.

Compared with the model (1), we prove that under some conditions, time delay can destabilize the stable equilibrium, and can even lead to the existence of periodic solutions. Especially, there exists a critical value τ_*. When the time delay is smaller than the critical value, prey and predator will coexist, and tend toward the coexisting equilibrium, and are evenly distributed homogeneous in the region; however, when the time delay crosses the critical value, the coexisting equilibrium is unstable, and Hopf bifurcation occurs. In this case, the prey and predator may also coexist, but they will coexist in the form of periodic oscillation. Further, diffusion may also cause inhomogeneous periodic solutions.

Unfortunately, we found the inhomogeneous periodic solution of our model is unstable and could not be shown through numerical simulations. In a future work, we will conduct a more general study, using a generalized logistic function, which allows us to study the Allee effect. That is relevant in several areas of application, namely biology and ecology.

Author Contributions: Writing—original draft preparation: R.Y. and X.Z.; writing—review and editing, funding acquisition: R.Y., X.Z. and Y.A.; methodology and supervision: R.Y. and Y.A. All authors have read and agreed to the published version of the manuscript.

Funding: This research is supported by Fundamental Research Funds for the Central Universities (No. 2572021DJ01), Postdoctoral program of Heilongjiang Province (No. LBH-Q21060), Natural Science Foundation of Heilongjiang Province (No. A2018001), and National Nature Science Foundation of China (No. 11601070).

Institutional Review Board Statement: Not applicable.

Informed Consent Statement: Not applicable.

Data Availability Statement: Not applicable.

Acknowledgments: The authors wish to express their gratitude to the editors and the reviewers for the helpful comments.

Conflicts of Interest: The authors declare that they have no conflict of interests.

References

1. Ford, J.K.; Reeves, R.R. Fight or flight: Antipredator strategies of baleen whales. *Mamm. Rev.* **2008**, *38*, 50–86. [CrossRef]
2. Ge, D.; Chesters, D.; Gomez-Zurita, J. Anti-predator defence drives parallel morphological evolution in flea beetles. *Proc. R. Soc. Lond. B Biol. Sci.* **2011**, *278*, 2133–2141. [CrossRef] [PubMed]
3. Lima, S.L. Nonlethal effectsin the ecology of predator-prey interactions. *Bioscience* **1998**, *48*, 25–34. [CrossRef]
4. Matassa, C.M.; Donelan, S.C.; Luttbeg, B. Resource levels and prey state influence antipredator behavior and the strength of nonconsumptive predator effects. *Oikos* **2016**, *125*, 1478–1488. [CrossRef]
5. Khater, M. Murariu, D.; Gras, R. Predation risk tradeoffs in prey: Effects on energy and behaviour. *Theor. Ecol.* **2016**, *9*, 251–268. [CrossRef]
6. Srinivasu, P.D.N.; Prasad, B.S.R.V.; Venkatesulu, M. Biological control through provision of additional food to predators: A theoretical study. *Theor. Popul. Biol.* **2007**, *72*, 111–120. [CrossRef]
7. Prasad, K.D.; Prasad, B.S.R.V. Qualitative analysis of additional food provided predator-prey system with anti-predator behaviour in prey. *Nonlinear Dyn.* **2019**, *96*, 1765–1793. [CrossRef]
8. Eskandari, Z.; Alidousti, J.; Avazzadeh, Z. Dynamics and bifurcations of a discrete-time prey-predator model with Allee effect on the prey population. *Ecol. Complex.* **2021**, *48*, 100962. [CrossRef]
9. Zhang, X.; Liu, Z. Hopf bifurcation analysis in a predator-prey model with predator-age structure and predator-prey reaction time delay. *Appl. Math. Model.* **2021**, *91*, 530–548. [CrossRef]
10. Duque, C.; Lizana, M. On the dynamics of a predator-prey model with nonconstant death rate and diffusion. *Nonlinear Anal. Real World Appl.* **2011**, *12*, 2198–2210. [CrossRef]
11. Gan, Q.; Xu, R.; Yang, P. Bifurcation and chaos in a ratio-dependent predator-prey system with time delay. *Chaos Solitons Fractals* **2009**, *39*, 1883–1895. [CrossRef]
12. Gilioli, G.; Pasquali, S.; Ruggeri, F. Nonlinear functional response parameter estimation in a stochastic predator-prey model. *Math. Biosci. Eng.* **2017**, *9*, 75–96.
13. Wang, M. Stability and Hopf bifurcation for a prey-predator model with prey-stage structure and diffusion. *Math. Biosci.* **2008**, *212*, 149–160. [CrossRef] [PubMed]
14. Guin, L.N.; Pal, S.; Chakravart, S. Pattern dynamics of a reaction-diffusion predator-prey system with both refuge and harvesting. *Int. J. Biomath.* **2021**, *14*, 2050084. [CrossRef]
15. Djilali, S.; Bentout, S.; Ghanbari, B. Spatial patterns in a vegetation model with internal competition and feedback regulation. *Eur. Phys. J. Plus* **2021**, *136*, 1–24. [CrossRef]
16. Souna, F.; Djilali, S.; Lakmeche, A. Spatiotemporal behavior in a predator–prey model with herd behavior and cross-diffusion and fear effect. *Eur. Phys. J. Plus* **2021** *136*, 1–21. [CrossRef]
17. Djilali, S.; Bentout, S. Pattern formations of a delayed diffusive predator–prey model with predator harvesting and prey social behavior. *Math. Methods Appl. Sci.* **2021**, *44*, 9128–9142. [CrossRef]
18. Wu, J. *Theory and Applications of Partial Functional Differential Equations*; Springer: Berlin, Germany, 1996.
19. Kreyszig, E. *Introductory Functional Analysis with Applications*; Wiley: New York, NY, USA, 1978; pp. 225–231.
20. Hale, J. *Theory of Functional Differential Equations*; Springer: Berlin, Germany, 1977.

mathematics

Article

Bifurcation Analysis of a Synthetic Drug Transmission Model with Two Time Delays

Hu Zhang [1], Anwar Zeb [2], Aying Wan [3,*] and Zizhen Zhang [1]

[1] School of Management Science and Engineering, Anhui University of Finance and Economics, Bengbu 233030, China; zhanghu2000@163.com (H.Z.); zzzhaida@163.com (Z.Z.)
[2] Department of Mathematics, Abbottabad Campus, COMSATS University Islamabad, Islamabad 22060, Pakistan; anwar@cuiatd.edu.pk
[3] School of Mathematics and Statistics, Hulunbuir University, Hulunbuir 021008, China
* Correspondence: wanaying1@aliyun.com

Abstract: Synthetic drugs are taking the place of traditional drugs and have made headlines giving rise to serious social issues in many countries. In this work, a synthetic drug transmission model incorporating psychological addicts with two time delays is being developed. Local stability and exhibition of Hopf bifurcation are established analytically and numerically by taking the combinations of the two time delays as bifurcation parameters. The exhibition of Hopf bifurcation shows that it is burdensome to eradicate the synthetic drugs transmission in the population.

Keywords: synthetic drugs transmission; time delays; Hopf bifurcation; local stability; period solutions

MSC: 34C23

Citation: Zhang, H.; Zeb, A.; Wan, A.; Zhang, Z. Bifurcation Analysis of a Synthetic Drug Transmission Model with Two Time Delays. *Mathematics* **2022**, *10*, 1532. https://doi.org/10.3390/math10091532

Academic Editors: Chunrui Zhang and Tudor Stefan Ratiu

Received: 8 March 2022
Accepted: 29 April 2022
Published: 3 May 2022

1. Introduction

In recent years, synthetic drugs which consist of a variety of psychoactive substances such as cocaine and marijuana compounds, are more and more popular due to the fact that they mainly appear in public places of entertainment frequented by young people. Synthetic drugs can bring about serious deleterious effects on a user's Central Nervous System (CNS) and make the users excited or inhibited [1]. Therefore, synthetic drugs are more addictive compared with traditional drugs. On the other hand, the manufacturing method of synthetic drugs is relatively simple and they are also easy to obtain. Accordingly, this leads to a sharp rise in the number of synthetic drug users around the globe. In China, for example, synthetic drug abuse had ranked first by the end of 2017 [2]. It is much worse that infectious diseases especially the spread of AIDS can be caused by synthetic drug abuse. In order to maintain social order, it is extremely urgent to control the spread of synthetic drug abuse.

A mathematical modelling approach has been utilized to solve social issues extensively since heroin addiction was considered an infectious disease [3]. Liu et al. [4,5] studied a heroin epidemic model with bilinear incidence rate. Ma et al. [6–8] discussed dynamics of a heroin model with nonlinear incidence rate. Yang et al. [9,10] considered an age-structured multi-group heroin epidemic model. There have been also some works about giving up smoking models [11–16], and drinking abuse models [17–20]. Motivated by the aforementioned works, some synthetic drug transmission models have been formulated by scholars. In [21], Das et al. proposed a fractional order synthetic drugs transmission model and decided stability of the model and formulated the optimal control of the model. In [22], Saha and Samanta proposed a synthetic drugs transmission model considering general rate. They proved local and global stability of the model and presented sensitivity analysis. Taking into account the relapse phenomenon in synthetic drug abuse, Liu et al. [23]

formulated a delayed synthetic drugs transmission model with relapse and analyzed stability of the model. Based on the work by Ma et al. [24] and in consideration of the effect of psychology and time delay, Zhang et al. [25] established the following synthetic drugs transmission model with time delay:

$$\begin{cases} \frac{dS(t)}{dt} &= A - dS(t) - \beta_1 S(t)P(t) - \beta_2 S(t)H(t), \\ \frac{dP(t)}{dt} &= \beta_1 S(t)P(t) + \beta_2 S(t)H(t) - \pi P(t) - (d+\gamma)P(t), \\ \frac{dH(t)}{dt} &= \pi P(t) + \theta T(t-\tau) - \sigma H(t) - dH(t), \\ \frac{dT(t)}{dt} &= \gamma P(t) + \sigma H(t) - \theta T(t-\tau) - dT(t), \end{cases} \tag{1}$$

where $S(t)$ denotes the number of the susceptible population at time t, $P(t)$ is the number of the psychological addicts at time t, $H(t)$ is the number of the physiological addicts at time t and $T(t)$ is the number of the drug-users in treatment at time t. A is the constant rate of entering the susceptible population; β_1 is the contact rate between the susceptible population and the psychological addicts; β_2 is the contact rate between the susceptible population and the physiological addicts; d is the natural mortality of all the populations; π is the escalation rate from the psychological addicts to the physiological addicts; γ is the treatment rate of the psychological addicts; σ is the treatment rate of the physiological addicts; θ is the relapse rate of the drug-users in treatment. The symbol τ is the relapse time period of the drug-users in treatment. Zhang et al. analyzed the effect of the time delay due to the relapse time period of the drug-users in treatment on the model (1).

Clearly, Zhang et al. considered that a drug-user in treatment usually needs a certain interval to become a physiological addict again. Likewise, we believe that both the psychological addicts and the physiological addicts need a period to accept treatment and come off drugs. In fact, the dynamical model with multiple time delays has been somewhat fruitful. Kundu and Maitra [26] formulated a three species predator-prey model with three delays and obtained the critical value of each time delay where the Hopf-bifurcation happened. Ren et al. [27] proposed a computer virus model with two time delays and found that a Hopf bifurcation may occur depending on the time delays. Xu et al. [28] investigated the influence of multiple time delays on bifurcation of a fractional-order neural network model through taking two different delays as bifurcation parameters. Motivated by the work above, we investigate the following synthetic drug transmission model with two time delays:

$$\begin{cases} \frac{dS(t)}{dt} &= A - dS(t) - \beta_1 S(t)P(t) - \beta_2 S(t)H(t), \\ \frac{dP(t)}{dt} &= \beta_1 S(t)P(t) + \beta_2 S(t)H(t) - \pi P(t) - dP(t) - \gamma P(t-\tau_2), \\ \frac{dH(t)}{dt} &= \pi P(t) + \theta T(t-\tau_1) - \sigma H(t-\tau_2) - dH(t), \\ \frac{dT(t)}{dt} &= \gamma P(t-\tau_2) + \sigma H(t-\tau_2) - \theta T(t-\tau_1) - dT(t), \end{cases} \tag{2}$$

where τ_1 is the time delay due to the relapse time period of the drug-users in treatment and τ_2 is the time delay due to the period that both the psychological addicts and the physiological addicts need to accept treatment and come off drugs.

The outline of this work is as follows. In the next Section, a series of sufficient criteria are derived by choosing four different combinations of the two time delays as bifurcation parameters. Moreover, direction and stability of the Hopf bifurcation are explored under the case when $\tau_1 \in (0, \tau_{10})$ and $\tau_2 > 0$ in Section 3. Numerical simulations are demonstrated to examine the validity of our theoretical findings in Section 4. Section 5 ends our work.

2. Positivity and Boundedness of the Solutions

Considering $\mathbb{R}^4_+ = \{(z_1, z_2, z_3, z_4) | z_j \geq 0, j = 1,2,3,4\}$ and $\tau = \max\{\tau_1, \tau_2\}$. The initial conditions for the model (2) are

$$S(\vartheta) = \xi_1(\vartheta), P(\vartheta) = \xi_2(\vartheta), H(\vartheta) = \xi_3(\vartheta), T(\vartheta) = \xi_4(\vartheta), \tag{3}$$

where $\xi_j(\vartheta) \geq 0$, $\xi(0) > 0$, $j = 1,2,3,4$; $\vartheta \in [-\tau, 0]$ and $(\xi_1, \xi_2, \xi_3, \xi_4) \in C([-\tau, 0], \mathbb{R}^4_+)$, where $C([-\tau, 0], \mathbb{R}^4_+)$ is the Banach Space of continuous functions from $[-\tau, 0]$ to $\mathbb{R}^4_+$.

It can be observed that all the solutions of the model (2) with the above initial conditions (3) are defined on $\mathbb{R}^4_+$ and remain positive $\forall t \geq 0$. We prove this by utilizing provided methods of Bodnar [28] and Yang et al. [29] . For this purpose we present the following result.

Theorem 1. *All the solution of model (2) with the positive initial condition (3) are positive for all $t > 0$.*

Proof. It is easy to verify for system (2) that by choosing that $S(t) = 0$ implies that $S'(t) = A > 0$ for all $t \geq 0$. Hence, $S(t) > 0$, for all $t \geq 0$.

Now, we let $\tau = \max\{\tau_1, \tau_2\}$. Suppose that there exists $t_1 \in [0, \tau]$ such that $P(t_1) = 0$ and $P'(t_1) < 0$, and $P(t) > 0$ for $t \in [0, t_1]$, and $H(t_1) > 0$, $T(t_1) > 0$, and $H(t) > 0$, $T(t) > 0$ for all $t \in [0, t_1]$, then we have

$$P'(t_1) = \beta_2 S(t_1) H(t_1) - \gamma P(t_1 - \tau_2),$$

Note that $t_1 - \tau_2 \in [-\tau_2, 0]$ therefore $P'(t_1) < 0$ not always holds (in this case for any initial condition). Therefore, we have a contradiction with $P'(t_1) < 0$. Therefore, $P(t) > 0$ for all $t \in [0, \tau]$.

Similarly, we assume that there exists $t_2 \in [0, \tau]$ such that $H(t_2) = 0$ and $H'(t_2) < 0$, and $H(t) > 0$ for $t \in [0, t_2]$, and $T(t_2) > 0$, and $T(t) > 0$ for all $t \in [0, t_2]$, then we have

$$H'(t) = \pi P(t_2) + \theta T(t_2 - \tau_1) - \sigma H(t - \tau_2).$$

Then, $t_2 - \tau_2 \in [-\tau_2, 0]$ therefore, $H'(t_2) < 0$ does not always hold, which is a contradiction. Therefore, $H(t) > 0$ for all $t \in [0, \tau]$. Using the same method we obtain $T(t) > 0$ for all $t \in [0, \tau]$. Therefore, the solution is positive for $t \in [0, \tau]$. By induction, we can show that the solution is positive for $t \in [n\tau, (n+1)\tau]$. Therefore, we deduce that the solution of the system (2) is positive under the given initial conditions (3) for all $t \geq 0$. □

Denote $N(t) = S(t) + P(t) + H(t) + T(t)$, then in view of the equations of the model (2), we obtain

$$\frac{d}{dt} N(t) = A - dN(t). \tag{4}$$

Solving Equation (4), yields

$$N(t) = \frac{A}{d} + (N(0) - \frac{A}{d}) e^{-dt}. \tag{5}$$

Accordingly, for $N(0) < \frac{A}{d}$, then we can know that $N(t) < \frac{A}{d}$ and $\lim_{t \to \infty} N(t) = \frac{A}{d}$. Conclusively, the set

$$\Delta = \{(S, P, H, T) \in \mathbb{R}^4_+ : S + P + H + T = \frac{A}{d}, S > 0, P > 0, H > 0, T > 0\}$$

is a bounded feasible region as well as positively invariant under the model (2).

3. Exhibition of the Hopf bifurcation

In this section, we shall explore the impact of the time delay τ_1 and τ_2 according to analysis of the distribution of the roots of associated characteristic equations, and using a similar process about delayed systems in [30–33].

According to the computation by Zhang et al. [25], we conclude that if the basic reproductive number $\Re_0 > 1$ then the model (2) is provided with a unique synthetic drug addiction equilibrium point $E_*(S_*, P_*, H_*, T_*)$, where

$$\begin{aligned} S_* &= \frac{(\pi+d+\gamma)P_*}{\beta_1 P_* + \beta_2 H_*}, P_* = \frac{d[(\Re_0-1)+U]}{\beta_1+\beta_2 V}, \\ H_* &= \frac{\pi P_* + \theta T_*}{\sigma+d}, T_* = \frac{[d(\gamma+\pi)+d\gamma]P_*}{d(\theta+\sigma+d)}, \end{aligned}$$

and

$$\begin{aligned} U &= \frac{A\beta_2\theta[\gamma(\sigma+d)+\pi\sigma]}{d^2(\sigma+d)(\theta+\sigma+d)(\pi+d+\gamma)}, \\ V &= \frac{\pi}{\sigma+d} + \frac{\theta[\gamma(\sigma+d)+\pi\sigma]}{d(\sigma+d)(\theta+\sigma+d)}, \\ \Re_0 &= \frac{A[\beta_1(\sigma+d)+\beta_2\pi]}{d(\sigma+d)(\pi+\gamma+d)}. \end{aligned}$$

The linearized section of the model (2) around the synthetic drug addiction equilibrium point $E_*(S_*, P_*, H_*, T_*)$ is

$$\begin{cases} \frac{dS(t)}{dt} &= x_{11}S(t) + x_{12}P(t) + x_{13}H(t), \\ \frac{dP(t)}{dt} &= x_{21}S(t) + x_{22}P(t) + x_{23}H(t) + z_{22}P(t-\tau_2), \\ \frac{dH(t)}{dt} &= x_{32}P(t) + x_{33}H(t) + z_{33}H(t-\tau_2) + y_{34}T(t-\tau_1), \\ \frac{dT(t)}{dt} &= x_{44}T(t) + z_{42}P(t-\tau_2) + z_{43}H(t-\tau_2) + y_{44}T(t-\tau_1), \end{cases} \tag{6}$$

with

$$\begin{aligned} x_{11} &= -(d+\beta_1 P_* + \beta_2 H_*), x_{12} = -\beta_1 S_*, x_{13} = -\beta_2 S_*, \\ x_{21} &= \beta_1 P_* + \beta_2 H_*, x_{22} = \beta_1 S_* - (\pi+d), x_{23} = \beta_2 S_*, z_{22} = -\gamma, \\ x_{32} &= \pi, x_{33} = -d, z_{33} = -\sigma, y_{34} = \theta, \\ x_{44} &= -d, y_{44} = -\theta, z_{42} = \gamma, z_{43} = \sigma. \end{aligned}$$

Then, we can obtain the corresponding characteristic equation about the synthetic drug addiction equilibrium point $E_*(S_*, P_*, H_*, T_*)$ as follows

$$\begin{aligned} \lambda^4 &+ X_{03}\lambda^3 + X_{02}\lambda^2 + X_{01}\lambda + X_{00} \\ &+ (Y_{03}\lambda^3 + Y_{02}\lambda^2 + Y_{01}\lambda + Y_{00})e^{-\lambda\tau_1} \\ &+ (Z_{03}\lambda^3 + Z_{02}\lambda^2 + Z_{01}\lambda + Z_{00})e^{-\lambda\tau_2} \\ &+ (A_{02}\lambda^2 + A_{01}\lambda + A_{00})e^{-\lambda(\tau_1+\tau_2)} \\ &+ (B_{02}\lambda^2 + B_{01}\lambda + B_{00})e^{-2\lambda\tau_2} \\ &+ (C_{01}\lambda + C_{00})e^{-\lambda(\tau_1+2\tau_2)} = 0, \end{aligned} \tag{7}$$

where

$$
\begin{aligned}
X_{00} &= x_{11}x_{33}x_{44}(x_{22}+z_{22}),\\
X_{01} &= -(x_{22}+z_{22})(x_{11}x_{33}+x_{11}x_{44}+x_{33}x_{44})-x_{11}x_{33}x_{44},\\
X_{02} &= x_{11}x_{33}+x_{11}x_{44}+x_{33}x_{44}+(x_{22}+z_{22})(x_{11}+x_{33}+x_{44}),\\
X_{03} &= -(x_{11}+x_{22}+x_{33}+x_{44}+z_{22}),\\
Y_{00} &= x_{11}x_{22}x_{33}y_{44},\\
Y_{01} &= -y_{44}(x_{11}x_{22}+x_{11}x_{33}+x_{22}x_{33}),\\
Y_{02} &= y_{44}(x_{11}+x_{22}+x_{33}), Y_{03}=-y_{44},\\
Z_{00} &= x_{11}x_{22}x_{44}z_{33},\\
Z_{01} &= -z_{33}(x_{11}x_{22}+x_{11}x_{44}+x_{22}x_{44}),\\
Z_{02} &= z_{33}(x_{11}+x_{22}+x_{44}), Z_{03}=-z_{33},\\
A_{00} &= x_{11}x_{22}(y_{34}z_{43}+y_{44}z_{33})-x_{21}y_{34}(x_{12}z_{43}+x_{13}z_{42})\\
&\quad +x_{11}(x_{33}y_{44}z_{22}+x_{23}y_{34}z_{42}),\\
A_{01} &= x_{23}y_{34}z_{42}-y_{44}z_{22}(x_{11}+x_{33})-(x_{11}+x_{22})(y_{34}z_{43}+y_{44}z_{33}),\\
A_{02} &= y_{34}z_{43}+y_{44}(z_{33}-z_{22}),\\
B_{00} &= x_{11}x_{44}z_{22}z_{33}, B_{01}=-z_{22}z_{33}(x_{11}+x_{44}), B_{02}=z_{22}z_{33},\\
C_{00} &= x_{11}z_{22}(y_{34}z_{43}+y_{44}z_{33}), C_{01}=-z_{22}(y_{34}z_{43}+y_{44}z_{33}).
\end{aligned}
$$

Case 1. $\tau_1=\tau_2=0$, Equation (7) equals

$$\lambda^4+X_{13}\lambda^3+X_{12}\lambda^2+X_{11}\lambda+X_{10}=0, \tag{8}$$

with

$$
\begin{aligned}
X_{10} &= X_{00}+Y_{00}+Z_{00}+A_{00}+B_{00}+C_{00},\\
X_{11} &= X_{01}+Y_{01}+Z_{01}+A_{01}+B_{01}+C_{01},\\
X_{12} &= X_{02}+Y_{02}+Z_{02}+A_{02}+B_{02},\\
X_{13} &= X_{03}+Y_{03}+Z_{03}.
\end{aligned}
$$

Following the work by Ma et al. [24] and the Routh-Hurwitz theorem, it can be seen that if $X_{10}>0$, $X_{13}>0$, $X_{12}X_{13}>X_{11}$ and $X_{11}X_{12}X_{13}>X_{10}X_{13}^2+X_{11}^2$, the model (2) is locally asymptotically stable.

Case 2. $\tau_1>0$ and $\tau_2=0$, Equation (7) becomes

$$\lambda^4+X_{23}\lambda^3+X_{22}\lambda^2+X_{21}\lambda+X_{20}+(Y_{23}\lambda^3+Y_{22}\lambda^2+Y_{21}\lambda+Y_{20})e^{-\lambda\tau_1}=0, \tag{9}$$

with

$$
\begin{aligned}
X_{20} &= X_{00}+Z_{00}+B_{00}, X_{21}=X_{01}+Z_{01}+B_{01},\\
X_{22} &= X_{02}+Z_{02}+B_{02}, X_{23}=X_{03}+Z_{03},\\
Y_{20} &= Y_{00}+A_{00}+C_{00}, Y_{21}=Y_{01}+A_{01}+C_{01},\\
Y_{22} &= Y_{02}+A_{02}, Y_{23}=Y_{03}.
\end{aligned}
$$

Let $\lambda=i\varsigma_1(\varsigma_1>0)$ be a root of Equation (9), then

$$
\begin{cases}
(Y_{21}\varsigma_1-Y_{23}\varsigma_1^3)\sin(\tau_1\varsigma_1)+(Y_{20}-Y_{22}\varsigma_1^2)\cos(\tau_1\varsigma_1)=X_{22}\varsigma_1^2-\varsigma_1^4-X_{20},\\
(Y_{21}\varsigma_1-Y_{23}\varsigma_1^3)\cos(\tau_1\varsigma_1)-(Y_{20}-Y_{22}\varsigma_1^2)\sin(\tau_1\varsigma_1)=X_{23}\varsigma_1^3-X_{21}\varsigma_1.
\end{cases} \tag{10}
$$

It follows from Equation (10) that

$$\varsigma_1^8+D_{23}\varsigma_1^6+D_{22}\varsigma_1^4+D_{21}\varsigma_1^2+D_{20}=0, \tag{11}$$

with

$$
\begin{aligned}
D_{20} &= X_{20}^2 - Y_{20}^2, \\
D_{21} &= X_{21}^2 + 2Y_{20}Y_{22} - Y_{21}^2, \\
D_{22} &= X_{22}^2 + 2X_{20} - 2X_{21}X_{23} - Y_{22}^2 + 2Y_{21}Y_{23}, \\
D_{23} &= X_{23}^2 - 2X_{22} - Y_{23}^2.
\end{aligned}
$$

Denote $\varsigma_1 = \vartheta_1$, then

$$\vartheta_1^4 + D_{23}\vartheta_1^3 + D_{22}\vartheta_1^2 + D_{21}\vartheta_1 + D_{20} = 0. \tag{12}$$

Distribution of the roots of Equation (12) has been discussed by Li and Wei [34]. Next, we suppose that Equation (12) has at least one positive root ϑ_{10} such that $\varsigma_{10} = \sqrt{\vartheta_{10}}$ ensuring that Equation (9) has a pair of purely imaginary roots $\pm i\varsigma_{10}$. For ς_{10}, from Equation (10), we have

$$\tau_{10} = \frac{1}{\varsigma_{10}} \times \arccos\left[\frac{E_{21}(\varsigma_{10})}{E_{22}(\varsigma_{10})}\right], \tag{13}$$

where

$$
\begin{aligned}
E_{21}(\varsigma_{10}) &= (Y_{22} - X_{23}Y_{23})\varsigma_{10}^6 + (X_{23}Y_{21} + X_{21}Y_{23} - Y_{20} - X_{22}Y_{22})\varsigma_{10}^4 \\
&\quad + (X_{22}Y_{20} - X_{21}Y_{21} + X_{20}Y_{22})\varsigma_{10}^2 - X_{20}Y_{20}, \\
E_{22}(\varsigma_{10}) &= Y_{23}^2\varsigma_{10}^6 + (Y_{22}^2 - 2Y_{21}Y_{23})\varsigma_{10}^4 + (Y_{21}^2 - 2Y_{20}Y_{22})\varsigma_{10}^2 + Y_{20}^2.
\end{aligned}
$$

By Equation (9), one has

$$
\begin{aligned}
\left[\frac{d\lambda}{d\tau}\right]^{-1} &= -\frac{4\lambda^3 + 3X_{23}\lambda^2 + 2X_{22}\lambda + X_{21}}{\lambda(\lambda^4 + X_{23}\lambda^3 + X_{22}\lambda^2 + X_{21}\lambda + X_{20})} \\
&\quad + \frac{3Y_{23}\lambda^2 + 2Y_{22}\lambda + Y_{21}}{\lambda(Y_{23}\lambda^3 + Y_{22}\lambda^2 + Y_{21}\lambda + Y_{20})} - \frac{\tau}{\lambda}
\end{aligned} \tag{14}
$$

Further,

$$Re\left[\frac{d\lambda}{d\tau}\right]^{-1}_{\lambda = i\varsigma_{10}} = \frac{f'(\vartheta_{10})}{E_{22}(\varsigma_{10})}, \tag{15}$$

where $f(\vartheta) = \vartheta_1^4 + D_{23}\vartheta_1^3 + D_{22}\vartheta_1^2 + D_{21}\vartheta_1 + D_{20}$ and $\vartheta_{10} = \varsigma_{10}^2$. It is apparent that if $f'(\vartheta_{10}) \neq 0$ holds, then the sufficient conditions for the appearance of a Hopf bifurcation at τ_{10} are satisfied. In conclusion, we have the following results in accordance with the Hopf bifurcation theorem in [35].

Theorem 2. *If $\Re_0 > 1$, then $E_*(S_*, P_*, H_*, T_*)$ of the model (2) is locally asymptotically stable whenever $\tau_1 \in [0, \tau_{10})$; while the model (2) exhibits a Hopf bifurcation near $E_*(S_*, P_*, H_*, T_*)$ when $\tau_1 = \tau_{10}$ and a group of periodic solutions appear around $E_*(S_*, P_*, H_*, T_*)$.*

Remark 1. *Actually, it should be pointed out that the impact of the time delay τ_1 has been analyzed in [25]. In what follows, we shall further analyze the impact of the time delay τ_2 and the combinations of the time delay τ_1 and τ_2, which has been neglected in [25].*

Case 3. $\tau_1 = 0$ and $\tau_2 > 0$, Equation (7) equals

$$\lambda^4 + X_{33}\lambda^3 + X_{32}\lambda^2 + X_{31}\lambda + X_{30} + (Z_{33}\lambda^3 + Z_{32}\lambda^2 + Z_{31}\lambda + Z_{30})e^{-\lambda\tau_2} + (B_{32}\lambda^2 + B_{31}\lambda + B_{30})e^{-2\lambda\tau_2} = 0, \tag{16}$$

with

$$\begin{aligned}X_{30} &= X_{00}+Y_{00}, X_{31}=X_{01}+Y_{01}, X_{32}=X_{02}+Y_{02}, X_{33}=X_{03}+Y_{03},\\ Z_{30} &= Z_{00}+A_{00}, Z_{31}=Z_{01}+A_{01}, Z_{32}=Z_{02}+A_{02}, Z_{33}=Z_{03},\\ B_{30} &= B_{00}+C_{00}, B_{31}=B_{01}+C_{01}, B_{32}=B_{02}.\end{aligned}$$

Multiplying by $e^{\lambda\tau_2}$ on left and right of Equation (16), then

$$Z_{33}\lambda^3+Z_{32}\lambda^2+Z_{31}\lambda+Z_{30}+(\lambda^4+X_{33}\lambda^3+X_{32}\lambda^2+X_{31}\lambda+X_{30})e^{\lambda\tau_2}+(B_{32}\lambda^2+B_{31}\lambda+B_{30})e^{-\lambda\tau_2}=0. \tag{17}$$

Let $\lambda = i\varsigma_2(\varsigma_2>0)$ be a root of Equation (17), then

$$\begin{cases} W_{31}(\varsigma_2)\cos(\tau_2\varsigma_2)-W_{32}(\varsigma_2)\sin(\tau_2\varsigma_2)=W_{33}(\varsigma_2),\\ W_{34}(\varsigma_2)\sin(\tau_2\varsigma_2)+W_{35}(\varsigma_2)\cos(\tau_2\varsigma_2)=W_{36}(\varsigma_2),\end{cases} \tag{18}$$

where

$$\begin{aligned}W_{31}(\varsigma_2) &= \varsigma_2^4-(X_{32}+B_{32})\varsigma_2^2+X_{30}+B_{30},\\ W_{32}(\varsigma_2) &= (X_{31}-B_{31})\varsigma_2-X_{33}\varsigma_2^3,\\ W_{33}(\varsigma_2) &= Z_{32}\varsigma_2^2-Z_{30},\\ W_{34}(\varsigma_2) &= \varsigma_2^4-(X_{32}-B_{32})\varsigma_2^2+X_{30}-B_{30},\\ W_{35}(\varsigma_2) &= (X_{31}+B_{31})\varsigma_2-X_{33}\varsigma_2^3,\\ W_{36}(\varsigma_2) &= Z_{33}\varsigma_2^3-Z_{31}\varsigma_2.\end{aligned}$$

Then, one has

$$\cos(\tau_2\varsigma_2)=\frac{E_{31}(\varsigma_2)}{E_{33}(\varsigma_2)}, \sin(\tau_2\varsigma_2)=\frac{E_{32}(\varsigma_2)}{E_{33}(\varsigma_2)},$$

with

$$\begin{aligned}E_{31}(\varsigma_2) &= (Z_{32}-X_{33}Z_{33})\varsigma_2^6+[Z_{33}(X_{31}-B_{31})+X_{33}Z_{31}-Z_{32}(X_{32}-B_{32})-Z_{30}]\varsigma_2^4\\ &\quad +[Z_{30}(X_{32}-B_{32})-Z_{31}(X_{31}-B_{31})]\varsigma_2^2-Z_{30}(X_{30}-B_{30}),\\ E_{32}(\varsigma_2) &= \varsigma_2^7+[X_{33}Z_{32}-Z_{31}-Z_{33}(X_{32}+B_{32})]\varsigma_2^5\\ &\quad +[Z_{33}(X_{30}+B_{30})+Z_{31}(X_{32}+B_{32})-Z_{32}(X_{31}+B_{31})-X_{33}Z_{30}]\varsigma_2^3\\ &\quad +[Z_{30}(X_{31}+B_{31})-Z_{31}(X_{30}+B_{30})]\varsigma_2,\\ E_{33}(\varsigma_2) &= \varsigma_2^8+(X_{33}^2-2X_{32})\varsigma_2^6+(X_{32}^2+2X_{30}-B_{32}^2-2X_{31}X_{33})\varsigma_2^4\\ &\quad +(2B_{30}B_{32}-2X_{30}X_{32}+X_{31}^2-B_{31}^2)\varsigma_2^2+X_{30}^2-B_{30}^2.\end{aligned}$$

Then, one can obtain the following relation about ς_2

$$E_{33}^2(\varsigma_2)-E_{31}^2(\varsigma_2)-E_{32}^2(\varsigma_2)=0. \tag{19}$$

It can be concluded that if we know all the values of parameters in the model (2), then all the roots of Equation (19) can be obtained with the help of Matlab software package. Therefore, we suppose that Equation (19) has at least one positive root ς_{20} such that Equation (17) has a pair of purely imaginary roots $\pm i\varsigma_{20}$. For ς_{20}, we have

$$\tau_{20}=\frac{1}{\varsigma_{20}}\times\arccos\left[\frac{E_{31}(\varsigma_{20})}{E_{33}(\varsigma_{20})}\right]. \tag{20}$$

Differentiating Equation (17) with respect to τ_2,

$$[\frac{d\lambda}{d\tau_2}]^{-1}=-\frac{U_{31}(\lambda)}{U_{32}(\lambda)}-\frac{\tau_2}{\lambda}, \tag{21}$$

where

$$\begin{aligned}
U_{31}(\lambda) &= 3Z_{33}\lambda^2 + 2Z_{32}\lambda + Z_{31} + (2B_{32}\lambda + B_{31})e^{-\lambda\tau_2} \\
&\quad + (4\lambda^3 + 3X_{33}\lambda^2 + 2X_{32}\lambda + X_{31})e^{\lambda\tau_2}, \\
U_{32}(\lambda) &= (\lambda^5 + X_{33}\lambda^4 + X_{32}\lambda^3 + X_{31}\lambda^2 + X_{30}\lambda)e^{\lambda\tau_2} \\
&\quad -(B_{32}\lambda^3 + B_{31}\lambda^2 + B_{30}\lambda)e^{-\lambda\tau_2}.
\end{aligned}$$

Thus,

$$Re[\frac{d\lambda}{d\tau_2}]^{-1}_{\lambda=i\varsigma_{20}} = \frac{\Xi_{31}\Pi_{31} + \Xi_{32}\Pi_{32}}{\Pi_{31}^2 + \Pi_{32}^2}, \tag{22}$$

with

$$\begin{aligned}
\Xi_{31} &= Z_{31} - 3Z_{33}\varsigma_{20}^2 + 2B_{32}\varsigma_{20}\sin(\tau_{20}\varsigma_{20}) + B_{31}\cos(\tau_{20}\varsigma_{20}) \\
&\quad + (X_{31} - 3X_{33}\varsigma_{20}^2)\cos(\tau_{20}\varsigma_{20}) - (2X_{32}\varsigma_{20} - 4\varsigma_{20}^3)\sin(\tau_{20}\varsigma_{20}), \\
\Xi_{32} &= 2Z_{32}\varsigma_{20} + 2B_{32}\varsigma_{20}\cos(\tau_{20}\varsigma_{20}) - B_{31}\sin(\tau_{20}\varsigma_{20}) \\
&\quad + (X_{31} - 3X_{33}\varsigma_{20}^2)\sin(\tau_{20}\varsigma_{20}) + (2X_{32}\varsigma_{20} - 4\varsigma_{20}^3)\cos(\tau_{20}\varsigma_{20}), \\
\Pi_{31} &= (X_{33}\varsigma_{20}^4 - X_{31}\varsigma_{20}^2)\cos(\tau_{20}\varsigma_{20}) - (\varsigma_{20}^5 - X_{32}\varsigma_{20}^3 + X_{30}\varsigma_{20})\sin(\tau_{20}\varsigma_{20}) \\
&\quad + (B_{32}\varsigma_{20}^3 - B_{30}\varsigma_{20})\sin(\tau_{20}\varsigma_{20}) + B_{31}\varsigma_{20}^2\cos(\tau_{20}\varsigma_{20}), \\
\Pi_{32} &= (X_{33}\varsigma_{20}^4 - X_{31}\varsigma_{20}^2)\sin(\tau_{20}\varsigma_{20}) + (\varsigma_{20}^5 - X_{32}\varsigma_{20}^3 + X_{30}\varsigma_{20})\cos(\tau_{20}\varsigma_{20}) \\
&\quad + (B_{32}\varsigma_{20}^3 - B_{30}\varsigma_{20})\cos(\tau_{20}\varsigma_{20}) - B_{31}\varsigma_{20}^2\sin(\tau_{20}\varsigma_{20}).
\end{aligned}$$

Therefore, if $\Xi_{31}\Pi_{31} + \Xi_{32}\Pi_{32} \neq 0$ then $Re[\frac{d\lambda}{d\tau_2}]^{-1}_{\lambda=i\varsigma_{20}} \neq 0$. In conclusion, we have the following theorem.

Theorem 3. *If $\Re_0 > 1$, then $E_*(S_*, P_*, H_*, T_*)$ of the model (2) is locally asymptotically stable whenever $\tau_2 \in [0, \tau_{20})$; while the model (2) exhibits a Hopf bifurcation near $E_*(S_*, P_*, H_*, T_*)$ when $\tau_2 = \tau_{20}$ and a group of periodic solutions appear around $E_*(S_*, P_*, H_*, T_*)$.*

Case 4. $\tau_1 > 0$ and $\tau_2 \in (0, \tau_{20})$. Let $\lambda = i\varsigma_1$ be a root of Equation (7), then

$$\begin{cases} W_{41}(\varsigma_1)\sin(\tau_1\varsigma_1) + W_{42}(\varsigma_1)\cos(\tau_1\varsigma_1) = W_{43}(\varsigma_1), \\ W_{41}(\varsigma_1)\cos(\tau_1\varsigma_1) - W_{42}(\varsigma_1)\sin(\tau_1\varsigma_1) = W_{44}(\varsigma_1), \end{cases} \tag{23}$$

where

$$\begin{aligned}
W_{41}(\varsigma_1) &= Y_{01}\varsigma_1 - Y_{03}\varsigma_1^3 + A_{01}\varsigma_1\cos(\tau_2\varsigma_1) - (A_{00} - A_{02}\varsigma_1^2)\sin(\tau_2\varsigma_1) \\
&\quad + C_{01}\varsigma_1\cos(2\tau_2\varsigma) - C_{00}\sin(2\tau_2\varsigma), \\
W_{42}(\varsigma_1) &= Y_{00} - Y_{02}\varsigma_1^2 + A_{01}\varsigma_1\sin(\tau_2\varsigma_1) + (A_{00} - A_{02}\varsigma_1^2)\cos(\tau_2\varsigma_1) \\
&\quad + C_{01}\varsigma_1\sin(2\tau_2\varsigma) + C_{00}\cos(2\tau_2\varsigma), \\
W_{43}(\varsigma_1) &= X_{02}\varsigma_1^2 - \varsigma_1^4 - X_{00} + (Z_{03}\varsigma_1^3 - Z_{01}\varsigma_1)\sin(\tau_2\varsigma_1) + (Z_{02}\varsigma_1^2 - Z_{00})\cos(\tau_2\varsigma_1) \\
&\quad - B_{01}\varsigma_1\sin(2\tau_2\varsigma_1) + (B_{02}\varsigma_1^2 - B_{00})\cos(2\tau_2\varsigma_1), \\
W_{44}(\varsigma_1) &= X_{03}\varsigma_1^3 - X_{01}\varsigma_1 + (Z_{03}\varsigma_1^3 - Z_{01}\varsigma_1)\cos(\tau_2\varsigma_1) - (Z_{02}\varsigma_1^2 - Z_{00})\sin(\tau_2\varsigma_1) \\
&\quad - B_{01}\varsigma_1\cos(2\tau_2\varsigma_1) - (B_{02}\varsigma_1^2 - B_{00})\sin(2\tau_2\varsigma_1).
\end{aligned}$$

Based on Equation (23), we obtain

$$\cos(\tau_1\varsigma_1) = \frac{E_{41}(\varsigma_1)}{E_{43}(\varsigma_1)}, \sin(\tau_1\varsigma_1) = \frac{E_{42}(\varsigma_1)}{E_{43}(\varsigma_1)},$$

where

$$\begin{aligned}
E_{41}(\varsigma_1) &= W_{41}(\varsigma_1)W_{44}(\varsigma_1) + W_{42}(\varsigma_1)W_{43}(\varsigma_1), \\
E_{42}(\varsigma_1) &= W_{41}(\varsigma_1)W_{43}(\varsigma_1) - W_{42}(\varsigma_1)W_{44}(\varsigma_1), \\
E_{43}(\varsigma_1) &= W_{41}^2(\varsigma_1) + W_{42}^2(\varsigma_1).
\end{aligned}$$

Then, we have the following relation about ς_1

$$E_{43}^2(\varsigma_1) - E_{41}^2(\varsigma_1) - E_{42}^2(\varsigma_1) = 0. \tag{24}$$

Similarly, we suppose that Equation (24) has at least one positive root ς_{1*} such that Equation (7) has a pair of purely imaginary roots $\pm i\varsigma_{1*}$. For ς_{1*}, we have

$$\tau_{1*} = \frac{1}{\varsigma_{1*}} \times \arccos\left[\frac{E_{41}(\varsigma_{1*})}{E_{43}(\varsigma_{1*})}\right]. \tag{25}$$

Differentiating Equation (7) with respect to τ_1, we have

$$[\frac{d\lambda}{d\tau_1}]^{-1} = \frac{U_{41}(\lambda)}{U_{42}(\lambda)} - \frac{\tau_1}{\lambda}, \tag{26}$$

where

$$\begin{aligned}
U_{41}(\lambda) &= 4\lambda^3 + 3X_{03}\lambda^2 + 2X_{02}\lambda + X_{01} + (3Y_{03}\lambda^2 + 2Y_{02}\lambda + Y_{01})e^{-\lambda\tau_1} \\
&\quad +(-\tau_2 Z_{03}\lambda^3 + (3Z_{03} - \tau_2 Z_{02})\lambda^2 + (2Z_{02} - \tau_2 Z_{01})\lambda + Z_{01} - \tau_2 Z_{00})e^{-\lambda\tau_2} \\
&\quad +(-\tau_2 A_{02}\lambda^2 + (2A_{02} - \tau_2 A_{01})\lambda + A_{01} - \tau_2 A_{00})e^{-\lambda(\tau_1+\tau_2)} \\
&\quad +(-2\tau_2 B_{02}\lambda^2 + (2B_{02} - 2\tau_2 B_{01})\lambda + B_{01} - 2\tau_2 B_{00})e^{-2\lambda\tau_2} \\
&\quad +(-2\tau_2 C_{01}\lambda + C_{01} - 2\tau_2 C_{00})e^{-\lambda(\tau_1+2\tau_2)}, \\
U_{42}(\lambda) &= (Y_{03}\lambda^4 + Y_{02}\lambda^3 + Y_{01}\lambda^2 + Y_{00}\lambda)e^{-\lambda\tau_1} \\
&\quad +(A_{02}\lambda^3 + A_{01}\lambda^2 + A_{00}\lambda)e^{-\lambda(\tau_1+\tau_2)} + (C_{01}\lambda^2 + C_{00}\lambda)e^{-\lambda(\tau_1+2\tau_2)}.
\end{aligned}$$

Further

$$Re[\frac{d\lambda}{d\tau_1}]^{-1}_{\lambda=i\varsigma_{1*}} = \frac{\Xi_{41}\Pi_{41} + \Xi_{42}\Pi_{42}}{\Pi_{41}^2 + \Pi_{42}^2}, \tag{27}$$

with

$$\begin{aligned}
\Xi_{41} &= X_{01} - 3X_{03}\varsigma_{1*}^2 + Y_{02}\varsigma_{1*}\sin(\tau_{1*}\varsigma_{1*}) + (Y_{01} - 3Y_{03}\varsigma_{1*}^2)\cos(\tau_{1*}\varsigma_{1*}) \\
&\quad +((2Z_{02} - \tau_2 Z_{01})\varsigma_{1*} + \tau_2 Z_{03}\varsigma_{1*}^3)\sin(\tau_2\varsigma_{1*}) \\
&\quad +(Z_{01} - \tau_2 Z_{00} - (3Z_{03} - \tau_2 Z_{02})\varsigma_{1*}^2)\cos(\tau_2\varsigma_{1*}) \\
&\quad +(2A_{02} - \tau_2 A_{01})\varsigma_{1*}\sin((\tau_{1*} + \tau_2)\varsigma_{1*}) \\
&\quad +(\tau_2 A_{02}\varsigma_{1*}^2 + A_{01} - \tau_2 A_{00})\cos((\tau_{1*} + \tau_2)\varsigma_{1*}) \\
&\quad +2(B_{02} - \tau_2 B_{01})\varsigma_{1*}\sin(2\tau_2\varsigma_{1*}) + (2\tau_2 B_{02}\varsigma_{1*}^2 + B_{01} - 2\tau_2 B_{00})\cos(2\tau_2\varsigma_{1*}) \\
&\quad -2\tau_2 C_{01}\varsigma_{1*}\sin((\tau_{1*} + 2\tau_2)\varsigma_{1*}) + (C_{01} - 2\tau_2 C_{00})\cos((\tau_{1*} + 2\tau_2)\varsigma_{1*}), \\
\Xi_{42} &= 2X_{02}\varsigma_{1*} - 4\varsigma_{1*}^3 + Y_{02}\varsigma_{1*}\cos(\tau_{1*}\varsigma_{1*}) - (Y_{01} - 3Y_{03}\varsigma_{1*}^2)\cos(\tau_{1*}\varsigma_{1*}) \\
&\quad +((2Z_{02} - \tau_2 Z_{01})\varsigma_{1*} + \tau_2 Z_{03}\varsigma_{1*}^3)\cos(\tau_2\varsigma_{1*}) \\
&\quad -(Z_{01} - \tau_2 Z_{00} - (3Z_{03} - \tau_2 Z_{02})\varsigma_{1*}^2)\sin(\tau_2\varsigma_{1*}) \\
&\quad +(2A_{02} - \tau_2 A_{01})\varsigma_{1*}\cos((\tau_{1*} + \tau_2)\varsigma_{1*}) \\
&\quad -(\tau_2 A_{02}\varsigma_{1*}^2 + A_{01} - \tau_2 A_{00})\sin((\tau_{1*} + \tau_2)\varsigma_{1*}) \\
&\quad +2(B_{02} - \tau_2 B_{01})\varsigma_{1*}\cos(2\tau_2\varsigma_{1*}) - (2\tau_2 B_{02}\varsigma_{1*}^2 + B_{01} - 2\tau_2 B_{00})\sin(2\tau_2\varsigma_{1*}) \\
&\quad -2\tau_2 C_{01}\varsigma_{1*}\cos((\tau_{1*} + 2\tau_2)\varsigma_{1*}) - (C_{01} - 2\tau_2 C_{00})\sin((\tau_{1*} + 2\tau_2)\varsigma_{1*}), \\
\Pi_{41} &= (Y_{00}\varsigma_{1*} - Y_{02}\varsigma_{1*}^3)\sin(\tau_{1*}\varsigma_{1*}) + (Y_{03}\varsigma_{1*}^4 - Y_{01}\varsigma_{1*}^2)\cos(\tau_{1*}\varsigma_{1*}) \\
&\quad +(A_{00}\varsigma_{1*} - A_{02}\varsigma_{1*}^3)\sin((\tau_{1*} + \tau_2)\varsigma_{1*}) - A_{01}\varsigma_{1*}^2\cos((\tau_{1*} + \tau_2)\varsigma_{1*}) \\
&\quad +C_{00}\varsigma_{1*}\sin((\tau_{1*} + 2\tau_2)\varsigma_{1*}) - C_{01}\varsigma_{1*}^2\cos((\tau_{1*} + 2\tau_2)\varsigma_{1*}), \\
\Pi_{42} &= (Y_{00}\varsigma_{1*} - Y_{02}\varsigma_{1*}^3)\cos(\tau_{1*}\varsigma_{1*}) - (Y_{03}\varsigma_{1*}^4 - Y_{01}\varsigma_{1*}^2)\sin(\tau_{1*}\varsigma_{1*}) \\
&\quad +(A_{00}\varsigma_{1*} - A_{02}\varsigma_{1*}^3)\cos((\tau_{1*} + \tau_2)\varsigma_{1*}) + A_{01}\varsigma_{1*}^2\sin((\tau_{1*} + \tau_2)\varsigma_{1*}) \\
&\quad +C_{00}\varsigma_{1*}\cos((\tau_{1*} + 2\tau_2)\varsigma_{1*}) + C_{01}\varsigma_{1*}^2\sin((\tau_{1*} + 2\tau_2)\varsigma_{1*}).
\end{aligned}$$

Clearly, if $\Xi_{41}\Pi_{41} + \Xi_{42}\Pi_{42} \neq 0$ then $Re[\frac{d\lambda}{d\tau_1}]^{-1}_{\lambda=i\varsigma_{1*}} \neq 0$. Then, we have the following theorem.

Theorem 4. *If $\Re_0 > 1$ and $\tau_2 \in (0, \tau_{20})$, then $E_*(S_*, P_*, H_*, T_*)$ of the model (2) is locally asymptotically stable whenever $\tau_1 \in [0, \tau_{1*})$; while the model (2) exhibits a Hopf bifurcation near $E_*(S_*, P_*, H_*, T_*)$ when $\tau_1 = \tau_{1*}$ and a group of periodic solutions appear around $E_*(S_*, P_*, H_*, T_*)$.*

Case 5. $\tau_1 \in (0, \tau_{10})$ and $\tau_2 > 0$. Multiplying $e^{\lambda\tau}$ on both sides of Equation (7), one can find

$$\begin{aligned} Z_{03}\lambda^3 &+ Z_{02}\lambda^2 + Z_{01}\lambda + Z_{00} \\ &+ (B_{02}\lambda^2 + B_{01}\lambda + B_{00})e^{-\lambda\tau_2} \\ &+ (\lambda^4 + X_{03}\lambda^3 + X_{02}\lambda^2 + X_{01}\lambda + X_{00})e^{\lambda\tau_2} \\ &+ (Y_{03}\lambda^3 + Y_{02}\lambda^2 + Y_{01}\lambda + Y_{00})e^{\lambda(\tau_2-\tau_1)} \\ &+ (A_{02}\lambda^2 + A_{01}\lambda + A_{00})e^{-\lambda\tau_1} \\ &+ (C_{01}\lambda + C_{00})e^{-\lambda(\tau_1+\tau_2)} = 0, \end{aligned} \tag{28}$$

Let $\lambda = i\varsigma_2$ be a root of Equation (7), then

$$\begin{cases} W_{51}(\varsigma_2)\sin(\tau_2\varsigma_2) + W_{52}(\varsigma_2)\cos(\tau_2\varsigma_2) = W_{53}(\varsigma_2), \\ W_{54}(\varsigma_2)\cos(\tau_2\varsigma_2) + W_{55}(\varsigma_2)\sin(\tau_2\varsigma_2) = W_{56}(\varsigma_2), \end{cases} \tag{29}$$

where

$$\begin{aligned} W_{51}(\varsigma_2) &= X_{03}\varsigma_2^3 + (B_{01} - X_{01})\varsigma_2 - (Y_{01}\varsigma_2 - Y_{03}\varsigma_2^3)\cos(\tau_1\varsigma_2) \\ &\quad + (Y_{00} - Y_{02}\varsigma_2^2)\sin(\tau_1\varsigma_2) + C_{01}\varsigma_2\cos(\tau_1\varsigma_2) - C_{00}\sin(\tau_1\varsigma_2), \\ W_{52}(\varsigma_2) &= \varsigma_2^4 - (B_{02} + X_{02})\varsigma_2^2 + B_{00} + X_{00} + (Y_{01}\varsigma_2 - Y_{03}\varsigma_2^3)\sin(\tau_1\varsigma_2) \\ &\quad + (Y_{00} - Y_{02}\varsigma_2^2)\cos(\tau_1\varsigma_2) + C_{01}\varsigma_2\sin(\tau_1\varsigma_2) + C_{00}\cos(\tau_1\varsigma_2), \\ W_{53}(\varsigma_2) &= Z_{02}\varsigma_2^2 - Z_{00} - A_{01}\varsigma_2\sin(\tau_1\varsigma_2) - (A_{00} - A_{02}\varsigma_2^2)\cos(\tau_1\varsigma_2), \\ W_{54}(\varsigma_2) &= (B_{01} + X_{01})\varsigma_2 - X_{03}\varsigma_2^3 + (Y_{01}\varsigma_2 - Y_{03}\varsigma_2^3)\cos(\tau_1\varsigma_2) \\ &\quad - (Y_{00} - Y_{02}\varsigma_2^2)\sin(\tau_1\varsigma_2) + C_{01}\varsigma_2\cos(\tau_1\varsigma_2) - C_{00}\sin(\tau_1\varsigma_2), \\ W_{55}(\varsigma_2) &= \varsigma_2^4 + (B_{02} - X_{02})\varsigma_2^2 - B_{00} + X_{00} + (Y_{01}\varsigma_2 - Y_{03}\varsigma_2^3)\sin(\tau_1\varsigma_2) \\ &\quad + (Y_{00} - Y_{02}\varsigma_2^2)\cos(\tau_1\varsigma_2) - C_{01}\varsigma_2\sin(\tau_1\varsigma_2) - C_{00}\cos(\tau_1\varsigma_2), \\ W_{56}(\varsigma_2) &= Z_{03}\varsigma_2^3 - Z_{01}\varsigma_2 - A_{01}\varsigma_2\cos(\tau_1\varsigma_2) + (A_{00} - A_{02}\varsigma_2^2)\sin(\tau_1\varsigma_2). \end{aligned}$$

Accordingly, one has

$$\cos(\tau_2\varsigma_2) = \frac{E_{51}(\varsigma_2)}{E_{53}(\varsigma_2)}, \sin(\tau_2\varsigma_2) = \frac{E_{51}(\varsigma_2)}{E_{53}(\varsigma_2)},$$

with

$$\begin{aligned} E_{51}(\varsigma_2) &= W_{51}(\varsigma_2)W_{56}(\varsigma_2) - W_{53}(\varsigma_2)W_{55}(\varsigma_2), \\ E_{52}(\varsigma_2) &= W_{53}(\varsigma_2)W_{54}(\varsigma_2) - W_{52}(\varsigma_2)W_{56}(\varsigma_2), \\ E_{53}(\varsigma_2) &= W_{51}(\varsigma_2)W_{54}(\varsigma_2) - W_{52}(\varsigma_2)W_{55}(\varsigma_2). \end{aligned}$$

Then, one has

$$E_{53}^2(\varsigma_1) - E_{51}^2(\varsigma_1) - E_{52}^2(\varsigma_1) = 0. \tag{30}$$

Next, we suppose that Equation (30) has at least one positive root ς_{2*} such that Equation (28) has a pair of purely imaginary roots $\pm i\varsigma_{2*}$. For ς_{2*}, we have

$$\tau_{2*} = \frac{1}{\varsigma_{2*}} \times \arccos\left[\frac{E_{51}(\varsigma_{2*})}{E_{53}(\varsigma_{2*})}\right]. \tag{31}$$

Differentiating Equation (28) regarding τ_2 and substituting $\lambda = i\varsigma_{2*}$, we have

$$Re[\frac{d\lambda}{d\tau_2}]^{-1}_{\lambda=i\varsigma_{2*}} = \frac{\Xi_{51}\Pi_{51} + \Xi_{52}\Pi_{52}}{\Pi_{51}^2 + \Pi_{52}^2}, \tag{32}$$

where

$$\begin{aligned}
\Xi_{51} &= Z_{01} - 3Z_{03}\varsigma_{2*}^2 + 2B_{02}\varsigma_{2*}\sin(\tau_{2*}\varsigma_{2*}) + B_{01}\cos(\tau_{2*}\varsigma_{2*}) \\
&\quad +(X_{01} - 3X_{03}\varsigma_{2*}^2)\cos(\tau_{2*}\varsigma_{2*}) - (2X_{02}\varsigma_{2*} - 4\varsigma_{2*}^3)\sin(\tau_{2*}\varsigma_{2*}) \\
&\quad +(Y_{01} - \tau_1 - (3Y_{03} - \tau_1 Y_{02})\varsigma_{2*}^2)\cos((\tau_{2*} - \tau_1)\varsigma_{2*}) \\
&\quad -((2Y_{02} - \tau_1 Y_{01})\varsigma_{2*} + \tau_1 Y_{03}\varsigma_{2*}^3)\sin((\tau_{2*} - \tau_1)\varsigma_{2*}) \\
&\quad +(2A_{02} - \tau_1 A_{01})\varsigma_{2*}\sin(\tau_{2*}\varsigma_{2*}) + (\tau_1 A_{02}\varsigma_{2*}^2 + A_{01} - \tau_1 A_{00})\cos(\tau_{2*}\varsigma_{2*}) \\
&\quad +(C_{01} - \tau_1 C_{00})\cos((\tau_1 + \tau_{2*})\varsigma_{2*}) - \tau_1 C_{01}\varsigma_{2*}\sin((\tau_1 + \tau_{2*})\varsigma_{2*}), \\
\Xi_{52} &= 2Z_{02}\varsigma_{2*} + 2B_{02}\varsigma_{2*}\cos(\tau_{2*}\varsigma_{2*}) - B_{01}\sin(\tau_{2*}\varsigma_{2*}) \\
&\quad +(X_{01} - 3X_{03}\varsigma_{2*}^2)\sin(\tau_{2*}\varsigma_{2*}) + (2X_{02}\varsigma_{2*} - 4\varsigma_{2*}^3)\cos(\tau_{2*}\varsigma_{2*}) \\
&\quad +(Y_{01} - \tau_1 - (3Y_{03} - \tau_1 Y_{02})\varsigma_{2*}^2)\sin((\tau_{2*} - \tau_1)\varsigma_{2*}) \\
&\quad +((2Y_{02} - \tau_1 Y_{01})\varsigma_{2*} + \tau_1 Y_{03}\varsigma_{2*}^3)\cos((\tau_{2*} - \tau_1)\varsigma_{2*}) \\
&\quad +(2A_{02} - \tau_1 A_{01})\varsigma_{2*}\cos(\tau_{2*}\varsigma_{2*}) - (\tau_1 A_{02}\varsigma_{2*}^2 + A_{01} - \tau_1 A_{00})\sin(\tau_{2*}\varsigma_{2*}) \\
&\quad -(C_{01} - \tau_1 C_{00})\sin((\tau_1 + \tau_{2*})\varsigma_{2*}) - \tau_1 C_{01}\varsigma_{2*}\cos((\tau_1 + \tau_{2*})\varsigma_{2*}), \\
\Pi_{51} &= (X_{03}\varsigma_{2*}^4 - X_{01}\varsigma_{2*}^2)\cos(\tau_{2*}\varsigma_{2*}) * -(\varsigma_{2*}^5 - X_{02}\varsigma_{2*}^3 + X_{00}\varsigma_{2*})\sin(\tau_{2*}\varsigma_{2*}) \\
&\quad +(Y_{03}\varsigma_{2*}^4 - Y_{01}\varsigma_{2*}^2)\cos((\tau_{2*} - \tau_1)\varsigma_{2*}) - (Y_{00}\varsigma_{2*} - Y_{02}\varsigma_{2*}^3)\sin((\tau_{2*} - \tau_1)\varsigma_{2*}) \\
&\quad +(B_{02}\varsigma_{2*}^3 - B_{00}\varsigma_{2*})\sin(\tau_{2*}\varsigma_{2*}) + B_{01}\varsigma_{2*}^2\cos(\tau_{2*}\varsigma_{2*}) \\
&\quad +C_{00}\varsigma_{2*}\sin((\tau_1 + \tau_{2*})\varsigma_{2*}) + C_{01}\varsigma_{2*}^2\cos((\tau_1 + \tau_{2*})\varsigma_{2*}), \\
\Pi_{52} &= (X_{03}\varsigma_{2*}^4 - X_{01}\varsigma_{2*}^2)\sin(\tau_{2*}\varsigma_{2*}) * +(\varsigma_{2*}^5 - X_{02}\varsigma_{2*}^3 + X_{00}\varsigma_{2*})\cos(\tau_{2*}\varsigma_{2*}) \\
&\quad +(Y_{03}\varsigma_{2*}^4 - Y_{01}\varsigma_{2*}^2)\sin((\tau_{2*} - \tau_1)\varsigma_{2*}) + (Y_{00}\varsigma_{2*} - Y_{02}\varsigma_{2*}^3)\cos((\tau_{2*} - \tau_1)\varsigma_{2*}) \\
&\quad +(B_{02}\varsigma_{2*}^3 - B_{00}\varsigma_{2*})\cos(\tau_{2*}\varsigma_{2*}) - B_{01}\varsigma_{2*}^2\sin(\tau_{2*}\varsigma_{2*}) \\
&\quad +C_{00}\varsigma_{2*}\cos((\tau_1 + \tau_{2*})\varsigma_{2*}) - C_{01}\varsigma_{2*}^2\sin((\tau_1 + \tau_{2*})\varsigma_{2*}).
\end{aligned}$$

Then, we can see that if $\Xi_{51}\Pi_{51} + \Xi_{52}\Pi_{52} \neq 0$ then $Re[\frac{d\lambda}{d\tau_2}]^{-1}_{\lambda=i\varsigma_{2*}} \neq 0$. Thus, we have the following theorem.

Theorem 5. *If $\Re_0 > 1$ and $\tau_1 \in (0, \tau_{10})$, then $E_*(S_*, P_*, H_*, T_*)$ of the model (2) is locally asymptotically stable whenever $\tau_2 \in [0, \tau_{2*})$; while the model (2) exhibits a Hopf bifurcation near $E_*(S_*, P_*, H_*, T_*)$ when $\tau_2 = \tau_{2*}$ and a group of periodic solutions appear around $E_*(S_*, P_*, H_*, T_*)$.*

4. Stability of the Periodic Solutions

In this section, we examine direction and stability of the Hopf bifurcation at τ_{2*} for the case $\tau_1 \in (0, \tau_{10})$ and $\tau_2 > 0$. Denote $v_1(t) = S(t) - S_*$, $v_2(t) = P(t) - P_*$, $v_3(t) = H(t) - H_*$, $v_4(t) = T(t) - T_*$, $\tau_2 = \tau_{2*} + \mu$ and $t \to (t/\tau_2)$. Suppose that $\tau_{10*} \in (0, \tau_{10}) < \tau_{2*}$ in this section. Thus, the model system (2) becomes Equation (33) in $C = C([-1, 0], R^4)$:

$$\dot{v}(t) = L_\mu(v_t) + F(\mu, v_t), \tag{33}$$

where

$$L_\mu\phi = (\tau_{2*} + \mu)\Big(L_1\phi(0) + L_2\phi(-\frac{\tau_{10*}}{\tau_{2*}}) + L_3\phi(-1)\Big), \tag{34}$$

and

$$F(\mu,\phi)=\begin{pmatrix}-\beta_1\phi_1(0)\phi_2(0)-\beta_2\phi_2(0)\phi_3(0)\\ \beta_1\phi_1(0)\phi_2(0)+\beta_2\phi_2(0)\phi_3(0)\\ 0\\ 0\end{pmatrix}, \tag{35}$$

with

$$L_1=\begin{pmatrix}x_{11}&x_{12}&x_{13}&0\\ x_{21}&x_{22}&x_{23}&0\\ 0&x_{32}&x_{33}&0\\ 0&0&0&x_{44}\end{pmatrix}, L_2=\begin{pmatrix}0&0&0&0\\ 0&0&0&0\\ 0&0&0&y_{34}\\ 0&0&0&y_{44}\end{pmatrix}, L_3=\begin{pmatrix}0&0&0&0\\ 0&z_{22}&0&0\\ 0&0&z_{33}&0\\ 0&z_{42}&z_{43}&0\end{pmatrix}.$$

Thus, there exists η function of ω and μ for $\omega\in[-1,0]$ fulfills

$$L_\mu\phi=\int_{-1}^{0}d\eta(\omega,\mu)\phi(\omega). \tag{36}$$

In fact,

$$\eta(\omega,\mu)=(\tau_{2*}+\mu)\begin{cases}(L_1+L_2+L_3), & \omega=0,\\ (L_2+L_3), & \omega\in[-\frac{\tau_{10*}}{\tau_{2*}},0),\\ L_2, & \omega\in(-1,-\frac{\tau_{10*}}{\tau_{2*}}),\\ 0, & \omega=-1,\end{cases} \tag{37}$$

For $\phi\in C([-1,0],R^4)$,

$$A(\mu)\phi=\begin{cases}\frac{d\phi(\omega)}{d\omega}, & -1\le\theta<0,\\ \int_{-1}^{0}d\eta(\omega,\mu)\phi(\omega), & \theta=0,\end{cases} \tag{38}$$

$$R(\mu)\phi=\begin{cases}0, & -1\le\omega<0,\\ F(\mu,\phi), & \omega=0,\end{cases} \tag{39}$$

Then system (33) equals

$$\dot{v}(t)=A(\mu)v_t+R(\mu)v_t. \tag{40}$$

For $\xi\in C^1([0,1],(R^4)^*)$,

$$A^*(\xi)=\begin{cases}-\frac{d\xi(s)}{ds}, & 0<s\le1,\\ \int_{-1}^{0}d\eta^T(s,0)\xi(-s), & s=0,\end{cases} \tag{41}$$

and

$$\langle\xi(s),\phi(\omega)\rangle=\bar{\xi}(0)\phi(0)-\int_{\omega=-1}^{0}\int_{\chi=0}^{\omega}\bar{\xi}(\chi-\omega)d\eta(\omega)\phi(\chi)d\chi, \tag{42}$$

an inner product form is defined in this form with $\eta(\omega)=\eta(\omega,0)$.

Denote that $\mathrm{Y}(\omega) = (1, \mathrm{Y}_2, \mathrm{Y}_3, \mathrm{Y}_4)^T e^{i\varsigma_{2*}\tau_{2*}\omega}$ is the eigenvector of $A(0)$ related with $+i\varsigma_{2*}\tau_{2*}$ and $\mathrm{Y}^*(s) = U(1, \mathrm{Y}_2^*, \mathrm{Y}_3^*, \mathrm{Y}_4^*)^T e^{i\varsigma_{2*}\tau_{2*}s}$ is the eigenvector of $A^*(0)$ related with $-i\varsigma_{2*}\tau_{2*}$, respectively. Then,

$$\begin{aligned}
\mathrm{Y}_2 &= \frac{x_{13}x_{21} + x_{23}(i\varsigma_{2*} - x_{11})}{x_{13}(i\varsigma_{2*} - x_{22} - z_{22}e^{-i\tau_{2*}\varsigma_{2*}}) + x_{12}x_{23}}, \\
\mathrm{Y}_3 &= \frac{i\varsigma_{2*} - x_{11} - x_{12}\mathrm{Y}_2}{x_{13}}, \\
\mathrm{Y}_4 &= \frac{(z_{42}\mathrm{Y}_2 + z_{43}\mathrm{Y}_3)e^{-i\tau_{2*}\varsigma_{2*}}}{i\varsigma_{2*} - x_{44} - y_{44}e^{-i\tau_{10*}\varsigma_{2*}}}, \\
\mathrm{Y}_2^* &= -\frac{i\omega_0 + l_{11} + l_{31}v_3}{l_{21}}, \\
\mathrm{Y}_2^* &= -\frac{i\varsigma_{2*} + x_{11}}{x_{21}}, \\
\mathrm{Y}_3^* &= -\frac{x_{13} + x_{23}\mathrm{Y}_2}{i\varsigma_{2*} + x_{33} + (z_{33} + z_{43}\mathrm{Y}_*)e^{i\tau_{2*}\varsigma_{2*}}}, \\
\mathrm{Y}_4^* &= \mathrm{Y}_*\mathrm{Y}_3^*, \mathrm{Y}_* = -\frac{y_{34}e^{i\tau_{10*}\varsigma_{2*}}}{i\varsigma_{2*} + x_{44} + y_{44}e^{i\tau_{10*}\varsigma_{2*}}}.
\end{aligned}$$

In view of Equation (42), one has

$$\begin{aligned}
\bar{U} &= [1 + \mathrm{Y}_2\bar{\mathrm{Y}}_2^* + \mathrm{Y}_3\bar{\mathrm{Y}}_3^* + \mathrm{Y}_4\bar{\mathrm{Y}}_4^* + (\mathrm{Y}_3\bar{\mathrm{Y}}_3^* + \mathrm{Y}_4\bar{\mathrm{Y}}_4^*)e^{-i\tau_{10*}\varsigma_{2*}} \\
&\quad + \mathrm{Y}_2(z_{22}\bar{\mathrm{Y}}_2^* + z_{42}\bar{\mathrm{Y}}_4^*)e^{-i\tau_{2*}\varsigma_{2*}} + \mathrm{Y}_3(z_{33}\bar{\mathrm{Y}}_3^* + z_{43}\bar{\mathrm{Y}}_4^*)e^{-i\tau_{2*}\varsigma_{2*}}]^{-1}.
\end{aligned} \tag{43}$$

Next, we can get the coefficients as follows by means of the method proposed in [35]:

$$\begin{aligned}
\Psi_{20} &= 2\tau_{2*}\bar{U}(\mathrm{Y}_2^* - 1)(\beta_1\mathrm{Y}_2 + \beta_2\mathrm{Y}_3), \\
\Psi_{11} &= \tau_{2*}\bar{U}(\mathrm{Y}_2^* - 1)(2\beta_1 Re\{\mathrm{Y}_2\} + 2\beta_2 Re\{\mathrm{Y}_3\}), \\
\Psi_{02} &= \bar{g}_{20}, \\
\Psi_{21} &= 2\tau_{2*}\bar{U}(\mathrm{Y}_2^* - 1)[\beta_1(Q_{11}^{(1)}(0)\mathrm{Y}_2 + \frac{1}{2}Q_{20}^{(1)}(0)\bar{\mathrm{Y}}_2 + Q_{11}^{(2)}(0) + \frac{1}{2}Q_{20}^{(2)}(0)) \\
&\quad + \beta_2(Q_{11}^{(1)}(0)\mathrm{Y}_3 + \frac{1}{2}Q_{20}^{(1)}(0)\bar{\mathrm{Y}}_3 + Q_{11}^{(3)}(0) + \frac{1}{2}Q_{20}^{(3)}(0))],
\end{aligned} \tag{44}$$

with

$$\begin{aligned}
Q_{20}(\omega) &= \frac{i\Psi_{20}}{\varsigma_{2*}\tau_{2*}}\mathrm{Y}(\omega) + \frac{i\bar{\Psi}_{02}}{3\varsigma_{2*}\tau_{2*}}\bar{\mathrm{Y}}(\omega) + J_1 e^{2i\varsigma_{2*}\tau_{2*}\omega}, \\
Q_{11}(\omega) &= -\frac{i\Psi_{11}}{\varsigma_{2*}\tau_{2*}}V(\theta) + \frac{i\bar{\Psi}_{11}}{\varsigma_{2*}\tau_{2*}}\bar{\mathrm{Y}}(\omega) + J_2.
\end{aligned}$$

where

$$J_1 = 2\begin{pmatrix} x_{11}^* & -x_{12} & -x_{13} & 0 \\ -x_{21} & x_{22}^* & -x_{23} & 0 \\ 0 & -x_{32} & x_{33}^* & y_{34}e^{-2i\varsigma_{2*}\tau_{10*}} \\ 0 & -z_{42}e^{-2i\varsigma_{2*}\tau_{2*}} & -z_{43}e^{-2i\varsigma_{2*}\tau_{2*}} & x_{44}^* \end{pmatrix}^{-1} \times \begin{pmatrix} -(\beta_1\mathrm{Y}_2 + \beta_2\mathrm{Y}_2) \\ \beta_1\mathrm{Y}_2 + \beta_2\mathrm{Y}_2 \\ 0 \\ 0 \end{pmatrix},$$

$$J_2 = \begin{pmatrix} x_{11} & x_{12} & x_{13} & 0 \\ x_{21} & x_{22} + z_{22} & x_{23} & 0 \\ 0 & x_{32} & x_{33} + z_{33} & y_{34} \\ 0 & z_{42} & z_{33} + z_{33} & x_{44} + y_{44} \end{pmatrix}^{-1} \times \begin{pmatrix} -(2\beta_1 Re\{\mathrm{Y}_2\} + 2\beta_2 Re\{\mathrm{Y}_3\}) \\ 2\beta_1 Re\{\mathrm{Y}_2\} + 2\beta_2 Re\{\mathrm{Y}_3\} \\ 0 \\ 0 \end{pmatrix},$$

with

$$
\begin{aligned}
x_{11}^* &= 2i\varsigma_{2*} - x_{11}, \\
x_{22}^* &= 2i\varsigma_{2*} - x_{22} - z_{22}e^{-2i\varsigma_{2*}\tau_{2*}}, \\
x_{33}^* &= 2i\varsigma_{2*} - x_{33} - z_{33}e^{-2i\varsigma_{2*}\tau_{2*}}, \\
x_{44}^* &= 2i\varsigma_{2*} - x_{44} - y_{44}e^{-2i\varsigma_{2*}\tau_{10*}}
\end{aligned} \tag{45}
$$

Then,

$$
\begin{aligned}
&C_1(0) = \frac{i}{2\tau_{2*}\varsigma_{2*}}\left(\Psi_{11}\Psi_{20} - 2|\Psi_{11}|^2 - \frac{|\Psi_{02}|^2}{3}\right) + \frac{\Psi_{21}}{2} \\
&\Lambda_1 = -\frac{Re\{C_1(0)\}}{Re\{\lambda'(\tau_{2*})\}}, \\
&\Lambda_2 = 2Re\{C_1(0)\}, \\
&\Lambda_3 = -\frac{Im\{C_1(0)\} + \Lambda_1 Im\{\lambda'(\tau_{2*})\}}{\tau_{2*}\varsigma_{2*}},
\end{aligned} \tag{46}
$$

Theorem 6. *For system (2), if $\Lambda_1 > 0$, then the Hopf bifurcation at τ_{2*} is supercritical (subcritical for $\Lambda_1 < 0$); if $\Lambda_2 < 0$, then bifurcating periodic solutions showing around $E_*(S_*, P_*H_*, T_*)$ are stable (unstable for $\Lambda_2 > 0$); if $\Lambda_3 > 0$, then bifurcating periodic solutions showing at $E_*(S_*, P_*H_*, T_*)$ increase (decrease for $\Lambda_3 < 0$).*

5. Numerical Example

In this section, we shall adopt a numerical example by extracting the same values of parameters as those in [25] to certify our obtained analytical results in previous sections. Then, the following numerical example model system is obtained:

$$
\left\{
\begin{aligned}
\frac{dS(t)}{dt} &= 2 - 0.02S(t) - 0.016S(t)P(t) - 0.028S(t)H(t), \\
\frac{dP(t)}{dt} &= 0.016S(t)P(t) + 0.028S(t)H(t) - 0.05P(t) - 0.095P(t-\tau_2), \\
\frac{dH(t)}{dt} &= 0.03P(t) + 0.5T(t-\tau_1) - 0.421H(t-\tau_2) - 0.02H(t), \\
\frac{dT(t)}{dt} &= 0.095P(t-\tau_2) + 0.421H(t-\tau_2) - 0.5T(t-\tau_1) - 0.02T(t),
\end{aligned}
\right. \tag{47}
$$

from which one has $\Re_0 = 12.3481 > 1$ and the unique synthetic drug addiction equilibrium point $E_*(1.3196, 13.6111, 45.6355, 39.4338)$.

For the case when $\tau_1 > 0$ and $\tau_2 = 0$, one has $\varsigma_{10} = 1.0902$ and $\tau_{10} = 9.7367$. In line with Theorem 1, $E_*(1.3196, 13.6111, 45.6355, 39.4338)$ is locally asymptotically stable in the interval $\tau_1 \in [0, \tau_{10} = 9.7367)$. Figure 1 shows the local asymptotical stability of the model system (47). Whereas, Figure 2 shows the exhibition of a Hopf bifurcation at $\tau_{10} = 9.7367$.

For $\tau_1 = 0$ and $\tau_2 > 0$, we have $\varsigma_{20} = 1.6264$ and $\tau_{20} = 20.8839$ based on some calculations. It can be observed that the model system (47) is locally asymptotically stable around $E_*(1.3196, 13.6111, 45.6355, 39.4338)$ when $\tau_2 = 18.6934 < \tau_{20} = 20.8839$, which is depicted in Figure 3. Nevertheless, $E_*(1.3196, 13.6111, 45.6355, 39.4338)$ loses its stability and the model system (47) experiences a Hopf bifurcation as the value of τ_2 crossed τ_{20}. The loss of stability dynamics of $E_*(1.3196, 13.6111, 45.6355, 39.4338)$ for $\tau_2 = 25.9358 > \tau_{20} = 20.8839$ is shown in Figure 4.

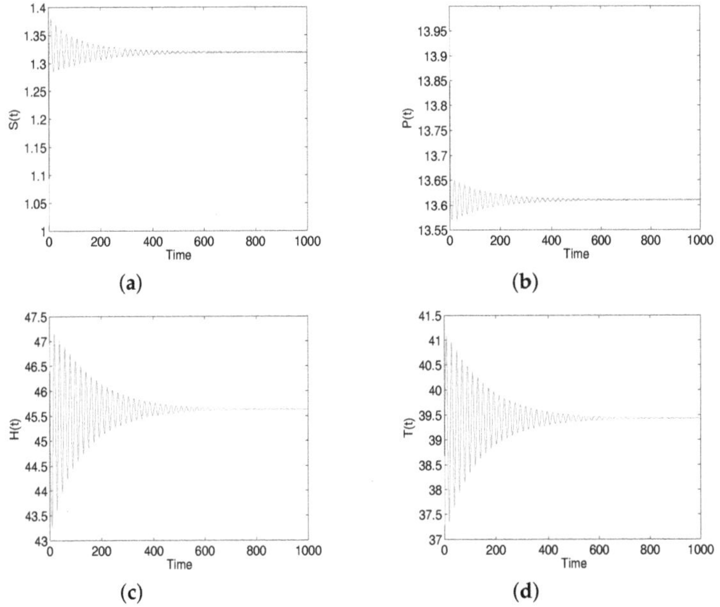

Figure 1. The time plot of (**a**) susceptible population, (**b**) psychological addicts, (**c**) physiological addicts and (**d**) drug-users in treatment for $\tau_1 = 8.2247 < \tau_{10} = 9.7367$ with $A = 2$, $d = 0.02$, $\beta_1 = 0.016$, $\beta_2 = 0.028$, $\pi = 0.03$, $\gamma = 0.095$, $\theta = 0.5$ and $\sigma = 0.21$.

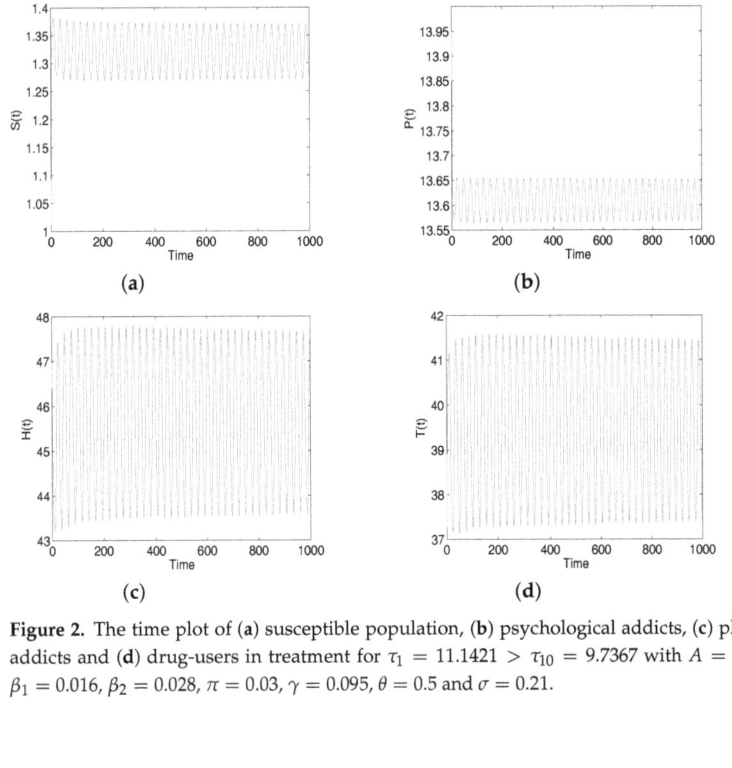

Figure 2. The time plot of (**a**) susceptible population, (**b**) psychological addicts, (**c**) physiological addicts and (**d**) drug-users in treatment for $\tau_1 = 11.1421 > \tau_{10} = 9.7367$ with $A = 2$, $d = 0.02$, $\beta_1 = 0.016$, $\beta_2 = 0.028$, $\pi = 0.03$, $\gamma = 0.095$, $\theta = 0.5$ and $\sigma = 0.21$.

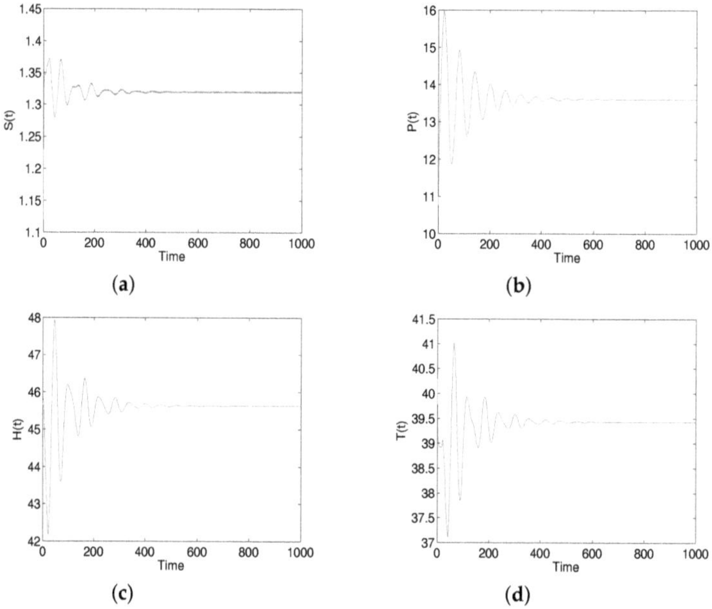

Figure 3. The time plot of (**a**) susceptible population, (**b**) psychological addicts, (**c**) physiological addicts and (**d**) drug-users in treatment for $\tau_2 = 18.6934 < \tau_{20} = 20.8839$ with $A = 2$, $d = 0.02$, $\beta_1 = 0.016$, $\beta_2 = 0.028$, $\pi = 0.03$, $\gamma = 0.095$, $\theta = 0.5$ and $\sigma = 0.21$.

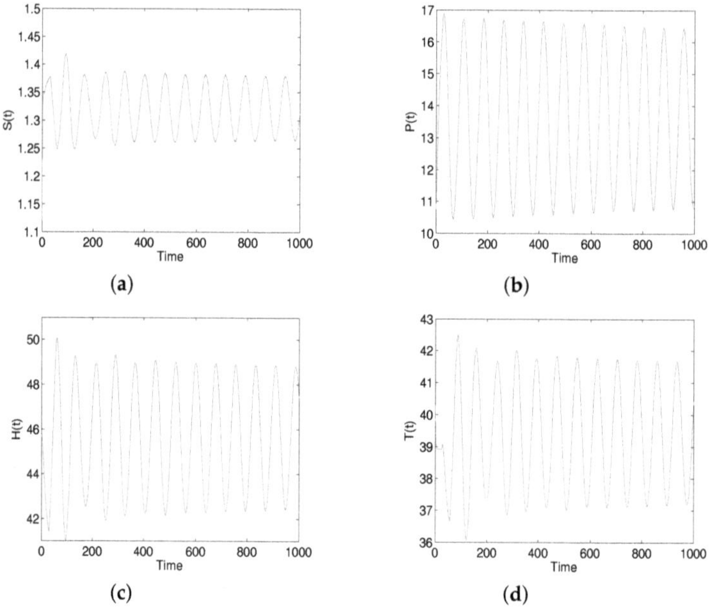

Figure 4. The time plot of (**a**) susceptible population, (**b**) psychological addicts, (**c**) physiological addicts and (**d**) drug-users in treatment for $\tau_2 = 25.9358 > \tau_{20} = 20.8839$ with $A = 2$, $d = 0.02$, $\beta_1 = 0.016$, $\beta_2 = 0.028$, $\pi = 0.03$, $\gamma = 0.095$, $\theta = 0.5$ and $\sigma = 0.21$.

For $\tau_1 > 0$ and $\tau_2 = 2.5 \in (0, \tau_{20})$ and supposing τ_1 as a parameter, we obtain $\varsigma_{1*} = 3.2156$ and $\tau_{1*} = 1.4096$ through some computations. In such a case, the model system (47) is locally asymptotically stable when $\tau_1 < \tau_{1*}$ but as τ_1 passes through τ_{1*} the model system (47) exhibits a Hopf bifurcation and the model system (47) loses stability. This property is depicted in Figures 5 and 6 for τ_1 = 1.3785 (<τ_{1*}) and τ_1 = 1.1.4308 (>τ_{1*}), respectively.

For $\tau_2 > 0$ and $\tau_1 = 1.5 \in (0, \tau_{10})$ and supposing τ_2 as a parameter, we get $\varsigma_{2*} = 0.7849$ and $\tau_{2*} = 8.9875$. The model system (47) is locally asymptotically stable for $\tau_2 < \tau_{2*}$ and unstable for $\tau_2 > \tau_{2*}$. Stability and instability behavior of the model system (47) is presented in Figures 7 and 8 for different values of τ_2, respectively.

In addition, for $\tau_1 = 1.5 \in (0, \tau_{10})$ and $\tau_2 > 0$, we obtain $\lambda'(\tau_{2*}) = 0.06568892 - 0.00081555i$ and $C_0 = -4.25450964 + 13.07154877i$. Thus, we have $\Lambda_1 = 64.76753827 > 0$, $\Lambda_2 = -8.50901928 < 0$ and $\Lambda_3 = -1.84550535 < 0$. Based on the Theorem 5, we can see that the Hopf bifurcation at $\tau_{2*} = 8.9875$ is supercritical; the bifurcating periodic solutions showing around $E_*(1.3196, 13.6111, 45.6355, 39.4338)$ are stable, and the bifurcating periodic solutions showing around $E_*(1.3196, 13.6111, 45.6355, 39.4338)$ are decreasing.

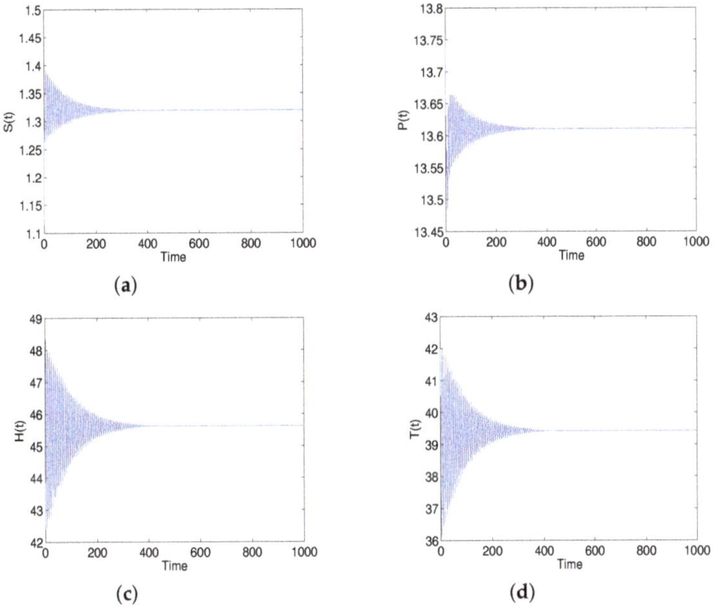

Figure 5. The time plot of (**a**) susceptible population, (**b**) psychological addicts, (**c**) physiological addicts and (**d**) drug-users in treatment for $\tau_1 = 1.3785 < \tau_{1*} = 1.4096$ and $\tau_2 = 2.5 \in (0, \tau_{20})$ with $A = 2$, $d = 0.02$, $\beta_1 = 0.016$, $\beta_2 = 0.028$, $\pi = 0.03$, $\gamma = 0.095$, $\theta = 0.5$ and $\sigma = 0.21$.

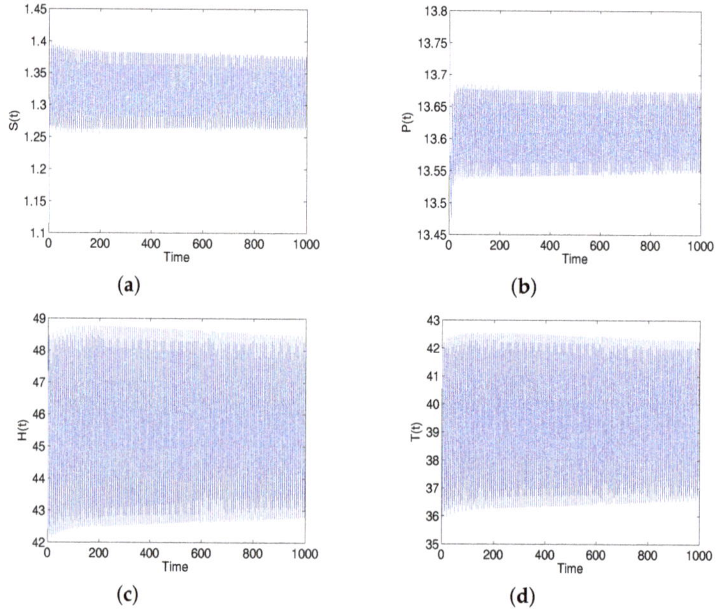

Figure 6. The time plot of (**a**) susceptible population, (**b**) psychological addicts, (**c**) physiological addicts and (**d**) drug-users in treatment for $\tau_1 = 1.4308 > \tau_{1*} = 1.4096$ and $\tau_2 = 2.5 \in (0, \tau_{20})$ with $A = 2, d = 0.02, \beta_1 = 0.016, \beta_2 = 0.028, \pi = 0.03, \gamma = 0.095, \theta = 0.5$ and $\sigma = 0.21$.

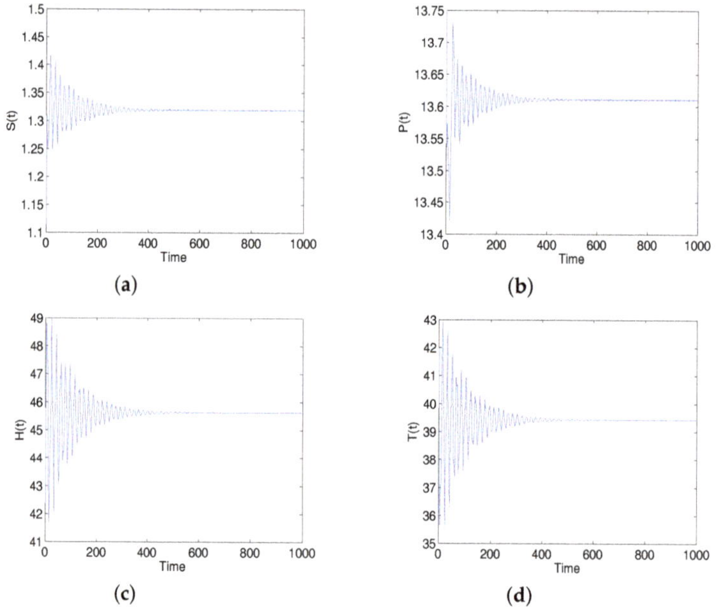

Figure 7. The time plot of (**a**) susceptible population, (**b**) psychological addicts, (**c**) physiological addicts and (**d**) drug-users in treatment for $\tau_2 = 8.2943 < \tau_{2*} = 8.9875$ and $\tau_1 = 1.5 \in (0, \tau_{10})$ with $A = 2, d = 0.02, \beta_1 = 0.016, \beta_2 = 0.028, \pi = 0.03, \gamma = 0.095, \theta = 0.5$ and $\sigma = 0.21$.

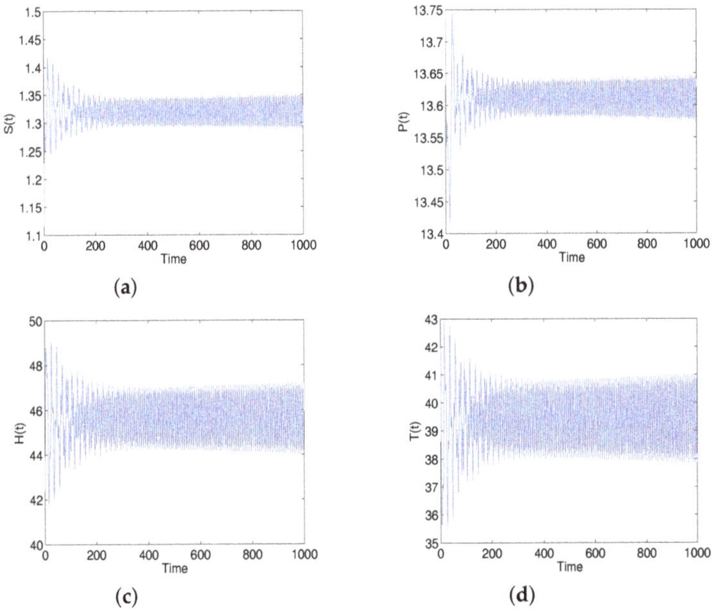

Figure 8. The time of (**a**) susceptible population, (**b**) psychological addicts, (**c**) physiological addicts and (**d**) drug-users in treatment plot for $\tau_2 = 9.3825 > \tau_{2*} = 8.9875$ and $\tau_1 = 1.5 \in (0, \tau_{10})$ with $A = 2, d = 0.02, \beta_1 = 0.016, \beta_2 = 0.028, \pi = 0.03, \gamma = 0.095, \theta = 0.5$ and $\sigma = 0.21$.

6. Conclusions

In this study, a synthetic drug transmission model with two time delays is proposed by introducing the time delay due to the period that both the psychological addicts and the physiological addicts need to accept treatment and come off drugs into the formulated model by in [25]. Through regarding the combinations of the two time delays as bifurcation parameters, sufficient criteria for local stability and exhibition of Hopf bifurcation are established. A crucial value point at which a Hopf bifurcation appears is calculated. Particularly, direction and stability of the model are explored with the aids of the normal form theory and center manifold theorem. Compared with the work in [25], we not only consider the impact of the time delay (τ_1) due to the relapse time period of the drug-users in treatment on the model system (2) but also the time delay (τ_2) due to the period that both the psychological addicts and the physiological addicts need to accept treatment and come off drugs on the model system. The results obtained in this study are supplements of the work in [25].

Author Contributions: All authors (H.Z., A.Z., A.W., Z.Z.) have equally contributed to this paper. All authors have read and agreed to the published version of the manuscript.

Funding: This research was supported by National Natural Science Foundation of China (12061033).

Institutional Review Board Statement: Not applicable

Informed Consent Statement: Not applicable

Data Availability Statement: Not applicable

Conflicts of Interest: The authors declare no conflict of interest.

References

1. Creagh, S.; Warden, D.; Latif, M.A.; Paydar, A. The new classes of synthetic illicit drugs can significantly harm the brain: A neuro imaging perspective with full review of MRI findings. *Clin. Imaging J.* **2018**, *2*, 000116.
2. China's Drug Situations Report in 2017. Available online: http://www.nncc626.com/2018-06/26/c_129901052.htm (accessed on 24 February 2022).
3. White, E.; Comiskey, C. Heroin epidemics, treatment and ODE modelling. *Math. Biosci.* **2007**, *208*, 312–324. [CrossRef] [PubMed]
4. Liu, J.L.; Zhang, T.L. Global behaviour of a heroin epidemic model with distributed delays. *Appl. Math. Lett.* **2011**, *24*, 1685–1692. [CrossRef]
5. Huang, G.; Liu, A.P. A note on global stability for a heroin epidemic model with distributed delay. *Appl. Math. Lett.* **2013**, *26*, 687–691. [CrossRef]
6. Liu, X.N.; Wang, J.L. Epidemic dynamics on a delayed multi-group heroin epidemic model with nonlinear incidence rate. *J. Nonlinear Sci. Appl.* **2016**, *9*, 2149–2160. [CrossRef]
7. Ma, M.J.; Liu, S.Y.; Li, J. Bifurcation of a heroin model with nonlinear incidence rate. *Nonlinear Dyn.* **2017**, *88*, 555–565. [CrossRef]
8. Djilali, S.; Touaoula, T.M.; Miri, S.E. A heroin epidemic model: Very general non linear incidence, treat-age, and global stability. *Acta Appl. Math.* **2017**, *152*, 171–194. [CrossRef]
9. Yang, J.Y.; Li, X.X.; Zhang, F.Q. Global dynamics of a heroin epidemic model with age structure and nonlinear incidence. *Int. J. Biomath.* **2016**, *9*, 1650033. [CrossRef]
10. Wang, J.L.; Wang, J.; Kuniya, T. Analysis of an age-structured multi-group heroin epidemic model. *Appl. Math. Comput.* **2019**, *347*, 78–100. [CrossRef]
11. Alzaid, S.S.; Alkahtani, B.S.T. Asymptotic analysis of a giving up smoking model with relapse and harmonic mean type incidence rate. *Results Phys.* **2021**, *28*, 104437. [CrossRef]
12. Sun, C.X.; Jia, J.W. Optimal control of a delayed smokingmodel with immigration. *J. Biol. Dyn.* **2019**, *13*, 447–460. [CrossRef] [PubMed]
13. Rahman, G.U.; Agarwal, R.P.; Din, Q. Mathematical analysis of giving up smoking model via harmonic mean type incidence rate. *Appl. Math. Comput.* **2019**, *354*, 128–148. [CrossRef]
14. Rahman, G.U.; Agarwal, R.P.; Liu, L.L.; Khan, A. Threshold dynamics and optimal control of an age-structured giving up smoking model. *Nonlinear Anal. Real World Appl.* **2018**, *43*, 96–120. [CrossRef]
15. Ucar, S.; Ucar, E.; Ozdemir, N.; Hammouch, Z. Mathematical analysis and numerical simulation for a smoking model with Atangana-Baleanu derivative. *Chaos Solitons Fractals* **2019**, *118*, 300–306. [CrossRef]
16. Hu, X.M.; Pratap, A.; Zhang, Z.Z.; Wan, A.Y. Hopf bifurcation and global exponential stability of an epidemiological smoking model with time delay. *Alex. Eng. J.* **2022**, *61*, 2096–2104. [CrossRef]
17. Zhang, Z.Z.; ur Rahman, G.; Nisar, K.S.; Agarwal, R.P. Incorporating convex incidence rate and public awareness program in modelling drinking abuse and novel control strategies with time delay. *Phys. Scr.* **2021**, *96*, 114006. [CrossRef]
18. Huo, H.F.; Chen, Y.L.; Xiang, H. Stability of a binge drinking model with delay. *J. Biol. Dyn.* **2017**, *11*, 210–225. [CrossRef]
19. Xiang, H.; Zhu, C.C.; Huo, H.F. Modelling the effect of immigration on drinking behavior. *J. Biol. Dyn.* **2017**, *11*, 275–298. [CrossRef]
20. Sharma, S.; Samanta, G.P. Analysis of a drinking epidemic model. *Int. J. Dyn. Control* **2015**, *3*, 288–305. [CrossRef]
21. Das, M.; Samanta, G.; Sen, M.D.L. Stability analysis and optimal control of a fractional order synthetic drugs transmission model. *Mathematics* **2021**, *9*, 703. [CrossRef]
22. Saha, S.; Samanta, G.P. Synthetic drugs transmission: Stability analysis and optimal control. *Lett. Biomath.* **2019**, *6*. [CrossRef]
23. Liu, P.; Zhang, L.; Xing, Y. Modelling and stability of a synthetic drugs transmission model with relapse and treatment. *J. Appl. Math. Comput.* **2019**, *60*, 465–484. [CrossRef]
24. Ma, M.J.; Liu, S.Y.; Xiang, H.; Li, J. Dynamics of synthetic drugs transmission model with psychological addicts and general incidence rate. *Phys. Stat. Mech. Appl.* **2018**, *491*, 641–649. [CrossRef]
25. Zhang, Z.Z.; Yang, F.F.; Xia, W.J. Influence of time delay on bifurcation of a synthetic drug transmission model with psychological addicts. *Adv. Differ. Equ.* **2020**, *144*, 15. [CrossRef]
26. Kundu, S.; Maitra, S. Dynamical behaviour of a delayed three species predator-prey model with cooperation among the prey species. *Nonlinear Dyn.* **2019**, *92*, 627–643. [CrossRef]
27. Ren, J.G.; Yang, X.F.; Yang, L.X.; Xu, Y.H.; Yang, F.Z. A delayed computer virus propagation model and its dynamics. *Chaos Solitons Fractals* **2012**, *45*, 74–79. [CrossRef]
28. Bodnar, M. The nonnegativity of solutions of delay differential equations. *Appl. Math. Lett.* **2000**, *13*, 91–95. [CrossRef]
29. Yang, X.; Chen, L.; Chen, J. Permanence and positive periodic solution for the single species nonautonomus delay diffusive model. *Comput. Math. Appl.* **1996**, *32*, 109–116. [CrossRef]
30. Xu, C.J.; Liao, M.X.; Li, P.L.; Guo, Y.; Xiao, Q.M.; Yuan, S. Influence of multiple time delays on bifurcation of fractional-order neural networks. *Appl. Math. Comput.* **2019**, *361*, 565–582. [CrossRef]
31. Duan, D.F.; Niu, B.; Wei, J.J. Local and global Hopf bifurcation in a neutral population model with age structure. *Math. Methods Appl. Sci.* **2019**, *42*, 4747–4764. [CrossRef]
32. Wang, Y.J.; Fan, D.J.; Wei, J.J. Stability and bifurcation analysis in a predator-prey model with age structure and two Delays. *Int. J. Biurcation Chaos* **2021**, *31*, 2150024. [CrossRef]

33. Wang, L.X.; Niu, B.; Wei, J.J. Dynamical analysis for a model of asset prices with two delays. *Phys. Stat. Mech. Appl.* **2016**, *447*, 297–313. [CrossRef]
34. Li, X.L.; Wei, J.J. On the zeros of a fourth degree exponential polynomial with applications to a neural network model with delays. *Chaos Solitons Fractals* **2005**, *26*, 519–526. [CrossRef]
35. Hassard, B.D.; Kazarinoff, N.D.; Wan, Y.H. *Theory and Applications of Hopf Bifurcation*; Cambridge University Press: Cambridge, UK, 1981.

mathematics MDPI

Article

Dynamic Analysis of a COVID-19 Vaccination Model with a Positive Feedback Mechanism and Time-Delay

Xin Ai [1], Xinyu Liu [1], Yuting Ding [1,*] and Han Li [2]

[1] Department of Mathematics, Northeast Forestry University, Harbin 150040, China; aixin010607@nefu.edu.cn (X.A.); lxy_lucky@nefu.edu.cn (X.L.)
[2] College of Economics and Management, Northeast Forestry University, Harbin 150040, China; li@nefu.edu.cn
* Correspondence: dingyt@nefu.edu.cn

Abstract: As the novel coronavirus pandemic has spread globally since 2019, most countries in the world are conducting vaccination campaigns. First, based on the traditional SIR infectious disease model, we introduce a positive feedback mechanism associated with the vaccination rate, and consider the time delay from antibody production to antibody disappearance after vaccination. We establish an UV_aV model for COVID-19 vaccination with a positive feedback mechanism and time-delay. Next, we verify the existence of the equilibrium of the formulated model and analyze its stability. Then, we analyze the existence of the Hopf bifurcation, and use the multiple time scales method to derive the normal form of the Hopf bifurcation, further determining the direction of the Hopf bifurcation and the stability of the periodic solution of the bifurcation. Finally, we collect the parameter data of some countries and regions to determine the reasonable ranges of multiple parameters to ensure the authenticity of simulation results. Numerical simulations are carried out to verify the correctness of the theoretical results. We also give the critical time for controllable widespread antibody failure to provide a reference for strengthening vaccination time. Taking two groups of parameters as examples, the time of COVID-19 vaccine booster injection should be best controlled before 38.5 weeks and 35.3 weeks, respectively. In addition, study the impact of different expiration times on epidemic prevention and control effectiveness. We further explore the impact of changes in vaccination strategies on trends in epidemic prevention and control effectiveness. It could be concluded that, under the same epidemic vaccination strategy, the existence level of antibody is roughly the same, which is consistent with the reality.

Keywords: COVID-19 model; vaccination willingness; failure time of vaccine antibody; Hopf bifurcation; multiple time scales method; normal form

MSC: 34K18; 37L10

Citation: Ai, X.; Liu, X.; Ding, Y.; Li, H. Dynamic Analysis of a COVID-19 Vaccination Model with a Positive Feedback Mechanism and Time-Delay. *Mathematics* **2022**, *10*, 1583. https://doi.org/10.3390/math10091583

Academic Editor: Dimplekumar N. Chalishajar

Received: 28 March 2022
Accepted: 3 May 2022
Published: 7 May 2022

1. Introduction

COVID-19 is ravaging the world, affecting 212 countries and territories around the world [1]. As of February 2022, it had infected more than 400 million people, with a mortality rate of about 6%. Within months of the coronavirus outbreak, there was effective control of epidemics in some countries through rigorous screening and quarantine strategies [2]. However, in some other countries, the novel coronavirus pandemic has spread rapidly and become a serious epidemic. The outbreak has not only affected human survival but also the global economy [3]. As a result, COVID-19 has become a hot topic in global research and has received wide attention worldwide.

At present, vaccines are currently the most effective strategy for preventing outbreaks [4]. However, vaccination varies from country to country around the world [5,6]. Booster shots are becoming widespread in developed economies, but basic immunization targets are not yet universally met in most emerging economies [7]. Since the outbreak in

2019, countries have attached great importance to the development of a vaccine. Currently, more than 160 candidate vaccines against SARS-CoV-2 are being developed globally. Results from the first human trial of a potential SARS-CoV-2 vaccine have been published [8]. Studies have shown that vaccines against COVID-19 in phase iii clinical trials have good safety and immunogenicity. However, attention should be paid to adverse reactions and long-term protection of the vaccine [9]. Among the four published vaccines, the protective efficacy of the inactivated vaccine was 79.34%, that of the vector vaccine was 62–90%, and that of the mRNA vaccine was all above 90% [10]. Therefore, there are still uncertainties about the protective efficacy and immune persistence of vaccines [11]. In the course of our study, the effectiveness of the vaccine is noteworthy.

In recent years, many scholars have studied the transmission mode of COVID-19 from different perspectives. In Olaniyi et al.'s study [12], an epidemic model based on a system of ordinary differential equations is formulated by taking into account the transmission routes from symptomatic, asymptomatic, and hospitalized individuals. Sensitivities of the model to changes in parameters are explored, and safe regions at certain threshold values of the parameters are derived. In addition, two time-dependent control variables, namely preventive and management measures, are considered to mitigate the damaging effects of the disease using Pontryagin's maximum principle. Abdy et al. [13] used fuzzy parameters to establish the SIR model of COVID-19. In the model analysis, the generation matrix method was used to obtain the stability of basic regeneration number and the model equilibrium. The evolution of diseases with extended incubation periods and the presence of asymptomatic patients such as COVID-19 have been modeled in Bardina's research [14]. In Ref. [15], Bardina et al. also developed a SEIR infectious disease model for COVID-19 based on some common control strategies. Algehyne et al. [16] investigated a new mathematical SQIR model for COVID-19 by means of four dimensions. In Ref. [17], Li et al. constructed a new (SEIHRD)-H-3-R-2 diffusion model was constructed in the literature to generate the most likely scenario of an epidemic. In Ref. [18], Li et al. proved the effectiveness of the EM algorithm by simulation. Peng et al. [19] plotted the causal cycle of the COVID-19 transmission transportation system dynamics model and analyzed the causal feedback loop. In particular, Cadoni et al. [20] investigated in detail how the size and timescale of the epidemic can be changed by acting on the parameters characterizing the model. In addition, they further compared the efficiency of different containment strategies for contrasting an epidemic diffusion.

In the process of COVID-19 vaccination, we believe that there is a time delay between antibody production and antibody disappearance. At present, some scholars have carried out certain studies on the COVID-19 epidemic model with time-delay. Yang et al. [21] considered that there were different infection delays among different populations, and established two different types of fractional order (Caputo and Caputo-Fabrizio) COVID-19 models with distributed time-delay. Radha et al. [22] investigated the effect of time delay in immune response based on the 2019 Universal SEIR model for coronavirus (COVID-19). Chang et al. [23] introduced the factor of policies and regulations with time-delay, and constructed an SIHRS model of COVID-19 pandemic with impulse and time-delay under media coverage. In Ref. [24], Zhu et al. obtained a delayed reaction–diffusion model that more closely approximates the actual spread of COVID-19 when the epidemic had entered the normalization stage. In Ref. [25], Yang et al. investigated a novel Susceptible-Exposed-Infected-Quarantined-Recovered (SEIQR) COVID-19 transmission model with two delays.

Novel coronavirus is a single-stranded plus strand RNA virus that can constantly mutate during the outbreak and development. A variety of novel coronavirus strains emerged in different countries and regions around the world. However, more transmissible and stealthy strains emerged [26], and questions such as the effectiveness and duration of vaccines become increasingly prominent [27,28]. In 2020, Beta, Lambda, Delta, Gamma, and other mutant strains emerged in various parts of the world [29], especially the Delta variant strain, which rapidly spread around the world and caused a new round of COVID-

19 outbreaks in many countries and regions, posing great challenges to global epidemic prevention and control [30,31]. More recently, there has been the Omicron variant, which appeared in several countries around the world [32]. The transmissibility of the virus also changes depending on the type of the novel coronavirus variant. The Delta variant is twice as transmissible as the original [33], and the infection rate of the Omicron variant is much higher than that of the Delta variant [34]. Therefore, considering the vaccination rate, failure rate, mortality rate, the time of the wide range of antibody failure and secondary vaccination rate, and discussing the impact of mutated strains of COVID-19, it is of great significance for epidemic prevention and control.

Therefore, the motivations of this study are as follows: first, different countries have different epidemic prevention strategies, population development trends and other indicators, and the epidemic prevention and control effects are also different, so it is of practical significance to study the impact of COVID-19 vaccination rate, failure rate and secondary vaccination rate on the epidemic prevention and control effects. Second, vaccination rate is affected by people's vaccination willingness, so it is of certain significance to study how vaccination willingness affects vaccination rate, and then how it affects the vaccination process. Third, there is a time delay between the generation of antibodies and the disappearance of antibodies after vaccination, so it is of great significance for epidemic prevention and control to provide a critical and controllable time for large-scale antibody failure, and also provides a reference for future booster vaccination cycle. Fourth, the novel coronavirus continues to mutate, giving rise to multiple mutated strains with higher transmissibility and mortality, so it is necessary to discuss the ability to cope with mutant strains under current control strategies. Based on the above questions, this paper studies a dynamic vaccination process (U-V_a-V) for COVID-19 vaccination, and introduces a positive feedback mechanism for vaccination rate, taking into account the time delay in the process from antibody generation to large-scale elimination of antibodies. In this paper, a novel dynamic differential equation model of COVID-19 vaccination with time delay is established, and numerical simulations are carried out using MATLAB.

The innovation of this paper are as follows: first, in this paper, our model is established by rational analysis. Second, we add the corresponding positive feedback mechanism to construct a dynamically changing vaccination rate in the process of considering the model parameters. Third, we include time delay regarding vaccine effectiveness and investigate the effect of critical time delay on the stability of the model. Finally, the model we built is generalizable within a reasonable range of parameters.

The remaining sections are arranged as follows: In Section 2, we present a time-delay differential equation for COVID-19 vaccination, taking into account the time for the large-scale failure of COVID-19 vaccines in the presence of antibodies. In Section 3, we study the stability of positive equilibrium and the existence of Hopf bifurcation of the system (1). In Section 4, we calculate the normal form of Hopf bifurcation of the formulated model by using the multiple time scales method. In Section 5, we perform data analysis on the parameters in the model and provide simulation results by substituting relevant parameters to verify the correctness of theoretical analysis. In addition, the critical time for controllable widespread antibody failure is given, and the influence of COVID-19 vaccination strategies and COVID-19 mutant strain on the epidemic prevention and control effect is discussed. Finally, conclusions are given in Section 6.

2. Mathematical Modeling

In Section 2, we will elaborate the model. The modeling in this paper is based on the dynamic process of COVID-19 vaccination.

First, we divide and explain the research object. When studying the process, we divide the sample population into three categories: The first type of sample U is an unvaccinated group, that is, the first type of population U is unvaccinated and does not have antibodies, which is recorded as unvaccinated population U. We do not consider that a small number of people have antibodies against COVID-19, so the second type of sample V_a is a vaccinated group, that is, the second type of population V_a is vaccinated and has antibodies, which is recorded as the vaccinated population V_a . The third type of sample V is the vaccine ineffective group, that is, the third type of population V has been vaccinated, but the antibody has disappeared, which is recorded as the ineffective population V .

Then, we briefly analyze the role relationship between the groups. Since COVID-19 antibodies have no maternal genetic characteristics, newborn population B is transferred to unvaccinated population U. Unvaccinated population U can become vaccinated population V_a by being vaccinated against COVID-19. The vaccinated population V_a may become ineffective population V due to the disappearance of antibodies after a period of time, and the vaccinated population V_a can be inoculated with booster injection to prolong the time of antibody disappearance. Ineffective population V can also become vaccinated population V_a through secondary vaccination with the COVID-19 vaccine. We assume that there is a vaccinated population V_a that may contract COVID-19 but not die. Thus, we obtain the relationship between three populations (unvaccinated population (U), vaccinated population (V_a), and ineffective population (V), as shown in Figure 1:

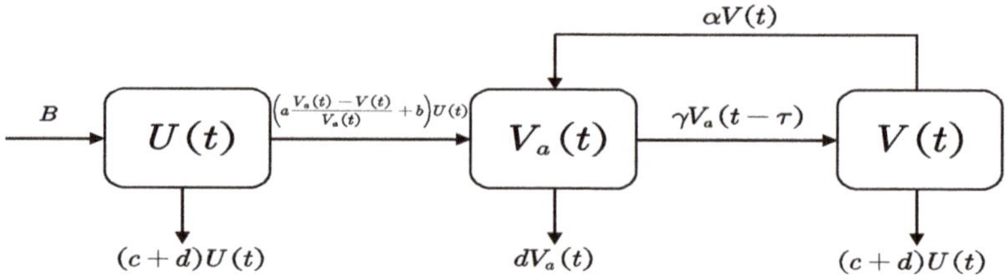

Figure 1. Flow chart for the UV_aV model.

In Figure 1, U, V_a, V represent the sample numbers of unvaccinated, vaccinated and antibody disappearance, respectively, and parameters B and d represent natural increase of population and death rate of the samples, respectively; c is mortality rate due to COVID-19; α represents the secondary vaccination rate from V to V_a; γ is the failure rate from V_a to V; a and b are the positive feedback coefficients and basic vaccination rate in the positive feedback mechanism from U to V_a. We need to emphasize that the parameters involved in Figure 1 are all normal numbers. Finally, it is important to note that there is $V_a > V$ in the vaccinated population.

Next, we analyze the meaning of time-delay τ. For the process from inoculated population V_a to ineffective population V, we analyze the existence of time delay from two aspects. On the one hand, the novel coronavirus we are working on is very close to influenza virus, and the half-life of influenza virus antibodies is only about six months [35]. On the other hand, studies have shown that the half-life of antibodies in patients with mild new coronations is only 36 days [36]. Therefore, it can be concluded that COVID-19 vaccine is a non-permanent immune vaccine and has the time τ of the wide range of antibody failure, that is to say, most recipients (γ) will have the situation of antibody disappearance after the time τ.

Furthermore, we construct a positive feedback mechanism on vaccine effectiveness to characterize a dynamic COVID-19 vaccination rate. For a vaccination rate from unvaccinated population U to vaccinated population V_a, we believe that a COVID-19 vaccination rate is affected by the willingness of the population to vaccinate. Li et al. [37] conducted a sample survey of patients in a tertiary hospital in a city, and concluded that worry about the safety and effectiveness of the vaccine was the main reason of the unwillingness for the vaccination. In Sarwar et al.'s [38] study, a multi-criteria decision-making method known as an analytical hierarchical method was applied to determine the COVID-19 vaccination willingness level of the public. The analysis revealed that the determinants of willingness to uptake the COVID-19 vaccine were individual decision, vaccine origin, adapting to change, and perceived barriers' high obstacles to vaccinating. In Liu et al.'s [39] article, it was shown that free vaccination significantly increased COVID-19 vaccination rates.

Referring to the literature above, we use the ratio of the current ineffective population V and the vaccinated population V_a to characterize the effectiveness and safety of COVID-19: a smaller ratio indicates that the vaccine is more effective and safe, whereas a larger ratio indicates that the vaccine is less effective. Moreover, we denote the influence factor of the effectiveness and safety of COVID-19 vaccines as a, and the combined influence of factors includes vaccine source, vaccine cost, and vaccination barriers as b, and we can regard it as the basic fixed vaccination rate b for a period of time. To sum up, we construct a positive feedback mechanism for U to V_a in the vaccination rate: $\frac{a(V_a-V)}{V_a}+b$.

Finally, combined with Figure 1, we give the following dynamic model of COVID-19 vaccination:

$$\begin{cases} \dot{U}(t) = B-(c+d)U(t)-\frac{aV_a(t)-aV(t)}{V_a(t)}U(t)-bU(t), \\ \dot{V}_a(t) = \frac{aV_a(t)-aV(t)}{V_a(t)}U(t)+bU(t)-dV_a(t)-\gamma V_a(t-\tau)+\alpha V(t), \\ \dot{V}(t) = \gamma V_a(t-\tau)-\alpha V(t)-(c+d)V(t). \end{cases} \tag{1}$$

where U, V_a, V are descriptive variables; B, a, b, c, d, α, γ are parameters; and τ is the time-delay. The specific definitions are given in Table 1.

Table 1. Descriptions of variables and parameters in the model (1).

Symbol	Descriptions
U	Number of unvaccinated individuals without antibodies
V_a	Number of vaccinated individuals who develop antibodies
V	Number of vaccinated individuals whose antibodies failed
B	Natural increase of population
a	Factor affecting vaccine safety and efficacy
d	Natural mortality rate
b	Basic fixed vaccination rate
c	Mortality rate due to COVID-19
α	Conversion rate from V to V_a, secondary vaccination rate for COVID-19 vaccine
γ	The conversion rate from V_a to V, the COVID-19 vaccine failure rate
τ	The time-delay between antibody production and antibody disappearance

3. Stability Analysis of Equilibrium and Existence of Hopf Bifurcation

In this section, we consider Equation (1) and determine the existence and stability of the positive equilibrium. We consider the following assumption:

(H1) $b(\alpha+c+d)+a(\alpha+c+d-\gamma)\geq 0$.

When **(H1)** holds, system (1) has one positive equilibrium $P(U^*, V_a^*, V^*)$, where

$$\begin{aligned} U^* &= \frac{B}{c+d}-\frac{B[b(\alpha+c+d)+a(\alpha+c+d-\gamma)]}{(c+d)[(\alpha+c+d)(b+c+d)+a(\alpha+c+d-\gamma)]}, \\ V_a^* &= \frac{(\alpha+c+d)V^*}{\gamma}, \\ V^* &= \frac{B\gamma[b(\alpha+c+d)+a(\alpha+c+d-\gamma)]}{[(\alpha+c+d)(b+c+d)+a(\alpha+c+d-\gamma)][(c+d)(d+\gamma)+\alpha d]}. \end{aligned} \tag{2}$$

We calculate the characteristic equation for equilibrium $P(U^*, V_a^*, V^*)$ as follows:

$$e^{-\lambda\tau}\left[A_1\lambda^2+B_1\lambda+C_1\right]+\lambda^3+D_1\lambda^2+E_1\lambda+F_1=0, \tag{3}$$

where

$$
\begin{aligned}
A_1 =&\gamma, \\
B_1 =&\left(\frac{aU^*\gamma}{V_a^*} + 2c\gamma + 2d\gamma + b\gamma + \frac{a\gamma(V_a^* - V^*)}{V_a^*}\right), \\
C_1 =&\left(c + d + b + \frac{a(V_a^* - V^*)}{V_a^*}\right)\left(\frac{aU^*\gamma}{V_a^*} + \gamma c + \gamma d\right) - \frac{aU^*\gamma}{V_a^*}\left(\frac{a(V_a^* - V^*)}{V_a^*} + b\right), \\
D_1 =&\left(2c + 3d + b + \alpha + \frac{a(V_a^* - V^*)}{V_a^*} - \frac{aU^*V^*}{(V_a^*)^2}\right), \\
E_1 =&\left(c + d + b + \frac{a(V_a^* - V^*)}{V_a^*}\right)\left(2d - \frac{aU^*V^*}{(V_a^*)^2} + \alpha + c\right) + \left(d - \frac{aU^*V^*}{(V_a^*)^2}\right)(\alpha + c + d) \\
&- \left(\frac{a(V_a^* - V^*)}{V_a^*} + b\right)\left(\frac{aU^*V^*}{(V_a^*)^2}\right), \\
F_1 =&\left(d - \frac{aU^*V^*}{(V_a^*)^2}\right)(\alpha + c + d)\left(c + d + b + \frac{a(V_a^* - V^*)}{V_a^*}\right) \\
&- \left(\frac{a(V_a^* - V^*)}{V_a^*} + b\right)\left[\frac{aU^*V^*}{(V_a^*)^2}(\alpha + c + d)\right],
\end{aligned}
$$

with U^*, V_a^*, V^* are given in Equation (2).

When $\tau = 0$, Equation (3) becomes

$$\lambda^3 + a_1\lambda^2 + a_2\lambda + a_3 = 0, \tag{4}$$

where

$$
\begin{aligned}
a_1 =& -\frac{aU^*V^*}{(V_a^*)^2} + \gamma + 3d + 2c + b + \frac{a(V_a^* - V^*)}{V_a^*} + \alpha, \\
a_2 =&\gamma\left(\frac{aU^*}{V_a^*} - \alpha\right) + \left(-\frac{aU^*V^*}{(V_a^*)^2} + 2d + \alpha + c + \gamma\right)\left(c + d + b + \frac{a(V_a^* - V^*)}{V_a^*}\right) \\
&- \frac{aU^*V^*}{(V_a^*)^2}\left(\frac{a(V_a^* - V^*)}{V_a^*} + b\right) + (\alpha + c + d)\left(d + \gamma - \frac{aV^*U^*}{(V_a^*)^2}\right), \\
a_3 =&\left(c + d + b + \frac{a(V_a^* - V^*)}{V_a^*}\right)\left[(\alpha + c + d)\left(d + \gamma - \frac{aU^*V^*}{(V_a^*)^2}\right) + \gamma\left(\frac{aU^*}{V_a^*} - \alpha\right)\right] \\
&- \left(\frac{a(V_a^* - V^*)}{V_a^*} + b\right)\left[\frac{a\gamma U^*}{V_a^*} + \frac{aU^*V^*}{(V_a^*)^2}(\alpha + c + d)\right].
\end{aligned}
$$

According to the Routh–Hurwitz criterion, we consider the following assumption:

(H2) $a_1 > 0, a_3 > 0, a_1a_2 - a_3 > 0$.

When **(H2)** holds, all the roots of Equation (4) have negative real parts, and the equilibrium $P(U^*, V_a^*, V^*)$ is locally asymptotically stable when $\tau = 0$.

When $\tau > 0$, let $\lambda = i\omega$ $(\omega > 0)$ be a root of Equation (3). Substituting $\lambda = i\omega$ $(\omega > 0)$ into Equation (3) and separating the real and imaginary parts, we have:

$$
\begin{cases}
\omega^2 D_1 - F_1 = -\omega^2 A_1 \cos(\omega\tau) + C_1 \cos(\omega\tau) + \omega B_1 \sin(\omega\tau), \\
\omega^3 - E_1\omega = \omega B_1 \cos(\omega\tau) + \omega^2 A_1 \sin(\omega\tau) - C_1 \sin(\omega\tau).
\end{cases} \tag{5}
$$

Equation (5) leads to

$$\begin{cases} \cos(\omega\tau) = \frac{m_2\omega^3+D_1m_1\omega^2-E_1m_2\omega-F_1m_1}{\gamma(m_1^2+m_2^2)}, \\ \sin(\omega\tau) = \frac{-m_1\omega^3+D_1m_2w^2+E_1m_1\omega-F_1m_2}{\gamma(m_1^2+m_2^2)}, \end{cases} \tag{6}$$

where $m_1 = \frac{-A_1\omega^2+C_1}{\gamma}$ and $m_2 = \frac{B_1\omega}{\gamma}$.

Adding the square of two equations of Equation (5) , and let $\omega^2 = z$, we can obtain

$$h(z) = z^3 + c_2z^2 + c_1z + c_0, \tag{7}$$

where $c_2 = (D_1^2 - 2E_1 - A_1^2), c_1 = -(2F_1D_1 - 2A_1C_1 + B_1^2 - E_1^2), c_0 = F_1^2 - C_1^2$.

We calculate the derivative of $h(z)$ to obtain $h'(z) = 3z^2 + 2c_2z + c_1$. When $\Delta = 4(c_2)^2 - 12c_1 > 0$, and letting $\tilde{z}_1, \tilde{z}_2$ be the root of $h'(z) = 3z^2 + 2c_2z + c_1 = 0$, suppose $\tilde{z}_1 < \tilde{z}_2$, thus $\tilde{z}_1 = \frac{-2c_2+\sqrt{c_2^2-3c_1}}{3}$ and $\tilde{z}_2 = \frac{-2c_2-\sqrt{c_2^2-3c_1}}{3}$.

Therefore, we give the following assumptions:

(H3) $c_0 < 0$, and satisfies $\Delta \le 0$ or $c_1 \le 0$ or $c_2 \ge 0$ or $h(\tilde{z}_1) \cdot h(\tilde{z}_2) \ge 0$.

If **(H3)** holds, then Equation (7) has only one positive root z_1.

(H4) $c_0 > 0, \Delta > 0, c_1 > 0, c_2 < 0, h(\tilde{z}_2) < 0$ or $c_0 > 0, \Delta > 0, c_1 < 0, h(\tilde{z}_2) < 0$.

If **(H4)** holds, then Equation (7) has two positive roots z_2 and z_3.

(H5) $c_0 < 0, \Delta > 0, c_1 > 0, c_2 < 0, h(\tilde{z}_1) \cdot h(\tilde{z}_2) < 0$.

If **(H5)** holds, then Equation (7) has three positive roots z_4, z_5 and z_6.

In general, substituting $\omega_k = \sqrt{z_k}$ $(k = 1, 2, \cdots, 6)$ into Equation (6), we obtain

$$\tau_k^{(j)} = \begin{cases} \frac{1}{\omega_k}[\arccos(P_k) + 2j\pi], & Q_k \ge 0, \\ \frac{1}{\omega_k}[2\pi - \arccos(P_k) + 2j\pi], & Q_k < 0, \ k = 1, 2, \cdots, 6; \ j = 0, 1, 2, \cdots, \end{cases} \tag{8}$$

where

$$Q_k = \sin(\omega_k\tau_k^{(j)}) = \frac{-m_1\omega_k^3 + D_1m_2w_k^2 + E_1m_1\omega_k - F_1m_2}{\gamma(m_1^2 + m_2^2)},$$

$$P_k = \cos(\omega_k\tau_k^{(j)}) = \frac{m_2\omega_k^3 + D_1m_1w_k^2 - E_1m_2\omega_k - F_1m_1}{\gamma(m_1^2 + m_2^2)}.$$

We discuss the number of positive roots of Equation (7) of the characteristic equation based on the above, and thus synthesize the following Lemma:

Lemma 1. *If* **(H3)** *or* **(H4)** *or* **(H5)** *holds, then Equation* (3) *has a pair of pure imaginary roots* $\pm i\omega_k$ *when* $\tau = \tau_k^{(j)}$ $(k = 1, 2, \cdots, 6; \ j = 0, 1, 2, \cdots)$, *and all the other roots of Equation* (3) *have nonzero real parts.*

Furthermore, let $\lambda(\tau) = \alpha(\tau) + i\omega(\tau)$ be the root of Equation (3) satisfying $\alpha(\tau_k^{(j)}) = 0$, $\omega(\tau_k^{(j)}) = \omega_k$ $(k = 1, 2, \cdots, 6; \ j = 0, 1, 2, \cdots)$. Then, we consider the transversality condition.

Next, we derive both sides of the characteristic Equation (3) with respect to τ and solve for

$$\mathrm{Re}(\frac{d\tau}{d\lambda}) = \frac{3z^2 + 2c_2z + c_1}{B_1^2z + (C_1 - A_1z)^2}.$$

which gives us $\mathrm{Re}(\frac{d\lambda}{d\tau})^{-1} = \mathrm{Re}(\frac{d\tau}{d\lambda})$. Then, we have the following Lemma:

Lemma 2. *If* **(H3)** *or* **(H4)** *or* **(H5)** *holds, and* $z_k = \omega_k^2$, $h'(z_k) \neq 0$, *then we have the following transversality conclusions:*

$$\mathrm{Re}\left(\frac{\mathrm{d}\lambda}{\mathrm{d}\tau}\right)^{-1}\Bigg|_{\tau=\tau_j^{(k)}} = \mathrm{Re}\left(\frac{\mathrm{d}\tau}{\mathrm{d}\lambda}\right)\Bigg|_{\tau=\tau_j^{(k)}} = \frac{h'(z_k)}{B_1^2 z_k + (C_1 - A_1 z_k)^2} \neq 0.$$

where $k = 1, 2, \cdots, 6$; $j = 0, 1, 2, \cdots$ *and* A_1, B_1 *and* C_1 *are given in Equation (3).*

Based on the above conclusions, Lemmas 1 and 2, we obtain the following Theorem:

Theorem 1. *Based on the assumptions* **(H1)** *and* **(H2)** *hold, we show the conclusion associated with the equilibrium* $P(U^*, V_a^*, V^*)$ *of the system* (1). *If one of three assumptions* **(H3), (H4),** *and* **(H5)** *holds, the equilibrium of system* (1) *undergoes the Hopf bifurcation at* $\tau = \tau_k^{(j)}$ $(k = 1, 2, \cdots, 6; j = 0, 1, 2, \cdots)$, *where* $\tau_k^{(j)}$ *is given by Equation* (8), *and*

(1) If the assumptions **(H1)** *and* **(H2)** *and* **(H3)** *hold,* $h(z)$ *has one positive root, then, when* $\tau \in [0, \tau_1^{(0)})$, *the equilibrium* $P(U^*, V_a^*, V^*)$ *is locally asymptotically stable, and the equilibrium* $P(U^*, V_a^*, V^*)$ *is unstable when* $\tau > \tau_1^{(0)}$.

(2) If the assumptions **(H1)** *and* **(H2)** *and* **(H4)** *hold,* $h(z)$ *has two positive roots, we suppose* $z_2 < z_3$, *then* $h'(z_2) < 0, h'(z_3) > 0$, *note that* $\tau_2^{(0)} > \tau_3^{(0)}$. *Then, there exists* $m \in N$ *such that* $0 < \tau_3^{(0)} < \tau_2^{(0)} < \tau_3^{(1)} < \tau_2^{(1)} < \cdots < \tau_2^{(m-1)} < \tau_3^{(m)} < \tau_3^{(m+1)}$. *When* $\tau \in [0, \tau_3^{(0)}) \cup \bigcup_{l=1}^{m} (\tau_2^{(l-1)}, \tau_3^{(l)})$, *the equilibrium* $P(U^*, V_a^*, V^*)$ *of the system* (1) *is locally asymptotically stable, and, when* $\tau \in \bigcup_{l=0}^{m-1} (\tau_3^{(l)}, \tau_2^{(l)}) \cup (\tau_3^{(m)}, +\infty)$, *the equilibrium* $P(U^*, V_a^*, V^*)$ *is unstable.*

(3) If the assumptions **(H1)** *and* **(H2)** *and* **(H5)** *hold,* $h(z)$ *has three positive roots, and system* (1) *will generate stability switches similar to the above case (2).*

4. Normal Form of Hopf Bifurcation

In this section, we calculate the normal form of Hopf bifurcation for the system (1) by using the multiple time scales method. In this paper, τ is the time delay between vaccination and vaccine failure, which has an important influence on model stability. Thus, we choose the time-delay τ as a bifurcation parameter, denoting $\tau = \tau_c + \varepsilon\tau_\varepsilon$, where τ_c is the critical value of Hopf bifurcation give in Equation (8), τ_ε is the disturbance parameter, and ε is the dimensionless scale parameter. Note that, when $\tau = \tau_c$, the characteristic Equation (3) has eigenvalue $\lambda = i\omega$, and system (1) undergoes a Hopf bifurcation near equilibrium $P(U^*, V_a^*, V^*)$.

The system (1) can be written as $\dot{X}(t) = AX(t) + BX(t-\tau) + F(X(t), X(t-\tau))$, and let $t \to t/\tau$, thus obtaining system (9):

$$\dot{X} = \tau AX + B\tau X(t-1) + \tau F(X, X(t-1)). \tag{9}$$

where $A := (a_{ij})_{3\times 3} = \begin{pmatrix} \frac{aV^*}{V_a^*} - a - b - c - d & -\frac{aV^*U^*}{(V_a^*)^2} & \frac{aU^*}{V_a^*} \\ a + b - \frac{aV^*}{V_a^*} & \frac{aU^*V^*}{(V_a^*)^2} - d & \alpha - \frac{aU^*}{V_a^*} \\ 0 & 0 & -(\alpha + c + d) \end{pmatrix}$,

$B = \begin{pmatrix} 0 & 0 & 0 \\ 0 & -\gamma & 0 \\ 0 & \gamma & 0 \end{pmatrix}$,

$$F(X(t), X(t-\tau)) := \begin{pmatrix} F_U \\ F_{V_a} \\ F_V \end{pmatrix}$$
$$= \begin{pmatrix} -\frac{V^*UV_a}{(V_a^*)^2} + \frac{aUV}{V_a^*} - \frac{aU^*V_aV}{(V_a^*)^2} + \frac{aV^*U^*V_a^2}{(V_a^*)^3} - \frac{aV^*U^*V_a^3}{(V_a^*)^4} + \frac{aV^*UV_a^2}{(V_a^*)^3} + \frac{aU^*VV_a^2}{(V_a^*)^3} - \frac{aUV_aV}{(V_a^*)^2} \\ \frac{V^*UV_a}{(V_a^*)^2} - \frac{aUV}{V_a^*} + \frac{aU^*V_aV}{(V_a^*)^2} - \frac{aV^*U^*V_a^2}{(V_a^*)^3} + \frac{aV^*U^*V_a^3}{(V_a^*)^4} - \frac{aV^*UV_a^2}{(V_a^*)^3} - \frac{aU^*VV_a^2}{(V_a^*)^3} + \frac{aUV_aV}{(V_a^*)^2} \\ 0 \end{pmatrix}.$$

We suppose h and h^* are the eigenvector of the corresponding eigenvalue $\lambda = \mathrm{i}\omega\tau_c, \lambda = -\mathrm{i}\omega\tau_c$, respectively, of system (1) for equilibrium P, and satisfies $\langle h^*, h\rangle = \overline{(h^*)^T} \cdot h = 1$. By simple calculation, we can obtain:

$$h := \begin{pmatrix} h_1 \\ h_2 \\ h_3 \end{pmatrix} = \begin{pmatrix} \frac{\left(\mathrm{i}\omega + \left(d - \frac{aV^*U^*}{(V_a^*)^2}\right)\tau_c + \gamma e^{-\mathrm{i}\omega}\tau_c\right)(i\omega + (\alpha + c + d)\tau_c) + \left(\frac{aU^*}{V_a^*} - \alpha\right)\gamma\tau_c^2 e^{-\mathrm{i}\omega}}{\gamma e^{-\mathrm{i}\omega}\left(a + b - \frac{aV^*}{V_a^*}\right)\tau_c^2} \\ \frac{i\omega + (\alpha + c + d)\tau_c}{\gamma e^{-\mathrm{i}\omega}\tau_c} \\ 1 \end{pmatrix},$$
$$h^* := \begin{pmatrix} h_1^* \\ h_2^* \\ h_3^* \end{pmatrix} = d_1 \begin{pmatrix} 1 \\ \frac{\mathrm{i}\omega - \left(a + b + c + d - \frac{aV^*}{V_a^*}\right)\tau_c}{\left(\frac{aV^*}{V_a^*} - a - b\right)\tau_c} \\ \frac{\left(\frac{aU^*}{V_a^*} - \alpha\right)\left(\mathrm{i}\omega - \left(a + b + c + d - \frac{aV^*}{V_a^*}\right)\tau_c\right) - \frac{aU^*\tau_c^2}{V_a^*}\left(\frac{aV^*}{V_a^*} - a - b\right)}{(\mathrm{i}\omega - (\alpha + c + d)\tau_c)\left(\frac{aV^*}{V_a^*} - a - b\right)\tau_c} \end{pmatrix}, \tag{10}$$

where

$$\lambda = \mathrm{i}\omega\tau_c,$$
$$d_1 = \frac{(\lambda - (\alpha + c + d)\tau_c)\left(\frac{aV^*}{V_a^*} - a - b\right)\gamma e^{\lambda}\tau_c}{v_1 + v_2 + v_3 + v_4},$$
$$v_1 = \left(-2\lambda + \left(a + b + c + 2d - \frac{aV^*U^*}{(V_a^*)^2} - \frac{aV^*}{V_a^*}\right)\tau_c + \gamma e^{\lambda}\right)(\lambda - (\alpha + c + d)\tau_c)^2,$$
$$v_2 = \gamma\tau_c e^{\lambda}\left(\alpha - \frac{aU^*}{V_a^*}\right)(\lambda - (\alpha + c + d)\tau_c),$$
$$v_3 = \gamma e^{\lambda}\left(\frac{aU^*}{V_a^*} - \alpha\right)\left(\lambda - \left(a + b + c + d - \frac{aV^*}{V_a^*}\right)\tau_c\right),$$
$$v_4 = -\frac{aU^*\tau_c^2\gamma e^{\lambda}}{V_a^*}\left(\frac{aV^*}{V_a^*} - a - b\right).$$

We suppose the solution of system (4.1) as follows:

$$X(t) = X(T_0, T_1, T_2, \cdots) = \sum_{k=1}^{\infty} \varepsilon^k X_k(T_0, T_1, T_2, \cdots). \tag{11}$$

The derivative with respect to t is transformed into:

$$\frac{d}{dt} = \frac{\partial}{\partial T_0} + \varepsilon\frac{\partial}{\partial T_1} + \varepsilon^2\frac{\partial}{\partial T_2} + \cdots = D_0 + \varepsilon D_1 + \varepsilon^2 D_2 + \cdots,$$

where $D_i = \frac{\partial}{\partial T_i}$, i = 0,1,2$\cdots$.

Note that

$$X_i = (U_i, V_{a_i}, V_i)^T = X_i\left(t, \varepsilon t, \varepsilon^2 t, \cdots\right),$$
$$X_{i1} = (U_{i1}, V_{a_{i1}}, V_{i1})^T = X_i\left(t-1, \varepsilon t, \varepsilon^2 t, \cdots\right), i = 1, 2, \cdots.$$

Then, we can obtain:

$$\dot{X}(t) = \varepsilon D_0 X_1 + \varepsilon^2 D_1 X_1 + \varepsilon^3 D_2 X_1 + \varepsilon^2 D_0 X_2 + \varepsilon^3 D_1 X_2 + \varepsilon^3 D_0 X_3 + \cdots. \tag{12}$$

By Taylor expansion of $X(t-1)$ at $X_i(t-1, \varepsilon t, \varepsilon^2 t, \cdots)$, we obtain that

$$X(t-1) = \varepsilon X_{11} + \varepsilon^2 (X_{21} - D_1 X_{11}) + \varepsilon^3 (X_{31} - D_1 X_{21} - D_2 X_{11}) + \cdots, \tag{13}$$

where $X_{i1} = X_i(T_0 - 1, T_1, T_2, \cdots)$, $i = 1, 2, 3, \cdots$.

We consider that τ is the bifurcation parameter, and we set $\tau = \tau_c + \varepsilon\tau_\varepsilon$, where $\tau_k^{(j)}$ is the critical value of the Hopf bifurcation, τ_ε is the perturbation parameter, and ε is the dimensionless parameter. Substituting Equations (11)–(13) into Equation (9), and comparing the coefficients before ε, we obtain the following equation:

$$\begin{aligned} &D_0 U_1 - \tau_c (a_{11} U_1 + a_{12} V_{a_1} + a_{13} V_1) = 0, \\ &D_0 V_{a_1} - \tau_c (a_{21} U_1 + a_{22} V_{a_1} + a_{23} V_1) + \tau_c V_{a_{11}} \gamma = 0, \\ &D_0 V_1 - \tau_c a_{33} V_1 - \tau_c V_{a_{11}} \gamma = 0. \end{aligned} \tag{14}$$

Then, we have the solution of Equation (14):

$$X_1(T_1, T_2, T_3, \cdots) = G(T_1, T_2, T_3, \cdots) e^{i\omega\tau_c T_0} h + \overline{G}(T_1, T_2, T_3, \cdots) e^{-i\omega\tau_c T_0} \overline{h}. \tag{15}$$

where h is given in Equation (10).

The expression of the coefficient before ε^2 is as follows:

$$\begin{aligned} &D_0 U_2 - \tau_c (a_{11} U_2 + a_{12} V_{a_2} + a_{13} V_2) \\ &= - D_1 U_1 + \tau_\varepsilon (a_{11} U_1 + a_{12} V_{a_1} + a_{13} V_1) - \frac{V^*}{(V_a^*)^2} U_1 V_{a_1} \tau_c \\ &+ \frac{a}{V_a^*} U_1 V_1 \tau_c - \frac{a U^*}{(V_a^*)^2} V_{a_1} V_1 \tau_c + \frac{a V^* U^*}{(V_a^*)^3} V_{a_1}^2 \tau_c, \\ &D_0 V_{a_2} - \tau_c (a_{21} U_2 + a_{22} V_{a_2} + a_{23} V_2) + \tau_c V_{a_{21}} \gamma \\ &= - D_1 V_{a_1} + \tau_c \left(\frac{V^* U_1 V_{a_1}}{(V_a^*)^2} - \frac{a U_1 V_1}{V_a^*} + \frac{a U^* V_{a_1} V_1}{(V_a^*)^2} - \frac{a V^* U^* V_{a_1}^2}{(V_a^*)^3} + \gamma D_1 V_{a_{11}} \right) \\ &+ \tau_\varepsilon (a_{21} U_1 + a_{22} V_{a_1} + a_{23} V_1 - \gamma V_{a_{11}}), \\ &D_0 U_2 - \tau_c a_{33} V_2 - \tau_c \gamma V_{a_{21}} = - D_1 V_1 + \tau_\varepsilon a_{33} V_1 - \tau_c \gamma D_1 V_{a_{11}} + \tau_\varepsilon \gamma V_{a_{11}}. \end{aligned} \tag{16}$$

Substituting Equation (15) into the right-hand side of Equation (16), the coefficient vector of $e^{i\omega T_0}$ is denoted by m_3. According to the solvability condition, the expression of $\frac{\partial G}{\partial T_1}$ can be obtained as follows:

$$\frac{\partial G}{\partial T_1} = K \tau_\varepsilon G, \tag{17}$$

where $K = \frac{a_{11} h_1 \overline{h_1^*} + a_{12} h_2 \overline{h_1^*} + a_{13} h_3 \overline{h_1^*} + a_{21} h_1 \overline{h_2^*} + a_{22} h_2 \overline{h_2^*} + a_{23} h_3 \overline{h_2^*} - \gamma e^{-i\omega\tau_c} h_2 \overline{h_2^*} + a_{33} h_3 \overline{h_3^*} + \gamma e^{-i\omega\tau_c} h_2 \overline{h_3^*}}{1 + \gamma\tau_c \left(h_2 \overline{h_3^*} - h_2 \overline{h_2^*}\right) e^{-i\omega\tau_c}}$.

τ_ε is a small disturbance parameter, and it has little effect on the high order. Thus, we only consider its effect on the linear part. We suppose the solution of Equation (16) is as follows:

$$\begin{aligned} U_2 &= g_1 e^{2i\omega\tau_c T_0} G^2 + \overline{g_1} e^{-2i\omega\tau_c T_0} \overline{G}^2 + l_1 G\overline{G}, \\ V_{a_2} &= g_2 e^{2i\omega\tau_c T_0} \overline{G}^2 + \overline{g_2} e^{-2i\omega\tau_c T_0} \overline{G}^2 + l_2 G\overline{G}, \\ V_2 &= g_3 e^{2i\omega\tau_c T_0} G^2 + \overline{g_3} e^{-2i\omega\tau_c T_0} \overline{G}^2 + l_3 G\overline{G}. \end{aligned} \quad (18)$$

Substituting Equation (18) into Equation (16), we obtain:

$$\begin{pmatrix} g_1 \\ g_2 \\ g_3 \end{pmatrix} = \frac{A_2^*}{|A_2|} \begin{pmatrix} y_1^1 \\ y_2^1 \\ y_3^1 \end{pmatrix}, \begin{pmatrix} l_1 \\ l_2 \\ l_3 \end{pmatrix} = \frac{A_3^*}{|A_3|} \begin{pmatrix} y_1^2 \\ y_2^2 \\ y_3^2 \end{pmatrix}, \quad (19)$$

where

$$\begin{aligned}
y_1^1 &= -\frac{V^*}{(V_a^*)^2} h_1 h_2 + \frac{a}{V_a^*} h_1 h_3 - \frac{aU^*}{(V_a^*)^2} h_2 h_3 + \frac{aV^*U^*}{(V_a^*)^3} h_1^2, \\
y_2^1 &= \frac{V^*}{(V_a^*)^2} h_1 h_2 - \frac{a}{V_a^*} h_1 h_3 + \frac{aU^*}{(V_a^*)^2} h_2 h_3 - \frac{aV^*U^*}{(V_a^*)^3} h_1^2, \\
y_3^1 &= 0. \\
y_1^2 &= \frac{V^*}{(V_a^*)^2} \left(h_1 \overline{h_2} + \overline{h_1} h_2\right) - \frac{a}{V_a^*} \left(h_1 \overline{h_3} + \overline{h_1} h_3\right) + \frac{aU^*}{(V_a^*)^2} \left(h_2 \overline{h_3} + \overline{h_2} h_3\right) - \frac{2aV^*U^*}{(V_a^*)^3} h_1 \overline{h_1}, \\
y_2^2 &= -\frac{V^*}{(V_a^*)^2} \left(h_1 \overline{h_2} + \overline{h_1} h_2\right) + \frac{a}{V_a^*} \left(h_1 \overline{h_3} + \overline{h_1} h_3\right) - \frac{aU^*}{(V_a^*)^2} \left(h_2 \overline{h_3} + \overline{h_2} h_3\right) + \frac{2aV^*U^*}{(V_a^*)^3} h_1 \overline{h_1}, \\
y_3^2 &= 0. \\
A_k &= \begin{pmatrix} x_{11}^k & x_{12}^k & x_{13}^k \\ x_{21}^k & x_{22}^k & x_{23}^k \\ x_{31}^k & x_{32}^k & x_{33}^k \end{pmatrix} \\
A_k^* &= \begin{pmatrix} x_{22}^k x_{33}^k - x_{32}^k x_{23}^k & -x_{21}^k x_{33}^k + x_{31}^k x_{23}^k & x_{21}^k x_{32}^k - x_{31}^k x_{22}^k \\ -x_{12}^k x_{33}^k + x_{32}^k x_{13}^k & x_{11}^k x_{33}^k - x_{31}^k x_{13}^k & -x_{11}^k x_{32}^k + x_{31}^k x_{12}^k \\ x_{12}^k x_{23}^k - x_{22}^k x_{13}^k & -x_{11}^k x_{23}^k + x_{21}^k x_{13}^k & x_{11}^k x_{22}^k - x_{21}^k x_{12}^k \end{pmatrix} \\
|A_k| &= x_{11}^k \left(x_{22}^k x_{33}^k - x_{32}^k x_{23}^k\right) - x_{12}^k \left(x_{21}^k x_{33}^k - x_{31}^k x_{23}^k\right) + x_{13}^k \left(x_{21}^k x_{32}^k - x_{31}^k x_{22}^k\right), \ k = 1, 2, 3.
\end{aligned}$$

with

$$\begin{aligned}
x_{11}^1 &= a + b + c + d - \frac{aV^*}{V_a^*} + i\omega, \ x_{12}^1 = \frac{aV^*U^*}{(V_a^*)^2}, \ x_{13}^1 = -\frac{aU^*}{V_a^*}, \\
x_{21}^1 &= \frac{aV^*}{V_a^*} - a - b, \ x_{22}^1 = d - \frac{aV^*U^*}{(V_a^*)^2} + i\omega + \gamma e^{-i\omega\tau_c}, \ x_{23}^1 = \frac{aU^*}{V_a^*} - \alpha, \\
x_{31}^1 &= 0, \ x_{32}^1 = -\gamma e^{-i\omega\tau_c}, \ x_{33}^1 = \alpha + c + d + i\omega, \\
x_{11}^2 &= a + b + c + d - \frac{aV^*}{V_a^*} + 2i\omega, \ x_{12}^2 = \frac{aV^*U^*}{(V_a^*)^2}, \ x_{13}^2 = -\frac{aU^*}{V_a^*}, \\
x_{21}^2 &= \frac{aV^*}{V_a^*} - a - b, \ x_{22}^2 = d - \frac{aV^*U^*}{(V_a^*)^2} + 2i\omega + \gamma e^{-2i\omega\tau_c}, \ x_{23}^2 = \frac{aU^*}{V_a^*} - \alpha,
\end{aligned}$$

$$x^2_{31} = 0,\ x^2_{32} = -\gamma e^{-2i\omega\tau_c},\ x^2_{33} = \alpha + c + d + 2i\omega,$$
$$x^3_{11} = \frac{aV^*}{V_a^*} - a - b - c - d,\ x^3_{12} = -\frac{aV^*U^*}{(V_a^*)^2},\ x^3_{13} = \frac{aU^*}{V_a^*},$$
$$x^3_{21} = a + b - \frac{aV^*}{V_a^*},\ x^3_{22} = \frac{aV^*U^*}{(V_a^*)^2} - d - \gamma,\ x^3_{23} = \alpha - \frac{aU^*}{V_a^*},$$
$$x^3_{31} = 0,\ x^3_{32} = \gamma,\ x^3_{33} = -\alpha - c - d.$$

The expression of the coefficient before ε^3 is:

$$\begin{aligned}
&D_0U_3 - \tau_c(a_{11}U_3 + a_{12}V_{a_3} + a_{13}V_3)\\
=& - D_1U_2D_2U_1 + \tau_\varepsilon(a_{11}U_2 + a_{12}V_{a_2} + a_{13}V_2) - \frac{V^*}{(V_a^*)^2}(U_1V_{a_1}\tau_\varepsilon + U_1V_{a_2}\tau_c + U_2V_{a_1}\tau_c)\\
&+ \frac{a}{V_a^*}(U_1V_1\tau_\varepsilon + U_1V_2\tau_c + U_2V_1\tau_c) - \frac{aU^*}{(V_a^*)^2}(V_{a_1}V_1\tau_\varepsilon + V_{a_1}V_2\tau_c + V_{a_2}V_1\tau_c) - \frac{aV^*U^*}{(V_a^*)^4}V_{a_1}^3\tau_c\\
&+ \frac{aV^*U^*}{(V_a^*)^3}\left(V_{a_1}^2\tau_\varepsilon + 2V_{a_1}V_{a_2}\tau_c\right) + \frac{aV^*}{(V_a^*)^3}U_1V_{a_1}^2\tau_c + \frac{aU^*}{(V_a^*)^3}V_{a_1}^2V_1\tau_c - \frac{a}{(V_a^*)^2}U_1V_{a_1}V_1\tau_c,\\
&D_0V_{a_3} - \tau_c(a_{21}U_3 + a_{22}V_{a_3} + a_{23}V_3) + \tau_cV_{a_{31}}\gamma\\
=& - D_1V_{a_2} - D_2V_{a_1} + \tau_\varepsilon(a_{21}U_2 + a_{22}V_{a_2} + a_{23}V_2) + \frac{V^*}{(V_a^*)^2}(U_1V_{a_1}\tau_\varepsilon + U_1V_{a_2}\tau_c + U_2V_{a_1}\tau_c)\\
&- \frac{a}{V_a^*}(U_1V_1\tau_\varepsilon + U_1V_2\tau_c + U_2V_1\tau_c) + \frac{aU^*}{(V_a^*)^2}(V_{a_1}V_1\tau_\varepsilon + V_{a_1}V_2\tau_c + V_{a_2}V_1\tau_c) + \frac{aV^*U^*}{(V_a^*)^4}V_{a_1}^3\tau_c\\
&- \frac{aV^*U^*}{(V_a^*)^3}\left(V_{a_1}^2\tau_\varepsilon + 2V_{a_1}V_{a_2}\tau_c\right) - \frac{aV^*}{(V_a^*)^3}U_1V_{a_1}^2\tau_c - \frac{aU^*}{(V_a^*)^3}V_{a_1}^2V_1\tau_c + \frac{a}{(V_a^*)^2}U_1V_{a_1}V_1\tau_c\\
&+ \tau_c\gamma D_1V_{a_{21}} + \tau_c\gamma D_2V_{a_{11}} - \tau_\varepsilon\gamma(V_{a_{21}} - D_1V_{a_{11}}),\\
&D_0V_3 - \tau_ca_{33}V_3 - \tau_c\gamma V_{a_{31}}\\
=& - D_1V_2D_2V_1 + \tau_\varepsilon a_{33}V_2 - \tau_c\gamma(D_1V_{a_{21}} + D_2V_{a_{11}}) + \tau_\varepsilon\gamma(V_{a_{21}} - D_1V_{a_{11}}).
\end{aligned} \tag{20}$$

Substituting Equations (15), (18) and (19) into the right-hand side of Equation (20), and m_4 denotes the coefficient vector of $e^{i\omega T_0}$. According to the solvability condition $\langle h^*, m_4\rangle = 0$, and noting that τ_ε^2 is small enough for small unfolding parameter τ_ε, we ignore the term $\tau_\varepsilon^2 G$. Then, we have:

$$\frac{\partial G}{\partial T_2} = HG^2\overline{G}, \tag{21}$$

where

$$\begin{aligned}
H =& \frac{\tau_c\left(\overline{h_1^*} - \overline{h_2^*}\right)\sum_{i=1}^4 H_i}{1 + \tau_c\gamma e^{-i\omega\tau_c}h_2\left(\overline{h_3^*} - \overline{h_2^*}\right)},\\
H_1 =& -\frac{V^*}{(V_a^*)^2}\left(h_1l_2 + g_2\overline{h_1} + h_2l_1 + \overline{h_2}G\right) + \frac{a}{V_a^*}\left(h_1l_3 + \overline{h_1}g_3 + h_3l_1 + \overline{h_3}G\right),\\
H_2 =& -\frac{aU^*}{(V_a^*)^2}\left(h_2l_3 + \overline{h_2}g_3 + h_3l_2 + \overline{h_3}g_2\right) + \frac{2aV^*U^*}{(V_a^*)^3}\left(h_2l_2 + \overline{h_2}g_2\right),\\
H_3 =& -\frac{3aV^*U^*}{(V_a^*)^4}h_2^2\overline{h_2} + \frac{aV^*}{(V_a^*)^3}\left(2h_1h_2\overline{h_2} + \overline{h_1}h_2^2\right),\\
H_4 =& \frac{aU^*}{(V_a^*)^3}\left(2h_2\overline{h_2}h_3 + h_2^2\overline{h_3}\right) - \frac{a}{(V_a^*)^2}\left(h_1h_2\overline{h_3} + h_1\overline{h_2}h_3 + \overline{h_1}h_2h_3\right),
\end{aligned}$$

where g_k ($k = 1,2,3$) and l_k ($k = 1,2,3$) are given in Equation (19), and h_j ($j = 1,2,3$) and h_j^* ($j = 1,2,3$) are given in Equation (10).

Letting $G \mapsto (G/\varepsilon)$, we can obtain the normal form of Hopf bifurcation of system (1) as:

$$\dot{G} = K\tau_\varepsilon G + HG^2\overline{G}, \quad (22)$$

where K is given in Equation (17), and H is given in Equation (21).

Letting $G = re^{i\theta}$ and substituting it into Equation (22), and we can obtain the normal form of the Hopf bifurcation in polar coordinates:

$$\begin{cases} \dot{r} = \mathrm{Re}(K)\tau_\varepsilon r + \mathrm{Re}(H)r^3, \\ \dot{\theta} = \mathrm{Im}(K)\tau_\varepsilon + \mathrm{Im}(H)r^2, \end{cases} \quad (23)$$

where K is expressed in Equation (17), and H is expressed in Equation (21).

According to the normal form of the Hopf bifurcation by polar coordinates, we just need to consider the first equation by system (23). Thus, there is the following theorem:

Theorem 2. *For system (23), when* $\frac{\mathrm{Re}(K)\tau_\varepsilon}{\mathrm{Re}(H)} < 0$, *there is a nontrivial fixed point* $r = \sqrt{-\frac{\mathrm{Re}(K)\tau_\varepsilon}{\mathrm{Re}(H)}} < 0$, *and system (1) has periodic solution:*

(1) If $\mathrm{Re}(K)\tau_\varepsilon < 0$, *then the periodic solution reduced on the center manifold is unstable.*

(2) If $\mathrm{Re}(K)\tau_\varepsilon > 0$, *then the periodic solution reduced on the center manifold is stable.*

5. Numerical Simulations

In this section, since different countries have different prevention and control strategies and basic national conditions, there are some differences in the parameters values taken in the corresponding models. We will complete the numerical simulations in two parts: the first part is the parameters analysis to estimate the required parameters range in the model and select two sets of parameters values within a reasonable parameters range; the second part is the numerical simulations and parameters discussion, using the two sets of reasonable parameters selected in the first part as an example and MATLAB for numerical simulations. In addition, based on the COVID-19 variant strains, the effect of each parameter on the critical time $\tau_1^{(0)}$ is discussed.

5.1. Parameter Analysis

In this part, we estimate some parameters used in numerical simulations to make them closer to the actual parameters. Then, we give estimates of natural birth rate B_r, disease-related death rate c, and natural death rate d. At the same time, we also made some reasonable assumptions about the large range of failure rate γ, the weight factor a, the fixed vaccination rate b, and the secondary vaccination rate α.

First, for the natural birth rate, we select the natural birth rate of some countries in a certain year of Central Intelligence Agency (CIA) as the study data, and after excluding the outliers, we analyze the range of natural birth rate values roughly: $Br \in (0.770, 1.250)$. Then, from the perspective of time change, we specifically analyze the change of natural birth rate B_r in China in recent years by using the data from the National Bureau of Statistics of the People's Republic of China (NBSPRC) as an example, and obtain that its mean value is within a reasonable interval. Analyze the world natural birth rate B_r from two dimensions of region and time. Finally, we consider the population base as unit 1, and the natural increase of population B and the natural birth rate B_r are numerically equal. Thus, the birth rate $B = 1.120\%$ is selected as the simulations parameter.

Second, for COVID-19 disease-related mortality c, we select the data of Johns Hopkins University (https://coronavirus.jhu.edu/map.html, accessed on 12 December 2021) to observe the mortality due to illness, and then we find that different countries have large fluctuations. Therefore, we select some representative countries in a balanced way and analyze the value range of disease-related mortality c. Here, the data mean is used as the parameters in the next section, and the disease-related mortality $c = 4.6550\%$ is obtained with general significance. It is important to note that the model applies equally to other reasonable values of the parameter c.

Next, as for the natural mortality rate d, the natural mortality rate of a country can be influenced by many aspects and varies greatly from country to country in practice. Therefore, when analyzing the natural mortality rate d, we select data from different countries in a balanced way for the analysis, and we take the data from the Intelligent Data Platform (https://mobile.hellobi.com, accessed on 14 December 2021) as an example, and excluding the abnormal mortality data in that year, we consider a reasonable interval for the natural mortality rate d: $d \in (4.5500, 14.5000)$. For a better fit, the birth rate B_r refers to the data from National Bureau of Statistics of the People's Republic of China (NBSPRC), so the mortality rate is also selected partially from NBSPRC, as shown in Figure 2. Due to the large range of intervals, we select $d = 0.6904\%$ and $d = 1.4170\%$ for subsequent numerical simulations.

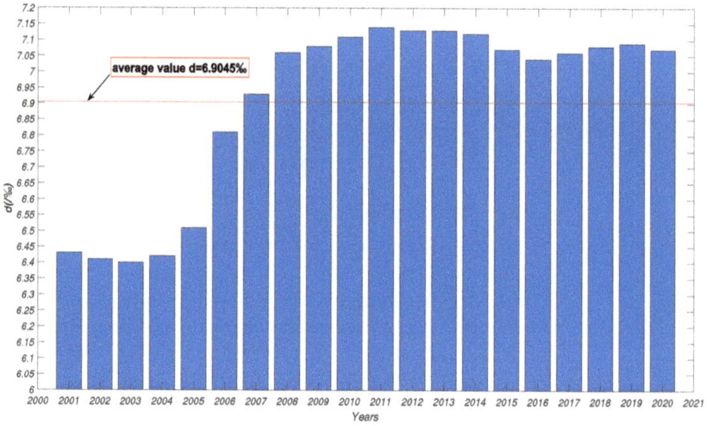

Figure 2. Annual natural mortality d in a low mortality country.

Finally, for parameters without numerical support, we select parameters values in the way of reasonable assumptions to carry out numerical simulations in the next section. In this model, for other assumed parameters, the model has stability and can give the model conclusion under reasonable parameters.

For large-range failure rate γ, the large-range is a catch-all term. Here, we believe that a failure rate greater than 0.5 and less than 1 is identified as a large-scale failure rate. In the future numerical simulations, we will take the vicinity of $\gamma = 0.67$ as an example for simulations.

As for the impact factor a and the fixed vaccination rate b, the values of a and b are greatly influenced by personal subjective consciousness and are also related to the publicity and encouragement policies of a country or region, but the relationship between a and b should be guaranteed: $a + b \leq 1$. In the following simulations, we take both a and b near 0.5 as an example.

For the secondary vaccination rate α, we can make assumptions, the significance of which is to study the epidemic prevention and control effects under different secondary vaccination rate α. In the simulations, we take α near 0.9 as an example for numerical simulations.

In summary, the two groups of parameters used in the simulations results in the next section are as follows:

$I: B = 0.0112, d = 0.0069, c = 0.04655, \gamma = 0.675, a = 0.49, b = 0.5, \alpha = 0.9.$

$II: B = 0.0112, d = 0.01417, c = 0.04655, \gamma = 0.685, a = 0.49, b = 0.5, \alpha = 0.92.$

5.2. Numerical Simulation Results

In this section, we take the two groups of parameters given in Section 5.1 as examples for numerical simulations, and analyze the epidemic prevention and control effects in the sense of this group of parameters, and then provide a critical time $\tau_1^{(0)}$ for controllable widespread antibody failure, which provides a reference for the inoculation time of booster injection. In order to explore the effect of different epidemic prevention and control measures, we discuss the influence of fixed vaccination rate b, secondary vaccination rate α and failure rate γ on the critical time $\tau_1^{(0)}$ of controllable widespread antibody failure. Finally, considering the frequent mutation of COVID-19 virus, we analyze the impact on epidemic prevention and control from the disease-related mortality rate c of the mutated strains.

For the first group parameters I:

$$B = 0.0112, d = 0.0069, c = 0.04655, \gamma = 0.675, a = 0.49, b = 0.5, \alpha = 0.9.$$

Obviously, the assumption **(H1)** holds, system (1) only has one nonnegative equilibrium P. After calculation, the assumption **(H2)** holds. Thus, the equilibrium $P = (U^*, V_a^*, V^*) \approx (0.016079, 0.231125, 0.163626)$ is locally asymptotically stable when $\tau = 0$.

Using MATLAB, we can obtain $\omega_0 = 0.005233, Q_0 \approx 0.225625, P_0 \approx 0.947214, \tau_1^{(0)} \approx 38.2901$ by plugging parameters group I into Equations (6)–(8). According to Theorem 1, the equilibrium P is locally asymptotically stable at $\tau \in [0, \tau_1^{(0)})$, and the Hopf bifurcation occurs near the equilibrium P when $\tau = \tau_1^{(0)}$. Then, we obtain $\mathrm{Re}(K) > 0, \mathrm{Re}(H) < 0$ from Equations (17) and (21). Thus, according to Theorem 2, the system (1) has forward periodic solution and the bifurcating periodic solution is stable when $\tau_\varepsilon > 0$.

When τ=0, we choose the initial value (0.02,0.2,0.2) and the equilibrium P of system (1) is locally asymptotically stable (see Figure 3).

When $\tau = 6 \in \left(0, \tau_1^{(0)}\right)$, we choose initial values $(0.015, 0.12, 0.2)$, and the equilibrium P of system (1) is locally asymptotically stable (see Figure 4).

When $\tau = 38.4 > \tau_1^{(0)} = 38.2901$ is near $\tau_1^{(0)}$, we choose initial values $(0.012, 0.232, 0.162)$, and system (1) has stable forward periodic solution near the equilibrium P (see Figure 5).

It can be seen from Figures 3–5, and the equilibrium P of system (1) is locally asymptotically stable when $\tau \in [0, \tau_1^{(0)})$ as shown in Figures 3 and 4. The periodic solution of system (1) near equilibrium P is stable when τ is near $\tau_1^{(0)}$ as shown in Figure 5. The equilibrium P of system (1) is unstable when $\tau \in (\tau_1^{(0)}, +\infty)$.

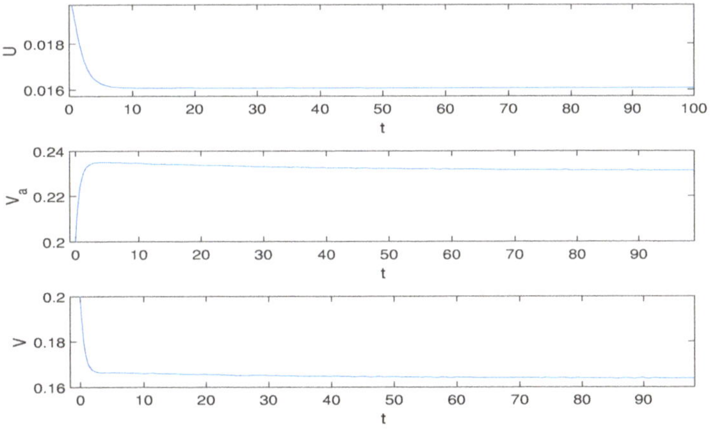

Figure 3. When τ = 0, the equilibrium P of system (1) is locally asymptotically stable.

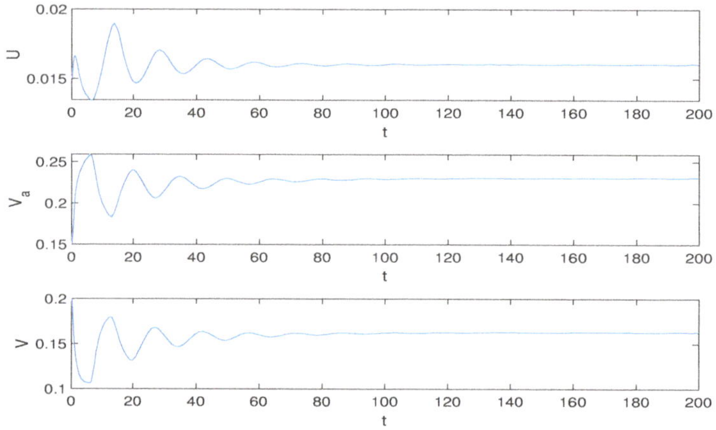

Figure 4. When $\tau = 4$, the equilibrium P of system (1) is locally asymptotically stable.

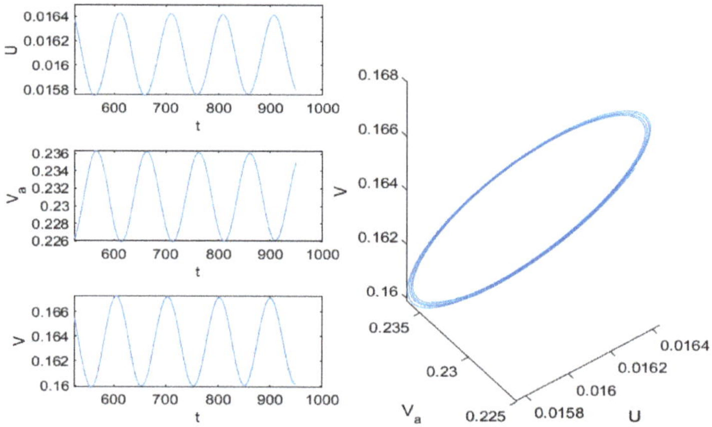

Figure 5. When $\tau = 38.4$, the periodic solution of system (1) near equilibrium P is stable.

Remark 1. *Under the first group parameters I, it can be found by numerical simulations that the time $\tau = 0$ of the wide range of antibody failure, that is, most people produce antibodies after vaccination and lose them in a short time. As the secondary vaccination rate α in the parameter is ideal, system (1) at this time is also stable, and the epidemic can be maintained even when the vaccine cost is high. When $\tau \in [0, \tau_1^{(0)})$, the shorter the time τ of the wide range of antibody failure is, the faster the antibody tends to stabilize, which also indicates that the number of secondary vaccinations is bigger, and the cost of controlling the epidemic is higher, but finally stabilizes near the equilibrium P. When $\tau > \tau_1^{(0)}$ is near $\tau_1^{(0)}$, the time τ of the wide range of antibody failure will change in a small range, and the antibody presence level will also show periodic changes. At this time, the epidemic prevention and control effect are controllable. When $\tau \in (\tau_1^{(0)}, +\infty)$, the antibody distribution level cannot be controlled effectively. The fluctuation range of antibody distribution increases with the increase of time. According to the actual situation, the effectiveness of vaccines will have a certain period of time; generally, there is no permanent effective situation. Therefore, the time τ of a wide range of antibody failure is finite. Although there are periods when the antibody level is ideal, there are also periods when the antibody level is low. In this case, the antibody level cannot be controlled to be stable, and the low antibody level may lead to the outbreak of the epidemic, and the epidemic prevention and control effect are not ideal. Based on the above analysis, we can* *conclude that the optimal time* $\tau_1^{(0)} = 38.2901$ *of controllable widespread antibody failure, which provides a reference for the second vaccination time of COVID-19 vaccine in medicine.*

Next, we consider a group of parameters with higher mortality. In order to compare with the first group parameters I, we also idealize the secondary vaccination rate α*, and select the secondary vaccination rate* α *under the future vaccination level. For the second group parameters II:*

$$B = 0.01231, d = 0.01417, c = 0.04655, \gamma = 0.685, a = 0.49, b = 0.5, \alpha = 0.92.$$

Obviously, the assumption **(H1)** *holds, substituting these parameters values into Equation* (2)*, we obtain that system* (1) *only has one nonnegative equilibrium* $P = (U^*, V_a^*, V^*) \approx (0.017375, 0.198918, 0.138938)$. *After calculation, the assumption f(H2) holds. Thus, the equilibrium P is locally asymptotically stable when* $\tau = 0$.

When $\tau = 0$, we choose the initial values $(0.01, 0.1, 0.2)$, and the equilibrium P of system (1) is locally asymptotically stable (see Figure 6).

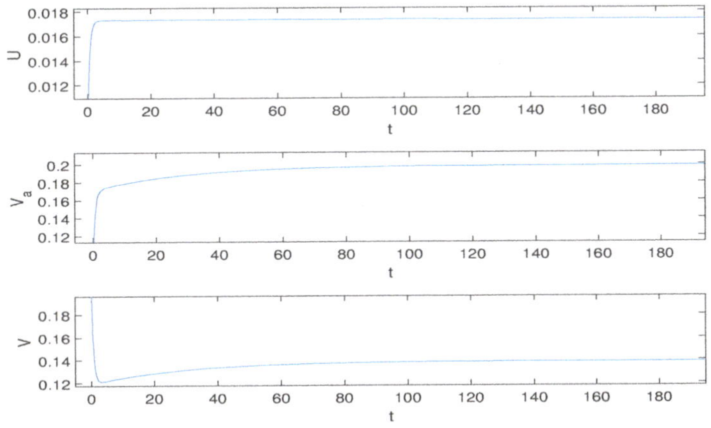

Figure 6. When τ=0, the equilibrium P of system (1) is locally asymptotically stable.

Substituting these parameters' values into Equation (7), we obtain $c_0 \approx -0.000081, c1 \approx 0.254617, c2 \approx 1.033500$. By derivation of Equation (7), $\Delta \approx 1.217044, \tilde{z}_1 \approx -0.505131, \tilde{z}_2 \approx -0.872863$, we further calculate $h(\tilde{z}_1) \approx 0.006119, h(\tilde{z}_2) \approx -0.099943$. It satisfies assumption **(H4)**. Using MATLAB, according to Equations (7) and (8), we obtain $\omega_1 \approx 0.017865, Q_0 \approx 0.62373, P_0 \approx 0.78164, \tau_1^{(0)} \approx 35.2992$.

Thus, according to Theorem 1, the equilibrium P is locally asymptotically stable when $\tau \in [0, \tau_1^{(0)})$, and the Hopf bifurcation occurs near the equilibrium P when $\tau_1^{(0)}$. According to Equation (17), Equation (21), and Theorem 2, we conclude that $\mathrm{Re}(K) > 0, \mathrm{Re}(H) < 0$; thus, system (1) has a forward periodic solution and the bifurcating periodic solution is stable when $\tau_\varepsilon > 0$.

When $\tau = 6 \in [0, \tau_1^{(0)})$, we choose the initial value $(0.01, 0.2, 0.2)$, and the equilibrium P of system (1) is locally asymptotically stable (see Figure 7).

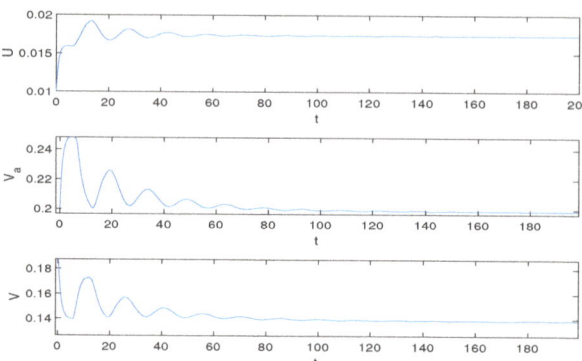

Figure 7. When $\tau = 6$, the equilibrium P of system (1) is locally asymptotically stable.

When $\tau = 35.5 > \tau_1^{(0)} = 35.2992$, we choose the initial value $(0.01, 0.2, 0.15)$, the model (1) has a stable forward periodic solution near the equilibrium P (see Figure 8).

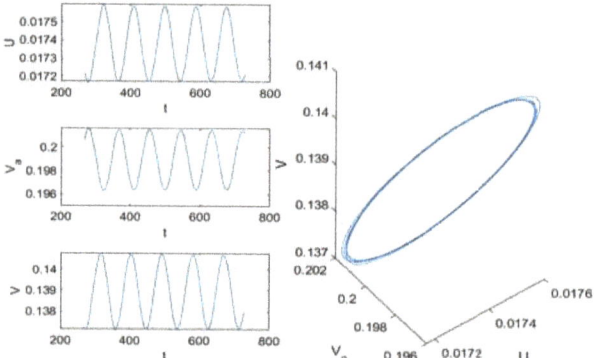

Figure 8. When $\tau = 35.5$, the periodic solution of system (1) near equilibrium P is stable.

It can be seen from Figures 6–8, the equilibrium P of system (1) is locally asymptotically stable as shown in Figures 6 and 7. The equilibrium P of system (1) is unstable when $\tau \in (\tau_1^{(0)}, +\infty)$. The equilibrium P of system (1) exhibits periodic fluctuation and bifurcates stable periodic solutions when τ approaches the critical time $\tau_1^{(0)}$ as shown in Figure 8. With the increase of τ, the fluctuation tendency of the system (1) at the same time level also increases.

Remark 2. *According to the above numerical simulations, it can be found that, when the time $\tau < \tau_1^{(0)}$ of the wide range of antibody failure, it will eventually stabilize to the same antibody presence level after a certain time. According to our analysis, the smaller the time delay τ is, the faster it tends to be stable. However, according to the actual situation, the smaller the failure time is, the more total inoculated doses will increase, resulting in the increase of epidemic prevention cost, and ultimately maintain the same epidemic effect. Therefore, the ideal situation of epidemic prevention and control is that antibody levels are stable and controllable, the validity of vaccines is longer, and the cost of epidemic prevention can be saved and the cost of epidemic prevention can be reduced. When $\tau \in (\tau_1^{(0)}, +\infty)$ and τ varies in a small range near $\tau_1^{(0)}$, the antibody levels will show periodic changes, but the overall situation of epidemic prevention and control is roughly stable. When $\tau > \tau_1^{(0)}$, the antibody presence level is high and low, and epidemic prevention and control is uncertain, which may lead to the outbreak of epidemic at the low antibody presence level.*

Remark 3. In the process of numerical simulations, we take the first group parameters I and the second group parameters II as examples and give the critical time $\tau_1^{(0)}$ of controllable widespread antibody failure of 38.5 weeks and 35.3 weeks, respectively, which can provide a reference for the vaccination time of COVID-19 vaccine booster injection in medical aspect to prolong the time of antibody disappearance.

Through the analysis of the simulations results of the two groups of parameters data, the antibody presence level is used to measure the epidemic prevention and control effect. Taking the time of six weeks of the wide range of antibody failure in the simulations as an example, the three groups population is roughly stable at $0.016, 0.231$, and 0.164 (unit: million) for the first group parameters I, while the three groups population is stable at $0.017, 0.624$, and 0.139 (unit: million) for the second group parameters II, and the proportions of antibody are 56.34% and 56.21%, respectively. It can be concluded that, under the same epidemic vaccination strategy, the existence level of antibody is roughly the same, which is consistent with the reality.

In terms of the critical time $\tau_1^{(0)}$ for controllable widespread antibody failure, the group with lower mortality has better critical time $\tau_1^{(0)}$ for controllable widespread antibody failure than the group with higher mortality. The shorter the time τ of the wide range of antibody failure, the more vaccinations per person, the higher the cost of quarantine, and the greater the impact on normal life. Through the above theoretical analysis, we can know that the antibody existence level will be the same if the antibody failure time τ is appropriately increased within the critical time τ for controllable widespread antibody failure. Therefore, we can achieve the ideal of epidemic prevention and control through more effective and longer-lasting vaccines.

Next, we discuss the impact of different epidemic prevention and control strategies on the epidemic prevention and control. We use the combination of discrete and continuous variables to investigated the influence on the critical time $\tau_1^{(0)}$ of controllable widespread antibody failure. We will discuss the effects of validity factor a, fixed vaccination rate b, failure rate γ, and disease-related mortality c on the critical time $\tau_1^{(0)}$ in detail below. Finally, the impact of a sudden increase in disease-related mortality c and antibody failure rate γ due to the emergence of a mutant strain of COVID-19 is analyzed.

We first analyze the impact factor a on vaccine effectiveness on the vaccination rate, and thus affect the critical time $\tau_1^{(0)}$ of controllable widespread antibody failure in system (1), and add the secondary vaccination rate α of a discrete case as shown in Figure 9:

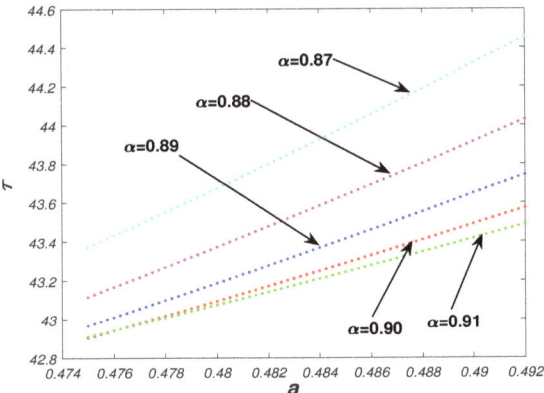

Figure 9. The influence of positive feedback factor a on the critical time $\tau_1^{(0)}$.

In Figure 9, it observes that the increase of influence factor a has a significant promoting effect on the critical time $\tau_1^{(0)}$, and the promoting relationship between them is approximately linear. Therefore, in the context of this discussion, we can promote the safety and effectiveness of COVID-19 vaccines by strengthening publicity, so as to improve the impact of vaccine effectiveness on vaccination, which also provides some suggestions for future epidemic prevention and control.

When other parameters are fixed, the influence of fixed vaccination rate b in the continuous case and secondary vaccination rate α in the discrete case on the critical time $\tau_1^{(0)}$ is investigated in Figure 10.

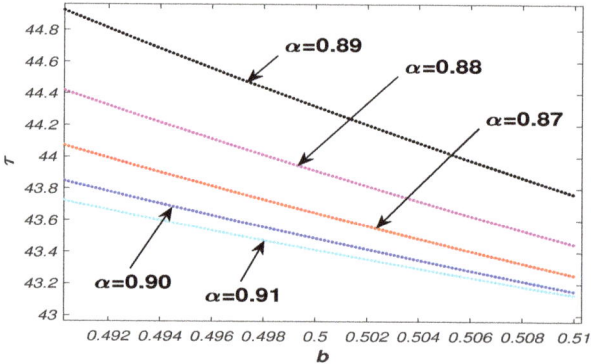

Figure 10. Influence of fixed vaccination rate b (continuous case) and secondary vaccination rate α (discrete case) on the critical time $\tau_1^{(0)}$.

In Figure 10, we find that the critical time $\tau_1^{(0)}$ will be suppressed by fixed vaccination rate b in a linear manner. In comparison with Figure 9, in order to increase the vaccination rate of COVID-19, to improve the final antibody presence level, and to promote the critical time $\tau_1^{(0)}$, we should properly regulate the vaccination strategy from two aspects: on the one hand, we should appropriately improve the role of effectiveness in vaccination willingness; on the other hand, the fixed vaccination rate b brought about by other factors should be appropriately reduced.

As the COVID-19 virus continues to mutate, it has created multiple mutated strains with higher transmissibility and mortality. Then, we consider the effects of the failure rate γ (see Figure 11) and mortality rate c (see Figure 12) on the critical time $\tau_1^{(0)}$.

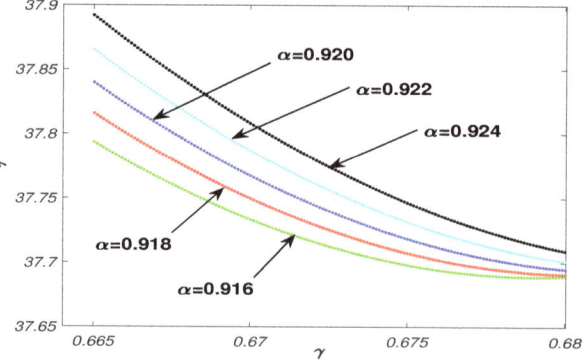

Figure 11. The influence of continuous antibody failure rate γ and discrete secondary vaccination rate α on the critical time $\tau_1^{(0)}$.

From Figure 11, it can be concluded that the smaller the antibody failure rate γ is, the larger the critical time $\tau_1^{(0)}$ is. The influence of failure rate γ on the critical time $\tau_1^{(0)}$ decreases with the increase of failure rate γ. When the failure rate $\gamma > 0.68$, the effect of γ on $\tau_1^{(0)}$ is almost zero. When the failure rate $\gamma < 0.68$, the smaller γ is, the more obvious the effect of increasing the critical time $\tau_1^{(0)}$ is. Therefore, from the perspective of epidemic control, we have confirmed the need to reduce the vaccine's own failure rate γ from the perspective of epidemic control.

Figure 12. The influence of continuous secondary vaccination rate α and discrete mortality rate c on the critical time $\tau_1^{(0)}$.

In the case of the COVID-19 mutant strains, the mutant strains cause a spike in antibody failure rate γ. If the failure rate γ of the primary antibody is less than 0.68, the γ surge will cause the shortening of the critical time $\tau_1^{(0)}$. If the failure rate γ of the original antibody is high, the effect of γ surge may be relatively small. Therefore, we should keep τ at a distance $\tau_1^{(0)}$ to prevent the risk of uncertainty due to mutant strains.

From Figure 12, comparing the influence of disease mortality rate c and secondary vaccination rate α on the critical time $\tau_1^{(0)}$, we can find that the influence of disease mortality rate c on the critical time $\tau_1^{(0)}$ is significantly higher than that of secondary vaccination rate α on the critical time $\tau_1^{(0)}$.

From the perspective of the COVID-19 mutant strains, the COVID-19 mutant strains may cause discrete changes in disease mortality rate c. We consider the effect of the discrete change of c on $\tau_1^{(0)}$ in Figure 12. Small changes in disease mortality rate c caused by the mutated strains may lead to large changes in the critical time $\tau_1^{(0)}$ of controllable widespread antibody failure, leading to instability in the vaccination system. After a certain period of time, antibody levels rise and fall, and the COVID-19 mutated strains may trigger a new outbreak. Therefore, we should pay attention to the variation trend of mutant strains and change the inoculation strategy in time when necessary. Before it becomes a mainstream mutant strain, countermeasures should be taken to ensure the effect of epidemic prevention and control.

Remark 4. *According to Figures 9–12, we find that the secondary vaccination rate α has a turning point α_0 around 0.91. In a certain range before α_0, as shown in Figures 9 and 10, the increase of the secondary vaccination rate α leads to the decrease of the critical time $\tau_1^{(0)}$, and the closer it is to 0.91, the less the effect is. In a certain range after α_0, the increase of secondary vaccination rate α will increase the critical time $\tau_1^{(0)}$, and the change relationship between the two is approximately linear, as shown in Figures 11 and 12.*

6. Conclusions

In this paper, an UV_aV vaccination model with time-delay was constructed for COVID-19 vaccination based on the transmission characteristics of COVID-19 vaccine antibodies. Compared with the traditional SIR model, this paper paid more attention to the presence of antibodies in the population and the vaccination situation of vaccines. At the same time, the effect of vaccination intention on vaccination rate was added into the model. We also analyzed the existence and stability of equilibrium, and studied the existence and stability of the Hopf bifurcation associated with existing equilibrium. Then, we derived the normal form of the Hopf bifurcation in the vaccination model by using the multiple time scales method. Finally, according to the parameters estimations and the data given in the literature, it was divided into two groups of parameters. One group is the small natural mortality parameters, and the other is the natural mortality parameters. Numerical simulations were carried out to verify the correctness of the theoretical analysis.

In [40], Lu et al. studied the impact of critical treatment time on epidemic prevention and control. In this paper, we considered the impact of the large-scale failure time of critical antibodies on epidemic prevention and control from the perspective of failure time. Numerical simulations showed that, when the time $\tau < \tau_1^{(0)}$ of the wide range of antibody failure was obtained in the sense of two parameters, after a certain time, the antibody would eventually approach the same level of existence, and the epidemic prevention and control effects were basically the same. Different failure time τ would produce different critical time $\tau_1^{(0)}$; the shorter the failure time τ, the faster the critical time $\tau_1^{(0)}$. However, the shorter the lapse, the greater the total number of vaccinations. Obviously, on the one hand, frequent vaccination would inevitably bring a great impact on people's life and work, but also seriously hindered the development of society and the country; on the other hand, frequent vaccinations increased the cost of prevention. When τ changed in a small range near $\tau_1^{(0)}$, we believed that the antibody level changed periodically and the epidemic prevention and control situation was under control. When $\tau > \tau_1^{(0)}$, the antibody presence level was high and low, and there was a risk of causing a new epidemic. Therefore, taking these two groups of parameters as examples, we gave the critical time $\tau_1^{(0)}$ of controllable widespread antibody failure of 38.5 weeks and 35.3 weeks, respectively, and the stability of the system would be greatly affected before and after the critical time $\tau_1^{(0)}$. This provided a medical reference for the time of COVID-19 vaccine booster injection to prolong the time of antibody disappearance.

In addition, according to Wang's et al. [41] research, the protection rate, the infection rate, and the average quarantine time had a significant impact on the prevention and the control of the epidemic. We discussed the impact of different vaccination strategies on the time $\tau_1^{(0)}$ for controllable widespread antibody failure, and considered the influence of COVID-19 mutated strains on epidemic prevention and control. We also provided some suggestions for epidemic prevention and control from the perspective of mathematical model and dynamic property analysis as follows:

(1): In the positive feedback mechanism, the effect factor a on vaccine effectiveness had a significant promoting effect on the critical time $\tau_1^{(0)}$. We can increase the impact of vaccine effectiveness on vaccination by increasing awareness about the safety and effectiveness of COVID-19 vaccines.

(2): In the positive feedback mechanism, the relatively fixed vaccination rate b inhibited the critical time $\tau_1^{(0)}$. Combined with (1), vaccination strategies were appropriately regulated from two aspects: on the one hand, the role of effectiveness in vaccination intention was appropriately increased; on the other hand, the fixed vaccination rate b brought about by other factors should be appropriately reduced.

(3): Considered that the mutant strains of COVID-19 may cause a sudden increase in the antibody failure rate γ and thus reduced the critical time $\tau_1^{(0)}$. In addition, the smaller the failure rate γ is, the more obvious the effect of critical time is. Therefore, from the perspective of model sensitivity, we confirmed the necessity of reducing vaccine failure rate γ.

(4): Considered that mutated strains of COVID-19 may caused mutations in disease-related mortality c. A small change in disease-related mortality c may cause a large change in the critical time $\tau_1^{(0)}$, which may change the system (1) stability. We should pay attention to the variation trend of mutant strains and change the inoculation strategy in time when necessary. Before the mutated strains cause a new outbreak, analysis showed that we can take measures such as vaccination boosters to reduce vaccine failure rates, thus reducing mortality due to disease and ensuring that the outbreak is within manageable limits.

Author Contributions: Writing—original draft preparation: X.A., X.L., Y.D. and H.L.; writing—review and funding acquisition: X.A., X.L. and Y.D.; methodology and supervision: X.A. and Y.D. All authors have read and agreed to the published version of the manuscript.

Funding: This research was funded by the Heilongjiang Provincial Natural Science Foundation of China (Grant No. LH2019A001) and College Students Innovations Special Project funded by Northeast Forestry University of China (No. 202110225003).

Institutional Review Board Statement: Not applicable.

Informed Consent Statement: Not applicable.

Data Availability Statement: The authors confirm that the data supporting the findings of this study are available within the article.

Acknowledgments: Authors are thankful to the handling editor and reviewers for their valuable comments and suggestions.

Conflicts of Interest: All authors declare no conflict of interest in this paper.

References

1. Maramattom B.V.; Bhattacharjee, S. Neurological complications with COVID-19: A contemporaneous review. *Ann. Indian Acad.* **2020**, *23*, 468–476. [CrossRef] [PubMed]
2. Zhao, D.H.; Lin, H.J.; Zhang, Z.R. Evidence-based framework and implementation of China's strategy in combating COVID-19. *Risk Manag. Healthc. Policy* **2020**, *13*, 1989–1998. [CrossRef] [PubMed]
3. Atalan, A. Is the lockdown important to prevent the COVID-19 pandemic? Effects on psychology, environment and economy-perspective. *Ann. Med. Surg.* **2012**, *56*, 38–42. [CrossRef] [PubMed]
4. Acharya, S.R.; Moon, D.H.; Shin, Y.C. Assessing attitude toward COVID-19 vaccination in South Korea. *Front. Psychol.* **2021**, *12*, 694151. [CrossRef] [PubMed]
5. Chakraborty, C.; Sharma, A.R.; Bhattacharya, M.; Agoramoorthy, G.; Lee, S.S. Asian-origin approved COVID-19 vaccines and current status of COVID-19 vaccination program in Asia: A critical analysis. *Vaccines* **2021**, *9*, 600. [CrossRef]
6. Tagoe, E.T.; Sheikh, N.; Morton, A.; Nonvignon, J.; Sarker, A.R.; Williams, L.; Megiddo, I. COVID-19 vaccination in lower-middle income countries: National stakeholder views on challenges, barriers and potential solutions. *Front. Public Health* **2021**, *9*, 709127. [CrossRef]
7. Van De Pas, R.; Van De Pas, M.A.; Ravinetto, R.; Srinivas, P.; Ochoa, T.J. COVID-19 vaccine equity: A health systems and policy perspective. *Expert Rev. Vaccines* **2021**, *21*, 25–36. [CrossRef]
8. Zhu, F.; Li, Y.; Guan, X.; Hou, L.; Wang, W.; Li, J.X.; Wu, S.P.; Wang, B.S.; Wang, Z.; Wang, L.; et al. Safety, tolerability and immunogenicity of a recombinant adenovirus type-5 vectored COVID-19 vaccine: A dose-escalation, open-label, non-randomised, first-in-human trial. *Lancet* **2020**, *395*, 1845–1854. [CrossRef]
9. Zhu, Y.; Wei, Y.; Sun, C.; He, H. Development of vaccines against COVID-19. *Prev. Med.* **2021**, *33*, 143–148.
10. Hodgson, S.H.; Mansatta, K.; Mallett, G.; Harris, V.; Emary, K.R.W.; Pollard, A.J. What defines an efficacious COVID-19 vaccine? A review of the challenges assessing the clinical efficacy of vaccines against SARS-CoV-2. *Lancet Infect. Dis.* **2021**, *21*, E26–E35. [CrossRef]
11. Grubaugh, N.D.; Hanage, W.P.; Rasmussen, A.L. Making sense of mutation: What D614G means for the COVID-19 pandemic remains unclear. *Cell* **2020**, *182*, 794–795. [CrossRef] [PubMed]
12. Olaniyi, S.; Obabiyi, O.S.; Okosun, K.O.; Oladipo, A.T.; Adewale, S.O. Mathematical modelling and optimal cost-effective control of COVID-19 transmission dynamics. *Eur. Phys. J. Plus* **2020**, *135*, 938. [CrossRef] [PubMed]
13. Abdy, M.; Side, S.; Annas, S.; Nur, W.; Sanusi, W. A SIR epidemic model for COVID-19 spread with fuzzy parameter: The case of Indonesia. *Adv. Differ. Equations* **2021**, *2021*, 105. [CrossRef] [PubMed]
14. Bardina, X.; Ferrante, M.; Rovira, C. A stochastic epidemic model of COVID-19 disease. *Aims Math.* **2020**, *5*, 7661–7677. [CrossRef]

15. He, S.B.; Peng, Y.X.; Sun, K.H. SEIR modeling of the COVID-19 and its dynamics. *Nonlinear Dynam.* **2020**, *101*, 1667–1680. [CrossRef] [PubMed]
16. Algehyne, E.A.; Din, R.U. On global dynamics of COVID-19 by using SQIR type model under nonlinear saturated incidence rate. *Alex. Eng. J.* **2021**, *60*, 393–399. [CrossRef]
17. Li, N.; Wang, Z.Y.; Pei, Z. Sequential resource planning decisions in an epidemic based on an innovative spread model. *IEEE T. Autom. Sci. Eng.* **2022**, *19*, 677–691. [CrossRef]
18. Li, M.Y.; Zhang, Y.J.; Zhou, X.H. Analysis of transimission pattern of COVID-19 based on EM algorithm and epidemiological data. *Acta Math. Appl. Sin.* **2020**, *43*, 427–439.
19. Chong, P.Y.; Yin, H. System dynamics simulation on spread of COVID-19 by traffic and transportation. *J. Traf. Trans. Eng.* **2020**, *20*, 100–109.
20. Cadoni, M.; Gaeta, G. Size and timescale of epidemics in the SIR framework. *Phys. D* **2020**, *411*, 132626. [CrossRef]
21. Yang, L.L.; Su, Y.M.; Zhuo, X.J. Comparison of two different types of fractional-order COVID-19 distributed time-delay models with real data application. *Int. J. Mod. Phys. B* **2021**, *35*, 2150219. [CrossRef]
22. Radha, M.; Radha, S. A study on COVID-19 transmission dynamics: Stability analysis of SEIR model with Hopf bifurcation for effect of time delay. *Adv. Differ. Equ.* **2020**, *1*, 523. [CrossRef] [PubMed]
23. Chang, X.H.; Wang, J.R.; Liu, M.X.; Jin, Z.; Han, D. Study on an SIHRS model of COVID-19 pandemic with impulse and time delay under media coverage. *IEEE Access* **2021**, *9*, 49387–49397. [CrossRef] [PubMed]
24. Zhu, C.C.; Zhu, J. Dynamic analysis of a delayed COVID-19 epidemic with home quarantine in temporal-spatial heterogeneous via global exponential attractor method. *Chaos Solitons Fract.* **2021**, *143*, 110546. [CrossRef] [PubMed]
25. Yang, F.F.; Zhang, Z.Z. A time-delay COVID-19 propagation model considering supply chain transmission and hierarchical quarantine rate. *Adv. Differ. Equ.* **2021**, *1*, 191. [CrossRef]
26. Hossain, M.K.; Hassanzadeganroudsari, M.; Apostolopoulos, V. The emergence of new strains of SARS-CoV-2. What does it mean for COVID-19 vaccines? *Expert Rev. Vaccines* **2021**, *20*, 635–638. [CrossRef]
27. Tartof, S.Y.; Slezak, J.M.; Fischer, H.; Hong, V.; Ackerson, B.K.; Ranasinghe, O.N.; Frankland, T.B.; Ogun, O.A.; Zamparo, J.M.; Gray, S.; et al. Effectiveness of mRNA BNT162b2 COVID-19 vaccine up to 6 months in a large integrated health system in the USA: A retrospective cohort study. *Lancet* **2021**, *398*, 1407–1416. [CrossRef]
28. Jara, A.; Undurraga, E.A.; Gonzalez, C.; Paredes, F.; Fontecilla, T.; Jara, G.; Pizarro, A.; Acevedo, J.; Leo, K.; Leon, F.; et al. Effectiveness of an inactivated SARS-CoV-2 vaccine in Chile. *N. Engl. J. Med.* **2021**, *385*, 875–884. [CrossRef]
29. Xiao, L.L.; Zhang, Y.; Hu, X.W.; Liu, T.; Liu, Y. Analysis of global prevalence of SARS-CoV-2 varia. *Chin. J. Front. Health Quar.* **2022**, *45*, 10–12.
30. Shi, Q.F.; Gao, X.D.; Hu, B.J. Research progress on characteristics, epidemiology and control measure of SARS-CoV-2 delta voc. *Chin. J. Nosocomiol.* **2021**, *31*, 3703–3707.
31. Raman, R.; Patel, K.; Ran, K. COVID-19: Unmasking emerging SARS-CoV-2 variants, vaccines and therapeutic strategies. *Biomolecules* **2021**, *11*, 993. [CrossRef] [PubMed]
32. Darvishi, M.; Rahimi, F.; Talebi, B.A. SARS-CoV-2 lambda (C.37): An emerging variant of concern. *Gene. Rep.* **2021**, *25*, 101378. [CrossRef] [PubMed]
33. Choi, J.Y.; Smith, D.M. SARS-CoV-2 variants of concern. *Yonsei Med. J.* **2021**, *62*, 961–968. [CrossRef] [PubMed]
34. Mohapatra, R.K.; Tiwari, R.; Sarangi, A.K.; Sharma, S.K.; Khandia, R. Twin combination of omicron and delta variants triggering a tsunami wave of ever high surges in COVID-19 cases: A challenging global threat with a special focus on the Indian subcontinent. *J. Med. Virol.* **2022**, *94*, 1761–1765. [CrossRef] [PubMed]
35. Zhao, X.H.; Ning, Y.L.; Chen, M.I.C.; Cook, A.R. Individual and population trajectories of influenza antibody titers over multiple seasons in a tropical country. *Am. J. Epidemiol.* **2018**, *187*, 135–143. [CrossRef] [PubMed]
36. Ibarrondo, F.J.; Fulcher, J.A.; Yang, O.O. Rapid decay of Anti-SARS-CoV-2 antibodies in persons with mild COVID-19. *N. Engl. J. Med.* **2020**, *383*, 1085–1087. [CrossRef] [PubMed]
37. Li, J.; Ao, N.; Yin, J.H. Willingness for COVID-19 vaccination and its influencing factors among outpatient clinic attendees in Kunming city. *China J. Public Health* **2021**, *37*, 411–414.
38. Sarwar, A.; Nazar, N.; Nazar, N.; Qadir, A. Measuring vaccination willingness in response to COVID-19 using a multi-criteria-decision-making method. *Hum. Vaccines* **2021**, *17*, 1–8. [CrossRef]
39. Liu, R.G.; Liu, Y.X.; Nicholas, S.; Leng, A.L.; Maitland, E.; Wang, J. COVID-19 vaccination willingness among Chinese adults under the free vaccination policy. *Vaccines* **2021**, *9*, 292. [CrossRef]
40. Lu, H.f.; Ding, Y.T.; Gong, S.L.; Wang, S.S. Mathematical modeling and dynamic analysis of SIQR model with delay for pandemic COVID-19. *Math. Biosci. Eng.* **2021**, *18*, 3197–3214. [CrossRef]
41. Wang, J.W.; Cui, Z.W; Dong, S. Simulation of COVID-19 propagation and transmission mechanism and intervention effect based on generalized SEIR model. *Sci. Technol. Rev.* **2020**, *38*, 130–138.

mathematics

Article

Stability and Numerical Simulations of a New $SVIR$ Model with Two Delays on COVID-19 Booster Vaccination

Xinyu Liu and Yuting Ding *

Department of Mathematics, Northeast Forestry University, Harbin 150040, China; lxy_lucky@nefu.edu.cn
* Correspondence: dingyt@nefu.edu.cn

Abstract: As COVID-19 continues to threaten public health around the world, research on specific vaccines has been underway. In this paper, we establish an $SVIR$ model on booster vaccination with two time delays. The time delays represent the time of booster vaccination and the time of booster vaccine invalidation, respectively. Second, we investigate the impact of delay on the stability of non-negative equilibria for the model by considering the duration of the vaccine, and the system undergoes Hopf bifurcation when the duration of the vaccine passes through some critical values. We obtain the normal form of Hopf bifurcation by applying the multiple time scales method. Then, we study the model with two delays and show the conditions under which the nontrivial equilibria are locally asymptotically stable. Finally, through analysis of official data, we select two groups of parameters to simulate the actual epidemic situation of countries with low vaccination rates and countries with high vaccination rates. On this basis, we select the third group of parameters to simulate the ideal situation in which the epidemic can be well controlled. Through comparative analysis of the numerical simulations, we concluded that the most appropriate time for vaccination is to vaccinate with the booster shot 6 months after the basic vaccine. The priority for countries with low vaccination rates is to increase vaccination rates; otherwise, outbreaks will continue. Countries with high vaccination rates need to develop more effective vaccines while maintaining their coverage rates. When the vaccine lasts longer and the failure rate is lower, the epidemic can be well controlled within 20 years.

Keywords: COVID-19 epidemic; booster vaccination; two delays; Hopf bifurcation; numerical simulations

MSC: 34K18

Citation: Liu, X.; Ding, Y. Stability and Numerical Simulations of a New $SVIR$ Model with Two Delays on COVID-19 Booster Vaccination. *Mathematics* **2022**, *10*, 1772. https://doi.org/10.3390/math10101772

Academic Editor: Alicia Cordero Barbero

Received: 20 April 2022
Accepted: 20 May 2022
Published: 23 May 2022

1. Introduction

1.1. Research Background

At present, the Coronavirus Disease 2019 (COVID-19) epidemic has not been completely controlled. The virus (SARS-CoV-2) is highly contagious, spreads by a wide range of routes, and constantly mutates as it spreads, making COVID-19 difficult to control [1]. Since there is no specific treatment for COVID-19, promoting a scale-up of vaccination and building herd immunity is the most effective measure to control the epidemic.

It has always been a hot topic to study the impact of vaccines on the spread of infectious diseases by analyzing the dynamic characteristics of the system [2–7]. Among them, De la Sen et al. [4] and Thater et al. [5] proposed different $SEIR$ models of disease transmission for vaccination and developed optimal vaccination strategies. Scherer et al. [6] calculated the threshold vaccination rate to eradicate an infection, and they explored the impact of vaccine-induced immunity that diminishes over time. Many researchers also considered vaccines in their models of COVID-19 epidemics. For example, Yang et al. [8] studied vaccination control in an epidemic model with time delay and applied it to COVID-19. These studies all have shown that vaccination has a significant effect on the control of diseases.

However, the level of neutralizing antibodies decreases over time, and the protective effect of the vaccine diminishes, which also needs to be considered in the model of COVID-19. For example, the $SVIR$ model developed by Duan et al. [9] takes into account that vaccines lose their protective properties over time, allowing vaccinated individuals to become susceptible again. Wald et al. [10] suggest it is necessary to reduce SARS-CoV-2 transmission and infection through enhanced vaccination. This suggests that an additional vaccination regime, called booster immunization, is needed to restore immunity in previously vaccinated populations. Salvagno et al. [11] found a significant decrease in antibodies 6 months after basic vaccination, which is consistent with the need for a vaccine booster. However, few studies have considered the COVID-19 booster vaccine in mathematical models, so we believe that dynamic analysis of the impact of the COVID-19 booster vaccine on epidemic control is needed at present.

There is always a considerable difference between the actual behavior of disease and the response of its mathematical model. In 1979, Cooke proposed the theory of "time delay" in his study of infectious disease transmission, which made the model more realistic [12]. Since then, many researchers have tried to take time delays into account in their models. Zhai et al. [13] studied studies a $SEIR$ epidemic model with time delay and vaccination control. In the infectious disease model for COVID-19, many studies consider a single time delay. For example, Rong et al. [14] studied the effect of delay in diagnosis on the transmission of COVID-19.

Much research shows two delays can reflect the actual problem more clearly. For instance, Song et al. [15] studied a new $SVEIRS$ infectious disease model with pulse and two time delays. In the study of Jiang et al. [16], a $SVEIRS$ epidemic model with two time delays and a nonlinear incidence rate was developed, and they analyzed the dynamic behavior of the model under pulse vaccination. An $SEIR$ epidemic model with two time delays and pulse vaccination was formulated in the study of Gao et al. [17]. However, there are few infectious disease models studying the novel coronavirus that consider two delays. Considering the characteristics of COVID-19 and vaccination, we believe that two time delays can better solve the problems existing in the actual COVID-19 epidemic; that is, we need to give booster shots at intervals after the basic vaccination and take into account the fact that the vaccine does not provide permanent immunity and will lose effectiveness some time after vaccination. Therefore, there are two time delays which cannot be ignored.

The stability of epidemic models and Hopf bifurcation analysis have always been the focus of this kind of epidemic model. In ref [18], Zhang et al. analyzed the stability and Hopf bifurcation of an $SVEIR$ epidemic model with vaccination and multiple time delays. The paper [19] written by Chen et al. mainly addressed stability analysis and estimation of the domain of attraction for the endemic equilibrium of a class of susceptible–exposed–infected–quarantine epidemic models. Li et al. [20] studied the stability and bifurcation analysis of an SIR epidemic model with logistic growth and saturation processing. In the study of Goel et al. [21], a time-delayed SIR epidemic model with a logistic growth of susceptibles was proposed and analyzed mathematically. The stability behavior of the model was analyzed for two equilibria: the disease-free equilibrium and the endemic equilibrium. Further, they investigated the stability behavior, demonstrating the occurrence of oscillatory and periodic solutions through Hopf bifurcation concerning every possible grouping of two time delays as the bifurcation parameter.

1.2. Research Motivation

The research motivation of this paper is as follows. There have been mass vaccine injections worldwide, but the level of antibodies in the receptor decreases over time, and the protective effect of the vaccine diminishes, so we also need to strengthen immunity to enhance the body's ability to resist SARS-CoV-2. In such cases, increasing the number of vaccinations is a measure to improve the level of immunity and increase protection. Therefore, the booster shot we are considering is a dose of vaccine that is administered again after the completion of the COVID-19 vaccine by antibody resolution in order to maintain immunity to COVID-19. Currently, the third dose of inactivated COVID-19 vaccine is the main booster vaccination in the world. The first and second doses of the COVID-19 vaccine are commonly referred to as basic vaccines. If the basic vaccine protection effect is still good, early booster vaccination wastes resources; if the interval between booster vaccination and basic vaccination is too long, it can cause the failure of herd immunity, and the epidemic will be out of control.

Thus, we first want to study the most appropriate time to give a booster vaccine. Therefore, we create a mathematical model that takes into account both basic and booster vaccination. Second, since the efficacy of the vaccine is unknown, we also consider the effect of the duration of the booster vaccine on the timing of the booster vaccination. We aim to develop a vaccine approach that can effectively help control the COVID-19 epidemic through dynamic analysis of the model that takes these two time delays into account. Third, different countries have different vaccine coverage rates and levels of concern. Our goal is to select different parameter groups to simulate the epidemic in different countries and to give the vaccination time requirements for epidemic control. At the same time, we select a set of ideal parameters that represent that the epidemic can be well controlled and compare them to the actual parameters to study what efforts we still need to make at present.

The structure of this paper is as follows. In Section 2, we establish an $SVIR$ booster vaccination model with two time delays. In Section 3, we analyze the existence and stability of non-negative equilibria and discuss the existence of Hopf bifurcation. We deduce the normal form of Hopf bifurcation in Section 4. In Section 5, we give some numerical simulations and get the conclusion of strengthening inoculation time. Finally, conclusions and suggestions are given in Section 6.

2. Mathematical Modeling

Different from the traditional infectious disease model, we redefined the cabin so that our model could better depict the relationship between basic vaccination and booster vaccination in order to study the role of booster vaccine in epidemic control. We divided COVID-19 susceptible people into two groups. One group involves people who have received basic but not booster shots (S), and the other group involves people who have completed all vaccinations (V); both groups are at risk of contracting COVID-19 through contact with infected people or other means and becoming infected (I). However, it should be noted that the infection rate of the susceptible in V is much lower than that of the susceptible in S. Some of the infected I will die of the disease, while others will recover (R) after treatment. However, their vaccine will be ineffective to varying degrees according to their conditions [22]. For people such as the elderly or those with underlying diseases who have recovered, the antibodies produced by the vaccine are almost completely disabled, and they need a basic injection to regain active antibodies. This group of people will become S. Otherwise, people who maintain some antibody activity in their bodies just need a booster shot to increase their resistance to SARS-CoV-2. They become V.

Taking all these factors into account, we get the concrete conversion between the four cabins shown in Figure 1.

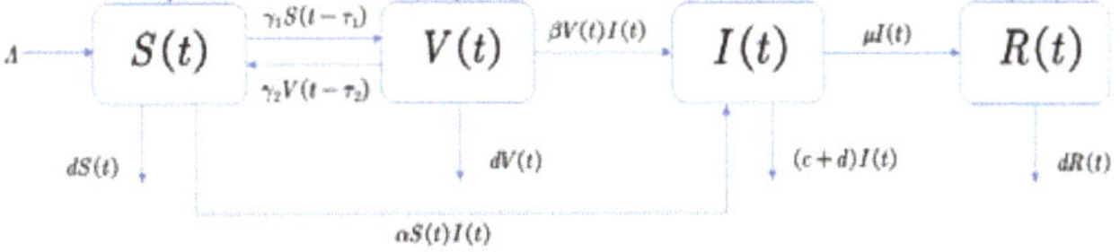

Figure 1. $SVIR$ Model diagram.

Table 1 shows specific definitions of variables and parameters. In this table, all parameters and variables are positive.

Table 1. Description of variables and parameters in the model

Symbol	Description
S	Number of susceptible persons who have received basic but not booster shots
V	Number of susceptible persons who have completed all vaccinations
I	Number of patients affected
R	Number of recovered persons
Λ	Inoculation rate of basic vaccine
α	Transition rate from S to I
β	Transition rate from V to I
γ_1	Transition rate from S to V
γ_2	Transition rate from V to S
μ	Transition rate from I to R; the cure rate of infected persons
σ_1	Transition rate from R to S
σ_2	Transition rate from R to V
c	National case fatality rate of COVID-19
d	Natural death rate of population
τ_1	Time-delay for people who received the basic vaccine to receive the booster vaccine
τ_2	Time-delay from people getting booster vaccination to their antibodies disappearing

For COVID-19 vaccines, susceptible people develop antibodies after vaccination, but the vaccine cannot provide long-term protection according to the background in Section 1.1. We assume that in our model, the basic vaccine's activity declines over time, but will become ineffective only if a person gets sick. Since the booster vaccine is only a supplement to the basic vaccine, the dose is less than the basic vaccine. We assume that over a long period, the potency of the antibody produced by the booster vaccine will gradually decline until it disappears. We define the time delay of the booster vaccine's failure in our model as τ_2. At the same time, as considered in Section 1.2, to keep the epidemic under control and to maximize the use of resources, those who receive only the basic vaccine need to receive booster shots after a certain time delay, as indicated by τ_1. In general, the duration of the vaccine's effective protection must be longer than the interval between vaccinations, so we specify $\tau_2 > \tau_1$ in our model. Therefore, we construct the following differential equation:

$$\begin{cases} \dfrac{dS(t)}{dt} =\Lambda - \gamma_1 S(t-\tau_1) + \gamma_2 V(t-\tau_2) - \alpha S(t)I(t) + \sigma_1 R(t) - dS(t), \\ \dfrac{dV(t)}{dt} =\gamma_1 S(t-\tau_1) - \gamma_2 V(t-\tau_2) - \beta V(t)I(t) + \sigma_2 R(t) - dV(t), \\ \dfrac{dI(t)}{dt} =\alpha S(t)I(t) + \beta V(t)I(t) - \mu I(t) - (c+d)I(t), \\ \dfrac{dR(t)}{dt} =\mu I(t) - \sigma_1 R(t) - \sigma_2 R(t) - dR(t). \end{cases} \tag{1}$$

The meanings of variables and parameters are given in Table 1. Timely booster vaccinations prevent inadequate antibody levels in individuals, which could lead to increased infection rates and the situation of the epidemic being out of control. Therefore, it is particularly important to choose the right timing for booster vaccination to control the epidemic.

3. Stability Analysis of Equilibria and Existence of Hopf Bifurcation

In this section, System (1) is considered. Obviously, System (1) has three equilibria:

$$E_1 = (S_1, V_1, 0, 0), E_{2_l} = (S_{2_l}, V_{2_l}, I_{2_l}, R_{2_l}), l = 1, 2 \tag{2}$$

where $S_1 = \frac{\Lambda}{\gamma_1 - \xi + d}$, $V_1 = \frac{\xi\Lambda}{(\gamma_1 - \xi + d)\gamma_2}$, with $\xi = \frac{\gamma_1\gamma_2}{\gamma_2 + d}$, and $R_{2_1} = \frac{-\Gamma_1 - \sqrt{\Gamma_2^2 - 4\Gamma_1\Gamma_3}}{2\Gamma_1}$, $R_{2_2} = \frac{-\Gamma_1 + \sqrt{\Gamma_2^2 - 4\Gamma_1\Gamma_3}}{2\Gamma_1}$, $S_{2_l} = b - ef - egR_{2_l}$, $V_{2_l} = f + gR_{2_l}$, $I_{2_l} = aR_{2_l}$, with $a = \frac{\sigma_1 + \sigma_2 + d}{\mu}$,

$b = \frac{\mu+c+d}{\alpha}, e = \frac{\beta}{\alpha}, f = \frac{\Lambda-bd}{d-ed}, g = \frac{\mu d+(c+d)(\sigma_1+\sigma_2+d)}{\mu(ed-d)}, \Gamma_1 = \beta ag, \Gamma_2 = dg - \sigma_2 + \beta fa + \gamma_2 g + eg\gamma_1, \Gamma_3 = df + \gamma_2 - \gamma_1(b - ef)$.

For equilibria E_1, E_{2_l}, we consider the following assumption:

Hypothesis 1 (H1). $\gamma_1 - \xi + d > 0$.

When (H1) holds, the equilibrium E_1 exists and is non-negative.

Hypothesis 2 (H2). $\Gamma_1 < 0, \Gamma_2 > 0, \Gamma_3 < 0$ *or* $\Gamma_1 < 0, \Gamma_2 > 0, \Gamma_3 > 0$.

When (H2) holds, the equilibrium E_{2_1} exists and is positive.

Hypothesis 3 (H3). $\Gamma_1 < 0, \Gamma_2 > 0, \Gamma_3 < 0$ *or* $\Gamma_1 < 0, \Gamma_2 < 0, \Gamma_3 > 0$.

When (H3) holds, the equilibrium E_{2_2} exists and is positive. We calculate the basic reproduction number R_0, the number of the suspected individuals who are infected by the same infectious individual, and can estimate the infectiousness of an infectious disease. According to System (1), we can get the new infections matrix $\mathcal{F}$ and the transition matrix $\mathcal{V}$.

$$\mathcal{F} = \begin{bmatrix} 0 \\ 0 \\ \alpha S(t)I(t) + \beta V(t)I(t) \\ 0 \end{bmatrix}, \mathcal{V} = \begin{bmatrix} -\Lambda + \gamma_1 S(t) - \gamma_2 V(t) - \sigma_1 R(t) + dS(t) + \alpha S(t)I(t) \\ -\gamma_1 S(t) + \gamma_2 V(t) + \beta V(t)I(t) - \sigma_2 R(t) + dV(t) \\ \mu I(t) + cI(t) + dI(t) \\ -\mu I(t) + \sigma_1 R(t) + \sigma_2 R(t) + dR(t) \end{bmatrix}.$$

Then, we make F_0 represent the derivative of $\mathcal{F}$ at E_1 and V_0 represent the derivative of $\mathcal{V}$ at E_1:

$$F_0 = \begin{bmatrix} 0 & 0 & 0 & 0 \\ 0 & 0 & 0 & 0 \\ 0 & 0 & \alpha S_1 + \beta V_1 & 0 \\ 0 & 0 & 0 & 0 \end{bmatrix}, V_0 = \begin{bmatrix} \gamma_1 + d & -\gamma_2 & \alpha S_1 & -\sigma_1 \\ -\gamma_1 & \gamma_2 + d & \beta V_1 & -\sigma_2 \\ 0 & -\varepsilon & \mu + c + d & 0 \\ 0 & -\gamma_1 & -\mu & \sigma_1 + \sigma_2 + d \end{bmatrix}.$$

We can obtain:

$$F_0 V_0^{-1} = \begin{bmatrix} 0 & 0 & 0 & 0 \\ 0 & 0 & 0 & 0 \\ 0 & 0 & \frac{\alpha S_1 + \beta V_1}{\mu + c + d} & 0 \\ 0 & 0 & 0 & 0 \end{bmatrix}.$$

The maximum eigenvalue of $F_0 V_0^{-1}$ is the basic regeneration number of System (1):

$$R_0 = \rho(F_0 V_0^{-1}) = \frac{\alpha S_1 + \beta V_1}{\mu + c + d}.$$

Transferring the equilibria $E_k, (k = 1, 2_1, 2_2)$ to the origin point: $\tilde{S} = S - S_k$, $\tilde{V} = V - V_k$, $\tilde{I} = I - I_k$, $\tilde{R} = R - R_k$ and linearizing System (1) around them. Renewedly denoting $\tilde{S}, \tilde{V}, \tilde{I}, \tilde{R}$ as S, V, I, R, we obtain the following model:

$$\begin{cases} \frac{dS}{dt} = -\gamma_1 S(t - \tau_1) + \gamma_2 V(t - \tau_2) - \alpha SI + \sigma_1 R - dS - \alpha S_k I - \alpha S I_k, \\ \frac{dV}{dt} = \gamma_1 S(t - \tau_1) - \gamma_2 V(t - \tau_2) - \beta VI - \beta V_k I - \beta V I_k + \sigma_2 R - dV, \\ \frac{dI}{dt} = \alpha SI + \alpha S_k I + \alpha S I_k + \beta VI + \beta V_k I + \beta V I_k - \mu I - (c + d)I, \\ \frac{dR}{dt} = \mu I - \sigma_1 R - \sigma_2 R - dR. \end{cases} \quad (3)$$

We can get the characteristic equation of the linearized system (1) as follows:

$$\begin{aligned}\sigma_1 e^{-\lambda\tau_1}\left(\lambda^3+B_1\lambda^2+C_1\lambda+D_1\right)+\sigma_2 e^{-\lambda\tau_2}\left(\lambda^3+B_2\lambda^2+C_2\lambda+D_2\right)\\ +\lambda^4+A_3\lambda^3+B_3\lambda^2+C_3\lambda+D_3=0,\end{aligned} \tag{4}$$

where

$$\begin{aligned}
B_1 &= \sigma_1+\sigma_2+3d+\mu+c+\beta I_k-\alpha S_k-\beta V_k,\\
C_1 &= (\sigma_1+\sigma_2+d)(2d+\mu+c+\beta I_k-\alpha S_k-\beta V_k)+(d+\mu+c)\beta I_k+d(d+\mu+c-\alpha S_k-\beta V_k),\\
D_1 &= (\sigma_1+\sigma_2+d)[(d+\mu+c)\beta I_k+d(d+\mu+c-\alpha S_k-\beta V_k)-\mu\sigma_1\beta I_k-\mu\sigma_2\beta I_k],\\
B_2 &= \sigma_1+\sigma_2+3d+\mu+c+\alpha I_k-\alpha S_k-\beta V_k,\\
C_2 &= (\sigma_1+\sigma_2+d)(2d+\mu+c+\alpha I_k-\alpha S_k-\beta V_k)+d(d+\mu+c-\alpha S_k-\beta V_k)+(d+\mu+c)\alpha I_k,\\
D_2 &= (\sigma_1+\sigma_2+d)[(d+\mu+c)\alpha I_k+d(d+\mu+c-\alpha S_k-\beta V_k)-\mu\sigma_1\alpha I_k-\mu\sigma_2\alpha I_k],\\
A_3 &= \sigma_1+\sigma_2+4d+\mu+c+\alpha I_k+\beta I_k-\alpha S_k-\beta V_k,\\
B_3 &=(\sigma_1+\sigma_2+d)(3d+\mu+c+\alpha I_k+\beta I_k-\alpha S_k-\beta V_k)+\big[(d+\alpha I_k)(2d+\mu+c+\beta I_k-\alpha S_k-\beta V_k)\\
&\quad+(d+\beta I_k)(d+\mu+c-\alpha S_k-\beta V_k)+\beta^2 I_k V_k+\alpha^2 I_k S_k\big],\\
C_3 &=(\sigma_1+\sigma_2+d)\big[(d+\alpha I_k)(2d+\mu+c+\beta I_k-\alpha S_k-\beta V_k)+(d+\beta I_k)(d+\mu+c-\alpha S_k-\beta V_k)\\
&\quad+\beta^2 I_k V_k+\alpha^2 I_k S_k\big]+\alpha^2 I_k S_k(d+\beta I_k)-\mu\sigma_1\alpha I_k-\mu\sigma_2\beta I_k,\\
D_3 &= \alpha^2 I_k S_k(d+\beta I_k)(\sigma_1+\sigma_2+d)-\mu\sigma_1\left(\alpha\beta I_k^2+\alpha d I_k\right)-\mu\sigma_2\left(\alpha\beta I_k^2+\beta d I_k\right), k=1,2_1,2_2.
\end{aligned}$$

3.1. *Analysis for Disease-Free Equilibrium E_1*

3.1.1. The Case for $\tau_1=0,\ \tau_2=0$

Firstly, we consider $R_0<1$. The characteristic equation of the linearized system (1) about E_1 is as follows:

$$(\lambda+\mu a)(\lambda+\mu+c+d-\beta V_1-\alpha S_1)\left[\left((\lambda+d)^2+(\lambda+d)\sigma_1 e^{-\lambda\tau_1}+(\lambda+d)\sigma_2 e^{-\lambda\tau_2}\right)\right]=0. \tag{5}$$

When $\tau_1=0,\ \tau_2=0$, it turns to

$$(\lambda+\sigma_1+\sigma_2+d)(\lambda+\mu+c+d-\beta V_1-\alpha S_1)(\lambda+d)(\lambda+d+\sigma_1+\sigma_2)=0. \tag{6}$$

Obviously, all the roots of Equation (6) have negative real parts due to $R_0<1, \sigma_1>0, \sigma_2>0, d>0$. We can conclude the disease-free equilibrium E_1 is locally asymptotically stable when $\tau_1=0, \tau_2=0$.

When $R_0>1$, Equation (6) has a positive root. Thus, the disease-free equilibrium E_1 is unstable when $\tau_1=0, \tau_2=0$.

3.1.2. The Case for $\tau_1=0,\ \tau_2>0$

When $\tau_2>0$, for equilibrium E_1, we simply need to think about the following equation

$$(\lambda+d)^2+(\lambda+d)\sigma_1+(\lambda+d)\sigma_2 e^{-\lambda\tau_2}=0. \tag{7}$$

To discuss the existence of Hopf bifurcation for E_1, we assume that $\lambda=i\omega_1\ (\omega_1>0)$ is a pure imaginary root of Equation (7). Substituting it into Equation (7) and separating the real and imaginary parts, we obtain:

$$\begin{cases}\gamma_2\omega_1\sin(\omega_1\tau_2)+d\gamma_2\cos(\omega_1\tau_2)=\omega_1^2-d^2-d\gamma_1\\ d\gamma_2\sin(\omega_1\tau_2)-\gamma_2\omega_1\cos(\omega_1\tau_2)=\omega_1(2d+\gamma_1)\end{cases} \tag{8}$$

Equation (8) derives to:

$$\begin{cases} \sin(\omega_1\tau_2) = \frac{\omega_1^3-(d^2+d\gamma_1)\omega_1+(2d^2\gamma_2+d\gamma_1\gamma_2)\omega_1}{\gamma_2(\omega_1^2+d^2)}, \\ \cos(\omega_1\tau_2) = \frac{-(d\gamma_2+\gamma_1\gamma_2)\omega_1^2-d^3\gamma_2-d^2\gamma_1\gamma_2}{\gamma_2(\omega_1^2+d^2)}. \end{cases} \tag{9}$$

Adding the square of two equations in Equation (8) and letting $z = \omega_1^2$, we get

$$h(z) = z^2 + c_1 z + c_0 = 0, \tag{10}$$

where $c_1 = \left[(2d+\gamma_1)^2 - \gamma_2^2 - 2(d^2+d\gamma_1)\right]$, $c_0 = \left(d^2+d\gamma_1\right)^2 - d^2\gamma_2^2$.

Therefore, we show the following assumptions:

Hypothesis 4 (H4). $c_0 < 0$;

Hypothesis 5 (H5). $c_1^2 - 4c_0 > 0, c_1 < 0, c_0 > 0$;

Hypothesis 6 (H6). $c_1^2 - 4c_0 < 0, c_0 > 0$ *or* $c_1^2 - 4c_0 > 0, c_1 > 0, c_0 > 0$.

Under (H4), Equation (10) has the unique positive root z_1. If (H5) holds, Equation (10) has two positive roots: z_2 and $z_3(z_2 < z_3)$. Under (H6), Equation (10) has no root. Substituting $\omega_{1k} = \sqrt{z_k}(k = 1,2,3)$ into Equation (9), we get the expression of τ_2:

$$\tau_{2k}^{(j)} = \begin{cases} \frac{1}{\omega_{1k}}[\arccos(P_k) + 2j\pi], & Q_k \geq 0, \\ \frac{1}{\omega_{1k}}[2\pi - \arccos(P_k) + 2j\pi], & Q_k < 0, \; k = 1,2,3 \; j = 0,1,2,\cdots, \end{cases} \tag{11}$$

where $Q_k = \sin(\omega_{1k}\tau_{2k}^{(j)}), P_k = \cos(\omega_{1k}\tau_{2k}^{(j)})$.

If $R_0 < 1$, when $\tau_2 = \tau_{2k}^{(j)}$ $(k = 1,2,3;\; j = 0,1,2,\cdots)$, then Equation (7) has a pair of pure imaginary roots $\pm i\omega_{1k}$, and all the other roots of Equation (7) have nonzero real parts. Furthermore, let $\lambda(\tau) = \alpha(\tau) + i\omega_1(\tau)$ be the root of Equation (7) satisfying $\alpha(\tau_k^{(j)}) = 0$, $\omega(\tau_k^{(j)}) = \omega_{1k}$ $(k = 1,2,3;\; j = 0,1,2,\cdots)$. Thus, $z_k = \omega_{1k}^2$, $h'(z_k) \neq 0$, where $h'(z)$ is the derivative of $h(z)$ with respect to z. Then, we have the following transversality condition:

$$\mathrm{Re}\left(\frac{d\tau}{d\lambda}\right)\Big|_{\tau=\tau_{2k}^{(j)}} = \mathrm{Re}\left(\frac{d\lambda}{d\tau}\right)^{-1}\Big|_{\tau=\tau_{2k}^{(j)}} = \frac{h'(\omega_{1k}^2)}{\gamma_2^2(\omega_{1k}^2 + d^2)} \neq 0, k = 1,2,3 \; j = 0,1,2,\cdots.$$

Lemma 1. *If $R_0 < 1$ holds, the equilibrium E_1 is stable and undergoes Hopf bifurcation at $\tau = \tau_{2k}^{(j)}$ $(k = 1,2,3;\; j = 0,1,2,\cdots)$, where $\tau_{2k}^{(j)}$ is given by Equation (11). Further, we denote the stable region of E_1 as I.*

3.1.3. The Case for $\tau_1 > 0, \tau_2 > 0$

With the above analysis, we choose $\tau_2 = \tau_{2*} \in$ I as a parameter; the characteristic equation of system (1) is rewritten as follows:

$$(\lambda + d)^2 + (\lambda + d)\sigma_1 e^{-\lambda\tau_1} + (\lambda + d)\sigma_2 e^{-\lambda\tau_{2*}} = 0.$$

Letting $\lambda = i\tilde{\omega}_1$ $(\tilde{\omega} > 0)$ be the root of the above equation, then separating the real and imaginary parts for the above equation, we get

$$\begin{cases} \tilde{\omega}_1^2 - d^2 - \gamma_2\tilde{\omega}_1\sin(\tilde{\omega}_1\tau_{2*}) - d\gamma_2\cos(\tilde{\omega}_1\tau_{2*}) = \gamma_1\tilde{\omega}_1\sin(\tilde{\omega}_1\tau_1) + d\gamma_1\cos(\tilde{\omega}_1\tau_1), \\ 2d\tilde{\omega}_1 - d\gamma_2\sin(\tilde{\omega}_1\tau_{2*}) + \gamma_2\tilde{\omega}_1\cos(\tilde{\omega}_1\tau_{2*}) = d\gamma_1\sin(\tilde{\omega}_1\tau_1) - \gamma_1\tilde{\omega}_1\cos(\tilde{\omega}_1\tau_1), \end{cases}$$

which leads to

$$\begin{aligned}F_1(\tilde{\omega}_1) =&\tilde{\omega}_1^4 + \left(2d^2 - \gamma_1^2 + \gamma_2^2\right)\tilde{\omega}_1^2 + d^4 - d^2\gamma_1^2 + d^2\gamma_2^2 \\ &- 2\left(\tilde{\omega}_1^2 - d^2\right)\left[\gamma_2 \sin\left(\tilde{\omega}_1\tau_{2*)}\right)\tilde{\omega}_1 + d\gamma_2\cos(\tilde{\omega}_1\tau_{2*})\right] \\ &+ 4d\tilde{\omega}_1[\gamma_2\tilde{\omega}_1\cos(\tilde{\omega}_1\tau_{2*}) - d\gamma_2\sin(\tilde{\omega}_1\tau_{2*})].\end{aligned} \tag{12}$$

Suppose

Hypothesis 7 (H7). *$d^4 - 2\gamma_2 d^3 - (\gamma_1^2 - \gamma_2^2)d^2 < 0$. Then, we have $F_1(0) < 0$ and $F_1(\infty) > 0$.*

Hence, $F_1(\tilde{\omega}_1) = 0$ has definite positive roots $\tilde{\omega}_{1k}, k = 0, 1, 2$. For every fixed $\tilde{\omega}_{1k}$, there is a sequence of τ_1 defined by:

$$\tau_{1k}^{(j)} = \begin{cases} \frac{1}{\tilde{\omega}_{1k}}[\arccos(P_{1k}) + 2j\pi], & Q_{1k} \geq 0, \\ \frac{1}{\tilde{\omega}_{1k}}[2\pi - \arccos(P_{1k}) + 2j\pi], & Q_{1k} < 0,\ k = 1, 2\ j = 0, 1, 2, \cdots, \end{cases} \tag{13}$$

where

$$\begin{cases} Q_{1k} \triangleq \sin\left(\tilde{\omega}_1\tau_{1k}^{(j)}\right) = \frac{\tilde{\omega}_1\left[\tilde{\omega}_1^2 - d^2 - \gamma_2\sin(\tilde{\omega}_1\tau_{2*})\tilde{\omega}_1 - d\gamma_2\cos(\tilde{\omega}_1\tau_{2*})\right] + d[2d\tilde{\omega}_1 + \gamma_2\tilde{\omega}_1\cos(\tilde{\omega}_1\tau_{2*}) - d\gamma_2\sin(\tilde{\omega}_1\tau_{2*})]}{\gamma_1\left(\tilde{\omega}_1^2 + d^2\right)}, \\ P_{1k} \triangleq \cos\left(\tilde{\omega}_1\tau_{1k}^{(j)}\right) = \frac{d\left[\tilde{\omega}_1^2 - d^2 - \gamma_2\sin(\tilde{\omega}_1\tau_{2*})\tilde{\omega}_1 - d\gamma_2\cos(\tilde{\omega}_1\tau_{2*})\right] - \tilde{\omega}_1[2d\tilde{\omega}_1 + \gamma_2\tilde{\omega}_1\cos(\tilde{\omega}_1\tau_{2*}) - d\gamma_2\sin(\tilde{\omega}_1\tau_{2*})]}{\gamma_1\left(\tilde{\omega}_1^2 + d^2\right)}. \end{cases}$$

Lemma 2. *Let $\tau_{1*} = min\tau_{1k}^{(j)}, i = 0, 1, 2, j = 0, 1, 2, \cdots$, when $\tau_1 = \tau_{1*}$, Equation (12) has a pair of purely imaginary roots $\pm i\tilde{\omega}_1$ for $\tau_2 \in I$. Assume $\mathrm{Re}(\frac{\mathrm{d}\tau}{\mathrm{d}\lambda})\Big|_{\tau=\tau_{1k}^{(j)}} \neq 0$. Thus, the equilibrium E_1 is locally asymptotically stable when $\tau_1 \in [0, \tau_{1*})$.*

Theorem 1. *For equilibrium E_1, we have the following conclusions.*
When (H1) does not hold or $R_0 > 1$ holds, equilibrium E_1 is unstable; When (H1) and $R_0 < 1$ hold,

(1) $\tau_1 = 0, \tau_2 = 0$
Equilibrium E_1 is locally asymptotically stable;

(2) $\tau_1 = 0, \tau_2 > 0$
- *(a)* *If (H4) holds, $h(z)$ has only one positive root z_1, when $\tau_1 \in [0, \tau_{21}^{(0)})$, the equilibrium E_1 is locally asymptotically stable;*
- *(b)* *If (H5) holds, $h(z)$ has two positive roots z_2 and z_3, then we suppose $z_2 < z_3$, and we get $h'(z_2) < 0, h'(z_3) > 0$. Then $\exists m \in N$, which can make $0 < \tau_{23}^{(0)} < \tau_{22}^{(0)} < \tau_{23}^{(1)} < \tau_{22}^{(1)} < \cdots < \tau_{23}^{(m)} < \tau_{23}^{(m+1)}$. When $\tau \in (0, \tau_{23}^{(0)}) \cup \bigcup_{l=1}^{m} (\tau_{22}^{(l-1)}, \tau_{23}^{(l)})$, the equilibrium E_1 of the model is locally asymptotically stable. When $\tau \in \bigcup_{l=0}^{m-1} (\tau_{23}^{(l)}, \tau_{22}^{(l)}) \cup (\tau_{23}^{(m)}, +\infty)$, the equilibrium E_1 is locally asymptotically unstable.*

(3) $\tau_1 > 0, \tau_2 > 0$
Under (H7), the equilibrium E_1 of system (1) is locally asymptotically stable when $\tau_1 \in [0, \tau_{1*})$ for the chosen τ_{2*} based on Lemma 2.

3.2. Analysis for Endemic Equilibrium E_{2_l}

3.2.1. The Case for $\tau_1 = 0, \tau_2 = 0$

When $R_0 > 1$ and (H2) or (H3) holds, the equilibrium E_1 is unstable and the other equilibrium E_{2_l} for System (2) exists and is positive. For the equilibrium E_{2_l}, Equation (4) is transformed into the following form when $\tau_1 = \tau_2 = 0$:

$$\lambda^4 + a_1\lambda^3 + a_2\lambda^2 + a_3\lambda + a_4 = 0, \tag{14}$$

where

$$a_1 = A_3 + \gamma_1 + \gamma_2,\ a_2 = B_3 + B_1\gamma_1 + B_2\gamma_2,$$
$$a_3 = C_3 + C_1\gamma_1 + C_2\gamma_2,\ a_4 = D_3 + D_1\gamma_1 + D_2\gamma_2.$$

According to the Routh–Hurwitz criterion, we show the following hypothesis:

Hypothesis 8 (H8). $a_1a_2 - a_3 > 0, a_3(a_1a_2 - a_3) > a_1^2a_4, a_4 > 0.$

If (H8) is satisfied, all eigenvalues of Equation (14) have negative real parts, the equilibrium E_{2_l} of model (1) is locally asymptotically stable when $\tau_1 = \tau_2 = 0$.

Lemma 3. *For equilibrium E_{2_l}, if $R_0 > 1$ and (H8) holds, equilibrium E_{2_l} is locally asymptotically stable. Further, when $R_0 < 1$ or (H8) does not hold, equilibrium E_{2_l} is unstable when $\tau_1 = \tau_2 = 0$.*

3.2.2. The Case for $\tau_1 = 0, \tau_2 > 0$

Similarly to the analysis of E_1, for the equilibrium E_{2_l}, the characteristic equation Equation (4) becomes the following form when $\tau_1 = 0$ and $\tau_2 > 0$:

$$\lambda^4 + q_1\lambda^3 + q_2\lambda^2 + q_3\lambda + q_4 + \gamma_2 e^{-\lambda\tau_2}\left(\lambda^3 + B_2\lambda^2 + C_2\lambda + D_2\right) = 0, \tag{15}$$

where

$$q_1 = A_3 + \gamma_1,\ q_2 = B_3 + B_1\gamma_1,\ q_3 = C_3 + C_1\gamma_1,\ q_4 = D_3 + D_1\gamma_1.$$

Assuming that $\lambda = i\omega_2(\omega_2 > 0)$ is a pure imaginary root of Equation (15), substituting it into Equation (15) and separating the real and imaginary parts, we have:

$$\begin{cases} {\omega_2}^4 - q_2{\omega_2}^2 + q_4 = \gamma_2\left(B_2{\omega_2}^2 - D_2\right)\cos(\omega_2\tau_2) + \gamma_2\left({\omega_2}^3 - C_2\omega_2\right)\sin(\omega_2\tau_2), \\ -q_1{\omega_2}^3 + q_3\omega_2 = \gamma_2\left(-B_2{\omega_2}^2 + D_2\right)\sin(\omega_2\tau_2) + \gamma_2\left({\omega_2}^3 - C_2\omega_2\right)\cos(\omega_2\tau_2). \end{cases} \tag{16}$$

Thus,

$$\begin{cases} \sin(\omega_2\tau_2) = \dfrac{(-q_1{\omega_2}^3 + q_3\omega_2)(-B_2{\omega_2}^2 + D_2) - ({\omega_2}^4 - q_2{\omega_2}^2 + q_4)(-{\omega_2}^3 + C_2\omega_2)}{\gamma_2(-B_2{\omega_2}^2 + D_2)^2 + \gamma_2(-{\omega_2}^3 + C_2\omega_2)^2}, \\ \cos(\omega_2\tau_2) = -\dfrac{({\omega_2}^4 - q_2{\omega_2}^2 + q_4)(-B_2{\omega_2}^2 + D_2) + (-q_1{\omega_2}^3 + q_3\omega_2)(-{\omega_2}^3 + C_2\omega_2)}{\gamma_2(-B_2{\omega_2}^2 + D_2)^2 + \gamma_2(-{\omega_2}^3 + C_2\omega_2)^2}. \end{cases} \tag{17}$$

Add the square of the two equations in Equation (17) and let $z = {\omega_2}^2$. So we get:

$$h(z) = z^4 + c_1z^3 + c_2z^2 + c_3z + c_4 = 0, \tag{18}$$

where

$$\begin{aligned} c_1 &= -2q_2 + q_1^2 - \gamma_2^2, \\ c_2 &= q_2^2 + 2q_4 - 2q_1q_3 - \gamma_2^2\left(B_2^2 - 2C_2\right), \\ c_3 &= -2q_2q_4 + q_3^2 - \gamma_2^2\left(-2B_2D_2 + C_2^2\right), \\ c_4 &= q_4^2 - \gamma_2^2 D_2^2. \end{aligned}$$

We hypothesize that Equation (18) has $l(l = 1, 2, 3, 4.)$ positive roots and mark as $z_1 > z_2 > z_3 > z_4$. Substituting $\omega_{2l} = \sqrt{z_l}$ into Equation (17), we get the expression of τ:

$$\tau_{22,l}^{(j)} = \begin{cases} \frac{1}{\omega_{2l}}[\arccos(P_{22,l}) + 2j\pi], & Q_{22,l} \geq 0, \\ \frac{1}{\omega_{2l}}[2\pi - \arccos(P_{22,l}) + 2j\pi], & Q_{22,l} < 0, \end{cases} \tag{19}$$

where $Q_{22,l} = \sin(\omega_{2l}\tau_{22,l}^{(j)})$, $P_{22,l} = \cos(\omega_{2l}\tau_{22,l}^{(j)})$.

Thus, we have the transversality condition:

$$\mathrm{Re}\left(\frac{d\lambda}{d\tau}\right)^{-1}\Bigg|_{\tau=\tau_{22,l}^{(j)}} = \mathrm{Re}\left(\frac{d\tau}{d\lambda}\right)\Bigg|_{\tau=\tau_{22,l}^{(j)}} = \frac{h'(\omega_{2l}^2)}{\gamma_2^2\left[\left(B_2\omega_{2l}^2 - D_2\right)^2 + \left(\omega_{2l}^3 - C_2\omega_{2l}\right)^2\right]} \neq 0 (j = 0, 1 \ldots).$$

Under this condition, we get the minimum critical deley $\tau = \tau_{22,l}$, and we suppose equilibrium E_{2_l} is stable in region I′ when $\tau_1 = 0$ and $\tau_2 > 0$.

3.2.3. The Case for $\tau_1 > 0$, $\tau_2 > 0$

For equilibrium E_{2_l}, similar to the analysis of E_1, we choose $\tau_2 = \tau_{22*} \in$ I′ as a parameter and let $\lambda = i\tilde{\omega}_2(\tilde{\omega}_2 > 0)$ be a pure imaginary root of characteristic equation Equation (4) and substitute it into this equation. Then, separating the real part and the imaginary part, we have:

$$\begin{cases} \tilde{\omega}_2^4 - B_3\tilde{\omega}_2^2 + D_3 + \gamma_2\cos(\tilde{\omega}_2\tau_{22*})\left(-B_2\tilde{\omega}_2^2 + D_2\right) + \gamma_2\sin(\tilde{\omega}_2\tau_{22*})\left(-\tilde{\omega}_2^3 + C_2\tilde{\omega}_2\right) \\ \quad = -\gamma_1\left(-B_1\tilde{\omega}_2^2 + D_1\right)\cos(\tilde{\omega}_2\tau_1) - \gamma_1\left(-\tilde{\omega}_2^3 + C_1\tilde{\omega}_2\right)\sin(\tilde{\omega}_2\tau_1), \\ -A_3\tilde{\omega}_2^3 + C_3\tilde{\omega}_2 + \gamma_2\cos(\tilde{\omega}_2\tau_{22*})\left(-\tilde{\omega}_2^3 + C_2\tilde{\omega}_2\right) - \gamma_2\sin(\tilde{\omega}_2\tau_{22*})\left(-B_2\tilde{\omega}_2^2 + D_2\right) \\ \quad = \gamma_1\left(-B_1\tilde{\omega}_2^2 + D_1\right)\sin(\tilde{\omega}_2\tau_1) - \gamma_1\left(-\tilde{\omega}_2^3 + C_1\tilde{\omega}_2\right)\cos(\tilde{\omega}_2\tau_1). \end{cases} \tag{20}$$

Then, we can obtain:

$$\begin{cases} \sin(\tilde{\omega}_2\tau_1) = \\ \frac{[\tilde{\omega}_2^4 - B_3\tilde{\omega}_2^2 + D_3 - \gamma_2\cos(\tilde{\omega}_2\tau_{22*})(B_2\tilde{\omega}_2^2 - D_2) - \gamma_2\sin(\tilde{\omega}_2\tau_{22*})(\tilde{\omega}_2^3 - C_2\tilde{\omega}_2)](\tilde{\omega}_2^3 - C_1\tilde{\omega}_2)}{\gamma_1\left[(-B_1\tilde{\omega}_2^2 + D_1)^2 + (-\tilde{\omega}_2^3 + C_1\tilde{\omega}_2)^2\right]} \\ - \frac{[-A_3\tilde{\omega}_2^3 + C_3\tilde{\omega}_2 - \gamma_2\cos(\tilde{\omega}_2\tau_{22*})(\tilde{\omega}_2^3 - C_2\tilde{\omega}_2) + \gamma_2\sin(\tilde{\omega}_2\tau_{22*})(B_2\tilde{\omega}_2^2 - D_2)](B_1\tilde{\omega}_2^2 - D_1)}{\gamma_1[(-B_1\tilde{\omega}_2^2 + D_1)^2 + (-\tilde{\omega}_2^3 + C_1\tilde{\omega}_2)^2}. \\ \cos(\omega\tau_1) = \\ \frac{[\tilde{\omega}_2^4 - B_3\tilde{\omega}_2^2 + D_3 - \gamma_2\cos(\tilde{\omega}_2\tau_{22*})(B_2\tilde{\omega}_2^2 - D_2) - \gamma_2\sin(\tilde{\omega}_2\tau_{22*})(\tilde{\omega}_2^3 - C_2\tilde{\omega}_2)](B_1\tilde{\omega}_2^2 - D_1)}{\gamma_1\left[(-B_1\tilde{\omega}_2^2 + D_1)^2 + (-\tilde{\omega}_2^3 + C_1\tilde{\omega}_2)^2\right]} \\ + \frac{[-A_3\tilde{\omega}_2^3 + C_3\tilde{\omega}_2 - \gamma_2\cos(\tilde{\omega}_2\tau_{22*})(\tilde{\omega}_2^3 - C_2\tilde{\omega}_2) + \gamma_2\sin(\tilde{\omega}_2\tau_{22*})(B_2\tilde{\omega}_2^2 - D_2)](\tilde{\omega}_2^3 - C_1\tilde{\omega}_2)}{\gamma_1\left[(-B_1\tilde{\omega}_2^2 + D_1)^2 + (-\tilde{\omega}_2^3 + C_1\tilde{\omega}_2)^2\right]}. \end{cases} \tag{21}$$

Adding the square of two equations in (20), we have:

$$\begin{aligned}F_2(\tilde{\omega}_2) &= \left(\tilde{\omega}_2^4 - B_3\tilde{\omega}_2^2 + D_3\right)^2 + \left(-A_3\tilde{\omega}_2^3 + C_3\tilde{\omega}_2\right)^2 + \gamma_2^2\left(-B_2\tilde{\omega}_2^2 + D_2\right)^2 + \gamma_2^2\left(-\tilde{\omega}_2^3 + C_2\tilde{\omega}_2\right)^2 \\ &+ 2\gamma_2\cos(\tilde{\omega}_2\tau_{22*})\left[\left(D_2 - B_2\tilde{\omega}_2^2\right)\left(\tilde{\omega}_2^4 - B_3\tilde{\omega}_2^2 + D_3\right) + \left(C_2\tilde{\omega}_2 - \tilde{\omega}_2^3\right)\left(C_3\tilde{\omega}_2 - A_3\tilde{\omega}_2^3\right)\right] \\ &+ 2\gamma_2\sin(\tilde{\omega}_2\tau_{22*})\left[\left(C_2\tilde{\omega}_2 - \tilde{\omega}_2^3\right)\left(\tilde{\omega}_2^4 - B_3\tilde{\omega}_2^2 + D_3\right) - \left(D_2 - B_2\tilde{\omega}_2^2\right)\left(C_3\tilde{\omega}_2 - A_3\tilde{\omega}_2^3\right)\right] \\ &- {\gamma_1}^2\left(-B_1\tilde{\omega}_2^2 + D_1\right)^2 - {\gamma_1}^2\left(-\tilde{\omega}_2^3 + C_1\tilde{\omega}_2\right)^2 = 0.\end{aligned} \quad (22)$$

Then, we give the following assumption:

Hypothesis 9 (H9). $D_3^2 + \gamma_2^2 {D_2}^2 + 2\gamma_2 D_2 D_3 - {\gamma_1}^2 D_1^2 < 0$

Under (H9), we can deduce $F_2(0) < 0$ and $F_2(\infty) > 0$. Thus, $F_2(\tilde{\omega}_2) = 0$ must have a positive root. We assume there are l positive roots of $F_2(\tilde{\omega}_2) = 0$ and denote as $\tilde{\omega}_{2l}$.

$$\tau_{12,l}^{(j)} = \begin{cases} \frac{1}{\tilde{\omega}_{2l}}[\arccos(P_{12,l}) + 2j\pi], & Q_{12,l} \geq 0, \\ \frac{1}{\tilde{\omega}_{2l}}[2\pi - \arccos(P_{12,l}) + 2j\pi], & Q_{12,l} < 0, \end{cases} \quad (23)$$

where

$$\begin{aligned}Q_{12,l} =& \frac{[\tilde{\omega}_2^4 - B_3\omega_0^2 + D_3 + \gamma_2\cos(\tilde{\omega}_2\tau_1^*)(D_2 - B_2\tilde{\omega}_2^2) + \gamma_2\sin(\tilde{\omega}_2\tau_1^*)(C_2\tilde{\omega}_2 - \tilde{\omega}_2^3)](\tilde{\omega}_2^3 - C_1\tilde{\omega}_2)}{\gamma_1\left[(-B_1\tilde{\omega}_2^2 + D_1)^2 + (-\tilde{\omega}_2^3 + C_1\tilde{\omega}_2)^2\right]} \\ &+ \frac{[C_3\tilde{\omega}_2 - A_3\tilde{\omega}_2^3 + \gamma_2\cos(\tilde{\omega}_2\tau_1^*)(C_2\tilde{\omega}_2 - \tilde{\omega}_2^3) - \gamma_2\sin(\tilde{\omega}_2\tau_1^*)(D_2 - B_2\tilde{\omega}_2^2)](D_1 - B_1\tilde{\omega}_2^2)}{\gamma_1[(-B_1\tilde{\omega}_2^2 + D_1)^2 + (-\tilde{\omega}_2^3 + C_1\tilde{\omega}_2)^2}, \\ P_{12,l} =& \frac{[\tilde{\omega}_2^4 - B_3\tilde{\omega}_2^2 + D_3 + \gamma_2\cos(\tilde{\omega}_2\tau_1^*)(D_2 - B_2\tilde{\omega}_2^2) + \gamma_2\sin(\tilde{\omega}_2\tau_1^*)(C_2\tilde{\omega}_2 - \tilde{\omega}_2^3)](B_1\tilde{\omega}_2^2 - D_1)}{\gamma_1\left[(-B_1\omega_0^2 + D_1)^2 + (-\tilde{\omega}_2^3 + C_1\tilde{\omega}_2)^2\right]} \\ &+ \frac{[C_3\tilde{\omega}_2 - A_3\tilde{\omega}_2^3 + \gamma_2\cos(\tilde{\omega}_2\tau_1^*)(C_2\tilde{\omega}_2 - \tilde{\omega}_2^3) - \gamma_2\sin(\tilde{\omega}_2\tau_1^*)(D_2 - B_2\tilde{\omega}_2^2)](\tilde{\omega}_2^3 - C_1\tilde{\omega}_2)}{\gamma_1\left[(-B_1\tilde{\omega}_2^2 + D_1)^2 + (-\tilde{\omega}_2^3 + C_1\tilde{\omega}_2)^2\right]}.\end{aligned}$$

Let $\tau_{12*} = \min\tau_{12,l}^{(j)}, j = 0, 1, 2, \ldots$; when $\tau_1 = \tau_{12*}$, Equation (22) has a pair of purely imaginary roots $\pm i\omega_{12*}$. Assume

Hypothesis 10 (H10). $\mathrm{Re}\left(\frac{d\lambda}{d\tau_1}\right)^{-1}\Big|_{\tau_1=\tau_{12*}} \neq 0$

Under (H10), the equilibrium E_{2_l} is locally asymptotically stable when $\tau_1 \in [0, \tau_{12*})$ and $\tau_2 = \tau_{22*}$.

Theorem 2. *For equilibrium E_{2_l}, we have the following conclusions.*
If (H2) or (H3) holds, the equilibrium E_{2_1} or E_{2_2} of the model is positive. Under this condition, we consider the following case.

(1) $\tau_1 = 0, \tau_2 = 0$

Based on Lemma 3, if $R_0 > 1$ and (H8) holds, equilibrium E_{2_l} is locally asymptotically stable. If $R_0 < 1$ or (H8) does not hold, equilibrium E_{2_l} is unstable.

(2) $\tau_1 = 0, \tau_2 > 0$

- *(a)* *If $h(z)$ of Equation (18) has no positive root, the equilibrium E_{2_l} is locally asymptotically stable when $\tau_2 > 0$;*

(b) *If $h(z)$ only has one positive root z_1, in System (1) Hopf bifurcation occurs at E_{2_l} when $\tau_2 = \tau_{22,1}^{(j)}$ and $h'(z_1) > 0$. We get $\forall 0 < \tau_2 < \tau_{22,1}^{(0)}$, the equilibrium E_{2_l} is asymptotically stable, and when $\forall\ \tau_2 > \tau_{22,1}^{(0)}$, the equilibrium E_{2_l} is unstable;*

(c) *If $h(z)$ has two positive roots z_1, z_2, in System (1) Hopf bifurcation occurs at E_{2_l} when $\tau_2 = \tau_{22,1}^{(j)}$ and $\tau_2 = \tau_{22,2}^{(j)}$. We assume $z_2 < z_1$, we get $h'(z_1) > 0, h'(z_2) < 0$. Thus, assuming $\tau_{22,1}^{(0)} < \tau_{22,2}^{(0)}$, there exists k, which makes: $0 < \tau_{22,1}^{(0)} < \tau_{22,2}^{(0)} < \tau_{22,1}^{(1)} < \tau_{22,2}^{(1)} < \cdots < \tau_{22,1}^{(k)} < \tau_{22,1}^{(k+1)}$. When $\tau_2 \in \left[0, \tau_{22,1}^{(0)}\right) \cup \bigcup_{i=1}^{k} (\tau_{22,2}^{(i-1)}, \tau_{22,1}^{(i)})$, the equilibrium is locally asymptotically stable. When $\tau_1 \in \bigcup_{i=0}^{k-1} (\tau_{22,1}^{(i)}, \tau_{22,2}^{(i)}) \cup (\tau_{22,1}^{(k)}, +\infty)$, the equilibrium is unstable;*

(d) *If $h(z)$ has three positive roots z_1, z_2, z_3, in System (1) Hopf bifurcation occurs at E_{2_l} when $\tau_2 = \tau_{22,l}^{(j)}, (l = 1,2,3)$. We assume $z_3 < z_2 < z_1$, so we have $h'(z_1) > 0, h'(z_2) < 0, h'(z_3) > 0$. Similar to the analysis of (c), the equilibrium E_{2_l} switches between stability and instability with the increase of τ_1. Finally, the equilibrium is unstable.*

(e) *If $h(z)$ has four positive roots z_1, z_2, z_3 and z_4, in System (1) Hopf bifurcation occurs at E_{2_l} when $\tau_2 = \tau_{22,l}^{(j)}, (l = 1,2,3,4)$. Assuming that $z_4 < z_3 < z_2 < z_1$, we can obtain $h'(z_1) > 0, h'(z_2) < 0, h'(z_3) > 0, h'(z_4) < 0$. Similar to the analysis of (c), the equilibrium E_{2_l} switches between stability and instability with the increase of τ_2. Finally, the equilibrium is unstable.*

(3) $\tau_1 > 0, \tau_2 > 0$

Under (H9) and (H10), the equilibrium E_{2_l} of system (1) is locally asymptotically stable when $\tau_1 \in [0, \tau_{12*})$ for the chosen τ_{22*} under the stable conditions of **(1)** *and* **(2)**.

4. Normal Form of Hopf Bifurcation

In this section, we derive the normal form of Hopf bifurcation for System (1) by using the multiple time scales method. We consider the delay for people having COVID-19 booster vaccination and the delay of vaccine failure. In order to find the most appropriate and effective booster vaccination time, we consider the time-delay τ_1 as a bifurcation parameter. Let $\tau_1 = \tau_c + \varepsilon\tau_\varepsilon$, where τ_c is the critical value of Hopf bifurcation given in Equation (13) or Equation (23), τ_ε is the disturbance parameter, and ε is the dimensionless scale parameter. Assuming that when $\tau_1 = \tau_c$, the characteristic equation Equation (4) has a pair of pure imaginary roots $\lambda = \pm i\omega_k$ at which System (1) undergoes Hopf bifurcation at equilibrium $E_k = (S_k, V_k, I_k, R_k), k = 1, 2_1, 2_2$. The details of the calculation of the normal form are in the Appendix A, and the normal form is as follows:

$$\dot{G} = M_k \tau_\varepsilon G_1 + H_k G_1^2 \bar{G}_1, \tag{24}$$

where M_k, H_k are given in Equation (A9) and Equation (A14).

Let $G = \gamma e^{i\theta}$ and substitute it into Equation (A15), we can obtain the normal form of Hopf bifurcation in polar coordinates:

$$\begin{cases} \dot{r} = \mathrm{Re}(M_k)\tau_\varepsilon r + \mathrm{Re}(H_k) r^3, \\ \dot{\theta} = \mathrm{Im}(M_k)\tau_\varepsilon + \mathrm{Im}(H_k) r^2. \end{cases} \tag{25}$$

Then, we have the theorem as follows.

Theorem 3. *If $\frac{Re(M_k)\tau_\varepsilon}{Re(H_k)\tau_c} < 0$ holds $(k = 1, 2_1, 2_2)$, System (1) has nontrivial fixed point $r^* = \sqrt{-\frac{Re(M_k)\tau_\varepsilon}{Re(H_k)\tau_c}}$, so System (1) has a periodic solution around the equilibrium E_k:*

(1) *If $\mathrm{Re}(M_k)\tau_\varepsilon < 0$, the periodic solution of System (1) is unstable.*

(2) *If $\mathrm{Re}(M_k)\tau_\varepsilon > 0$, the periodic solution of System (1) is stable.*

5. Numerical Simulations

In this section, we carry out numerical simulations to verify our theoretical analysis. In order to simulate the optimal time of booster vaccination both in countries with low vaccination rates and high vaccination rates, we choose two groups of actual parameters under different vaccination rates according to official data. We also study the impact of vaccine effectiveness on the epidemic by adding a third set of parameters. Then, we calculate the equilibria and critical values of time delay through MATLAB. After that, we simulate the change of the epidemic with different booster vaccination times. According to the results, we give the conclusion on the most suitable booster vaccination time and give some reasonable suggestions for epidemic control.

5.1. Determination for Parameter Values

In this section, we use statistical methods to analyze the values of parameters according to the actual data obtained from several official websites. Then, we select three groups of parameters with the highest research significance.

(1) COVID-19 mortality rate: c

Based on data from the official website of The World Health Organization (https://www.who.int/, accessed on 14 March 2022), we can obtain the COVID-19 mortality rates of different countries. In order to ensure that the data can reflect the average, we take representative data and eliminate outliers. Finally, we screen the death rates due to disease for 29 countries. According to the data, we make a bar chart, which is presented in Figure 2.

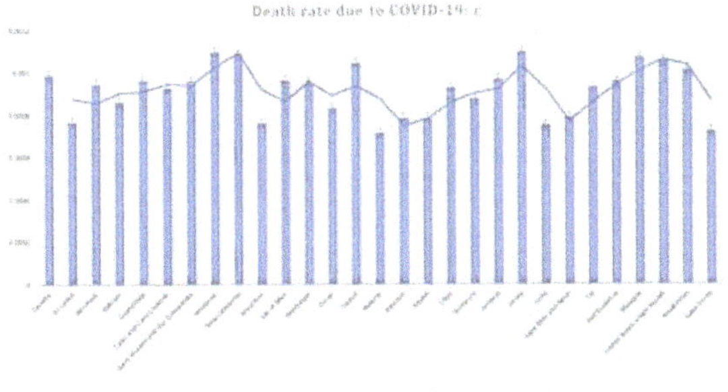

Figure 2. COVID-19 mortality rates of 29 countries.

From Figure 2, it is easy to find that the COVID-19 mortality rates of these countries are mostly in the range of 0.0008 to 0.001, so we choose the mean value of 0.0009 as the value of c.

(2) Cure rate: μ

We obtained the cure rates of COVID-19 in different countries from the website of the WHO. By eliminating the missing values and outliers, we obtain the cure rates of 62 countries (such as the USA, Japan, Germany, Austria, Italy, Canada, South Africa, France and so on) and plot the scatter diagram in Figure 3.

As for cure rates μ, we can clearly see that it is almost at the same level through the dotted line in Figure 3, so we figure out the average rate of 62 countries: 0.861 as the value of μ.

(3) Infection rate: α, β

Infection rates can vary from country to country because of the spread of the disease and the level of government concern. In addition, while antibodies are produced in vaccinated people, an immune barrier is not yet fully formed. So they also have some rate of transmission, but obviously, the people who get the booster vaccine have a lower rate of infection than the people who just get the basic vaccine. We consult the relevant data from the Centers for Disease Control and Prevention (https://www.cdc.gov/coronavirus/2019

-ncov/index.html, accessed on 14 March 2022) and determine the values or range of α and β in light of the actual situation. Then, we choose $\alpha = 0.007$ and $\beta = 0.0002$.

(4) Re-vaccination rate: σ_1, σ_2

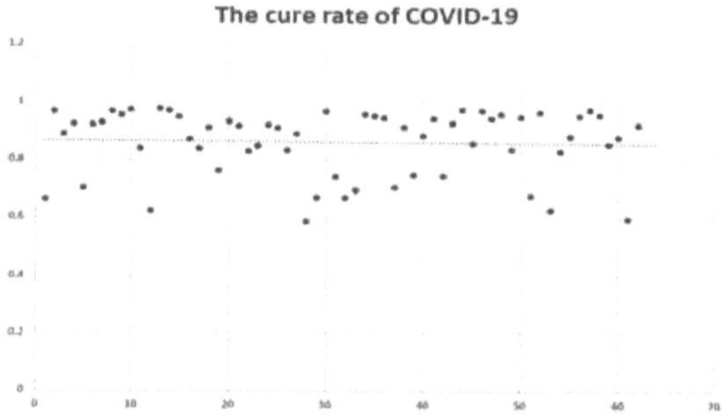

Figure 3. Cure rates of COVID-19 of 62 countries.

As we mentioned in the modeling, the level of antibody production after vaccination depends on the individual [22]. For people such as the elderly or those with underlying diseases who have recovered, the antibodies produced by the vaccine are almost completely disabled, and they need a basic injection to regain active antibodies at a conversion rate of σ_1 from R to S. In addition, some people still have some antibody activity in their bodies, and they only need to inject enhancers to increase their resistance to SARS-CoV-2 at a conversion rate of σ_2 from R to V. We think the difference is related to the age structure of the infected person (see Figure 4).

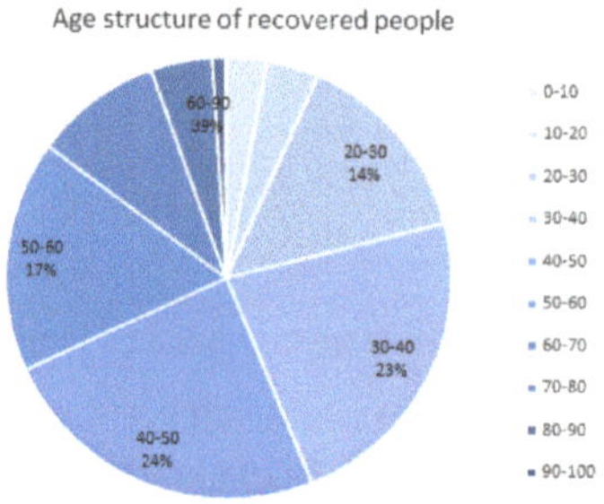

Figure 4. Age structure of recovered people.

We find that recovered people between 20 and 50 years old account for 61% of the total, and we assume that this group has better physical fitness than other age groups. So we consider $\frac{\sigma_2}{\sigma_1} = 1.6$, and choose $\sigma_1 = 0.2, \sigma = 0.32$.

(5) Natural mortality rate: d

In order to find the value of natural mortality rate d, we select population data from the National Bureau of Statistics (http://www.stats.gov.cn/enGliSH/, accessed on 14 March 2022) from 2006 to 2019, and we forecast a natural mortality rate $d = 0.00707$ in 2022 based on trends (see Figure 5).

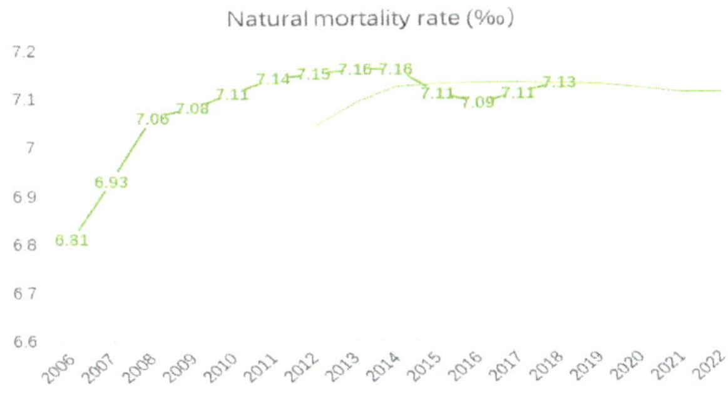

Figure 5. Natural mortality rate.

(6) Basic vaccination rate: Λ

Due to limited vaccine resources in some countries or insufficient attention to the epidemic, vaccination rates vary significantly among countries. We classify countries in terms of high and low vaccination rates and discuss the impact of booster vaccination on epidemic control in both groups.

As we can see in Figures 6 and 7, we classify the data provided by the WHO and select reasonable data to draw scatter plots. For countries with low vaccination rates, we find vaccination rates are around 0.8, so we select $\Lambda = 0.8$ for the first set of parameters. For countries with high vaccination rates, in which people recognize the effectiveness of vaccines for epidemic control, vaccination rates reach 10, so we select $\Lambda = 10$.

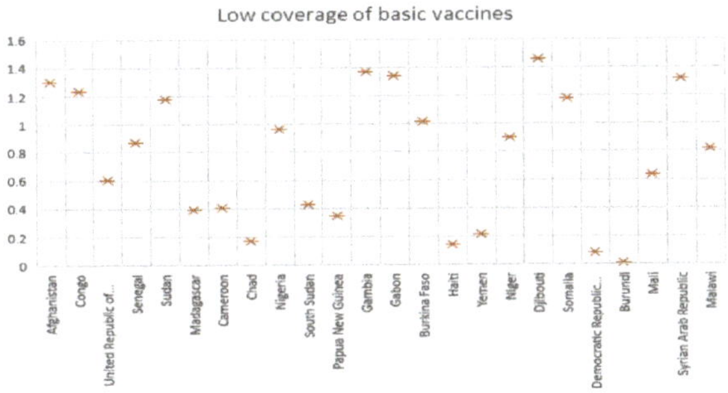

Figure 6. The basic vaccination rates of 24 countries with low vaccination rates.

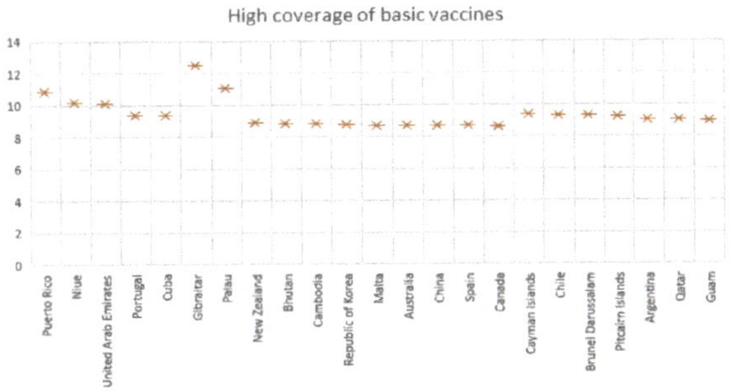

Figure 7. The basic vaccination rates of 23 countries with high vaccination rates.

(7) Booster vaccination rate: γ_1

For booster vaccination, although the vaccination process is still going on and the rate of booster vaccination is still a variable, we can still analyze it based on the available data from the WHO because the level of national interest in vaccines does not change very much (see Figures 8 and 9).

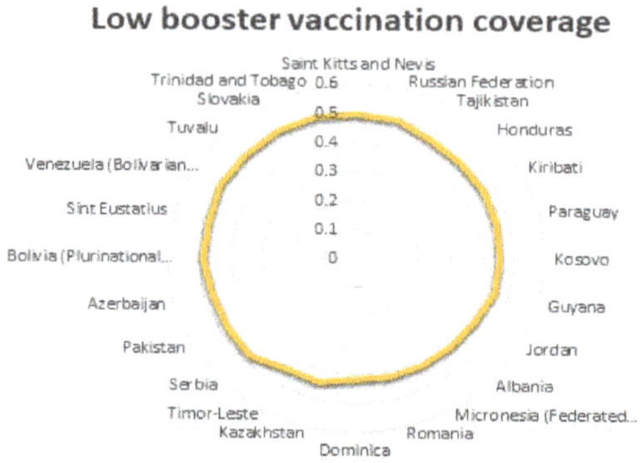

Figure 8. The booster vaccination rates of 24 countries with low vaccination rates.

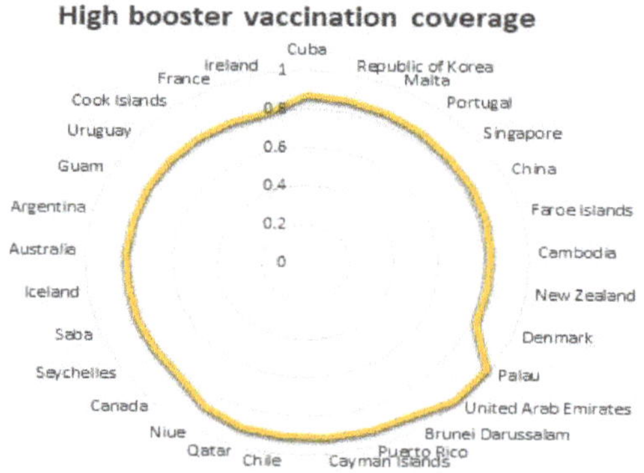

Figure 9. The booster vaccination rates of 29 countries with high vaccination rates.

It is clear that the low booster vaccination rate is between 0.4 and 0.5, so we choose $\gamma_1 = 0.45$ as the booster vaccination rate for countries with low vaccination rates. In Figure 9, an average of 0.864 is selected as the booster vaccination rate for countries with high vaccination rates.

(8) The failure rate of booster vaccination: γ_2

As for γ_2, since the booster vaccine has just been developed, there is no exact failure rate and expiry time. Therefore, we refer to other vaccine-related data from the official website and select $\gamma_2 = 0.25$ as the failure rate of vaccines in countries with high vaccination rates and $\gamma_2 = 0.5$ as the failure rate of vaccines in countries with low vaccination rates, according to some experts' prediction of the effectiveness of COVID-19 booster vaccines. To study the impact of a lower vaccine failure rate on epidemic control, we select $\gamma_2 = 0.15$ in the third group of parameters. This is consistent with the fact that the higher the failure rate, the less willing people are to be vaccinated.

Based on the above consideration, we take the following two groups of parameters (our parameters are all dimensionless):
(I): $\Lambda = 0.8, d = 0.00707, \mu = 0.861, c = 0.0009, \alpha = 0.007, \beta = 0.0002, \gamma_1 = 0.45, \gamma_2 = 0.5, \sigma_1 = 0.2, \sigma_2 = 0.32$;
(II): $\Lambda = 10, d = 0.00707, \mu = 0.861, c = 0.0009, \alpha = 0.007, \beta = 0.0002, \gamma_1 = 0.864, \gamma_2 = 0.25, \sigma_1 = 0.2, \sigma_2 = 0.32$;

(III): $\Lambda = 10, d = 0.00707, \mu = 0.861, c = 0.0009, \alpha = 0.007, \beta = 0.0002, \gamma_1 = 0.864, \gamma_2 = 0.15, \sigma_1 = 0.246, \sigma_2 = 0.22$.

Parameter (I) simulates countries with low vaccination rates and low vaccine effectiveness, probably due to limited national resources and low level of development; Parameter (II) simulates countries with high vaccination rates and average vaccine effectiveness, which is consistent with the current reality of most countries; In order to study methods that can better control the epidemic, we select a third group of parameters (III), which reduced the failure rate compared with the second group of parameters.

5.2. Simulations and Verification

For the group of parameters (I):

$$\Lambda = 0.8, d = 0.00707, \mu = 0.861, c = 0.0009, \alpha = 0.007,$$
$$\beta = 0.0002, \gamma_1 = 0.45, \gamma_2 = 0.5, \sigma_1 = 0.2, \sigma_2 = 0.32.$$

This represents countries with low vaccination rates. We calculate the disease-free equilibrium $E_1 = [59.95, 53.20, 0, 0]$. Under this group of parameters, $R_0 < 1$, so equilibria E_{2_l} do not exist, and $E_1 = [59.95, 53.20, 0, 0]$ is locally asymptotically stable when $\tau_1 = \tau_2 = 0$ according to Theorem 1 and Theorem 2. When $\tau_1 > 0, \tau_2 = 0$, $h(z)$ only has one positive root, and $\omega_{11} = 0.0724$, $\sin(\omega_{11}\tau_{21}^{(0)}) = 0.1448$, $\cos(\omega_{11}\tau_{21}^{(0)}) = -0.9141$, $\tau_{21}^{(0)} = 37.62$. We choose $\tau_2 = \tau_{2*} = 24$ and substitute it into Equations (12) and (13); we get $\tilde{\omega}_{11} = 0.3814$, $\sin(\tilde{\omega}_{11}\tau_{11}^{(0)}) = 0.5218$, $\cos(\tilde{\omega}_{11}\tau_{11}^{(0)}) = 0.8530$, $\tau_{11}^{(0)} = 1.44$. If (H5) holds, the equilibrium E_1 is locally asymptotically stable when $\tau_1 \in [0, \tau_{1*})$.

When $\tau_{2*} = 24 \in (0, \tau_{21}^{(0)}) = (0, 37.62)$, $\tau_{1*} = 1 \in (0, \tau_{11}^{(0)}) = (0, 1.44)$, the equilibrium E_1 is locally asymptotically stable according to Theorem 1; $\tau_{2*} = 24$ means the vaccine will fail 24 months after injection and $\tau_{1*} = 1$ means that people begin to inject booster vaccinations after 1 month to cope with the decrease of vaccine effectiveness. We choose initial values [50, 50, 10, 10] and picture the number of people in different cabins changing over time in Figure 10.

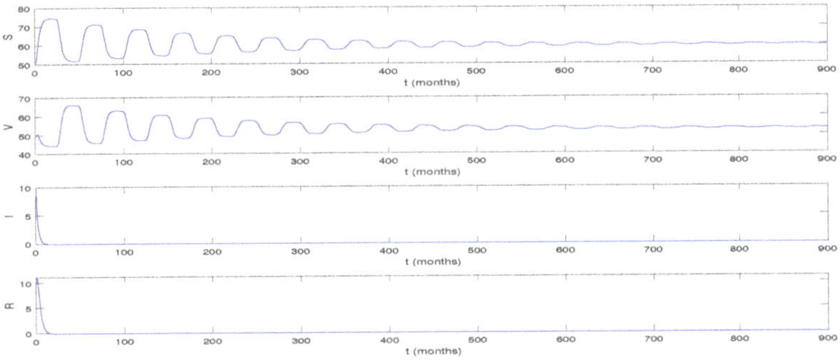

Figure 10. When $\tau_{2*} = 24, \tau_{1*} = 1$, equilibrium E_1 of System (1) is locally asymptotically stable.

The figure above shows that when the vaccine is available for two years, people who get a booster vaccine within a month of getting the basic vaccine can get rid of all infections within 20 months. In other words, herd immunity is achieved before the vaccine wears off. S and V will stabilize after 400 months, and the epidemic will completely disappear.

Remark 1: *Our simulations show that for low-coverage countries, when the vaccine is valid for two years, people need to receive the booster vaccine promptly within one and a half months of receiving the basic vaccine. After 1.5 months, an outbreak will occur. Further, the faster people are vaccinated, the more effectively the epidemic is contained. However, it became clear that getting a booster vaccine after a month would not meet the requirements of the vaccine for the human body. Most of these countries are currently experiencing outbreaks. This is consistent with our simulation results.*

For the group of parameters (II):

$$\Lambda = 10, d = 0.00707, \mu = 0.861, c = 0.0009, \alpha = 0.007,$$
$$\beta = 0.0002, \gamma_1 = 0.864, \gamma_2 = 0.25, \sigma_1 = 0.2, \sigma_2 = 0.32.$$

This represents the situation for countries with high vaccination rates and average vaccine effectiveness. We find $R_0 > 1$, so equilibrium E_{2_1} make sense and is [104.47, 688.37, 255.14, 367.79]. Equilibrium E_1 is unstable. Substituting this group of parameters into Equation (14), (H6) is satisfied, so equilibrium E_{2_1} is locally asymptotically stable when $\tau_1 = \tau_2 = 0$ according to Theorem 2. When $\tau_1 = 0, \tau_2 > 0, h(z)$ only has one positive root, and $\omega_{21} = 0.0805$, $\tau_{22,1}^{(0)} = 28.50$. Selecting $\tau_{2*} = 25$, we obtain $\tilde{\omega}_{21} = 0.2157$, $\sin(\tilde{\omega}_{21}\tau_{12,1}^{(0)}) = 0.8118$, $\cos(\tilde{\omega}_{21}\tau_{12,1}^{(0)}) = -0.5840$, $\tau_{12,1}^{(0)} = 10.17$. Substituting the parameters (II) into Equations (A9) and (A14), we have $\text{Re}(M_k) > 0, \text{Re}(H_k) < 0$. According to Theorem 3, we can deduce $\tau_\varepsilon > 0$, $\text{Re}(M_k)\tau_\varepsilon > 0$; the periodic solution is stable. This means that the epidemic will fluctuate greatly over time, and people's means of controlling the epidemic have no obvious effect on controlling the epidemic. However, there will not be a sudden increase in the number of infected people at a certain moment, and the epidemic situation will not be uncontrollable.

Considering the vaccine developed at present is not an instantaneous failure, and vaccines cannot be administered in a short time, $\tau_1 = \tau_2 = 0$ is impossible.

According to existing medical research, we believe that the validity period of the vaccine is 23–32 months, so we choose $\tau_{2*} = 25$ as the validity period of a booster vaccine. Our purpose is to study the impact of different booster vaccine inoculation times on the epidemic situation. Through our simulation under this set of parameters, we find two important time nodes—6 months and 10 months—to get booster vaccination after basic vaccination. Vaccination after 10 months will lead to an outbreak, which is consistent with our theoretical analysis. Vaccination within six months makes a difference in the epidemic compared to the situation in which people get vaccinated after 6 months.

When $\tau_{2*} = 25, \tau_{1*} = 7$ that means the vaccine will expire after 25 months and booster vaccination will be carried out after 7 months. We still choose [100, 500, 200, 300] as the initial values; the epidemic situation is shown in Figure 11.

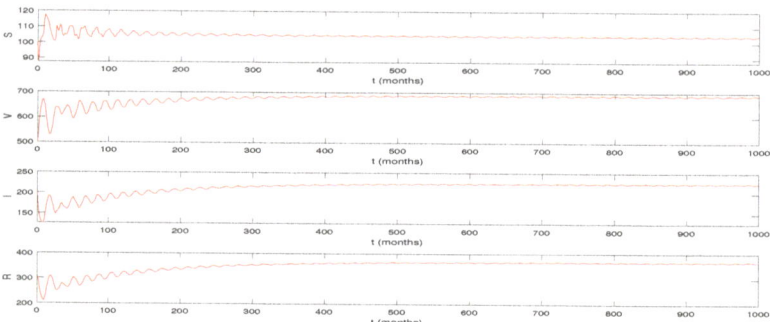

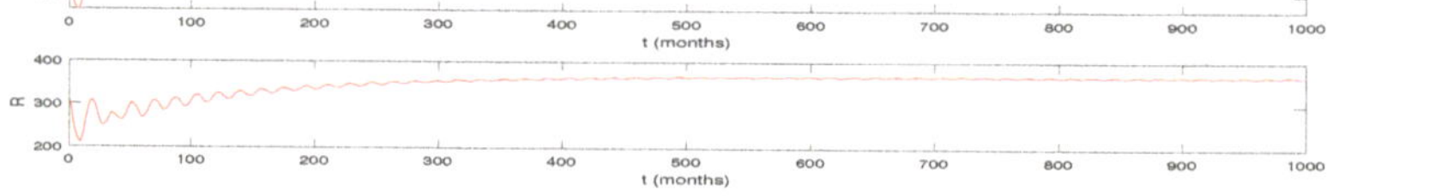

Figure 11. $\tau_{2*} = 25, \tau_{1*} = 7$, equilibrium E_{2_1} of System (1) is locally asymptotically stable.

While the vaccine is still valid for 25 months, people getting booster shots within 7 months will have an overall increase in infections for 500 months, meaning that the number of infections will be high for a long time. This situation can only keep the epidemic under control but does not reduce the number of infected people.

When $\tau_{2*} = 25 \in (0, \tau_{22,1}^{(0)}) = (0, 28.5)$, $\tau_{1*} = 6 \in (0, \tau_{12,1}^{(0)}) = (0, 10.17)$ that means the vaccine expire after 25 months, and we inject the booster vaccine after 6 months; we choose [100, 500, 200, 300] as the initial values (see Figure 12).

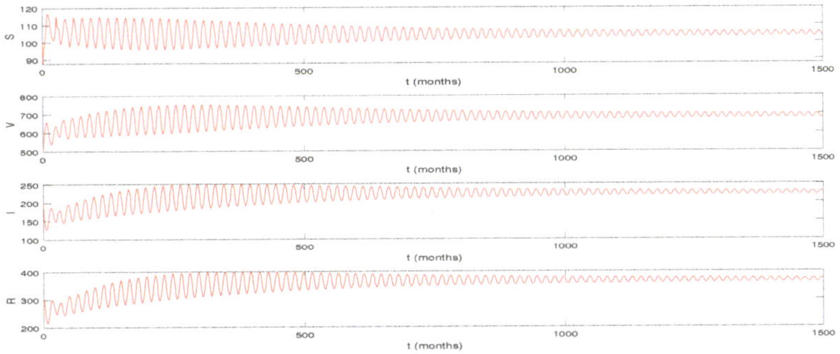

Figure 12. $\tau_{2*} = 25$, $\tau_{1*} = 6$, equilibrium E_{2_1} of System (1) is locally asymptotically stable.

We can see that the epidemic has fluctuated over 500 months. This is consistent with our reality. Currently, we are required to get a booster shot six months after the basic vaccine. Even then, the epidemic does not disappear completely. There are periodic fastigiums in the number of infections. However, by vaccinating we can prevent the number of infections from increasing or staying high and stabilize the epidemic over many years. That is, the booster vaccination has a positive effect on the development of the epidemic, and the trend will be better with the booster vaccination in time.

Remark 2: *This means that under this set of parameters, people will inevitably live with the virus for a long time, and a booster vaccination at the right time will only have a temporary effect on reducing the number of infections.*

For the group of parameters (III):

$$\Lambda = 10, d = 0.00707, \mu = 0.861, =0.0009, \alpha = 0.007,$$
$$\beta = 0.0002, \gamma_1 = 0.864, \gamma_2 = 0.15, \sigma_1 = 0.246, \sigma_2 = 0.22.$$

This set of parameters represents the ideal situation in which the outbreak can be well contained. We find $R_0 > 1$, so equilibrium E_{2_1} makes sense and is [100.92, 812.57, 169.97, 309.34]. Equilibrium E_1 is unstable. Substituting this group of parameters into Equation (14), (H6) is satisfied, so equilibrium E_{2_1} is locally asymptotically stable when $\tau_1 = \tau_2 = 0$ according to Theorem 2. When $\tau_1 = 0, \tau_2 > 0$, $h(z)$ only has one positive root, and $\omega_{21} = 0.0576$, $\tau_{22,1}^{(0)} = 38.78$. Selecting $\tau_{2*} = 32$, we obtain $\tilde{\omega}_{21} = 0.1152$, $\sin(\tilde{\omega}_{21}\tau_{12,1}^{(0)}) = 0.7078$, $\cos(\tilde{\omega}_{21}\tau_{12,1}^{(0)}) = -0.7064$, $\tau_{12,1}^{(0)} = 20.44$. Substituting the parameters (II) into Equations (A9) and (A14), we have $\mathrm{Re}(M_k) > 0, \mathrm{Re}(H_k) < 0$. According to Theorem 3, we can deduce $\tau_\varepsilon > 0$, $\mathrm{Re}(M_k)\tau_\varepsilon > 0$, which means under this set of parameters, if the equilibrium E_{2_1} is unstable, a stable Hopf bifurcation periodic solution will appear. This means that although there will not be a large number of people infected with the novel coronavirus and the number of cases will surge, people's methods are still ineffective, and people need to find better ways to control the epidemic.

When $\tau_{2*} = 32 \in (0, \tau_{22,1}^{(0)}) = (0, 38.78), \tau_{1*} = 6 \in (0, \tau_{12,1}^{(0)}) = (0, 20.44)$ that means the vaccine expires after 32 months and people inject the booster vaccine after 6 months, we choose [100, 1000, 200, 300] as the initial values (see Figure 13).

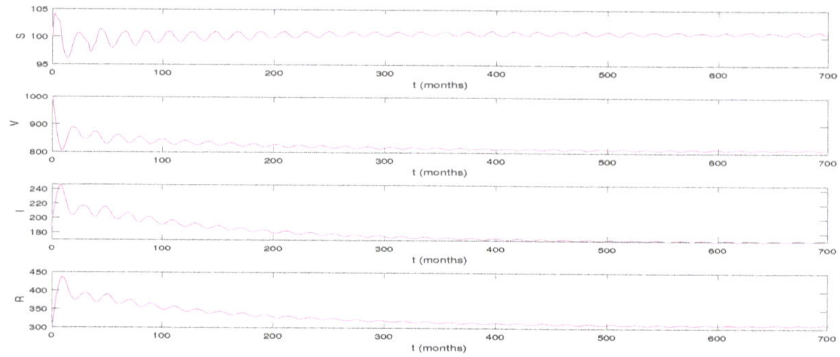

Figure 13. $\tau_{2*} = 32$, $\tau_{1*} = 6$, equilibrium E_{2_1} of System (1) is locally asymptotically stable.

Figure 13 shows a declining trend in the number of infections under the third set of parameters, which stabilizes and approaches almost zero after two decades. This suggests that when the validity of the vaccine is increased to 32 months and the vaccine failure rate is reduced to 0.15, people who receive the booster vaccine 6 months after the basic vaccine can control the outbreak more effectively without long-term coexistence with the virus. In other words, if the vaccine is effective enough, we can expect to be free of COVID-19 by 2042 or earlier. However, this is a relatively ideal situation because many factors in reality can cause the values of parameters in the model to change at any time, and our simulation is based on only a set of constant parameters.

To make the simulation results closer to reality, we can change the value of parameters in real-time according to the actual situation of the epidemic development and use our model to predict the development of the epidemic under different factors such as infection rate, cure rate and vaccine effectiveness. We can provide ideas for the country to control the epidemic by analyzing the simulation results.

When $\tau_{2*} = 32$, $\tau_{1*} = 14.5$ that means the vaccine expires after 32 months, but people inject the booster vaccine after 14.5 months; we choose [100, 1000, 200, 300] as the initial values (see Figure 14).

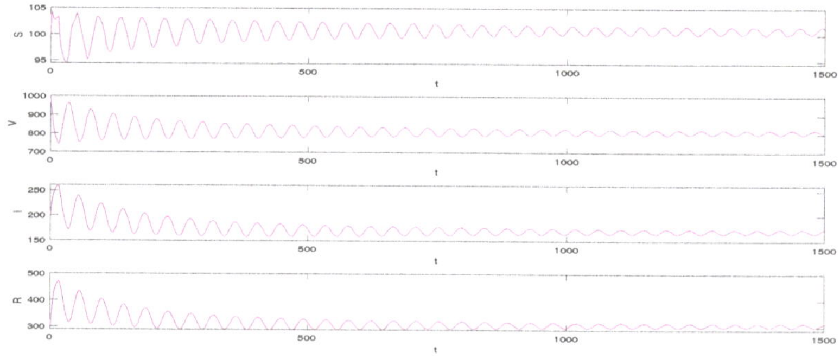

Figure 14. $\tau_{2*} = 32$, $\tau_{1*} = 14.5$, equilibrium E_{2_1} of System (1) is locally asymptotically stable.

Remark 3: *Comparing Figure 13 with Figure 14, it can be found that when the booster vaccination time is 14.5 months, although the system fluctuation trend becomes smaller and the number of infected people also decreases, it takes longer for the system to stabilize than when the booster vaccination time is 6 months. As shown in Figure 14, the system is not stable after 500 months, which has a bad impact on the country's economy and development. Therefore, it is necessary to implement the booster vaccine as soon as the effectiveness of the vaccine is certain.*

5.3. Analysis of Simulations

Based on the above simulations, we have the following conclusions:

(1) When the time of vaccine expiration is determined, the less time people have between a basic vaccine and a booster, the better the outbreak will be contained in both low and high coverage countries, and when the time of booster vaccination exceeds the critical value, System (1) will be unstable and the epidemic will be out of control. The critical time for the booster vaccination is 1.4 months for countries with low vaccination rates and 10.17 months for countries with high vaccination rates. It is clear that increasing vaccination rates have had a positive impact on epidemic control.

(2) We select the parameters (I) and (II) closest to the current epidemic situation, and the simulation results are consistent with the real situation. Due to limited vaccine resources or other reasons, some countries have low vaccination rates. For them, booster vaccination is not completed effectively and on time. As for the critical time of 1.44 months in our simulation results, it is impossible to complete in reality. We look at the epidemic status of most countries with low vaccination rates and found that most of them are in an uncontrolled state of the epidemic, which is consistent with our simulations. For countries with high vaccination rates, we found that the critical time for booster vaccination is 10.17 months, which can be achieved in reality. Given the physical demands of vaccination, most countries require people to receive the booster vaccine promptly 6 months after receiving the basic vaccine. In our simulations, 6 months is also considered to be the most suitable optimal time for booster vaccination. In this case, there will be some fluctuations in the current epidemic, but the number of infections will not be at a high level all the time, and people will be able to control the epidemic within a certain range and eventually stabilize it. When the inoculation time is 7 months, although the epidemic does not fluctuate greatly in the near stage and eventually tends to stabilize, the number of infected people will remain at a high level. This means that under the second set of parameters, the effectiveness of the vaccine will not be enough to eliminate the epidemic, and even if people are actively vaccinated and have high vaccination rates, they will inevitably live with COVID-19 for a long time.

(3) Due to the short development time of the vaccine, its effectiveness is still unclear. In our numerical simulations, different parameters are used to study the impact of vaccine effectiveness on the epidemic. We choose parameters (III) to simulate a better epidemic scenario. Compared with the groups of parameters (I) and (II), the third group has a higher vaccination rate and lower vaccine failure rate, the basal shot is less likely to fail, and the proportion of recovered patients who retain antibodies from the basal shot increased. Through our simulation, we found that under the third set of parameters, when the validity of the vaccine is 32 months and the booster vaccination time is controlled within 20 months, the number of infections decreased and eventually approached zero, the system stabilized, and the epidemic almost disappeared. Changing the timing of the booster vaccine, we found that when the booster vaccine is given at 6 months, the epidemic could be virtually eliminated by 2042. Even though the parameters can change over time in the real world, and this is an ideal situation for us to simulate with a constant set of parameters, we can still conclude that the longer the interval between actual vaccinations, the longer it takes for the epidemic to stabilize. Therefore, considering the economic level of the country and the requirements of the vaccine for the human body, we believe that under the third group of parameters we selected, timely vaccination after 6 months is the ideal epidemic control means.

Compared with the second group of parameters (II), the failure rate of the third group (III) of enhanced vaccines is reduced, the validity period is longer, and the epidemic can be effectively controlled, or even almost disappear. Under the second set of parameters (II), the vaccine is not effective enough, and the epidemic continues. This shows the importance of vaccine effectiveness in controlling outbreaks. In order to better control the epidemic, we need to work to develop a more effective vaccine.

(4) In our simulations above, we select parameters consistent with the current epidemic situation in 2022 and obtain simulation results consistent with the real situation. In fact, our simulations can change with reality, which means that our models are very broad. For example, if a country wants to study epidemic prevention and control strategies for itself, we can bring in the country's data, take into account the comprehensive strength of the country and the requirements of economic development, analyze the data and select reasonable parameters for simulation to obtain the best time for strengthening vaccination and provide targeted strategies for epidemic control. Our model can also simulate the situation as the virus mutates by changing the infection rate α and β. Global vaccination is still ongoing, so vaccination rates are constantly changing, and we can change the vaccination rates in the parameters to change our conclusions in real-time. Once the parameters are determined, we can calculate the corresponding critical booster timing and make recommendations that are appropriate to the current epidemic situation.

5.4. Recommendations for Countries

(i) For countries with low vaccination rates:

Based on our simulations, it is clear that good control of the epidemic requires people to get the booster vaccine within 1.5 months of getting the basic vaccine. However, a 1.5-month interval between basic and booster vaccination is not feasible in real life given the requirements of the vaccine for people's health conditions. That means it is very difficult to control COVID-19 in these countries. Therefore, we call on countries with low vaccination rates to increase their vaccination rates as soon as possible so that people pay enough attention to COVID-19;otherwise, it will be difficult to control the epidemic.

(ii) For countries with high vaccination rates:

(1) It is clear that timely booster vaccination has a positive impact on controlling the outbreak. Controlling booster vaccination time within a critical period (10.2 months) can make sure the epidemic is under control. Considering the requirements of booster vaccination on the body, we believe that 6 months is the most appropriate time for booster vaccination.

(2) In countries that are already able to get the majority of people who get the basic vaccine on time to get the booster vaccine 6 months later, we can see that there is an upper bound in the number of infections in those countries, which means that the epidemic is contained, and the number of infections does not peak all the time. However, the epidemic is not completely under control. In these countries, the epidemic is cyclical at this stage, with the number of cases going up and down. However, when we improve the effectiveness of the vaccine, which means the duration of the vaccine is longer and the failure rate of the vaccine is lower, the epidemic will be better controlled. The number of cases tends to decrease and almost stabilize after 20 years. So we suggest that research into an effective vaccine should continue, both to increase its longevity and to reduce the vaccine failure rate.

(3) Considering that the virus is still mutating, we suggest that countries make timely policy changes based on the real-time situation of the epidemic.

6. Conclusions

In this paper, we have established an $SVIR$ model on booster vaccination with two time delays to study the most suitable time for booster vaccination. We have studied the impact of the timing of booster vaccination and the expiration of booster vaccine on outbreaks. We studied the stability of the equilibria of System (1) and determine the stability and direction of the periodic bifurcation solution using the multi-time scale method and obtain the standard form of Hopf bifurcation. Then we have carried out some numerical simulations to verify the analytic results and give some reasonable suggestions to control the epidemic.

We have found that high vaccination rates are necessary for the current epidemic situation and that current vaccines are not effective as a specific method of controlling the epidemic. As well as improving vaccination rates, there are other measures that need to be taken, such as reducing social interaction. Further, we have specific recommendations for different countries as well.

Author Contributions: Writing—original draft preparation: X.L.; funding acquisition: X.L. and Y.D.; methodology and supervision: X.L. and Y.D. All authors have read and agreed to the published version of the manuscript.

Funding: This study was funded by the Heilongjiang Provincial Natural Science Foundation of China (Grant No. LH2019A001) and College Students Innovations Special Project funded by Northeast Forestry University of China (No. 202110225003).

Institutional Review Board Statement: Not applicable.

Informed Consent Statement: Not applicable.

Data Availability Statement: Not applicable.

Conflicts of Interest: All authors declare no conflict of interest in this paper.

Appendix A

System (3) can be written as:

$$X'(t) = AX(t) + BX(t-\tau_1) + CX(t-\tau_2) + F[X(t), X(t-\tau_1), X(t-\tau_2)], \tag{A1}$$

where $X(t) = (S_k, V_k, I_k, R_k)^T, X(t-\tau_1) = (S_k(t-\tau_1), V_k(t-\tau_1), I_k(t-\tau_1), R_k(t-\tau_1))^T$, $X(t-\tau_2) = (S_k(t-\tau_2), V_k(t-\tau_2), I_k(t-\tau_2), R_k(t-\tau_2))^T$, and

$$A = \begin{pmatrix} -\alpha I_k - d & 0 & -\alpha S_k & \sigma_1 \\ 0 & -d-\beta I_k & -\beta V_k & \sigma_2 \\ \alpha I_k & \beta I_k & \alpha S_k + \beta V_k - \mu - c - d & 0 \\ 0 & 0 & \mu & -\sigma_1 - \sigma_2 - d \end{pmatrix},$$

$$B = \begin{pmatrix} -\gamma_1 & 0 & 0 & 0 \\ \gamma_1 & 0 & 0 & 0 \\ 0 & 0 & 0 & 0 \\ 0 & 0 & 0 & 0 \end{pmatrix}, C = \begin{pmatrix} 0 & \gamma_2 & 0 & 0 \\ 0 & -\gamma_2 & 0 & 0 \\ 0 & 0 & 0 & 0 \\ 0 & 0 & 0 & 0 \end{pmatrix}, F = \begin{pmatrix} -\alpha SI \\ -\beta VI \\ \alpha SI + \beta VI \\ 0 \end{pmatrix}.$$

We suppose $h_k = (h_{k1}, h_{k2}, h_{k3}, h_{k4})^T$ is the eigenvector of the linear operator corresponding to the eigenvalue $i\omega$, and let $h_k{}^* = (h^*_{k1}, h^*_{k2}, h^*_{k3}, h^*_{k4})^T$ be the normalized eigenvector of the adjoint operator of the linear operator corresponding to the eigenvalues $-i\omega$ satisfying the inner product $< h_k{}^*, h_k >= 1$, with $h^*_{kj} = d_k \bar{h}^*_{kj}$. By a simple calculation, we can obtain:

$$
\begin{aligned}
h_{k3} &= 1, \\
h_{k4} &= \frac{\mu}{i\omega+\sigma_1+\sigma_2+d}, \\
h_{k2} &= \frac{(i\omega-\alpha S^*-\beta V^*+\mu+c+d)(i\omega+d+\alpha I^*+\gamma_1 e^{-i\omega\tau_1})}{\gamma_2\gamma_1 e^{-i\omega(\tau_1+\tau_2)}-(i\omega+d+\alpha I^*+\gamma_1 e^{-i\omega\tau_1})(i\omega+d+\beta I^*+\gamma_2 e^{-i\omega\tau_2})} \\
&\quad+\frac{\alpha S^*\gamma_1 e^{-i\omega\tau_1}-(\sigma_1\gamma_1 e^{-i\omega\tau_1}+(i\omega+d+\alpha I^*+\gamma_1 e^{-i\omega\tau_1})\sigma_2)h_{k4}}{\gamma_2\gamma_1 e^{-i\omega(\tau_1+\tau_2)}-(i\omega+d+\alpha I^*+\gamma_1 e^{-i\omega\tau_1})(i\omega+d+\beta I^*+\gamma_2 e^{-i\omega\tau_2})}, \\
h_{k1} &= \frac{-(i\omega-\alpha S^*-\beta V^*+\mu+c+d)+\beta I^* h_{k2}}{-\alpha I^*}, \\
\tilde{h}^*_{k3} &= 1, \\
\tilde{h}^*_{k1} &= \frac{(-i\omega+d+\alpha I^*+\gamma_1 e^{-i\omega\tau_1})(-\beta I^*)-\alpha I^*\gamma_2 e^{-i\omega\tau_2}}{\gamma_2\gamma_1 e^{-i\omega(\tau_1+\tau_2)}-(-i\omega+d+\alpha I^*+\gamma_1 e^{-i\omega\tau_1})(-i\omega+d+\beta I^*+\gamma_2 e^{-i\omega\tau_2})}, \\
\tilde{h}^*_{k2} &= \frac{\gamma_1 e^{-i\omega\tau_1}\beta I^*+\alpha I^*(-i\omega+d+\beta I^*+\gamma_2 e^{-i\omega\tau_2})}{(-i\omega+d+\alpha I^*+\gamma_1 e^{-i\omega\tau_1})(-i\omega+d+\beta I^*+\gamma_2 e^{-i\omega\tau_2})-\gamma_2\gamma_1 e^{-i\omega(\tau_1+\tau_2)}}, \\
\tilde{h}^*_{k4} &= \frac{\sigma_1\tilde{h}^*_{k1}+\sigma_2\tilde{h}^*_{k2}}{-i\omega+\sigma_1+\sigma_2+d},
\end{aligned}
\tag{A2}
$$

where $d_k = \frac{1}{h_{k1}\bar{\tilde{h}}^*_{k1}+h_{k2}\bar{\tilde{h}}^*_{k2}+h_{k3}\bar{\tilde{h}}^*_{k3}+h_{k4}\bar{\tilde{h}}^*_{k4}}, (k=1,2_1,2_2, j=1,2,3,4.)$.

$X(t)$ can be written as:

$$
X(t) = X(T_0, T_1, T_2, \cdots) = \sum_{k=1}^{\infty} \varepsilon^k X_k(T_0, T_1, T_2, \cdots), \tag{A3}
$$

$X'(t)$ can be written as:

$$
\begin{aligned}
X'(t) =& \frac{dX(t)}{dt} = \varepsilon\frac{dX_1}{dt}+\varepsilon^2\frac{dX_2}{dt}+\varepsilon^3\frac{dX_3}{dt}+\cdots \\
=&\varepsilon(\frac{\partial X_1}{\partial T_0}+\varepsilon\frac{\partial X_1}{\partial T_1}+\varepsilon^2\frac{\partial X_1}{\partial T_2})+\varepsilon^2(\frac{\partial X_2}{\partial T_0}+\varepsilon\frac{\partial X_2}{\partial T_1})+\varepsilon^3\frac{\partial X_3}{\partial T_0}+\cdots \\
=&\varepsilon D_0X_1+\varepsilon^2 D_1X_1+\varepsilon^3 D_2X_1+\varepsilon^2 D_0X_2+\varepsilon^3 D_1X_2+\varepsilon^3 D_0X_3+\cdots.
\end{aligned}
\tag{A4}
$$

where $D_i = \frac{\partial}{\partial T_i}(i=1,2,3,\cdots)$ is a differential operator.

Since we are more concerned about the influence of booster vaccination time, we take τ_1 as the bifurcation parameter. We let $\tau_1 = \tau_c + \varepsilon\tau_\varepsilon$, where τ_c is the critical time delay given in Equation (13) or Equation (23), τ_ε is the disturbance parameter and ε is the dimensionless scale parameter. Using Taylor expansion of $X(t-\tau_2)$ and $X(t-\tau_1)$, respectively, we have:

$$
\begin{aligned}
X(t-\tau_2) =& \varepsilon X_{1,\tau_2}+\varepsilon^2(X_{2,\tau_2}-D_1X_{1,\tau_2})+\varepsilon^3(X_{3,\tau_2}-D_1X_{2,\tau_2}-D_2X_{1,\tau_2})+\cdots, \\
X(t-\tau_1) =& = \varepsilon X_{1,\tau_c}+\varepsilon^2 X_{2,\tau_c}+\varepsilon^3 X_{3,\tau_c}-\varepsilon^2\tau_\varepsilon D_0X_{1,\tau_c}-\varepsilon^3\tau_\varepsilon D_0X_{2,\tau_c}-\varepsilon^2\tau_c D_1X_{1,\tau_c} \\
&-\varepsilon^3\tau_\varepsilon D_1X_{1,\tau_c}-\varepsilon^3\tau_c D_2X_{1,\tau_c}-\varepsilon^3\tau_c D_1X_{2,\tau_c}+\cdots,
\end{aligned}
\tag{A5}
$$

where $X_{j,\tau_2} = X_j(T_0-\tau_2, T_1, T_2, \cdots)$, $X_{j,\tau_c} = X_j(T_0-\tau_c, T_1, T_2, \cdots)$, j=1,2,3. Then, we substitute Equations (A3)–(A5) into Equation (A1). For the ε-order terms, we have:

$$
\begin{cases}
D_0S_1+\gamma_1 S_{1,\tau_c}-\gamma_2 V_{1,\tau_2}-\sigma_1 R_1+dS_1+\alpha S_1 I^*+\alpha S^* I_1 = 0, \\
D_0V_1-\gamma_1 S_{1,\tau_c}+\gamma_2 V_{1,\tau_2}+\beta V_1 I^*+\beta V^* I_1-\sigma_2 R_1-dV_1 = 0, \\
D_0I_1-\alpha S_1 I^*-\alpha S^* I_1-\beta V_1 I^*-\beta V^* I_1+\mu I_1+cI_1+dI_1 = 0, \\
D_0R_1-\mu I_1+\sigma_1 R_1+\sigma_2 R_1+dR_1 = 0.
\end{cases}
\tag{A6}
$$

Since $\pm i\omega_k^*(k=1,2)$ are the eigenvalues of the linear part of Equation (A1), the solution of Equation (A6) can be expressed in the following form:

$$X_1(T_1,T_2,T_3,\cdots)=G(T_1,T_2,T_3,\cdots)e^{i\omega_k^* T_0}h_k+\bar{G}(T_1,T_2,T_3,\cdots)e^{-i\omega_k^* T_0}\bar{h}_k, k=1,2. \quad (A7)$$

where h_k is given in Equation (A2).

For the ε^2-order terms, we obtain:

$$\begin{cases} D_0S_2+\gamma_1 S_{2,\tau_c}-\gamma_2 V_{2,\tau_2}-\sigma_1 R_2+dS_2+\alpha S_2 I^*+\alpha S^* I_2 \\ \qquad =-D_1S_1+\gamma_1(\tau_\varepsilon D_0 S_{1,\tau_c}+\tau_c D_1 S_{1,\tau_c})-\gamma_2 D_1 V_{1,\tau_2}-\alpha S_1 I_1, \\ D_0V_2-\gamma_1 S_{2,\tau_c}+\gamma_2 V_{2,\tau_2}+\beta V_2 I^*+\beta V^* I_2-\sigma_2 R_2-dV_2 \\ \qquad =-D_1V_1-\gamma_1(\tau_\varepsilon D_0 S_{1,\tau_c}+\tau_c D_1 S_{1,\tau_c})+\gamma_2 D_1 V_{1,\tau_2}-\beta V_1 I_1, \\ D_0I_2-\alpha S_2 I^*-\alpha S^* I_2-\beta V_2 I^*-\beta V^* I_2+\mu I_2+cI_2+dI_2=-D_1I_1+\alpha S_1 I_1+\beta V_1 I_1, \\ D_0R_2-\mu I_2+\sigma_1 R_2+\sigma_2 R_2+dR_2=-D_1R_1. \end{cases} \quad (A8)$$

Then we substitute Equation (A7) into the right side of Equation (A8) and mark the coefficient before $e^{i\omega T_0}$ as vector m_1. In accordance with the solvability condition: $<h_k^*, m_1>=0$, we can obtain the expression of $\frac{\partial G}{\partial T_1}$:

$$\frac{\partial G}{\partial T_1}=M_k\tau_\varepsilon G, \quad (A9)$$

where $M_k=\frac{\gamma_1 i\omega\left(h_{k1}\bar{h}_{k1}^*-h_{k1}\bar{h}_{k2}^*\right)}{1+\gamma_2 e^{-i\omega\tau_2}\left(h_{k2}\bar{h}_{k1}^*-h_{k2}\bar{h}_{k2}^*\right)+\gamma_1\tau_c e^{-i\omega\tau_c}\left(h_{k1}\bar{h}_{k2}^*-h_{k1}\bar{h}_{k1}^*\right)}, k=1,2.$

We assume the solution of Equation (A8) is the following form:

$$\begin{aligned} S_{2,k}=&g_{k1}e^{2i\omega_k\tau_c T_0}G^2+\bar{g}_{k1}e^{-2i\omega_k\tau_c T_0}\bar{G}^2+l_{k1}G\bar{G}, \\ V_{2,k}=&g_{k2}e^{2i\omega_k\tau_c T_0}G^2+\bar{g}_{k2}e^{-2i\omega_k\tau_c T_0}\bar{G}^2+l_{k2}G\bar{G}, \\ I_{2,k}=&g_{k3}e^{2i\omega_k\tau_c T_0}G^2+\bar{g}_{k3}e^{-2i\omega_k\tau_c T_0}\bar{G}^2+l_{k3}G\bar{G}, \\ R_{2,k}=&g_{k4}e^{2i\omega_k\tau_c T_0}G^2+\bar{g}_{k4}e^{-2i\omega_k\tau_c T_0}\bar{G}^2+l_{k4}G\bar{G}. \end{aligned} \quad (A10)$$

Substituting them into Equation (A8), we can solve the expression of $g_1,g_2,g_3,g_4,l_1,l_2,l_3,l_4$ from the following equations.

$$\begin{bmatrix} (2i\omega+\eta_1) & -\gamma_2 e^{-i\omega\tau_2} & \alpha S^* & -\sigma_1 \\ -\gamma_1 e^{-i\omega\tau_c} & (2i\omega+\eta_2) & \beta V^* & -\sigma_2 \\ 0 & -\alpha I^*-\beta I^* & (2i\omega+\eta_3) & 0 \\ 0 & 0 & -\mu & (2i\omega+\eta_4) \end{bmatrix}\begin{bmatrix} g_1 \\ g_2 \\ g_3 \\ g_4 \end{bmatrix}=\begin{bmatrix} -\alpha h_1 h_3 \\ -\beta h_2 h_3 \\ \alpha h_2 h_3+\beta h_1 h_3 \\ 0 \end{bmatrix}, \quad (A11)$$

$$\begin{bmatrix} \eta_1 & -\gamma_2 & \alpha S^* & -\sigma_1 \\ -\gamma_1 & \eta_2 & \beta V^* & -\sigma_2 \\ 0 & -\alpha I^*-\beta I^* & \eta_3 & 0 \\ 0 & 0 & -\mu & \eta_4 \end{bmatrix}\begin{bmatrix} l_1 \\ l_2 \\ l_3 \\ l_4 \end{bmatrix}=\begin{bmatrix} -\alpha h_1\bar{h}_3-\alpha\bar{h}_1 h_3 \\ -\beta\bar{h}_2 h_3-\beta h_2\bar{h}_3 \\ \alpha h_1\bar{h}_3+\alpha\bar{h}_1 h_3+\beta\bar{h}_2 h_3+\beta h_2\bar{h}_3 \\ 0 \end{bmatrix}, \quad (A12)$$

where

$$\eta_1=\gamma_1 e^{-i\omega\tau_c}-d+\alpha I^*,\ \eta_2=\gamma_2 e^{-i\omega\tau_2}+\beta I^*-d,$$
$$\eta_3=-\alpha S^*-\beta V^*+\mu+c+d,\ \eta_4=\sigma_1+\sigma_2+d.$$

For ε^3-term, we have:

$$\left\{\begin{array}{l} D_0S_3+\gamma_1 S_{3,\tau_c}-\gamma_2 V_{3,\tau_2}-\sigma_1 R_3+dS_3+\alpha S_3 I^*+\alpha S^* I_3 \\ =-D_2S_1-D_1S_2+\gamma_1(\tau_\varepsilon D_0 S_{2,\tau_c}+\tau_c D_1 S_{1,\tau_c}+\tau_\varepsilon D_1 S_{1,\tau_c}+\tau_c D_2 S_{1,\tau_c}) \\ -\gamma_2(D_2 V_{1,\tau_2}+D_1 V_{2,\tau_2})-\alpha(S_2 I_1+S_1 I_2), \\ D_0 V_3-\gamma_1 S_{3,\tau_c}+\gamma_2 V_{3,\tau_2}+\beta V_3 I^*+\beta V^* I_3-\sigma_2 R_3-dV_3 \\ =-D_1V_2-D_2V_1-\gamma_1(\tau_\varepsilon D_0 S_{2,\tau_c}+\tau_c D_1 S_{1,\tau_c}+\tau_\varepsilon D_1 S_{1,\tau_c}+\tau_c D_2 S_{1,\tau_c}) \\ +\gamma_2(D_2 V_{1,\tau_2}+D_1 V_{2,\tau_2})-\beta(V_2 I_1+V_1 I_2), \\ D_0 I_3-\alpha S_3 I^*-\alpha S^* I_3-\beta V_3 I^*-\beta V^* I_3+\mu I_3+cI_3+dI_3 \\ =-D_2 I_1-D_1 I_2+\alpha(S_1 I_2+S_2 I_1)+\beta(V_1 I_2+V_2 I_1), \\ D_0 R_3-\mu I_3+\sigma_1 R_3+\sigma_2 R_3+dR_3 \\ =-D_1 R_2-D_2 R_1. \end{array}\right. \tag{A13}$$

We substitute Equations (A7), (A9) and (A10) into the right expression of Equation (A13) and note the coefficient of $e^{i\omega_k T_0}$ as vector m_2. According to solvability condition $< h_k^*, m_2 >= 0$, we have the expression of $\frac{\partial G}{\partial T_2}$. Since τ_ε^2 has less impact on normal form, we can ignore the $\tau_\varepsilon^2 G$ term. Thus, we can obtain:

$$\frac{\partial G}{\partial T_2}=H_k G^2\bar{G}, \tag{A14}$$

where

$$H_k=\frac{\partial G_1}{\partial T_2}=\frac{\alpha(h_1 l_3+\bar{h}_1 g_3+h_3 l_1+\bar{h}_3 g_1)(\bar{h}_3^*-\bar{h}_1^*)+\beta(h_2 l_3+\bar{h}_2 g_3+h_3 l_2+\bar{h}_3 g_2)(\bar{h}_3^*-\bar{h}_2^*)}{1+\gamma_2(h_2\bar{h}_1^*-h_2\bar{h}_2^*)e^{-i\omega\tau_2}+\gamma_1\tau_c e^{-i\omega\tau_c}(h_1\bar{h}_2^*-h_1\bar{h}_1^*)}.$$

Then, we let $G\to G/\varepsilon$. Therefore, we get the normal form of Hopf bifurcation for System (1):

$$\dot{G}=M_k\tau_\varepsilon G_1+H_k G_1^2\bar{G}_1, \tag{A15}$$

where M_k, H_k are given in Equation (A9) and Equation (A14).

References

1. Nathan, D.G; Emma, B.H.; Joseph, R.F; Alexandra, L.P.; MugeCevik Public health actions to control new SARS-CoV-2 variants. *Cell* **2021**, *184*, 1127–1132.
2. Pei, Y.Z.; Li, S.P.; Li, C.G.; Chen, S.Z. The effect of constant and pulse vaccination on an SIR epidemic model with infectious period. *Appl. Math. Model.* **2011**, *35*, 3866–3878.
3. Cao, B.Q.; Shan, M.J.; Zhang, Q.M.; Wang, W.M. A stochastic SIS epidemic model with vaccination. *Physica A* **2017**, *486*, 127–143. [CrossRef]
4. De la Sen, M.; Alonso-Quesada, S. Vaccination strategies based on feedback control techniques for a general SEIR-epidemic model. *Appl. Math. Comput.* **2011**, *218*, 3888–3904. [CrossRef]
5. Khyar, O.; Allali, K. Optimal vaccination strategy for an SEIR model of infectious diseases with Logistic growth. *Math. Biosci. Eng.* **2017**, *15*, 485–505.
6. Scherer, A.; McLean, A. Mathematical models of vaccination. *Brit. Med. Bull.* **2002**, *62*, 187–199. [CrossRef]
7. Bjornstad, O.N.; Shea, K.; Krzywinski, M.; Altman, N. The SEIRS model for infectious disease dynamics. *Nat. Methods* **2020**, *17*, 557–558. [CrossRef]
8. Yang, B.; Yu, Z.H.; Cai, Y.L. The impact of vaccination on the spread of COVID-19: Studying by a mathematical model. *Nonlinear Dyn.* **2022**, *590*, 126717. [CrossRef]
9. Duan, X.C.; Yuan, S.l.; Li, X.Z. Global stability of an SVIR model with age of vaccination. *Appl. Math Comput.* **2014**, *226*, 528–540. [CrossRef]
10. Anna, W. Booster Vaccination to Reduce SARS-CoV-2 Transmission and Infection. *JAMA-J. Am. Med. Assoc.* **2012**, *327*, 327–328.
11. Salvagno, G.L.; Henry, B.M.; Pighi, L.D.N.; Simone, D.N.; Gianluca.G.; Giuseppe, L. The pronounced decline of anti-SARS-CoV-2 spike trimeric IgG and RBD IgG in baseline seronegative individuals six months after BNT162b2 vaccination is consistent with the need for vaccine boosters. *Clin. Chem. Lab. Med.* **2022**, *60*, E29–E31. [CrossRef] [PubMed]
12. Cooke, K.L. Stability analysis for a vector disease model. *J. Math. Biol.* **1996**, *35*, 240–260. [CrossRef] [PubMed]
13. Zhai, S.D.; Luo, G.Q.; Huang, T.; Wang, X.; Tao, J.L.; Zhou, P. Vaccination control of an epidemic model with time delay and its application to COVID-19. *Nonlinear Dyn.* **2021**, *106*, 1279–1292. [CrossRef] [PubMed]

14. Rong, X.M.; Yang, L.; Chu, H.D.; Fan, M. Effect of delay in diagnosis on transmission of COVID-19. *Math. Biosci. Eng.* **2020**, *17*, 2725–2740. [CrossRef]
15. Song, X.Y.; Jiang, Y.; Wei, H.M. Analysis of a saturation incidence SVEIRS epidemic model with pulse and two time delays. *Appl. Math. Comput.* **2009**, *214*, 381–390. [CrossRef]
16. Jiang, Y.; Mei, L.Q.; Song, X.Y. Global analysis of a delayed epidemic dynamical system with pulse vaccination and nonlinear incidence rate. *Appl. Math. Model.* **2011**, *35*, 4865–4876. [CrossRef]
17. Gao, S.J.; Teng, Z.D.; Xie, D.H. The effects of pulse vaccination on SEIR model with two time delays. *Appl. Math. Comput.* **2008**, *201*, 282–292. [CrossRef]
18. Zhang, Z.Z.; Kundu, S.; Tripathi,J.P.; Bugalia, S. Stability and Hopf bifurcation analysis of an SVEIR epidemic model with vaccination and multiple time delays. *Chaos Soliton Fract.* **2020**, *131*, 109483. [CrossRef]
19. Chen, X.Y.; Cao, J.D.; Park, J.H.; Qiu,J.L. Stability analysis and estimation of domain of attraction for the endemic equilibrium of an SEIQ epidemic model. *Nonlinear Dynam.* **2018**, *87*, 975–985. [CrossRef]
20. Li, J.H.; Teng, Z.D.; Wang, G.Q.; Zhang, L.; Hu, C. Stability and bifurcation analysis of an SIR epidemic model with logistic growth and saturated treatment. *Chaos Soliton Fract.* **2017**, *99*, 63–71. [CrossRef]
21. Goel, K.; Kumar, A.; Nilam Stability analysis of a logistic growth epidemic model with two explicit time-delays, the nonlinear incidence and treatment rates. *J. Appl. Math. Comput.* **2021**, 389–402.
22. Hye, K.L.; Ludwig, K.; Ludwig, K.S.; Sebastian, K.; Birgit, P. Robust immune response to the BNT162b mRNA vaccine in an elderly population vaccinated 15 months after recovery from COVID-19. *MedRxiv Preprint* **2021**, *5*. [CrossRef]

mathematics

Article

Stability and Optimal Control of Tree-Insect Model under Forest Fire Disturbance

Xiaoxiao Liu [1] and Chunrui Zhang [2,*]

[1] College of Mechanical and Electrical Engineering, Northeast Forestry University, Harbin 150040, China; liuxiaoxiao1994@nefu.edu.cn
[2] College of Science, Northeast Forestry University, Harbin 150040, China
* Correspondence: math@nefu.edu.cn

Abstract: In this article, we propose a mathematical model for insect outbreaks coupled with wildfire disturbances and an optimization model for finding suitable wildfire frequencies. We use a refined Holling II function as a model for the nonlinear response of fire frequency against trees and insects. The results show that for the tree–insect–wildfire model, there is a coexistence equilibrium in the system. Sensitivity analysis is performed to determine the effect of wildfire on trees in the optimization model. The results show that forest fires have a significant impact on the equilibrium mechanism of tree–insect coexistence. Numerical simulations suggest that in some areas of high fire intensity, there may be positive feedback between disturbances from wildfires and insect outbreaks. The result is consistent with the present theory in this field.

Keywords: forest fire; tree–beetle system; stability; sensitivity analysis; optimal control

MSC: 34C23; 35K57

Citation: Liu, X.; Zhang, C. Stability and Optimal Control of Tree-Insect Model under Forest Fire Disturbance. *Mathematics* **2022**, *10*, 2563. https://doi.org/10.3390/math10152563

Academic Editor: Irina Bashkirtseva

Received: 8 June 2022
Accepted: 19 July 2022
Published: 22 July 2022

1. Introduction

Disturbance interactions are receiving increasing attention in today's ecological studies [1,2]. Ecologists now have a much better understanding of individual disturbances, recognizing that natural ecosystems are affected by many types of natural disturbances, and studies have found significant interactions between these disturbances [3]. These disturbances are divided into natural and anthropogenic. Natural disturbances include wildfires, hurricanes, insect pests, diseases, floods, droughts, etc. Anthropogenic disturbances include artificial logging, water pollution, air pollution, etc. Among them, wildfires and pests are the two main natural disruptions of forest grassland. The synergistic relationship between wildfires and insects has been clearly described in previous studies. The study concluded that the massive tree mortality caused by insect outbreaks was an important cause of subsequent wildfires [4]. Correspondingly, the damage and death caused by the fire will produce focus trees that attract more beetles [5]. In separate studies, McHugh [6] and Cunningham [7] followed tree mortality and beetle infestation in a forest for three years following a wildfire and found that fire damage resulted in a higher probability of beetle attacks on trees. Similar results have been found in other studies of wildfires and pests (Bradley and Tueller [8]). However, some other studies have shown that beetles do not prioritize attacking trees with fire-damaged trunks, but that focal trees have a higher success rate of attack when beetle numbers are low (Elkin and Reid [9]). Furthermore, Sanchez-Martinez and Wagner [10] found that bark beetle numbers are at low levels regardless of the number of trees in the forest, including a large number of trees destroyed by wildfire. These results confirm the complexity of the link between insects and fire when assessed on a long-term and large-scale basis. Fleming et al. [11] took a statistical approach to examine the interaction between spruce budworm damage and forest fire risk. In their paper, they use a GIS overlay of the fire and spruce budworm histories in Ontario in order to define polygons with unique histories of forest fire and insect damage. McHugh et al. [12] measured insect abundance in several burned stands in Northern Arizona and found that trees targeted by insects had more canopy damage from fires compared to trees that were not targeted. Santoro et al. [13] found increased post-fire populations of the pine engraver (Ips pini) despite also measuring increased insects. Bebi et al. [14] found that forests burned in 1879 during the spruce beetle explosion were less affected by the infestation than old-growth forests that had not been burned in the 1940s. Historically, insect pests and wildfires have had a predominant impact on evolutionary progression in the forests of the American West. In the last 100 years, fire suppression has led to larger and more serious wildfire and insect outbreaks. In the year 2002, more than 50,000 acres of land in three northeastern provinces of China were damaged by wildfires and about 800,000 acres were damaged by insects such as bark beetles and pine wood nematodes. The relationship between fires and insect outbreaks is often described as a mutual and synergistic one. Although there are underlying feedbacks between these two natural disturbances, consensus on responses is lacking in the accepted papers, with some published studies recording substantial impacts on fires and burning from trees killed by beetles, while others report none or diminished impacts. The temporal dynamics of the B. Chen Charpentier model is consistent with the assumed two-stage model of beetle demography (also known as the binary theory) [15] and is able to fit the existing data. In particular, the model consists of the thoughts of the classical model described and developed by Safranyik [16]. The optimal control model is sufficiently accurate to allow an analytical characterization of the dynamic behavior. At the same time, this model extends the tree–beetle system model to include average wildfire disturbance and its interaction dynamics with insect outbreaks. Fire can simultaneously slay beetles and trees and can also diminish the defenses of surviving trees against beetle invasion.

The structure of this paper is as follows: In Section 2, based on the work of reference [17], a tree–beetle–fire model is considered. The threshold value of boundary equilibrium point stability is obtained, and the internal equilibrium point global stability is proved. In Section 3, the optimal control strategy of wildfire frequency is considered by optimizing and rewriting the model to find the appropriate frequency of wildfire occurrence to minimize the damage to trees. Using the optimization model to simulate the reported forest fire data from State Forestry Administration 2004 to 2017 and predict the development trend of a forest area after the occurrence of forest fires. The sensitivity analysis is used to identify the intensity of forest fires in Section 4, and the results show that the frequency of forest fires had a great influence on the tree–insect coexistence mechanism.

2. Deterministic Model for Tree–Beetle–Fire System

In this section, based on the work of reference [17], we describe the formulation of the deterministic model for the tree–beetle–fire system introduced. Positive feedback may occur between forest fires and beetle outbreaks, which will enhance the frequencies and severities of these two types of naturally occurring disturbances so that it includes the mortality of trees caused by fire. By considering an ordinary differential equation model, we propose the following

$$\begin{cases} \frac{dV}{dt} = r_v V(1 - \frac{V}{K_v} - f_k \frac{B}{r+B}) - P\frac{V}{K_v} M_v V, \\ \frac{dB}{dt} = r_b B(1 - \frac{B}{K_e}) - \frac{\alpha B}{1+\beta B} - M_b P \frac{V}{K_v} M_v V. \end{cases} \quad (1)$$

The variables are V and B, indicating a number of vulnerable trees and mountain pine beetles in each tree. The constant r_v is the inherent percentage of growth of vulnerable trees (1/time) and the constant r_b is the inherent percentage of growth of vulnerable beetles (1/time). K_v represents the carrying capacity of the system. K_e is the carrying capacity of the beetles per tree. α represents the defense rate of the pine tree, and β represents the reciprocal of beetle density. When the pine tree is saturated with defense, f_k is the fraction of trees killed by successful attacks and r represents the threshold value of the number of beetles successfully attacked (beetles per tree). The special relationship models the reality that the increased death rate of trees due to beetle existence is linearly related to B when the beetle population is small, and it reaches saturation at f_k when the beetle population is extremely high. As described above, the equation is an extension of the logistic type of growth, which includes the host pine's defense against the beetle, described by the Holling II functional response. The constant M_v represents the percentage of trees lost/damaged in the fire. The constant M_b represents the effect of forest fires on beetles, and c is the defense parameter of fire weakening pine against beetles. The term $0 \leq P(\frac{V}{K_v}) \leq 1$ is the frequency of fire or probability of fire, and we assume that it is proportional to the population of trees within the forest. The constant P is a measure of the average intensity of vegetation feedback to the fire for different thermogenic properties and $0 < f_k < 1, 0 < M_v < 1, 0 < c < 1, 0 < M_b < 1, t > 0$. We define

$$v = \frac{V}{K_v}, b = \frac{B}{K_v}, r_1 = \frac{r_b}{r_v}, \beta_1 = \beta K_e^2, K = f_k K_e, m_v = \frac{M_v P}{K_v}, m_b = \frac{M_b M_v P}{K_v}, \alpha_f = \frac{\alpha(1 - cM_v)K_e}{r_v}, \tag{2}$$

which then can be rewritten as $(1 + m_v) < m_b, m_b > m_v$

$$\begin{cases} \frac{dv}{dt} = v(1 - v - \frac{Kb}{r+K_e b} - m_v v), \\ \frac{db}{dt} = b[r_1(1-b) - \frac{\alpha_f}{1+\beta_1 b} - m_b v]. \end{cases} \tag{3}$$

The parameters of the above two systems are all positive.

Existence and Stability of Equilibrium

In this subsection, we demonstrate the existence of the equilibria. According to the biological meaning, we need all equilibria to be nonnegative. By using system (3), the equilibrium satisfies the following equations:

$$\begin{cases} v(1 - v - \frac{Kb}{r+K_e b} - m_v v) = 0, \\ b[r_1(1-b) - \frac{\alpha_f}{1+\beta_1 b} - m_b v] = 0. \end{cases} \tag{4}$$

Consequently, we can immediately calculate that system (4) has only one boundary equilibrium $E^0 = (\frac{1}{m_v+1}, 0)$.

We next consider the coexistence equilibrium $E^* = (v_*, b_*)$ such that $v_* > 0, b_* > 0$. By using the first equation of system (4), we obtain

$$v = \frac{r + (K_e - K)b}{(1 + m_v)(r + K_e b)}. \tag{5}$$

Substituting (5) into the second equation of system (4), we obtain

$$H(b) = c_1 b^3 + c_2 b^2 + c_3 b + c_4 = 0, \tag{6}$$

where

$$\begin{aligned} c_1 &= -\beta_1 K_e r_1 (1 + m_v), \\ c_2 &= [K m_b - r r_1 (1 + m_v)]\beta_1 + K_e[(1 + m_v)(-1 + \beta_1) r_1 - m_b \beta_1], \\ c_3 &= (1 + m_v)[-K_e \alpha_f + r_1[K_e + r(-1 + \beta_1)] + m_b(K - K_e - r\beta_1)], \\ c_4 &= r[(r_1 - \alpha_f)(1 + m_v) - m_b]. \end{aligned}$$

Suppose $(r_1 - \alpha_f)(1 + m_v) > m_b$, then $H(0) > 0$. Since $\beta_1, K_e, r_1, m_v > 0$, then $c_1 < 0$ and $H(+\infty)) = -\infty$. From the real continuation method, there exist $b_* > 0$ and $H(b_*) = 0$. Since $0 < f_k < 1$ and $K_e f_k = K$, then $K_e - K > 0$, hence

$$v = \frac{r + (K_e - K)b_*}{(1 + m_v)(r + K_e b_*)} > 0.$$

Summarizing the above discussions, when $(r_1 - \alpha_f)(1 + m_v) > m_b$, the system (3) has at least one coexistence equilibrium $E^* = (v_*, b_*)$.

In the following, we consider the stability of the equilibria. To determine the local stability of these equilibria, we consider the Jacobian matrix of system (3):

$$J = \begin{pmatrix} 1 - 2v - \frac{bK}{r+K_e b} - 2m_v v & \frac{K_e K v b}{(r+K_e b)^2} - \frac{Kv}{r+K_e b} \\ -m_b b & r_1(1-2b) - m_b v + \frac{b\alpha_f \beta_1}{(1+b\beta_1)^2} - \frac{\alpha_f}{1+b\beta_1} \end{pmatrix}. \quad (7)$$

The Jacobian matrix of system (3) at $E^0 = (\frac{1}{m_v+1}, 0)$ is

$$J^0 = \begin{pmatrix} m_1 & m_2 \\ n_1 & n_2 \end{pmatrix}.$$

where $m_1 = -1 < 0, m_2 = -\frac{K}{r(1+m_v)}, n_1 = 0, n_2 = r_1 - \alpha_f - \frac{m_b}{1+m_v}$. The eigenvalues of $J^0 : |\lambda E - J^0| = \lambda^2 - TR_1 + DET_1 = 0$, can be determined by

$$\begin{cases} TR_1 = n_2 + m_1, \\ DET_1 = -m_2 n_1 + m_1 n_2 = m_1 n_2. \end{cases}$$

Summing up the above discussions, we obtain the following Theorem 1.

Theorem 1. *Let $r_1, m_b, \alpha_f, m_v, K, r$ be positive parameters. Then we have*

(1) *If $(r_1 - \alpha_f)(1 + m_v) < m_b$, boundary equilibrium E^0 of system (3) is local asymptotically stable.*

(2) *If $(r_1 - \alpha_f)(1 + m_v) > m_b$, boundary equilibrium E^0 of system (3) is unstable.*

Remark 1. *Let $r_1 > \alpha_f$. Defining threshold $R^* = \frac{(r_1-\alpha_f)(1+m_v)}{m_b}$. Then if $R^* < 1$ boundary equilibrium E^0 is asymptotically stable; if $R^* > 1$, and boundary equilibrium E^0 is unstable, coexistence equilibrium E^* exists.*

Remark 2.

$$\begin{aligned} R^* &= \frac{(r_1 - \alpha_f)(1 + m_v)}{m_b} \\ &= \frac{1}{m_b}[(r_1 - \frac{\alpha K_e}{m_v}) + (r_1 - \frac{\alpha K_e}{r_v} + \frac{\alpha r c K_e^2}{r_v P})m_v + \frac{\alpha r c K_e^2}{r_v P} m_v^2]. \end{aligned}$$

Defining $m_b = (r_1 - \frac{\alpha K_e}{m_v}) + (r_1 - \frac{\alpha K_e}{r_v} + \frac{\alpha r c K_e^2}{r_v P})m_v + \frac{\alpha r c K_e^2}{r_v P} m_v^2$. The properties of R^* can be seen in Figure 1.

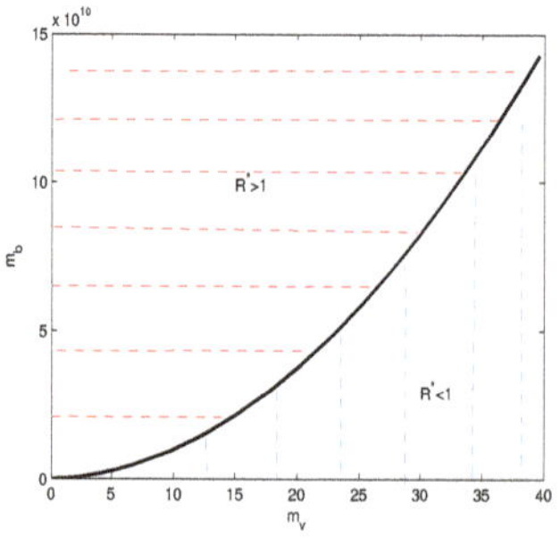

Figure 1. The properties of the threshold R^*.

In the following, we consider the properties of $E^* = (v_*, b_*)$. The Jacobian matrix of system (3) at $E^* = (v_*, b_*)$ is

$$J^1 = \begin{pmatrix} p_1 & p_2 \\ s_1 & s_2 \end{pmatrix}.$$

where $p_1 = -(1 + m_v)v_* < 0, p_2 = -\frac{Krv_*}{(r+K_e b_*)^2} < 0, s_1 = -m_b b_* < 0, s_2 = r_1(1 - 2b_*) - \frac{\alpha_f}{(1+\beta_1 b_*)^2} - m_b v_*$. Take the eigenvalues of J^1 can be determined by $|\lambda E - J^1| = \lambda^2 - TR_2 + DET_2 = 0$, where

$$\begin{cases} TR_2 = s_2 + p_1, \\ DET_2 = -p_2 s_1 + p_1 s_2. \end{cases}$$

Summarizing the above discussions, we obtain the following Theorem 2.

Theorem 2. *Let $r_1, m_b, \alpha_f, m_v, K, r, K_e$ be positive parameters and $R^* > 1$.*

(1) If $s_2 < \frac{p_2 s_1}{p_1}$, coexistence equilibrium E^* of system (3) is local asymptotically stable.

(2) If $\frac{p_2 s_1}{p_1} < s_2 < 0$, coexistence equilibrium E^* of system (3) is unstable.

In order to verify the asymptotic stability of the forest fire-forest beetle outbreak model system, numerical simulation is performed on the model (3). Using the parameter value in [16]: $m_b = 366.75$, $m_v = 75$, $\beta_1 = 156.9398$, $\alpha_f = 699.3189$, $r_1 = 33.75$, $r = 9.1$, $K = 1467$, and $c = 0.5$, $r_v = 0.08$, $K_e = 1956$, $K_v = 100$, $P = 0.1$, $\alpha = 0.04086$, we obtain positive equilibrium points $(v_*, b_*) \approx (0.00334654, 0.799878)$. These parameter values satisfy the conditions of the theorem analyzed above. The above analysis shows that the system is asymptotically stable, as shown in Figure 2. The figure on the left shows the tree's endemic state for fire, and the figure on the right shows the beetle's endemic state for fire.

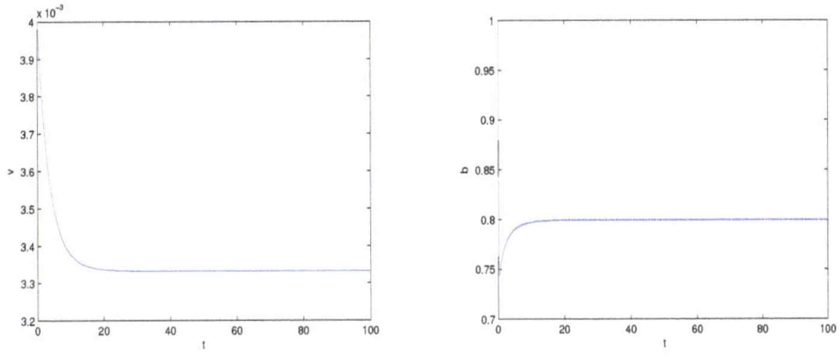

Figure 2. Tree's and beetle's endemic state.

Next we derive some basic properties of solutions to system (3), such as the nonexistence of limit cycles. According to the biological setting of the model described above, we define

$$\Omega = \{(v, b) : v > 0, b > 0\}. \quad (8)$$

Then, we have

Theorem 3. *Let Ω be defined as in system (3), suppose that $r_1 > \alpha_f \beta_1$, system (3) has no periodic orbits in Ω.*

Proof of Theorem 3. We define $\Omega = \frac{1}{vb} > 0$, then we have

$$\begin{cases} QF \triangleq \frac{1}{vb}[v(1 - v - \frac{Kb}{r+K_e b} - m_v v)], \\ QG \triangleq \frac{1}{v}[r_1(1 - b) - \frac{\alpha_f}{1+\beta_1 b} - m_b v]. \end{cases} \quad (9)$$

an easy computation yields that

$$\frac{\partial QF}{\partial v} = \frac{1}{b}(-1 - m_v) < 0, b \in \Omega.$$

and

$$\frac{\partial QG}{\partial b} = \frac{1}{v}(-r_1 + \frac{\alpha_f \beta_1}{(1+\beta_1)^2}) < \frac{1}{v}(-r_1 + \alpha_f \beta_1).$$

Suppose that $r_1 > \alpha_f \beta_1$, then $\frac{\partial QG}{\partial b} < 0$. For $(v, b) \in \Omega$, we have

$$\frac{\partial QF}{\partial v} + \frac{\partial QG}{\partial b} < 0.$$

Therefore, the Dulac criterion can be applied to system (3) in Ω and there exist no periodic orbits in Ω. According to the above analysis, E^* is globally approaching stability. □

According to Theorems 2 and 3, we have the following Theorem 4:

Theorem 4. *Suppose $R^* > 1$ and $r_1, m_b, \alpha_f, m_v, K, r, K_e$ are positive parameters. If $r_1 > \alpha_f \beta_1$, then the internal positive equilibrium point is globally asymptotically stable.*

3. Optimal Control Strategy

There are potential interactions between insect outbreaks and wildfire disturbances in forests. Wildfires are a potential threat to tree growth, and they also kill beetles. Therefore, it is an optimization problem to find the suitable frequency of wildfire so that there is little damage to trees and the beetles can be destroyed. Optimization has always played a critical part in the management of forests and pests in the design and operation. In the paragraphs below, we discuss optimal control strategies for wildfire frequency. The m_v in system (3) is set to be time-dependent $m_v(t)$, describing the time-varying wildfire intensity, and there exists $\overline{m_v}$ such that $0 \leq m_v(t) \leq \overline{m_v}$. Within the fixed time $[0, T]$ with $T > 0$, the constraint set reads

$$U = \{m_v(t) | 0 \leq m_v(t) \leq m_v, 0 \leq t \leq T, m_v(t) \text{ are Lebesgue measurable}\}. \quad (10)$$

The optimal objectives are to minimize the number of insects and the wildfire frequency. We rewrite system (3) as

$$\begin{cases} \frac{dv}{dt} = v(1 - v - \frac{Kb}{r+K_e b} - m_v v), \\ \frac{db}{dt} = b[r_1(1-b) - \frac{\alpha_1}{1+\beta_1 b} + \frac{\alpha_2 m_v}{1+\beta_1 b} - \alpha_3 m_v v]. \end{cases} \quad (11)$$

The quadratic optimal objective function reads:

$$J(m_v) = \int_0^T (\frac{1}{2} b^2(t) + \frac{1}{2} m_v^2(t)) dt$$

with $b(0) = b_0, v(0) = v_0$. The optimal control problem rewrites

$$J^*(m_v^{**}(\cdot)(t)) = \min_{m_v(t) \in U} J(m_v(t)). \quad (12)$$

Using the method in [18], we check the existence of optimal control $m_v(t)$ by satisfied H1–H4 the following:

Hypothesis 1 (H1). *The set of state and control variables are nonempty;*

Hypothesis 2 (H2). *The set U of the control variables is closed and convex;*

Hypothesis 3 (H3). *The right side of each equation in control problem (11) is continuous with a bounded sum of controls and states above, which can be written as a linear function of U with coefficients depending on time and state [19];*

Hypothesis 4 (H4). *There exists constants $\alpha_1, \alpha_2, \alpha_3 > 0$ such that the integrand $L(m_v(t))$ of the objective functional J is convex and satisfied.*

The Hypothesis H4 can be obtained since $L(m_v(t)) = \frac{1}{2}(b^2(t) + m_v^2(t))$. Using the Hypothesis (H1–H4), we have

Theorem 5. *For the optimal control problem (10)–(12), there exists an optimal control m_v^{**} such that $J^*(m_v^{**}(\cdot)(t)) = \min_{m_v(t)\in U} J(m_v(t))$.*

We give the Hamiltonian function to obtain the minimum value of (12).

$$H = \frac{1}{2}(b^2 + m_v^2) + \lambda_1[v(1 - v - \frac{Kb}{r + K_e b} - m_v v)] + \lambda_2[b(r_1(1-b) - \frac{\alpha_1}{1+\beta_1 b} + \frac{\alpha_2 m_v}{1+\beta_1 b} - \alpha_3 m_v v)].$$

Using Pontryagin's Maximum Principle, the optimal solution of (10)–(12) can be obtained as follows

$$\begin{cases} \frac{\partial H}{\partial m_v}|_{(m_v^{**},\lambda_1,\lambda_2,t)} = 0, \\ \frac{\partial \lambda_1}{\partial m_v}|_{(m_v^{**},\lambda_1,\lambda_2,t)} = -\dot{\lambda}_1, \lambda_1 = 0, \\ \frac{\partial \lambda_2}{\partial m_v}|_{(m_v^{**},\lambda_1,\lambda_2,t)} = -\dot{\lambda}_2, \lambda_2 = 0. \end{cases}$$

Theorem 6. *The optimal control of (10)–(12) is given by*

$$m_v^{**} = \min\{\overline{m_v}, \max\{\lambda_1 vb + \lambda_2\alpha_3 vb - \frac{\lambda_2\alpha_2 b^2}{1+\beta_1 b}, 0\}\}. \tag{13}$$

where λ_1, λ_2 are the adjoint variables satisfying (13).

Proof of Theorem 6. By Pontryagin's Maximum Principle, finding the optimal control of (10)–(12) is equivalent to minimizing the following Hamiltonian function H above. The optimal control

$\frac{\partial H}{\partial m_v}|_{(m_v^{**},\lambda_1,\lambda_2,t)} = 0$ gives $m_v^{**} - \lambda_1 vb - \lambda_2\alpha_3 vb + \frac{\lambda_2\alpha_2 b^2}{1+\beta_1 b} = 0$, where the adjoint variables are satisfied. Furthermore,

$\dot{\lambda_1} = -\frac{\partial H}{\partial b}|_{(m_v^{**},\lambda_1,\lambda_2,t)} = -b + \frac{\lambda_1 vKr}{(r+K_e b)^2} - \lambda_2[r_1 - r_1 b - \frac{\alpha_1}{(1+\beta_1 b)^2} + \frac{\alpha_2 m_v}{(1+\beta_1 b)^2} - \alpha_3 m_v v]$

$\dot{\lambda_2} = -\frac{\partial H}{\partial b}|_{(m_v^{**},\lambda_1,\lambda_2,t)} = -\lambda_1(1 - 2v - \frac{Kb}{r+K_e b} - m_v) + \lambda_2\alpha_3 m_v$ and the transversality conditions $\lambda_1(T) = 0, \lambda_2(T) = 0$.

Moreover, since $m_v^{**} \in U$, using the lower and upper bounds of $\overline{m_b}(t)$, the optimal m_v^{**} can be characterized by (13). □

On the basis of model (11), we discuss the influence of different m_v on the model. We define $\alpha_1 = \frac{\alpha K_e}{r_v}, \alpha_2 = \frac{\alpha c K_e}{r_v}, \alpha_3 = M_b$. Using the wildfire and beetle data from some provinces in China (Heilongjiang, Jilin, Inner Mongolia. et al. [20]). With these data, the averages of these parameters from 2004 to 2017 are obtained for 11 provinces, see Table 1. The curves in Figure 3 show the influence of m_v on trees and beetles. Figure 4 magnifies the function image of beetle time to see the change trend of the beetle more clearly.

Table 1. The parameter and values to be used in the model (11).

Parameter	M_v	r_v	m_v	α_1	α_2
Beijing	0.764572	0.048204	158.611171	1657.993	828.9964
Tianjin	0.445343	0.021843	203.882824	3658.925	1829.463
Hebei	0.154946	0.023128	66.995922	3455.703	1727.852
Shanxi	0.252996	0.036412	69.4821260	2194.957	1097.479
Inner Mongoria	0.561737	0.045826	122.5812760	1744.046	872.0231
Liaoning	0.337569	0.016873	200.0673550	4736.759	2368.379
Jilin	0.38393	0.006038	635.8630730	13236.66	6618.332
Heilongjiang	0.239552	0.008569	279.546910	9326.556	4663.278
Shandong	0.524125	0.024039	218.031458	3324.691	1662.345
Henan	0.258396	0.046559	55.498005	1716.561	858.2804

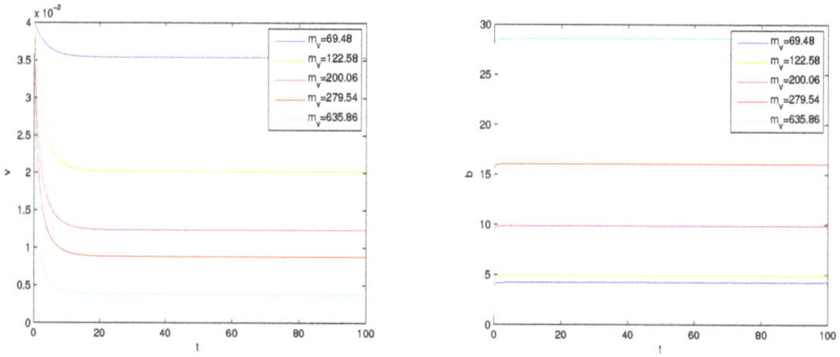

Figure 3. Effects of m_v on trees and beetles. Shanxi $m_v = 69.48$, Inner Mongoria $m_v = 122.58$, Liaoning $m_v = 200.06$, Heilongjiang $m_v = 279.54$, Jilin $m_v = 635.86$.

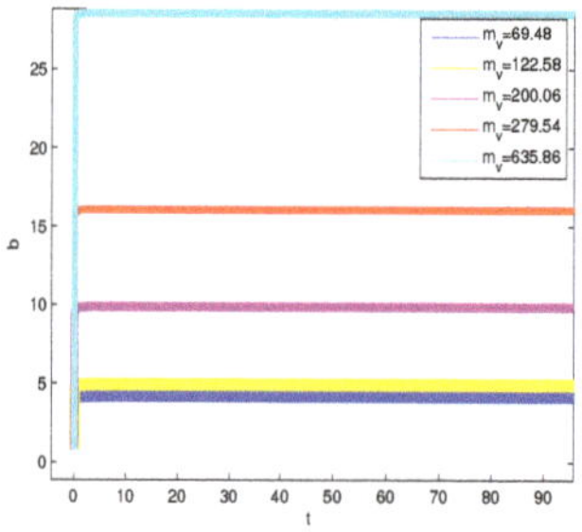

Figure 4. Local view of effects of m_v on beetles in Figure 3.

Sensitivity Analysis and Numerical Simulations

In this section, we first use (11) to simulate the reported forest fire data from 2004 to 2017 and predict the development trend of the forest area after the occurrence of a forest fire. Then, we conduct a sensitivity analysis for some critical parameters, perform the numerical simulation for optimal control, and search for some valid control and preventive measures. The forest area data of forest fires are extracted from the State Forestry Administration (See Table 2).

Table 2. Annual forest area data of forest fires in each province (unit: ten thousand hectares).

Year	2004	2008	2009	2010	2011	2012	2013	2014	2015	2016	2017
Shanxi	0.18412	0.1013	0.3149	0.0499	0.6372	0.048	0.2145	0.076	0.0814	0.0272	0.0299
Inner Mongoria	0.51265	1.5358	1.7764	0.9129	0.1741	0.4464	0.0826	0.595	0.3847	0.1622	2.4805
Liaoning	0.04303	0.1249	0.1424	0.0404	0.0577	0.0374	0.0143	0.1045	0.1922	0.1706	0.0802
Jilin	0.03272	0.0445	0.0351	0.0084	0.024	0.0178	0.0063	0.0134	0.0541	0.0123	0.045
Heilong jiang	18.55472	1.8402	9.9819	1.3779	0.1741	0.1046	0.0106	0.0301	0.0787	0.064	0.0883
Hebei	0.13467	0.033	0.0443	0.0221	0.2169	0.2112	0.0422	0.1168	0.0471	0.0573	0.1157

Based on the data of the forest fire area in Table 2, we calculate v and the parameter $K_v = 100$ in the model (11). For numerical simulation, most parameters of (11) were obtained from the literature. The influence trend of forest fires on forest areas in six provinces (Heilongjiang, Jilin, Liaoning, etc.) was predicted by fitting (11) with the data from 2004 to 2017. A numerical simulation shows that the model (11) with reasonable parameter values agrees well with the measured data. From 2004 to 2017, the area of forest fires in the same province decreased year by year. In order to better study the impact of forest fire on forest trees, we conduct a study. The key parameters are analyzed by sensitivity; Figure 5a–f show the forecast figures of Shanxi, Inner Mongolia, Liaoning, Jilin, Heilongjiang and Hebei, respectively.

With the help of model (11), we fit it to the data from 2004 to 2017 to predict the dynamics of trees and insects in the presence of fire (Figure 5). A numerical simulation shows that model (11) and reasonable parameter values can match the reported data well. From 2004 to 2017, the area of forest affected by fires decreased year by year and stabilized. Then, the rationality of the parameters selected by the model (11) is verified.

The accuracy of the original data or the stability of the optimal solution when the system changes is an important step in model optimization [21]. In the process of model optimization, sensitivity analysis is the most commonly used test method. Sensitivity analysis can quickly identify a few key factors from a large number of parameters and input states in the power system, but usually, it is not necessary to calculate the sensitivity coefficient of each parameter, and only those parameters with great uncertainty can be selected for sensitivity analysis. Based on the sensitivity analysis results of the tree–beetle–fire model, it is shown that the intensity of forest fire is the key factor in controlling and predict the mechanism of tree–beetle coexistence. To better understand the impact of fire on forests and insects, we conduct a study by analyzing the impact of key parameters m_v in sensitivity characterization.

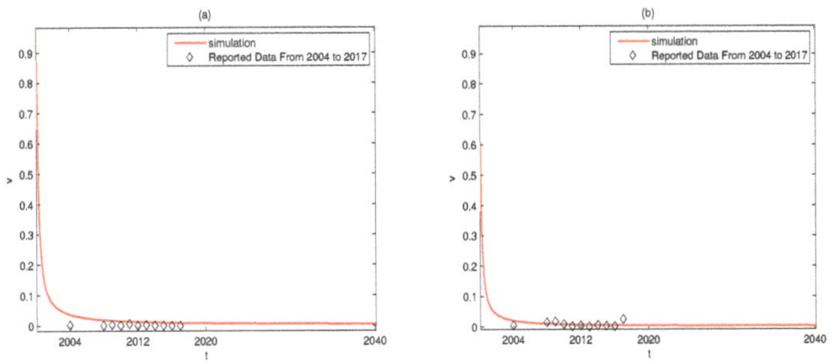

Figure 5. *Cont.*

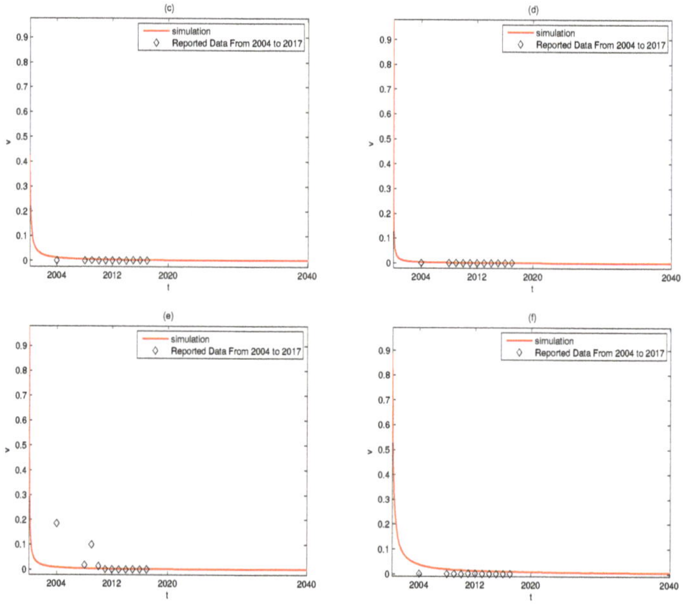

Figure 5. Predicted tendency of forest fire in HeiLongJiang, Inner Mongolia, JiLin, etc. (**a**) Number of forests in ShanXi. (**b**) Number of forests in LiaoNing. (**c**) Number of forests in JiLin. (**d**) Number of forests in Inner Mongolia. (**e**) Number of forests in HeiLongJiang. (**f**) Number of forests in HeBei.

The specific steps of the sensitivity coefficient algorithm are as follows. We consider function $y(t) = f(t, y, p)$, the absolute sensitivity of variable y_i to parameter P:

$$S_i(t) = \frac{\partial y_i(t.P)}{\partial P}, i = v, b.$$

We denote the relative sensitivity of a variable to a parameter:

$$s_i(t) = \frac{\partial y_i(t.P)}{\partial P}\frac{P}{y_i}, i = v, b,$$

the absolute sensitivity equation of parameter S_i:

$$\dot{S_i} = \frac{\partial f}{\partial y}S_i + \frac{\partial f}{\partial p}, i = v, b.$$

Next, the sensitivity of forest fire frequency and the impact of forest fires on trees to various variables in the system is discussed through sensitivity analysis and relative sensitivity analysis. The sensitivity equation of the system contains four equations for parameter m_v.

$$\begin{cases} \dot{v} = v(1 - v - \frac{Kb}{r+K_eb} - m_v v), \\ \dot{b} = b[r_1(1-b) - \frac{\alpha_1}{1+\beta_1 b} + \frac{\alpha_2 m_v}{1+\beta_1 b} - \alpha_3 m_v v], \\ \dot{S_v} = S_v(1 - 2v - \frac{Kb}{r+K_eb} - 2m_v v) - S_b\frac{Krv}{r+K_eb} - v^2, \\ \dot{S_b} = S_b(r_1 - 2r_1 b - \frac{\alpha_1}{(1+\beta_1 b)^2} + \frac{\alpha_2 m_v}{(1+\beta_1 b)^2} - \alpha_3 m_v v) - S_v\alpha_3 m_v b + \frac{\alpha_2 b}{1+\beta_1 b} - \alpha_3 vb. \end{cases} \tag{14}$$

The Rk-4 method was used to calculate the system, and the sensitivity and relative sensitivity analysis of forest fire intensity and the impact of forest fires on trees were obtained. The conclusions obtained can reflect the impact intensity of each variable in the system, as shown in the figure.

As shown in Figures 6 and 7, both the sensitivity and relative sensitivity of m_v to $v(t)$ show a trend less than 0, indicating that the increase in m_v will lead to the decrease in $v(t)$, and when $t = 10$, $S_v = -1.109 < 10^{-6} < 0$, $\frac{m_v S_v}{v} = -0.02485 < 0$. That means that when m_v increases by 10%, trees will decrease by 0.2485%. The sensitivity and relative sensitivity of m_v to $b(t)$ show a trend greater than 0, indicating that the increase in m_v will lead to the decrease in $b(t)$. When $b(t)$, $S_b = 0.001797 > 0$ and $\frac{m_v S_b}{v} = 0.2593 > 0$. That means that when m_v increases by 10%, beetles will increase by 2.593%. Ecologically speaking, we assume that the beetle–tree system has been exposed to sequential fires of constant intensity. This means that a sufficiently intense fire will result in a large number of trees being burned and weaken the defenses of living trees, thus allowing beetle epidemics (beetle outbreaks) to become established in the forest. With our results, there may be positive feedback between disturbances between wildfires and insect outbreaks, which would enhance the frequency and severity of forest damage from these two natural disturbances. This situation is consistent with current theories in the field.

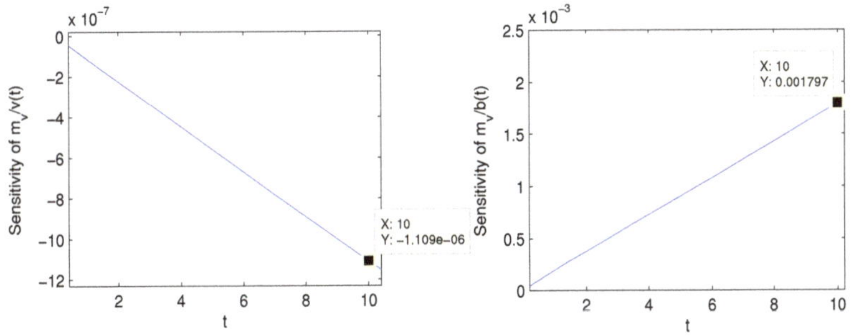

Figure 6. Sensitivity of $m_v(t)$ to $v(t)$ and $b(t)$.

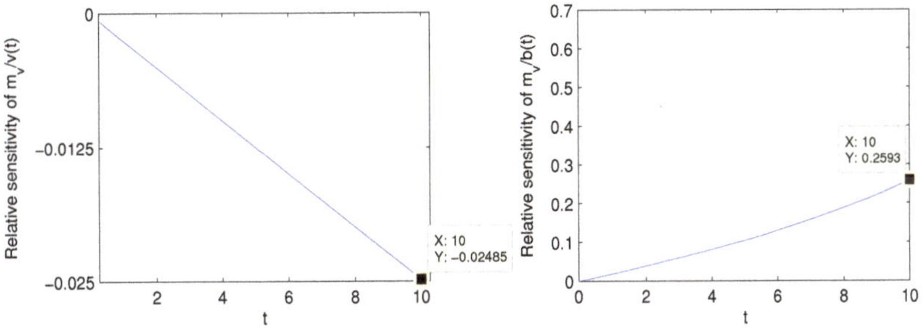

Figure 7. Relative sensitivity of $m_v(t)$ to $v(t)$ and $b(t)$.

4. Discussion

We present mathematical models with generalizations that provide a basis for exploring the disturbance effects of wildfires and insect outbreaks on forests. Current research reports show that there is a lack of proof of the global stability of the model, as well as analysis and fitting of actual data; see [17]. In Section 2, we prove the coexistence equilibrium is globally stable under certain conditions. In this paper, the tree–insect–fire model is optimized and rewritten. The optimal control strategy for the frequency of wildfire occurrence is discussed. In order to find the appropriate wildfire occurrence frequency and reduce the loss of trees. Based on the forest fire data from 2004 to 2017 provided by the State Forestry Administration, the development trend of a forest area after a forest fire is predicted. The sensitivity analysis is used to identify the frequency and intensity of forest fires, and the results show that the frequency of forest fires greatly influenced the tree–insect coexistence mechanism, or to be more precise, when the beetle–tree system is exposed to continuous fires of constant intensity. Intense fires will result in the burning of large amounts of forest and, in the process, also weaken the defense systems of living trees, thus allowing beetle epidemics to become established in the forest, which is consistent with the subsequent research theory in Reference [17].

Author Contributions: Formal analysis, C.Z.; Writing—original draft, X.L. and C.Z. All authors have read and agreed to the published version of the manuscript.

Funding: This research received no external funding.

Institutional Review Board Statement: Not applicable.

Informed Consent Statement: Not applicable.

Data Availability Statement: Not applicable.

Conflicts of Interest: The authors declare no conflict of interest.

References

1. Amman, G.D.; Schmitz, R.F. Mountain Pine Beetle: Lodgepole Pine Interactions and Strategies for Reducing Tree Losses. *Ambio* **1988**, *17*, 62–68.
2. Green, P.W.; James, J.M. Mountain Pine Beetle-Induced Changes to Selected Lodgepole Pine Fuel Complexes within the Intermountain Region. *For. Sci.* **2007**, *4*, 507–518.
3. Bigler, C.; Kulakoswki, D.; Veblen, T.T. Multiple disturbance interactions and drought influence fire severity in Rocky Mountain subalpine forests. *Ecology* **2005**, *86*, 3018–3029.
4. Geiszler, D.R.; Gara, R.I.; Driver, C.H.; Gallucci, V.F.; Martin, R.E. Fire, Fungi, and Beetle Influences on a Lodgepole Pine Ecosystem of South-Central Oregon. *Oecologia* **1980**, *46*, 239–243. [PubMed]
5. Mcculllough, D.G. Fire and Insects in Northern and Boreal Forest Ecosystems of North Americal. *Annu. Rev. Entomol.* **1998**, *43*, 107–127. [PubMed]
6. Forthofer, J.M.; Butler, B.W.; McHugh, C.W.; Finney, M.A. A comparison of three approaches for simulating fine-scale surface winds in support of wildland fire management. Part II. An exploratory study of the effect of simulated winds on fire growth simulations. *Int. J. Wildland Fire* **2014**, *23*, 969–981.
7. Barclay, H.J.; Li, C.; Benson, L.; Taylor, S.; Shore, T. Effects of fire return rates on traversability of lodgepole pine forests for mountain pine beetle (Coleoptera: Scolytidae) and the use of patch metrics to estimate traversability. *Can. Entomol.* **2005**, *137*, 566–583.
8. Bradley, T.; Tueller, P. Effects of fire on bark beetle presence on Jeffrey pine in the Lake Tahoe Basin. *For. Ecol. Manag.* **2001**, *142*, 205–214.
9. Elkin, C.M.; Reid, M.L. Attack and Reproductive Success of Mountain Pine Beetles (Coleoptera: Scolytidae) in Fire-Damaged Lodgepole Pines. *Environ. Entomol.* **2004**, *4*, 1070–1080.
10. Mart, G.S.; Wagner, M.R. Bark beetle community structure under four ponderosa pine forest stand conditions in northern Arizona. *For. Ecol. Manag.* **2002**, *170*, 145–160.
11. Fleming, R.A.; Candau, J.N.; Mcalpine, R.S. Landscape-Scale Analysis of Interactions between Insect Defoliation and Forest Fire in Central Canada. *Clim. Chang.* **2002**, *55*, 251–272.
12. Mchugh, C.W.; Kolb, T.E.; Wilson, J.L. Bark Beetle Attacks on Ponderosa Pine Following Fire in Northern Arizona. *Environ. Entomol.* **2003**, *32*, 510–522.
13. Santoro, A.E.; Lombardero, M.J.; Ayres, M.P.; Ruel, J.J. Interactions between fire and bark beetles in an old growth pine forest. *For. Ecol. Manag.* **2001**, *144*, 245–254.
14. Bebi, P.; Kulakowski, D.; Veblen, T. Interactions between fire and spruce beetles in a subalpine Rocky Mountain forest landscape Ecology. *For. Ecol. Manag.* **2003**, *84*, 362–371.
15. Heimann,B.; Fleming, W.H.; Rishel, R.W. Deterministic and Stochastic Optimal Control. *J. Appl. Math. Mech.* **1979**, *59*, 494
16. Safranyik, L.; Wilson, W.R. *The Mountain Pine Beetle: A Synthesis of Biology, Management and Impacts on Lodgepole Pine*; Safranyik, L., Wilson, B., Eds.; Canadian Forest Service Publications: Ottawa, ON, Canada, 2007; p. 299.
17. Charpentier, B.C.; Leite, M. A model for coupling fire and insect outbreak in forests. *Ecol. Model.* **2014**, *286*, 26–36. [CrossRef]
18. Zhou, L.; Fan, M.; Hou, Q.; Jin, Z.; Sun, X. Transmission dynamics and optimal control of brucellosis in Inner Mongolia of China. *Math. Biosci. Eng.* **2018**, *15*, 543–567. [CrossRef]
19. Martin, R.H. Logarithmic norms and projections applied to linear differential systems. *J. Math. Anal. Appl.* **1974**, *45*, 432–454.
20. Zhang, J.L. *China Forestry Statisitical Yearbook*; China Forestry Publishing House: Beijing, China, 2017; pp. 5–396.
21. Bonnans, J.F.; Shapiro, A. *Perturbation Analysis of Optimization Problems Stability and Sensitivity Analysis*; Springer: New York, NY, USA, 2000; Volume 4, pp. 260–400.

mathematics

Article

Modeling Nonlinear Hydroelastic Response for the Endwall of the Plane Channel Due to Its Upper-Wall Vibrations

Marina Barulina [1,2], Loredana Santo [3,*], Victor Popov [1,4], Anna Popova [4] and Dmitry Kondratov [1,2,4]

1 Institute of Precision Mechanics and Control of the Russian Academy of Sciences, 24, Rabochaya Street, 410028 Saratov, Russia
2 Faculty of Computer Science and Information Technology, Saratov National Research State University Named after N.G. Chernyshevsky, 83, St. Astrakhanskaya, 410012 Saratov, Russia
3 Department of Industrial Engineering, University of Rome tor Vergata, via del Politecnico 1, 00133 Rome, Italy
4 Department of Applied Mathematics and System Analysis, Yuri Gagarin State Technical University of Saratov, 77, Politechnicheskaya Street, 410054 Saratov, Russia
* Correspondence: loredana.santo@uniroma2.it

Abstract: A mathematical model for studying the nonlinear response of the endwall of a narrow channel filled with a viscous fluid to the vibration of the channel's upper wall was formulated. The channel, formed by two parallel, rigid walls, was investigated. The right end-channel wall was supported by a nonlinear spring. At the end of the left channel, the fluid flowed into a cavity with constant pressure. The upper channel wall oscillated according to a given law. As a result of the interaction between the endwall and the upper wall via a viscous fluid, the forced, nonlinear oscillations of the channel endwall arose. The fluid motion was considered in terms of the hydrodynamic lubrication theory. The endwall was studied as a spring-mass system with a nonlinear cubic restoring force. The coupled hydroelasticity problem was formulated, and it was shown that the problem under consideration was reduced to a single equation in the form of the Duffing equation. The nonlinear hydroelastic response of the end wall was determined by means of the harmonic balance method. The results of numerical experiments on nonlinear hydroelastic response behavior and a comparison with the case when the support spring is linear were presented. The obtained results are of a fundamental nature and can be used in modeling various devices and systems that have narrow channels filled with viscous fluid and are subjected to vibrations on one side of the channel. For example, coolant pipes are subjected to vibrations from the engine. Of particular interest is the application of the presented solution to the mathematical modeling of nano- and micro-spacecraft systems with fluids since the proposed decision allows for the consideration of some boundary effects, which is important for nano- and micro-spacecraft due to their small size.

Keywords: hydroelastic response; viscous fluid; nonlinear oscillations

MSC: 74F10

Citation: Barulina, M.; Santo, L.; Popov, V.; Popova, A.; Kondratov, D. Modeling Nonlinear Hydroelastic Response for the Endwall of the Plane Channel Due to Its Upper-Wall Vibrations. *Mathematics* **2022**, *10*, 3844. https://doi.org/10.3390/math10203844

Academic Editor: Chunrui Zhang

Received: 7 September 2022
Accepted: 14 October 2022
Published: 17 October 2022

1. Introduction

Mechanical systems, which are elastic structures that interact with a fluid, are currently actively used in mechanical engineering and aircraft-building. Such structures can be systems of rigid bodies on an elastic suspension [1,2] or linear, or nonlinear, plates and shells, with or without geometrical irregularity [3–5]. In particular, Indeitsev et al. [1] studied the interaction of a vibrating stamp supported by a spring and an ideal fluid with a free surface located in a plane of an infinitely long channel of small depth. A study of the longitudinal oscillations of the plate excited by an oncoming flow of a viscous fluid in a channel with parallel walls was carried out by Kurzin et al. [2] Kurzin et al. considered the case when the plate's end is fixed on a spring and the plate itself performs forced transverse oscillations. The influence of a liquid's viscosity leads to the complete damping of the free vibrations of such elastic structural elements over time, which allows us to consider only the forced vibrations arising from various causes.

There are a fair number of publications devoted to studying the interaction of fluid and elastic elements. For example, in [6], Bochkarev et al. carried out experimental studies to determine the natural frequencies of the oscillations of rectangular plates that interact with the free surface of water. For this, various types of supports at the ends of the plates were considered. Amabile et al. [7,8] engaged in research on the state of shells that contained a flow of an inviscid and incompressible fluid. For example, the response of such shells to harmonic excitation in the spectral vicinity of one of the lowest natural frequencies was studied in [7], and the stability of a circular, cross-sectional cylindrical shell with hinged ends was studied in [8] using the Galerkin method. The effect of viscous structural damping was introduced in [8] to account for energy dissipation.

Numerical modeling of the stability of the gap between two shells was carried out in [9,10] using the finite element method for different values of the stiffness of the outer shell and the fluid flow parameters. A mathematical model was considered to predict the hydroelastic response of a mechanical system consisting of a multilayer, circular plate that forms the wall of a narrow channel filled with viscous fluid [11]. Kondratov et al. [12] constructed a mathematical model for the two-dimensional problem of the hydroelastic interaction between the channel wall and the end seal through a pulsating layer of a viscous fluid. The end seal was considered as a linear elastic suspension.

Kheiri et al. [13] studied the dynamics and stability of a pipe conveying fluid in the case when the restrained end supports of the pipe are flexible. Barman et al. [14] studied the effect of an elastic bottom in the interaction of a two-layer fluid with a caisson-type, multi-chamber, porous breakwater fitted with a perforated frontwall. In addition, Barman et al. [14] showed that shear force and bottom deflection, and accordingly the elastic parameters of the seafloor, affect wave scattering.

The evaluation of the Duffing equation parameters is one of the most important tasks that should be resolved for solving the above problems. There are a number of works that are devoted to the experimental determination of the parameters of the Duffing equation, for example [15,16]. However, the experimental data must be processed by numerical methods, and this introduces an additional error in determining the values of the parameters.

In the model proposed in this work, the damping coefficient is determined analytically from the solution of the coupled hydroelasticity problem. This coefficient is determined by the physical parameters of the liquid and the geometric dimensions of the channel. However, there are no studies of the hydroelastic response of the channel endwall suspended on a nonlinear spring due to the interaction of the endwall with the vibrating wall of the channel through the viscous fluid that fills it. At the same time, the solution to this theoretical problem is required to solve such practical problems as studying the vibrations of bellows made of nonlinear materials or located on a nonlinear foundation; studying the oscillations of sensitive elements of pressure sensors (piezoelectric elements) mounted on a non-linear substrate; the study and control of the state of the channel with liquid according to the parameters of the vibration of its mechanical seal; etc. For example, the results of the proposed theoretical study can be useful for such problems as the hydroelastic analysis of a moored, floating, and submerged flexible, porous plate [17], the investigation of the effect of a flexible, floating plate on the dynamics of fluid flow over a mild slope [18], the analysis of the hydroelastic response of a moored, floating, flexible plate [19], etc. [20–23]. The future perspective is the application of the presented solution to the mathematical modeling of nano- and micro-spacecraft systems with fluids. Such an application is related to space sustainability, which is a new topic that involves knowledge in different fields aimed at the conscious use of space and its transportations and facilities for future life in space and on new planets [24].

Thus, it can be noted that the problem that is proposed in the paper for a solution is relevant to modern practical problems of technology and therefore requires a solution. This fact determines the scientific novelty and relevance of this study.

2. Problem Statement

Consider a narrow channel formed by two parallel, rigid walls (Figure 1). The channel-wall dimensions in the plan are $2\ell \times b$. The center of the Cartesian coordinate system xyz is located at the center of the inner surface of the lower fixed wall. We are studying a two-dimensional problem, so the change in the hydrodynamic parameters of the fluid along the y axis is neglected, which is equivalent to condition $2\ell << b$.

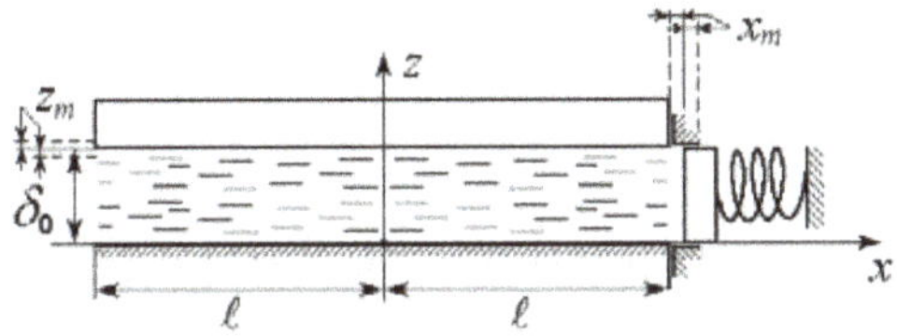

Figure 1. Scheme of a two-dimensional channel with an endwall supported by a spring.

The upper-channel wall oscillates in the direction of the *z-axis* according to a given harmonic law. The initial distance between the upper and lower walls is δ_0, and, since the channel is narrow, $2\ell >> \delta_0$. The channel is completely filled with a viscous fluid, the compressibility of which is neglected. The amplitude of the oscillations of the upper wall is $z_m << \delta_0$. At the left end of the channel, it is assumed that the pressure p_0 is constant, which is equivalent to the free outflow of fluid into a large cavity. Starting at this point in time, the value of this pressure is taken as the reference value and set equal to zero. The right channel-end is a mechanical seal in the form of a rigid wall supported by a spring with rigid cubic nonlinearity. That means the spring has the nonlinear characteristic of the restoring force, which changes symmetrically depending on its tension–compression, and the spring stiffness increases during compression. The rigid wall at the end of the right channel can move in the direction of the axis with the amplitude $x_m << \ell$. At the right end, we assume that the fluid flow rate coincides with the flow rate due to its displacement by the endwall, so no leaks are present. Moreover, we take into account that the transient processes decay due to the viscosity of the liquid. So, we study the steady, nonlinear, forced vibrations of the endwall of the channel, i.e., the anharmonic vibrations [25,26].

It should be noted that, since the problem is symmetrical about the Oy axis, it is sufficient to consider this problem in the two-dimensional case. This approach is widely used in solving practical problems.

Let the law of motion of the upper wall be harmonic, and it can be expressed in the following form:

$$z = z_m f_z(\omega t),\ f_z(\omega t) = \sin(\omega t), \tag{1}$$

where ω is the frequency of harmonic oscillations, and t is the time.

The equations of motion for a viscous fluid in the narrow channel are the Navier–Stokes equations and the continuity equation, written for a plane problem of hydromechanics [27,28]:

$$\begin{aligned} \frac{\partial u_x}{\partial t} + u_x\frac{\partial u_x}{\partial x} + u_z\frac{\partial u_x}{\partial z} &= -\frac{1}{\rho}\frac{\partial p}{\partial x} + \nu\left(\frac{\partial^2 u_x}{\partial x^2} + \frac{\partial^2 u_x}{\partial z^2}\right), \\ \frac{\partial u_z}{\partial t} + u_x\frac{\partial u_z}{\partial x} + u_z\frac{\partial u_z}{\partial z} &= -\frac{1}{\rho}\frac{\partial p}{\partial z} + \nu\left(\frac{\partial^2 u_z}{\partial x^2} + \frac{\partial^2 u_z}{\partial z^2}\right), \\ \frac{\partial u_x}{\partial x} + \frac{\partial u_z}{\partial z} &= 0, \end{aligned} \tag{2}$$

where u_x, u_z are the projections of the fluid velocity vector on the coordinate axes, p is the pressure, ρ is the density, and ν is the fluid kinematic viscosity.

The boundary conditions of Equation (2) are the non-slip conditions for the liquid at the upper and lower walls of the channel. They are expressed in the coincidence of the velocities of the fluid and the channel walls:

$$\begin{array}{c} u_x = 0,\ u_z = 0 \text{ at } z = 0, \\ u_x = 0,\ u_z = \frac{dz_*}{dt} \text{ at } z = z_*, \end{array} \tag{3}$$

For the right and left channels, two different types of conditions should be formulated. The first one is the condition that the pressure at the left end coincides with the reference value of pressure. The second is the condition that the fluid flow rate at the channel end coincides with the flow rate because of its displacement by the endwall. These conditions can be written as follow:

$$\begin{array}{c} p = p_0 = 0 \text{ at } x = -\ell, \\ \int_0^{z_*} u_x dz = \delta_0 \frac{dx_*}{dt} \text{ at } x = x_*, \end{array} \tag{4}$$

where z_* is the motion predetermined law of the upper channel wall, x_* is the motion law of the channel endwall, and p_0 is the reference pressure value.

Note that the wall displacements in the x and z directions are represented as $x_* = \ell + x_m f_x(\eta t)$ and $z_* = \delta_0 + z_m f_z(\omega t)$ in expressions (3) and (4). Additionally, η is the characteristic frequency of the nonlinear oscillations of the endwall.

The equation of motion for the endwall as a nonlinear spring-mass system has the following form:

$$m\frac{d^2x}{dt^2} + n_1 x + n_3 x^3 = b\int_0^{z_*} p|_{x=x_*} dz, \tag{5}$$

where m is the endwall mass, n_1 is the coefficient of rigidity of the support spring attached to the linear term, and $n_3 > 0$ is the stiffness coefficient of the support spring attached to the nonlinear cubic term.

3. Determination of Endwall Response

Let us introduce the dimensionless variables and small parameters of the problem:

$$\begin{array}{c} \psi = \frac{\delta_0}{\ell} << 1,\ \lambda = \frac{z_m}{\delta_0} << 1,\ \xi = \frac{x}{\ell},\ \zeta = \frac{z}{\delta_0},\ u_x = \frac{z_m \omega}{\psi} U_\xi, \\ u_z = z_m \omega U_\zeta,\ \ p = p_0 + \frac{\rho \nu z_m \omega}{\delta_0 \psi^2} P, \end{array} \tag{6}$$

where ψ, λ are the small parameters that characterize the problem; also, we will consider that, in the formulation under consideration, $x_m/\ell << 1$ and $x_m\psi/z_m = O(1)$.

Studying the equations of fluid dynamics, we take into account those for narrow gaps; as follows from the theory of hydrodynamic lubrication [27,28], the motion of the fluid can be considered as creeping; that is, the inertial terms in these equations can be neglected. Then, taking into account the variables (6), Equation (2) has the form

$$\begin{array}{c} -\frac{\partial P}{\partial \xi} + \psi^2 \frac{\partial^2 U_\xi}{\partial \xi^2} + \frac{\partial^2 U_\xi}{\partial \zeta^2} = 0, \\ -\frac{\partial P}{\partial \zeta} + \psi^2 \left[\psi^2 \frac{\partial^2 U_\zeta}{\partial \xi^2} + \frac{\partial^2 U_\zeta}{\partial \zeta^2} \right] = 0, \\ \frac{\partial U_\xi}{\partial \xi} + \frac{\partial U_\zeta}{\partial \zeta} = 0. \end{array} \tag{7}$$

The boundary conditions for Equation (7) in dimensionless variables (5), according to Equations (3) and (4), are written as follows:

$$\begin{array}{c} U_\xi = U_\zeta = 0 \text{ at } \zeta = 0, \\ U_\xi = 0,\ U_\zeta = \frac{1}{\omega}\frac{df_z(\omega t)}{dt} \text{ at } \zeta = 1 + \lambda f_z(\omega t), \\ P = 0 \ \text{ at } \xi = -1, \\ \int_0^{1+\lambda f_z} U_\xi d\zeta = \frac{x_m \psi}{z_m}\frac{1}{\omega}\frac{df_x(\eta t)}{dt} \ \text{ at } \xi = 1 + (x_m/\ell) f_x(\eta t). \end{array} \tag{8}$$

Note that there are regular perturbations in the proposed formulation of the problem. This means that each subsequent term of the asymptotic decomposition in a small parameter will be significantly lesser than the previous ones. Additionally, that will be true in the entire range of changes in the problem's independent variables and physical parameters. Using this approach, we have, in Equation (7) and the boundary conditions (8), $\psi = o(1)$, $\lambda = x_m/\ell = o(1)$, $x_m\psi/z_m = O(1)$, and the terms at λ, x_m/ℓ, ψ, and ψ^2 can be omitted [29]. As a result, for the case of creeping fluid motion in a narrow channel, we obtain the following equations for its dynamics:

$$\begin{aligned} -\frac{\partial P}{\partial \xi} + \frac{\partial^2 U_\xi}{\partial \zeta^2} = 0, \\ \frac{\partial P}{\partial \zeta} = 0, \\ \frac{\partial U_\xi}{\partial \xi} + \frac{\partial U_\zeta}{\partial \zeta} = 0. \end{aligned} \quad (9)$$

Taking into account the above remarks, the boundary conditions (8) have the following form:

$$\begin{aligned} U_\xi = U_\zeta = 0 \text{ at } \zeta = 0, \\ U_\xi = 0,\ U_\zeta = \tfrac{1}{\omega}\tfrac{df_z(\omega t)}{dt} \text{ at } \zeta = 1, \\ P = 0 \text{ at } \xi = -1, \\ \textstyle\int_0^1 U_\xi d\zeta = \tfrac{x_m\psi}{z_m}\tfrac{1}{\omega}\tfrac{df_x(\eta t)}{dt} \text{ at } \xi = 1. \end{aligned} \quad (10)$$

According to the second equation in Equation (9), the pressure does not depend on the coordinate ζ. Therefore, Equation (5), taking into account Equation (6), is written as

$$m\frac{d^2x}{dt^2} + n_1x + n_3x^3 = \delta_0 b\rho\nu z_m\omega\left(\delta_0\psi^2\right)^{-1} P|_{\xi=1}. \quad (11)$$

Solving Equation (9) with boundary conditions (10), we find that

$$\begin{aligned} U_\xi = \tfrac{\zeta^2-\zeta}{2}\tfrac{\partial P}{\partial \xi}, \\ U_\zeta = \tfrac{1}{12}\tfrac{\partial^2 P}{\partial \xi^2}\left(3\zeta^2 - 2\zeta^3\right), \\ P = \tfrac{6}{\omega}\tfrac{df(\omega t)_z}{dt}\left(\xi^2 - 1\right) - 12\left(\tfrac{1}{\omega}\tfrac{df_z(\omega t)}{dt} + \tfrac{x_m\psi}{z_m}\tfrac{1}{\omega}\tfrac{df_x(\eta t)}{dt}\right)(\xi + 1). \end{aligned} \quad (12)$$

Then, the pressure in the channel cross-section at its right end is equal to

$$P|_{\xi=1} = -24\left(\frac{1}{\omega}\frac{df_z(\omega t)}{dt} + \frac{x_m\psi}{z_m}\frac{1}{\omega}\frac{df_x(\eta t)}{dt}\right). \quad (13)$$

Taking into account Equation (13), we write Equation (11) as

$$m\frac{d^2x}{dt^2} + K_x\frac{dx}{dt} + n_1x + n_3x^3 = -K_z\frac{dz}{dt} \quad (14)$$

and taking into account the predetermined law of the movement of the upper wall (1), this equation can be written in the following form:

$$m\frac{d^2x}{dt^2} + K_x\frac{dx}{dt} + n_1x + n_3x^3 = -z_m\omega K_z\cos\omega t, \quad (15)$$

where $K_x = 24b\ell\rho\nu/\delta_0$ and $K_z = 24b\ell^2\rho\nu/\delta_0^2$ are the damping coefficients due to the viscous fluid influence.

The multiplier $-z_m\omega$ represents the amplitude of the vibration velocity of the upper channel wall. The right side of Equation (15) is the driving force, which varies according to the harmonic law with amplitude $-z_m\omega K_z$. Therefore, Equation (15) is the Duffing oscillator equation. Furthermore, we assume that the vibration velocity amplitude $z_m\omega$ is set on the basis of a velocity of 1 m/s, i.e., $z_m\omega = k \cdot 1$ (m/s), where k is the coefficient determining vibration overload by speed. It is known [25,26] that the solution of the Duffing equation for small oscillation amplitudes and damping coefficients is an anharmonic oscillation.

As is known [25,26], the Duffing equation (Equation (15)) can be solved using the harmonic balance method. Further study is limited by the research of the main hydroelastic response of the channel endwall at a frequency close to the driving force frequency. The frequency of the forced vibrations of the endwall is assumed to be equal to the frequency of the driving force in this method, and the desired solution is represented as a harmonic one, that is $\eta \approx \omega$ and $x = x_m\cos(\omega t - \varphi)$. When we perform the linearization procedure for Equation (15) by the harmonic balance method [25,26], we obtain the following algebraic system:

$$\begin{aligned} x_m\left(n_1 - m\omega^2\right) + \tfrac{3}{4}n_3x_m^3 &= -z_m\omega K_z\cos\varphi, \\ K_x\omega x_m &= -z_m\omega K_z\sin\varphi. \end{aligned} \tag{16}$$

Squaring the right and left parts of these equations and then adding them, we obtain an equation for determining the primary hydroelastic response of the endwall:

$$\left(\left(n_1 - m\omega^2\right) + \frac{3}{4}n_3x_m^2\right)^2 x_m^2 + (K_x\omega x_m)^2 = (z_m\omega K_z)^2. \tag{17}$$

From Equation (17), taking into account our previous remarks, we can write the primary hydroelastic response of the channel endwall, which is supported on the spring with cubic nonlinearity and performs nonlinear oscillations with the frequency of the driving force, i.e., its nonlinear amplitude-frequency response:

$$x_m = \frac{kK_z/m}{\sqrt{\left(\omega_*^2 - \omega^2\right)^2 + (K_x\omega/m)^2}}, \quad \omega_*^2(x_m) = (n_1/m) + (3/4)x_m^2n_3/m, \tag{18}$$

which, by solving it for ω, can be reduced to the form:

$$\omega^2 = \omega_*^2 - \frac{1}{2}\left(\frac{K_x}{m}\right)^2 \pm \sqrt{\left(\frac{kK_z}{x_m m}\right)^2 - \omega_*^2\left(\frac{K_x}{m}\right)^2 - \frac{1}{4}\left(\frac{K_x}{m}\right)^4}. \tag{19}$$

The first term ω_* in Equation (19) defines the so-called skeletal curve, which corresponds to the Duffing equation, from which the damping term and driving force are excluded, i.e., for the problem under consideration, in Equation (15) (or in Equation (19)) $K_z = K_x = 0$ is set. In other words, the skeletal curve is the curve of the natural undamped oscillations of a nonlinear conservative system with cubic nonlinearity.

In addition, from Equation (16), the phase characteristic of the considered channel wall can be obtained:

$$tg\varphi = \frac{K_x\omega/m}{\omega_*^2 - \omega^2}. \tag{20}$$

The right and left parts of expression (18) include the amplitude of the endwall vibrations, making it difficult to use this expression directly. However, the nonlinear hydroelastic response can be constructed numerically using expression (19). Note that we have the case of supporting the endwall of the channel on a linear spring for which $n_3 = 0$. In this case, the endwall will undergo harmonic oscillations excited by the vibration of the upper wall of the channel, and expression (18) will be a linear amplitude characteristic that unambiguously connects the amplitude and frequency of the oscillations of the endwall.

Some numerical experiments were conducted to illustrate the results obtained. The nonlinear and linear hydroelastic responses of the channel endwall were calculated according to (19) and (18) for $z_m\omega = 1$ m/s, $k = 1.5$ with the following geometric and physical–mechanical parameters: $\ell = 0.1$ m, $\delta_0 = 0.05$ m, $b = 0.5$ m, $m = 0.5$ kg, $n_1 = 10^7$ kg/s^2, $n_3 = 9 \times 10^{12}$ kg/(m^{2}s^2), $\rho = 1.84 \times 10^3$ kg/m^3, and $\nu = 2.53 \times 10^{-4}$ m^2/s. The calculated curves of the hydroelastic response of the channel wall are shown in Figure 2.

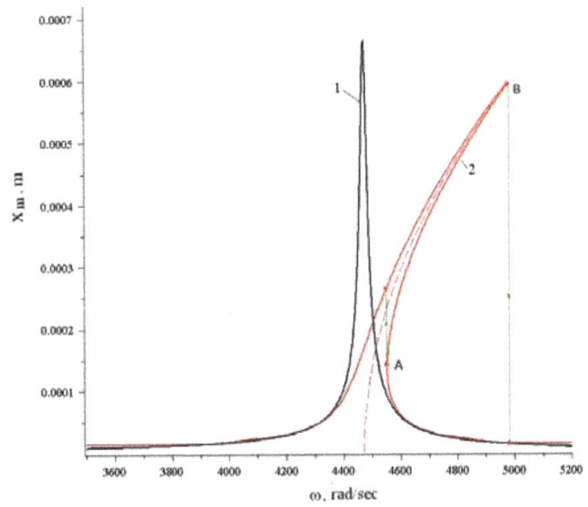

Figure 2. Hydroelastic response of the channel wall: 1: linear support spring: black line ($n_3 = 0$), 2: spring with strong cubic nonlinearity: red line ($n_3 > 0$); the dotted line shows the skeletal curve ω; A and B—frequencies at which the amplitudes of nonlinear oscillations can change abruptly; green lines with arrows—directions of amplitude change.

4. Discussion

As can be seen from the presented calculations, the curvature of the amplitude characteristic at the primary resonance is observed when the cubic nonlinearity of the end-support spring is considered. Moreover, the constructed mathematical model makes it possible to determine the frequencies at which the amplitudes of nonlinear oscillations can change abruptly. As shown in Figure 2, these frequencies are in the range between points A and B. A jump change in the oscillations' amplitude of the endwall is observed at these points when the frequency of oscillations of the upper wall changes. It is known [25,26] that the lower part of the nonlinear hydroelastic response curve between points A and B is unstable. Arrows indicate the directions of the jumps in amplitude. An increase in the amplitude of the vibration velocity of the upper wall will lead to a rise in the range of these frequencies.

To verify the constructed mathematical model, the experimental results obtained by Jiao et al. [23] can be used. Jiao et al. studied the longitudinal vibrations of the bellows, considering the damping properties of a viscous fluid in a linear formulation using the following parameters:

$$\ell = 0.05 \text{ m}, \delta_0 = 0.0065 \text{ m}, b = 0.038\pi \text{ m}, n_1 = 10.13 \times 10^3 \text{ kg/s}^2, \rho = 9.03 \times 10^2 \text{ kg/m}^3, \nu = 10^{-4} \text{ m}^2/\text{s}.$$

The calculated theoretical value of the damping factor in the longitudinal direction is equal to $K_x = 2$ Ns/m (see Formula (15)) for a system with the parameters presented above. The experimentally determined damping coefficient in the longitudinal direction was 3.547 Ns/m.

Furthermore, the linear hydroelastic response of the bellows was calculated using Formula (18), assuming $n_3 = 0$, to reduce the proposed model to a linear one. The calculation result is shown in Figure 3.

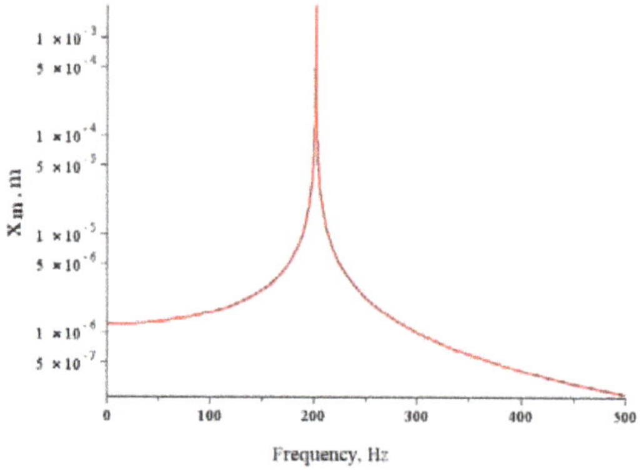

Figure 3. Hydroelastic response of the channel wall. The theoretical curve is based on experimental data [23].

The experimental data presented above were obtained at a resonance frequency of 200 Hz, as stated in [23]. The resonant frequency calculated according to the proposed model is equal to 201.3 Hz. So, theoretical and experimental results are in good agreement for the linear case.

The above comparison shows that the proposed model is quite adequate for the process under study and expands the possibility of its use in the case when taking into account the nonlinear properties of the bellows material.

Thus, the proposed model can evaluate vibrations of sensitive elements mounted on nonlinear elastic foundations and those in contact with a layer of viscous fluid, as used, for example, in pressure sensors.

5. Conclusions

Since the developed mathematical model is fundamental in nature, it can be used in modeling various devices and systems which have narrow channels filled with a viscous fluid and which are subjected to vibrations on one side of the channel.

For example, the mathematical model developed can be used in the aerospace field to model the dynamics of fluid-based angular rate sensors [30], for instance, for the rate-integrating gyroscope, when we are considering the nonlinearity of the end seal (bellows) of the sensor cavity where the float is located.

Another example would be coolant pipes that are subjected to vibration from the engine. Of particular interest is the application of the presented solution to the mathematical modeling of nano- and micro-spacecraft systems with fluids since the proposed model allows the consideration of some boundary effects, which is important for nano- and micro-spacecraft due to their small size.

Thus, in this paper, a new mathematical model for studying nonlinear hydroelastic oscillations of a channel endwall supported by a spring with strong cubic nonlinearity is proposed. It is shown that, for a narrow channel filled with a viscous incompressible fluid, the equation of motion for its endwall is reduced to the Duffing equation, with the damping coefficient determined by the viscosity of the fluid and the geometric dimensions of the channel.

Author Contributions: Conceptualization, M.B. and V.P.; methodology, D.K. and L.S.; validation, V.P., A.P., and D.K.; formal analysis, V.P.; investigation, A.P. and D.K.; resources, M.B. and L.S.; writing—original draft preparation, V.P. and D.K.; writing—review and editing, M.B. and L.S.; visualization, V.P. and A.P.; supervision, M.B., V.P. and D.K.; project administration, L.S. All authors have read and agreed to the published version of the manuscript.

Funding: This research received no external funding.

Data Availability Statement: Not applicable.

Conflicts of Interest: The authors declare no conflict of interest.

References

1. Indeitsev, D.A.; Osipova, E.V. Nonlinear effects in trapped modes of standing waves on the surface of shallow water. *Tech. Phys.* **2000**, *45*, 1513–1517. [CrossRef]
2. Kurzin, V.B. Streamwise vibrations of a plate in a viscous fluid flow in a channel, induced by forced transverse vibrations of the plate. *J. Appl. Mech. Tech. Phys.* **2011**, *52*, 459–463. [CrossRef]
3. Païdoussis, M.P.; Price, S.J.; De Langre, E. *Fluid-Structure Interactions: Cross-Flow-Induced Instabilities*; Cambridge University Press: Cambridge, UK, 2010.
4. Amabili, M. *Nonlinear Vibrations and Stability of Shells and Plates*; Cambridge University Press: Cambridge, UK, 2008.
5. Kalinina, A.; Kondratov, D.; Kondratova, Y.; Mogilevich, L.; Popov, V. Investigation of hydroelasticity coaxial geometrically irregular and regular shells under vibration. In Recent Research in Control Engineering and Decision Making, Proceedings of the International Conference on Information Technologies, Saratov, Russia, 7–8 February 2019; Springer: Cham, Switzerland, 2019; pp. 125–137.
6. Bochkarev, S.A.; Kamenskikh, A.O.; Lekomtsev, S.V. Experimental investigation of natural and harmonic vibrations of plates interacting with air and fluid. *Ocean Eng.* **2020**, *206*, 107341. [CrossRef]
7. Amabili, M.; Pellicano, F.; Païdoussis, M.P. Non-linear dynamics and stability of circular cylindrical shells containing flowing fluid. Part III: Truncation effect without flow and experiments. *J. Sound Vib.* **2000**, *237*, 617–640. [CrossRef]
8. Amabili, M.; Pellicano, F.; Païdoussis, M.P. Non-linear dynamics and stability of circular cylindrical shells conveying flowing fluid. *Comput. Struct.* **2002**, *80*, 899–906. [CrossRef]
9. Bochkarev, S.A.; Matveenko, V.P. Stability analysis of loaded coaxial cylindrical shells with internal fluid flow. *Mech. Solids* **2010**, *45*, 789–802. [CrossRef]
10. Bochkarev, S.A.; Lekomtsev, S.V.; Matveenko, V. Parametric investigation of the stability of coaxial cylindrical shells containing flowing fluid. *Eur. J. Mech. -A/Solids* **2014**, *47*, 174–181. [CrossRef]
11. Kondratov, D.V.; Mogilevich, L.I.; Popov, V.S.; Popova, A.A. Hydroelastic Vibrations of Circular Sandwich Plate Under Inertial Excitation. In *Nonlinear Mechanics of Complex Structures*; Springer: Cham, Switzerland, 2021; pp. 227–242.
12. Kondratov, D.V.; Popov, V.S.; Popova, A.A. Modeling the end seal oscillations of the channel filled with pulsating viscous fluid. In Proceedings of the 6th International Conference on Industrial Engineering, Sochi, Russia, May 2021; pp. 665–672.
13. Kheiri, M.; Païdoussis, M.; Del Pozo, G.C.; Amabili, M. Dynamics of a pipe conveying fluid flexibly restrained at the ends. *J. Fluids Struct.* **2014**, *49*, 360–385. [CrossRef]
14. Barman, K.K.; Bora, S.N. Elastic bottom effects on ocean water wave scattering by a composite caisson-type breakwater placed upon a rock foundation in a two-layer fluid. *Int. J. Appl. Mech.* **2021**, *13*, 2150114. [CrossRef]
15. Khatiry Goharoodi, S.; Dekemele, K.; Dupre, L.; Loccufier, M.; Crevecoeur, G. Sparse Identification of Nonlinear Duffing Oscillator from Measurement Data. *IFAC-PapersOnLine* **2018**, *51*, 162–167. [CrossRef]
16. Silva, C.E.; Gibert, J.M.; Maghareh, A.; Dyke, S.J. Dynamic study of a bounded cantilevered nonlinear spring for vibration reduction applications: A comparative study. *Nonlinear Dyn.* **2020**, *101*, 893–909. [CrossRef]
17. Mohapatra, S.; Guedes Soares, C. Hydroelastic Response to Oblique Wave Incidence on a Floating Plate with a Submerged Perforated Base. *J. Mar. Sci. Eng.* **2022**, *10*, 1205. [CrossRef]
18. Selvan, S.; Ghosh, S.; Behera, H.; Meylan, M. Hydroelastic response of a floating plate on the falling film: A stability analysis. *Wave Motion* **2021**, *104*, 102749. [CrossRef]
19. Mohapatra, S.C.; Soares, C.G. Effect of Mooring Lines on the Hydroelastic Response of a Floating Flexible Plate Using the BIEM Approach. *J. Mar. Sci. Eng.* **2021**, *9*, 941. [CrossRef]
20. Varney, P.; Green, I. Impact Phenomena in a Noncontacting Mechanical Face Seal. *J. Tribol.* **2017**, *139*, 022201. [CrossRef]
21. Velmisov, P.A.; Pokladova, Y.V. Mathematical modelling of the "Pipeline–pressure sensor" system. *J. Phys. Conf. Ser.* **2019**, *1353*, 01208. [CrossRef]
22. Antsiferov, S.A.; Kondratov, D.V.; Mogilevich, L.I. Perturbing Moments in a Floating Gyroscope with Elastic Device Housing on a Vibrating Base in the Case of a Nonsymmetric End Outflow. *Mech. Solids* **2009**, *44*, 352–360. [CrossRef]
23. Jiao, X.; Zhang, J.; Zhao, H.; Yan, Y. Research on dynamic stiffness of the damping element in bellows-type fluid viscous damper by a simplified model. *Eng. Comput.* **2021**, *38*, 413–441. [CrossRef]
24. Santo, L. Space sustainability, advanced materials and micro/nanotechnologies for future life in outer Space. *Emergent Mater.* **2022**, *5*, 237–240. [CrossRef]
25. Nayfeh, A.H.; Mook, D.T. *Nonlinear Oscillations*; John Wiley & Sons: Hoboken, NJ, USA, 2008.
26. Krack, M.; Gross, J. *Harmonic Balance for Nonlinear Vibration Problems*; Springer International Publishing: Cham, Switzerland, 2019; Volume 1.
27. Lamb, H. *Hydrodynamics*, 6th ed.; Dover Publications Inc.: New York, NY, USA, 1945.
28. Loitsyanskii, L.G. *Mechanics of Liquids and Gases*; Pergamon Press: Oxford, UK, 1966.

29. Van Dyke, M. *Perturbation Methods in Fluid Mechanics;* Parabolic Press: Stanford, CA, USA, 1975.
30. El-Sheimy, N.; Youssef, A. Inertial sensors technologies for navigation applications: State of the art and future trends. *Satell. Navig.* **2020**, *1*, 2. [CrossRef]

mathematics

Article

A New Fractal-Fractional Version of Giving up Smoking Model: Application of Lagrangian Piece-Wise Interpolation along with Asymptotical Stability

Sina Etemad [1,*], Albert Shikongo [2], Kolade M. Owolabi [3], Brahim Tellab [4], İbrahim Avcı [5], Shahram Rezapour [1,6,*] and Ravi P. Agarwal [7,*]

1 Department of Mathematics, Azarbaijan Shahid Madani University, Tabriz 3751-71379, Iran
2 Engineering Mathematics, School of Engineering, University of Namibia, Windhoek 13301, Namibia
3 Department of Mathematical Sciences, Federal University of Technology, Akure PMB 704, Nigeria
4 Laboratory of Applied Mathematics, Kasdi Merbah University, Ouargla 30000, Algeria
5 Department of Computer Engineering, Faculty of Engineering, Final International University, via Mersin 10, Kyrenia 99300, Northern Cyprus, Turkey
6 Department of Medical Research, China Medical University Hospital, China Medical University, Taichung 40402, Taiwan
7 Department of Mathematics, Texas A&M University-Kingsville, Kingsville, TX 78363, USA
* Correspondence: sina.etemad@azaruniv.ac.ir (S.E.); sh.rezapour@azaruniv.ac.ir (S.R.); ravi.agarwal@tamuk.edu (R.P.A.)

Abstract: In this paper, a new kind of mathematical modeling is studied by providing a five-compartmental system of differential equations with respect to new hybrid generalized fractal-fractional derivatives. For the first time, we design a model of giving up smoking to analyze its dynamical behaviors by considering two parameters of such generalized operators; i.e., fractal dimension and fractional order. We apply a special sub-category of increasing functions to investigate the existence of solutions. Uniqueness property is derived by a standard method based on the Lipschitz rule. After proving stability property, the equilibrium points are obtained and asymptotically stable solutions are studied. Finally, we illustrate all analytical results and findings via numerical algorithms and graphs obtained by Lagrangian piece-wise interpolation, and discuss all behaviors of the relevant solutions in the fractal-fractional system.

Keywords: hybrid fractal-fractional derivative; smoking model; approximate solution; stability; sensitivity analysis; Lagrangian piece-wise interpolation

MSC: 34A08; 65P99; 49J15

Citation: Etemad, S.; Shikongo, A.; Owolabi, K.M.; Tellab, B.; Avcı, İ.; Rezapour, S.; Agarwal, R.P. A New Fractal-Fractional Version of Giving up Smoking Model: Application of Lagrangian Piece-Wise Interpolation along with Asymptotical Stability. *Mathematics* **2022**, *10*, 4369. https://doi.org/10.3390/math10224369

Academic Editor: Chunrui Zhang

Received: 22 September 2022
Accepted: 15 November 2022
Published: 20 November 2022

1. Introduction

Smoking has always been one of the known causes of many human diseases, which threatens the physical health of a large part of the world's population (both smokers and non-smokers). The impact of tobacco abuse, especially cigarettes, on different parts of the human body can be seen so clearly that one of its primary effects is the death of more than 5,000,000 people per year. If we want to make a comparison between smokers and non-smokers, we can refer to the results of medical reports in hospitals around the world, in which the rate of heart attacks and the prevalence of lung cancer in smokers compared to non-smokers are more than 70% and 10%, respectively. Even based on the reports of WHO, the lifespan of non-smokers has been reported to be 10 to 13 years longer than that of smokers. Smoking in the short term can cause bad breath, yellowing of teeth, wrinkled skin, persistent cough, and high blood pressure. In the long term, this bad habit causes dangerous diseases such as stomach ulcers, heart diseases and cancers such as lung, mouth and gums, and throat.

Due to the widespread use of tobacco among teenagers and even children, every year the World Health Organization requests researchers and doctors to study its effects on people's health and present the results in the form of detailed reports and charts and tables. Recently, using the data and numerical results of such studies, researchers have done mathematical modeling of the process of smoking in various statistical societies, and using mathematical algorithms and computer calculations, they are trying to provide methods to control and optimize the outputs. In this direction, researchers turned to mathematical tools and models, and tried to simulate the dynamics of processes and phenomena with the help of differential equations (ordinary and partial) and to get accurate solutions by solving them. Zaman [1] in 2011 designed a model of giving up smoking and analyzed the system qualitatively. In 2008, Sharomi et al. [2] proposed a system of curtailing smoking in the form of four differential equations and investigated stable and unstable solutions. After that, Alkhudhari et al. [3] suggested a four-compartmental system of smoking and checked the effect of smokers on temporary quitters based on the equlibrium criteria. Rahman et al. [4] studied an age-structured model of giving up smoking and conducted an optimal analysis. In addition, in another work, Rahman et al. [5] extended their model of giving up smoking by considering the harmonic mean incidence rate. Other full studies can be found in this regard such as Refs. [6,7].

Due to the weakness of classical operators, generalized fractional operators (Caputo–Fabrizio [8] and Atangana–Baleanu [9]) quickly attracted the attention of many researchers. The non-locality property of the new operators along with their memory property narrowed the field to classical operators such as Riemann–Liouville and Caputo [10]. Of course, there were still those who used classical operators for their modeling to study the dynamics of smoking. For instances, Erturk et al. [11] constructed a five-compartmental fractional giving up smoking model (based on the standard model [12]) via the singular Caputo derivative, and by using the MSGDT method, derived the approximate solutions and lastly, compared their results with the data obtained by the Runge–Kutta algorithm. Zeb et al. [13] gave another fractional model of such a phenomena and analyzed it via the HAM technique. Finally, the giving up smoking and smoking cessation models have been evaluated with various parameters and control tools in different mathematical models with new nonsingular operators, among which we can refer to the research articles published in Refs. [14–16].

More recently, another class of hybrid two-parametric operators was given by Atangaga, for which we can derive more accurate numerical outputs in comparison to both fractional and integer-order operators [17,18]. Due to the effect of fractal dimension and fractional order in the final result, these operators are called "Fractal-Fractional Operators". In the structure of these operators, the role of fractal derivative is essential, and by considering the kernels, these operators divide into three types called the Power law, exponential decay law, and generalized Mittag–Leffler law-type fractal-fractional operators. For more information, one can refer to [17,18]. The effectiveness and efficiency of new operators in obtaining accurate results can be seen in a large number of relevant studies [19–29].

To state the contribution of our work, as we said above, we know that the classical standard time-derivatives are local operators and have some weaknesses in the prediction of the dynamics of a phenomenon. Even a well-known fractional derivative such as the Caputo–Liouville has its own limitations. Since its kernel has a weak memory effect in comparison to the newly-defined fractal-fractional derivatives, this type of derivative cannot precisely describe the full effect of the memory. Hence, due to the strong memory effect, complex dynamics, and non-locality of the generalized hybrid fractal-fractional operators, our main objective in the present research is to use the novel two-parametric power-law type $(\varkappa_1, \varkappa_2)$-fractal-fractional derivative to model the giving up smoking efficiently. In addition, dynamics of the supposed fractal-fractional model is predicted by a numerical scheme with respect to two fractional and fractal parameters continuously for which we can analyze some behaviors of the system accurately.

The rest of the paper is organized as follows. Section 2 deals with preliminaries and Section 3 describes the extended model. Mathematical analysis is carried out in Section 4, whereas in Section 6, the numerical simulations are done based on the algorithms derived in Section 5. Section 7 concludes the paper.

2. Preliminaries

In this section, we recall some basic definitions and theorems about fixed point theory and fractal-fractional calculus that are needed in the sequel.

Let Φ denotes a family of non-decreasing functions $\phi : [0, \infty) \to [0, \infty)$ such that

$$\sum_{m=1}^{\infty} \phi^m(\mathrm{t}) < \infty, \ \forall \mathrm{t} > 0,$$

and

$$\phi(\mathrm{t}) < \mathrm{t}, \ \forall \mathrm{t} > 0.$$

Definition 1 ([30]). *Let $\mathcal{X}$ be a metric space, $\psi : \mathcal{X}^2 \to \mathbb{R}^+ \cup \{0\}$, and $\mathcal{V} : \mathcal{X} \to \mathcal{X}$ be a selfmap.*

(1) *$\mathcal{V}$ is called ψ-ϕ-contraction if for each $z_1, z_2 \in \mathcal{X}$,*

$$\psi(z_1, z_2)\mathbf{d}(\mathcal{V}z_1, \mathcal{V}z_2) \le \phi(\mathbf{d}(z_1, z_2)),$$

where $\mathbf{d}$ denotes the metric function.

(2) *$\mathcal{V}$ is called ψ-admissible if $\psi(z_1, z_2) \ge 1$ gives $\psi(\mathcal{V}z_1, \mathcal{V}z_2) \ge 1$.*

Now, we will state two theorems in relation to the existence of a fixed point for such special contractions, which is used in the following sections.

Theorem 1 ([30]). *Assume that $(\mathcal{X}, \mathbf{d})$ is a complete metric space, $\psi : \mathcal{X} \times \mathcal{X} \to \mathbb{R}$, $\phi \in \Phi$, and $\mathcal{V} : \mathcal{X} \to \mathcal{X}$ is an ψ-ϕ-contraction such that*

(1) *$\mathcal{V}$ is ψ-admissible;*
(2) *There is $z_0 \in \mathcal{X}$ such that $\psi(z_0, \mathcal{V}z_0) \ge 1$;*
(3) *For every sequence $\{z_n\}$ in $\mathcal{X}$ with $z_n \to z$ and $\psi(z_n, z_{n+1}) \ge 1$ for all $n \ge 1$, we have $\psi(z_n, z) \ge 1$ for all $n \ge 1$.*

Then, $\mathcal{V}$ has at least a fixed point.

In addition, the following theorem is another theorem that is used for existence results in the sequel.

Theorem 2 (Leray–Schauder [31]). *Assume that $\mathcal{X}$ is a Banach space, $\mathbb{A}$ is a convex, bounded and closed set in $\mathcal{X}$, $\mathbb{G}$ is an open subset of $\mathbb{A}$ such that $0 \in \mathbb{G}$, and $\mathcal{Y} : \bar{\mathbb{G}} \to \mathbb{A}$ is a compact and continuous map. Then either:*

(i) *There is $z \in \bar{\mathbb{G}}$ such that $\mathcal{Y}(z) = z$, or;*
(ii) *There are $z \in \partial\mathbb{G}$ and $\alpha \in (0, 1)$ so that $z = \alpha\mathcal{Y}(z)$.*

Now, we recall fractal-fractional operators.

Definition 2 ([17]). *Let $a, b \in \mathbb{R}$ with $a < b$. Assume that a continuous real-valued function $\mathcal{V}$ is a fractal differentiable on (a, b) from the dimension $\varkappa_2$. Then the power-law type $(\varkappa_1, \varkappa_2)$-fractal-fractional derivative of $\mathcal{V}$ in the Riemann–Liouville sense is defined by*

$${}^{\mathbb{FFP}}\mathfrak{D}_{a,\mathrm{t}}^{\varkappa_1,\varkappa_2}\mathcal{V}(\mathrm{t}) = \frac{1}{\Gamma(n-\varkappa_1)}\frac{\mathrm{d}}{\mathrm{d}\mathrm{t}^{\varkappa_2}}\int_a^{\mathrm{t}} (\mathrm{t}-\mathrm{u})^{n-\varkappa_1-1}\mathcal{V}(\mathrm{u})\,\mathrm{d}\mathrm{u}, \quad (n-1 < \varkappa_1, \varkappa_2 \le n \in \mathbb{N}),$$

where $\mathrm{t} \in (a, b)$ and $\dfrac{\mathrm{d}\mathcal{V}(\mathrm{u})}{\mathrm{d}\mathrm{u}^{\varkappa_2}} = \lim_{\mathrm{t}\to\mathrm{u}} \dfrac{\mathcal{V}(\mathrm{t}) - \mathcal{V}(\mathrm{u})}{\mathrm{t}^{\varkappa_2} - \mathrm{u}^{\varkappa_2}}$ is the fractal derivative.

If $\varkappa_2 = 1$, then ${}^{\mathbb{FFP}}\mathfrak{D}_{a,t}^{\varkappa_1,\varkappa_2}$ reduces to the Riemann–Liouville fractional derivative ${}^{\mathbb{RLV}}\mathfrak{D}_{a,t}^{\varkappa_1}$ of order $\varkappa_1$.

Definition 3 ([17]). *Let $a, b \in \mathbb{R}$ with $a < b$. Assume that the real-valued function $\mathcal{V}$ is continuous on (a, b). The power-law type $(\varkappa_1, \varkappa_2)$-fractal-fractional integral of $\mathcal{V}$ is defined by*

$$ {}^{\mathbb{FFP}}\mathfrak{I}_{a,t}^{\varkappa_1,\varkappa_2}\mathcal{V}(t) = \frac{\varkappa_2}{\Gamma(\varkappa_1)} \int_a^t u^{\varkappa_2-1}(t-u)^{\varkappa_1-1}\mathcal{V}(u)\, du, \tag{1} $$

where $t \in (a, b)$.

3. Description of the Giving up Smoking Model

This section is devoted to introducing a new generalized version of the giving up smoking model conducted by Singh, Kumar, Al Qurashi, and Baleanu in [14]. The total population in this model is illustrated by $\mathcal{N}(t)$ at every time $t \in [0, T]$. This general class $\mathcal{N}(t)$ is divided into five subclasses; i.e., we have three types of smokers, such as potential, occasional, and heavy smokers denoted by $\mathcal{P}(t)$, $\mathcal{O}(t)$ and $\mathcal{H}(t)$, respectively. In addition, we have two other groups such as temporary quitters denoted by $\mathcal{Q}(t)$ and those smokers who quit permanently denoted by $\mathcal{R}(t)$. Therefore, $\mathcal{N}(t) = \mathcal{P}(t) + \mathcal{O}(t) + \mathcal{H}(t) + \mathcal{Q}(t) + \mathcal{R}(t)$. By the above assumptions, the mentioned model is designed by:

$$ \begin{cases} \dfrac{d\mathcal{P}(t)}{dt} = \upsilon - \vartheta\mathcal{P}(t) - \omega\mathcal{P}(t)\mathcal{O}(t), \\ \dfrac{d\mathcal{O}(t)}{dt} = -\vartheta\mathcal{O}(t) + \omega\mathcal{P}(t)\mathcal{O}(t) - \gamma\mathcal{O}(t)\mathcal{H}(t), \\ \dfrac{d\mathcal{H}(t)}{dt} = (-(\vartheta+\theta) + \gamma\mathcal{O}(t))\mathcal{H}(t) + \zeta\mathcal{Q}(t), \\ \dfrac{d\mathcal{Q}(t)}{dt} = -(\vartheta+\zeta)\mathcal{Q}(t) + \theta(1-q)\mathcal{H}(t), \\ \dfrac{d\mathcal{R}(t)}{dt} = -\vartheta\mathcal{R}(t) + q\theta\mathcal{H}(t). \end{cases} \tag{2} $$

In view of the widespread use of tobacco among teenagers and children coupled with the weakness of classical and generalized fractional operators in description of such phenomena, by considering the effect of fractal dimension and fractional order in the final result on modeling dynamical systems, the above model is extended by replacing the classical time-derivative with the generalized new hybrid $(\varkappa_1, \varkappa_2)$-fractal-fractional derivative as follows

$$ \begin{cases} {}^{\mathbb{FFP}}\mathfrak{D}_{0,t}^{\varkappa_1,\varkappa_2}\mathcal{P}(t) = \upsilon - \vartheta\mathcal{P}(t) - \omega\mathcal{P}(t)\mathcal{O}(t), \\ {}^{\mathbb{FFP}}\mathfrak{D}_{0,t}^{\varkappa_1,\varkappa_2}\mathcal{O}(t) = -\vartheta\mathcal{O}(t) + \omega\mathcal{P}(t)\mathcal{O}(t) - \gamma\mathcal{O}(t)\mathcal{H}(t), \\ {}^{\mathbb{FFP}}\mathfrak{D}_{0,t}^{\varkappa_1,\varkappa_2}\mathcal{H}(t) = (-(\vartheta+\theta) + \gamma\mathcal{O}(t))\mathcal{H}(t) + \zeta\mathcal{Q}(t), \\ {}^{\mathbb{FFP}}\mathfrak{D}_{0,t}^{\varkappa_1,\varkappa_2}\mathcal{Q}(t) = -(\vartheta+\zeta)\mathcal{Q}(t) + \theta(1-q)\mathcal{H}(t), \\ {}^{\mathbb{FFP}}\mathfrak{D}_{0,t}^{\varkappa_1,\varkappa_2}\mathcal{R}(t) = -\vartheta\mathcal{R}(t) + q\theta\mathcal{H}(t), \end{cases} \tag{3} $$

subject to initial conditions

$$ \mathcal{P}(0) = \mathcal{P}_0 \geq 0, \ \mathcal{O}(0) = \mathcal{O}_0 \geq 0, \ \mathcal{H}(0) = \mathcal{H}_0 \geq 0, $$
$$ \mathcal{Q}(0) = \mathcal{Q}_0 \geq 0, \ \mathcal{R}(0) = \mathcal{R}_0 \geq 0, $$

where ${}^{\mathbb{FFP}}\mathfrak{D}_{0,t}^{\varkappa_1,\varkappa_2}$ is the power-law type $(\varkappa_!, \varkappa_2)$-fractal-fractional derivative with $\varkappa_1, \varkappa_2 \in (0,1]$.

In (3), we have some non-negative parameters that we here aim to introduce:

(1) ω: the contact rate between the potential smokers and smokers who smoke occasionally;
(2) γ: the rate of contact between occasional smokers and heavy smokers;
(3) ζ: the rate at which temporary quitters return back to smoking;
(4) ϑ: the rate of natural death;
(5) θ: the rate of giving up smoking;
(6) $(1-q)$: (at a rate θ) the fraction of smokers who temporarily give up smoking;
(7) q: (at a rate θ) the remaining fraction of smokers who give up smoking forever;
(8) v: the rate of becoming a potential smoker.

The main point of difference of our contribution about the model derived in Ref. [14] is that the first equation in Ref. [14] is somehow confusing and ineffective. Therefore, one of our major contributions is to modify it with the constant influx of potential smokers.

4. Mathematical Analysis

In this section, the existence of unique solution, stability analysis for the fractal-fractional operator, equilibrium point, sensitivity analysis and asymptotic stability analysis are carried out.

4.1. Existence of Solutions

In real cases, the existence of such dynamical systems is an important question before every analysis and simulation. To answer such a question, we apply fixed point theory. We guarantee this existence in this section. For conducting a qualitative analysis, we consider the Banach space $\mathcal{X} = \mathbb{U}^5$, where $\mathbb{U} = C(\mathbb{J}, \mathbb{R})$, and the norm

$$\|\Lambda\|_{\mathcal{X}} = \|(\mathcal{P}, \mathcal{O}, \mathcal{H}, \mathcal{Q}, \mathcal{R})\|_{\mathcal{X}} = \max\{|\mathcal{P}(t)| + |\mathcal{O}(t)| + |\mathcal{H}(t)| + |\mathcal{Q}(t)| + |\mathcal{R}(t)| : \ t \in \mathbb{J}\}.$$

At first, the model (3) can be rewritten by follows

$$\begin{cases} \mathcal{V}_1(t, \mathcal{P}(t), \mathcal{O}(t), \mathcal{H}(t), \mathcal{Q}(t), \mathcal{R}(t)) = v - \vartheta\mathcal{P}(t) - \omega\mathcal{P}(t)\mathcal{O}(t), \\ \mathcal{V}_2(t, \mathcal{P}(t), \mathcal{O}(t), \mathcal{H}(t), \mathcal{Q}(t), \mathcal{R}(t)) = -\vartheta\mathcal{O}(t) + \omega\mathcal{P}(t)\mathcal{O}(t) - \gamma\mathcal{O}(t)\mathcal{H}(t), \\ \mathcal{V}_3(t, \mathcal{P}(t), \mathcal{O}(t), \mathcal{H}(t), \mathcal{Q}(t), \mathcal{R}(t)) = (-(\vartheta + \theta) + \gamma\mathcal{O}(t))\mathcal{H}(t) + \zeta\mathcal{Q}(t), \\ \mathcal{V}_4(t, \mathcal{P}(t), \mathcal{O}(t), \mathcal{H}(t), \mathcal{Q}(t), \mathcal{R}(t)) = -(\vartheta + \zeta)\mathcal{Q}(t) + \theta(1-q)\mathcal{H}(t), \\ \mathcal{V}_5(t, \mathcal{P}(t), \mathcal{O}(t), \mathcal{H}(t), \mathcal{Q}(t), \mathcal{R}(t)) = -\vartheta\mathcal{R}(t) + q\theta\mathcal{H}(t). \end{cases} \quad (4)$$

Hence, it becomes

$$\begin{cases} {}^{\mathbb{RLV}}\mathfrak{D}_{0,t}^{\varkappa_1}\mathcal{P}(t) = \varkappa_2 t^{\varkappa_2 - 1}\mathcal{V}_1(t, \mathcal{P}(t), \mathcal{O}(t), \mathcal{H}(t), \mathcal{Q}(t), \mathcal{R}(t)), \\ {}^{\mathbb{RLV}}\mathfrak{D}_{0,t}^{\varkappa_1}\mathcal{O}(t) = \varkappa_2 t^{\varkappa_2 - 1}\mathcal{V}_2(t, \mathcal{P}(t), \mathcal{O}(t), \mathcal{H}(t), \mathcal{Q}(t), \mathcal{R}(t)), \\ {}^{\mathbb{RLV}}\mathfrak{D}_{0,t}^{\varkappa_1}\mathcal{H}(t) = \varkappa_2 t^{\varkappa_2 - 1}\mathcal{V}_3(t, \mathcal{P}(t), \mathcal{O}(t), \mathcal{H}(t), \mathcal{Q}(t), \mathcal{R}(t)), \\ {}^{\mathbb{RLV}}\mathfrak{D}_{0,t}^{\varkappa_1}\mathcal{Q}(t) = \varkappa_2 t^{\varkappa_2 - 1}\mathcal{V}_4(t, \mathcal{P}(t), \mathcal{O}(t), \mathcal{H}(t), \mathcal{Q}(t), \mathcal{R}(t)), \\ {}^{\mathbb{RLV}}\mathfrak{D}_{0,t}^{\varkappa_1}\mathcal{R}(t) = \varkappa_2 t^{\varkappa_2 - 1}\mathcal{V}_5(t, \mathcal{P}(t), \mathcal{O}(t), \mathcal{H}(t), \mathcal{Q}(t), \mathcal{R}(t)). \end{cases} \quad (5)$$

By (5), we can write a mini-compact system of IVPs (3) as

$$\begin{cases} {}^{\mathbb{RLV}}\mathfrak{D}_{0,t}^{\varkappa_1}\Lambda(t) = \varkappa_2 t^{\varkappa_2-1}\mathcal{V}(t,\Lambda(t)), \quad \varkappa_1,\varkappa_2 \in (0,1], \\ \Lambda(0) = \Lambda_0, \end{cases} \tag{6}$$

where

$$\Lambda(t) = \big(\mathcal{P}(t), \mathcal{O}(t), \mathcal{H}(t), \mathcal{Q}(t), \mathcal{R}(t)\big)^T, \qquad \Lambda_0 = \big(\mathcal{P}_0, \mathcal{O}_0, \mathcal{H}_0, \mathcal{Q}_0, \mathcal{R}_0\big)^T, \tag{7}$$

and

$$\mathcal{V}(t,\Lambda(t)) = \begin{cases} \mathcal{V}_1(t,\mathcal{P}(t),\mathcal{O}(t),\mathcal{H}(t),\mathcal{Q}(t),\mathcal{R}(t)), \\ \mathcal{V}_2(t,\mathcal{P}(t),\mathcal{O}(t),\mathcal{H}(t),\mathcal{Q}(t),\mathcal{R}(t)), \\ \mathcal{V}_3(t,\mathcal{P}(t),\mathcal{O}(t),\mathcal{H}(t),\mathcal{Q}(t),\mathcal{R}(t)), \\ \mathcal{V}_4(t,\mathcal{P}(t),\mathcal{O}(t),\mathcal{H}(t),\mathcal{Q}(t),\mathcal{R}(t)), \\ \mathcal{V}_5(t,\mathcal{P}(t),\mathcal{O}(t),\mathcal{H}(t),\mathcal{Q}(t),\mathcal{R}(t)). \end{cases} \tag{8}$$

By properties of the hybrid $(\varkappa_1, \varkappa_2)$-fractal-fractional integral, the solution of the mini-compact system of IVP (6) is given by

$$\Lambda(t) = \Lambda(0) + \frac{\varkappa_2}{\Gamma(\varkappa_1)} \int_0^t u^{\varkappa_2-1}(t-u)^{\varkappa_1-1}\mathcal{V}(u,\Lambda(u))\,du. \tag{9}$$

Now, we extend the above compact $(\varkappa_1, \varkappa_2)$-fractal-fractional integral equation to a system of $(\varkappa_1, \varkappa_2)$-fractal-fractional integral equations as

$$\begin{cases} \mathcal{P}(t) = \mathcal{P}_0 + \frac{\varkappa_2}{\Gamma(\varkappa_1)} \int_0^t u^{\varkappa_2-1}(t-u)^{\varkappa_1-1}\mathcal{V}_1(u,\mathcal{P}(u),\mathcal{O}(u),\mathcal{H}(u),\mathcal{Q}(u),\mathcal{R}(u))\,du, \\ \mathcal{O}(t) = \mathcal{O}_0 + \frac{\varkappa_2}{\Gamma(\varkappa_1)} \int_0^t u^{\varkappa_2-1}(t-u)^{\varkappa_1-1}\mathcal{V}_2(u,\mathcal{P}(u),\mathcal{O}(u),\mathcal{H}(u),\mathcal{Q}(u),\mathcal{R}(u))\,du, \\ \mathcal{H}(t) = \mathcal{H}_0 + \frac{\varkappa_2}{\Gamma(\varkappa_1)} \int_0^t u^{\varkappa_2-1}(t-u)^{\varkappa_1-1}\mathcal{V}_3(u,\mathcal{P}(u),\mathcal{O}(u),\mathcal{H}(u),\mathcal{Q}(u),\mathcal{R}(u))\,du, \\ \mathcal{Q}(t) = \mathcal{Q}_0 + \frac{\varkappa_2}{\Gamma(\varkappa_1)} \int_0^t u^{\varkappa_2-1}(t-u)^{\varkappa_1-1}\mathcal{V}_4(u,\mathcal{P}(u),\mathcal{O}(u),\mathcal{H}(u),\mathcal{Q}(u),\mathcal{R}(u))\,du, \\ \mathcal{R}(t) = \mathcal{R}_0 + \frac{\varkappa_2}{\Gamma(\varkappa_1)} \int_0^t u^{\varkappa_2-1}(t-u)^{\varkappa_1-1}\mathcal{V}_5(u,\mathcal{P}(u),\mathcal{O}(u),\mathcal{H}(u),\mathcal{Q}(u),\mathcal{R}(u))\,du. \end{cases} \tag{10}$$

Our aim in this step is to transform the problem (3) into a fixed point problem. Define $\mathcal{Y} : \mathcal{X} \to \mathcal{X}$ by

$$\mathcal{Y}(\Lambda(t)) = \Lambda(0) + \frac{\varkappa_2}{\Gamma(\varkappa_1)} \int_0^t u^{\varkappa_2-1}(t-u)^{\varkappa_1-1}\mathcal{V}(u,\Lambda(u))\,du, \tag{11}$$

for each $t \in \mathbb{J}$ and $\Lambda \in \mathcal{X}$.

Theorem 3. *There are $\kappa : \mathbb{R} \times \mathbb{R} \to \mathbb{R}$, $\mathcal{V} \in C(\mathbb{J} \times \mathcal{X}, \mathcal{X})$ and an increasing function $\phi \in \Phi$ such that*
$(\mathfrak{H}_1)$ *for any $\Lambda_1, \Lambda_2 \in \mathcal{X}$ and $t \in \mathbb{J}$,*

$$\big|\mathcal{V}(t,\Lambda_1(t)) - \mathcal{V}(t,\Lambda_2(t))\big| \le \delta\phi(|\Lambda_1(t) - \Lambda_2(t)|),$$

where $\delta = \dfrac{\Gamma(\varkappa_2 + \varkappa_1)}{T^{\varkappa_2+\varkappa_1-1}\Gamma(\varkappa_2+1)}$, *and* $\kappa(\Lambda_1(t), \Lambda_2(t)) \geq 0$.
$(\mathfrak{H}_2)$ *There is* $\Lambda_0 \in \mathcal{X}$ *such that for all* $t \in \mathbb{J}$,

$$\kappa(\Lambda_0(t), \mathcal{Y}(\Lambda_0(t))) \geq 0,$$

and the inequality

$$\kappa(\Lambda_1(t), \Lambda_2(t)) \geq 0,$$

implies that

$$\kappa(\mathcal{Y}(\Lambda_1(t)), \mathcal{Y}(\Lambda_2(t))) \geq 0,$$

for any $\Lambda_1, \Lambda_2 \in \mathcal{X}$ *and* $t \in \mathbb{J}$.
$(\mathfrak{H}_3)$ *For every sequence* $\{\Lambda_n\}_{n\geq 1}$ *in* $\mathcal{X}$ *converging to* Λ *and for each* $t \in \mathbb{J}$,

$$\kappa(\Lambda_n(t), \Lambda_{n+1}(t)) \geq 0,$$

gives

$$\kappa(\Lambda_n(t), \Lambda(t)) \geq 0.$$

Then, there is at least a solution for the fractal-fractional hybrid model of giving up smoking (3).

Proof. Let Λ_1 and Λ_2 belong to $\mathcal{X}$ with $\kappa(\Lambda_1(t), \Lambda_2(t)) \geq 0$ for each $t \in \mathbb{J}$. In this case, the Euler Beta function gives

$$\begin{aligned}
|\mathcal{Y}(\Lambda_1(t)) - \mathcal{Y}(\Lambda_2(t))| &\leq \frac{\varkappa_2}{\Gamma(\varkappa_1)} \int_0^t u^{\varkappa_2-1}(t-u)^{\varkappa_1-1} |\mathcal{V}(u, \Lambda_1(u)) - \mathcal{V}(u, \Lambda_2(u))| du \\
&\leq \frac{\varkappa_2 \delta}{\Gamma(\varkappa_1)} \int_0^t u^{\varkappa_2-1}(t-u)^{\varkappa_1-1} \phi(|\Lambda_1(u) - \Lambda_2(u)|) du \\
&\leq \frac{\varkappa_2 \delta \phi(\|\Lambda_1 - \Lambda_2\|_{\mathcal{X}})}{\Gamma(\varkappa_1)} \int_0^t u^{\varkappa_2-1}(t-u)^{\varkappa_1-1} du \\
&\leq \frac{\varkappa_2 \delta T^{\varkappa_2+\varkappa_1-1} \mathcal{B}(\varkappa_2, \varkappa_1)}{\Gamma(\varkappa_1)} \phi(\|\Lambda_1 - \Lambda_2\|_{\mathcal{X}}) \\
&= \phi(\|\Lambda_1 - \Lambda_2\|_{\mathcal{X}}).
\end{aligned}$$

Thus,

$$\|\mathcal{Y}(\Lambda_1) - \mathcal{Y}(\Lambda_2)\|_{\mathcal{X}} \leq \phi(\|\Lambda_1 - \Lambda_2\|_{\mathcal{X}}).$$

Now, for each $\Lambda_1, \Lambda_2 \in \mathcal{X}$, we define a function $\psi : \mathcal{X} \times \mathcal{X} \to [0, +\infty)$ as

$$\psi(\Lambda_1, \Lambda_2) = \begin{cases} 1 & \text{if } \kappa(\Lambda_1(t), \Lambda_2(t)) \geq 0, \\ 0 & \text{otherwise,} \end{cases}$$

Then, for every $\Lambda_1, \Lambda_2 \in \mathcal{X}$, we will obtain

$$\psi(\Lambda_1, \Lambda_2) \mathbf{d}(\mathcal{Y}(\Lambda_1), \mathcal{Y}(\Lambda_2)) \leq \phi(\mathbf{d}(\Lambda_1, \Lambda_2)).$$

Hence, $\mathcal{Y}$ is an $\psi - \phi-$contraction. To show that $\mathcal{Y}$ is $\psi-$admissible, let $\Lambda_1, \Lambda_2 \in \mathcal{X}$ be arbitrary with $\psi(\Lambda_1, \Lambda_2) \geq 1$. From property of ψ, it yields

$$\kappa(\Lambda_1(t), \Lambda_2(t)) \geq 0.$$

Then, the condition $(\mathfrak{H}_2)$ gives

$$\kappa(\mathcal{Y}(\Lambda_1(t)), \mathcal{Y}(\Lambda_2(t))) \geq 0.$$

Once again, by property of ψ, we follow that $\psi(\mathcal{Y}(\Lambda_1), \mathcal{Y}(\Lambda_2)) \geq 1$. Therefore, $\mathcal{Y}$ is $\psi-$admissible on $\mathcal{X}$.

The condition $(\mathfrak{H}_2)$ ensures the existence of $\Lambda_0 \in \mathcal{X}$, which satisfies

$$\kappa(\Lambda_0(\mathrm{t}), \mathcal{Y}(\Lambda_0(\mathrm{t}))) \geq 0,$$

for each $\mathrm{t} \in \mathbb{J}$. Evidently, $\psi(\Lambda_0, \mathcal{Y}(\Lambda_0)) \geq 1$,

Now, suppose that $\{\Lambda_n\}_{n\geq 1}$ is a sequence defined in $\mathcal{X}$ converging to Λ and for all $n \geq 1$, $\psi(\Lambda_n, \Lambda_{n+1}) \geq 1$. From the property of ψ, we obtain

$$\kappa(\Lambda_n(\mathrm{t}), \Lambda_{n+1}(\mathrm{t})) \geq 0.$$

Thus, the condition $(\mathfrak{C}_3)$ gives us that

$$\kappa(\Lambda_n(\mathrm{t}), \Lambda(\mathrm{t})) \geq 0.$$

This implies $\psi(\Lambda_n, \Lambda) \geq 1$ for all $n \geq 1$. Thus the item (3) of Theorem 1 is valid. Therefore, Theorem 1 is valid. In consequence, $\mathcal{Y}$ has a fixed point $\Lambda^* \in \mathcal{X}$. Hence $\Lambda^* = (\mathcal{P}^*, \mathcal{O}^*, \mathcal{H}^*, \mathcal{Q}^*, \mathcal{R}^*)^T$ is a solution of the fractal-fractional model of giving up smoking (3). □

Theorem 4. *Let $\mathcal{V} \in C(\mathbb{J} \times \mathcal{X}, \mathcal{X})$.*

$(\mathcal{D}_1)$ There are $K \in L^1(\mathbb{J}, [0, +\infty))$ and an increasing function $B \in C([0, +\infty), (0, +\infty))$ provided that

$$|B(\mathrm{t}, \Lambda(\mathrm{t}))| \leq K(\mathrm{t}) B(|\Lambda(\mathrm{t})|), \ \forall \mathrm{t} \in \mathbb{J}, \ \text{and} \ \Lambda \in \mathcal{X};$$

$(\mathcal{D}_2)$ There is $b > 0$ such that

$$b > \Lambda_0 + \frac{T^{\varkappa_2+\varkappa_1-1}\Gamma(\varkappa_2+1)}{\Gamma(\varkappa_2+\varkappa_1)} K_0^* B(b), \tag{12}$$

where $K_0^* = \sup\limits_{\mathrm{t}\in\mathbb{J}} |K(\mathrm{t})|$.

Then, there is a solution for the fractal-fractional model of giving up smoking (3).

Proof. To complete the proof, we consider $\mathcal{Y}$ defined in (11), and the closed ball

$$\mathbf{N}_L = \{\Lambda \in \mathcal{X} : \ \|\Lambda\|_{\mathcal{X}} \leq L\}.$$

The continuity of $\mathcal{V}$ implies that of $\mathcal{Y}$. Now, by $(\mathcal{D}_1)$ and for $\Lambda \in \mathbf{N}_L$, we estimate

$$\begin{aligned} |\mathcal{Y}(\Lambda(\mathrm{t}))| &\leq |\Lambda(0)| + \frac{\varkappa_2}{\Gamma(\varkappa_1)} \int_0^{\mathrm{t}} \mathrm{u}^{\varkappa_2-1}(\mathrm{t}-\mathrm{u})^{\varkappa_1-1} |\mathcal{V}(\mathrm{u}, \Lambda(\mathrm{u}))| d\mathrm{u} \\ &\leq \Lambda_0 + \frac{\varkappa_2}{\Gamma(\varkappa_1)} \int_0^{\mathrm{t}} \mathrm{u}^{\varkappa_2-1}(\mathrm{t}-\mathrm{u})^{\varkappa_1-1} K(\mathrm{u}) B(|\Lambda(\mathrm{u})|) d\mathrm{u} \\ &\leq \Lambda_0 + \frac{\varkappa_2 T^{\varkappa_2+\varkappa_1-1}\mathfrak{B}(\varkappa_2, \varkappa_1)}{\Gamma(\varkappa_1)} K_0^* B(\|\Lambda\|_{\mathcal{X}}) \\ &\leq \Lambda_0 + \frac{T^{\varkappa_2+\varkappa_1-1}\Gamma(\varkappa_2+1)}{\Gamma(\varkappa_2+\varkappa_1)} K_0^* B(L). \end{aligned}$$

Consequently, we get

$$\|\mathcal{Y}\Lambda\|_{\mathcal{X}} \leq \Lambda_0 + \frac{T^{\varkappa_2+\varkappa_1-1}\Gamma(\varkappa_2+1)}{\Gamma(\varkappa_2+\varkappa_1)} K_0^* B(L) < +\infty. \tag{13}$$

Thus, $\mathcal{Y}$ is uniformly bounded on $\mathcal{X}$. Next, we choose arbitrarily $t, \tau \in [0, T]$ with $t < \tau$ and $\Lambda \in \mathbf{N}_L$. By

$$\mathcal{V}^* = \sup_{(t,\Lambda)\in\mathbb{J}\times\mathbf{N}_L} |\mathcal{V}(t, \Lambda(t))| < +\infty,$$

we find

$$\begin{aligned} |\mathcal{Y}(\Lambda(\tau)) - \mathcal{Y}(\Lambda(t))| &= \left| \frac{\varkappa_2}{\Gamma(\varkappa_1)} \int_0^\tau u^{\varkappa_2-1}(t-u)^{\varkappa_1-1}\mathcal{V}(u,\Lambda(u))du \right. \\ &\quad \left. - \frac{\varkappa_2}{\Gamma(\varkappa_1)} \int_0^t u^{\varkappa_2-1}(t-u)^{\varkappa_1-1}\mathcal{V}(u,\Lambda(u))du \right| \\ &\leq \frac{\varkappa_2 \mathcal{V}^*}{\Gamma(\varkappa_1)} \left| \int_0^\tau u^{\varkappa_2-1}(t-u)^{\varkappa_1-1}du - \int_0^t u^{\varkappa_2-1}(t-u)^{\varkappa_1-1}du \right| \\ &\leq \frac{\varkappa_2 \mathcal{V}^* B(\varkappa_2,\varkappa_1)}{\Gamma(\varkappa_1)} \left(\tau^{\varkappa_2+\varkappa_1-1} - t^{\varkappa_2+\varkappa_1-1} \right) \\ &= \frac{\mathcal{V}^*\Gamma(\varkappa_2+1)}{\Gamma(\varkappa_2+\varkappa_1)} \left(\tau^{\varkappa_2+\varkappa_1-1} - t^{\varkappa_2+\varkappa_1-1} \right). \end{aligned} \tag{14}$$

Note that from the above computations, the right-hand side of (14) is not dependent on Λ and also converges to 0 as $t \to \tau$. So

$$\|\mathcal{Y}(\Lambda(\tau)) - \mathcal{Y}(\Lambda(t))\|_{\mathcal{X}} \to 0,$$

as $t \to \tau$, which shows the equicontinuity of $\mathcal{Y}$. By referring to the Arzelà–Ascoli theorem, $\mathcal{Y}$ is compact on $\mathbf{N}_L$. Now, Theorem 2 is valid on $\mathcal{Y}$. We have one of the consequences (i) or (ii). We know that from $(\mathcal{D}_2)$, there exists $b > 0$ such that

$$\Lambda_0 + \frac{T^{\varkappa_2+\varkappa_1-1}\Gamma(\varkappa_2+1)}{\Gamma(\varkappa_2+\varkappa_1)} K_0^* B(b) < b. \tag{15}$$

Then, we consider

$$\mathbb{G} = \{\Lambda \in \mathcal{X} : \ \|\Lambda\|_{\mathcal{X}} < b\}.$$

By assuming the existence of $\Lambda \in \partial\mathbb{G}$ and $\alpha \in (0,1)$ such that $\Lambda = \alpha\mathcal{Y}(\Lambda)$, we can write

$$\begin{aligned} b = \|\Lambda\|_{\mathcal{X}} = \alpha\|\mathcal{Y}\Lambda\|_{\mathcal{X}} &< \Lambda_0 + \frac{T^{\varkappa_2+\varkappa_1-1}\Gamma(\varkappa_2+1)}{\Gamma(\varkappa_2+\varkappa_1)} K_0^* B(\|\Lambda\|_{\mathcal{X}}) \\ &< \Lambda_0 + \frac{T^{\varkappa_2+\varkappa_1-1}\Gamma(\varkappa_2+1)}{\Gamma(\varkappa_2+\varkappa_1)} K_0^* B(b) < b, \end{aligned}$$

by (15). However, this is impossible. Thus (ii) does not hold and by Theorem 2, $\mathcal{Y}$ has a fixed point in $\overline{\mathbb{G}}$ which is considered as a solution of the fractal-fractional model of giving up smoking (3). □

4.2. Unique Solution

To prove the uniqueness of the solution in the model of giving up smoking (3), we use the Lipschitz property under the functions $\mathcal{V}_i, (i = 1, \dots 5)$ defined by (4).

Lemma 1. *Let the functions $\mathcal{P}, \mathcal{O}, \mathcal{H}, \mathcal{Q}, \mathcal{R}, \mathcal{P}^*, \mathcal{O}^*, \mathcal{H}^*, \mathcal{Q}^*, \mathcal{R}^* \in \mathbb{U} = C(\mathbb{J}, \mathbb{R})$ and assume that* $(\mathcal{P}_1)$ $\|\mathcal{P}\| \leq \gamma_1, \|\mathcal{O}\| \leq \gamma_2, \|\mathcal{H}\| \leq \gamma_3, \|\mathcal{Q}\| \leq \gamma_4, \|\mathcal{R}\| \leq \gamma_5$ *for some positive constants* $\gamma_1, \gamma_2, \gamma_3, \gamma_4, \gamma_5$.

Then, the functions $\mathcal{V}_1, \mathcal{V}_2, \mathcal{V}_3, \mathcal{V}_4, \mathcal{V}_5$ defined by (4) satisfy the Lipschitz property with respect to the corresponding components if

$$\delta_1 = \vartheta + \omega\gamma_2, \quad \delta_2 = \vartheta + \omega\gamma_1 + \gamma\gamma_3,$$

$$\delta_3 = \vartheta + \theta + \gamma\gamma_2, \quad \delta_4 = \vartheta + \zeta, \quad \delta_5 = \vartheta. \tag{16}$$

Proof. We begin with function $\mathcal{V}_1$. For other solution functions, the proof is similar. For any functions $\mathcal{P}, \mathcal{P}^* \in \mathbb{U} = C(\mathbb{J}, \mathbb{R})$, we get

$$\begin{aligned} & \left\| \mathcal{V}_1\big(t, \mathcal{P}(t), \mathcal{O}(t), \mathcal{H}(t), \mathcal{Q}(t), \mathcal{R}(t)\big) - \mathcal{V}_1\big(t, \mathcal{P}^*(t), \mathcal{O}^*(t), \mathcal{H}^*(t), \mathcal{Q}^*(t), \mathcal{R}^*(t)\big) \right\| \\ = & \left\| \big(\vartheta - \vartheta\mathcal{P}(t) - \omega\mathcal{P}(t)\mathcal{O}(t)\big) - \big(\vartheta - \vartheta\mathcal{P}^*(t) - \omega\mathcal{P}^*(t)\mathcal{O}(t)\big) \right\| \\ \leq & \ \big(\vartheta + \omega\|\mathcal{O}(t)\|\big)\|\mathcal{P}(t) - \mathcal{P}^*(t)\| \\ \leq & \ \big(\vartheta + \omega\gamma_2\|\big)\|\mathcal{P}(t) - \mathcal{P}^*(t)\| \\ = & \ \delta_1\|\mathcal{P}(t) - \mathcal{P}^*(t)\|. \end{aligned}$$

This shows that $\mathcal{V}_1$ is a Lipschitz function with respect to $\mathcal{P}$ with the Lipschitz constant $\delta_1 > 0$. By continuing similar proofs, we see that the functions $\mathcal{V}_2, \mathcal{V}_3, \mathcal{V}_4, \mathcal{V}_5$ are Lipschitiz with respect to the corresponding components with the Lipschitz constants $\delta_2, \delta_3, \delta_4, \delta_5 > 0$, respectively. □

Theorem 5. *By considering the condition* $(\mathcal{P}_1)$*, the fractal-fractional model of giving up smoking* (3) *has a unique solution if*

$$\frac{T^{\varkappa_2+\varkappa_1-1}\Gamma(\varkappa_2+1)}{\Gamma(\varkappa_2+\varkappa_1)}\delta_i < 1, \quad i \in \{1, \dots, 5\}. \tag{17}$$

Proof. Let us consider the fact that the conclusion is not to be held. That is, there exists another solution. Assume that $(\mathcal{P}^*, \mathcal{O}^*, \mathcal{H}^*, \mathcal{Q}^*, \mathcal{R}^*)$ is another solution with initial condition $(\mathcal{P}_0, \mathcal{O}_0, \mathcal{H}_0, \mathcal{Q}_0, \mathcal{R}_0)$ such that by (10), we have

$$\begin{aligned} \mathcal{P}^*(t) &= \mathcal{P}_0 + \frac{\varkappa_2}{\Gamma(\varkappa_1)}\int_0^t u^{\varkappa_2-1}(t-u)^{\varkappa_1-1}\mathcal{V}_1\big(u, \mathcal{P}^*(u), \mathcal{O}^*(u), \mathcal{H}^*(u), \mathcal{Q}^*(u), \mathcal{R}^*(u)\big)\,du, \\ \mathcal{O}^*(t) &= \mathcal{O}_0 + \frac{\varkappa_2}{\Gamma(\varkappa_1)}\int_0^t u^{\varkappa_2-1}(t-u)^{\varkappa_1-1}\mathcal{V}_2\big(u, \mathcal{P}^*(u), \mathcal{O}^*(u), \mathcal{H}^*(u), \mathcal{Q}^*(u), \mathcal{R}^*(u)\big)\,du, \\ \mathcal{H}^*(t) &= \mathcal{H}_0 + \frac{\varkappa_2}{\Gamma(\varkappa_1)}\int_0^t u^{\varkappa_2-1}(t-u)^{\varkappa_1-1}\mathcal{V}_3\big(u, \mathcal{P}^*(u), \mathcal{O}^*(u), \mathcal{H}^*(u), \mathcal{Q}^*(u), \mathcal{R}^*(u)\big)\,du, \\ \mathcal{Q}^*(t) &= \mathcal{Q}_0 + \frac{\varkappa_2}{\Gamma(\varkappa_1)}\int_0^t u^{\varkappa_2-1}(t-u)^{\varkappa_1-1}\mathcal{V}_4\big(u, \mathcal{P}^*(u), \mathcal{O}^*(u), \mathcal{H}^*(u), \mathcal{Q}^*(u), \mathcal{R}^*(u)\big)\,du, \\ \mathcal{R}^*(t) &= \mathcal{R}_0 + \frac{\varkappa_2}{\Gamma(\varkappa_1)}\int_0^t u^{\varkappa_2-1}(t-u)^{\varkappa_1-1}\mathcal{V}_5\big(u, \mathcal{P}^*(u), \mathcal{O}^*(u), \mathcal{H}^*(u), \mathcal{Q}^*(u), \mathcal{R}^*(u)\big)\,du. \end{aligned}$$

Now, we can estimate

$$\begin{aligned} \big|\mathcal{P}(t) - \mathcal{P}^*(t)\big| &\leq \frac{\varkappa_2}{\Gamma(\varkappa_1)}\int_0^t u^{\varkappa_2-1}(t-u)^{\varkappa_1-1}\Big|\mathcal{V}_1\big(u, \mathcal{P}(u), \mathcal{O}(u), \mathcal{H}(u), \mathcal{Q}(u), \mathcal{R}(u)\big) \\ &\quad -\mathcal{V}_1\big(u, \mathcal{P}^*(u), \mathcal{O}^*(u), \mathcal{H}^*(u), \mathcal{Q}^*(u), \mathcal{R}^*(u)\big)\Big|\,du \\ &\leq \frac{\varkappa_2}{\Gamma(\varkappa_1)}\delta_1\|\mathcal{P} - \mathcal{P}^*\|\int_0^t u^{\varkappa_2-1}(t-u)^{\varkappa_1-1}\,du \\ &\leq \frac{T^{\varkappa_2+\varkappa_1-1}\Gamma(\varkappa_2+1)}{\Gamma(\varkappa_2+\varkappa_1)}\delta_1\|\mathcal{P} - \mathcal{P}^*\|. \end{aligned}$$

This gives

$$\left[1 - \frac{T^{\varkappa_2+\varkappa_1-1}\Gamma(\varkappa_2+1)}{\Gamma(\varkappa_2+\varkappa_1)}\delta_1\right]\|\mathcal{P} - \mathcal{P}^*\| \leq 0.$$

Then from (17), it follows that $\|\mathcal{P} - \mathcal{P}^*\| = 0$, and accordingly $\mathcal{P} = \mathcal{P}^*$. Similarly, we get

$$\left[1 - \frac{T^{\varkappa_2+\varkappa_1-1}\Gamma(\varkappa_2+1)}{\Gamma(\varkappa_2+\varkappa_1)}\delta_2\right]\|\mathcal{O} - \mathcal{O}^*\| \leq 0,$$

which gives that $\|\mathcal{O} - \mathcal{O}^*\| = 0$, and so $\mathcal{O} = \mathcal{O}^*$. By the same arguments, we obtain

$$\left[1 - \frac{T^{\varkappa_2+\varkappa_1-1}\Gamma(\varkappa_2+1)}{\Gamma(\varkappa_2+\varkappa_1)}\delta_3\right]\|\mathcal{H}_-\mathcal{H}^*\| \leq 0.$$

Therefore, $\|\mathcal{H} - \mathcal{H}^*\| = 0$, and so $\mathcal{H} = \mathcal{H}^*$. In a similar way, we immediately get

$$\left[1 - \frac{T^{\varkappa_2+\varkappa_1-1}\Gamma(\varkappa_2+1)}{\Gamma(\varkappa_2+\varkappa_1)}\delta_4\right]\|\mathcal{Q} - \mathcal{Q}^*\| \leq 0,$$

and

$$\left[1 - \frac{T^{\varkappa_2+\varkappa_1-1}\Gamma(\varkappa_2+1)}{\Gamma(\varkappa_2+\varkappa_1)}\delta_5\right]\|\mathcal{R} - \mathcal{R}^*\| \leq 0,$$

The last two inequalities give $\|\mathcal{Q} - \mathcal{Q}^*\| = 0$ and $\|\mathcal{R} - \mathcal{R}^*\| = 0$, respectively. Thus, $\mathcal{Q} = \mathcal{Q}^*$ and $\mathcal{R} = \mathcal{R}^*$. Consequently, we find that

$$(\mathcal{P}, \mathcal{O}, \mathcal{H}, \mathcal{Q}, \mathcal{R}) = (\mathcal{P}^*, \mathcal{O}^*, \mathcal{H}^*, \mathcal{Q}^*, \mathcal{R}^*).$$

This shows that the fractal-fractional model of giving up smoking (3) has a unique solution. □

4.3. Stability Criterion

In this section, we aim to study the stability property based on the definition of Ulam–Hyers. This definition has applicable significance since it states that if we are studying an Ulam–Hyers stable system then we do not have to obtain the exact solution. Therefore, by proving the stability of the solutions of the given system, we can confidently focus on its approximate solutions in the next sections. More precisely, we are here to study the stability property for solutions of the fractal-fractional model of giving up smoking (3). The main focus is on the Ulam–Hyers and Ulam–Hyers–Rassias stability. For more information, we refer to Refs. [32,33].

Definition 4. *The fractal-fractional model of of giving up smoking (3) is Ulam–Hyers stable if there are real constants $\mathbb{M}_{\mathcal{V}_i} > 0$, $i \in \{1, \ldots, 5\}$ such that for all $L_i > 0$ and for all $(\mathcal{P}^*, \mathcal{O}^*, \mathcal{H}^*, \mathcal{Q}^*, \mathcal{R}^*) \in \mathcal{X}$ satisfying*

$$\begin{cases} \left|{}^{\mathbb{FFP}}\mathfrak{D}_{0,t}^{\varkappa_1,\varkappa_2}\mathcal{P}^*(t) - \mathcal{V}_1(t, \mathcal{P}^*(t), \mathcal{O}^*(t), \mathcal{H}^*(t), \mathcal{Q}^*(t), \mathcal{R}^*(t))\right| < L_1, \\ \left|{}^{\mathbb{FFP}}\mathfrak{D}_{0,t}^{\varkappa_1,\varkappa_2}\mathcal{O}^*(t) - \mathcal{V}_2(t, \mathcal{P}^*(t), \mathcal{O}^*(t), \mathcal{H}^*(t), \mathcal{Q}^*(t), \mathcal{R}^*(t))\right| < L_2, \\ \left|{}^{\mathbb{FFP}}\mathfrak{D}_{0,t}^{\varkappa_1,\varkappa_2}\mathcal{H}^*(t) - \mathcal{V}_3(t, \mathcal{P}^*(t), \mathcal{O}^*(t), \mathcal{H}^*(t), \mathcal{Q}^*(t), \mathcal{R}^*(t))\right| < L_3, \\ \left|{}^{\mathbb{FFP}}\mathfrak{D}_{0,t}^{\varkappa_1,\varkappa_2}\mathcal{Q}^*(t) - \mathcal{V}_4(t, \mathcal{P}^*(t), \mathcal{O}^*(t), \mathcal{H}^*(t), \mathcal{Q}^*(t), \mathcal{R}^*(t))\right| < L_4, \\ \left|{}^{\mathbb{FFP}}\mathfrak{D}_{0,t}^{\varkappa_1,\varkappa_2}\mathcal{R}^*(t) - \mathcal{V}_5(t, \mathcal{P}^*(t), \mathcal{O}^*(t), \mathcal{H}^*(t), \mathcal{Q}^*(t), \mathcal{R}^*(t))\right| < L_5, \end{cases} \tag{18}$$

there is $(\mathcal{P}, \mathcal{O}, \mathcal{H}, \mathcal{Q}, \mathcal{R}) \in \mathcal{X}$ *satisfying the fractal-fractional hybrid model of giving up smoking* (3) *such that*

$$\begin{cases} \left|\mathcal{P}^*(t) - \mathcal{P}(t)\right| \leq \mathbb{M}_{\mathcal{V}_1} L_1, \\ \left|\mathcal{O}^*(t) - \mathcal{O}(t)\right| \leq \mathbb{M}_{\mathcal{V}_2} L_2, \\ \left|\mathcal{H}^*(t) - \mathcal{H}(t)\right| \leq \mathbb{M}_{\mathcal{V}_3} L_3, \\ \left|\mathcal{Q}^*(t) - \mathcal{Q}(t)\right| \leq \mathbb{M}_{\mathcal{V}_4} L_4, \\ \left|\mathcal{R}^*(t) - \mathcal{R}(t)\right| \leq \mathbb{M}_{\mathcal{V}_5} L_5, \quad \forall t \in \mathbb{J}. \end{cases} \tag{19}$$

Definition 5. *The fractal-fractional model of giving up smoking* (3) *is generalized Ulam–Hyers stable if there are real constants* $\mathbb{M}_{\mathcal{V}_i} \in C(\mathbb{R}^+, \mathbb{R}^+)$, $(i \in \{1, \ldots, 5\})$ *with* $\mathbb{M}_{\mathcal{V}_i}(0) = 0$ *such that for all* $L_i > 0$ *and for all* $(\mathcal{P}^*, \mathcal{O}^*, \mathcal{H}^*, \mathcal{Q}^*, \mathcal{R}^*) \in \mathcal{X}$ *satisfying* (18), *there is* $(\mathcal{P}, \mathcal{O}, \mathcal{H}, \mathcal{Q}, \mathcal{R}) \in \mathcal{X}$ *as a solution of the fractal-fractional hybrid model of giving up smoking* (3) *such that*

$$\begin{cases} \left|\mathcal{P}^*(t) - \mathcal{P}(t)\right| \leq \mathbb{M}_{\mathcal{V}_1}(L_1), & \left|\mathcal{O}^*(t) - \mathcal{O}(t)\right| \leq \mathbb{M}_{\mathcal{V}_2}(L_2), \\ \left|\mathcal{H}^*(t) - \mathcal{H}(t)\right| \leq \mathbb{M}_{\mathcal{V}_3}(L_3), & \left|\mathcal{Q}^*(t) - \mathcal{Q}(t)\right| \leq \mathbb{M}_{\mathcal{V}_4}(L_4), \\ \left|\mathcal{R}^*(t) - \mathcal{R}(t)\right| \leq \mathbb{M}_{\mathcal{V}_5}(L_5), \quad \forall t \in \mathbb{J}. \end{cases}$$

Note that Definition 4 is obtained from Definition 5.

Remark 1. *Notice that* $(\mathcal{P}^*, \mathcal{O}^*, \mathcal{H}^*, \mathcal{Q}^*, \mathcal{R}^*) \in \mathcal{X}$ *is called a solution for inequalities* (4) *if and only if there are* $\hbar_1, \hbar_2, \hbar_3, \hbar_4, \hbar_5 \in C([0, T], \mathbb{R})$ *(depending on* $\mathcal{P}^*, \mathcal{O}^*, \mathcal{H}^*, \mathcal{Q}^*, \mathcal{R}^*$*, respectively) so that for each* $t \in \mathbb{J}$,
(i) $|\hbar_i(t)| < L_i$, $(i \in \{1, \ldots, 5\})$,
(ii) We have

$$\begin{cases} {}^{\mathbb{FFP}}\mathfrak{D}_{0,t}^{\varkappa_1,\varkappa_2}\mathcal{P}^*(t) = \mathcal{V}_1(t, \mathcal{P}^*(t), \mathcal{O}^*(t), \mathcal{H}^*(t), \mathcal{Q}^*(t), \mathcal{R}^*(t)) + \hbar_1(t), \\ {}^{\mathbb{FFP}}\mathfrak{D}_{0,t}^{\varkappa_1,\varkappa_2}\mathcal{O}^*(t) = \mathcal{V}_2(t, \mathcal{P}^*(t), \mathcal{O}^*(t), \mathcal{H}^*(t), \mathcal{Q}^*(t), \mathcal{R}^*(t)) + \hbar_2(t), \\ {}^{\mathbb{FFP}}\mathfrak{D}_{0,t}^{\varkappa_1,\varkappa_2}\mathcal{H}^*(t) = \mathcal{V}_3(t, \mathcal{P}^*(t), \mathcal{O}^*(t), \mathcal{H}^*(t), \mathcal{Q}^*(t), \mathcal{R}^*(t)) + \hbar_3(t), \\ {}^{\mathbb{FFP}}\mathfrak{D}_{0,t}^{\varkappa_1,\varkappa_2}\mathcal{Q}^*(t) = \mathcal{V}_4(t, \mathcal{P}^*(t), \mathcal{O}^*(t), \mathcal{H}^*(t), \mathcal{Q}^*(t), \mathcal{R}^*(t)) + \hbar_4(t), \\ {}^{\mathbb{FFP}}\mathfrak{D}_{0,t}^{\varkappa_1,\varkappa_2}\mathcal{R}^*(t) = \mathcal{V}_5(t, \mathcal{P}^*(t), \mathcal{O}^*(t), \mathcal{H}^*(t), \mathcal{Q}^*(t), \mathcal{R}^*(t)) + \hbar_5(t). \end{cases}$$

Definition 6. *The fractal-fractional model of giving up smoking* (3) *is Ulam–Hyers–Rassias stable with respect to the functions* β_i, $(i \in \{1, \ldots, 5\})$, *if there are constants* $0 < \mathbb{M}_{(\mathcal{V}_i, \beta_i)} \in \mathbb{R}$ *so that for each* $L_i > 0$ *and for each* $(\mathcal{P}^*, \mathcal{O}^*, \mathcal{H}^*, \mathcal{Q}^*, \mathcal{R}^*) \in \mathcal{X}$ *satisfying*

$$\begin{cases} \left|{}^{\mathbb{FFP}}\mathfrak{D}_{0,t}^{\varkappa_1,\varkappa_2}\mathcal{P}^*(t) - \mathcal{V}_1(t, \mathcal{P}^*(t), \mathcal{O}^*(t), \mathcal{H}^*(t), \mathcal{Q}^*(t), \mathcal{R}^*(t))\right| < L_1\beta_1(t), \\ \left|{}^{\mathbb{FFP}}\mathfrak{D}_{0,t}^{\varkappa_1,\varkappa_2}\mathcal{O}^*(t) - \mathcal{V}_2(t, \mathcal{P}^*(t), \mathcal{O}^*(t), \mathcal{H}^*(t), \mathcal{Q}^*(t), \mathcal{R}^*(t))\right| < L_2\beta_2(t), \\ \left|{}^{\mathbb{FFP}}\mathfrak{D}_{0,t}^{\varkappa_1,\varkappa_2}\mathcal{H}^*(t) - \mathcal{V}_3(t, \mathcal{P}^*(t), \mathcal{O}^*(t), \mathcal{H}^*(t), \mathcal{Q}^*(t), \mathcal{R}^*(t))\right| < L_3\beta_3(t), \\ \left|{}^{\mathbb{FFP}}\mathfrak{D}_{0,t}^{\varkappa_1,\varkappa_2}\mathcal{Q}^*(t) - \mathcal{V}_4(t, \mathcal{P}^*(t), \mathcal{O}^*(t), \mathcal{H}^*(t), \mathcal{Q}^*(t), \mathcal{R}^*(t))\right| < L_4\beta_4(t), \\ \left|{}^{\mathbb{FFP}}\mathfrak{D}_{0,t}^{\varkappa_1,\varkappa_2}\mathcal{R}^*(t) - \mathcal{V}_5(t, \mathcal{P}^*(t), \mathcal{O}^*(t), \mathcal{H}^*(t), \mathcal{Q}^*(t), \mathcal{R}^*(t))\right| < L_5\beta_5(t), \end{cases} \tag{20}$$

there is $(\mathcal{P}, \mathcal{O}, \mathcal{H}, \mathcal{Q}, \mathcal{R}) \in \mathcal{X}$ *satisfying the fractaional-fractal hybrid model of giving up smoking* (3) *such that*

$$\begin{cases} \left|\mathcal{P}^*(t) - \mathcal{P}(t)\right| \leq L_1 \mathbb{M}_{(\mathcal{V}_1,\beta_1)} \beta_1(t), \\ \left|\mathcal{O}^*(t) - \mathcal{O}(t)\right| \leq L_2 \mathbb{M}_{(\mathcal{V}_2,\beta_2)} \beta_2(t), \\ \left|\mathcal{H}^*(t) - \mathcal{H}(t)\right| \leq L_3 \mathbb{M}_{(\mathcal{V}_3,\beta_3)} \beta_3(t), \\ \left|\mathcal{Q}^*(t) - \mathcal{Q}(t)\right| \leq L_4 \mathbb{M}_{(\mathcal{V}_4,\beta_4)} \beta_4(t), \\ \left|\mathcal{R}^*(t) - \mathcal{R}(t)\right| \leq L_5 \mathbb{M}_{(\mathcal{V}_5,\beta_5)} \beta_5(t), \quad \forall t \in \mathbb{J}. \end{cases}$$

Definition 7. *The fractal-fractional model of giving up smoking* (3) *is generalized Ulam–Hyers–Rassias stable with respect to* β_i, $(i \in \{1, \ldots, 5\})$, *if there are constants* $0 < \mathbb{M}_{(\mathcal{V}_i,\beta_i)} \in \mathbb{R}$ *so that for each* $(\mathcal{P}^*, \mathcal{O}^*, \mathcal{H}^*, \mathcal{Q}^*, \mathcal{R}^*) \in \mathcal{X}$ *satisfying*

$$\begin{cases} \left|{}^{\mathbb{FFP}}\mathfrak{D}_{0,t}^{\varkappa_1,\varkappa_2}\mathcal{P}^*(t) - \mathcal{V}_1\big(t, \mathcal{P}^*(t), \mathcal{O}^*(t), \mathcal{H}^*(t), \mathcal{Q}^*(t), \mathcal{R}^*(t)\big)\right| < \beta_1(t), \\ \left|{}^{\mathbb{FFP}}\mathfrak{D}_{0,t}^{\varkappa_1,\varkappa_2}\mathcal{O}^*(t) - \mathcal{V}_2\big(t, \mathcal{P}^*(t), \mathcal{O}^*(t), \mathcal{H}^*(t), \mathcal{Q}^*(t), \mathcal{R}^*(t)\big)\right| < \beta_2(t), \\ \left|{}^{\mathbb{FFP}}\mathfrak{D}_{0,t}^{\varkappa_1,\varkappa_2}\mathcal{H}^*(t) - \mathcal{V}_3\big(t, \mathcal{P}^*(t), \mathcal{O}^*(t), \mathcal{H}^*(t), \mathcal{Q}^*(t), \mathcal{R}^*(t)\big)\right| < \beta_3(t), \\ \left|{}^{\mathbb{FFP}}\mathfrak{D}_{0,t}^{\varkappa_1,\varkappa_2}\mathcal{Q}^*(t) - \mathcal{V}_4\big(t, \mathcal{P}^*(t), \mathcal{O}^*(t), \mathcal{H}^*(t), \mathcal{Q}^*(t), \mathcal{R}^*(t)\big)\right| < \beta_4(t), \\ \left|{}^{\mathbb{FFP}}\mathfrak{D}_{0,t}^{\varkappa_1,\varkappa_2}\mathcal{R}^*(t) - \mathcal{V}_5\big(t, \mathcal{P}^*(t), \mathcal{O}^*(t), \mathcal{H}^*(t), \mathcal{Q}^*(t), \mathcal{R}^*(t)\big)\right| < \beta_5(t), \end{cases}$$

there is $(\mathcal{P}, \mathcal{O}, \mathcal{H}, \mathcal{Q}, \mathcal{R}) \in \mathcal{X}$ *satisfying the fractal-fractional hybrid model of giving up smoking* (3) *such that*

$$\begin{cases} \left|\mathcal{P}^*(t) - \mathcal{P}(t)\right| \leq \mathbb{M}_{(\mathcal{V}_1,\beta_1)} \beta_1(t), \\ \left|\mathcal{O}^*(t) - \mathcal{O}(t)\right| \leq \mathbb{M}_{(\mathcal{V}_2,\beta_2)} \beta_2(t), \\ \left|\mathcal{H}^*(t) - \mathcal{H}(t)\right| \leq \mathbb{M}_{(\mathcal{V}_3,\beta_3)} \beta_3(t), \\ \left|\mathcal{Q}^*(t) - \mathcal{Q}(t)\right| \leq \mathbb{M}_{(\mathcal{V}_4,\beta_4)} \beta_4(t), \\ \left|\mathcal{R}^*(t) - \mathcal{R}(t)\right| \leq \mathbb{M}_{(\mathcal{V}_5,\beta_5)} \beta_5(t), \quad \forall t \in \mathbb{J}. \end{cases}$$

Remark 2. *Notice that* $(\mathcal{P}^*, \mathcal{O}^*, \mathcal{H}^*, \mathcal{Q}^*, \mathcal{R}^*) \in \mathbb{X}$ *is called a solution for inequalities* (5) *if and only if there are* $\hbar_1, \hbar_2, \hbar_3, \hbar_4, \hbar_5 \in C([0, T], \mathbb{R})$ *(depending on* $\mathcal{P}^*, \mathcal{O}^*, \mathcal{H}^*, \mathcal{Q}^*, \mathcal{R}^*$*, respectively) such that for each* $t \in \mathbb{J}$,

(i) $\left|\hbar_i(t)\right| < L_i\beta_i(t), \quad (i \in \{1, \ldots, 5\})$,

(ii) We have

$$\begin{cases} {}^{\mathbb{FFP}}\mathfrak{D}_{0,t}^{\varkappa_1,\varkappa_2}\mathcal{P}^*(t) = \mathcal{V}_1\big(t, \mathcal{P}^*(t), \mathcal{O}^*(t), \mathcal{H}^*(t), \mathcal{Q}^*(t), \mathcal{R}^*(t)\big) + \hbar_1(t), \\ {}^{\mathbb{FFP}}\mathfrak{D}_{0,t}^{\varkappa_1,\varkappa_2}\mathcal{O}^*(t) = \mathcal{V}_2\big(t, \mathcal{P}^*(t), \mathcal{O}^*(t), \mathcal{H}^*(t), \mathcal{Q}^*(t), \mathcal{R}^*(t)\big) + \hbar_2(t), \\ {}^{\mathbb{FFP}}\mathfrak{D}_{0,t}^{\varkappa_1,\varkappa_2}\mathcal{H}^*(t) = \mathcal{V}_3\big(t, \mathcal{P}^*(t), \mathcal{O}^*(t), \mathcal{H}^*(t), \mathcal{Q}^*(t), \mathcal{R}^*(t)\big) + \hbar_3(t), \\ {}^{\mathbb{FFP}}\mathfrak{D}_{0,t}^{\varkappa_1,\varkappa_2}\mathcal{Q}^*(t) = \mathcal{V}_4\big(t, \mathcal{P}^*(t), \mathcal{O}^*(t), \mathcal{H}^*(t), \mathcal{Q}^*(t), \mathcal{R}^*(t)\big) + \hbar_4(t), \\ {}^{\mathbb{FFP}}\mathfrak{D}_{0,t}^{\varkappa_1,\varkappa_2}\mathcal{R}^*(t) = \mathcal{V}_5\big(t, \mathcal{P}^*(t), \mathcal{O}^*(t), \mathcal{H}^*(t), \mathcal{Q}^*(t), \mathcal{R}^*(t)\big) + \hbar_5(t). \end{cases}$$

Theorem 6. *If the condition* $(\mathcal{P}_1)$ *holds, then the fractal-fractional model of giving up smoking* (3) *is Ulam–Hyers and generalized Ulam–Hyers stable such that*

$$\frac{T^{\varkappa_2+\varkappa_1-1}\Gamma(\varkappa_2+1)}{\Gamma(\varkappa_2+\varkappa_1)}\delta_i < 1, \quad i \in \{1,\ldots,5\},$$

where δ_i*'s are defined by* (16).

Proof. Let $L_1 > 0$ and $\mathcal{P}^* \in \mathbb{U}$ be arbitrary so that

$$\left|{}^{\mathrm{FFP}}\mathfrak{D}_{0,t}^{\varkappa_1,\varkappa_2}\mathcal{P}^*(t) - \mathcal{V}_1(t,\mathcal{P}^*(t),\mathcal{O}^*(t),\mathcal{H}^*(t),\mathcal{Q}^*(t),\mathcal{R}^*(t))\right| < L_1.$$

Then, in view of Remark 1, we can find a function $\hbar_1(t)$ satisfying

$${}^{\mathrm{FFP}}\mathfrak{D}_{0,(t)}^{\varkappa_1,\varkappa_2}\mathcal{P}^*(t) = \mathcal{V}_1(t,\mathcal{P}^*(t),\mathcal{O}^*(t),\mathcal{H}^*(t),\mathcal{Q}^*(t),\mathcal{R}^*(t)) + \hbar_1(t),$$

with $|\hbar_1(t)| \leq L_1$. It follows that

$$\begin{aligned}\mathcal{P}^*(t) &= \mathcal{P}_0 + \frac{\varkappa_2}{\Gamma(\varkappa_1)}\int_0^t u^{\varkappa_2-1}(t-u)^{\varkappa_1-1}\mathcal{V}_1(u,\mathcal{P}^*(u),\mathcal{O}^*(u),\mathcal{H}^*(u),\mathcal{Q}^*(u),\mathcal{R}^*(u))\,du \\ &\quad + \frac{\varkappa_2}{\Gamma(\varkappa_1)}\int_0^t u^{\varkappa_2-1}(t-u)^{\varkappa_1-1}\hbar_1(u)\,du.\end{aligned}$$

By using Theorem 5, let $\mathcal{P} \in \mathbb{U}$ be a unique solution of the fractal-fractional model of giving up smoking (3). Then $\mathcal{P}(t)$ is given by

$$\mathcal{P}(t) = \mathcal{P}_0 + \frac{\varkappa_2}{\Gamma(\varkappa_1)}\int_0^t u^{\varkappa_2-1}(t-u)^{\varkappa_1-1}\mathcal{V}_1(u,\mathcal{P}(u),\mathcal{O}(u),\mathcal{H}(u),\mathcal{Q}(u),\mathcal{R}(u))\,du.$$

Then

$$\begin{aligned}|\mathcal{P}^*(t) - \mathcal{P}(t)| &\leq \frac{\varkappa_2}{\Gamma(\varkappa_1)}\int_0^t u^{\varkappa_2-1}(t-u)^{\varkappa_1-1} \\ &\times |\mathcal{V}_1(u,\mathcal{P}^*(u),\mathcal{O}^*(u),\mathcal{H}^*(u),\mathcal{Q}^*(u),\mathcal{R}^*(u)) \\ &\quad -\mathcal{V}_1(u,\mathcal{P}(u),\mathcal{O}(u),\mathcal{H}(u),\mathcal{Q}(u),\mathcal{R}(u))|\,du \\ &\quad + \frac{\varkappa_2}{\Gamma(\varkappa_1)}\int_0^t u^{\varkappa_2-1}(t-u)^{\varkappa_1-1}|\hbar_1(u)|\,du \\ &\leq \frac{T^{\varkappa_2+\varkappa_1-1}\Gamma(\varkappa_2+1)}{\Gamma(\varkappa_2+\varkappa_1)}\delta_1\|\mathcal{P}^*-\mathcal{P}\| + \frac{T^{\varkappa_2+\varkappa_1-1}\Gamma(\varkappa_2+1)}{\Gamma(\varkappa_2+\varkappa_1)}L_1.\end{aligned}$$

Hence, we get

$$\|\mathcal{P}^*-\mathcal{P}\| \leq \frac{T^{\varkappa_2+\varkappa_1-1}\Gamma(\varkappa_2+1)}{\Gamma(\varkappa_2+\varkappa_1) - T^{\varkappa_2+\varkappa_1-1}\Gamma(\varkappa_2+1)\delta_1}L_1.$$

If we let $\mathbb{M}_{\mathcal{V}_1} = \dfrac{T^{\varkappa_2+\varkappa_1-1}\Gamma(\varkappa_2+1)}{\Gamma(\varkappa_2+\varkappa_1) - T^{\varkappa_2+\varkappa_1-1}\Gamma(\varkappa_2+1)\delta_1}$, then we obtain $\|\mathcal{P}^*-\mathcal{P}\| \leq \mathbb{M}_{\mathcal{V}_1}L_1$. Again, we find that

$$\begin{aligned}&\|\mathcal{O}^*-\mathcal{O}\| \leq \mathbb{M}_{\mathcal{V}_2}L_2, \quad \|\mathcal{H}^*-\mathcal{H}\| \leq \mathbb{M}_{\mathcal{V}_3}L_3, \quad \|\mathcal{Q}^*-\mathcal{Q}\| \leq \mathbb{M}_{\mathcal{V}_4}L_4, \\ &\|\mathcal{R}^*-\mathcal{R}\| \leq \mathbb{M}_{\mathcal{V}_5}L_5,\end{aligned}$$

where

$$\mathbb{M}_{\mathcal{V}_i} = \frac{T^{\varkappa_2+\varkappa_1-1}\Gamma(\varkappa_2+1)}{\Gamma(\varkappa_2+\varkappa_1) - T^{\varkappa_2+\varkappa_1-1}\Gamma(\varkappa_2+1)\delta_i}, \quad (i \in \{2,\ldots,5\}).$$

Thus, the Ulam–Hyers stability of the fractal-fractional model of giving up smoking (3) is fulfilled. Now, set

$$\mathbb{M}_{\mathcal{V}_i}(L_i) = \frac{T^{\varkappa_2+\varkappa_1-1}\Gamma(\varkappa_2+1)L_i}{\Gamma(\varkappa_2+\varkappa_1) - T^{\varkappa_2+\varkappa_1-1}\Gamma(\varkappa_2+1)\delta_i}, \quad (i \in \{1,\ldots,5\}).$$

Thus, $\mathbb{M}_{\mathcal{V}_i}(0) = 0$. Hence, the generalized Ulam–Hyers stability is satisfied for the mentioned model (3). □

Theorem 7. *Assume that the condition $(\mathcal{P}_1)$ holds and,*

$(\mathcal{P}_2)$ There are increasing functions $\beta_i \in C([0,T],\mathbb{R})$ and $\Omega_{\beta_i} > 0$ $(i \in \{1,\ldots,5\})$ such that for each $t \in \mathbb{J}$,

$$^{\mathbb{FFP}}\mathfrak{I}_{0,t}^{\varkappa_1,\varkappa_2}\beta_i(t) < \Omega_{\beta_i}\beta_i(t), \quad (i \in \{1,\ldots,5\}). \tag{21}$$

Then, the fractal-fractional model of giving up smoking (3) is Ulam–Hyers–Rassias and generalized Ulam–Hyers–Rassias stable.

Proof. For each constant $L_1 > 0$ and for each $\mathcal{P}^* \in \mathbb{U}$ satisfying

$$\left|^{\mathbb{FFP}}\mathfrak{D}_{0,t}^{\varkappa_1,\varkappa_2}\mathcal{P}^*(t) - \mathcal{V}_1(t,\mathcal{P}^*(t),\mathcal{O}^*(t),\mathcal{H}^*(t),\mathcal{Q}^*(t),\mathcal{R}^*(t))\right| < L_1\beta_1(t),$$

we can find the function $\hbar_1(t)$ such that

$$^{\mathbb{FFP}}\mathfrak{D}_{0,(t)}^{\varkappa_1,\varkappa_2}\mathcal{P}^*(t) = \mathcal{V}_1(t,\mathcal{P}^*(t),\mathcal{O}^*(t),\mathcal{H}^*(t),\mathcal{Q}^*(t),\mathcal{R}^*(t)) + \hbar_1(t),$$

with $|\hbar_1(t)| < L_1\beta_1(t)$. It follows that

$$\begin{aligned}\mathcal{P}^*(t) &= \mathcal{P}_0 + \frac{\varkappa_2}{\Gamma(\varkappa_1)}\int_0^t u^{\varkappa_2-1}(t-u)^{\varkappa_1-1}\mathcal{V}_1(u,\mathcal{P}^*(u),\mathcal{O}^*(u),\mathcal{H}^*(u),\mathcal{Q}^*(u),\mathcal{R}^*(u))\,du \\ &\quad + \frac{\varkappa_2}{\Gamma(\varkappa_1)}\int_0^t u^{\varkappa_2-1}(t-u)^{\varkappa_1-1}\hbar_1(u)\,du.\end{aligned}$$

By using Theorem 5, let $\mathcal{P} \in \mathbb{U}$ be a unique solution of the fractal-fractional model of giving up smoking (3). Then $\mathcal{P}(t)$ is formulated as

$$\mathcal{P}(t) = \mathcal{P}_0 + \frac{\varkappa_2}{\Gamma(\varkappa_1)}\int_0^t u^{\varkappa_2-1}(t-u)^{\varkappa_1-1}\mathcal{V}_1(u,\mathcal{P}(u),\mathcal{O}(u),\mathcal{H}(u),\mathcal{Q}(u),\mathcal{R}(u))\,du.$$

Then, by (21), we get

$$\begin{aligned}|\mathcal{P}^*(t) - \mathcal{P}(t)| &\le \frac{\varkappa_2}{\Gamma(\varkappa_1)}\int_0^t u^{\varkappa_2-1}(t-u)^{\varkappa_1-1} \\ &\quad \times \big|\mathcal{V}_1(u,\mathcal{P}^*(u),\mathcal{O}^*(u),\mathcal{H}^*(u),\mathcal{Q}^*(u),\mathcal{R}^*(u)) \\ &\quad -\mathcal{V}_1(u,\mathcal{P}(u),\mathcal{O}(u),\mathcal{H}(u),\mathcal{Q}(u),\mathcal{R}(u))\big|\,du \\ &\quad + \frac{\varkappa_2}{\Gamma(\varkappa_1)}\int_0^t u^{\varkappa_2-1}(t-u)^{\varkappa_1-1}\beta_1(u)\,du \\ &\le L_1\Omega_{\beta_1}\beta_1(t) + \frac{T^{\varkappa_2+\varkappa_1-1}\Gamma(\varkappa_2+1)}{\Gamma(\varkappa_2+\varkappa_1)}\delta_1\|\mathcal{P}^* - \mathcal{P}\|.\end{aligned}$$

Accordingly, it gives

$$\|\mathcal{P}^* - \mathcal{P}\| \leq \frac{L_1\Gamma(\varkappa_2+\varkappa_1)\Omega_{\beta_1}}{\Gamma(\varkappa_2+\varkappa_1) - T^{\varkappa_2+\varkappa_1-1}\Gamma(\varkappa_2+1)\delta_1}\beta_1(\mathrm{t}).$$

If we let

$$\mathbb{M}_{(\mathcal{V}_1,\beta_1)} = \frac{\Gamma(\varkappa_2+\varkappa_1)\Omega_{\beta_1}}{\Gamma(\varkappa_2+\varkappa_1) - T^{\varkappa_2+\varkappa_1-1}\Gamma(\varkappa_2+1)\delta_1},$$

then, we obtain $\|\mathcal{P}^* - \mathcal{P}\| \leq L_1\mathbb{M}_{(\mathcal{V}_1,\beta_1)}\beta_1(\mathrm{t})$. In a similar way, we also have

$$\begin{aligned}
&\|\mathcal{O}^* - \mathcal{O}\| \leq L_2\mathbb{M}_{(\mathcal{V}_2,\beta_2)}\beta_2(\mathrm{t}), \quad \|\mathcal{H}^* - \mathcal{H}\| \leq L_3\mathbb{M}_{(\mathcal{V}_3,\beta_3)}\beta_3(\mathrm{t}),\\
&\|\mathcal{Q}^* - \mathcal{Q}\| \leq L_4\mathbb{M}_{(\mathcal{V}_4,\beta_4)}\beta_4(\mathrm{t}), \quad \|\mathcal{R}^* - \mathcal{R}\| \leq L_5\mathbb{M}_{(\mathcal{V}_5,\beta_5)}\beta_5(\mathrm{t}),
\end{aligned}$$

where

$$\mathbb{M}_{(\mathcal{V}_i,\beta_i)} = \frac{\Gamma(\varkappa_2+\varkappa_1)\Omega_{\beta_i}}{\Gamma(\varkappa_2+\varkappa_1) - T^{\varkappa_2+\varkappa_1-1}\Gamma(\varkappa_2+1)\delta_i}, \quad (i \in \{2,\ldots,5\}).$$

Therefore, the fractal-fractional model of giving up smoking (3) is Ulam–Hyers–Rassias stable. If $L_i = 1, \ (i \in \{1,\ldots,5\})$, then the fractal-fractional model of giving up smoking (3) is generalized Ulam–Hyers–Rassias stable. □

4.4. Equilibrium Points

When

$${}^{\mathbb{FFP}}\mathfrak{D}^{\varkappa_1,\varkappa_2}_{0,\mathrm{t}}\mathcal{P}(\mathrm{t}) = {}^{\mathbb{FFP}}\mathfrak{D}^{\varkappa_1,\varkappa_2}_{0,\mathrm{t}}\mathcal{O}(\mathrm{t}) = {}^{\mathbb{FFP}}\mathfrak{D}^{\varkappa_1,\varkappa_2}_{0,\mathrm{t}}\mathcal{H}(\mathrm{t}) = {}^{\mathbb{FFP}}\mathfrak{D}^{\varkappa_1,\varkappa_2}_{0,\mathrm{t}}\mathcal{Q}(\mathrm{t}) = {}^{\mathbb{FFP}}\mathfrak{D}^{\varkappa_1,\varkappa_2}_{0,\mathrm{t}}\mathcal{R}(\mathrm{t}) = 0,$$

we can find the following results from the fractal-fractional model of giving up smoking (3).

Theorem 8. *The fractal-fractional model of giving up smoking (3) has at most three equilibrium points, namely the smoking-free equilibrium point* $(\frac{v}{\vartheta},0,0,0,0)$ *and smoking equilibrium points*

$$\begin{cases}
\left(\frac{v}{\vartheta+\omega\bar{\mathcal{O}}}, \frac{v}{\vartheta+\omega\bar{\mathcal{O}}}, \frac{\omega v-\vartheta^2-\vartheta\omega\bar{\mathcal{O}}}{\gamma\vartheta+\gamma\omega\bar{\mathcal{O}}}, \frac{(\vartheta+\theta)}{\zeta}\bar{\mathcal{H}}, \frac{q\theta}{\vartheta}\bar{\mathcal{H}}\right),\\
\text{and}\\
\left(\frac{v}{\vartheta}, \frac{v}{\vartheta+\omega\bar{\mathcal{O}}}, \frac{\omega v-\vartheta^2-\vartheta\omega\bar{\mathcal{O}}}{\gamma\vartheta+\gamma\omega\bar{\mathcal{O}}}, \frac{\theta(1-q)}{(\vartheta+\zeta)}\bar{\mathcal{H}}, \frac{q\theta}{\vartheta}\bar{\mathcal{H}}\right).
\end{cases}$$

Proof. Let $(\bar{\mathcal{P}},\bar{\mathcal{O}},\bar{\mathcal{H}},\bar{\mathcal{Q}},\bar{\mathcal{R}})$ denote the equilibrium point for the fractal-fractional model of giving up smoking (3). When $\bar{\mathcal{O}} = \bar{\mathcal{H}} = \bar{\mathcal{Q}} = \bar{\mathcal{R}} = 0$, then from the first equation in (3), we find that

$$\bar{\mathcal{P}} = \frac{v}{\vartheta},$$

whereas, if $\bar{\mathcal{O}} \neq 0, \ \bar{\mathcal{H}} \neq 0, \ \bar{\mathcal{Q}} \neq 0, \ \bar{\mathcal{R}} \neq 0$, then, we obtain

$$\bar{\mathcal{P}} = \frac{v}{\vartheta+\omega\bar{\mathcal{O}}},$$

which is substituted into the second equation in (3) to give

$$\bar{\mathcal{H}} = \frac{\omega v - \vartheta^2 - \vartheta\omega\bar{\mathcal{O}}}{\gamma\vartheta + \gamma\omega\bar{\mathcal{O}}}.$$

Consequently, it follows trivially from the remaining subsequent equations that

$$\bar{\mathcal{Q}} = \frac{(\vartheta+\theta)}{\zeta}\bar{\mathcal{H}} \text{ or } \bar{\mathcal{Q}} = \frac{\theta(1-q)}{(\vartheta+\zeta)}\bar{\mathcal{H}} \ \& \ \bar{\mathcal{R}} = \frac{q\theta}{\vartheta}\bar{\mathcal{H}},$$

and it completes the proof. □

4.5. Time-Dependent Basic Reproduction Number

In view of the derivation of the model in Equation (3), the basic reproduction number, henceforth denoted as R_0 is expected to define the expected number of secondary cases produced, in a completely potential population, by a typical smoking individual [34]. Therefore, the progression from $\mathcal{O}$ to $\mathcal{H}$ and failure to quit smoking are not considered to be new cases, but rather the progression of a smoking individual through various compartments. Hence, the following results are stated. Moreover, time-dependent variations in the transmission potential of infectious diseases are of practical importance. Consequently, in Ref. [35] it is reported that time-dependent reproduction number $R(t)$ measures the disease transmissibility, which can be estimated over the course of disease progression. Thus, $R(t)$ has been particularly useful for monitoring epidemic trends by measuring the progress of interventions over time and for providing parameters for mathematical phenomena. Hence, by following [36], one can find the following results.

Theorem 9. *The time-dependent basic reproduction number for the fractal-fractional model of giving up smoking* (3) *is*

$$R(t) = \frac{\mathcal{S}(t)}{\mathcal{S}(0)} R_0, \text{ where, } R_0 = \frac{\omega v}{\vartheta^2}.$$

Proof. It suffices to derive the R_0. Then, the remaining part of the proof is followed easily. The respective vectors for the rate of appearance of new smokers and transfer of individuals in the model (3) are

$$\mathcal{F} = \begin{pmatrix} \omega \mathcal{P}\mathcal{O} \\ 0 \\ 0 \\ 0 \\ 0 \end{pmatrix} \ \& \ \mathcal{V} = \begin{pmatrix} \vartheta \mathcal{P} + \omega \mathcal{P}\mathcal{O} - v \\ \vartheta \mathcal{O} + \gamma \mathcal{O}\mathcal{H} \\ (\vartheta + \theta)\mathcal{H} - \gamma \mathcal{O}(t)\mathcal{H}(t) - \zeta \mathcal{Q}(t) \\ (\vartheta + \zeta)\mathcal{Q}(t) - \theta(1-q)\mathcal{H}(t) \\ \vartheta \mathcal{R}(t) - q\theta \mathcal{H}(t). \end{pmatrix}.$$

Based on the smoking compartments, i.e., $\mathcal{O}, \mathcal{H}, \mathcal{Q}$ and free-smoking equilibrium, we find that

$$F = \begin{pmatrix} \frac{\omega v}{\vartheta} & 0 & 0 \\ 0 & 0 & 0 \\ 0 & 0 & 0 \end{pmatrix} \ \& \ V = \begin{pmatrix} \vartheta & 0 & 0 \\ 0 & (\vartheta + \theta) & -\zeta \\ 0 & -\theta(1-q) & (\vartheta + \zeta) \end{pmatrix}.$$

It gives

$$V^{-1} = \frac{1}{\vartheta[(\vartheta+\theta)(\vartheta+\zeta) - \zeta\theta(1-q)]} \begin{pmatrix} (\vartheta+\theta)(\vartheta+\zeta) - \zeta\theta(1-q) & 0 & 0 \\ 0 & \vartheta(\vartheta+\zeta) & \vartheta\theta(1-q) \\ 0 & \vartheta\zeta & \vartheta(\vartheta+\zeta) \end{pmatrix}.$$

Thus, by Ref. [37], the basic reproduction number is followed easily. □

4.6. Sensitivity Analysis

In view of theorem 9, one can see that the sensitivity analysis of $R(t)$ depends mainly on R_0. Thus, in what follows, the analysis is therefore curtailed to the sensitivity of R_0. By recalling that the sensitivity analysis enables us to predict which parameters have a high impact on the basic reproduction number [38], one of the main objectives is therefore to suggest strategies to ensure that the necessary control measures are taken to stop smoking and prevent a possible increase in the number of smokers in the future. Such attempts are, of course, attained in the direction of supporting the efforts of lowering the value of the basic reproduction number. Considering that there are many negative conditions brought about by smoking, together with the challenge of completely eliminating the smoking epidemic in a population in a short time, attempts to reduce the spread of smoking are therefore very important. Thus, lowering the value R_0 is one of the most fundamental issues, as it possesses a major influence on the effect of parameters on the change of R_0. To this end, we will evaluate the influence aspects of the parameters that affect R_0 by determining the normalized forward sensitivity index of it [38]. Starting with the first to the last parameter listed under model in Equation (2), the normalized forward sensitivity index of the variable R_0 yields the following results.

Theorem 10. *The parameters $\gamma, \zeta, \vartheta, q$ are likely to bring about the decrease in the time-dependent basic reproduction number.*

Proof. It follows trivially through R_0 that

$$\begin{cases} \frac{\partial R_0}{\partial \omega} \times \frac{\omega}{R_0} = \frac{\partial\left[\frac{\omega v}{\vartheta^2}\right]}{\partial \omega} \times \frac{\omega}{\frac{\omega v}{\vartheta^2}} = \frac{v}{\vartheta^2}\frac{\vartheta^2}{\omega v} = \omega^{-1} > 0, \\ \frac{\partial R_0}{\partial \gamma} \times \frac{\gamma}{R_0} = \frac{\partial\left[\frac{\omega v}{\vartheta^2}\right]}{\partial \gamma} \times \frac{\gamma}{\frac{\omega v}{\vartheta^2}} = 0, \\ \frac{\partial R_0}{\partial \zeta} \times \frac{\zeta}{R_0} = \frac{\partial\left[\frac{\omega v}{\vartheta^2}\right]}{\partial \zeta} \times \frac{\zeta}{\frac{\omega v}{\vartheta^2}} = 0, \\ \frac{\partial R_0}{\partial \vartheta} \times \frac{\vartheta}{R_0} = \frac{\partial\left[\frac{\omega v}{\vartheta^2}\right]}{\partial \vartheta} \times \frac{\vartheta}{\frac{\omega v}{\vartheta^2}} = -2 < 0, \\ \frac{\partial R_0}{\partial \theta} \times \frac{\theta}{R_0} = \frac{\partial\left[\frac{\omega v}{\vartheta^2}\right]}{\partial \theta} \times \frac{\theta}{\frac{\omega v}{\vartheta^2}} = 0, \\ \frac{\partial R_0}{\partial q} \times \frac{q}{R_0} = \frac{\partial\left[\frac{\omega v}{\vartheta^2}\right]}{\partial q} \times \frac{q}{\frac{\omega v}{\vartheta^2}} = 0, \\ \frac{\partial R_0}{\partial v} \times \frac{v}{R_0} = \frac{\partial\left[\frac{\omega v}{\vartheta^2}\right]}{\partial v} \times \frac{v}{\frac{\omega v}{\vartheta^2}} = \vartheta^{-1} > 0, \end{cases}$$

which concludes the proof. □

4.7. Asymptotically Stability Analysis

To investigate the local asymptotic stability for the fractal-fractional model of giving up smoking (3), one requires the Jacobian matrix [39] computed at the equilibrium points and associated characteristic equation. Let $\mathcal{E} := (\bar{\mathcal{P}}, \bar{\mathcal{O}}, \bar{\mathcal{H}}, \bar{\mathcal{Q}}, \bar{\mathcal{R}})$. Thus, the non-zero entries of the Jacobian matrix are

$$J(\mathcal{E})_{(1,1)} = -(\vartheta + \omega\bar{\mathcal{O}}),\ J(\mathcal{E})_{(1,2)} = -\omega\bar{\mathcal{P}},\ J(\mathcal{E})_{(2,2)} = \omega\bar{\mathcal{P}} - \vartheta - \gamma\bar{\mathcal{H}},$$

$$J(\mathcal{E})_{(3,2)} = \gamma\bar{\mathcal{H}},\ J(\mathcal{E})_{(3,3)} = -(\theta + \vartheta),\ J(\mathcal{E})_{(3,4)} = \zeta,\ J(\mathcal{E})_{(4,3)} = -\theta(q-1),$$

$$J(\mathcal{E})_{(4,4)} = -(\vartheta + \zeta),\ J(\mathcal{E})_{(5,3)} = q\theta,\ J(\mathcal{E})_{(5,5)} = -\vartheta,$$

and the associated characteristic equation [40] is

$$\lambda^5 - a_4\lambda^4 - a_3\lambda^3 - a_2\lambda^2 - a_1\lambda - a_0 = 0,$$

where,

$$
\begin{cases}
a_4 = \gamma\bar{\mathcal{O}} - 5\vartheta - \zeta - \gamma\bar{\mathcal{H}} - \theta - \omega\bar{\mathcal{O}} + \omega\bar{\mathcal{P}}, \\
a_3 = 4\bar{\mathcal{O}}\gamma\vartheta - 4\vartheta\zeta - 10\vartheta^2 - \bar{\mathcal{H}}\gamma\theta - 4\bar{\mathcal{H}}\gamma\vartheta - \bar{\mathcal{H}}\gamma\zeta - 4\theta\vartheta + \bar{\mathcal{O}}\gamma\zeta - \bar{\mathcal{O}}\omega\theta + \bar{\mathcal{P}}\omega\theta \\
\quad -4\bar{\mathcal{O}}\omega\vartheta + 4\bar{\mathcal{P}}\omega\vartheta - \bar{\mathcal{O}}\omega\zeta + \bar{\mathcal{P}}\omega\zeta - q\theta\zeta + \bar{\mathcal{O}}^2\gamma\omega - \bar{\mathcal{H}}\bar{\mathcal{O}}\gamma\omega - \bar{\mathcal{O}}\bar{\mathcal{P}}\gamma\omega, \\
a_2 = 6\bar{\mathcal{O}}\gamma\vartheta^2 - 6\vartheta^2\zeta - 10\vartheta^3 - 6\bar{\mathcal{H}}\gamma\vartheta^2 - 6\theta\vartheta^2 - 6\bar{\mathcal{O}}\omega\vartheta^2 + 6\bar{\mathcal{P}}\omega\vartheta^2 + 3\bar{\mathcal{O}}\gamma\vartheta\zeta - 3\bar{\mathcal{O}}\omega\theta\vartheta \\
\quad +3\bar{\mathcal{P}}\omega\theta\vartheta - 3\bar{\mathcal{O}}\omega\vartheta\zeta + 3\bar{\mathcal{P}}\omega\vartheta\zeta - 3q\theta\vartheta\zeta + 3\bar{\mathcal{O}}^2\gamma\omega\vartheta + \bar{\mathcal{O}}^2\gamma\omega\zeta - 3\bar{\mathcal{H}}\gamma\theta\vartheta - 3\bar{\mathcal{H}}\gamma\vartheta\zeta \\
\quad -\bar{\mathcal{H}}\bar{\mathcal{O}}\gamma\omega\theta - 3\bar{\mathcal{H}}\bar{\mathcal{O}}\gamma\omega\vartheta - \bar{\mathcal{H}}\bar{\mathcal{O}}\gamma\omega\zeta - 3\bar{\mathcal{O}}\bar{\mathcal{P}}\gamma\omega\vartheta - \bar{\mathcal{O}}\bar{\mathcal{P}}\gamma\omega\zeta - \bar{\mathcal{H}}\gamma q\theta\zeta - \bar{\mathcal{O}}\omega q\theta\zeta + \bar{\mathcal{P}}\omega q\theta\zeta, \\
a_1 = 4\bar{\mathcal{O}}\gamma\vartheta^3 - 4\vartheta^3\zeta - 5\vartheta^4 - 4\bar{\mathcal{H}}\gamma\vartheta^3 - 4\theta\vartheta^3 - 4\bar{\mathcal{O}}\omega\vartheta^3 + 4\bar{\mathcal{P}}\omega\vartheta^3 - 3\bar{\mathcal{H}}\gamma\theta\vartheta^2 - 3\bar{\mathcal{H}}\gamma\vartheta^2\zeta \\
\quad +3\bar{\mathcal{O}}\gamma\vartheta^2\zeta - 3\bar{\mathcal{O}}\omega\theta\vartheta^2 + 3\bar{\mathcal{P}}\omega\theta\vartheta^2 - 3\bar{\mathcal{O}}\omega\vartheta^2\zeta + 3\bar{\mathcal{P}}\omega\vartheta^2\zeta - 3q\theta\vartheta^2\zeta + 3\bar{\mathcal{O}}^2\gamma\omega\vartheta^2 \\
\quad -3\bar{\mathcal{H}}\bar{\mathcal{O}}\gamma\omega\vartheta^2 - 3\bar{\mathcal{O}}\bar{\mathcal{P}}\gamma\omega\vartheta^2 + 2\bar{\mathcal{O}}^2\gamma\omega\vartheta\zeta - 2\bar{\mathcal{H}}\bar{\mathcal{O}}\gamma\omega\theta\vartheta - 2\bar{\mathcal{H}}\bar{\mathcal{O}}\gamma\omega\vartheta\zeta - 2\bar{\mathcal{O}}\bar{\mathcal{P}}\gamma\omega\vartheta\zeta - 2\bar{\mathcal{H}}\gamma q\theta\vartheta\zeta \\
\quad -2\bar{\mathcal{O}}\omega q\theta\vartheta\zeta + 2\bar{\mathcal{P}}\omega q\theta\vartheta\zeta - \bar{\mathcal{H}}\bar{\mathcal{O}}\gamma\omega q\theta\zeta, \\
a_0 = \bar{\mathcal{O}}\gamma\vartheta^4 - \vartheta^4\zeta - \vartheta^5 - \bar{\mathcal{H}}\gamma\vartheta^4 - \theta\vartheta^4 - \bar{\mathcal{O}}\omega\vartheta^4 + \bar{\mathcal{P}}\omega\vartheta^4 - \bar{\mathcal{H}}\gamma\theta\vartheta^3 - \bar{\mathcal{H}}\gamma\vartheta^3\zeta + \bar{\mathcal{O}}\gamma\vartheta^3\zeta \\
\quad -\bar{\mathcal{O}}\omega\theta\vartheta^3 + \bar{\mathcal{P}}\omega\theta\vartheta^3 - \bar{\mathcal{O}}\omega\vartheta^3\zeta + \bar{\mathcal{P}}\omega\vartheta^3\zeta - q\theta\vartheta^3\zeta + \bar{\mathcal{O}}^2\gamma\omega\vartheta^3 + \bar{\mathcal{O}}^2\gamma\omega\vartheta^2\zeta - \bar{\mathcal{H}}\bar{\mathcal{O}}\gamma\omega\vartheta^3 \\
\quad -\bar{\mathcal{O}}\bar{\mathcal{P}}\gamma\omega\vartheta^3 - \bar{\mathcal{H}}\bar{\mathcal{O}}\gamma\omega\theta\vartheta^2 - \bar{\mathcal{H}}\bar{\mathcal{O}}\gamma\omega\vartheta^2\zeta - \bar{\mathcal{O}}\bar{\mathcal{P}}\gamma\omega\vartheta^2\zeta - \bar{\mathcal{H}}\gamma q\theta\vartheta^2\zeta - \bar{\mathcal{O}}\omega q\theta\vartheta^2\zeta \\
\quad +\bar{\mathcal{P}}\omega q\theta\vartheta^2\zeta - \bar{\mathcal{H}}\bar{\mathcal{O}}\gamma\omega q\theta\vartheta\zeta.
\end{cases}
$$

Thus, if

(a) $5\vartheta + \zeta + \theta > \frac{\omega\upsilon}{\vartheta}$,
(b) $q\theta\zeta + 4\vartheta\zeta + 10\vartheta^2 + 4\theta\vartheta > (\theta + 4\vartheta + \zeta)\frac{\omega\upsilon}{\vartheta}$,
(c) $6\vartheta^2\zeta + 10\vartheta^3 + 6\theta\vartheta^2 + 3q\theta\vartheta\zeta > (6\vartheta^2 + 3\theta\vartheta + 3\vartheta\zeta + q\theta\zeta)\frac{\omega\upsilon}{\vartheta}$,
(d) $4\vartheta^2\zeta + 5\vartheta^3 + 4\theta\vartheta^2 + 3q\theta\vartheta\zeta > (4\vartheta^2 + 3\theta\vartheta + 3\vartheta\zeta + 2q\theta\zeta)\frac{\omega\upsilon}{\vartheta}$,
(e) $\vartheta^2\zeta + \vartheta^3 + \theta\vartheta^2 + q\theta\vartheta\zeta > (\vartheta^2 + \theta\vartheta + \vartheta\zeta + q\theta\zeta)\frac{\omega\upsilon}{\vartheta}$,

in that case, the smoking-free equilibrium point is locally stable if the equilibrium points are positive [41].

Similarly, one finds that if

(a)

$$5\vartheta + \zeta + \gamma\bar{\mathcal{H}} + \theta + \omega\bar{\mathcal{O}} > \gamma\bar{\mathcal{O}} + \omega\bar{\mathcal{P}},$$

(b)

$$
\begin{cases}
4\bar{\mathcal{O}}\omega\vartheta + \bar{\mathcal{O}}\omega\zeta + q\theta\zeta + \bar{\mathcal{H}}\bar{\mathcal{O}}\gamma\omega + \bar{\mathcal{O}}\bar{\mathcal{P}}\gamma\omega + 4\vartheta\zeta + 10\vartheta^2 + \bar{\mathcal{H}}\gamma\theta \\
+4\bar{\mathcal{H}}\gamma\vartheta + \bar{\mathcal{H}}\gamma\zeta + 4\theta\vartheta + \bar{\mathcal{O}}\omega\theta > 4\bar{\mathcal{O}}\gamma\vartheta + \bar{\mathcal{O}}\gamma\zeta + \bar{\mathcal{P}}\omega\theta + 4\bar{\mathcal{P}}\omega\vartheta + \bar{\mathcal{P}}\omega\zeta + \bar{\mathcal{O}}^2\gamma\omega,
\end{cases}
$$

(c)

$$
\begin{cases}
6\vartheta^2\zeta + 10\vartheta^3 + 6\bar{\mathcal{H}}\gamma\vartheta^2 + 6\theta\vartheta^2 + 6\bar{\mathcal{O}}\omega\vartheta^2 + 3\bar{\mathcal{O}}\omega\theta\vartheta + 3\bar{\mathcal{O}}\omega\vartheta\zeta + 3q\theta\vartheta\zeta \\
+3\bar{\mathcal{H}}\gamma\theta\vartheta + 3\bar{\mathcal{H}}\gamma\vartheta\zeta + \bar{\mathcal{H}}\bar{\mathcal{O}}\gamma\omega\theta + 3\bar{\mathcal{H}}\bar{\mathcal{O}}\gamma\omega\vartheta + \bar{\mathcal{H}}\bar{\mathcal{O}}\gamma\omega\zeta + 3\bar{\mathcal{O}}\bar{\mathcal{P}}\gamma\omega\vartheta + \bar{\mathcal{O}}\bar{\mathcal{P}}\gamma\omega\zeta \\
+\bar{\mathcal{H}}\gamma q\theta\zeta + \bar{\mathcal{O}}\omega q\theta\zeta > 6\bar{\mathcal{O}}\gamma\vartheta^2 + 6\bar{\mathcal{P}}\omega\vartheta^2 + 3\bar{\mathcal{O}}\gamma\vartheta\zeta + 3\bar{\mathcal{P}}\omega\theta\vartheta + 3\bar{\mathcal{P}}\omega\vartheta\zeta + 3\bar{\mathcal{O}}^2\gamma\omega\vartheta, \\
+\bar{\mathcal{O}}^2\gamma\omega\zeta + \bar{\mathcal{P}}\omega q\theta\zeta,
\end{cases}
$$

(d)

$$\begin{cases} 4\vartheta^3\zeta + 5\vartheta^4 + 4\bar{\mathcal{H}}\gamma\vartheta^3 + 4\theta\vartheta^3 + 4\bar{\mathcal{O}}\omega\vartheta^3 + 3\bar{\mathcal{H}}\gamma\theta\vartheta^2 + 3\bar{\mathcal{H}}\gamma\vartheta^2\zeta \\ +3\bar{\mathcal{O}}\omega\theta\vartheta^2 + 3\bar{\mathcal{O}}\omega\vartheta^2\zeta + 3q\theta\vartheta^2\zeta + 3\bar{\mathcal{H}}\bar{\mathcal{O}}\gamma\omega\vartheta^2 + 3\bar{\mathcal{O}}\bar{\mathcal{P}}\gamma\omega\vartheta^2 \\ +2\bar{\mathcal{H}}\bar{\mathcal{O}}\gamma\omega\theta\vartheta + 2\bar{\mathcal{H}}\bar{\mathcal{O}}\gamma\omega\vartheta\zeta + 2\bar{\mathcal{O}}\bar{\mathcal{P}}\gamma\omega\vartheta\zeta - 2\bar{\mathcal{H}}\gamma q\theta\vartheta\zeta \\ +2\bar{\mathcal{O}}\omega q\theta\vartheta\zeta + \bar{\mathcal{H}}\bar{\mathcal{O}}\gamma\omega q\theta\zeta > 4\bar{\mathcal{O}}\gamma\vartheta^3 + 4\bar{\mathcal{P}}\omega\vartheta^3 \\ +3\bar{\mathcal{O}}\gamma\vartheta^2\zeta + 3\bar{\mathcal{P}}\omega\theta\vartheta^2 + 3\bar{\mathcal{P}}\omega\vartheta^2\zeta + 3\bar{\mathcal{O}}^2\gamma\omega\vartheta^2 \\ +2\bar{\mathcal{O}}^2\gamma\omega\vartheta\zeta + 2\bar{\mathcal{P}}\omega q\theta\vartheta\zeta, \end{cases}$$

(e)

$$\begin{cases} \vartheta^4\zeta + \vartheta^5 + \bar{\mathcal{H}}\gamma\vartheta^4 + \theta\vartheta^4 + \bar{\mathcal{O}}\omega\vartheta^4 + \bar{\mathcal{H}}\gamma\theta\vartheta^3 + \bar{\mathcal{H}}\gamma\vartheta^3\zeta \\ +\bar{\mathcal{O}}\omega\theta\vartheta^3 + \bar{\mathcal{O}}\omega\vartheta^3\zeta + q\theta\vartheta^3\zeta + \bar{\mathcal{H}}\bar{\mathcal{O}}\gamma\omega\vartheta^3 + \bar{\mathcal{O}}\bar{\mathcal{P}}\gamma\omega\vartheta^3 + \bar{\mathcal{H}}\bar{\mathcal{O}}\gamma\omega\theta\vartheta^2 \\ +\bar{\mathcal{H}}\bar{\mathcal{O}}\gamma\omega\vartheta^2\zeta + \bar{\mathcal{O}}\bar{\mathcal{P}}\gamma\omega\vartheta^2\zeta + \bar{\mathcal{H}}\gamma q\theta\vartheta^2\zeta + \bar{\mathcal{O}}\omega q\theta\vartheta^2\zeta + \bar{\mathcal{H}}\bar{\mathcal{O}}\gamma\omega q\theta\vartheta\zeta \\ > \bar{\mathcal{O}}\gamma\vartheta^4 + \bar{\mathcal{P}}\omega\vartheta^4 + \bar{\mathcal{O}}\gamma\vartheta^3\zeta + \bar{\mathcal{P}}\omega\theta\vartheta^3 + \bar{\mathcal{P}}\omega\vartheta^3\zeta + \bar{\mathcal{O}}^2\gamma\omega\vartheta^3 \\ +\bar{\mathcal{O}}^2\gamma\omega\vartheta^2\zeta + \bar{\mathcal{P}}\omega q\theta\vartheta^2\zeta, \end{cases}$$

then the smoking equilibrium point is locally stable if the equilibrium points are positive [41].

Lemma 2. *The time-dependent basic reproduction number $R(t) < 1$ is globally stable in $\mathcal{X}$, whereas, if $R(t) > 1$, the unique smoking equilibrium point is globally asymptotically stable in the interior of $\mathcal{X}$.*

Proof. The proof of lemma 2 is similar to the proof established in [42]. □

5. Numerical Algorithm

In this section, we describe the numerical algorithm for the fractal-fractional model of giving up smoking (3). To do this, we apply the technique based on the fractal-fractional derivative operator [18]. To begin this process, we note that the system of fractal-fractional derivatives in the Riemann–Liouville sense in Equation (3) can be converted to

$$\begin{cases} {}^{RL}\mathfrak{D}_{0,t}^{\varkappa_1}\mathcal{P}(t) = \varkappa_2\tau^{\varkappa_2-1}[v - \vartheta\mathcal{P}(t) - \omega\mathcal{P}(t)\mathcal{O}(t)], \\ {}^{RL}\mathfrak{D}_{0,t}^{\varkappa_1}\mathcal{O}(t) = \varkappa_2\tau^{\varkappa_2-1}[-\vartheta\mathcal{O}(t) + \omega\mathcal{P}(t)\mathcal{O}(t) - \gamma\mathcal{O}(t)\mathcal{H}(t)], \\ {}^{RL}\mathfrak{D}_{0,t}^{\varkappa_1}\mathcal{H}(t) = \varkappa_2\tau^{\varkappa_2-1}[(-(\vartheta+\theta) + \gamma\mathcal{O}(t))\mathcal{H}(t) + \zeta\mathcal{Q}(t)], \\ {}^{RL}\mathfrak{D}_{0,t}^{\varkappa_1}\mathcal{Q}(t) = \varkappa_2\tau^{\varkappa_2-1}[-(\vartheta+\zeta)\mathcal{Q}(t) + \theta(1-q)\mathcal{H}(t)], \\ {}^{RL}\mathfrak{D}_{0,t}^{\varkappa_1}\mathcal{R}(t) = \varkappa_2\tau^{\varkappa_2-1}[-\vartheta\mathcal{R}(t) + q\theta\mathcal{H}(t)]. \end{cases} \quad (22)$$

By applying the Riemann–Liouville fractional integral on both sides of equation in (22) one obtains

$$
\begin{cases}
\mathcal{P}(t) = \mathcal{P}(0) + \frac{\varkappa_2}{\Gamma(\varkappa_1)} \int_0^t \iota^{\varkappa_2 - 1}(t-\iota)^{\varkappa_1 - 1}[\upsilon - \vartheta\mathcal{P}(\iota) - \omega\mathcal{P}(\iota)\mathcal{O}(\iota)]d\iota, \\
\mathcal{O}(t) = \mathcal{O}(0) + \frac{\varkappa_2}{\Gamma(\varkappa_1)} \int_0^t \iota^{\varkappa_2 - 1}(t-\iota)^{\varkappa_1 - 1}[-\vartheta\mathcal{O}(\iota) + \omega\mathcal{P}(\iota)\mathcal{O}(\iota) - \gamma\mathcal{O}(\iota)\mathcal{H}(\iota)]d\iota, \\
\mathcal{H}(t) = \mathcal{H}(0) + \frac{\varkappa_2}{\Gamma(\varkappa_1)} \int_0^t \iota^{\varkappa_2 - 1}(t-\iota)^{\varkappa_1 - 1}[(-(\vartheta+\theta) + \gamma\mathcal{O}(\iota))\mathcal{H}(\iota) + \zeta\mathcal{Q}(\iota)]d\iota, \\
\mathcal{Q}(t) = \mathcal{Q}(0) + \frac{\varkappa_2}{\Gamma(\varkappa_1)} \int_0^t \iota^{\varkappa_2 - 1}(t-\iota)^{\varkappa_1 - 1}[-(\vartheta+\zeta)\mathcal{Q}(\iota) + \theta(1-q)\mathcal{H}(\iota)]d\iota, \\
\mathcal{R}(t) = \mathcal{R}(0) + \frac{\varkappa_2}{\Gamma(\varkappa_1)} \int_0^t \iota^{\varkappa_2 - 1}(t-\iota)^{\varkappa_1 - 1}[-\vartheta\mathcal{R}(\iota) + q\theta\mathcal{H}(\iota)]d\iota.
\end{cases} \tag{23}
$$

Using a new approach at t_{n+1}, (where n denotes the denotes the number of subintervals) we discretize the mentioned Equation (23) for $t = t_{n+1}$, and we get

$$
\begin{cases}
\mathcal{P}(t_{n+1}) = \mathcal{P}_0 + \frac{\varkappa_2}{\Gamma(\varkappa_1)} \int_0^{t_{n+1}} \iota^{\varkappa_2 - 1}(t_{n+1}-\iota)^{\varkappa_1 - 1}[\upsilon - \vartheta\mathcal{P}(\iota) - \omega\mathcal{P}(\iota)\mathcal{O}(\iota)]d\iota, \\
\mathcal{O}(t_{n+1}) = \mathcal{O}_0 + \frac{\varkappa_2}{\Gamma(\varkappa_1)} \int_0^{t_{n+1}} \iota^{\varkappa_2 - 1}(t_{n+1}-\iota)^{\varkappa_1 - 1}[-\vartheta\mathcal{O}(\iota) + \omega\mathcal{P}(\iota)\mathcal{O}(\iota) - \gamma\mathcal{O}(\iota)\mathcal{H}(\iota)]d\iota, \\
\mathcal{H}(t_{n+1}) = \mathcal{H}_0 + \frac{\varkappa_2}{\Gamma(\varkappa_1)} \int_0^{t_{n+1}} \iota^{\varkappa_2 - 1}(t_{n+1}-\iota)^{\varkappa_1 - 1}[(-(\vartheta+\theta) + \gamma\mathcal{O}(\iota))\mathcal{H}(\iota) + \zeta\mathcal{Q}(\iota)]d\iota, \\
\mathcal{Q}(t_{n+1}) = \mathcal{Q}_0 + \frac{\varkappa_2}{\Gamma(\varkappa_1)} \int_0^{t_{n+1}} \iota^{\varkappa_2 - 1}(t_{n+1}-\iota)^{\varkappa_1 - 1}[-(\vartheta+\zeta)\mathcal{Q}(\iota) + \theta(1-q)\mathcal{H}(\iota)]d\iota, \\
\mathcal{R}(t_{n+1}) = \mathcal{R}_0 + \frac{\varkappa_2}{\Gamma(\varkappa_1)} \int_0^{t_{n+1}} \iota^{\varkappa_2 - 1}(t_{n+1}-\iota)^{\varkappa_1 - 1}[-\vartheta\mathcal{R}(\iota) + q\theta\mathcal{H}(\iota)]d\iota.
\end{cases} \tag{24}
$$

Approximating the obtained integrals in Equation (24), we obtain

$$
\begin{cases}
\mathcal{P}(t_{n+1}) = \mathcal{P}_0 + \frac{\varkappa_2}{\Gamma(\varkappa_1)} \sum_{i=0}^{n} \int_{t_i}^{t_{i-1}} \iota^{\varkappa_2 - 1}(t_{n+1}-\iota)^{\varkappa_1 - 1}[\upsilon - \vartheta\mathcal{P}(\iota) - \omega\mathcal{P}(\iota)\mathcal{O}(\iota)]d\iota, \\
\mathcal{O}(t_{n+1}) = \mathcal{O}_0 + \frac{\varkappa_2}{\Gamma(\varkappa_1)} \sum_{i=0}^{n} \int_{t_i}^{t_{i-1}} \iota^{\varkappa_2 - 1}(t_{n+1}-\iota)^{\varkappa_1 - 1}[-\vartheta\mathcal{O}(\iota) + \omega\mathcal{P}(\iota)\mathcal{O}(\iota) - \gamma\mathcal{O}(\iota)\mathcal{H}(\iota)]d\iota, \\
\mathcal{H}(t_{n+1}) = \mathcal{H}_0 + \frac{\varkappa_2}{\Gamma(\varkappa_1)} \sum_{i=0}^{n} \int_{t_i}^{t_{i-1}} \iota^{\varkappa_2 - 1}(t_{n+1}-\iota)^{\varkappa_1 - 1}[(-(\vartheta+\theta) + \gamma\mathcal{O}(\iota))\mathcal{H}(\iota) + \zeta\mathcal{Q}(\iota)]d\iota, \\
\mathcal{Q}(t_{n+1}) = \mathcal{Q}_0 + \frac{\varkappa_2}{\Gamma(\varkappa_1)} \sum_{i=0}^{n} \int_{t_i}^{t_{i-1}} \iota^{\varkappa_2 - 1}(t_{n+1}-\iota)^{\varkappa_1 - 1}[-(\vartheta+\zeta)\mathcal{Q}(\iota) + \theta(1-q)\mathcal{H}(\iota)]d\iota, \\
\mathcal{R}(t_{n+1}) = \mathcal{R}_0 + \frac{\varkappa_2}{\Gamma(\varkappa_1)} \sum_{i=0}^{n} \int_{t_i}^{t_{i-1}} \iota^{\varkappa_2 - 1}(t_{n+1}-\iota)^{\varkappa_1 - 1}[-\vartheta\mathcal{R}(\iota) + q\theta\mathcal{H}(\iota)]d\iota.
\end{cases} \tag{25}
$$

Applying the Lagrangian piece-wise interpolation [43] to each functions

$$
\begin{cases}
\iota^{\varkappa_2 - 1}(t_{n+1}-\iota)^{\varkappa_1 - 1}[\upsilon - \vartheta\mathcal{P}(\iota) - \omega\mathcal{P}(\iota)\mathcal{O}(\iota)], \\
\iota^{\varkappa_2 - 1}(t_{n+1}-\iota)^{\varkappa_1 - 1}[-\vartheta\mathcal{O}(\iota) + \omega\mathcal{P}(\iota)\mathcal{O}(\iota) - \gamma\mathcal{O}(\iota)\mathcal{H}(\iota)], \\
\iota^{\varkappa_2 - 1}(t_{n+1}-\iota)^{\varkappa_1 - 1}[(-(\vartheta+\theta) + \gamma\mathcal{O}(\iota))\mathcal{H}(\iota) + \zeta\mathcal{Q}(\iota)], \\
\iota^{\varkappa_2 - 1}(t_{n+1}-\iota)^{\varkappa_1 - 1}[-(\vartheta+\zeta)\mathcal{Q}(\iota) + \theta(1-q)\mathcal{H}(\iota)], \\
\iota^{\varkappa_2 - 1}(t_{n+1}-\iota)^{\varkappa_1 - 1}[-\vartheta\mathcal{R}(\iota) + q\theta\mathcal{H}(\iota)],
\end{cases} \tag{26}
$$

we find

$$\begin{cases} \iota^{\varkappa_2-1}(t_{n+1}-\iota)^{\varkappa_1-1}[\upsilon-\vartheta\mathcal{P}(\iota)-\omega\mathcal{P}(\iota)\mathcal{O}(\iota)] \\ =\frac{\iota-t_{i-1}}{t_i-t_{i-1}}t_i^{\varkappa_2-1}[\upsilon-\vartheta\mathcal{P}(t_i)-\omega\mathcal{P}(t_i)\mathcal{O}(t_i)] \\ \quad -\frac{\iota-t_i}{t_i-t_{i-1}}t_{i-1}^{\varkappa_2-1}[\upsilon-\vartheta\mathcal{P}(t_{i-1})-\omega\mathcal{P}(t_{i-1})\mathcal{O}(t_{i-1})], \\ \iota^{\varkappa_2-1}(t_{n+1}-\iota)^{\varkappa_1-1}[-\vartheta\mathcal{O}(\iota)+\omega\mathcal{P}(\iota)\mathcal{O}(\iota)-\gamma\mathcal{O}(\iota)\mathcal{H}(\iota)] \\ =\frac{\iota-t_{i-1}}{t_i-t_{i-1}}t_i^{\varkappa_2-1}[-\vartheta\mathcal{O}(t_i)+\omega\mathcal{P}(t_i)\mathcal{O}(t_i)-\gamma\mathcal{O}(t_i)\mathcal{H}(t_i)] \\ \quad -\frac{\iota-t_i}{t_i-t_{i-1}}t_{i-1}^{\varkappa_2-1}[-\vartheta\mathcal{O}(t_{i-1})+\omega\mathcal{P}(t_{i-1})\mathcal{O}(t_{i-1})-\gamma\mathcal{O}(t_{i-1})\mathcal{H}(t_{i-1})], \\ \iota^{\varkappa_2-1}(t_{n+1}-\iota)^{\varkappa_1-1}[(-(\vartheta+\theta)+\gamma\mathcal{O}(\iota))\mathcal{H}(\iota)+\zeta\mathcal{Q}(\iota)] \\ =\frac{\iota-t_{i-1}}{t_i-t_{i-1}}t_i^{\varkappa_2-1}[(-(\vartheta+\theta)+\gamma\mathcal{O}(t_i))\mathcal{H}(t_i)+\zeta\mathcal{Q}(t_i)] \\ \quad -\frac{\iota-t_i}{t_i-t_{i-1}}t_{i-1}^{\varkappa_2-1}[(-(\vartheta+\theta)+\gamma\mathcal{O}(t_{i-1}))\mathcal{H}(t_{i-1})+\zeta\mathcal{Q}(t_{i-1})], \\ \iota^{\varkappa_2-1}(t_{n+1}-\iota)^{\varkappa_1-1}[-(\vartheta+\zeta)\mathcal{Q}(\iota)+\theta(1-q)\mathcal{H}(\iota)] \\ =\frac{\iota-t_{i-1}}{t_i-t_{i-1}}t_i^{\varkappa_2-1}[-(\vartheta+\zeta)\mathcal{Q}(t_i)+\theta(1-q)\mathcal{H}(t_i)] \\ \quad -\frac{\iota-t_i}{t_i-t_{i-1}}t_{i-1}^{\varkappa_2-1}[-(\vartheta+\zeta)\mathcal{Q}(t_{i-1})+\theta(1-q)\mathcal{H}(t_{i-1})], \\ \iota^{\varkappa_2-1}(t_{n+1}-\iota)^{\varkappa_1-1}[-\vartheta\mathcal{R}(\iota)+q\theta\mathcal{H}(\iota)]=\frac{\iota-t_{i-1}}{t_i-t_{i-1}}t_i^{\varkappa_2-1}[-\vartheta\mathcal{R}(t_i)+q\theta\mathcal{H}(t_i)] \\ \quad -\frac{\iota-t_i}{t_i-t_{i-1}}t_{i-1}^{\varkappa_2-1}[-\vartheta\mathcal{R}(t_{i-1})+q\theta\mathcal{H}(t_{i-1})]. \end{cases} \tag{27}$$

Consequently,

$$\begin{aligned} \mathcal{P}(t_{n+1}) &= \mathcal{P}_0+\frac{\varkappa_2}{\Gamma(\varkappa_1)}\sum_{i=0}^{n}\int_{t_i}^{t_{i-1}}\iota^{\varkappa_2-1}(t_{n+1}-\iota)^{\varkappa_1-1}[\frac{\iota-t_{i-1}}{t_i-t_{i-1}}t_i^{\varkappa_2-1}[\upsilon-\vartheta\mathcal{P}(t_i)-\omega\mathcal{P}(t_i)\mathcal{O}(t_i)] \\ &\quad -\frac{\iota-t_i}{t_i-t_{i-1}}t_{i-1}^{\varkappa_2-1}[\upsilon-\vartheta\mathcal{P}(t_{i-1})-\omega\mathcal{P}(t_{i-1})\mathcal{O}(t_{i-1})]]d\iota, \\ \mathcal{O}(t_{n+1}) &= \mathcal{O}_0+\frac{\varkappa_2}{\Gamma(\varkappa_1)}\sum_{i=0}^{n}\int_{t_i}^{t_{i-1}}\iota^{\varkappa_2-1}(t_{n+1}-\iota)^{\varkappa_1-1}[-\vartheta\mathcal{O}(\iota)+\omega\mathcal{P}(\iota)\mathcal{O}(\iota)-\gamma\mathcal{O}(\iota)\mathcal{H}(\iota)]d\iota \\ &= \frac{\iota-t_{i-1}}{t_i-t_{i-1}}t_i^{\varkappa_2-1}[-\vartheta\mathcal{O}(t_i)+\omega\mathcal{P}(t_i)\mathcal{O}(t_i)-\gamma\mathcal{O}(t_i)\mathcal{H}(t_i)] \\ &\quad -\frac{\iota-t_i}{t_i-t_{i-1}}t_{i-1}^{\varkappa_2-1}[-\vartheta\mathcal{O}(t_{i-1})+\omega\mathcal{P}(t_{i-1})\mathcal{O}(t_{i-1})-\gamma\mathcal{O}(t_{i-1})\mathcal{H}(t_{i-1})]d\iota, \\ \mathcal{H}(t_{n+1}) &= \mathcal{H}_0+\frac{\varkappa_2}{\Gamma(\varkappa_1)}\sum_{i=0}^{n}\int_{t_i}^{t_{i-1}}\iota^{\varkappa_2-1}(t_{n+1}-\iota)^{\varkappa_1-1}[(-(\vartheta+\theta)+\gamma\mathcal{O}(\iota))\mathcal{H}(\iota)+\zeta\mathcal{Q}(\iota)]d\iota \\ &= \frac{\iota-t_{i-1}}{t_i-t_{i-1}}t_i^{\varkappa_2-1}[(-(\vartheta+\theta)+\gamma\mathcal{O}(t_i))\mathcal{H}(t_i)+\zeta\mathcal{Q}(t_i)] \\ &\quad -\frac{\iota-t_i}{t_i-t_{i-1}}t_{i-1}^{\varkappa_2-1}[(-(\vartheta+\theta)+\gamma\mathcal{O}(t_{i-1}))\mathcal{H}(t_{i-1})+\zeta\mathcal{Q}(t_{i-1})]d\iota, \\ \mathcal{Q}(t_{n+1}) &= \mathcal{Q}_0+\frac{\varkappa_2}{\Gamma(\varkappa_1)}\sum_{i=0}^{n}\int_{t_i}^{t_{i-1}}\iota^{\varkappa_2-1}(t_{n+1}-\iota)^{\varkappa_1-1}[-(\vartheta+\zeta)\mathcal{Q}(\iota)+\theta(1-q)\mathcal{H}(\iota)]d\iota \end{aligned} \tag{28}$$

$$= \frac{\iota - t_{i-1}}{t_i - t_{i-1}} t_i^{\varkappa_2 - 1}[-(\vartheta + \zeta)\mathcal{Q}(t_i) + \theta(1-q)\mathcal{H}(t_i)]$$

$$- \frac{\iota - t_i}{t_i - t_{i-1}} t_{i-1}^{\varkappa_2 - 1}[-(\vartheta + \zeta)\mathcal{Q}(t_{i-1}) + \theta(1-q)\mathcal{H}(t_{i-1})]d\iota,$$

$$\mathcal{R}(t_{n+1}) = \mathcal{R}_0 + \frac{\varkappa_2}{\Gamma(\varkappa_1)} \sum_{i=0}^{n} \int_{t_i}^{t_{i-1}} \iota^{\varkappa_2 - 1}(t_{n+1} - \iota)^{\varkappa_1 - 1}[-\vartheta\mathcal{R}(t_i) + q\theta\mathcal{H}(t_i)]d\iota$$

$$- \frac{\iota - t_i}{t_i - t_{i-1}} t_{i-1}^{\varkappa_2 - 1}[-\vartheta\mathcal{R}(t_{i-1}) + q\theta\mathcal{H}(t_{i-1})]d\iota.$$

The equations in (28) are equivalent to

$$\begin{cases} \mathcal{P}(t_{n+1}) = \mathcal{P}_0 + \frac{\varkappa_2(\Delta t)^{\varkappa_1}}{\Gamma(\varkappa_1+2)} \sum_{i=0}^{n} t_i^{\varkappa_2-1}[\upsilon - \vartheta\mathcal{P}(t_i) - \omega\mathcal{P}(t_i)\mathcal{O}(t_i)] \\ \quad \times [(n+1-i)^{\varkappa_1}(n-i+2+\varkappa_1) - (n-i)^{\varkappa_1}(n-i+2+2\varkappa_1)] \\ \quad - t_{i-1}^{\varkappa_2-1}[\upsilon - \vartheta\mathcal{P}(t_{i-1}) - \omega\mathcal{P}(t_{i-1})\mathcal{O}(t_{i-1})] \\ \quad \times [(n+1-i)^{\varkappa_1+1} - (n-i)^{\varkappa_1}(n-i+1+\varkappa_1)], \end{cases} \tag{29}$$

and

$$\begin{cases} \mathcal{O}(t_{n+1}) = \mathcal{O}_0 + \frac{\varkappa_2(\Delta t)^{\varkappa_1}}{\Gamma(\varkappa_1+2)} \sum_{i=0}^{n} t_i^{\varkappa_2-1}[-\vartheta\mathcal{O}(t_i) + \omega\mathcal{P}(t_i)\mathcal{O}(t_i) - \gamma\mathcal{O}(t_i)\mathcal{H}(t_i)] \\ \quad \times [(n+1-i)^{\varkappa_1}(n-i+2+\varkappa_1) - (n-i)^{\varkappa_1}(n-i+2+2\varkappa_1)] \\ \quad - t_{i-1}^{\varkappa_2-1}[-\vartheta\mathcal{O}(t_{i-1}) + \omega\mathcal{P}(t_{i-1})\mathcal{O}(t_{i-1}) - \gamma\mathcal{O}(t_{i-1})\mathcal{H}(t_{i-1})] \\ \quad \times [(n+1-i)^{\varkappa_1+1} - (n-i)^{\varkappa_1}(n-i+1+\varkappa_1)], \end{cases} \tag{30}$$

and

$$\begin{cases} \mathcal{H}(t_{n+1}) = \mathcal{H}_0 + \frac{\varkappa_2(\Delta t)^{\varkappa_1}}{\Gamma(\varkappa_1+2)} \sum_{i=0}^{n} t_i^{\varkappa_2-1}[(-(\vartheta+\theta) + \gamma\mathcal{O}(t_i))\mathcal{H}(t_i) + \zeta\mathcal{Q}(t_i)] \\ \quad \times [(n+1-i)^{\varkappa_1}(n-i+2+\varkappa_1) - (n-i)^{\varkappa_1}(n-i+2+2\varkappa_1)] \\ \quad - t_{i-1}^{\varkappa_2-1}[(-(\vartheta+\theta) + \gamma\mathcal{O}(t_{i-1}))\mathcal{H}(t_{i-1}) + \zeta\mathcal{Q}(t_{i-1})] \\ \quad \times [(n+1-i)^{\varkappa_1+1} - (n-i)^{\varkappa_1}(n-i+1+\varkappa_1)], \end{cases} \tag{31}$$

and

$$\begin{cases} \mathcal{Q}(t_{n+1}) = \mathcal{Q}_0 + \frac{\varkappa_2(\Delta t)^{\varkappa_1}}{\Gamma(\varkappa_1+2)} \sum_{i=0}^{n} t_i^{\varkappa_2-1}[-(\vartheta+\zeta)\mathcal{Q}(t_i) + \theta(1-q)\mathcal{H}(t_i)] \\ \quad \times [(n+1-i)^{\varkappa_1}(n-i+2+\varkappa_1) - (n-i)^{\varkappa_1}(n-i+2+2\varkappa_1)] \\ \quad - t_{i-1}^{\varkappa_2-1}[-(\vartheta+\zeta)\mathcal{Q}(t_{i-1}) + \theta(1-q)\mathcal{H}(t_{i-1})]] \\ \quad \times [(n+1-i)^{\varkappa_1+1} - (n-i)^{\varkappa_1}(n-i+1+\varkappa_1)], \end{cases} \tag{32}$$

and

$$\begin{cases} \mathcal{R}(t_{n+1}) = \mathcal{R}_0 + \frac{\varkappa_2(\Delta t)^{\varkappa_1}}{\Gamma(\varkappa_1+2)} \sum_{i=0}^{n} t_i^{\varkappa_2-1}[-\vartheta\mathcal{R}(t_i) + q\theta\mathcal{H}(t_i)] \\ \quad \times [(n+1-i)^{\varkappa_1}(n-i+2+\varkappa_1) - (n-i)^{\varkappa_1}(n-i+2+2\varkappa_1)] \\ \quad - t_{i-1}^{\varkappa_2-1}[-\vartheta\mathcal{R}(t_{i-1}) + q\theta\mathcal{H}(t_{i-1})]] \\ \quad \times [(n+1-i)^{\varkappa_1+1} - (n-i)^{\varkappa_1}(n-i+1+\varkappa_1)]. \end{cases} \tag{33}$$

We refer to equations in (29)–(33) as the numerical scheme for the solutions of the fractal-fractional model of giving up smoking (3).

6. Simulations and Discussion

Simulation and discussion on the behavior of the fractal-fractional model of giving up smoking (3) are implemented in this section according to the parameters computed in Ref. [14]. Based on this source, we assume $v = 0.2$, $\vartheta = 0.04$, $\gamma = 0.3$, $\zeta = 0.25$, $\omega = 0.23$, $\theta = 2$, $q = 0.4$. The initial values are:

$$\mathcal{P}_0 = 0.60301, \quad \mathcal{O}_0 = 0.24000, \quad \mathcal{H}_0 = 0.10628, \quad \mathcal{Q}_0 = 0.03260, \quad \mathcal{R}_0 = 0.01811.$$

As a first step, to compare the best fitting parameters with our assumption parameters [14], we regenerate the total population ($\mathcal{N} = \mathcal{P} + \mathcal{O} + \mathcal{H} + \mathcal{Q} + \mathcal{R}$) by adding white Gaussian noise. Then, we apply the well-known least square technique for the regenerated total population and find the curve of best fit for the new data. The comparative results including the approximate $\mathcal{N}(t)$ by the Adams–Bashforth technique (blue dashed line), regenerated $\mathcal{N}(t)$ with noise (blue dots), and the curve of best fit for the new data (red line) are graphically represented in Figure 1. From this graphical illustration, we can observe the great agreement between the Adams–Bashforth solution of $\mathcal{N}(t)$ and the curve of best fit created from the regenerated data with white Gaussian noise. In addition, obtained root mean square error for the best fit, which is a criterion to see the goodness of the fit, is produced as 0.3198.

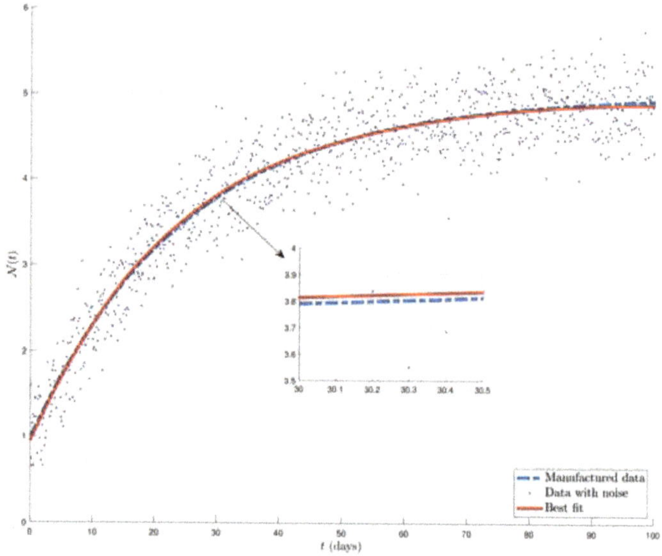

Figure 1. Comparison between the approximate total population $\mathcal{N}(t)$ with noise data and curve of best fit.

In Figure 2, we illustrate the obtained dynamics of all five state functions $\mathcal{P}, \mathcal{O}, \mathcal{H}, \mathcal{Q}, \mathcal{R}$ via the numerical technique introduced in Section 5.

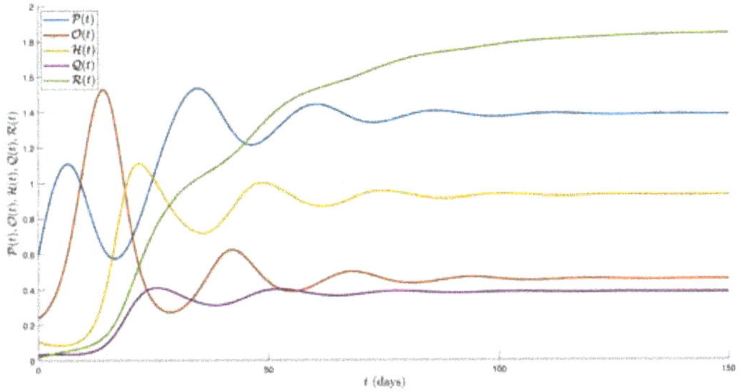

Figure 2. Behaviors of five sub-classes under fractal-fractional order $\varkappa_1 = \varkappa_2 = 1.00$.

In Figures 3–7, we illustrate the behaviors of five state functions $\mathcal{P}(t), \mathcal{O}(t), \mathcal{H}(t), \mathcal{Q}(t), \mathcal{R}(t)$, respectively, when the Adams–Bashforth technique is applied under the fractal-fractional orders $\varkappa_1 = \varkappa_2 = 0.95, 0.96, 0.97, 0.98, 1.00$. From these illustrations, we can observe that while the fractal-fractional order gets closer to the integer case, the density of each state function is increasing at about the same rate. In addition, it can be said that the fractal-fractional orders have an effect on the trajectories regarding converging to a more stable case.

In Figures 8–11, the behaviors of approximate solutions of some pairs of the state functions such as a) $\mathcal{P}(t) - \mathcal{O}(t)$, b) $\mathcal{P}(t) - \mathcal{R}(t)$, c) $\mathcal{O}(t) - \mathcal{H}(t)$, and d) $\mathcal{H}(t) - \mathcal{Q}(t)$ under the integer-order are graphically illustrated where the time $t \in [0, 150]$ and step size $h = 0.1$.

In Figures 12–14, to observe the effects of contact rates on the sub-classes, we illustrate the behaviors of approximate solutions of state functions $\mathcal{P}(t)$, $\mathcal{H}(t)$ and $\mathcal{Q}(t)$ versus the different values of contact rates γ, ω, ζ.

From Figure 12, we can observe that decreasing the contact rate between occasionally smokers and heavy smokers (γ) has a positive effect on the population of potential smokers $\mathcal{P}$; that is, the density of the potential smokers is decreasing at about the same rate. Similarly, when the contact rate between the potential smokers and occasional smokers (ω) decreases, from Figure 13, we can see that the population of heavy smokers $\mathcal{H}$ also decreases. Figure 14 shows us that increasing the contact rate between heavy smokers and temporary quitters who return back to smoking (ζ), has an effect on decreasing the population of temporary quitters who return back to smoking $\mathcal{Q}$.

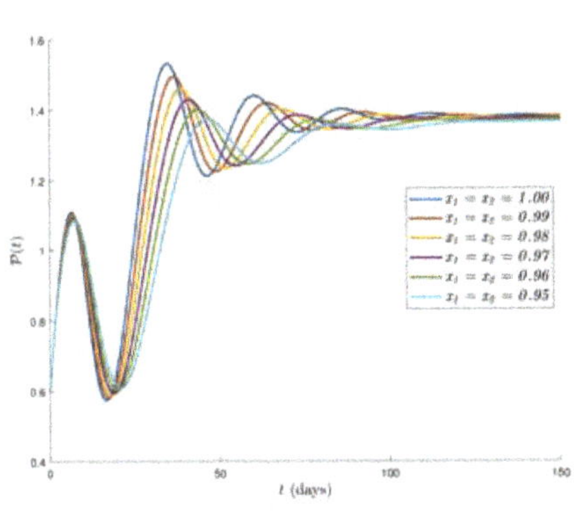

Figure 3. Behaviors of $\mathcal{P}(t)$.

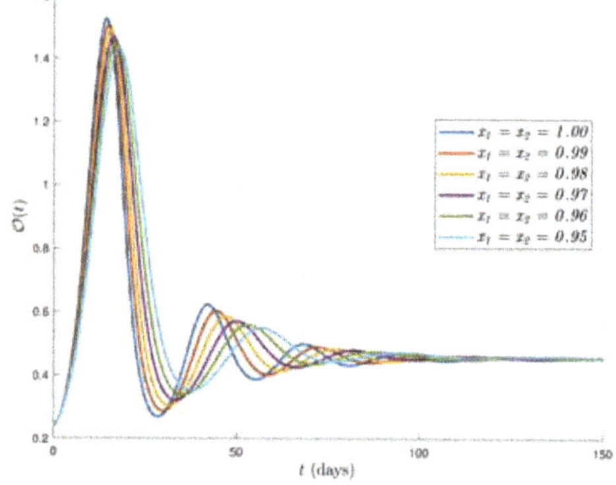

Figure 4. Behaviors of $\mathcal{O}(t)$.

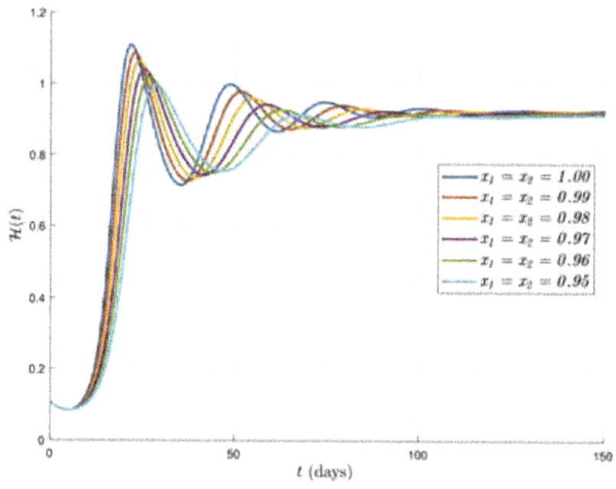

Figure 5. Behaviors of $\mathcal{H}(t)$.

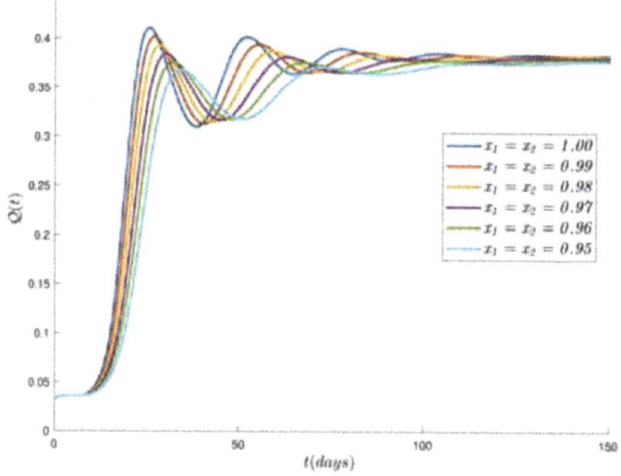

Figure 6. Behaviors of $\mathcal{Q}(t)$.

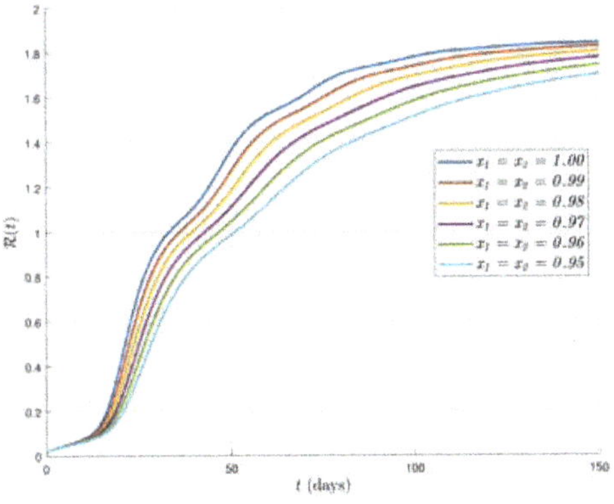

Figure 7. Behaviors of $\mathcal{R}(t)$.

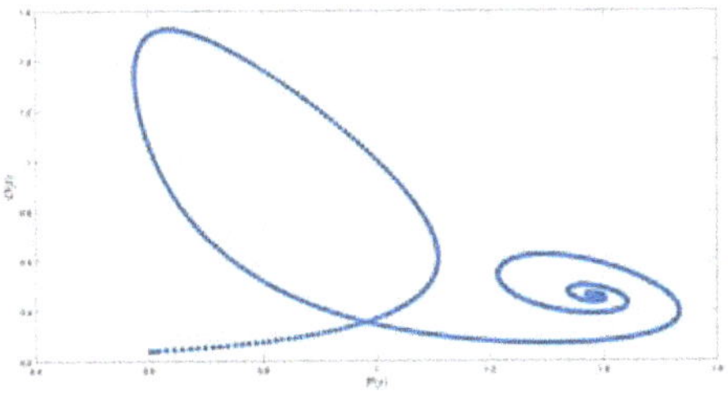

Figure 8. Behaviors of pair of sub-classes $\mathcal{P}(t) - \mathcal{O}(t)$.

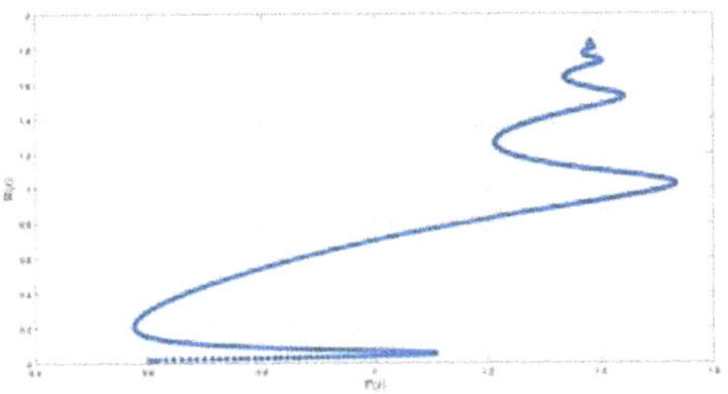

Figure 9. Behaviors of pair of sub-classes $\mathcal{P}(t) - \mathcal{R}(t)$.

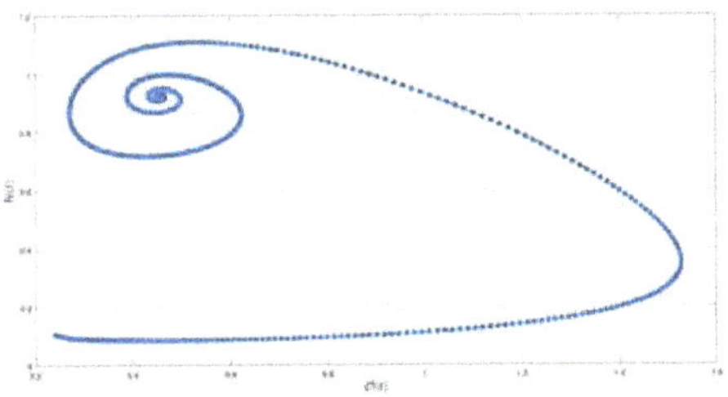

Figure 10. Behaviors of pair of sub-classes $\mathcal{O}(t) - \mathcal{H}(t)$.

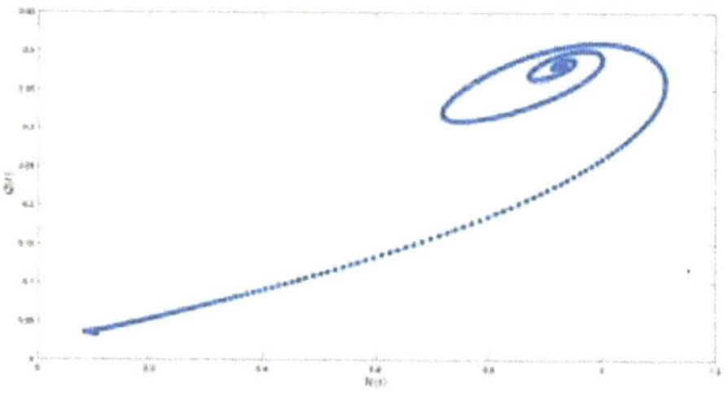

Figure 11. Behaviors of pair of sub-classes $\mathcal{H}(t) - \mathcal{Q}(t)$.

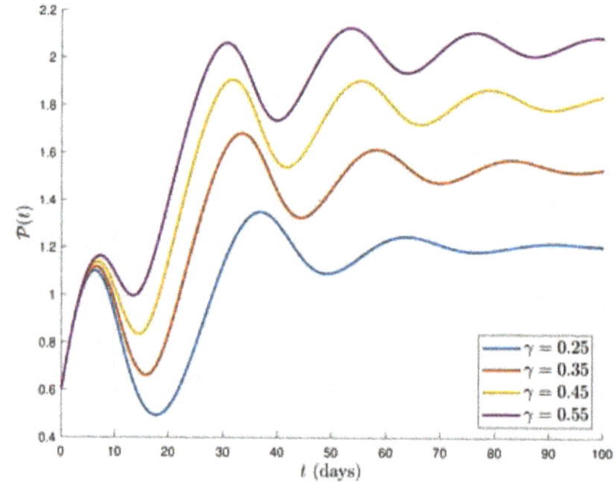

Figure 12. Effects of contact rates on state functions: $\mathcal{P}(t)$ versus γ.

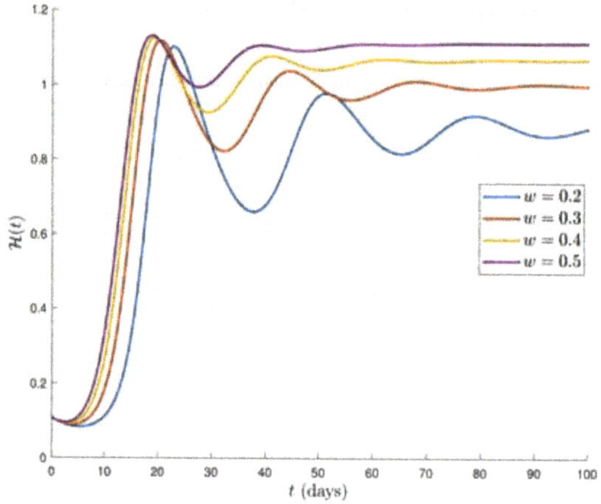

Figure 13. Effects of contact rates on state functions: $\mathcal{H}(t)$ versus ω.

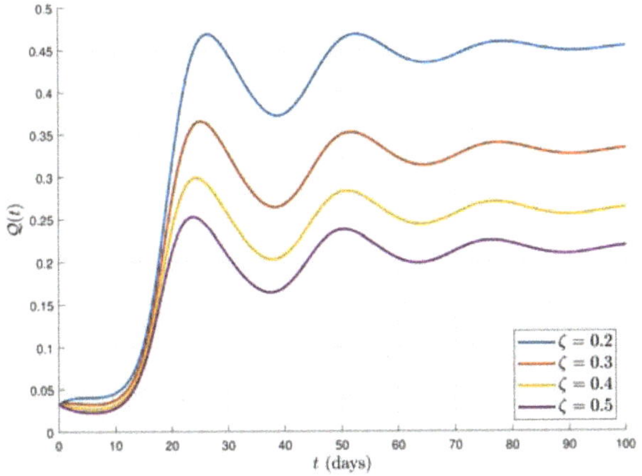

Figure 14. Effects of contact rates on state functions: $\mathcal{Q}(t)$ versus ζ.

7. Conclusions

In this research, a new mathematical model of giving up smoking was designed by defining a five-compartmental system of differential equations based on the new hybrid generalized fractal-fractional derivatives. The properties of solutions to this fractal-fractional model of giving up smoking were discussed from several points of view. A special sub-class of increasing functions along with a special kind of contractions was used to complete the existing section about the solutions.Steady-state analysis was conducted for this model and we derived a numerical scheme for the fractal-fractional model of giving up smoking by terms of fractal and fractional parameters. In other words, we derived approximate solutions of the system (3) via the Adams–Bashforth method and simulated the behaviors of each sub-classes from several aspects such as variations of fractal-fractional dimension-orders. From the illustrated results, we can see that by increasing the fractal-fractional orders, the density of each sub-population also increases. We also observed and discussed the effects of contact rates γ, ω, ζ on the behaviors of sub-classes in Section 6. All the approximate results and calculations are obtained with the help of MATLAB version R2019A. These simulations and graphs show that if we control the contact rate in each sub-class, then we can obtain significant results in reducing the number of people who quit smoking. New directions can be extended by considering other generalized kernels in the fractal-fractional operators in future research projects.

Author Contributions: Conceptualization, S.E., S.R. and R.P.A.; formal analysis, S.E., A.S., K.M.O., B.T., İ.A., S.R. and R.P.A.; methodology, S.E., A.S., K.M.O., B.T., İ.A., S.R. and R.P.A.; software, S.E., K.M.O. and İ.A. All authors have read and agreed to the published version of the manuscript.

Funding: This research received no funding.

Institutional Review Board Statement: Not applicable.

Informed Consent Statement: Not applicable.

Data Availability Statement: Data sharing is not applicable to this article as no datasets were generated nor analyzed during the current study.

Acknowledgments: The first and sixth authors would like to thank Azarbaijan Shahid Madani University. The second author would like to thank University of Namibia. In addition, the third author author would like to thank Federal University of Technology Akure.

Conflicts of Interest: The authors declare no conflict of interest.

References

1. Zaman, G. Qualitative behavior of giving up smoking models. *Bull. Malays. Math. Soc.* **2011**, *34*, 403–415.
2. Sharomi, O.; Gumel, A.B.; Curtailing smoking dynamics: a mathematical modeling approach. *Appl. Math. Comput.* **2008**, *195*, 475–499. [CrossRef]
3. Alkhudhari, Z.; Al-Sheikh, S.; Al-Tuwairqi, S. Global dynamics of a mathematical model on smoking. *Appl. Math.* **2014**, *2014*, 847075. [CrossRef]
4. Rahman, G.U.; Agarwal, R.P.; Liu, L.; Khan, A. Threshold dynamics and optimal control of an age-structured giving up smoking model. *Nonlinear Anal. Real World Appl.* **2018**, *43*, 96–120. [CrossRef]
5. Rahman, G.U.; Agarwal, R.P.; Din, Q. Mathematical analysis of giving up smoking model via harmonic mean type incidence rate. *Appl. Math. Comput.* **2019**, *354*, 128–148. [CrossRef]
6. Zhang, Z.; Rahman, G.U.; Agarwal, R.P.; Harmonic mean type dynamics of a delayed giving up smoking model and optimal control strategy via legislation. *J. Franklin Ins.* **2020**, *357*, 10669–10690. [CrossRef]
7. Li, X.; Agarwal, R.P.; Gomez-Aguilar, J.F.; Badshah, Q.; Rahman, G.U. Threshold dynamics: Formulation, stability & sensitivity analysis of co-abuse model of heroin and smoking. *Chaos, Solitons Fractals* **2022**, *161*, 112373.
8. Caputo, M.; Fabrizio, M. A new definition of fractional derivative without singular kernel. *Prog. Fract. Differ. Appl.* **2015**, *1*, 73–85.
9. Atangana, A.; Baleanu, D. New fractional derivatives with non-local and non-singular kernel: Theory and application to heat transfer model. *Therm. Sci.* **2016**, *20*, 763–769. [CrossRef]
10. Podlubny, I. *Fractional Differential Equations*; Academic Press: Cambridge, MA, USA, 1999.
11. Erturk, V.S.; Zaman, G.; Momani, S. A numeric analytic method for approximating a giving up smoking model containing fractional derivatives. *Comput. Math. Appl.* **2012**, *64*, 3068–3074. [CrossRef]
12. Zaman, G.; Islam, S. A non-standard numerical method for a giving-up smoking model. *Nonlinear Sci. Lett. A* **2010**, *4*, 397–402.
13. Zeb, A.; Chohan, I.; Zaman, G. The homotopy analysis method for approximating of giving up smoking model in fractional order. *Appl. Math.* **2012**, *3*, 914–919. [CrossRef]
14. Singh, J.; Kumar, D.; Qurashi, M.A.; Baleanu, D. A new fractional model for giving up smoking dynamics. *Adv. Differ. Equ.* **2017**, *2017*, 88. [CrossRef]
15. Ahmad, A.; Farman, M.; Ghafar, A.; Inc, M.; Ahmad, M.O.; Sene, N. Analysis and simulation of fractional order smoking epidemic model. *Comput. Math. Meth. Med.* **2022**, *2022*, 9683187. [CrossRef] [PubMed]
16. Ucar, S.; Ucar, E.; Ozdemir, N.; Hammouch, Z. Mathematical analysis and numerical simulation for a smoking model with Atangana–Baleanu derivative. *Chaos Solitons Fractals* **2019**, *118*, 300–306. [CrossRef]
17. Atangana, A. Fractal-fractional differentiation and integration: connecting fractal calculus and fractional calculus to predict complex system. *Chaos Solitons Fractals* **2017**, *102*, 396–406. [CrossRef]
18. Atangana, A.; Qureshi, S.; Modeling attractors of chaotic dynamical systems with fractal-fractional operators. *Chaos, Solitons Fractals* **2019**, *123*, 320–337. [CrossRef]
19. Khan, H.; Ahmad, F.; Tunc, O.; Idrees, M. On fractal-fractional Covid-19 mathematical model. *Chaos, Solitons Fractals* **2022**, *157*, 111937. [CrossRef]
20. Khan, H.; Alzabut, J.; Shah, A.; Etemad, S.; Rezapour, S.; Park, C. A study on the fractal-fractional tobacco smoking model. *AIMS Math.* 2022, *7*, 13887–13909. [CrossRef]
21. Najafi, H.; Etemad, S.; Patanarapeelert, N.; Asamoah, J.K.K.; Rezapour, S.; Sitthiwirattham, T. A study on dynamics of $CD4^{+}$ T-cells under the effect of HIV-1 infection based on a mathematical fractal-fractional model via the Adams-Bashforth scheme and Newton polynomials. *Mathematics* **2022**, *10*, 1366. [CrossRef]
22. Abro, K.A.; Atangana, A. Numerical and mathematical analysis of induction motor by means of AB-fractal-fractional differentiation actuated by drilling system. *Numer. Meth. Partial Differ. Equ.* **2022**, *38*, 293–307. [CrossRef]
23. Saad, K.M.; Alqhtani, M.; Gomez-Aguilar, J.F. Fractal-fractional study of the hepatitis C virus infection model. *Res. Phys.* **2020**, *19*, 103555. [CrossRef]
24. Etemad, S.; Avcı, İ.; Kumar, P.; Baleanu, D.; Rezapour, S. Some novel mathematical analysis on the fractal–fractional model of the AH1N1/09 virus and its generalized Caputo-type version. *Chaos Solitons Fractals* **2022**, *162*, 112511. [CrossRef]
25. Asamoah, J.K.K. Fractal-fractional model and numerical scheme based on Newton polynomial for Q fever disease under Atangana-Baleanu derivative. *Res. Phys.* **2022**, *34*, 105189. [CrossRef]
26. Khan, H.; Alam, K.; Gulzar, H.; Etemad, S.; Rezapour, S. A case study of fractal-fractional tuberculosis model in China: Existence and stability theories along with numerical simulations. *Math. Comput. Simul.* **2022**, *198*, 455–473. [CrossRef]
27. Mohammadi, H.; Kumar, S.; Rezapour, S.; Etemad, S. A theoretical study of the Caputo-Fabrizio fractional modeling for hearing loss due to Mumps virus with optimal control. *Chaos, Solitons Fractals* **2021**, *144*, 110668. [CrossRef]
28. Owolabi, K.M.; Shikongo, A. Fractal Fractional Operator Method on HER2+ Breast Cancer Dynamics. *Int. J. Appl. Comput. Math.* **2021**, *7*, 85. [CrossRef]
29. Owolabi, K.M.; Shikongo, A.; Atangana, A. Fractal Fractional Derivative Operator Method on MCF-7 Cell Line Dynamics. In *Methods of Mathematical Modelling and Computation for Complex Systems. Studies in Systems, Decision and Control*; Singh, J., Dutta, H., Kumar, D., Baleanu, D., Hristov, J., Eds.; Springer: Cham, Switzerland, 2022; Volume 373.
30. Samet, B.; Vetro, C.; Vetro, P. Fixed point theorems for α-ψ-contractive type mappings. *Nonlinear Anal.* **2012**, *75*, 2154–2165. [CrossRef]

31. Granas, A.; Dugundji, J. *Fixed Point Theory*; Springer: New York, NY, USA, 2003.
32. Rassias, T.M. On the stability of the linear mapping in Banach spaces. *Proc. Amer. Math. Soc.* **1978**, *72*, 297–300. [CrossRef]
33. Cho, Y.J.; Park, C.; Rassias, T.M.; Saadati, R. *Stability of Functional Equations in Banach Algebras*; Springer: Cham, Switzerland, 2015.
34. den Driessche, P.V.; Watmough, J. Reproduction numbers and sub-threshold endemic equilibria for compartmental models of disease transmission. *Math. Biosci.* **2002**, *180*, 29–48. [CrossRef]
35. Arruda, A.G.; Alkhamis, M.A.; VanderWaal, K.; Morrison, R.B.; Perez, A.M. Estimation of time-dependent reproduction numbers for porcine reproductive and respiratory syndrome across different regions and production systems of the US. *Front. Vet. Sci.* **2017**, *4*, 46. [CrossRef] [PubMed]
36. Diekmann, O.; Heesterbeek, J.A.P. *Mathematical Epidemiology of Infectious Diseases*; Model Building, Analysis and Interpretation; John Wiley and Sons: New York, NY, USA, 2000.
37. Diekmann, O.; Heesterbeek, J.A.P.; Metz, J.A.J. On the definition and the computation of the basic reproduction ratio R_0 in models for infectious diseases in heterogeneous populations. *J. Math. Biol.* **1990**, *28*, 365–382. [CrossRef]
38. Chitnis, N.; Hyman, J.M.; Cushing, J.M. Determining important parameters in the spread of malaria through the sensitivity analysis of a mathematical model. *Bull. Math. Biol.* **2008**, *70*, 1272–1296. [CrossRef]
39. Mathai, A.M. *Jobians of Matrix Transformation and Functions of Matrix Arguments*; World Scientific Publishing: Hackensack, NJ, USA, 1997.
40. Bretscher, O. *Linear Algebra with Applications-Pearson*; Cambridge University Press: New York, NY, USA, 1974.
41. Kim, J.-H.; Su, W.; Song, Y.J. On stability of a polynomial. *J. Appl. Math. Inform.* **2018**, *36*, 231–236.
42. Li, M.Y.; Wang, L. Global stability in some seir epidemic models. In *Mathematical Approaches for Emerging and Reemerging Infectious Diseases: Models, Methods, and Theory*; Castillo-Chavez, C., Blower, S., van den Driessche, P., Kirschner, D., Yakubu, AA. Eds.; Springer, New York, NY, USA, 2002.
43. Burden, R.L.; Faires, J.D. *Numerical Analysis*; Brooks/Cole: Pacific Grove, CA, USA, 2011.

mathematics MDPI

Article

Hopf Bifurcation in a Predator–Prey Model with Memory Effect in Predator and Anti-Predator Behaviour in Prey

Wenqi Zhang, Dan Jin * and Ruizhi Yang

Department of Mathematics, Northeast Forestry University, Harbin 150040, China
* Correspondence: jindan720@163.com or jindan@nefu.edu.cn

Abstract: In this paper, a diffusive predator–prey model with a memory effect in predator and anti-predator behaviour in prey is studied. The stability of the coexisting equilibrium and the existence of Hopf bifurcation are analysed by analysing the distribution of characteristic roots. The property of Hopf bifurcation is investigated by the theory of the centre manifold and normal form method. Through the numerical simulations, it is observed that the anti-predator behaviour parameter η, the memory-based diffusion coefficient parameter d, and memory delay τ can affect the stability of the coexisting equilibrium under some parameters and cause the spatially inhomogeneous oscillation of prey and predator's densities.

Keywords: memory effect; anti-predator behaviour; delay; Hopf bifurcation

MSC: 34K18; 35B32

Citation: Zhang, W.; Jin, D.; Yang, R. Hopf Bifurcation in a Predator–Prey Model with Memory Effect in Predator and Anti-Predator Behaviour in Prey. *Mathematics* **2023**, *11*, 556. https://doi.org/10.3390/math11030556

Academic Editor: Ioannis K. Argyros

Received: 26 December 2022
Revised: 17 January 2023
Accepted: 18 January 2023
Published: 20 January 2023

1. Introduction

The predator–prey model has attracted the attention of many scholars [1–3]. Traditional predator–prey models often label animals as predator and prey; this is based on the assumptions that predators feed on prey [4–6]. However, sometimes, anti-predator behaviour in prey may occur [7,8]. Experiments show that anti-predator behaviour in prey can be divided into two cases [9]: (a) morphological changes or through changes in behaviour [10,11] or (b) the preys attack their predators [12,13].

B. Tang and Y. Xiao [9] proposed the following model:

$$\begin{cases} \frac{du}{dt} = ru(1-\frac{u}{K}) - \frac{\beta uv}{a+u^2}, \\ \frac{dv}{dt} = \frac{\mu\beta uv}{a+u^2} - cv - \eta uv. \end{cases} \tag{1}$$

All the parameters are positive. r, K, β, a, μ, and c represent the growth rate, carrying capacity, capture rate, handling time, conversion rate, and death rate, respectively. The term ηuv represents the anti-predator behaviour in prey. The function response $\frac{\beta u}{a+u^2}$ is the simplified Monod–Haldane function, which is also called the Holling type IV functional response. They mainly studied the bifurcations, including saddle–node bifurcation, Hopf bifurcation, homoclinic bifurcation, and a Bogdanov–Takens bifurcation of codimension 2, and showed that anti-predator behaviour is a benefit for the prey population [9].

Motivated by the work of [9], some scholars have studied the predator–prey models using anti-predator behaviour [14–17]. Wang et al. studied a predator–prey model with a stage structure for the prey and anti-predator behaviour and mainly focused on the stability and Hopf bifurcation [15]. J. Liu and X. Zhang considered a delayed reaction–diffusion predator–prey model with anti-predator behaviour and a Holling II functional response [16]. They mainly studied the Turing instability and Hopf bifurcation. R. Yang and J. Ma studied a diffusive predator–prey model with anti-predator behaviour and a Beddington–DeAngelis functional response and showed that the Turing instability induced by diffusion and Hopf bifurcation were induced by time delay [17]. Although it is shown in the literature [16,17] that there may be spatially inhomogeneous periodic solutions caused by time delay, no examples of spatially inhomogeneous periodic solutions are provided in numerical simulations.

In the real world, prey and predators are not static in space and they often engender self-diffusion. Therefore, many scholars use a reaction diffusion equation to describe the growth law of populations [18,19]. In addition, smart predators also have memory effect and cognitive behaviour [20]. For example, blue whales migrate by memory. Another example is that animals in polar regions usually determine their spatial movement by judging their footprints, which record the history of species' distributions and movements, including time delay. Obviously, highly developed animals can even remember their historical distribution or cluster of species in space. Great progress has been made in the implicit integration of spatial cognition or memory [21–23]. Some scholars have studied spatial memory in population models by introducing an additional delayed diffusion term [24–26]. In [22], the authors studied a memory-based reaction–diffusion equation with nonlocal maturation delay and a homogeneous Dirichlet boundary condition and mainly considered the local stability and Hopf bifurcation. In [25], Song et al. provided a normal form theory for Turing–Hopf bifurcation in the general reaction–diffusion equation with memory-based diffusion and a nonlocal reaction. In [26], Song et al. obtained the normal form of the Hopf bifurcation in the predator–prey model with a memory effect.

In this paper, assuming the predator has spatial-memory diffusion, we study the following model:

$$\begin{cases} \dfrac{\partial u(x,t)}{\partial t} = d_1\Delta u + ru(1-\dfrac{u}{K}) - \dfrac{\beta uv}{a+u^2}, \\ \dfrac{\partial v(x,t)}{\partial t} = -d\nabla(v\nabla u(t-\tau)) + d_2\Delta v + \dfrac{\mu\beta uv}{a+u^2} - cv - \eta uv, \ \ x\in\Omega,\ t>0 \\ \dfrac{\partial u(x,t)}{\partial \bar{v}} = \dfrac{\partial v(x,t)}{\partial \bar{v}} = 0, \ \ x\in\partial\Omega,\ t>0 \\ u(x,\theta) = u_0(x,\theta)\geq 0, v(x,\theta) = v_0(x,\theta)\geq 0, \ \ x\in\bar{\Omega}, \theta\in[-\tau,0]. \end{cases} \tag{2}$$

where d_1 and d_2 are self-diffusion parameters. The term $-d\nabla(v\nabla u(t-\tau))$ is the memory-based diffusion effect. d is the memory-based diffusion co-efficient and the time delay $\tau > 0$ is the averaged memory period of the predator. If we assume the region the prey and predator live in is closed, then the Neumann boundary condition is used. For the convenience of calculation, we use $\Omega = (0, l\pi)$. As far as we know, no one has studied the model (2) at present. The aim of this paper is to study the effect of the memory delay, the memory-based diffusion, and the anti-predator behaviour on the model (2) from the perspective of stability and Hopf bifurcation.

The paper is arranged as follows. In Section 2, we studied the stability and the existence of Hopf bifurcation. In Section 3, we analysed the property of Hopf bifurcation. In Section 4, we provide some numerical simulations. In Section 5, we obtain a short conclusion.

2. Stability Analysis

The existence of equilibria has been studied in [9]. For the sake of completeness, we just provide the following lemma; the proof is available in [9].

Lemma 1. *The existence of equilibria for model (2) is as follows.*

- *The model (2) always has two boundary equilibriums $(0,0)$ and $(K,0)$.*
- **Case I:** *$a\eta - \beta\mu \geq 0$. The model (2) always has no positive equilibrium.*
- **Case II:** *$a\eta - \beta\mu < 0$.*
  - ⋆ **Subcase I:** *The model (2) always has no positive equilibrium when $f(u_c) > 0$.*
  - ⋆ **Subcase II:** *The model (2) has two positive equilibria (u_-, v_-) and (u_+, v_+) when $f(u_c) < 0$ and $f(K) > 0$.*

- ⋆ **Subcase III:** *The model* (2) *has a unique positive equilibrium* (u_-, v_-) *when* $f(u_c) < 0$ *and* $f(K) \le 0$.
- ⋆ **Subcase IV:** *The model* (2) *has a unique positive equilibrium* $(u_-, v_-)=(u_+, v_+)$ *when* $f(u_c) = 0$.

where $u_c = \frac{-c+\sqrt{c^2-3\eta(a\eta-\beta\mu)}}{3\eta}$, $f(u_c) = \frac{1}{27\eta^2}\left(2c^3 + 9c\eta(2a\eta+\beta\mu) - 2(c^2+3\eta(-a\eta+\beta\mu))^{3/2}\right)$, $f(u) = u^3\eta + cu^2 + u(a\eta-\beta\mu) + ac = 0$, $u_\pm = \frac{-c+\sqrt{A}(\cos[\frac{\theta}{3}]\pm\sqrt{3}\sin[\frac{\theta}{3}])}{3\eta}$, $v_\pm = \frac{r(K-u_\pm)(a+u_\pm^2)}{K\beta}$, $A = c^2 - 3\eta(\eta a - \beta\mu)$, $B = c(\eta a - \beta\mu) - 9\eta ac$, $T = \frac{(2Ac-3\eta B)}{2\sqrt{A^3}}$, $\theta = \arccos[T]$.

In the following, we just assume the model (2) has a positive equilibrium $E_*(u_*, v_*)$. In particular, the model (2) may have two positive equilibria. Then, we can use the same method to study the property for different positive equilibria. The linear system of (2) at $E_*(u_*, v_*)$ is

$$\frac{\partial u}{\partial t}\begin{pmatrix} u(x,t) \\ u(x,t) \end{pmatrix} = J_1\begin{pmatrix} \Delta u(t) \\ \Delta v(t) \end{pmatrix} + J_2\begin{pmatrix} \Delta u(t-\tau) \\ \Delta v(t-\tau) \end{pmatrix} + L\begin{pmatrix} u(x,t) \\ v(x,t) \end{pmatrix}, \tag{3}$$

where

$$J_1 = \begin{pmatrix} d_1 & 0 \\ 0 & d_2 \end{pmatrix}, \quad J_2 = \begin{pmatrix} 0 & 0 \\ -dv_* & 0 \end{pmatrix}, \quad L = \begin{pmatrix} \alpha_1 & \alpha_2 \\ \beta_1 & 0 \end{pmatrix},$$

and $\alpha_1 = -\frac{ru_*}{K(a+u_*^2)}(a - 2Ku_* + 3u_*^2)$, $\alpha_2 = -\frac{u_*\beta}{a+u_*^2} < 0$, $\beta_1 = v_*\left(\frac{(a-u_*^2)\beta\mu}{(a+u_*^2)^2} - \eta\right)$.

The characteristic equations are:

$$\lambda^2 + \kappa_n\lambda + \nu_n + \varrho_n e^{-\lambda\tau} = 0, \quad n \in \mathbb{N}_0, \tag{4}$$

where

$$\kappa_n = (d_1+d_2)\mu_n - \alpha_1, \quad \nu_n = -\alpha_2\beta_1 - \alpha_1 d_2\mu_n + d_1 d_2\mu_n^2, \quad \varrho_n = -\alpha_2 dv_*\mu_n, \quad \mu_n = \frac{n^2}{l^2}.$$

2.1. $\tau = 0$

The characteristic Equations (4) are:

$$\lambda^2 + \kappa_n\lambda + \nu_n + \varrho_n = 0, \quad n \in \mathbb{N}_0, \tag{5}$$

where $\nu_n + \varrho_n = -\alpha_2\beta_1 - (\alpha_2 dv_* + \alpha_1 d_2)\mu_n + d_1 d_2\mu_n^2$. We propose the following hypothesis:

Hypothesis 1 (H1).

$$a\eta - \beta\mu < 0, \quad K < \frac{a+3u_*^2}{2u_*}, \quad \eta < \frac{(a-u_*^2)\beta\mu}{(a+u_*^2)^2}.$$

In particular, in **(H1)**, $K < \frac{a+3u_*^2}{2u_*}$ implies $\alpha_1 < 0$, and $\eta < \frac{(a-u_*^2)\beta\mu}{(a+u_*^2)^2}$ implies $\beta_1 > 0$. We should notice that u_* is related to parameter η, so $\eta < \frac{(a-u_*^2)\beta\mu}{(a+u_*^2)^2}$ is very complicated. Then we can obtain the following theorem.

Theorem 1. *For system* (2) *with* $\tau = 0$, $E_*(u_*, v_*)$ *is locally stable under* **(H1)**.

2.2. $\tau > 0$

Assume **(H1)** holds and let $i\omega$ ($\omega > 0$) be a solution of (4), then:

$$-\omega^2 + \kappa_n i\omega + \nu_n + \varrho_n(\cos\omega\tau - i\sin\omega\tau) = 0.$$

We can obtain $\cos\omega\tau = \frac{\omega^2 - \nu_n}{\varrho_n}$, $\sin\omega\tau = \frac{\kappa_n\omega}{\varrho_n} > 0$ under hypothesis (**H1**). It leads to:

$$\omega^4 + \left(\kappa_n^2 - 2\nu_n\right)\omega^2 + \nu_n^2 - \varrho_n^2 = 0. \tag{6}$$

Let $p = \omega^2$, then (6) becomes:

$$p^2 + \left(\kappa_n^2 - 2\nu_n\right)p + \nu_n^2 - \varrho_n^2 = 0, \tag{7}$$

and the roots of (7) are $p_n^{\pm} = \frac{1}{2}[-(\kappa_n^2 - 2\nu_n) \pm \sqrt{(\kappa_n^2 - 2\nu_n)^2 - 4(\nu_n^2 - \varrho_n^2)}]$. By direct computation, we have:

$$\begin{cases} \kappa_n^2 - 2\nu_n = (d_1^2 + d_2^2)\mu_n^2 - 2\alpha_1 d_1 \mu_n + \alpha_1^2 + 2\alpha_2\beta_1, \\ \nu_n - \varrho_n = d_1 d_2 \frac{n^4}{l^4} + (\alpha_2 d v_* - \alpha_1 d_2)\mu_n - \alpha_2\beta_1, \end{cases}$$

and $\nu_n + \varrho_n > 0$ under hypothesis (**H1**). Define $\eta_{\pm} = \frac{-(\alpha_2 d v_* - \alpha_1 d_2) \pm \sqrt{(\alpha_2 d v_* - \alpha_1 d_2)^2 - 4 d_1 d_2 (-\alpha_2\beta_1)}}{2 d_1 d_2}$, $d_* = \frac{\alpha_1 d_2}{\alpha_2 v_*} + \frac{2}{v_*}\sqrt{-\frac{b_1 d_1 d_2}{\alpha_2}}$, and $\mathbb{S} = \{n | \frac{n^2}{l_2} \in (\eta_-, \eta_+),\ n \in \mathbb{N}_0\}$. Then:

$$\begin{cases} \nu_n - \varrho_n > 0, & \text{for } d \le d_*,\ n \in \mathbb{N}_0, \\ \nu_n - \varrho_n > 0, & \text{for } d > d_*,\ n \notin \mathbb{S}, \\ \nu_n - \varrho_n < 0, & \text{for } d > d_*,\ n \in \mathbb{S}. \end{cases} \tag{8}$$

The existence of purely imaginary roots of Equation (4) can be divided into the following two cases.

Case 1: $\alpha_1^2 + 2\alpha_2\beta_1 > 0$. We can obtain $\kappa_n^2 - 2\nu_n > \alpha_1^2 + 2\alpha_2 b_1 > 0$. For $d > d_*$ and $n \in \mathbb{S}$, then Equation (4) has a pair of purely imaginary roots $\pm i\omega_n^+$ at $\tau_n^{j,+}$ for $j \in \mathbb{N}_0$ and $n \in \mathbb{S}$. Otherwise, Equation (4) does not have characteristic roots with zero real parts.

Case 2: $\alpha_1^2 + 2\alpha_2\beta_1 < 0$. Divide this case into the following two subcases.

- For $d \le d_*$ and $n \in \mathbb{S}_1 := \{n | \kappa_n^2 - 2\nu_n < 0,\ (\kappa_n^2 - 2\nu_n)^2 - 4(\nu_n^2 - \varrho_n^2) > 0,\ n \in \mathbb{N}_0\}$, then Equation (4) has two pairs of purely imaginary roots $\pm i\omega_n^{\pm}$ at $\tau_n^{j,\pm}$ for $j \in \mathbb{N}_0$ and $n \in \mathbb{S}_1$. Otherwise, Equation (4) does not have characteristic roots with zero real parts.
- For $d > d_*$ and $n \in \mathbb{S}_2 := \{n | \kappa_n^2 - 2\nu_n < 0,\ (\kappa_n^2 - 2\nu_n)^2 - 4(\nu_n^2 - \varrho_n^2) > 0,\ n \in \mathbb{N}_0,\ n \notin \mathbb{S}\}$, then Equation (4) has two pairs of purely imaginary roots $\pm i\omega_n^{\pm}$ at $\tau_n^{j,\pm}$ for $j \in \mathbb{N}_0$ and $n \in \mathbb{S}_1$. For $d > d_*$ and $n \in \mathbb{S}$, then Equation (4) has a pair of purely imaginary roots $\pm i\omega_n^+$ at $\tau_n^{j,+}$ for $j \in \mathbb{N}_0$ and $n \in \mathbb{S}$. Otherwise, Equation (4) does not have characteristic roots with zero real parts.

  Where

$$\omega_n^{\pm} = \sqrt{p_n^{\pm}}, \quad \tau_n^{j,\pm} = \frac{1}{\omega_n^{\pm}} \arccos\left(\frac{(\omega_n^{\pm})^2 - \nu_n}{\varrho_n}\right) + 2j\pi. \tag{9}$$

Define $\mathbb{M} = \{\tau_n^{j,+}$ or $\tau_n^{j,-} |$. Equation (4) has purely imaginary roots $\pm i\omega_n^+$ or $\pm i\omega_n^-$ when $\tau = \tau_n^{j,+}$ or $\tau_n^{j,-}\}$.

Lemma 2. *Assume (H1) holds. Then,* $Re(\frac{d\lambda}{d\tau})|_{\tau=\tau_n^{j,+}} > 0$, $Re(\frac{d\lambda}{d\tau})|_{\tau=\tau_n^{j,-}} < 0$ *for* $\tau_n^{j,\pm} \in \mathbb{S}$ *and* $j \in \mathbb{N}_0$.

Proof. By (4), we have:

$$\left(\frac{d\lambda}{d\tau}\right)^{-1} = \frac{2\lambda + \kappa_n}{\varrho_n \lambda e^{-\lambda\tau}} - \frac{\tau}{\lambda}.$$

Then:

$$
\begin{aligned}
[\mathrm{Re}(\frac{d\lambda}{d\tau})^{-1}]_{\tau=\tau_n^{j,\pm}} &= \mathrm{Re}[\frac{2\lambda+\kappa_n}{\varrho_n\lambda e^{-\lambda\tau}} - \frac{\tau}{\lambda}]_{\tau=\tau_n^{j,\pm}} \\
&= [\frac{1}{\kappa_n^2\omega^2+(\nu_n-\omega)^2}(2\omega^2+\kappa_n^2-2\nu_n)]_{\tau=\tau_n^{j,\pm}} \\
&= \pm[\frac{1}{\kappa_n^2\omega^2+(\nu_n-\omega)^2}\sqrt{(\kappa_n^2-2\nu_n)^2-4(\nu_n^2-\varrho_n^2)}]_{\tau=\tau_n^{j,\pm}}.
\end{aligned}
$$

Therefore, $\mathrm{Re}(\frac{d\lambda}{d\tau})|_{\tau=\tau_n^{j,+}} > 0$, $\mathrm{Re}(\frac{d\lambda}{d\tau})|_{\tau=\tau_n^{j,-}} < 0$. □

Denote $\tau_* = min\{\tau_n^{0,\pm} | \tau_n^{0,\pm} \in \mathbb{M}\}$.

Theorem 2. *For the model (2), assume (**H1**) holds.*

- $E_*(u_*, v_*)$ *is locally stable for* $\tau > 0$ *when* $\mathbb{M} = \varnothing$.
- $E_*(u_*, v_*)$ *is locally stable for* $\tau \in [0, \tau_*)$ *when* $\mathbb{M} \neq \varnothing$.
- $E_*(u_*, v_*)$ *is unstable for* $\tau \in (\tau_*, \tau_* + \epsilon)$ *for some* $\epsilon > 0$ *when* $\mathbb{M} \neq \varnothing$.
- $\tau = \tau_n^{j,+}$ $(\tau = \tau_n^{j,-})$, $j \in \mathbb{N}_0$, $\tau_n^{j,\pm} \in \mathbb{M}$ *are Hopf bifurcation points.*

3. Property of Hopf Bifurcation

By the algorithm in [26], we provide the normal form of Hopf bifurcation as follows. The detail computation is provided in Appendix A.

$$
\dot{z} = Bz + \frac{1}{2}\begin{pmatrix} B_1 z_1 \varepsilon \\ \bar{B}_1 z_2 \varepsilon \end{pmatrix} + \frac{1}{3!}\begin{pmatrix} B_2 z_1^2 z_2 \varepsilon \\ \bar{B}_2 z_1 z_2^2 \varepsilon \end{pmatrix} + O(|z|\varepsilon^2 + |z^4|), \tag{10}
$$

where

$$
B_1 = 2i\tilde{\omega}\psi^T\phi, \ B_2 = B_{21} + \frac{3}{2}(B_{22} + B_{23}).
$$

By coordinate transformation $z_1 = \omega_1 - i\omega_2$, $z_2 = \omega_1 + i\omega_2$, and $\omega_1 = \rho\cos\xi$, $\omega_2 = \rho\sin\xi$, the normal form (10) can be rewritten as:

$$
\dot{\rho} = K_1\varepsilon\rho + K_2\rho^3 + O(\rho\varepsilon^2 + |(\rho,\varepsilon)|^4), \tag{11}
$$

where $K_1 = \frac{1}{2}\mathrm{Re}(B_1)$, $K_2 = \frac{1}{3!}\mathrm{Re}(B_2)$.

From [26], we have the following theorem:

Theorem 3. *If* $K_1K_2 < 0(> 0)$, *the Hopf bifurcation is supercritical (subcritical) and the bifurcating periodic solutions is stable (unstable) for* $K_2 < 0(> 0)$.

4. Numerical Simulations

Fix the following parameters:

$$
c = 0.05,\ r = 0.5,\ a = 1,\ \mu = 0.8,\ \beta = 0.4,\ K = 3,\ d_1 = 0.1,\ d_2 = 0.2,\ l = 2. \tag{12}
$$

4.1. The Effect of Anti-Predator Behaviour

We know that the system (2) has a positive equilibrium when $\eta \leq 0.1560$. Especially, the system (2) has a unique positive equilibrium (u_-, v_-) when $\eta \leq 0.0153$ (Figure 1 left) and has two positive equilibria, (u_-, v_-) and (u_+, v_+), when $0.0153 < \eta < 0.1560$ (Figure 1 right). However, when $\eta \approx 0.1560$, (u_-, v_-) and (u_+, v_+) coincide into one positive equilibrium (Figure 1 right).

Through analysis, we can obtain (u_+, v_+), which is always unstable when it exists. Then, we mainly study the dynamics at (u_-, v_-). The parameters α_1 and β_1 with parameter η at (u_-, v_-) are provided in Figure 2. It shows that (u_-, v_-) is always unstable when $\tau = 0$ and anti-predator behaviour parameter η is larger than some critical value. To guarantee assumption $(\mathbf{H_1})$ is true, $\alpha_1 < 0$ and $\beta_1 >$ should hold.

The bifurcation diagram of system (2) with parameter η when $d = 0.7$ is provided in Figure 3 left. When parameter η increases, the stability interval of (u_-, v_-) becomes smaller. This implies that increasing the anti-predator behaviour parameter η is not beneficial to the uniform distribution of predator and prey and will cause inhomogeneous oscillations of the population's density.

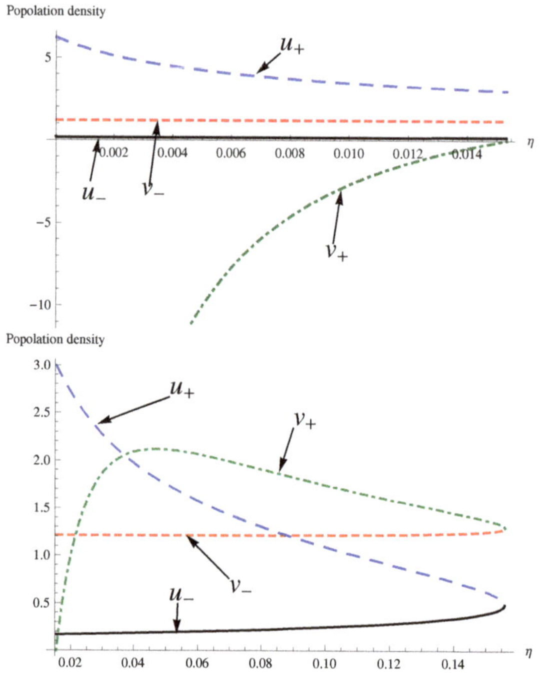

Figure 1. The existence of positive equilibrium with parameter η.

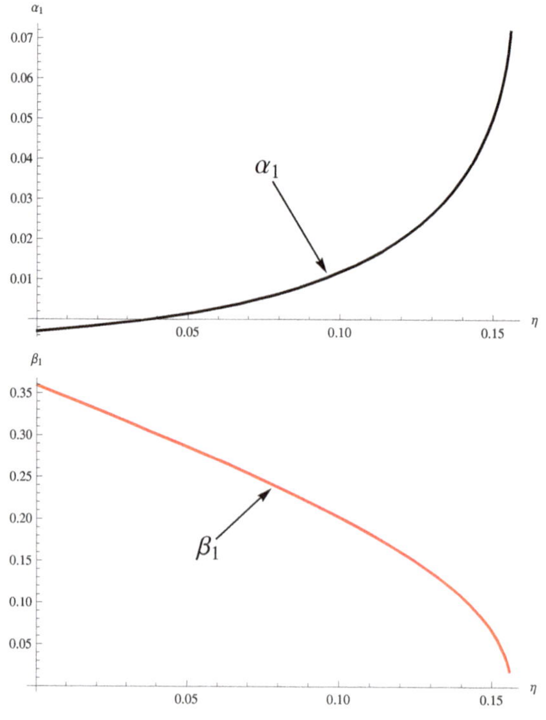

Figure 2. α_1 and β_1 with parameter η at (u_-, v_-).

4.2. The Effect of Memory-Based Diffusion

We also provide the bifurcation diagram of system (2) with parameter d when $\eta = 0.01$ (Figure 3 right). When parameter $d < d_*$, (u_-, v_-) is always stable. When we increase parameter d until $d > d_*$, the Hopf bifurcating curves emerge. When parameter d increases, the stability interval of (u_-, v_-) becomes smaller. This implies that increasing the memory-based diffusion coefficient parameter d is not beneficial to the uniform distribution of predators and prey when $d > d_*$ and will cause spatial oscillations of the population's density.

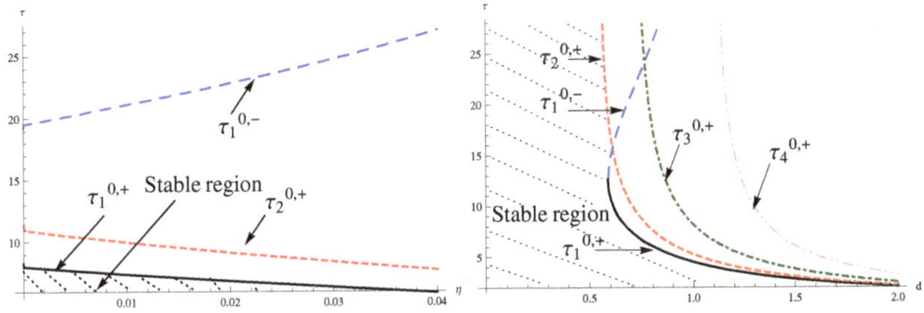

$d = 0.7$ $\eta = 0.01$

Figure 3. Bifurcation diagram of system (2) with parameter η (**Left**) and d (**Right**).

4.3. The Effect of Memory Delay

Especially, we choose $\eta = 0.01$, then $(u_-, v_-) \approx (0.1658, 1.2134)$ is the unique positive equilibrium. From direct calculation, we have $\alpha_1^2 + 2\alpha_2\beta_1 \approx -0.0446 < 0$, and $d_* \approx 0.5452$. Choose $d = 0.7 > d_*$, then $\mathbb{S}_2 = \{1\}$, $\mathbb{S} = \{2\}$, $\tau_* = \tau_1^{0,+} \approx 7.3983 < \tau_2^{0,+} \approx 10.0126 < \tau_1^{0,-} \approx 21.1518$ and $K_1 \approx 0.04689 > 0$, $K_2 \approx -0.0708 < 0$. Then (u_-, v_-) is locally stable when $\tau \in [0, \tau_*)$ (Figure 4) and unstable when $\tau > \tau_*$. We can see from Figure 4 that when the time delay is less than the critical value, the density of the prey and predator will be evenly distributed in space and tend to the coexisting equilibrium. In addition, the stable bifurcating periodic orbits with mode-1 and exists for $\tau > \tau_*$ (Figure 5). At this time, when the time delay is greater than the critical value, the density of prey and predator will produce periodic oscillation and the spatial distribution is uneven. This means that the delay in the averaged memory period of the predator may affect the stability of (u_-, v_-) and induce the spatial oscillations of the population's density under some parameters.

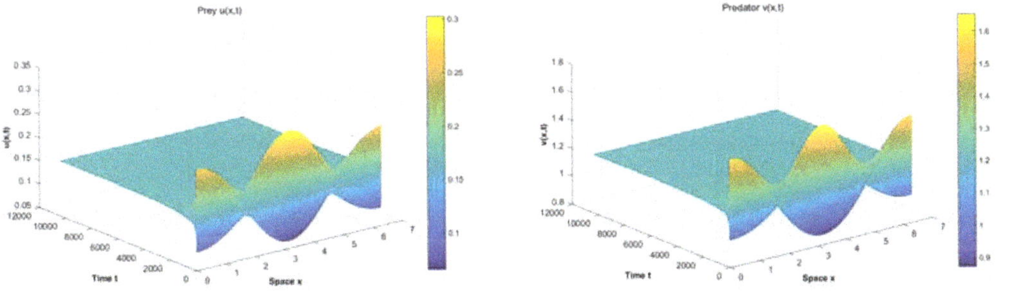

Prey $u(x,t)$ Predator $v(x,t)$

Figure 4. The numerical simulations of system (2) with $d = 0.7$ and $\tau = 7$.

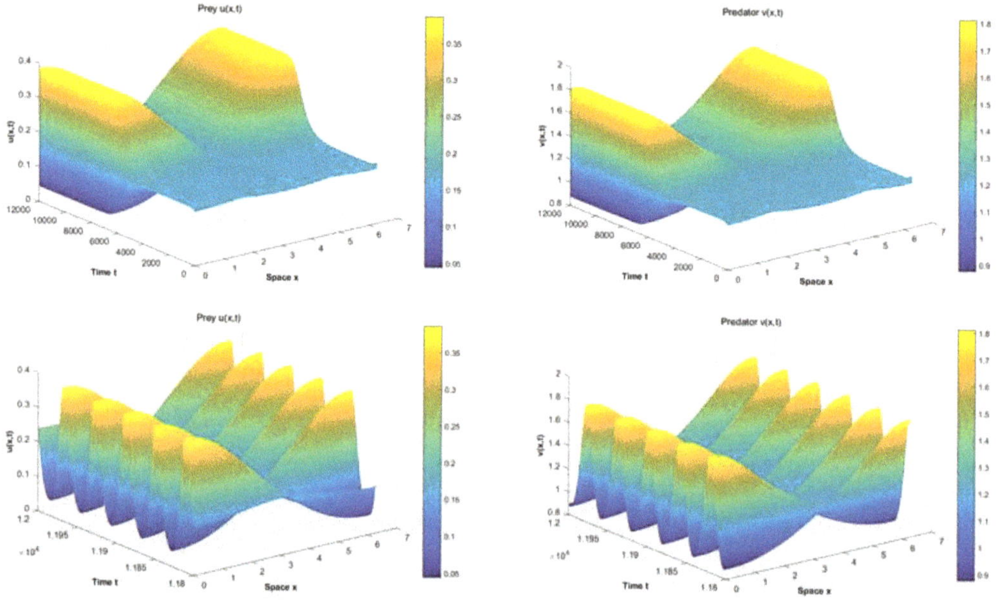

Prey $u(x,t)$ Predator $v(x,t)$

Figure 5. The numerical simulations of system (2) with $d = 0.7$ and $\tau = 8$. The time scale of the top two figures is from 0 to 12,000. The time scales of the two figures below are from 11,800 to 12,000.

5. Conclusions

We incorporate the predator's memory effect and the prey's anti-predator behaviour into a predator–prey model. We mainly study the stability of the coexisting equilibrium and memory delay inducing Hopf bifurcation. Through the method in [26], we provide the normal form of Hopf bifurcation at the coexisting equilibrium that can be used to determine the direction and stability of the bifurcating period solutions. Through numerical simulations, we obtain that the anti-predator behaviour parameter η can affect the existence and stability of the coexisting equilibrium. Furthermore, increasing the anti-predator behaviour parameter η is not beneficial to the stability of the coexisting equilibrium and will cause spatial inhomogeneous periodic oscillation of the prey and predator's densities. In addition, the memory-based diffusion coefficient parameter d can also affect the stability of the coexisting equilibrium when it is larger than the critical value d_*. At last, the memory delay has the destabilizing effect on the coexisting equilibrium and induces spatial inhomogeneous periodic oscillation of prey and predator's densities.

Author Contributions: W.Z., D.J. and R.Y. contributed to the study conception and design. Material preparation, data collection, and analysis were performed by D.J. All authors read and approved the final manuscript.

Funding: This research is supported by the Fundamental Research Funds for the Central Universities (Grant No. 2572022BC01), and College Students Innovations Special Project funded by Northeast Forestry University.

Data Availability Statement: Data sharing is not applicable to this article as no datasets were generated or analyzed during the current study.

Conflicts of Interest: The authors declare no conflict of interest.

Appendix A. Computation of Normal Form

In this section, we use the algorithm in [26] to compute the normal form of the Hopf bifurcation. We denote the critical value of the Hopf bifurcation as $\tilde{\tau}$ and that Equation (4) has a pair of purely imaginary roots: $\pm i\omega_n$. Let $\bar{u}(x,t) = u(x,\tau t) - u_*$ and $\bar{v}(x,t) = v(x,\tau t) - v_*$. Drop the bar, (2) can be written as:

$$\begin{cases} \dfrac{\partial u}{\partial t} = \tau\left[d_1\Delta u + r(u+u_*)\left(1 - \dfrac{u+u_*}{K}\right) - \dfrac{\beta(u+u_*)(v+v_*)}{a+(u+u_*)^2}\right], \\ \dfrac{\partial v}{\partial t} = \tau\left[-d\nabla((v+v_*)\nabla(u(t-1)+u_*)) + d_2\Delta v + \dfrac{\mu\beta(u+u_*)(v+v_*)}{a+(u+u_*)^2} - c(v+v_*) - \eta(u+u_*)(v+v_*)\right]. \end{cases} \tag{A1}$$

Define the real-valued Sobolev space $\mathbb{X} = \left\{U = (u,v)^T \in W^{2,2}(0,l\pi)^2,\ (\frac{\partial u}{\partial x}, \frac{\partial v}{\partial x})|_{x=0,l\pi} = 0\right\}$, the inner product:

$$[U,V] = \int_0^{l\pi} U^T V dx, \text{ for } U,\ V \in \mathbb{X},$$

and $\mathbb{C} = C([-1,0];\mathbb{X})$. Set $\tau = \tilde{\tau} + \varepsilon$, where ε is small perturbation. Then system (A1) is rewritten as

$$\frac{dU(t)}{dt} = d(\varepsilon)\Delta(U_t) + L(\varepsilon)(U_t) + F(U_t,\varepsilon), \tag{A2}$$

where for $\varphi = (\varphi,\varphi_2)^T \in \mathbb{C}$, $d(\varepsilon)\Delta$, $L(\varepsilon) : \mathbb{C} \to \mathbb{X}$, $F : \mathbb{C} \times \mathbb{R}^2 \to \mathbb{X}$. They are defined as:

$$d(\varepsilon)\Delta(\varphi) = d_0\Delta(\varphi) + F^d(\varphi,\varepsilon),\ L(\varepsilon)(\varphi) = (\tilde{\tau}+\varepsilon)A\varphi(0),$$

$$F(\varphi,\varepsilon) = (\tilde{\tau}+\varepsilon)\begin{pmatrix} f(\phi^{(1)}(0)+u_*, \phi^{(2)}(0)+v_*) \\ g(\phi^{(1)}(0)+u_*, \phi^{(2)}(0)+v_*) \end{pmatrix} - L(\varepsilon)(\varphi),$$

and

$$d_0\Delta(\varphi) = \tilde{\tau}J_1\varphi_{xx}(0) + \tilde{\tau}J_2\varphi_{xx}(-1),$$

$$F^d(\varphi,\varepsilon) = -d(\tilde{\tau}+\varepsilon)\begin{pmatrix} 0 \\ \phi_x^{(1)}(-1)\phi_x^{(2)}(0) + \phi_{xx}^{(1)}(-1)\phi^{(2)}(0) \end{pmatrix} + \varepsilon\begin{pmatrix} d_1\phi_{xx}^{(1)}(0) \\ -dv_*\phi_{xx}^{(1)}(-1) + d_2\phi_{xx}^{(2)}(0) \end{pmatrix}.$$

Denote $L_0(\varphi) = \tilde{\tau}A\varphi(0)$ and rewrite (A2) as:

$$\frac{dU(t)}{dt} = d_0\Delta(U_t) + L_0(U_t) + \tilde{F}(U_t,\varepsilon), \tag{A3}$$

where: $\tilde{F}(\varphi,\varepsilon) = \varepsilon A\varphi(0) + F(\varphi,\varepsilon) + F^d(\varphi,\varepsilon)$. The characteristic equation for the linearized equation $\frac{dU(t)}{dt} = d_0\Delta(U_t) + L_0(U_t)$ is $\tilde{\Gamma}_n(\lambda) = det(\tilde{M}_n((\lambda)))$, where

$$\tilde{M}_n((\lambda) = \lambda I_2 + \tilde{\tau}\mu_n D_1 + \tilde{\tau}e^{-\lambda}\mu_n D_2 - \tilde{\tau}A. \tag{A4}$$

The eigenvalue problem:

$$-z(x)'' = \nu z(x),\ x \in (0,l\pi);\ z(0)' = z(l\pi)' = 0,$$

has eigenvalues μ_n and normalized eigenfunctions:

$$z_n(x) = \frac{\cos\frac{nx}{l}}{||\cos\frac{nx}{l}||_{2,2}} = \begin{cases} \frac{1}{l\pi} & n = 0, \\ \frac{\sqrt{2}}{l\pi}\cos\frac{nx}{l} & n \neq 0, \end{cases} \tag{A5}$$

Set $\beta_n^{(j)} = z_n(x)e_j$, $j = 1,2$, where $e_1 = (1,0)^T$ and $e_2 = (0,1)^T$. Define $\eta_n(\theta) \in BV([-1,0],\mathbb{R}^2)$, such that:

$$\int_{-1}^0 d\eta^n(\theta)\phi(\theta) = L_0^d(\varphi(\theta)) + L_0(\varphi(\theta)),\ \varphi \in C,$$

$C = C([-1,0],\mathbb{R}^2)$, $C^* = C([0,1],\mathbb{R}^{2*})$, and:

$$<\psi(s),\varphi(\theta)> = \psi(0)\varphi(0) - \int_{-1}^0\int_0^\theta \psi(\xi-\theta)d\eta^n(\theta)\varphi(\xi)d\xi,\ \psi \in C^*,\ \varphi \in C. \tag{A6}$$

Let $\Lambda = \{i\tilde{\omega}, -i\tilde{\omega}\}$, the eigenspace P, and corresponding adjoint space P^*. Decompose $C = P \oplus Q$, where $Q = \{\varphi \in C :< \psi, \varphi >= 0, \forall \psi \in P^*\}$. Choose $\Phi(\theta) = (\phi(\theta), \bar{\phi}(\theta))$, $\Psi(\theta) = col(\psi^T(s), \bar{\psi}^T(s))$, where:

$$\phi(\theta) = \phi e^{i\tilde{\omega}\theta} := \begin{pmatrix} \phi_1(\theta) \\ \phi_2(\theta) \end{pmatrix}, \ \psi(s) = \psi e^{-i\tilde{\omega}s} := \begin{pmatrix} \psi_1(s) \\ \psi_2(s) \end{pmatrix},$$

$$\phi = \begin{pmatrix} 1 \\ \frac{1}{\alpha_2}(-\alpha_1 + d_1\mu_n + i\tilde{\omega}) \end{pmatrix}, \quad \psi = M\begin{pmatrix} 1 \\ \frac{\alpha_2}{d_2\mu_n + i\tilde{\omega}} \end{pmatrix},$$

and

$$M = \left(-\frac{\alpha_1 l^2 - d_1 n^2 - d_2 n^2 - \alpha_2 d v_* e^{-i\tilde{\omega}} n^2 \tilde{\tau} - 2il^2\tilde{\omega}}{d_2 n^2 + il^2\tilde{\omega}} \right)^{-1}.$$

Then, $\phi(\theta)$ and $\psi(s)$ are the bases of P and P^*, respectively. Furthermore, such that $< \phi, \psi >= I_2$.

By direct computation, we have:

$$f_{20} = \begin{pmatrix} f_{20}^{(1)} \\ f_{20}^{(2)} \end{pmatrix}, \ f_{11} = \begin{pmatrix} f_{11}^{(1)} \\ f_{11}^{(2)} \end{pmatrix}, \ f_{02} = \begin{pmatrix} f_{02}^{(1)} \\ f_{02}^{(2)} \end{pmatrix},$$

$$f_{30} = \begin{pmatrix} f_{30}^{(1)} \\ f_{30}^{(2)} \end{pmatrix}, \ f_{21} = \begin{pmatrix} f_{21}^{(1)} \\ f_{21}^{(2)} \end{pmatrix}, \ f_{12} = \begin{pmatrix} f_{12}^{(1)} \\ f_{12}^{(2)} \end{pmatrix}, \ f_{03} = \begin{pmatrix} f_{03}^{(1)} \\ f_{03}^{(2)} \end{pmatrix},$$

where $f_{20}^{(1)} = -\frac{2u_*(-3a+u_*^2)v_*\beta}{(a+u_*^2)^3} - \frac{2r}{K}$, $f_{11}^{(1)} = \frac{(-a+u_*^2)\beta}{(a+u_*^2)^2}$, $f_{02}^{(1)} = 0$, $f_{30}^{(1)} = \frac{6(a^2-6au_*^2+u_*^4)v_*\beta}{(a+u_*^2)^4}$, $f_{21}^{(1)} = -\frac{2u_*(-3a+u_*^2)\beta}{(a+u_*^2)^3}$, $f_{12}^{(1)} = 0$, $f_{03}^{(1)} = 0$, $f_{20}^{(2)} = \frac{2(-3au_*+u_*^3)v_*\beta\mu}{(a+u_*^2)^3}$, $f_{11}^{(2)} = -\eta + \frac{(a-u_*^2)\beta\mu}{(a+u_*^2)^2}$, $f_{02}^{(2)} = 0$, $f_{30}^{(2)} = -\frac{6(a^2-6au_*^2+u_*^4)v_*\beta\mu}{(a+u_*^2)^4}$, $f_{21}^{(2)} = \frac{2(-3au_*+u_*^3)\beta\mu}{(a+u_*^2)^3}$, $f_{12}^{(2)} = 0$, $f_{03}^{(2)} = 0$. We can computation the following parameters:

$$\begin{aligned} A_{20} &= f_{20}\phi_1(0)^2 + f_{02}\phi_2(0)^2 + 2f_{11}\phi_1(0)\phi_2(0) = \overline{A}_0 2, \\ A_{11} &= 2f_{20}\phi_1(0)\bar{\phi}_1(0) + 2f_{02}\phi_2(0)\bar{\phi}_2(0) + 2f_{11}(\phi_1(0)\bar{\phi}_2(0) + \bar{\phi}_1(0)\phi_2(0)), \\ A_{21} &= 3f_{30}\phi_1(0)^2\bar{\phi}_1(0) + 3f_{03}\phi_2(0)^2\bar{\phi}_2(0) + 3f_{21}\left(\phi_1(0)^2\bar{\phi}_2(0) + 2\phi_1(0)\bar{\phi}_1(0)\phi_2(0)\right) \\ &\quad + 3f_{12}\left(\phi_2(0)^2\bar{\phi}_1(0) + 2\phi_2(0)\bar{\phi}_2(0)\phi_1(0)\right), \end{aligned} \tag{A7}$$

$$A_{20}^d = -2d\tau\begin{pmatrix} 0 \\ \phi_1(0)(-1)\phi_2(0)(0) \end{pmatrix} = \bar{A_{02}^d}, \ A_{11}^d = -2d\tau\begin{pmatrix} 0 \\ 2\mathrm{Re}[\phi_1(-1)\bar{\phi}_2(0)] \end{pmatrix},$$

and $\widetilde{A}_{j_1j_2} = A_{j_1j_2} - 2\mu_n A_{j_1j_2}^d$ for $j_1, j_2 = 0, 1, 2$, $j_1 + j_2 = 2$. In addition, $h_{0,20}(\theta) = \frac{1}{l\pi}(\widetilde{M}_0(2i\tilde{\omega}))^{-1} A_{20}e^{2i\tilde{\omega}\theta}$, $h_{0,11}(\theta) = \frac{1}{l\pi}(\widetilde{M}_0(0))^{-1}A_{11}$, $h_{2n,20}(\theta) = \frac{1}{2l\pi}(\widetilde{M}_{2n}(2i\tilde{\omega}))^{-1}\widetilde{A}_{20}e^{2i\tilde{\omega}\theta}$, $h_{2n,11}(\theta) = \frac{1}{l\pi}(\widetilde{M}_{2n}(0))^{-1}\widetilde{A}_{11}$.

$$S_2(\phi(\theta), h_{n,q_1q_2}(\theta)) = 2\phi_1 h_{n,q_1q_2}^{(1)} f_{20} + 2\phi_2 h_{n,q_1q_2}^{(2)} f_{02} + 2(\phi_1 h_{n,q_1q_2}^{(2)} + \phi_2 h_{n,q_1q_2}^{(1)}) f_{11},$$

$$S_2(\bar{\phi}(\theta), h_{n,q_1q_2}(\theta)) = 2\bar{\phi}_1 h_{n,q_1q_2}^{(1)} f_{20} + 2\bar{\phi}_2 h_{n,q_1q_2}^{(2)} f_{02} + 2(\bar{\phi}_1 h_{n,q_1q_2}^{(2)} + \bar{\phi}_2 h_{n,q_1q_2}^{(1)}) f_{11},$$

$$S_2^{d,1}(\phi(\theta), h_{0,11}(\theta)) = -2d\tilde{\tau}\begin{pmatrix} 0 \\ \phi_1(-1)h_{0,11}^{(2)}(0) \end{pmatrix}, \ S_2^{d,1}(\bar{\phi}(\theta), h_{0,11}(\theta)) = -2d\tilde{\tau}\begin{pmatrix} 0 \\ \bar{\phi}_1(-1)h_{0,20}^{(2)}(0) \end{pmatrix},$$

$$S_2^{d,1}(\phi(\theta), h_{2n,11}(\theta)) = -2d\tilde{\tau}\begin{pmatrix} 0 \\ \phi_1(-1)h_{2n,11}^{(2)}(0) \end{pmatrix}, \ S_2^{d,1}(\bar{\phi}(\theta), h_{2n,20}(\theta)) = -2d\tilde{\tau}\begin{pmatrix} 0 \\ \bar{\phi}_1(-1)h_{2n,20}^{(2)}(0) \end{pmatrix},$$

$$S_2^{d,2}(\phi(\theta), h_{2n,11}(\theta)) = -2d\tilde{\tau}\begin{pmatrix} 0 \\ \phi_1(-1)h_{2n,11}^{(2)}(0) \end{pmatrix} - 2d\tilde{\tau}\begin{pmatrix} 0 \\ \phi_2(0)h_{2n,11}^{(1)}(-1) \end{pmatrix},$$

$$S_2^{d,2}(\bar{\phi}(\theta), h_{2n,20}(\theta)) = -2d\tilde{\tau}\begin{pmatrix} 0 \\ \bar{\phi}_1(-1)h_{2n,20}^{(2)}(0) \end{pmatrix} - 2d\tilde{\tau}\begin{pmatrix} 0 \\ \bar{\phi}_2(0)h_{2n,20}^{(1)}(-1) \end{pmatrix},$$

$$S_2^{d,3}(\phi(\theta),h_{2n,11}(\theta)) = -2d\tilde{\tau}\begin{pmatrix} 0 \\ \phi_2(0)h^{(1)}_{2n,11}(-1) \end{pmatrix},\ S_2^{d,3}(\bar{\phi}(\theta),h_{2n,20}(\theta)) = -2d\tilde{\tau}\begin{pmatrix} 0 \\ \bar{\phi}_1(0)h^{(2)}_{2n,20}(-1) \end{pmatrix}.$$

Then, we have:

$$\begin{aligned}
B_{21} =& \frac{3}{2l\pi}\psi^T A21, \\
B_{22} =& \frac{1}{l\pi}\psi^T(S_2(\phi(\theta),h_{0,11}(\theta)) + S_2(\bar{\phi}(\theta),h_{0,20}(\theta))) + \frac{1}{2l\pi}\psi^T(S_2(\phi(\theta),h_{2n,11}(\theta)) + S_2(\bar{\phi}(\theta),h_{2n,20}(\theta))), \\
B_{23} =& -\frac{1}{l\pi}\mu_n\psi^T(S_2^{d,1}(\phi(\theta),h_{0,11}(\theta)) + S_2^{d,1}(\bar{\phi}(\theta),h_{0,20}(\theta))) \\
&+ \frac{1}{2l\pi}\psi^T\sum_{j=1,2,3} b^{(j)}_{2n}(S_2^{d,j}(\phi(\theta),h_{2n,11}(\theta)) + S_2^{d,j}(\bar{\phi}(\theta),h_{2n,20}(\theta))),
\end{aligned}$$

where $b^{(1)}_{2n} = -\mu_n, b^{(2)}_{2n} = -2\mu_n, b^{(3)}_{2n} = -4\mu_n$.

References

1. Yang, R.; Nie, C.; Jin, D. Spatiotemporal dynamics induced by nonlocal competition in a diffusive predator-prey system with habitat complexity. *Nonlinear Dyn.* **2022**, *110*, 879–900. [CrossRef]
2. Yang, R.; Wang, F.; Jin, D. Spatially inhomogeneous bifurcating periodic solutions induced by nonlocal competition in a predator-prey system with additional food. *Math. Methods Appl. Sci.* **2022**, *45*, 9967–9978. [CrossRef]
3. Tan, Y.; Cai, Y.; Yao, R.; Hu, M.; Wang, W. Complex dynamics in an eco-epidemiological model with the cost of anti-predator behaviors. *Nonlinear Dyn.* **2022**, *107*, 3127–3141. [CrossRef]
4. Xiang, A.; Wang, L. Boundedness of a predator-prey model with density-dependent motilities and stage structure for the predator. *Electron. Res. Arch.* **2022**, *30*, 1954–1972. [CrossRef]
5. Shang, Z.; Qiao, Y. Bifurcation analysis of a Leslie-type predator-prey system with simplified Holling type IV functional response and strong Allee effect on prey. *Nonlinear Anal. Real World Appl.* **2022**, *64*, 103453. [CrossRef]
6. Yang, R.; Jin, D.; Wang, W. A diffusive predator-prey model with generalist predator and time delay. *Aims Math.* **2022**, *7*, 4574–4591. [CrossRef]
7. Tripathi, J.P.; Bugalia, S.; Jana, D.; Gupta, N.; Tiwari, V.; Li, J.; Sun, G.-Q. Modeling the cost of anti-predator strategy in a predator-prey system: The roles of indirect effect. *Math. Methods Appl. Sci.* **2021**, *45*, 4365–4396. [CrossRef]
8. Pimenov, A.; Kelly, T.C.; Korobeinikov, A.; O'Callaghan, M.J.; Rachinskii, D. Memory and adaptive behavior in population dynamics: Anti-predator behavior as a case study. *J. Math. Biol.* **2017**, *74*, 1533–1559. [CrossRef]
9. Tang, B.; Xiao, Y. Bifurcation analysis of a predator-prey model with anti-predator behaviour. *Chaos Solitons Fractals* **2015**, *70*, 58–68. [CrossRef]
10. Lima, S.L. Stress and decision-making under the risk of predation: Recent developments from behavioral, reproductive, and ecological perspectives. *Adv. Study Behav.* **1998**, *27*, 215–290.
11. Relyea, R.A. How prey respond to combined predators: A review and an empirical test. *Ecology* **2003**, *84*, 1827–1839. [CrossRef]
12. Choh, Y.; Lgnacio, M.; Sabelis, M.W.; Janssen, A. Predator-prey role reversals, juvenile experience and adult antipredator behaviour. *Sci. Rep.* **2012**, *2*, 728. [CrossRef]
13. Saitō, Y. Prey kills predator: Counter-attack success of a spider mite against its specific phytoseiid predator. *Exp. Appl. Acarol.* **1986**, *2*, 47–62. [CrossRef]
14. Prasad, K.D.; Prasad, B.S.R.V. Qualitative analysis of additional food provided predator-prey system with anti-predator behaviour in prey. *Nonlinear Dyn.* **2019**, *96*, 1765–1793. [CrossRef]
15. Wang, L.; Zhang, M.; Jia, M. A delayed predator-prey model with prey population guided anti-predator behaviour and stage structure. *J. Appl. Anal. Comput.* **2021**, *11*, 1811–1824. [CrossRef]
16. Liu, J.; Zhang, X. Stability and Hopf bifurcation of a delayed reaction-diffusion predator-prey model with anti-predator behaviour. *Nonlinear Anal. Model. Control* **2019**, *24*, 387–406. [CrossRef]
17. Yang, R.; Ma, J. Analysis of a diffusive predator-prey system with anti-predator behaviour and maturation delay. *Chaos Solitons Fractals* **2018**, *109*, 128–139. [CrossRef]
18. Yang, R.; Zhao, X.; An, Y. Dynamical Analysis of a Delayed Diffusive Predator-Prey Model with Additional Food Provided and Anti-Predator Behavior. *Mathematics* **2022**, *10*, 469. [CrossRef]
19. Yang, R.; Song, Q.; An, Y. Spatiotemporal Dynamics in a Predator-Prey Model with Functional Response Increasing in Both Predator and Prey Densities. *Mathematics* **2022**, *10*, 17. [CrossRef]
20. Fagan, W.F.; Lewis, M.A.; Auger-Méthé, M.; Avgar, T.; Benhamou, S.; Breed, G.; LaDage, L.; Schlägel, U.E.; Tang, W.-W.; Papastamatiou, Y.P.; et al. Spatial memory and animal movement. *Ecol. Lett.* **2014**, *16*, 1316–1329. [CrossRef]
21. Shi, J.; Wang, C.; Wang, H.; Yan, X. Diffusive Spatial Movement with Memory. *J. Dyn. Differ. Equ.* **2020**, *32*, 979–1002. [CrossRef]
22. An, Q.; Wang, C.; Wang, H. Analysis of a spatial memory model with nonlocal maturation delay and hostile boundary condition. *Discret. Contin. Dyn. Syst.* **2020**, *40*, 5845–5868. [CrossRef]

23. Shi, J.; Wang, C.; Wang, H. Diffusive spatial movement with memory and maturation delays. *Nonlinearity* **2019**, *32*, 3188–3208. [CrossRef]
24. Shi, Q.; Shi, J.; Wang, H. Spatial movement with distributed delay. *J. Math. Biol.* **2021**, *82*, 33. [CrossRef] [PubMed]
25. Song, Y.; Wu, S.; Wang, H. Spatiotemporal dynamics in the single population model with memory-based diffusion and nonlocal effect. *J. Differ. Equ.* **2019**, *267*, 6316–6351. [CrossRef]
26. Song, Y.; Peng, Y.; Zhang, T. The spatially inhomogeneous Hopf bifurcation induced by memory delay in a memory-based diffusion system. *J. Differ. Equ.* **2021**, *300*, 597–624. [CrossRef]

Σ mathematics

MDPI

Article

Diffusion-Induced Instability of the Periodic Solutions in a Reaction-Diffusion Predator-Prey Model with Dormancy of Predators

Mi Wang [1,2]

[1] College of Intelligent Systems Science and Engineering, Harbin Engineering University, Harbin 150001, China; nefulxywangmi@163.com
[2] College of Mathematical Sciences, Harbin Engineering University, Harbin 150001, China

Abstract: A reaction-diffusion predator-prey model with the dormancy of predators is considered in this paper. We are concerned with the long-time behaviors of the solutions of this system. We divided our investigations into two cases: for the ODEs system, we study the existence and stability of the equilibrium solutions and derive precise conditions on system parameters so that the system can undergo Hopf bifurcations around the positive equilibrium solution. Moreover, the properties of Hopf bifurcation are studied in detail. For the reaction-diffusion system, we are able to derive conditions on the diffusion coefficients so that the spatially homogeneous Hopf bifurcating periodic solutions can undergo diffusion-triggered instability. To support our theoretical analysis, we also include several numerical results.

Keywords: predator-prey interactions; dormancy of predators; stability; hopf bifurcations; diffusion-induced instability

MSC: 34C23; 35B32; 37G10; 37L110; 37M20; 35K57

Citation: Wang, M. Diffusion-Induced Instability of the Periodic Solutions in a Reaction-Diffusion Predator-Prey Model with Dormancy of Predators. *Mathematics* **2023**, *11*, 1875. https://doi.org/10.3390/math11081875

Academic Editor: Chunrui Zhang

Received: 30 March 2023
Revised: 12 April 2023
Accepted: 13 April 2023
Published: 15 April 2023

1. Introduction

Interactions between predator and prey can generate rich dynamics and have engaged numerous investigators' attention. In the existing literature, the following homogeneous diffusive predator-prey model has been extensively considered:

$$\begin{cases} \dfrac{\partial U}{\partial s} = D_1\Delta U + AU\Big(1-\dfrac{U}{N}\Big) - \dfrac{BUV}{C+U}, & x\in\Omega, s>0,\\ \dfrac{\partial V}{\partial s} = D_2\Delta V + \dfrac{EUV}{C+U} - FV, & x\in\Omega, s>0,\\ \dfrac{\partial U}{\partial \nu} = \dfrac{\partial V}{\partial \nu} = 0, & x\in\partial\Omega, s\geq 0,\\ U(x,0)=U(x_0), V(x,0)=V(x_0), & x\in\Omega, \end{cases} \tag{1}$$

where Ω is an open bounded domain in $\mathbf{R}^N$ with $N\geq 1$; ν is the outer unit normal to the boundary $\partial\Omega$, which is assumed to be sufficiently smooth; $U(s,t)$ and $V(s,t)$ are the population densities of the prey and the predator at time s and position $x\in\Omega$, respectively; D_1 and D_2 are the diffusion coefficients of U and V, respectively; A,B,C,E,F are all of the positive constants; A is the intrinsic growth rate; N is the carrying capacity; B and E are the strength of the relative effect on the two species in the interaction; $U/(C+U)$ is the functional response of the predator to the prey density; C is the "saturation" effect; and F is the death rate of V.

Then, by a non-dimensionalized change of variables (see also [1]):

$$t=As, u=\frac{U}{C}, v=\frac{BV}{EC}, d_1=\frac{D_1}{A}, d_2=\frac{D_2}{A}, k=\frac{N}{C}, m=\frac{E}{A}, \theta=\frac{F}{A},$$

we can reduce the system (1) to the simplified dimensionless form as follows:

$$\begin{cases} \dfrac{\partial u}{\partial t} = d_1 \Delta u + u\left(1 - \dfrac{u}{k}\right) - \dfrac{muv}{1+u}, & x \in \Omega, t > 0, \\ \dfrac{\partial v}{\partial t} = d_2 \Delta v + \dfrac{muv}{1+u} - \theta v, & x \in \Omega, t > 0, \\ \dfrac{\partial u}{\partial \nu} = \dfrac{\partial v}{\partial \nu} = 0, & x \in \partial\Omega, t \geq 0, \\ u(x,0) = u(x_0), v(x,0) = v(x_0), & x \in \Omega, \end{cases} \tag{2}$$

where u and v are the scaled densities of the prey and predator, respectively; $u(1 - u/k)$ is the growth rate of u in the absence of the predator; θ is the death rate of the predator; $mu/(1+u)$ is the functional response determining the predator's consumption of the prey's abundance; k is the fraction of the prey's biomass, which can be transformed into the predator's biomass; and d_1 and d_2 are the diffusion coefficients of u and v, respectively.

System (2) and the like have been studied extensively in the existing literature. For example, for the corresponding ODE system of (2), Hsu [2] showed that the local stability of the positive equilibrium solution can also indicate its global asymptotic stability. In [3], Hsu and Shi studied the relaxation oscillations of (2), while in [4], Cheng observed that the periodic solution of the ODEs in system (2) is unique and stable. For the reaction-diffusion system of system (2), in [5], Ko and Ryu not only studied the existence of non-constant positive equilibrium solutions but also investigated the local existence of periodic solutions. In [1], Yi, Wei, and Shi performed steady-state bifurcation and Hopf bifurcation analysis of the system. In [6], Peng and Shi considered global steady-state bifurcations of the system, and their results proved that the global bifurcation of steady-state solutions comprises bounded loops .

In this paper, we mainly consider the following reaction-diffusion predator-prey system with dormancy:

$$\begin{cases} \dfrac{\partial u}{\partial t} = d_1 \Delta u + u\left(1 - \dfrac{u}{k}\right) - \dfrac{muv}{1+u}, & x \in \Omega, t > 0, \\ \dfrac{\partial v}{\partial t} = d_2 \Delta v + \dfrac{\mu muv}{1+u} + \alpha w - \theta v, & x \in \Omega, t > 0, \\ \dfrac{\partial w}{\partial t} = d_3 \Delta w + \dfrac{(1-\mu)muv}{1+u} - \alpha w, & x \in \Omega, t > 0, \\ \dfrac{\partial u}{\partial \nu} = \dfrac{\partial v}{\partial \nu} = \dfrac{\partial w}{\partial \nu} = 0, & x \in \partial\Omega, t \geq 0, \\ u(x,0) = u(x_0), v(x,0) = v(x_0), w(x,0) = w(x_0), & x \in \Omega, \end{cases} \tag{3}$$

where $\mu \in (0,1)$, $\alpha > 0$, $m > 0$, $\theta > 0$, $d_1 > 0$, $d_2 > 0$, and $d_3 \geq 0$; w is the predator' density with a dormant state or resting eggs; μ and $1 - \mu$ denote the proportion of reproduction effects on predators between active and dormant states, respectively; and α stands for the hatching of dormant predators or the average dormancy period.

In [7], Kuwamura showed that the hatching of resting eggs can keep the population dynamics stable when the switching between non-resting and resting eggs is sharp. In [8], Kuwamura, Nakazawa, and Ogawa studied the stationary and oscillatory diffusion-induced instabilities of the constant equilibrium solutions.

For system (3), we are mainly interested in the influence of the dormancy of the predators on the dynamics of the system. In particular, we focus on the diffusion-induced instability of the Hopf bifurcating periodic solutions of the system, which is less understood for this particular model in the existing literature [9–18]. We shall prove that from suitable conditions on the diffusion rates d_1, d_2, d_3, the spatially homogeneous periodic solution can undergo diffusion-induced instability and can induce the new spatiotemporal patterns emerging consequently. We would like to remark that for the system without the dormancy of predators (e.g., system (2)), Yi, Wei, and Shi proposed that under suitable conditions, once the periodic solution is stable with respect to the ODEs, it is still stable with respect to the PDEs; thus, there is no diffusion-induced instability of the periodic solutions. Based on this, we shall present a quite interesting difference between the system with the dormancy of predators and the system without the dormancy of predators.

The rest of this paper is organized in the following way. In Section 2, we consider the dynamics of the ODEs system; in Section 3, we consider the diffusion-induced instability of the periodic solutions bifurcating from Hopf bifurcations; in Section 4, we present some numerical simulations to illustrate our theoretical analysis; and in Section 5, we draw some conclusions.

2. The Dynamical Behaviors of the Kinetic System

In this section, we consider the following kinetic system:

$$\begin{cases} \dfrac{du}{dt} = u\left(1 - \dfrac{u}{k}\right) - \dfrac{muv}{1+u}, \\ \dfrac{dv}{dt} = \dfrac{\mu muv}{1+u} + \alpha w - \theta v, \\ \dfrac{dw}{dt} = \dfrac{(1-\mu)muv}{1+u} - \alpha w. \end{cases} \tag{4}$$

2.1. The Auxiliary System: The Predator-Prey System without Dormancy of Predators

To begin with, we consider the following kinetic system of system (2):

$$\frac{du}{dt} = u\left(1 - \frac{u}{k}\right) - \frac{muv}{1+u}, \quad \frac{dv}{dt} = \frac{muv}{1+u} - \theta v. \tag{5}$$

System (5) has a trivial solution $(0,0)$, a semi-trivial solution $(k,0)$, and a unique positive equilibrium solution under certain conditions stated below.

We now state the following results on system (5) due to Hsu [2] (see also [1]):

Lemma 1 ([1,2]). *The following conclusions hold true:*

1. *Suppose that either* $m \le \theta$ *or* $\dfrac{mk}{1+k} \le \theta < m$ *holds. Then, system* (5) *has no positive equilibrium solutions; in this case,* $(0,0)$ *is unstable, while* $(k,0)$ *is globally asymptotically stable;*
2. *Suppose that* $\dfrac{mk}{1+k} > \theta$ *holds. Then, system* (5) *has a unique positive equilibrium solution* (τ, v_τ)*, where*

$$\tau := \frac{\theta}{m-\theta}, \; v_\tau := \frac{\tau(k-\tau)}{k\theta}. \tag{6}$$

In this case, both $(0,0)$ *and* $(k,0)$ *are unstable,* (τ, v_τ) *is globally asymptotically stable if either* $0 < k \le 1$ *and* $\tau \in (0,k)$ *or* $k > 1$ *and* $\tau \in \left(\dfrac{k-1}{2}, k\right)$ *holds, while* (τ, v_τ) *is unstable if* $k > 1$ *and* $\lambda \in \left(0, \dfrac{k-1}{2}\right)$. *In particular, the loss of the stability of* (τ, v_τ) *leads to a Hopf bifurcation at* $\tau = \dfrac{k-1}{2}$.

2.2. The Predator-Prey Model with Dormancy of Predators

In this subsection, we study the predator-prey system with dormancy, which is system (4). Clearly, system (4) has $(0,0,0)$ and $(k,0,0)$ as its equilibrium solutions. We have the following results:

Theorem 1. *The following conclusions hold true:*

1. $(0,0,0)$ *is always unstable in* (4).
2. $(k,0,0)$ *is locally asymptotically stable in* (4) *when* $\theta > \dfrac{mk}{1+k}$, *while it is unstable when* $\theta < \dfrac{mk}{1+k}$.

Proof. The Jacobian matrix of system (4) evaluated at $(0,0,0)$ is given by

$$J(0,0,0) := \begin{bmatrix} 1 & 0 & 0 \\ 0 & -\theta & \alpha \\ 0 & 0 & -\alpha \end{bmatrix},$$

which has three eigenvalues: $\beta_1 = 1 > 0,\ \beta_2 = -\theta < 0,\ \beta_3 = -\alpha < 0$. Thus, $(0,0,0)$ is unstable with respect to (4).

The Jacobian matrix of system (4) evaluated at $(k,0,0)$ is given by

$$J(k,0,0) := \begin{bmatrix} -1 & -\frac{mk}{1+k} & 0 \\ 0 & \frac{\mu mk}{1+k} - \theta & \alpha \\ 0 & \frac{mk(1-\mu)}{1+k} & -\alpha \end{bmatrix}.$$

The characteristic equation of $J_2(k,0,0)$ is given by

$$(\beta+1)\left[\beta^2 + (\alpha - \frac{\mu mk}{1+k} + \theta)\beta + \alpha\left(\theta - \frac{mk}{1+k}\right)\right] = 0. \tag{7}$$

If $\theta > \frac{mk}{1+k}$, for $(k,0,0)$, all of the eigenvalues of (7) have negative real parts. Thus, $(k,0,0)$ is stable.

If $\theta < \frac{mk}{1+k} < m$, then (7) has a positive eigenvalue. Thus, $(k,0,0)$ is unstable. □

Clearly, if (τ, v_τ) is a positive equilibrium solution of (5), then (τ, v_τ, w_τ) is a positive equilibrium solution of (4), where

$$\tau := \frac{\theta}{m-\theta},\ v_\tau := \frac{\tau(k-\tau)}{k\theta},\ w_\tau := \frac{\tau(1-\mu)(k-\tau)}{k\alpha}. \tag{8}$$

Then, by Lemma 1, we have the following results on the existence of positive equilibrium solution of system (4).

Theorem 2. *Suppose that $\frac{mk}{1+k} > \theta$ holds. Then, system (4) has a unique positive equilibrium solution (τ, v_τ, w_τ), which is defined by (8).*

Next, we study the stability of (τ, v_τ, w_τ) in system (4).

We choose α as the bifurcation parameter. Linearizing system (4) at (τ, v_τ, w_τ), we obtain its Jacobian matrix:

$$J(\alpha) := \begin{bmatrix} -A & -\theta & 0 \\ \mu B & (\mu-1)\theta & \alpha \\ (1-\mu)B & (1-\mu)\theta & -\alpha \end{bmatrix}, \tag{9}$$

where

$$A := \frac{\tau(2\tau+1-k)}{k(1+\tau)},\ B := \frac{k-\tau}{k(1+\tau)}. \tag{10}$$

The characteristic equation of $J(\alpha)$ is

$$\beta^3 + M_2(\alpha)\beta^2 + M_1(\alpha)\beta + M_0(\alpha) = 0, \tag{11}$$

where

$$M_0(\alpha) := \alpha\theta B,\ M_1(\alpha) :=A\big(\alpha + (1-\mu)\theta\big) + \mu\theta B,\ M_2(\alpha) := \alpha + (1-\mu)\theta + A. \tag{12}$$

To study the stability of (τ, v_τ, w_τ), by Appendix of [19] (see also Lemma 2 below), we need to know the signs of $M_0(\alpha)$, $M_1(\alpha)$, $M_2(\alpha)$ and $M_2(\alpha)M_1(\alpha) - M_0(\alpha)$.

We make the following assumptions:

(H) Suppose that either (1): $0 < k \le 1$ and $\tau \in (0, k)$ or (2): $k > 1$ and $\tau \in \left(\frac{k-1}{2}, k\right)$ holds so that (τ, v_τ) is stable in system (5).

Under assumption (H), we have $A > 0$ and $B > 0$. Thus, $M_0(\alpha) > 0$, $M_1(\alpha) > 0$, and $M_2(\alpha) > 0$ for all $\alpha > 0$ and $\mu \in (0, 1)$.

Thus, to study the stability of (τ, v_τ, w_τ), it remains to study the sign of $M_2(\alpha)M_1(\alpha) - M_0(\alpha)$, which takes the following form:

$$M_2(\alpha)M_1(\alpha) - M_0(\alpha) = A\alpha^2 + \rho_1\alpha + \rho_0, \tag{13}$$

where

$$\rho_1 := A^2 + \theta(1-\mu)\big[2A - B\big],\ \rho_0 := \theta\big[(1-\mu)\theta + A\big]\big[(1-\mu)A + \mu B\big]. \tag{14}$$

Clearly, under assumption (H), we have $\rho_0 > 0$. We now consider the sign of ρ_1.

We can check that

$$2A - B = \frac{4\tau^2 + (3-2k)\tau - k}{k(1+\tau)},$$

which has a unique positive root, denoted by $\hat{\tau}$, which is given by

$$\hat{\tau} := \frac{2k - 3 + \sqrt{4k^2 + 4k + 9}}{8}. \tag{15}$$

It can be directly checked that

$$\hat{\tau} \in \begin{cases} (0, k), & \text{if } 0 < k \le 1, \\ \left(\frac{k-1}{2}, k\right), & \text{if } k > 1. \end{cases} \tag{16}$$

Clearly, $2A - B < 0$ for $\tau \in (0, \hat{\tau})$, while $2A - B > 0$ for $\tau > \hat{\tau}$.

Then, for any $\tau \in [\hat{\tau}, k)$, $\mu \in (0, 1)$ and $\theta > 0$, $\rho_1 > 0$. Therefore, for any $\alpha > 0$, $M_2(\alpha)M_1(\alpha) - M_0(\alpha) > 0$. By Appendix of [19], (τ, v_τ, w_τ) is locally asymptotically stable in system (4).

In what follows, we study the case when $\tau \in (\tau_0, \hat{\tau})$ so that $2A - B < 0$, where

$$\tau_0 := \begin{cases} 0, & \text{if } 0 < k \le 1, \\ \frac{k-1}{2}, & \text{if } k > 1. \end{cases} \tag{17}$$

If we regard A and B as the functions of τ, we can check that $A = A(\tau)$ is increasing and $B = B(\tau)$ is decreasing in τ. Moreover, $A - B < 0$ for $\tau \in (\tau_0, \hat{\tau})$.

One can check that for any $\tau \in (\tau_0, \hat{\tau})$, $\rho_1 = 0$ (resp., $\rho_1 < 0$) is equivalent to

$$\mu = \hat{\mu}(\tau) := \frac{A^2}{\theta(2A - B)} + 1,\ (\text{resp., } \mu < \hat{\mu}(\tau)). \tag{18}$$

Then, we have

$$\hat{\mu}'(\tau) = \frac{2AA'(A-B) + A^2B'}{\theta(2A-B)^2} < 0. \tag{19}$$

When $\tau \to \widehat{\tau}$, $2A - B \to 0^-$, $A^2 \to A^2(\widehat{\tau}) \neq 0$, then $\widehat{\mu}(\tau) \to -\infty$ as $\tau \to \widehat{\tau}$; When $\tau \to \tau_0^+$, since $A^2 \to 0, 2A - B \neq 0$, we have $\widehat{\mu}(\tau) \to 1$ as $\tau \to \tau_0^+$. Then, for any $\tau \in (\tau_0, \widehat{\tau})$, we have $\widehat{\mu}(\tau) \in (-\infty, 1)$. Since $\widehat{\mu}'(\tau) < 0$, a unique $\tau^* \in (\tau_0, \widehat{\tau})$ exists such that

$$\widehat{\mu}(\tau)\begin{cases} \in (0,1), & \text{if } \tau \in (\tau_0, \tau^*), \\ = 0, & \text{if } \tau = \tau^*, \\ \in (-\infty, 0), & \text{if } \tau \in (\tau^*, \widehat{\tau}). \end{cases} \tag{20}$$

If $\tau \in [\tau^*, \widehat{\tau})$, then for any $\mu \in (0,1)$, it always holds true that $\mu > \widehat{\mu}(\tau)$, which means that $\rho_1 > 0$. Thus, $M_2(\alpha)M_1(\alpha) - M_0(\alpha) > 0$ for any $\alpha > 0$, (τ, v_τ, w_τ) is locally stable in system (4).

If $\tau \in (\tau_0, \tau^*)$, then $\widehat{\mu}(\tau) \in (0,1)$. Therefore, for any $\mu \in (0,1)$, a unique $\tau_\mu \in (\tau_0, \tau^*)$ exists, satisfying

$$\begin{cases} \widehat{\mu}(\tau) > \mu, & \text{if } \tau \in (\tau_0, \tau_\mu), \\ \widehat{\mu}(\tau) = \mu, & \text{if } \tau = \tau_\mu, \\ \widehat{\mu}(\tau) < \mu, & \text{if } \tau \in (\tau_\mu, \tau^*), \end{cases} \tag{21}$$

or equivalently

$$\begin{cases} \rho_1 < 0, & \text{if } \tau \in (\tau_0, \tau_\mu), \\ \rho_1 = 0, & \text{if } \tau = \tau_\mu, \\ \rho_1 > 0, & \text{if } \tau \in (\tau_\mu, \tau^*). \end{cases}$$

Then, for any $\tau \in [\tau_\mu, \tau^*)$, (τ, v_τ, w_τ) is locally stable in system (4).

Next, we assume the case of $\tau \in (\tau_0, \tau_\mu)$, in which $\rho_1 < 0$. Regarding $M_2(\alpha)M_1(\alpha) - M_0(\alpha) = \alpha^2 + \rho_1\alpha + \rho_0$ as the quadratic function τ, we can obtain its discriminant

$$\Delta_\alpha := \theta^2 B^2 \mu^2 + 2\theta B(2\theta A - \theta B - A^2)\mu + A^4 - 2\theta A^2 B - 4\theta^2 AB + \theta^2 B^2. \tag{22}$$

Assume that for some $\theta > 0$, we have $\Delta_\alpha < 0$. Then, for any $\alpha > 0$, we have $M_2(\alpha)M_1(\alpha) - M_0(\alpha) = \alpha^2 + \rho_1\alpha + \rho_0 > 0$. Hence, for any $\alpha > 0$, (τ, v_τ, w_τ) is locally stable in system (4).

Assume that for some $\theta > 0$, we have $\Delta_\alpha > 0$. Then, $M_2(\alpha)M_1(\alpha) - M_0(\alpha) = A\alpha^2 + \rho_1\alpha + \rho_0 = 0$ has two distinct positive solutions given by

$$\alpha_1 := \frac{-\rho_1 - \sqrt{\Delta_\alpha}}{2A} > 0,\ \alpha_2 := \frac{-\rho_1 + \sqrt{\Delta_\alpha}}{2A} > 0. \tag{23}$$

Thus, for any $\alpha \in (0, \alpha_1) \cup (\alpha_2, \infty)$, we have $M_2(\alpha)M_1(\alpha) - M_0(\alpha) = A\alpha^2 + \rho_1\alpha + \rho_0 > 0$. Then, (τ, v_τ, w_τ) is locally stable in system (4). While if $\alpha \in (\alpha_1, \alpha_2)$, we have $M_2(\alpha)M_1(\alpha) - M_0(\alpha) = A\alpha^2 + \rho_1\alpha + \rho_0 < 0$. Then, (τ, v_τ, w_τ) is unstable in system (4).

We are now in the position to state the stability results of (τ, v_τ, w_τ):

Theorem 3. *Suppose that either $0 < k \leq 1$ but $\tau \in (0, k)$ or $k > 1$ but $\tau \in \left(\frac{k-1}{2}, k\right)$ holds so that (τ, v_τ) is stable in system (5). Let $\widehat{\tau}$, τ_0, τ^*, and τ_μ be defined in (16), (17), (20) and (21), respectively. Then, we have $\tau_0 < \tau_\mu < \tau^* < \widehat{\tau} < k$. In particular,*

1. *Suppose that $\tau \in (\tau_0, \tau_\mu)$ holds. Let Δ_α be defined by (22).*
   - *(a) If, additionally, $\Delta_\alpha < 0$, then for any $\alpha > 0$, (τ, v_τ, w_τ) is locally asymptotically stable in system (4);*
   - *(b) If, additionally, $\Delta_\alpha > 0$, then for any $\alpha \in (0, \alpha_1) \cup (\alpha_2, +\infty)$, (τ, v_τ, w_τ) is locally asymptotically stable in (4), while for $\alpha \in (\alpha_1, \alpha_2)$, (τ, v_τ, w_τ) is unstable in system (4).*
2. *Suppose that $\tau \in [\tau_\mu, k)$ holds. Then, for any $\alpha > 0$, (τ, v_τ, w_τ) is locally asymptotically stable in system (4).*

Remark 1.

1. *We would like to remark that it is analytically demanding to analyze the sign of Δ_α. Indeed, we need to resort to numerical simulations to determine when $\Delta_\alpha > 0$ or $\Delta_\alpha < 0$. It is found from numerical simulations that for some θ, we have $\Delta_\alpha < 0$, while for the other θ, $\Delta_\alpha > 0$;*
2. *We assume that either $0 < k \leq 1$ but $\tau \in (0, k)$ or $k > 1$ but $\tau \in \left(\frac{k-1}{2}, k\right)$ holds so that (τ, v_τ) is stable in system (5). However, for case of 2(b), when $\alpha \in (\alpha_1, \alpha_2)$, (τ, v_τ, w_τ) is unstable. From this, we can see a difference between the system without dormancy and the system with dormancy.*

Theorem 4. *Suppose that either $0 < k \leq 1$ but $\tau \in (0, k)$ or $k > 1$ but $\tau \in \left(\frac{k-1}{2}, k\right)$ holds, so that (τ, v_τ) is stable in system (5). Let $\tau \in (\tau_0, \tau_\mu)$ and $\Delta_\alpha > 0$ so that α_1 and α_2 are well-defined. Then, at $\alpha = \overline{\alpha}$, the Hopf bifurcation around (τ, v_τ, w_τ) occurs. Moreover, at $\alpha = \overline{\alpha}$, the Hopf bifurcating periodic solution is stable and the bifurcation direction is forward if* $\mathrm{Re}(c_1(\overline{\alpha})) < 0$, *while the Hopf bifurcating periodic solution is unstable and the bifurcation direction is backward if* $\mathrm{Re}(c_1(\overline{\alpha})) > 0$, *where $\overline{\alpha} = \alpha_1$ or α_2, and* $\mathrm{Re}(c_1(\overline{\alpha}))$ *is defined by (26).*

Proof. 1. The proof of the existence of Hopf bifurcations at $\alpha = \alpha_1$ and α_2. By the aforementioned analysis, at $\alpha = \alpha_1$ and α_2, we have $M_2(\alpha)M_1(\alpha) - M_0(\alpha) = 0$. Thus, at $\alpha = \alpha_1$ and α_2, the eigenvalue problem has a pair of purely imaginary roots and a negative root. Furthermore, according to Theorem 3, we have

$$M_1'(\overline{\alpha}_1)M_2(\overline{\alpha}_1) + M_1(\overline{\alpha}_1)M_2'(\overline{\alpha}_1) - M_0'(\overline{\alpha}_1) < 0,$$
$$M_1'(\overline{\alpha}_2)M_2(\overline{\alpha}_2) + M_1(\overline{\alpha}_2)M_2'(\overline{\alpha}_2) - M_0'(\overline{\alpha}_2) > 0.$$

Therefore, by the Hopf bifurcation theorem, at $\alpha = \alpha_1$ and α_2, the Hopf bifurcation around (τ, v_τ, w_τ) occurs.

2. Now, we derive conditions to determine the bifurcation direction and the stability of the periodic solutions.

By Theorem A.1 of [19] (or see also Lemma 2 below), the bifurcation direction (forward or backward) and the stability/instability of the periodic solutions can be determined by the sign of $\mathrm{Re}(c_1(\overline{\alpha}))(2\overline{\alpha}A + \rho_1)$, where $\overline{\alpha} = \alpha_1$ or α_2, and ρ_1 is defined in (14).

By using the framework of Theorem A.1 of [19], we need to calculate the term $\mathrm{Re}(c_1(\overline{\alpha}))$. To that end, we define the matrix P in the following way:

$$P(\alpha) = \begin{pmatrix} 1 & 0 & 1 \\ p_{21} & p_{22} & p_{23} \\ p_{31} & p_{32} & p_{33} \end{pmatrix}, \tag{24}$$

where

$$p_{21}(\alpha) := -\frac{A}{\theta},\ p_{22}(\alpha) := -\frac{\sqrt{M_1(\alpha)}}{\theta},\ p_{23}(\alpha) := \frac{\alpha + (1-\mu)\theta}{\theta},\ p_{31}(\alpha) := \frac{A}{\theta},$$
$$p_{32}(\alpha) := \frac{\sqrt{M_1(\alpha)}(A - \theta(1-\mu))}{\alpha\theta},\ p_{33}(\alpha) := -\frac{(\alpha + (1-\mu)\theta)(A+\alpha) + \mu\theta B}{\alpha\theta}.$$

Then, we can calculate

$$\begin{aligned} h_1(\alpha, y_1, y_2, y_3) &= \frac{(p_{22}p_{33} - p_{23}p_{32})g_1 + p_{32}g_2 - p_{22}g_3}{\det(P)}, \\ h_2(\alpha, y_1, y_2, y_3) &= \frac{(p_{31}p_{23} - p_{21}p_{33})g_1 + (p_{33} - p_{31})g_2 + (p_{21} - p_{23})g_3}{\det(P)}, \\ h_3(\alpha, y_1, y_2, y_3) &= \frac{(p_{21}p_{32} - p_{22}p_{31})g_1 - p_{32}g_2 + p_{22}g_3}{\det(P)}, \end{aligned} \tag{25}$$

where the determinant of P denotes as $\det(P)$ and

$$\begin{aligned} g_1 :=& \frac{(y_1+y_3)^2}{k} - \frac{m(y_1+y_3)(p_{21}y_1+p_{22}y_2+p_{23}y_3)}{1+y_1+y_3}, \\ g_2 :=& \frac{\mu m(y_1+y_3)(p_{21}y_1+p_{22}y_2+p_{23}y_3)}{1+y_1+y_3}, \\ g_3 :=& \frac{(1-\mu)m(y_1+y_3)(p_{21}y_1+p_{22}y_2+p_{23}y_3)}{1+y_1+y_3}, \end{aligned}$$

and y_1, y_2, y_3 denote the transformation from the variables u, v, w. Then, by (A.17) in Appendix of [19], we have

$$\begin{aligned} \mathrm{Re}(c_1(\overline{\alpha})) =& \frac{1}{16\sqrt{M_1(\overline{\alpha})}}\big((h_1)_{y_1y_1}(h_2)_{y_1y_1} - (h_1)_{y_1y_1}(h_1)_{y_1y_2} + (h_2)_{y_1y_1}(h_2)_{y_1y_2}\big) \\ &+ \frac{1}{16}\big((h_1)_{y_1y_1y_1} + (h_2)_{y_1y_1y_2}\big) + \frac{1}{8M_2(\overline{\alpha})}(h_3)_{y_1y_1}\big((h_1)_{y_1y_3} + (h_2)_{y_2y_3}\big) \\ &+ \frac{M_2(\overline{\alpha})}{16\big(M_2(\overline{\alpha})^2 + 4M_1(\overline{\alpha})\big)}(h_3)_{y_1y_1}\big((h_1)_{y_1y_3} - (h_2)_{y_2y_3}\big) \\ &+ \frac{M_2(\overline{\alpha})}{8\big(M_2(\overline{\alpha})^2 + 4M_1(\overline{\alpha})\big)}(h_3)_{y_1y_2}\big((h_1)_{y_2y_3} + (h_2)_{y_1y_3}\big) \\ &+ \frac{\sqrt{M_1(\overline{\alpha})}}{8\big(M_2(\overline{\alpha})^2 + 4M_1(\overline{\alpha})\big)}(h_3)_{y_1y_1}\big((h_2)_{y_1y_3} + (h_1)_{y_2y_3}\big) \\ &- \frac{\sqrt{M_1(\overline{\alpha})}}{4\big(M_2(\overline{\alpha})^2 + 4M_1(\overline{\alpha})\big)}(h_3)_{y_1y_2}\big((h_1)_{y_1y_3} - (h_2)_{y_2y_3}\big), \end{aligned} \tag{26}$$

where h_1, h_2, and h_3 are defined in (25).

By Theorem A.1 of [19] (see also Lemma 2 below), we can draw the following conclusions: at $\overline{\alpha} = \alpha_1$, the bifurcating periodic solution is unstable and the bifurcation occurs for $\alpha \in (\alpha_1 - \epsilon, \alpha_1)$ for sufficiently small $\epsilon > 0$ if $\mathrm{Re}(c_1(\overline{\alpha}_1)) > 0$, and the bifurcating periodic solution is stable and the bifurcation occurs for $\alpha \in (\alpha_1, \alpha_1 + \epsilon)$ for sufficiently small $\epsilon > 0$ if $\mathrm{Re}(c_1(\overline{\alpha}_1)) < 0$ holds. On the other hand, at $\overline{\alpha} = \alpha_2$, the bifurcating periodic solution is unstable and the bifurcation occurs for $\alpha \in (\alpha_2, \alpha_2 + \epsilon)$ for sufficiently small $\epsilon > 0$ if $\mathrm{Re}(c_1(\overline{\alpha}_2)) > 0$, and the bifurcating periodic solution is stable and the bifurcation occurs for $\alpha \in (\alpha_2 - \epsilon, \alpha_2)$ for sufficiently small $\epsilon > 0$ if $\mathrm{Re}(c_1(\overline{\alpha}_2)) < 0$ holds. □

Remark 2.

1. *It is analytically demanding to obtain a explicit expression of* $\mathrm{Re}(c_1(\overline{\alpha}))$, *and we shall resort to numerical tools to calculate it in the part of numerical simulations;*
2. *For simplicity, we denote* $(u_p(t), v_p(t), w_p(t))$, *and* P *by the Hopf bifurcating periodic solution and its minimum period.*

3. Diffusion-Induced Instability of the Bifurcating Periodic Solutions

In this section, we shall consider diffusion-induced instability of the periodic solutions obtained in the last section. About diffusion-induced instability, we can see [20].

3.1. Preliminaries

We recall the following results of [19] on diffusion-induced instability of the bifurcating periodic solutions for the general reaction-diffusion system

$$\begin{cases} \dfrac{\partial u_1}{\partial t} = d_1 \Delta u_1 + f_1(\alpha, u_1, u_2, u_3), x \in \Omega, t > 0, \\ \dfrac{\partial u_2}{\partial t} = d_2 \Delta u_2 + f_2(\alpha, u_1, u_2, u_3), x \in \Omega, t > 0, \\ \dfrac{\partial u_3}{\partial t} = d_3 \Delta u_3 + f_3(\alpha, u_1, u_2, u_3), x \in \Omega, t > 0, \\ \partial_\nu u_1 = \partial_\nu u_2 = \partial_\nu u_3 = 0, x \in \partial\Omega, \end{cases} \tag{27}$$

where $f_1, f_2, f_3 \in C^3$, and for any $\alpha > 0$, $(0,0,0)$ is always the constant equilibrium solution; $d_1 > 0, d_2 > 0$, and $d_3 > 0$; $\Omega := \{\ell y : y \in \Omega_*\}$ is star-shaped centered by the origin; $0 < \ell < \infty$; and Ω_* is a bounded domain in $\mathbf{R}^n$ $(n \geq 1)$ with sufficiently smooth boundary $\partial\Omega_*$.

The ODE system of system (27) is given by:

$$\frac{du_1}{dt} = f_1(\alpha, u_1, u_2, u_3), \ \frac{du_2}{dt} = f_2(\alpha, u_1, u_2, u_3), \ \frac{du_3}{dt} = f_3(\alpha, u_1, u_2, u_3), \tag{28}$$

where f_i $(i = 1,2,3)$ are defined in (27).

The linearized operator of (28) at $(\alpha, 0, 0, 0)$ can be evaluated as follows:

$$J(\alpha) := \begin{pmatrix} a_{11}(\alpha) & a_{12}(\alpha) & a_{13}(\alpha) \\ a_{21}(\alpha) & a_{22}(\alpha) & a_{23}(\alpha) \\ a_{31}(\alpha) & a_{32}(\alpha) & a_{33}(\alpha) \end{pmatrix}, \tag{29}$$

where $a_{ij}(\alpha) := \partial f_i(\alpha, 0, 0, 0)/\partial u_j$, for $i, j = 1,2,3$. Rewrite the system (28) in the following form:

$$\begin{pmatrix} u_1' \\ u_2' \\ u_3' \end{pmatrix} = J(\alpha) \begin{pmatrix} u_1 \\ u_2 \\ u_3 \end{pmatrix} + \begin{pmatrix} g_1(\alpha, u_1, u_2, u_3) \\ g_2(\alpha, u_1, u_2, u_3) \\ g_3(\alpha, u_1, u_2, u_3) \end{pmatrix},$$

where $' := d/dt$, and for $\delta = 1,2,3$,

$$\begin{aligned} g_\delta(\alpha, u_1, u_2, u_3) =& \frac{1}{2}\Big(\sum_{k=1}^{3} \frac{\partial^2 f_\delta}{\partial u_k^2} + 2 \sum_{1 \leq i < j \leq 3} \frac{\partial^2 f_\delta}{\partial u_i \partial u_j} \Big) \\ &+ \frac{1}{6}\Big(\sum_{k=1}^{3} \frac{\partial^3 f_\delta}{\partial u_k^3} + 3 \sum_{1 \leq i < j \leq 3}^{3} \Big(\frac{\partial^2 f_\delta}{\partial u_i^2 \partial u_j} + \frac{\partial^2 f_\delta}{\partial u_i \partial u_j^2} \Big) + 6 \frac{\partial^3 f_\delta}{\partial u_1 \partial u_2 \partial u_3} \Big) + o, \end{aligned}$$

where o is the higher order terms of $g_\delta(\alpha, u_1, u_2, u_3)$.

The eigenvalue problem of $J(\alpha)$ is governed by the following equation:

$$\mu^3 + M_2(\alpha)\mu^2 + M_1(\alpha)\mu + M_0(\alpha) = 0, \tag{30}$$

where

$$M_2(\alpha) := -\sum_{i=1}^{3} a_{ii}(\alpha), \ M_1(\alpha) := \sum_{i=1}^{3} A_{ii}(\alpha), \ M_0(\alpha) := -\det(J(\alpha)), \tag{31}$$

where $a_{ij}(\alpha)$ is defined in (29), $A_{ij}(\alpha)$ represents the algebraic cofactor of $a_{ij}(\alpha)$, and $\det(\cdot)$ is the determinant of a matrix.

In [19], Wang and Yi obtained the following results:

Lemma 2. *Assume that there exists a positive* $\overline{\alpha}$*, such that* $M_0(\overline{\alpha}) > 0, M_1(\overline{\alpha}) > 0, M_2(\overline{\alpha}) > 0$*, and that*

$$M_1(\overline{\alpha})M_2(\overline{\alpha}) - M_0(\overline{\alpha}) = 0, \; M_1(\overline{\alpha})M_2'(\overline{\alpha}) + M_1'(\overline{\alpha})M_2(\overline{\alpha}) - M_0'(\overline{\alpha}) \neq 0. \tag{32}$$

Then, we have

1. *For* $\alpha \in (\overline{\alpha}, \overline{\alpha} + \epsilon)$*, the steady state* $(0,0,0)$ *is locally asymptotically stable, while it is unstable for* $\alpha \in (\overline{\alpha} - \epsilon, \overline{\alpha})$ *provided that*

$$M_1(\overline{\alpha})M_2'(\overline{\alpha}) + M_1'(\overline{\alpha})M_2(\overline{\alpha}) - M_0'(\overline{\alpha}) > 0,$$

where $\epsilon > 0$ *is the sufficiently small number.*

2. *For* $\alpha \in (\overline{\alpha}, \overline{\alpha} + \epsilon)$*, the steady state* $(0,0,0)$ *is unstable, while it is locally asymptotically stable for* $\alpha \in (\overline{\alpha} - \epsilon, \overline{\alpha})$ *provided that*

$$M_1(\overline{\alpha})M_2'(\overline{\alpha}) + M_1'(\overline{\alpha})M_2(\overline{\alpha}) - M_0'(\overline{\alpha}) < 0,$$

where $\epsilon > 0$ *is the sufficiently small number.*

3. *At* $\alpha = \overline{\alpha}$*, near* $(0,0,0)$*, system (28) will experience Hopf bifurcations. The Hopf bifurcating periodic solution is stable if* $\mathrm{Re}(c_1(\overline{\alpha})) < 0$*, while it is unstable if* $\mathrm{Re}(c_1(\overline{\alpha})) > 0$*. The bifurcation direction is backward if*

$$\mathrm{Re}(c_1(\overline{\alpha}))\Big(M_1(\overline{\alpha})M_2'(\overline{\alpha}) + M_1'(\overline{\alpha})M_2(\overline{\alpha}) - M_0'(\overline{\alpha})\Big) < 0,$$

while the bifurcation direction is forward if

$$\mathrm{Re}(c_1(\overline{\alpha}))\Big(M_1(\overline{\alpha})M_2'(\overline{\alpha}) + M_1'(\overline{\alpha})M_2(\overline{\alpha}) - M_0'(\overline{\alpha})\Big) > 0,$$

where $c_1(\overline{\alpha})$ *denotes the first Lyapunov coefficient and* $\mathrm{Re}(c_1(\overline{\alpha}))$ *represents the real parts of* $c_1(\overline{\alpha})$*.*

Moreover, Wang and Yi [19] also provide conditions on d_1, d_2, d_3 so that diffusion-induced instability of the periodic solutions occurs, which methods and theories base on [21–25].

Lemma 3. *Let* α *be fixed to be sufficiently close to* $\overline{\alpha}$ *such that* $(u_1^p(t), u_2^p(t), u_3^p(t))$ *is a stable bifurcating periodic solution of system (28) described in Lemma 2. Then,* $(u_1^p(t), u_2^p(t), u_3^p(t))$ *is unstable in system (27) if the constant* ℓ *is sufficiently large, and*

$$\begin{aligned} &M_1(\overline{\alpha})\Big(\big(a_{11}(\overline{\alpha})Q(\overline{\alpha}) - 1\big)d_1 + \big(a_{22}(\overline{\alpha})Q(\overline{\alpha}) - 1\big)d_2 + \big(a_{33}(\overline{\alpha})Q(\overline{\alpha}) - 1\big)d_3\Big) \\ &\quad + \Big(M_2(\overline{\alpha})Q(\overline{\alpha}) + 1\Big)\Big(A_{11}(\overline{\alpha})d_1 + A_{22}(\overline{\alpha})d_2 + A_{33}(\overline{\alpha})d_3\Big) > 0, \end{aligned} \tag{33}$$

where

$$Q(\overline{\alpha}) := \frac{\sqrt{M_1(\overline{\alpha})}}{M_1(\overline{\alpha}) + M_2^2(\overline{\alpha})} \frac{\mathrm{Im}(c_1(\overline{\alpha}))}{\mathrm{Re}(c_1(\overline{\alpha}))} - \frac{M_2(\overline{\alpha})}{M_1(\overline{\alpha}) + M_2^2(\overline{\alpha})}. \tag{34}$$

3.2. Diffusion-Induced Instability of the Periodic Solutions for Predator-Prey System

In this subsection, we shall utilize the abstract contents in preliminaries to study the diffusion-induced instability of the periodic solution $(u_p(t), v_p(t), w_p(t))$ as defined in Section 2.

Suppose that either (1): $0 < k \leq 1$ and $\tau \in (0, k)$ or (2): $k > 1$ and $\tau \in \left(\frac{k-1}{2}, k\right)$ holds so that (τ, v_τ) is stable in system (5).

Let $\tau \in (\tau_0, \tau_\mu)$ and $\Delta_\alpha > 0$ so that α_1 and α_2 are well-defined. Then, at $\alpha = \alpha_1$ and $\alpha = \alpha_2$, the Hopf bifurcation around (τ, v_τ, w_τ) occurs. Moreover, we assume that $\mathrm{Re}(c_1(\alpha_1)) < 0$ (resp., $\mathrm{Re}(c_1(\alpha_2)) < 0$) so that the periodic solution which bifurcating from Hopf bifurcating at (α_1, τ, v_τ) (resp., (α_2, τ, v_τ)) is orbitally asymptotically stable.

According to Lemma 3, to study the diffusion-induced instability of the periodic solution $(u_p(t), v_p(t), w_p(t))$, we need to compute $\mathrm{Im}(c_1(\overline{\alpha}))$, where $\overline{\alpha} = \alpha_1$ or α_2. Then, by using the method in Appendix of [19], we can obtain

$$\begin{aligned}
\mathrm{Im}(c_1(\overline{\alpha})) =& \frac{1}{32\sqrt{M_1(\overline{\alpha})}}\left((h_1)^2_{y_1y_1} - (h_2)^2_{y_1y_1} + 2(h_1)_{y_1y_2}(h_2)_{y_1y_1}\right) \\
&- \frac{1}{16\sqrt{M_1(\overline{\alpha})}}\left(\left((h_1)_{y_1y_1} + (h_1)_{y_2y_2}\right)^2 + \left((h_2)_{y_1y_1} + (h_2)_{y_2y_2}\right)^2\right) \\
&- \frac{1}{96\sqrt{M_1(\overline{\alpha})}}\Big(\left((h_1)_{y_1y_1} - (h_1)_{y_2y_2} - 2(h_2)_{y_1y_2}\right)^2 + \left((h_2)_{y_1y_1} - (h_2)_{y_2y_2} + 2(h_1)_{y_1y_2}\right)^2\Big) \\
&+ \frac{1}{8M_2(\overline{\alpha})}(h_3)_{y_1y_1}\left((h_2)_{y_1y_3} - (h_1)_{y_2y_3}\right) + \frac{1}{16}\left((h_2)_{y_1y_1y_1} - (h_1)_{y_1y_1y_2}\right) \\
&+ \frac{M_2(\overline{\alpha})}{16(M_2(\overline{\alpha})^2 + 4M_1(\overline{\alpha}))}(h_3)_{y_1y_1}\left((h_2)_{y_1y_3} + (h_1)_{y_2y_3}\right) \\
&- \frac{M_2(\overline{\alpha})}{8(M_2(\overline{\alpha})^2 + 4M_1(\overline{\alpha}))}(h_3)_{y_1y_2}\left((h_1)_{y_1y_3} - (h_2)_{y_2y_3}\right) \\
&- \frac{\sqrt{M_1(\overline{\alpha})}}{8(M_2(\overline{\alpha})^2 + 4M_1(\overline{\alpha}))}(h_3)_{y_1y_1}\left((h_1)_{y_1y_3} + (h_2)_{y_2y_3}\right) \\
&- \frac{\sqrt{M_1(\overline{\alpha})}}{4(M_2(\overline{\alpha})^2 + 4M_1(\overline{\alpha}))}(h_3)_{y_1y_2}\left((h_2)_{y_1y_3} + (h_1)_{y_2y_3}\right).
\end{aligned} \tag{35}$$

Then, from Lemma 3, we now state our main results.

Theorem 5. *Let α be fixed to be close to $\overline{\alpha}$, where $\overline{\alpha} = \alpha_1$ or α_2, and $\mathrm{Re}(c_1(\overline{\alpha})) < 0$ so that $(u_p(t), v_p(t), w_p(t))$ is stable in the kinetic system (4). Then, $(u_p(t), v_p(t), w_p(t))$ is able to experience diffusion-induced instability provided that the constant ℓ is large enough and*

$$\begin{aligned}
&M_1(\overline{\alpha})\Big(\left(-AQ(\overline{\alpha}) - 1\right)d_1 + \left((\mu - 1)\theta Q(\overline{\alpha}) - 1\right)d_2 - \left(\overline{\alpha}Q(\overline{\alpha}) + 1\right)d_3\Big) \\
&+ \left(M_2(\overline{\alpha})Q(\overline{\alpha}) + 1\right)\Big(d_2 A\overline{\alpha} + d_3\theta(A(1-\mu) + \mu B)\Big) > 0,
\end{aligned} \tag{36}$$

where A, B, $M_1(\alpha)$, $M_2(\alpha)$ are set in (9) and (11); moreover,

$$Q(\overline{\alpha}) := \frac{\sqrt{M_1(\overline{\alpha})}}{M_1(\overline{\alpha}) + M_2(\overline{\alpha})^2}\frac{\mathrm{Im}(c_1(\overline{\alpha}))}{\mathrm{Re}(c_1(\overline{\alpha}))} - \frac{M_2(\overline{\alpha})}{M_1(\overline{\alpha}) + M_2(\overline{\alpha})^2},$$

where $\mathrm{Re}(c_1(\overline{\alpha}))$ is described in (26).

Remark 3. *It is analytically demanding to obtain a explicit expression of $\mathrm{Re}(c_1(\overline{\alpha}))$, $\mathrm{Im}(c_1(\overline{\alpha}))$ and $Q(\overline{\alpha})$. We shall resort to numerical tools to calculate it in the part of numerical simulations.*

4. Numerical Examples

In this section, we present some numerical examples. We divided our numerical simulations into two parts: "larger"μ (μ is very close to 1) and "smaller"μ (μ is very close to 0).

Case 1 ("larger"μ). We set $m = 100$, $\theta = 10$, $k = 1.1$, and $\mu = 0.8$. In this case, we have

$$\overline{\alpha}_1 = 8.8542, \overline{\alpha}_2 = 132.771, \mathrm{Re}(c_1(\overline{\alpha}_1)) = -11.6638 < 0, \mathrm{Re}(c_1(\overline{\alpha}_2)) = -14.3536 < 0.$$

By Theorem 4, at $\alpha = 8.8542$ and $\alpha = 132.771$, the supercritical Hopf bifurcation occurs around $(\tau, v_\tau, w_\tau) = (0.1111, 0.01, 0.1769)$. That is, the bifurcating periodic solution, denoted by $(u_p(t), v_p(t), w_p(t))$, is stable in the ODEs system.

At $\alpha = \overline{\alpha}_1 = 8.8542$,

$$\mathrm{Re}(c_1(\overline{\alpha}_1))\big(M_1(\overline{\alpha}_1)M_2'(\overline{\alpha}_1) + M_1'(\overline{\alpha}_1)M_2(\overline{\alpha}_1) - M_0'(\overline{\alpha}_1)\big) < 0,$$

which indicates that Hopf bifurcation direction is backward. Set $\alpha = 8.7542$, $\Omega = (0, 1000)$, $u_0(x) = \tau + 0.001$, $v_0(x) = v_\tau + 0.001$, $w_0(x) = w_\tau + 0.0001$.

Firstly, we set $d_1 = d_2 = d_3 = 1$. Numerical simulation shows that $(u_p(t), v_p(t), w_p(t))$ remains stable in the diffusive system. No diffusion-induced instability of $(u_p(t), v_p(t), w_p(t))$ occurs (see Figure 1).

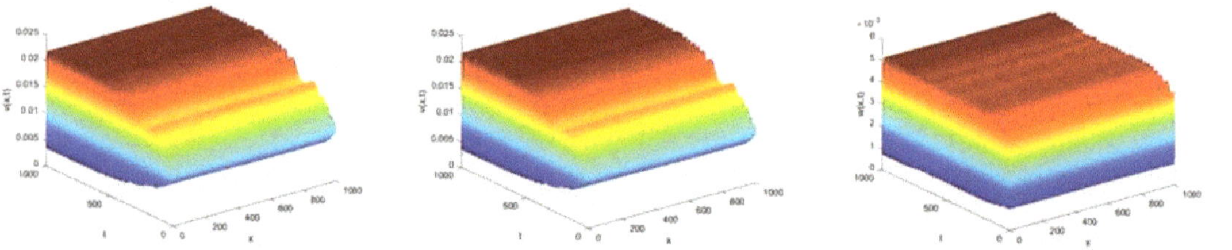

(**a**) u(x,t) (**b**) v(x,t) (**c**) w(x,t)

Figure 1. When $d_1 = d_2 = d_3$, $(u_p(t), v_p(t), w_p(t))$ remains stable in the diffusive system (3).

Secondly, we set $d_1 = 1$, $d_2 = 5$, $d_3 = 30$; $\Omega = (0, 1000)$; $u_0(x) = \tau + 0.001\sin(x)$, $v_0(x) = v_\tau + 0.001\sin(3x)$, $w_0(x) = w_\tau + 0.001\sin(0.005x)$. By Theorem 5, $(u_p(t), v_p(t), w_p(t))$ becomes diffusion-induced unstable in diffusive system (3). This is demonstrated by Figure 2.

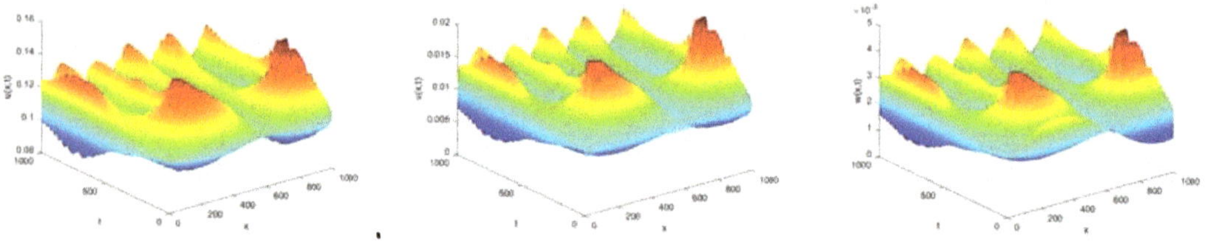

(**a**) u(x,t) (**b**) v(x,t) (**c**) w(x,t)

Figure 2. $(u_p(t), v_p(t), w_p(t))$ becomes diffusion-induced unstable, and the emerging spatiotemporal patterns can be observed.

At $\alpha = \overline{\alpha}_2 = 132.771$, we have

$$\mathrm{Re}(c_1(\overline{\alpha}_2))\Big(M_1(\overline{\alpha}_2)M_2'(\overline{\alpha}_2) + M_1'(\overline{\alpha}_2)M_2(\overline{\alpha}_2) - M_0'(\overline{\alpha}_2)\Big) > 0,$$

which implies that the bifurcating direction is forward. Then, we choose $\alpha = 132.871$, $\Omega = (0, 1000)$, $u_0(x) = \tau + 0.001$, $v_0(x) = v_\tau + 0.001$, $w_0(x) = w_\tau + 0.0001$. In this case, there is a stable periodic solution in the system (4) and denoted by $(u_p(t), v_p(t), w_p(t))$.

First, we set $d_1 = d_2 = d_3 = 1$. $\Omega = (0, 1000)$, $u_0(x) = \tau + 0.001\sin(x)$, $v_0(x) = v_\tau + 0.001\sin(3x)$, $w_0(x) = w_\tau + 0.0001\sin(0.5x)$. In this case, $(u_p(t), v_p(t), w_p(t))$

remains stable in system (3). No diffusion-induced instability of $(u_p(t), v_p(t), w_p(t))$ occurs. This is demonstrated by Figure 3.

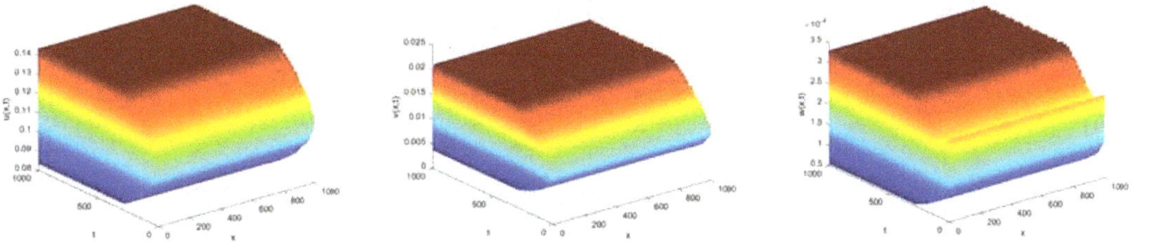

(**a**) u(x,t) (**b**) v(x,t) (**c**) w(x,t)

Figure 3. For $d_1 = d_2 = d_3$, $(u_p(t), v_p(t), w_p(t))$ is still stable in system (3).

Secondly, we set $d_1 = 1$, $d_2 = 5$, $d_3 = 30$, $\Omega = (0, 1000)$, $u_0(x) = \tau + 0.001\sin(x)$, $v_0(x) = v_\tau + 0.001\sin(3x)$, $w_0(x) = w_\tau + 0.0001\sin(0.005x)$. In this case, by theorem 5, $(u_p(t), v_p(t), w_p(t))$ becomes diffusion-induced unstable in system (3). This is demonstrated by Figure 4.

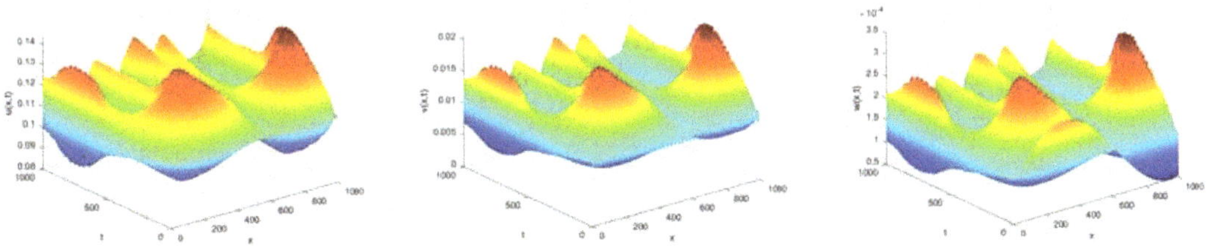

(**a**) u(x,t) (**b**) v(x,t) (**c**) w(x,t)

Figure 4. $(u_p(t), v_p(t), w_p(t))$ becomes diffusion-induced unstable, and the emerging spatiotemporal patterns can be simulated.

Case 2 ("smaller"μ). We set $m = 100$, $\theta = 10$, $k = 1.1$ and $\mu = 0.1$. In this case, we have

$$\overline{\alpha}_1 = 1.1589, \overline{\alpha}_2 = 636.1936, \mathrm{Re}(c_1(\overline{\alpha}_1)) = -0.4907 < 0, \mathrm{Re}(c_1(\overline{\alpha}_2)) = -14.3536 < 0.$$

According to Theorem 4, at $\alpha = \overline{\alpha}_1$ or $\alpha = \overline{\alpha}_2$, the supercritical Hopf bifurcation occurs around $(\tau, v_\tau, w_\tau) = (0.1111, 0.01, 0.1042)$. That is, the bifurcating periodic solution, denoted by $(u_p(t), v_p(t), w_p(t))$, is asymptotically stable in the ODEs system.

At $\alpha = \overline{\alpha}_1 = 1.1589$,

$$\mathrm{Re}(c_1(\overline{\alpha}_1))\big(M_1(\overline{\alpha}_1)M_2'(\overline{\alpha}_1) + M_1'(\overline{\alpha}_1)M_2(\overline{\alpha}_1) - M_0'(\overline{\alpha}_1)\big) < 0,$$

which indicates that the Hopf bifurcation direction is backward. Set $\alpha = 1.0589$, $\Omega = (0, 1000)$, $u_0(x) = \tau + 0.001$, $v_0(x) = v_\tau + 0.001$, and $w_0(x) = w_\tau + 0.0001$. System (4) has a stable periodic solution, denoted by $(u_p(t), v_p(t), w_p(t))$.

First, we set $d_1 = d_2 = d_3 = 1$. $\Omega = (0, 1000)$. No diffusion-induced instability of $(u_p(t), v_p(t), w_p(t))$ occurs. This is demonstrated by Figure 5.

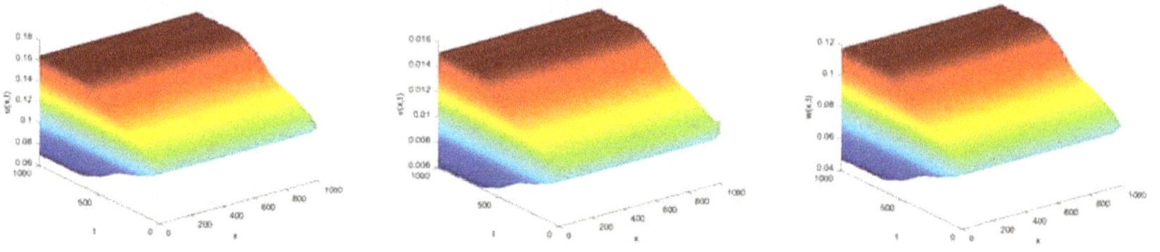

(**a**) u(x,t) (**b**) v(x,t) (**c**) w(x,t)

Figure 5. When $d_1 = d_2 = d_3$, $(u_p(t), v_p(t), w_p(t))$ remains stable in system (3).

Secondly, we set $d_1 = 1, d_2 = 5, d_3 = 30$. $\Omega = (0, 1000)$, and $u_0(x) = \tau + 0.001\sin(x)$, $v_0(x) = v_\tau + 0.001\sin(3x)$, $w_0(x) = w_\tau + 0.001\sin(0.005x)$. By Theorem 5, $(u_p(t), v_p(t), w_p(t))$ becomes diffusion-induced unstable and the emerging spatiotemporal patterns can be found. This is demonstrated by Figure 6.

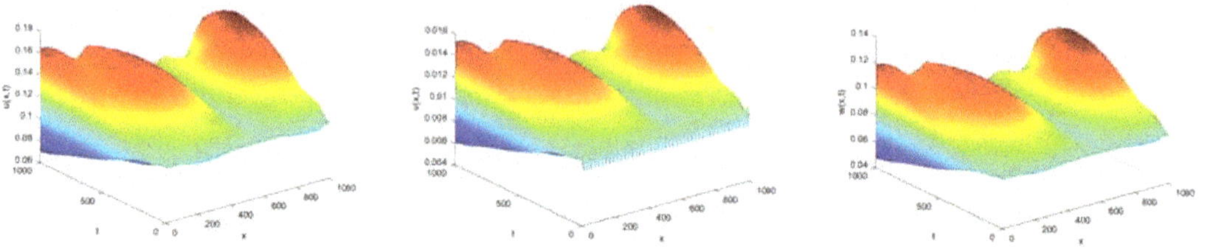

(**a**) u(x,t) (**b**) v(x,t) (**c**) w(x,t)

Figure 6. $(u_p(t), v_p(t), w_p(t))$ becomes diffusion-induced unstable, and the emerging spatiotemporal patterns are observed.

At $\alpha = \overline{\alpha}_2$, we have

$$\mathrm{Re}(c_1(\overline{\alpha}_2))\Big(M_1(\overline{\alpha}_2)M_2'(\overline{\alpha}_2) + M_1'(\overline{\alpha}_2)M_2(\overline{\alpha}_2) - M_0'(\overline{\alpha}_2)\Big) > 0,$$

which confirms that the Hopf bifurcation is forward. We set $\alpha = 636.2936$, $\Omega = (0, 1000)$, $u_0(x) = \tau + 0.001$, $v_0(x) = v_\tau + 0.001$, $w_0(x) = w_\tau + 0.0002$. Then, the kinetic system (4) possesses a periodic solution $(u_p(t), v_p(t), w_p(t))$, which is stable.

First, we set $d_1 = d_2 = d_3 = 1$. $\Omega = (0, 1000)$. The diffusion-induced instability of $(u_p(t), v_p(t), w_p(t))$ cannot be found. This is demonstrated by Figure 7.

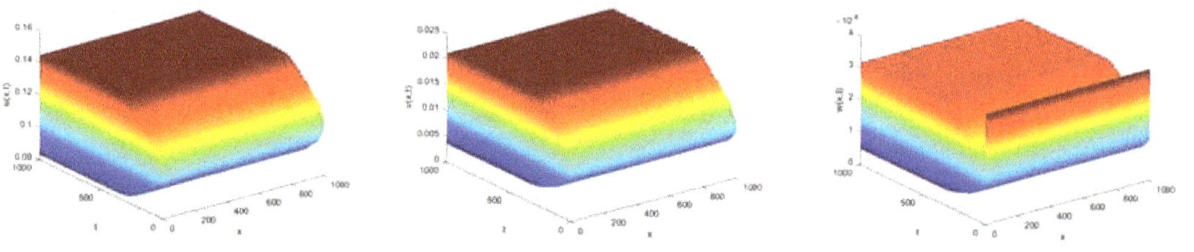

(**a**) u(x,t) (**b**) v(x,t) (**c**) w(x,t)

Figure 7. When $d_1 = d_2 = d_3$, $(u_p(t), v_p(t), w_p(t))$ remains stable in system (3).

Secondly, let $d_1 = 1$, $d_2 = 5$, $d_3 = 30$. $\Omega = (0, 1000)$, and $u_0(x) = \tau + 0.001\sin(x)$, $v_0(x) = v_\tau + 0.001\sin(3x)$, $w_0(x) = w_\tau + 0.001\sin(0.005x)$. By Theorem 5, $(u_p(t), v_p(t), w_p(t))$ becomes diffusion-induced unstable and the emerging spatiotemporal patterns can be observed. This is demonstrated by Figure 8.

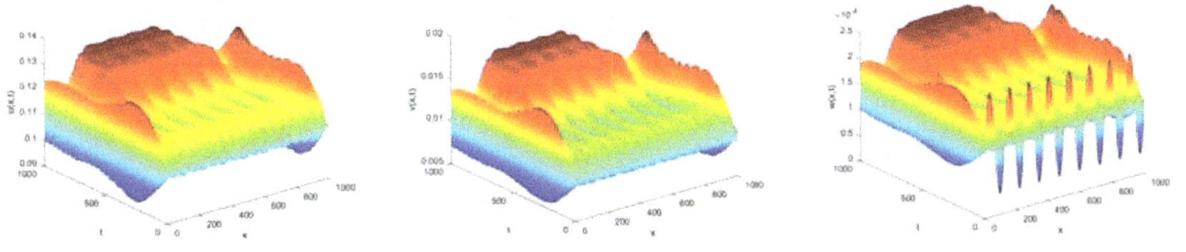

(**a**) u(x,t) (**b**) v(x,t) (**c**) w(x,t)

Figure 8. $(u_p(t), v_p(t), w_p(t))$ becomes diffusion-induced unstable, and the emerging spatiotemporal patterns can be observed.

5. Concluding Remarks

In this paper, a homogeneous diffusive predator-prey system with the dormancy of predators is mainly considered. It concentrates on the diffusion-induced instability of the Hopf bifurcating periodic solutions.

Without regard to the dormancy effect, the predator-prey system is a system with two components. Motivated by [2,3], we choose the first component τ of the positive equilibrium solution (τ, v_τ) as the bifurcation parameter. We assume that the unique positive equilibrium solution of the system (the 2-component predator-prey system) is stable with respect to the corresponding ODEs system, say

$$\text{either } 0 < k \leq 1 \text{ but } \tau \in (0, k), \text{ or } k > 1 \text{ but } \tau \in \left(\frac{k-1}{2}, k\right)$$

holds so that (τ, v_τ) is stable in system (5). By [2], (τ, v_τ) is globally asymptotically stable in system (5).

In the presence of the dormancy effect, the predator-prey system becomes a system with 3-components. Our results indicated that for some θ, if $\Delta_\alpha > 0$, then for suitable τ and α (say, $\tau \in (\tau_0, \tau_\mu)$, $\alpha = \alpha_1$ and $\alpha = \alpha_2$), the ODEs predator-prey system might exhibit temporal oscillations. This suggests that the dormancy effects can favor the emergence of temporal oscillatory patterns. Precisely, the smaller μ (the modeling the strengthen of the dormancy effect) is, the larger stability range of τ is. At $\alpha = \alpha_1$ and $\alpha = \alpha_2$, Hopf bifurcations around (τ, v_τ, w_τ) occur. By calculating the first Lyapunov coefficients, we can derive conditions to determine the stability of the periodic solutions.

When diffusions are introduced into the predator-prey system with dormancy, we can deduce the reaction-diffusion equations with the 3-components system. Referring to the abstract results in [19], we are able to expound some precise conditions on the diffusion coefficients to determine the diffusion-induced instability of the periodic solutions.

Funding: This research was supported by the National Natural Science Foundation of China (11371108, 11971088).

Data Availability Statement: Not applicable.

Acknowledgments: The author wish to thank the editors and reviewers for their helpful comments.

Conflicts of Interest: The authors declare no conflict of interest.

References

1. Yi, F.; Wei, J.; Shi, J. Bifurcation and spatiotemporal patterns in a homogenous diffusive predator-prey system. *J. Differ. Equ.* **2009**, *246*, 1944–1977. [CrossRef]
2. Hsu, S. On global stability of a predator-prey system. *Math. Biosci.* **1978**, *39*, 1–10. [CrossRef]
3. Hsu, S.; Shi, J. Relaxation oscillator profile of limit cycle in predator-prey system. *Discrete Contin. Dyn. Syst.-Ser. B* **2009**, *11*, 893–911.
4. Cheng, K. Uniqueness of a limit cycle for a predator-prey system. *SIAM J. Math. Anal.* **1981**, *12*, 541–548. [CrossRef]
5. Ko, W.; Ryu, K. Qualitative analysis of a predator-prey model with Holling type II functional response incorporating a prey refuge. *J. Differ. Equ.* **2006**, *231*, 534–550. [CrossRef]
6. Peng, R.; Shi, J. Non-existence of non-constant positive steady states of two Holling type-II predator–prey systems: Strong interaction case. *J. Differ. Equ.* **2009**, *247*, 866–886. [CrossRef]
7. Kuwamura, M.; Nakazawa, T.; Ogawa, T. A minimum model of prey-predator system with dormancy of predators and the paradox of enrichment. *J. Math. Biol.* **2008**, *58*, 459–479. [CrossRef]
8. Kuwamura, M. Turing instabilities in prey-predator systems with dormancy of predators. *J. Math. Biol.* **2015**, *71*, 125–149. [CrossRef]
9. Yi, F. Turing instability of the periodic solutions for general reaction-diffusion system with cross-diffusion and the patch model with cross-diffusion-like coupling. *J. Differ. Equ.* **2021**, *281*, 397–410. [CrossRef]
10. Conway, E.; Hoff, D.; Smoller, J. Large time behavior of solutions of systems of nonlinear reaction-diffusion equations. *SIAM J. Appl. Math.* **1978**, *35*, 1–16. [CrossRef]
11. Hasting, S.; Murray, J. The existence of oscillatory solutions in the Field-Noyes model for the Belousov-Zhabontinskii reaction. *SIAM J. Appl. Math* **1975**, *28*, 678–688. [CrossRef]
12. Klaasen, G.; Troy, W. The existence, uniqueness and instability of spherically symmetric solutions of a system of reaction-diffusion equations. *J. Differ. Equ.* **1984**, *52*, 91–115. [CrossRef]
13. Maginu, K. Stability of spatially homogeneous periodic solutions of reaction-diffusion equations. *J. Differ. Equ.* **1979**, *31*, 130–138. [CrossRef]
14. Murray, J. On a model for the temporal oscillations in the Belousov-Zhabotinsky reaction. *J. Chem. Phys.* **1974**, *61*, 3610–3613. [CrossRef]
15. Qian, H.; Murray, J. A simple method of parameter space determination for diffusion-driven instability with three species. *Appl. Math. Lett.* **2001**, *14*, 405–411. [CrossRef]
16. Ruan, S. Diffusion-driven instability in the Gierer-Meinhardt model of morphogenesis. *Nat. Resour. Model.* **1998**, *11*, 131–142. [CrossRef]
17. Ruan, W.; Pao, C. Asymptotic behavior and positive solutions of a chemical reaction diffusion system. *J. Math. Anal. Appl.* **1992**, *169*, 157–178. [CrossRef]
18. Yi, F.; Liu, S.; Tuncer, N. Spatiotemporal patterns of a reaction-diffusion substrate-inhibition Seelig model. *J. Dyn. Differ. Equ.* **2017**, *29*, 219–241.
19. Wang, M.; Yi, F. On the dynamics of the diffusive Field-Noyes model for the Belousov-Zhabotinskii reaction. *J. Differ. Equ.* **2022**, *318*, 443–479. [CrossRef]
20. Turing, A. The chemical basis of morphogenesis. *Phil. Trans. R. Soc. London.* **1952**, *B237*, 37–72.
21. Coddington, E.; Levinson, N. *Theory of Ordinary Differential Equations*; McGraw-Hill: New York, NY, USA, 1955.
22. Friedman, A. *Partial Differential Equations of Parabolic Type*; Prentice-Hall: Englewood Cliffs, NJ, USA, 1964.
23. Hassard, B.; Kazarinoff, N.; Wan, Y. *Theory and Application of Hopf Bifurcation*; Cambridge University Press: New York, NY, USA, 1981.
24. Wiggins, S. *Introduction to Applied Nonlinear Dynamical Systems and Chaos*; Springer: New York, NY, USA, 1990.
25. Weinberger, H. Invariant sets for weakly coupled parabolic and elliptic systems. *Rend. Mat.* **1975**, *8*, 295–310.

Disclaimer/Publisher's Note: The statements, opinions and data contained in all publications are solely those of the individual author(s) and contributor(s) and not of MDPI and/or the editor(s). MDPI and/or the editor(s) disclaim responsibility for any injury to people or property resulting from any ideas, methods, instructions or products referred to in the content.

mathematics

Article

Neimark–Sacker Bifurcation of a Discrete-Time Predator–Prey Model with Prey Refuge Effect

Binhao Hong and Chunrui Zhang *

College of Science, Northeast Forestry University, Harbin 150040, China
* Correspondence: math@nefu.edu.cn

Abstract: In this paper, we deduce a predator–prey model with discrete time in the interior of $\mathbb{R}^2_+$ using a new discrete method to study its local dynamics and Neimark–Sacker bifurcation. Compared with continuous models, discrete ones have many unique properties that help to understand the changing patterns of biological populations from a completely new perspective. The existence and stability of the three equilibria are analyzed, and the formation conditions of Neimark–Sacker bifurcation around the unique positive equilibrium point are established using the center manifold theorem and bifurcation theory. An attracting closed invariant curve appears, which corresponds to the periodic oscillations between predators and prey over a long period of time. Finally, some numerical simulations and their biological meanings are given to reveal the complex dynamical behavior.

Keywords: predator–prey model; Neimark–Sacker bifurcation; refuge

MSC: 26D15; 33C20; 33C47; 33E20; 60E05

Citation: Hong, B.; Zhang, C. Neimark–Sacker Bifurcation of a Discrete-Time Predator–Prey Model with Prey Refuge Effect. *Mathematics* **2023**, *11*, 1399. https://doi.org/10.3390/math11061399

Academic Editor: Carmen Chicone

Received: 24 February 2023
Revised: 7 March 2023
Accepted: 10 March 2023
Published: 14 March 2023

1. Introduction

Theoretical ecology aims to give reasonable explanations for the interactions among biological populations in nature with the help of dynamical models to predict the distribution and population structure of communities. Since the pioneers Lotka [1] and Volterra [2] constructed the famous Lotka–Volterra ecosystem model [3], the use of mathematical models to explain complex ecological properties has been common in biology (see [4–8]). Among them, predator–prey systems, which can explain predation relationships, have been intensively studied and made great progress in the 1980s [9,10].

Brauer, F. and Sanchez, D. A. studied a predator–prey system with constant harvest and storage rates. They found novel dynamical properties, such as the stability of equilibrium points and existence of limit loops [11]. There are many predator–prey systems related to the Allee effect and fear effect [12–14]. These articles not only give the stability of the equilibrium point and bifurcation categories but, more importantly, describe the influence of the Allee effect and fear effect on the final density of the population. In addition, the dynamic predation behavior of predators in ecosystems strongly depends on functional responses.

One of the most common functional responses in predator–prey systems is the well-known Holling type-II response. Kuznetsov, Y.A. studied a food chain model composed of logistic prey and Holling type II predators and superpredators and gave several types of bifurcations with their chaotic behaviors [15]. Aziz-Alaoui, MA. and Okiye, MD. presented a two-dimensional predator–prey food chain continuous model with a Holling type-II response. They concluded with global stability of the coexisting interior equilibrium using a Lyapunov function [16].

In natural predator–prey interactions, failure to protect prey is likely to cause their extinction, which is detrimental to biodiversity. Chen, LD., Chen, LJ., Xie, XD. proposed a Leslie–Gower predator–prey model incorporating a prey refuge, where the analysis showed that increasing the amount of refuge increased prey densities [17]. Therefore, models that consider prey refuges can more accurately respond to interspecific relationships in nature than can general models.

In the ecological community, many populations do not vary in numbers continuously. Therefore, it is particularly important to study discrete models. A discrete model has multiple periodic bifurcations, chaotic properties and generate periodic orbits, while a continuous one produces only simple S-shaped curves [18,19]. Normally, the discretization method given by Euler is used in most studies [20,21]. Since the accuracy of the Euler method is determined by the step size, it has low accuracy and stability. However, the semi-discrete method can achieve higher accuracy and stability with suitable choices of schemes.

In this paper, we modify a continuous predator–prey model with the prey refuge effect using a semi-discrete method in Section 2. In Section 3, we determine the existence and stability of three equilibria and focus on the local dynamics about the unique positive equilibrium point. In Section 4, we study Neimark–Sacker bifurcation when bifurcation parameter γ varies in a small neighborhood of the positive equilibrium point. In Section 5, some numerical simulations for Neimark–Sacker bifurcation are given by phase diagrams to verify our results. Finally, our conclusions and biological meanings are given in Section 6.

2. Preliminaries and Notation

Ghosh J., Sahoo B. and Poria S. constructed a predator–prey model with a logical growth rate and prey refuge in the presence of additional food for predator based on the Holling type-II functional response, which is given as follows [22].

$$\begin{cases} \frac{dN}{dT} = rN\left(1-\frac{N}{K}\right) - \frac{c'(1-c)e_1NP}{a+h_2e_2A+h_1e_1N} \\ \frac{dP}{dT} = \frac{b((1-c)e_1N+e_2A)P}{a+h_2e_2A+h_1e_1N} - mP \end{cases}$$

where $F(N) = \frac{c'(1-c)e_1N}{a+h_2e_2A+h_1e_1N}$ is the functional response in the presence of prey refuge c and additional food for predator A. N and P indicate the biomass of the prey and predator, respectively. e_1 and h_1 represent the ability of the predator to detect prey and the handling time of the predator per prey item, respectively. e_2 and h_2 denote the ability to detect additional food and the handling time of additional food biomass, respectively. r and K, respectively, represent the intrinsic growth rate and environmental carrying capacity of the prey.

To simplify the parameters, we denote $x = \frac{e_1h_1}{a}N$, $y = \frac{c'e_1}{ar}P$, $\alpha = \frac{h_2}{h_1}$, $\xi = \frac{e_2h_1A}{a}$, $\beta = \frac{b}{h_1r}$, $\delta = \frac{m}{r}$, and $t = rT$. Subsequently, the simplified model is given by [22]:

$$\begin{cases} \frac{dx}{dt} = x\left(1-\frac{x}{\gamma}\right) - \frac{(1-c)xy}{1+\alpha\xi+x} \\ \frac{dy}{dt} = \frac{\beta((1-c)x+\xi)y}{1+\alpha\xi+x} - \delta y \end{cases} \tag{1}$$

Based on the model (1) already constructed by Ghosh J., Sahoo B. and Poria S. and the significant work given by Gladkov, S.O. who demonstrated a method for obtaining any dynamic equations describing various biological systems, including considering the heterogeneous distribution of populations [23], we used the semi-discrete method [24,25] for model (1) modification.

We divide the continuous time t into small parts (i.e., $t \in [n\,, n+1)\,,\ n \in \mathbb{N}^+$) and integrate over the unit time period.

$$\int_n^{n+1} \frac{1}{x(t)}dx(t) = \int_n^{n+1} \left[x(t)\left(1-\frac{x(t)}{\gamma}\right) - \frac{(1-c)x(t)y(t)}{1+\alpha\xi+x(t)}\right]dt$$

$$\ln x_{n+1} - \ln x_n = x_n\left(1-\frac{x_n}{\gamma}\right) - \frac{(1-c)x_ny_n}{1+\alpha\xi+x_n}$$

Using the same discrete method in the second equation, we obtained the following discrete-time system:

$$\begin{cases} x_{n+1} = x_n e^{1-\frac{x_n}{\gamma}-\frac{(1-c)y_n}{1+\alpha\xi+x_n}} \\ y_{n+1} = y_n e^{\frac{\beta(1-c)x_n+\xi}{1+\alpha\xi+x_n}-\delta} \end{cases} \tag{2}$$

3. Existence and Stability of Equilibria

Initially, the existence and stability of the equilibrium points of system (2) are analyzed. By calculating system (2), clearly, trivial and boundary equilibria $E_1 = (0,0)$, $E_2 = (\gamma, 0)$ are obtained. In the following research, we focus on studying the local dynamics around the unique positive equilibrium point $E_3 = (x^*, y^*) = \left(\frac{\delta+(\alpha\delta-\beta)\xi}{\beta(1-c)-\delta}, \left(\frac{1+\alpha\xi+x^*}{1-c}\right)\left(1-\frac{x^*}{\gamma}\right) \right)$.

The Jacobi matrix of the linear system of (2) at any equilibrium point (x, y) can be obtained as

$$J(x,y) = \begin{pmatrix} \left(1 + x\left(-\frac{1}{\gamma} + \frac{(1-c)y}{(1+\alpha\xi+x)^2}\right)\right) e^{\left(1-\frac{x}{\gamma}-\frac{(1-c)y}{1+\alpha\xi+x}\right)} & -\frac{(1-c)x}{1+\alpha\xi+x} e^{\left(1-\frac{x}{\gamma}-\frac{(1-c)y}{1+\alpha\xi+x}\right)} \\ \frac{((1-c)(1+\alpha\xi)-\xi)\beta y}{(1+\alpha\xi+x)^2} e^{\left(\frac{((1-c)x+\xi)\beta}{1+\alpha\xi+x}-\delta\right)} & e^{\left(\frac{((1-c)x+\xi)\beta}{1+\alpha\xi+x}-\delta\right)} \end{pmatrix}$$

Now, we give some dynamical properties about three equilibria.

Theorem 1. *The following results hold for system (2):*

(*i*) *The trivial equilibrium E_1 is a saddle point if and only if $\frac{\beta\xi}{1+\alpha\xi} < \delta$, and it is a source if and only if $\frac{\beta\xi}{1+\alpha\xi} > \delta$.*

(*ii*) *The boundary equilibrium E_2 is a sink if and only if $\frac{\beta((1-c)\gamma+\xi)}{1+\alpha\xi+\gamma} < \delta$, it is a saddle point if and only if $\frac{\beta((1-c)\gamma+\xi)}{1+\alpha\xi+\gamma} > \delta$, and transcritical bifurcation occurs at E_2 if and only if $\frac{\beta((1-c)\gamma+\xi)}{1+\alpha\xi+\gamma} = \delta$.*

Proof. (*i*) First, the Jacobian matrix of (2) at point $E_1 = (0,0)$ is given by:

$$J(E_1) = \begin{pmatrix} e & 0 \\ 0 & e^{\frac{\beta\xi}{1+\alpha\xi}-\delta} \end{pmatrix}$$

Then, eigenvalues of $J(E_1)$ are $\lambda_1 = e > 1$ and $\lambda_2 = e^{\frac{\beta\xi}{1+\alpha\xi}-\delta}$. Therefore, E_1 is a saddle point if and only if $\frac{\beta\xi}{1+\alpha\xi} < \delta$, and it is a source if and only if $\frac{\beta\xi}{1+\alpha\xi} > \delta$.

(*ii*) Secondly, the Jacobian matrix of (2) at point $E_2 = (\gamma, 0)$ is given by:

$$J(E_2) = \begin{pmatrix} 0 & -\frac{(1-c)\gamma}{1+\alpha\xi+\gamma} \\ 0 & e^{\frac{\beta((1-c)\gamma+\xi)}{1+\alpha\xi+\gamma}-\delta} \end{pmatrix}$$

Then, eigenvalues of $E_2 = (\gamma, 0)$ are $\lambda_1 = 0 < 1$ and $\lambda_2 = e^{\frac{\beta((1-c)\gamma+\xi)}{1+\alpha\xi+\gamma}-\delta}$. Therefore, E_2 is a sink if and only if $\frac{\beta((1-c)\gamma+\xi)}{1+\alpha\xi+\gamma} < \delta$, it is a saddle point if and only if $\frac{\beta((1-c)\gamma+\xi)}{1+\alpha\xi+\gamma} > \delta$, and transcritical bifurcation occurs at E_2 if and only if $\frac{\beta((1-c)\gamma+\xi)}{1+\alpha\xi+\gamma} = \delta$.

□

Next, we study the dynamics of system (2) at its unique positive internal equilibrium point $E_3 = (x^*, y^*) = \left(\frac{\delta+(\alpha\delta-\beta)\xi}{\beta(1-c)-\delta}, \left(\frac{1+\alpha\xi+x^*}{1-c}\right)\left(1-\frac{x^*}{\gamma}\right) \right)$.

Theorem 2. *The following results hold for system (2):*

(*i*) *The positive equilibrium* E_3 *is a sink if*

$$\begin{cases} 4+\frac{2x^*}{\gamma}\left(\frac{\gamma-x^*}{1+\alpha\xi+x^*}-1\right)+\frac{\beta(1-c)((1-c)(1+\alpha\xi)-\xi)x^*y^*}{(1+\alpha\xi+x^*)^3}>0 \\ c<1-\frac{\xi}{1+\alpha\xi} \\ \frac{x^*}{\gamma}\left(\frac{\gamma-x^*}{1+\alpha\xi+x^*}-1\right)+\frac{\beta(1-c)((1-c)(1+\alpha\xi)-\xi)x^*y^*}{(1+\alpha\xi+x^*)^3}<0 \end{cases}$$

(*ii*) *The positive equilibrium* E_3 *is a saddle point if*

$$\begin{cases} c<1-\frac{\xi}{1+\alpha\xi} \\ 4+\frac{2x^*}{\gamma}\left(\frac{\gamma-x^*}{1+\alpha\xi+x^*}-1\right)+\frac{\beta(1-c)((1-c)(1+\alpha\xi)-\xi)x^*y^*}{(1+\alpha\xi+x^*)^3}<0 \end{cases}$$

(*iii*) *The positive equilibrium* E_3 *is a source if*

$$\begin{cases} 4+\frac{2x^*}{\gamma}\left(\frac{\gamma-x^*}{1+\alpha\xi+x^*}-1\right)+\frac{\beta(1-c)((1-c)(1+\alpha\xi)-\xi)x^*y^*}{(1+\alpha\xi+x^*)^3}>0 \\ c<1-\frac{\xi}{1+\alpha\xi} \\ \frac{x^*}{\gamma}\left(\frac{\gamma-x^*}{1+\alpha\xi+x^*}-1\right)+\frac{\beta(1-c)((1-c)(1+\alpha\xi)-\xi)x^*y^*}{(1+\alpha\xi+x^*)^3}>0 \end{cases}$$

(*iv*) *Transcritical bifurcation occurs at* E_3 *if*

$$\begin{cases} c=1-\frac{\xi}{1+\alpha\xi} \\ -2<\frac{x^*}{\gamma}\left(\frac{\gamma-x^*}{1+\alpha\xi+x^*}-1\right)<0 \end{cases}$$

(*v*) *Flip bifurcation occurs at* E_3 *if*

$$\begin{cases} 4+\frac{2x^*}{\gamma}\left(\frac{\gamma-x^*}{1+\alpha\xi+x^*}-1\right)+\frac{\beta(1-c)((1-c)(1+\alpha\xi)-\xi)x^*y^*}{(1+\alpha\xi+x^*)^3}=0 \\ -4<\frac{x^*}{\gamma}\left(\frac{\gamma-x^*}{1+\alpha\xi+x^*}-1\right)<-2 \end{cases}$$

(*vi*) *Neimark–Sacker bifurcation occurs at* E_3 *if*

$$\begin{cases} \frac{x^*}{\gamma}\left(\frac{\gamma-x^*}{1+\alpha\xi+x^*}-1\right)+\frac{\beta(1-c)((1-c)(1+\alpha\xi)-\xi)x^*y^*}{(1+\alpha\xi+x^*)^3}=0 \\ -4<\frac{x^*}{\gamma}\left(\frac{\gamma-x^*}{1+\alpha\xi+x^*}-1\right)<0 \end{cases}$$

Proof. The Jacobian matrix $J(x^*,\ y^*)$ of system (2) is given by:

$$J(x^*,y^*)=\begin{pmatrix} \frac{x^*}{\gamma}\left(\frac{\gamma-x^*}{1+\alpha\xi+x^*}-1\right)+1 & -\frac{(1-c)x^*}{1+\alpha\xi+x^*} \\ \frac{((1-c)(1+\alpha\xi)-\xi)\beta y^*}{(1+\alpha\xi+x^*)^2} & 1 \end{pmatrix}$$

The characteristic polynomial of $J(x^*,\ y^*)$ is given by:

$$P(\lambda)=\lambda^2-\left(2+\frac{x^*}{\gamma}\left(\frac{\gamma-x^*}{1+\alpha\xi+x^*}-1\right)\right)\lambda+\frac{x^*}{\gamma}\left(\frac{\gamma-x^*}{1+\alpha\xi+x^*}-1\right)+\frac{\beta(1-c)((1-c)(1+\alpha\xi)-\xi)x^*y^*}{(1+\alpha\xi+x^*)^3}+1$$

Then, eigenvalues of $J(x^*,\ y^*)$ are

$$\lambda_1=\frac{1+M+\sqrt{(1-M)^2+4BC}}{2},\quad \lambda_2=\frac{1+M-\sqrt{(1-M)^2+4BC}}{2},$$

where $M=1+\frac{x^*}{\gamma}\left(\frac{\gamma-x^*}{1+\alpha\xi+x^*}-1\right)$ and $BC=-\frac{\beta(1-c)((1-c)(1+\alpha\xi)-\xi)x^*y^*}{(1+\alpha\xi+x^*)^3}$.

(i) E_3 is a sink with the eigenvalues $|\lambda_1| < 1$ and $|\lambda_2| < 1$, which is equivalent to $BC < 0$, $2M - BC + 2 > 0$, and $1 - M + BC > 0$.
(ii) E_3 is a saddle point with the eigenvalues $|\lambda_1| < 1$ and $|\lambda_2| > 1$ ($|\lambda_1| > 1$ and $|\lambda_2| < 1$), which is equivalent to $BC < 0$ and $2M - BC + 2 < 0$.
(iii) E_3 is a source with the eigenvalues $|\lambda_1| > 1$ and $|\lambda_2| > 1$, which is equivalent to $2M - BC + 2 > 0$, $BC < 0$, and $1 - M + BC < 0$.
(iv) Transcritical bifurcation occurs with the eigenvalues $\lambda_1 = 1$, $|\lambda_2| < 1$ or $\lambda_2 = 1$, $|\lambda_1| < 1$, which is equivalent to $BC = 0$ and $|M| < 1$.
(v) Flip bifurcation occurs with the eigenvalues $\lambda_1 = -1$, $|\lambda_2| < 1$ or $\lambda_2 = -1$, $|\lambda_1| < 1$, which is equivalent to $2M - BC + 2 = 0$ and $|M + 2| < 1$.
(vi) Neimark–Sacker bifurcation occurs with the eigenvalues $\lambda_1\lambda_2 = 1$ and $|\lambda_1 + \lambda_2| < 2$, which is equivalent to $M - BC = 1$ and $|M + 1| < 2$.

□

In practical biological applications, we can artificially control whether the system ends up being stable or unstable based on inequalities of the variables given in Theorems 1 and 2, which means that the biomass of predators and prey can be regulated. Therefore, this is significant for predicting future biomass trends of populations and for taking conservation measures in advance for endangered species to maintain biodiversity.

4. Neimark–Sacker Bifurcation at (x_0, y_0)

Bifurcation is a phenomenon in nonlinear dynamical systems where a small perturbation of a parameter can cause a sudden qualitative change in its dynamic behavior. From bifurcations, several consequences can be obtained, such as the emergence of periodic probits and limit cycles. In this section, we study the Neimark–Sacker bifurcation at (x_0, y_0).

To simplify the system for ease of study, we assume that the parameter $A = 0$, which means that zero additional food biomass and only the influence of prey refuge c on the model is considered. Then, system (2) turns into system (3):

$$\begin{cases} x_{n+1} = x_n e^{1 - \frac{x_n}{\gamma} - \frac{(1-c)y_n}{1+\alpha\xi+x_n}} \\ y_{n+1} = y_n e^{\frac{\beta(1-c)x_n+\xi}{1+\alpha\xi+x_n} - \delta} \end{cases} \tag{3}$$

Its positive equilibrium (x^*, y^*) turns into $(x_0, y_0) = \left(\frac{\delta}{\beta(1-c)-\delta}, \frac{1+x_0}{1-c}\left(1 - \frac{x_0}{\gamma}\right)\right)$.

In this section, we discuss how system (3) undergoes Neimark–Sacker bifurcation around its positive equilibrium (x_0, y_0) when γ is chosen as a bifurcation parameter. The necessary conditions for Neimark–Sacker bifurcation to occur are given by the following curve:

$$S = \left\{(c, \beta, \delta) \in \mathbb{R}^3_+ : \gamma = \gamma^* = \frac{\delta + \beta(1-c) + \delta(\beta(1-c) - \delta)}{(\beta(1-c) - \delta)^2 + (\beta(1-c) - \delta)}, |D| < 2\right\} \tag{4}$$

where

$$D = \frac{x^*}{\gamma}\left(\frac{\gamma - x^*}{1 + x^*} - 1\right) + 2.$$

4.1. Existence Condition of Neimark–Sacker Bifurcation at (x_0, y_0)

The Jacobian matrix $J(x_0, y_0)$ of system (3) is given by:

$$J(x_0, y_0) = \begin{pmatrix} \left(1 + \frac{\delta}{\beta(1-c)}\right)\left(1 - \frac{\delta}{\gamma(\beta(1-c)-\delta)}\right) & -\frac{\delta}{\beta} \\ \frac{\gamma(\beta(1-c)-\delta)}{\gamma(1-c)} & 1 \end{pmatrix}$$

The characteristic polynomial of $J(x_0, y_0)$ is given by:

$$Q(\lambda) = \lambda^2 - \left(\left(1+\frac{\delta}{\beta(1-c)}\right)\left(1-\frac{\delta}{\gamma(\beta(1-c)-\delta)}\right)+1\right)\lambda + \left(1+\frac{\delta}{\beta(1-c)}\right)\left(1-\frac{\delta}{\gamma(\beta(1-c)-\delta)}\right) - \frac{\delta(\gamma(\beta(1-c)-\delta)-\delta)}{\beta\gamma(c-1)}$$

For the emergence of Neimark–Sacker bifurcation around positive equilibrium (x_0, y_0) of system (3), two roots of $Q(\lambda)$ must be complex conjugates with a unit modulus. Therefore, it is easy to obtain the bifurcation parameter $\gamma^* = \frac{\delta+\beta(1-c)+\delta(\beta(1-c)-\delta)}{(\beta(1-c)-\delta)^2+(\beta(1-c)-\delta)}$.

Consider parameter γ with a small perturbation ε, i.e., $\gamma = \gamma^* + \varepsilon$, where $|\varepsilon| \ll 1$ and $\gamma^* = \frac{\delta+\beta(1-c)+\delta(\beta(1-c)-\delta)}{(\beta(1-c)-\delta)^2+(\beta(1-c)-\delta)}$, then system (3) becomes

$$\begin{cases} x_{n+1} = x_n e^{1-\frac{x_n}{\gamma^*+\varepsilon}-\frac{(1-c)y_n}{1+x_n}} \\ y_{n+1} = y_n e^{\frac{\beta(1-c)x_n}{1+x_n}-\delta} \end{cases} \tag{5}$$

The characteristic equation of $J\left(\frac{\delta}{\beta(1-c)-\delta}, \frac{1+x_0}{1-c}\left(1-\frac{x_0}{\gamma^*+\varepsilon}\right)\right)$ is given by:

$$\lambda^2 + p(\varepsilon)\lambda + q(\varepsilon) = 0,$$

where

$$p(\varepsilon) = \left(1+\frac{\delta}{k+\delta}\right)\left(1-\frac{\delta}{(\gamma^*+\varepsilon)k}\right)+1$$
$$q(\varepsilon) = \left(1+\frac{\delta}{k+\delta}\right)\left(1-\frac{\delta}{(\gamma^*+\varepsilon)k}\right) - \frac{\delta((\gamma^*+\varepsilon)k-\delta)}{\beta(c-1)(\gamma^*+\varepsilon)}$$
$$k = \beta(1-c)-\delta.$$

The roots of characteristic equation of $J\left(\frac{\delta}{\beta(1-c)-\delta}, \frac{1+x_0}{1-c}\left(1-\frac{x_0}{\gamma^*+\varepsilon}\right)\right)$ are

$$\lambda_1 = \frac{p(\varepsilon)+i\sqrt{4q(\varepsilon)-p(\varepsilon)^2}}{2}, \quad \lambda_2 = \frac{p(\varepsilon)-i\sqrt{4q(\varepsilon)-p(\varepsilon)^2}}{2}$$

Additionally,

$$|\lambda_{1,2}| = \sqrt{q(\varepsilon)}, \ \frac{d|\lambda_{1,2}|}{d\varepsilon}|_{\varepsilon=0} = \frac{\delta k(k+1)^2}{(k+\delta)(k+2\delta+\delta k)} > 0$$

We require that, when $\varepsilon = 0$, $p(0) \neq 0, 1$, i.e., $\frac{\delta k}{(k+\delta)(k+2\delta+\delta k)} \neq 1, 2$. Therefore, $\lambda_{1,2}^n \neq 1$, $n = 1, 2, 3, 4$.

The transversal condition at (x_0, y_0) is given by

$$\begin{aligned} \frac{d|\lambda_1|^2}{d\varepsilon}|_{\varepsilon=0} &= \left(\lambda_1\frac{d\lambda_2}{d\varepsilon}+\lambda_2\frac{d\lambda_1}{d\varepsilon}\right)|_{\varepsilon=0} \\ &= -\frac{\delta^2 m^2}{2k}\frac{1}{\gamma^{*3}} + \frac{\delta(m\beta(c-1)(m+2)-2k)}{2k\beta(c-1)}\frac{1}{\gamma^{*2}} - \frac{\delta^2 m^2}{2k^2}\frac{1}{\gamma^*} + \frac{\delta^2 m^2}{2k}, \end{aligned}$$

where $m = \frac{k+2\delta}{k+\delta}$.

If $\frac{d|\lambda_1|^2}{d\varepsilon}|_{\varepsilon=0} \neq 0$, then Neimark–Sacker bifurcation will occur at (x_0, y_0).

4.2. The Direction of Neimark–Sacker Bifurcation at (x_0, y_0)

We consider the translations $\overline{x_n} = x_n - x_0$, $\overline{y_n} = y_n - y_0$ for shifting (x_0, y_0) to the origin. Through calculating, we obtain

$$\begin{cases} \overline{x_{n+1}} = (\overline{x_n} + x_0)e^{1-\frac{(\overline{x_n}+x_0)}{\gamma^*+\varepsilon}-\frac{(1-c)(\overline{y_n}+y_0)}{1+(\overline{x_n}+x_0)}} - x_0 \\ \overline{y_{n+1}} = (\overline{y_n} + y_0)e^{\frac{\beta(1-c)(\overline{x_n}+x_0)}{1+(\overline{x_n}+x_0)}-\delta} - y_0 \end{cases} \tag{6}$$

Expanding (6) up to the third order at the origin using a Taylor series, we obtain

$$\begin{pmatrix} \overline{x_{n+1}} \\ \overline{y_{n+1}} \end{pmatrix} = \begin{pmatrix} a_{11} & a_{12} \\ b_{11} & b_{12} \end{pmatrix} \begin{pmatrix} \overline{x_n} \\ \overline{y_n} \end{pmatrix} + \begin{pmatrix} f(\overline{x_n}, \overline{y_n}) \\ g(\overline{x_n}, \overline{y_n}) \end{pmatrix}, \tag{7}$$

where

$$f(\overline{x_n}, \overline{y_n}) = a_{13}\overline{x_n}^3 + a_{14}\overline{x_n}^2 + a_{15}\overline{x_n}\,\overline{y_n} + a_{16}\overline{x_n}^2\overline{y_n} + a_{17}\overline{x_n}\,\overline{y_n}^2 + a_{18}\overline{y_n}^2 + a_{19}\overline{y_n}^3 + O\left((|\overline{x_n}| + |\overline{y_n}|)^3\right)$$

$$g(\overline{x_n}, \overline{y_n}) = b_{13}\overline{x_n}^3 + b_{14}\overline{x_n}^2 + b_{15}\overline{x_n}\,\overline{y_n} + b_{16}\overline{x_n}^2\overline{y_n} + O\left((|\overline{x_n}| + |\overline{y_n}|)^3\right)$$

$$a_1 = \frac{y_0(c-1)}{(x_0+1)^2},\quad a_2 = \frac{y_0(c-1)}{(x_0+1)^3},\quad a_3 = \frac{y_0(c-1)}{(x_0+1)^4},\quad b_1 = \frac{x_0(1-c)}{(x_0+1)^2},\quad b_2 = \frac{x_0(1-c)}{(x_0+1)^3},\quad b_3 = \frac{x_0(1-c)}{(x_0+1)^4},$$

$$a_{11} = \left(1 + \frac{\delta}{k+\delta}\right)\left(1 - \frac{\delta}{k(\gamma^*+\varepsilon)}\right),\quad a_{12} = -\frac{\delta}{\beta},\quad b_{11} = \frac{(\gamma^*+\varepsilon)k-\delta}{(\gamma^*+\varepsilon)(1-c)},\quad b_{12} = 1,$$

$$a_{13} = \frac{1}{2}\left(\frac{1}{(\gamma^*+\varepsilon)} + a_1\right)^2 + a_2 - x_0\left(\left(\frac{1}{(\gamma^*+\varepsilon)} + a_1\right)\left(\frac{1}{6}\left(\frac{1}{(\gamma^*+\varepsilon)} + a_1\right)^2 + \frac{1}{2}a_2\right) + a_3 + \frac{1}{2}a_2\left(\frac{1}{(\gamma^*+\varepsilon)} + a_1\right)\right)$$

$$a_{14} = -\frac{1}{(\gamma^*+\varepsilon)} - a_1 + x_0\left(\frac{1}{2}\left(\frac{1}{(\gamma^*+\varepsilon)} + a_1\right)^2 + a_2\right),\quad a_{15} = -x_0\left(\frac{a_1}{y_0} + \frac{c-1}{x_0+1}\left(\frac{1}{(\gamma^*+\varepsilon)} + a_1\right)\right) + \frac{c-1}{x_0+1},$$

$$a_{16} = -\frac{a_1}{y_0} - \frac{c-1}{x_0+1}\left(\frac{1}{(\gamma^*+\varepsilon)} + a_1\right) + x_0\left(\frac{a_2}{y_0} + \frac{a_1}{2y_0}\left(\frac{1}{(\gamma^*+\varepsilon)} + a_1\right) + \frac{a_3(c-1)}{2} + \left(\frac{a_1}{2y_0} + \frac{c-1}{3(x_0+1)}\left(\frac{1}{(\gamma^*+\varepsilon)} + a_1\right)\right.\right.$$
$$\left.\left. - \frac{c-1}{x_0+1}\left(\frac{1}{6}\left(\frac{1}{(\gamma^*+\varepsilon)} + a_1\right)^2 + \frac{1}{2}a_2\right)\right)\left(\frac{1}{(\gamma^*+\varepsilon)} + a_1\right)\right),$$

$$a_{17} = \frac{a_1(c-1)}{2y_0} - x_0\left(\frac{a_2(c-1)}{2y_0} + \frac{c-1}{x_0+1}\left(\frac{a_1}{2y_0} + \frac{c-1}{3(x_0+1)}\left(\frac{1}{(\gamma^*+\varepsilon)} + a_1\right) + \frac{a_1(c-1)}{6y_0}\left(\frac{1}{(\gamma^*+\varepsilon)} + a_1\right)\right)\right),$$

$$a_{18} = \frac{x_0(c-1)^2}{2(x_0+1)^2},\quad a_{19} = \frac{x_0(c-1)^3}{6(x_0+1)^3},$$

$$b_{13} = -y_0\left(\beta\left(b_3 + \frac{a_2}{y_0}\right) + \frac{\beta^2}{2}\left(b_1 + \frac{c-1}{x_0+1}\right)\left(b_2 + \frac{a_1}{y_0}\right) + \beta\left(\frac{\beta^2}{6}\left(b_1 + \frac{c-1}{x_0+1}\right)^2 + \frac{\beta}{2}\left(b_2 + \frac{a_1}{y_0}\right)\right)\left(b_1 + \frac{c-1}{x_0+1}\right)\right),$$

$$b_{14} = y_0\left(\frac{\beta^2}{2}\left(b_1 + \frac{c-1}{x_0+1}\right)^2 + \beta\left(b_2 + \frac{a_1}{y_0}\right)\right),\quad b_{15} = -\beta\left(b_1 + \frac{c-1}{x_0+1}\right),$$

$$b_{16} = \frac{\beta^2}{2}\left(b_1 + \frac{c-1}{x_0+1}\right)^2 + \beta\left(b_2 + \frac{a_1}{y_0}\right)$$

Next, by using the center manifold theorem and normal form theories, the direction of Neimark–Sacker bifurcation at (x_0, y_0) is given.

$$\Psi = -\mathrm{Re}\left(\frac{(1-2\lambda_1)\lambda_2^2}{1-\lambda_1}\theta_{11}\theta_{20}\right) - \frac{1}{2}|\theta_{11}|^2 - |\theta_{02}|^2 + \mathrm{Re}(\lambda_2\theta_{21})$$

where the parameters $\theta_{02}, \theta_{11}, \theta_{20}$ and θ_{21} are determined by coefficients in (7).

Theorem 3. *If $\Psi \neq 0$, then the unique positive equilibrium point (x_0, y_0) of system (3) undergoes Neimark–Sacker bifurcation when the bifurcation parameter γ varies in a small neighborhood of $\gamma^* = \frac{\delta+\beta(1-c)+\delta(\beta(1-c)-\delta)}{(\beta(1-c)-\delta)^2+(\beta(1-c)-\delta)}$. Additionally, if $\Psi < 0$, then the curve generates attraction near the equilibrium point for $\varepsilon > 0$. Furthermore, if $\Psi > 0$, then the curve generates repulsion near the equilibrium point for $\varepsilon < 0$.*

Proof. Now, let

$$\eta = \frac{p(0)}{2},\quad \tau = \frac{\sqrt{4q(0) - p(0)^2}}{2}$$

The invertible matrix T is given by

$$T = \begin{pmatrix} a_{12} & 0 \\ \eta - a_{11} & -\tau \end{pmatrix}$$

Using the following translation

$$\begin{pmatrix} \overline{x_n} \\ \overline{y_n} \end{pmatrix} = \begin{pmatrix} a_{12} & 0 \\ \eta - a_{11} & -\tau \end{pmatrix} \begin{pmatrix} u_n \\ v_n \end{pmatrix}$$

Then, (7) turns into

$$\begin{pmatrix} u_{n+1} \\ v_{n+1} \end{pmatrix} = \begin{pmatrix} \eta & -\tau \\ \tau & \eta \end{pmatrix} \begin{pmatrix} u_n \\ v_n \end{pmatrix} + \begin{pmatrix} P(u_n, v_n) \\ Q(u_n, v_n) \end{pmatrix}$$

where

$$P(u_n, v_n) = l_{11}u_n^3 + l_{12}u_n^2 + l_{13}u_n v_n + l_{14}u_n^2 v_n + l_{15}u_n v_n^2 + l_{16}v_n^2 + l_{17}v_n^3 + O\Big((|u_n| + |v_n|)^3\Big)$$

$$Q(u_n, v_n) = l_{21}u_n^3 + l_{22}u_n^2 + l_{23}u_n v_n + l_{24}u_n^2 v_n + l_{25}u_n v_n^2 + l_{26}v_n^2 + l_{27}v_n^3 + O\Big((|u_n| + |v_n|)^3\Big)$$

$$l_{11} = a_{12}^2 a_{13} + a_{12}a_{16}(\eta - a_{11}) + a_{17}(\eta - a_{11})^2 + \tfrac{a_{19}(\eta - a_{11})^3}{a_{12}},$$

$$l_{12} = a_{12}a_{14} + a_{15}(\eta - a_{11}) + \tfrac{a_{18}(\eta - a_{11})^2}{a_{12}}, \qquad l_{13} = -a_{15}\tau - \tfrac{2a_{18}\tau(\eta - a_{11})}{a_{12}},$$

$$l_{14} = -a_{12}a_{16}\tau - 2a_{17}\tau - \tfrac{3a_{19}\tau(\eta - a_{11})^2}{a_{12}}, \qquad l_{15} = a_{17}\tau^2 + \tfrac{3a_{19}\tau^2(\eta - a_{11})}{a_{12}},$$

$$l_{16} = \tfrac{a_{18}\tau^2}{a_{12}}, \qquad l_{17} = -\tfrac{a_{19}\tau^3}{a_{12}},$$

$$l_{21} = \tfrac{1}{\tau}\Big(a_{12}^2 a_{13}(\eta - a_{11}) + a_{12}a_{16}(\eta - a_{11})^2 + a_{17}(\eta - a_{11})^3 + \tfrac{a_{19}(\eta - a_{11})^4}{a_{12}} - b_{13}a_{12}^3 - b_{16}a_{12}^2(\eta - a_{11})\Big),$$

$$l_{22} = \tfrac{1}{\tau}\Big(a_{12}a_{14}(\eta - a_{11}) + a_{15}(\eta - a_{11})^2 + \tfrac{a_{18}(\eta - a_{11})^3}{a_{12}} - b_{14}a_{12}^2 - b_{15}a_{12}(\eta - a_{11})\Big),$$

$$l_{23} = -a_{15}(\eta - a_{11}) - \tfrac{2a_{18}(\eta - a_{11})}{a_{12}} + b_{15}a_{12},$$

$$l_{24} = -a_{12}a_{16}(\eta - a_{11}) - 2a_{17}(\eta - a_{11}) - \tfrac{3a_{19}(\eta - a_{11})^3}{a_{12}} + b_{16}a_{12}^2,$$

$$l_{25} = a_{17}\tau(\eta - a_{11}) + \tfrac{3a_{19}\tau(\eta - a_{11})^2}{a_{12}}, \qquad l_{26} = \tfrac{a_{18}\tau(\eta - a_{11})}{a_{12}}, \qquad l_{27} = -\tfrac{a_{19}\tau^2(\eta - a_{11})}{a_{12}}$$

According to the normal form theories related to bifurcation analysis, we require the following quantity at $(u, v, \varepsilon) = (0, 0, 0)$:

$$\Psi = -\text{Re}\left(\frac{(1 - 2\lambda_1)\lambda_2^2}{1 - \lambda_1}\theta_{11}\theta_{20}\right) - \frac{1}{2}|\theta_{11}|^2 - |\theta_{02}|^2 + \text{Re}(\lambda_2\theta_{21})$$

where

$$\theta_{20} = \tfrac{1}{8}(P_{uu} - P_{vv} + 2Q_{uv} + i(Q_{uu} - Q_{vv} - 2P_{uv}))$$

$$\theta_{11} = \tfrac{1}{4}(P_{uu} + P_{vv} + i(Q_{uu} + Q_{vv}))$$

$$\theta_{02} = \tfrac{1}{8}(P_{uu} - P_{vv} + 2Q_{uv} + i(Q_{uu} - Q_{vv} + 2P_{uv}))$$

$$\theta_{21} = \tfrac{1}{16}(P_{uuu} + P_{uvv} + Q_{uuv} + Q_{vvv} + i(Q_{uuu} + Q_{uvv} - P_{uuv} - P_{vvv}))$$

$P_{uuu} = 6l_{11}$, $P_{uu} = 2l_{12}$, $P_{uv} = l_{13}$, $P_{uuv} = 2l_{14}$, $P_{uvv} = 2l_{15}$, $P_{vv} = 2l_{16}$, $P_{vvv} = 6l_{17}$, $Q_{uuu} = 6l_{21}$, $Q_{uu} = 2l_{22}$, $Q_{uv} = l_{23}$, $Q_{uuv} = 2l_{24}$, $Q_{uvv} = 2l_{25}$, $Q_{vv} = 2l_{26}$, $Q_{vvv} = 6l_{27}$

□

5. Numerical Simulation

In this section, numerical simulations are presented to verify the theories given above. Since our model is difference equations, and the iterative expressions are already given, there is no need to create novel calculations, such as interpolation methods in the case of differential equations. We assume that $(\beta, c, \delta) = (0.2, 0.3, 0.08)$ and $\gamma \in (3.3, 3.7)$, then system (3) undergoes Neimark–Sacker bifurcation around its positive equilibrium $(x_0, y_0) = (1.3333333, 2.0759193)$ when γ passes through the critical value $\gamma^* = 3.2345912$. At $(\beta, c, \delta, \varepsilon) = (0.2, 0.3, 0.08, 3.2345912)$, the eigenvalues of system (3) are $\lambda_1 = 0.9893238 + 0.1457338i$ and $\lambda_2 = 0.9893238 - 0.1457338i$ with $|\lambda_1| = |\lambda_2| = 1$.

From Figure 1, it can be seen that the model has a limit loop at (x_0, y_0) as γ changes, which means that the biomass of predators and prey will eventually form a cycle. From Figure 2, it is clear that, when γ is chosen as the bifurcation parameter, (x_0, y_0) of system (3) is locally focused when $\gamma < \gamma^*$. Furthermore, when $\gamma > \gamma^*$, there exist attracting closed invariant curves.

We assume that the parameters β and δ are constant during the increasing of γ, which means that the growth rate of prey and the death rate of predators are unchangeable. Since γ is proportional to the refuge parameter c (4), it is clear that, with the improvement of refuge ability, the quantitative relationship between predator and prey changes from constant to regular periodic.

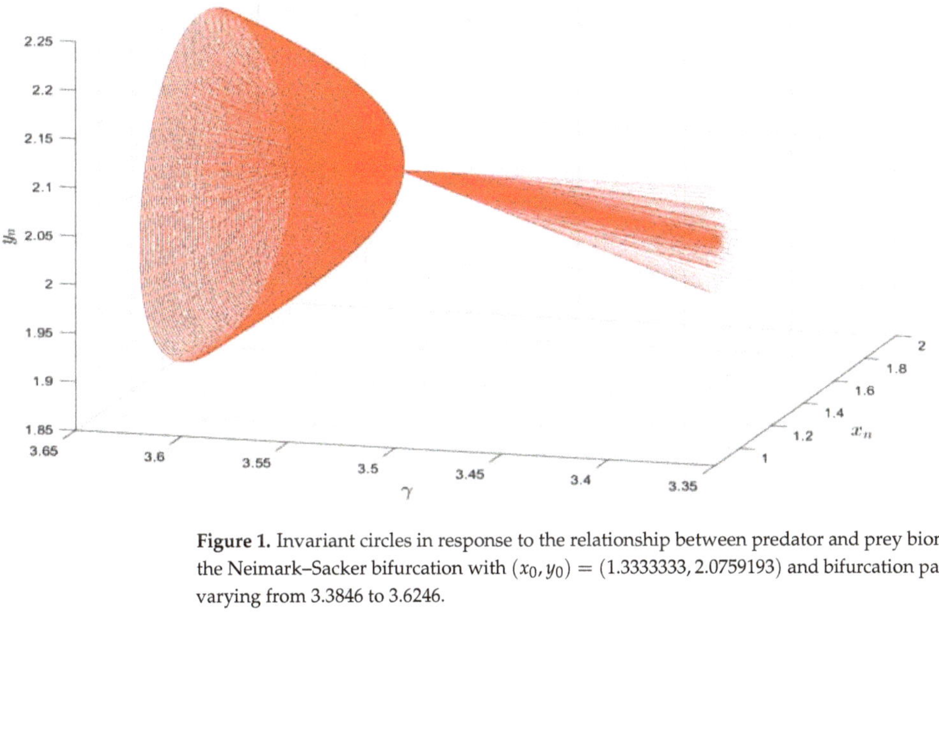

Figure 1. Invariant circles in response to the relationship between predator and prey biomass from the Neimark–Sacker bifurcation with $(x_0, y_0) = (1.3333333, 2.0759193)$ and bifurcation parameter γ varying from 3.3846 to 3.6246.

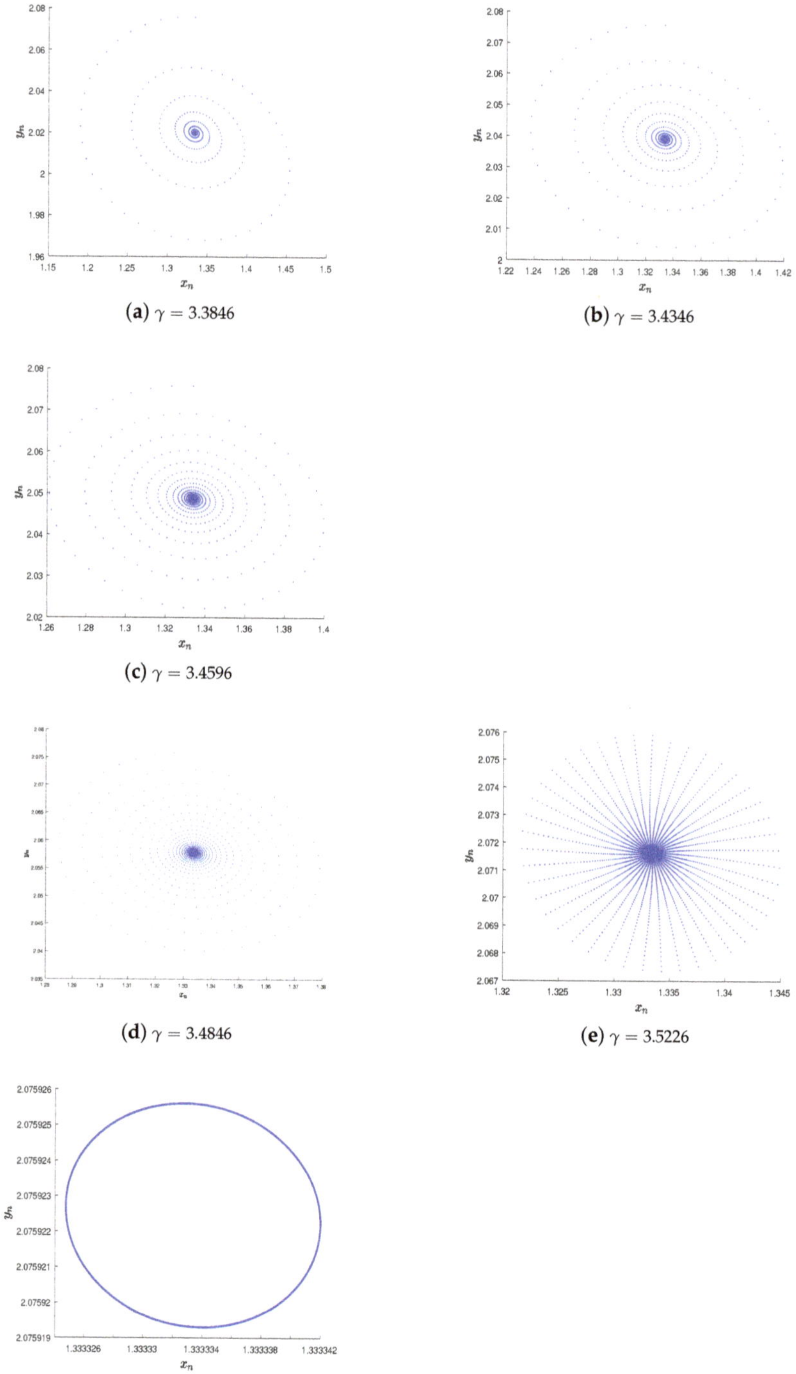

(a) $\gamma = 3.3846$ **(b)** $\gamma = 3.4346$

(c) $\gamma = 3.4596$

(d) $\gamma = 3.4846$ **(e)** $\gamma = 3.5226$

(f) $\gamma = 3.5346$

Figure 2. *Cont.*

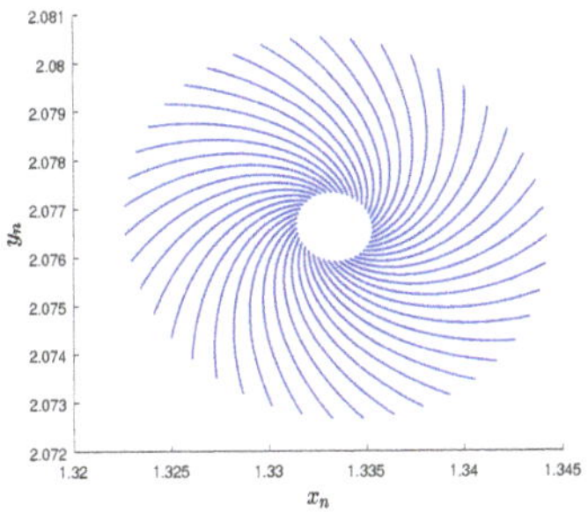

Figure 2. Phase diagrams of system (3) with parameters $(\beta, c, \delta) = (0.2, 0.3, 0.08)$ and $(x_0, y_0) = (1.3333333, 2.0759193)$ and with different values of γ.

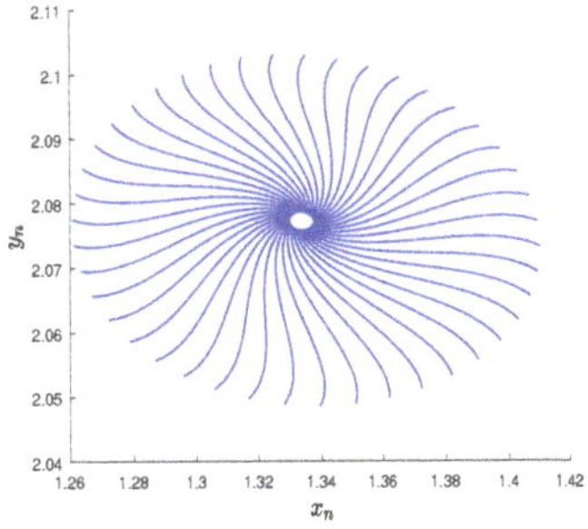

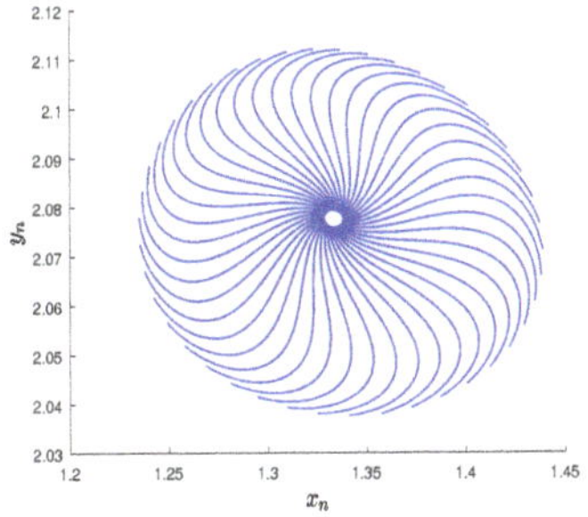

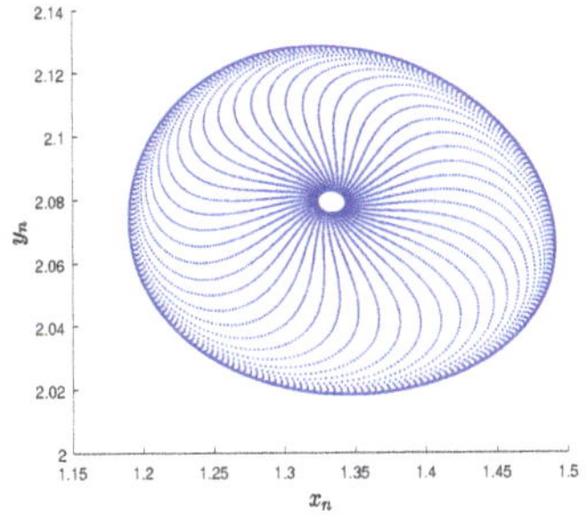

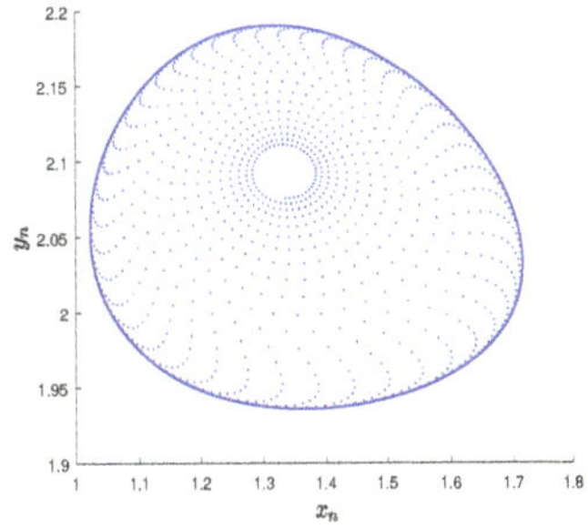

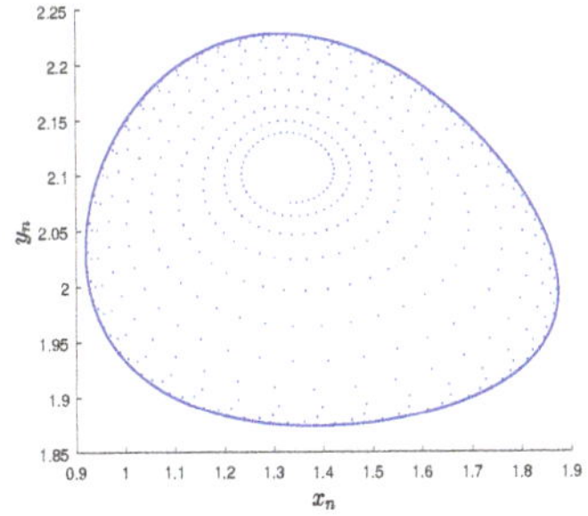

6. Conclusions

Our work deals with the study of the local dynamical properties of a predator–prey system with discrete time (2) and Neimark–Sacker bifurcation associated with the periodic solution of system (3) improved by system (2). We proved that system (2) has three equilibria, and we provided their dynamical properties. Particularly, we focused on the stability and bifurcation situations of its unique positive equilibrium $(x^*, y^*) = \left(\frac{\delta+(\alpha\delta-\beta)\xi}{\beta(1-c)-\delta}, \left(\frac{1+\alpha\xi+x^*}{1-c}\right)\left(1-\frac{x^*}{\gamma}\right)\right)$ and presented a specific form of resolution and proof.

In addition, we proved that system (3) undergoes Neimark–Sacker bifurcation around its interior fixed point (x_0, y_0) when the bifurcation curve is given as $S = \left\{(c,\beta,\delta) \in \mathbb{R}^3_+ : \gamma = \gamma^* = \frac{\delta+\beta(1-c)+\delta(\beta(1-c)-\delta)}{(\beta(1-c)-\delta)^2+(\beta(1-c)-\delta)}, |D| < 2\right\}$, where $D = \frac{x^*}{\gamma}\left(\frac{\gamma-x^*}{1+x^*} - 1\right) + 2$. In order to verify the theoretical discussion, we also provided a numerical simulation at (x_0, y_0) when the parameter is varied in a small neighborhood of $\gamma = \gamma^*$. When $\gamma > \gamma^*$, there exist attracting closed invariant curves from the positive equilibrium, which indicates that predators and prey can coexist under the periodic oscillations for an extended period of time.

In biology, with the improvement of refuge ability c, the quantitative relationship between predator and prey changes from constant to regular periodic, which means that slight growth of the refuge ability c destroys the original balance and better explains population attributes in nature. It appears that prey refuges not only ensure that prey do not become extinct but also promote interactions with predators and enhance population activity on a periodic scale. Therefore, we can precisely change the biological density of predators and prey to achieve the desired goal by regulating the number of refuge parameters c in relation to other variables according to one's needs.

In subsequent work, other parameters can be considered for bifurcation studies to obtain conclusions of different biological significance. Alternatively, other discrete methods can be used to improve the model.

Author Contributions: Writing—review & editing, B.H. and C.Z. All authors have read and agreed to the published version of the manuscript.

Funding: This research received no external funding.

Data Availability Statement: Not applicable.

Acknowledgments: The authors wish to thank the editors and reviewers for their helpful comments.

Conflicts of Interest: The authors declare that they have no competing interests.

References

1. Lotka, A.J. Analytical Note on Certain Rhythmic Relations in Organic Systems. *Proc. Natl. Acad. Sci. USA* **1920**, *6*, 410–415. [CrossRef] [PubMed]
2. Volterra, V. Variazioni e Fluttuazioni del Numero d'Individui in Specie Animali Conviventi. *Mem. R. Accad. Naz. Lincei. Ser. VI* **1926**, *2*, 31–113.
3. Lotka, A.J. Contribution to the Mathematical Theory of Capture. *Proc. Natl. Acad. Sci. USA* **1932**, *18*, 172–178. [CrossRef]
4. Liu, C.; Zhang, Q.L.; Huang, J.; Tang, W.S. Dynamical Behavior of a Harvested Prey-Predator Model with Stage Structure and Discrete Time Delay. *J. Biol. Syst.* **2009**, *17*, 759–777. [CrossRef]
5. Samuelson, P.A. Generalized Predator-Prey Oscillations in Ecological and Economic Equilibrium. *Proc. Natl. Acad. Sci. USA* **1971**, *68*, 980–983. [CrossRef]
6. Liu, X.X.; Zhang, C.R. Stability and Optimal Control of Tree-Insect Model under Forest Fire Disturbance. *Mathematics* **2022**, *10*, 2563. [CrossRef]
7. Chen, H.Y.; Zhang, C.R. Dynamic analysis of a Leslie–Gower-type predator–prey system with the fear effect and ratio-dependent Holling III functional response. *Nonlinear Anal. Model. Control.* **2022**, *27*, 1–23. [CrossRef]
8. Liu, X.L.; Xiao, D.M. Complex dynamic behaviors of a discrete-time predator–prey system. *Chaos Solitons Fractals* **2007**, *32*, 80–94. [CrossRef]
9. Beretta, E.; Capasso, V.; Rinaldi, F. Global stability results for a generalized Lotka-Volterra system with distributed delays. *J. Math. Biol.* **1988**, *26*, 661–688. [CrossRef]
10. Hofbauer, J.; Thus, J.W. Multiple limit cycles for predator-prey models. *Math. Biosci.* **1990**, *99*, 71–75. [CrossRef] [PubMed]

11. Brauer, F.; Sánchez, D.A. Constant rate population harvesting: Equilibrium and stability. *Theor. Popul. Biol.* **1975**, *8*, 12–30. [CrossRef]
12. Cheng, L.F.; Cao, H.J. Bifurcation analysis of a discrete-time ratio-dependent predator–prey model with Allee Effect. *Commun. Nonlinear Sci. Numer. Simul.* **2016**, *38*, 288–302. [CrossRef]
13. Lai, L.Y.; Zhu, Z.L.; Chen, F.D. Stability and Bifurcation in a Predator-Prey Model with the Additive Allee Effect and the Fear Effect dagger. *Mathematics* **2020**, *8*, 1280. [CrossRef]
14. Sasmal, S.K. Population dynamics with multiple allee effects induced by fear factors—A mathematical study on prey-predator interactions. *Appl. Math. Model.* **2018**, *64*, 1–14. [CrossRef]
15. Kuznetsov, Y.A.; Rinaldi, S. Remarks on food chain dynamics. *Math. Biosci.* **1996**, *134*, 1–33. [CrossRef]
16. Aziz-Alaoui, M.A.; Okiye, M.D. Boundedness and global stability for a predator-prey model with modi-fied Leslie-Gower and Holling-type II schemes. *Appl. Math. Lett.* **2003**, *16*, 1069–1075. [CrossRef]
17. Chen, F.D.; Chen, L.J.; Xie, X.D. On a Leslie-Gower predator-prey model incorporating a prey refuge. *Nonlinear Anal. Real World Appl.* **2009**, *10*, 2905–2908. [CrossRef]
18. Hung, K.-C.; Wang, S.-H. A theorem on S-shaped bifurcation curve for a positone problem with convex–concave nonlinearity and its applications to the perturbed Gelfand problem. *J. Differ. Equ.* **2011**, *251*, 223–237. [CrossRef]
19. Hu, Z.Y.; Teng, Z.D.; Zhang, L. Stability and bifurcation analysis of a discrete predator–prey model with nonmonotonic functional response. *Nonlinear Anal. Real World Appl.* **2011**, *12*, 2356–2377. [CrossRef]
20. Zhang, C.R.; Zheng, B. Stability and bifurcation of a two-dimension discrete neural network model with multi-delays. *Chaos Solitons Fractals* **2007**, *31*, 1232–1242. [CrossRef]
21. Abdelaziz, M.A.M.; Ismail, A.I.; Abdullah, F.A.; Mohd, M.H. Bifurcations and chaos in a discrete SI epi-demic model with fractional order. *Adv. Differ. Equ.***2018**, *2018*, 1–19. [CrossRef]
22. Ghosh, J.; Sahoo, B.; Poria, S. Prey-predator dynamics with prey refuge providing additional food to predator. *Chaos Solitons Fractals* **2017**, *96*, 110–119. [CrossRef]
23. Gladkov, S.O. On the Question of Self-Organization of Population Dynamics on Earth. *Biophysics* **2021**, *66*, 858–866. [CrossRef]
24. Li, W.; Li, X.Y. Neimark–Sacker Bifurcation of a Semi-Discrete Hematopoiesis Model. *J. Appl. Anal. Comput.* **2018**, *8*, 1679–1693. [CrossRef]
25. Li, X.Y.; Shao, X.M. Flip bifurcation and Neimark–Sacker bifurcation in a discrete predator-prey model with Michaelis-Menten functional response. *Electron. Res. Arch.* **2023**, *31*, 37–57. [CrossRef]

mathematics

MDPI

Article

Stability Analysis and Hopf Bifurcation of a Delayed Diffusive Predator–Prey Model with a Strong Allee Effect on the Prey and the Effect of Fear on the Predator

Yining Xie [1], Jing Zhao [1] and Ruizhi Yang [2,*]

[1] School of Mechanical and Electrical Engineering, Northeast Forestry University, Harbin 150040, China; yiningxie@nefu.edu.cn (Y.X.)
[2] Department of Mathematics, Northeast Forestry University, Harbin 150040, China
* Correspondence: yangrz@nefu.edu.cn

Abstract: In this paper, we propose a diffusive predator–prey model with a strong Allee effect and nonlocal competition in the prey and a fear effect and gestation delay in the predator. We mainly study the local stability of the coexisting equilibrium and the existence and properties of Hopf bifurcation. We provide bifurcation diagrams with the fear effect parameter (s) and the Allee effect parameter (a), showing that the stable region of the coexisting equilibrium increases (or decreases) with an increase in the fear effect parameter (s) (or the Allee effect parameter (a)). We also show that gestation delay (τ) can affect the local stability of the coexisting equilibrium. When the delay (τ) is greater than the critical value, the coexistence equilibrium loses its stability, and bifurcating periodic solutions appear. Whether the bifurcated periodic solution is spatially homogeneous or inhomogeneous depends on the fear effect parameter (s) and the Allee effect parameter (a). These results show that the fear effect parameter (s), the Allee effect parameter (a), and gestation delay (τ) can be used to control the growth of prey and predator populations.

Keywords: delay; Hopf bifurcation; predator–prey; Allee effect

MSC: 34K18; 35B32

Citation: Xie, Y.; Zhao, J.; Yang, R. Stability Analysis and Hopf Bifurcation of a Delayed Diffusive Predator–Prey Model with a Strong Allee Effect on the Prey and the Effect of Fear on the Predator. *Mathematics* **2023**, *11*, 1996. https://doi.org/10.3390/math11091996

Academic Editor: Irina Bashkirtseva

Received: 16 March 2023
Revised: 17 April 2023
Accepted: 19 April 2023
Published: 23 April 2023

1. Introduction

Scholars have long been committed to using mathematical methods to explain and predict biological phenomena [1–4]. The analysis of predator–prey models is a research subject that has recently attracted considerable attention [5–8] from mathematicians and biologists. In order to better describe the law of changes in a population, many scholars have used differential equations to build predator–prey models and have introduced different parameters in order to consider biological factors. Considering that the internal mating of a population affects the law of change in that population when the population density is low, W. Allee proposed the famous Allee effect [9]. If the population density is too sparse, then mating between populations becomes difficult, and Allee effects may occur when the population density is under a specific threshold. Thus, Allee effects are strongly related to the vulnerability of populations to extinction [10–12]. For example, if pressure from the harvesting of bluefin tuna (Thunnus thynnus) is too strong, the population will collapse [11]. At a very small population size, the probability of finding an acceptable mate for some endangered species, such as lakapo (Strigos habroptilus), is very low [11].

The earliest single-population model exhibiting the Allee effect is as follows [13]:

$$\frac{du(t)}{dt} = r_1 u(t)\left(1 - \frac{u(t)}{K}\right)(u(t) - a_0),$$

where $u(t)$ represents the density of prey at time t, and r_1 and K are the prey's intrinsic growth rate and carrying capacity, respectively. The parameter a_0 denotes the Allee threshold, and the term $(u(t) - a_0)$ denotes the Allee effect. It must be noted that the Allee threshold is the critical population size or density below which the per capita population growth rate becomes negative. A strong Allee effect is an Allee effect at the Allee threshold. Whether the Allee effect is weak or strong depends on the opposing strengths of positive and negative density dependence. After the introduction of this model, many researchers began to pay attention to predator–prey models with strong Allee effects.

In nature, the influence of predators on prey species is not mediated only by simple predatory behavior. Since the prey has memory, the presence of predators has an inevitable impact on the behavior and psychology of the prey. For example, when a predator appears, the prey will be vigilant and will stop eating and breeding. This indirect effect on prey populations is known as the fear effect, and it is found widely in nature. Many researchers have focused on predator–prey models with the fear effect [14–16]. However, these models describe the prey as having a fear effect in connection with the predator, which affects the growth law of the prey. In nature, predators also have fear effects. For example, scientists have used the barking of dogs on a tape to simulate a scene of fear in raccoons. In this way, raccoons reduce their frequency and time of foraging; this protects the raccoons' prey to maintain a balance in the ecosystem. In [17], T. Liu et al. proposed a predator–prey model with a fear effect on the predator and a strong Allee effect on the prey:

$$\begin{cases} \frac{du(t)}{dt} = r_1 u(t)\left(1 - \frac{u(t)}{K}\right)(u(t) - a_0) - \frac{\lambda u(t)v(t)}{1+kv(t)}, \\ \frac{dv(t)}{dt} = \frac{r_2 v(t)}{1+kv(t)}\left(1 - \frac{v(t)}{qu(t)}\right). \end{cases} \tag{1}$$

where $u(t)$ and $v(t)$ represent the densities of the prey and predator, respectively; and r_1, K, a_0, λ, k, r_2, and q are the prey's intrinsic growth rate, the carrying capacity, the strong Allee effect, the capture rate, a measure of the fear effect, the predator's intrinsic growth rate, and a measure of food quality for the predator, respectively. More explanations of the parameters can be found in [17]. By setting $\tilde{u} = \frac{u}{K}$, $\tilde{v} = \frac{v}{Kq}$, $\tilde{t} = \frac{t}{Kr_1}$, $a = \frac{a_0}{K}$, $c = \frac{\lambda q K}{r_1}$, $s = kqK$, and $r = \frac{r_2}{r_1 K}$ and dropping "~", model (1) is changed into

$$\begin{cases} \frac{du(t)}{dt} = u(t)\left((1 - u(t))(u(t) - a) - \frac{cv(t)}{1+sv(t)}\right), \\ \frac{dv(t)}{dt} = \frac{rv(t)}{1+sv(t)}\left(1 - \frac{v(t)}{u(t)}\right). \end{cases} \tag{2}$$

The authors mainly studied model (2) from the perspective of bifurcation, such as Hopf bifurcation and Bogdanov–Takens bifurcation [17]. Research has shown that increasing the fear effect on the predator is conducive to protecting prey populations.

We assume that the concentration distribution of species is uniform in model (2), but this is not always the actual situation in nature. In real nature, due to widespread self-diffusion phenomena, few populations of species have a homogeneous spatial distribution [18–20]. This is precisely because of the existence of diffusion phenomena; population models often show some more abundant dynamic phenomena, such as spatially inhomogeneous periodic solutions, spatial patterns, etc. In addition, time delays also exist [21–23], such as time delays in maturity, gestation, and predation. Time delays often affect the stability of the constant steady-state solution, and they cause periodic oscillations in the population density. Therefore, we introduce self-diffusion and time delay into model (2) as follows.

$$\begin{cases} \frac{\partial u(x,t)}{\partial t} = d_1 \Delta u(x,t) + u(x,t)\left((1 - u(x,t))(u(x,t) - a) - \frac{cv(x,t)}{1+sv(x,t)}\right), \\ \frac{\partial v(x,t)}{\partial t} = d_2 \Delta v(x,t) + \frac{rv(x,t)}{1+sv(x,t)}\left(1 - \frac{v(x,t-\tau)}{u(x,t-\tau)}\right). \end{cases} \tag{3}$$

where d_1, $d_2 > 0$ represent the self-diffusion coefficients of the prey and predator, respectively, and τ is the gestation delay in the predator. The growth law of the predator (the second equation in (3)) can be considered a logistic growth law, where $(u(t-\tau)$ is the carrying capacity of the environment. An increase in density of predators at time t already exists for predators at time $t-\tau$, where τ is the gestation time of predators. Therefore, the negative feedback of the density of the predator at time t is related to the relationship between the predator and the prey at time $t-\tau$.

In nature, animals in the same area usually compete for a common but limited resource; due to the depletion of resources, intraspecies competition effects should depend on the average population density in the neighborhood of the current location. In [24,25], the author suggested that internal competition within the population is often spatially inhomogeneous and measured this effect by weighting and integration, modifying the $\frac{u}{K}$ as $\frac{1}{K}\int_\Omega G(x,y)u(y,t)dy$. $G(x,y)$ is a kernel function. In [26], Geng et al. studied Hopf, Turing, double-Hopf, and Turing–Hopf bifurcations of a diffusive predator–prey model with nonlocal competition. In [27], Liu et al. studied a diffusive predator–prey model with nonlocal competition and time delay. These works show that spatially inhomogeneous bifurcating periodic solutions are stable, in contrast to models without nonlocal competition. A predator–prey model with nonlocal competition can produce complex dynamics, such as spatiotemporal patterns and stably spatially inhomogeneous periodic solutions [26–29].

Based on the above considerations, we introduce nonlocal competition among prey into model (3) as follows.

$$\begin{cases} \frac{\partial u(x,t)}{\partial t} = d_1\Delta u(x,t) + u(x,t)\Big((1-\int_\Omega G(x,y)u(y,t)dy)(u(x,t)-a) - \frac{cv(x,t)}{1+sv(x,t)}\Big), \\ \frac{\partial v(x,t)}{\partial t} = d_2\Delta v(x,t) + \frac{rv(x,t)}{1+sv(x,t)}(1-\frac{v(x,t-\tau)}{u(x,t-\tau)}), \ x\in\Omega,\ t>0 \\ \frac{\partial u(x,t)}{\partial \bar{v}} = \frac{\partial v(x,t)}{\partial \bar{v}} = 0, \ x\in\partial\Omega,\ t>0 \\ u(x,\theta)=u_0(x,\theta)\geq 0, v(x,\theta)=v_0(x,\theta)\geq 0, \ x\in\bar{\Omega}, \theta\in[-\tau,0]. \end{cases} \tag{4}$$

The integral term $\int_\Omega G(x,y)u(y,t)dy$ in the first equation of (4) accounts for nonlocal competition among the prey individuals. The kernel function is of the following form:

$$G(x,y) = \frac{1}{|\Omega|} = \frac{1}{l\pi}, \ x,y\in\Omega,$$

which can be regarded as a measurement of the competition pressure at location x from the individuals at another location (y), which is widely used by some scholars [26–28]. The region $\Omega=(0,l\pi)$ with $l>0$ is used for the convenience of calculation. In this case, the strength of the competition among all prey individuals is the same across the habitat.

The aim of this paper is to consider the dynamics of model (4) from the perspective of stability and Hopf bifurcation and to study the effects of the Allee effect and fear effect on population growth law using numerical simulation. This article is structured as follows. In Section 2, we analyze the stability of the coexisting equilibrium and the existence of Hopf bifurcation. In Section 3, we analyze the properties of Hopf bifurcation. In Section 4, we perform some numerical simulations and analyze the results. In Section 5, we provide a brief conclusion.

2. Stability Analysis

In [17], the authors found that system (4) had no less than one equilibrium, which was noted as $E_*(u_*,v_*)$. We can obtain the concrete form of u_* by calculating the positive root of the following equation:

$$su^3-(as+s-1)u^2+(as+c-a-1)u+a=0=0. \tag{5}$$

For the completeness of the article, we provide the following lemma and a numerical simulation (see Figure 1). In Figure 1, we can see that with the increase in parameter a, the two positive equilibrium points degenerate into one positive equilibrium point. However, when parameter a is greater than a certain critical value, the positive equilibrium point disappears.

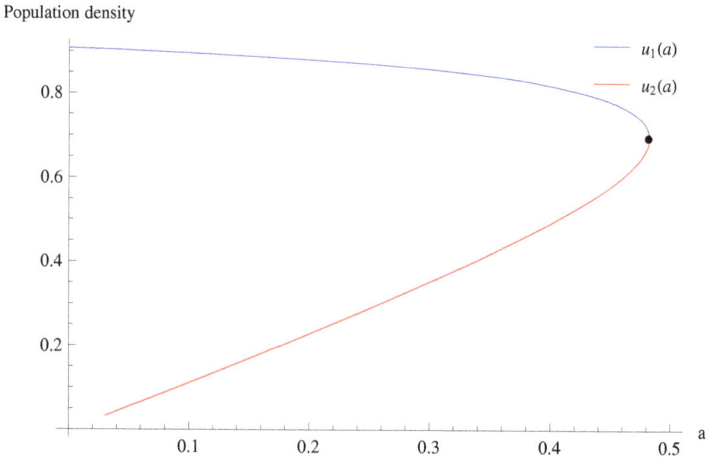

Figure 1. Positive roots of (5) with a under the following parameter settings: $s = 0.1$, $c = 0.1$, and $r = 0.25$.

Lemma 1. *If support* $(\mathbf{H_1})$ *holds, the following results are true for system* (4).

1. *If* $c < a(1-s)$ *or* $c > a(1-s)+1$, $s(a+1) > 1$:
   (a). *If* $D < 0$, *there are two distinct positive equilibria;*
   (b). *If* $D = 0$,
      (ib). *if* $A > 0$, *there exists a unique positive equilibrium;*
      (iib). *if* $A = 0$, *there exists no positive equilibrium;*
   (c). *If* $D > 0$, *there exists no positive equilibrium.*
2. *If* $c \geq a(1-s)$, $s(a+1) \leq 1$, *there exists no positive equilibrium.*

$$\begin{aligned} A &= (as+s-1)^2 - 3s(as+c-a-1), \\ B &= -(as+s-1)(as+c-a-1) - 9as, \\ C &= (as+c-a-1)^2 + 3a(as+s-1), \\ D &= -B^2 - 4AC. \end{aligned} \tag{6}$$

According to [17], (u_2, v_2) is always the saddle point under this set of parameters. We mainly study the stability and Hopf bifurcation of the equilibrium ((u_1, v_1)) in the following.

We linearize system (4) at $E_*(u_*, v_*)$:

$$\frac{\partial}{\partial t}\begin{pmatrix} u(x,t) \\ u(x,t) \end{pmatrix} = D\begin{pmatrix} \Delta u(x,t) \\ \Delta v(x,t) \end{pmatrix} + L_1\begin{pmatrix} u(x,t) \\ v(x,t) \end{pmatrix} + L_2\begin{pmatrix} u(x,t-\tau) \\ v(x,t-\tau) \end{pmatrix} + L_3\begin{pmatrix} \hat{u}(x,t) \\ \hat{v}(x,t) \end{pmatrix}, \tag{7}$$

where

$$D = \begin{pmatrix} d_1 & 0 \\ 0 & d_2 \end{pmatrix}, \quad L_1 = \begin{pmatrix} a_1 & a_2 \\ 0 & 0 \end{pmatrix}, \quad L_2 = \begin{pmatrix} 0 & 0 \\ b_1 & -b_1 \end{pmatrix}, \quad L_3 = \begin{pmatrix} \hat{a} & 0 \\ 0 & 0 \end{pmatrix},$$

$$a_1 = (1-u_*)u_* > 0, \ a_2 = -\frac{cu_*}{(1+su_*)^2} < 0, \ b_1 = \frac{r}{1+su_*} > 0, \ \hat{a} = -u_*(u_*-a) < 0, \tag{8}$$

and $\hat{u} = \frac{1}{l\pi} \int_0^{l\pi} u(y,t)dy$.

Then, the characteristic equations of (7) are

$$\lambda^2 + P_n\lambda + Q_n + (R_n + b_1\lambda)e^{-\lambda\tau} = 0, \ \ n \in \mathbb{N}_0, \tag{9}$$

where

$$\begin{aligned} &P_0 = -\hat{a} - a_1, \ \ Q_0 = 0, \ \ R_0 = -(\hat{a} + a_1 + a_2)b_1, \\ &P_n = (d_1 + d_2)\frac{n^2}{l^2} - a_1, \ \ Q_n = d_2\frac{n^2}{l^2}\left(d_1\frac{n^2}{l^2} - a_1\right), \\ &R_n = b_1\left(d_1\frac{n^2}{l^2} - (a_1 + a_2)\right), \ \ n \in \mathbb{N}. \end{aligned} \tag{10}$$

Let $\tau = 0$; Equation (9) becomes

$$\lambda^2 + (P_n + b_1)\lambda + Q_n + R_n = 0, \quad n \in \mathbb{N}_0. \tag{11}$$

We make the following hypothesis:

$$(\mathbf{H_1}) \qquad P_n + b_1 > 0, \ Q_n + R_n > 0, \text{ for } n \in \mathbb{N}_0.$$

Under this hypothesis $(\mathbf{H_1})$, $E_*(u_*, v_*)$ is locally asymptotically stable when $\tau = 0$. Next, we will discuss the case of $\tau > 0$.

Lemma 2. *If support* $(\mathbf{H_1})$ *holds, the following results are true for Equation* (9):

1. *There exists a pair of purely imaginary roots:* $\pm i\omega_n^+$ *at* $\tau_n^{j,+}$ *for* $j \in \mathbb{N}_0$ *and* $n \in \mathbb{W}_1$;
2. *There are two pairs of purely imaginary roots:* $\pm i\omega_n^\pm$ *at* $\tau_n^{j,\pm}$ *for* $j \in \mathbb{N}_0$ *and* $n \in \mathbb{W}_2$;
3. *There exists no purely imaginary root for* $n \in \mathbb{W}_3$,

where $\pm i\omega_n^\pm$, $\tau_n^{j,\pm}$, $\mathbb{W}_1$, $\mathbb{W}_2$, *and* $\mathbb{W}_3$ *are defined in* (14) *and* (15).

Proof. Let $i\omega$ $(\omega > 0)$ be a solution of Equation (9). Then,

$$-\omega^2 + i\omega P_n + Q_n + (R_n + b_1 i\omega)(\cos\omega\tau - i\sin\omega\tau) = 0, \ \ n \in \mathbb{N}_0.$$

Obviously, $\cos\omega\tau = \frac{\omega^2(R_n - b_1P_n) - Q_nR_n}{R_n^2 + b_1^2\omega^2}$, $\sin\omega\tau = \frac{\omega\left(P_nR_n - b_1(\omega^2 - Q_n)\right)}{R_n^2 + b_1^2\omega^2}$. This leads to

$$\omega^4 + \omega^2\left(P_n^2 - 2Q_n - b_1^2\right) + Q_n^2 - R_n^2 = 0, \ \ n \in \mathbb{N}_0. \tag{12}$$

Let $z = \omega^2$; then, (12) becomes

$$z^2 + z\left(P_n^2 - 2Q_n - b_1^2\right) + Q_n^2 - R_n^2 = 0, \ \ n \in \mathbb{N}_0. \tag{13}$$

Let $H_n = P_n^2 - 2Q_n - b_1^2$, $J_n = Q_n + R_n$, and $K_n = Q_n - R_n$. Then, $z^\pm = \frac{1}{2}[-H_n \pm \sqrt{H_n^2 - 4J_nK_n}]$ are the roots of (13). If $(\mathbf{H_1})$ holds, $J_n > 0$ $(n \in \mathbb{N}_0)$. Then, we can obtain

$$\begin{aligned} &H_0 = (\hat{a} + a_1)^2 - b_1^2, \\ &H_k = \left(a_1 - d_1\frac{k^2}{l^2}\right)^2 + d_2^2\frac{k^4}{l^4} - b_1^2, \quad \text{for } k \in \mathbb{N} \\ &K_0 = b_1(\hat{a} + a_1 + a_2) < 0, \\ &K_k = d_1d_2\frac{k^4}{l^4} - (b_1d_1 + a_1d_2)\frac{k^2}{l^2} + (a_1 + a_2)b_1, \quad \text{for } k \in \mathbb{N}. \end{aligned}$$

We define

$$\begin{aligned}\mathbb{S}_1 &= \{n|K_n < 0,\ n \in \mathbb{N}_0\},\\ \mathbb{S}_2 &= \{n|K_n > 0,\ H_n < 0,\ H_n^2 - 4J_nK_n > 0,\ n \in \mathbb{N}\},\\ \mathbb{S}_3 &= \{n|K_n > 0,\ H_n^2 - 4J_nK_n < 0,\ n \in \mathbb{N}\},\end{aligned} \tag{14}$$

and

$$\omega_n^{\pm} = \sqrt{z_n^{\pm}},\quad \tau_n^{j,\pm} = \begin{cases} \frac{1}{\omega_n^{\pm}}\arccos(V_{cos}^{(n,\pm)}) + 2j\pi, & V_{sin}^{(n,\pm)} \geq 0,\\ \frac{1}{\omega_n^{\pm}}\left[2\pi - \arccos(V_{cos}^{(n,\pm)})\right] + 2j\pi, & V_{sin}^{(n,\pm)} < 0.\end{cases}$$
$$V_{cos}^{(n,\pm)} = \frac{(\omega_n^{\pm})^2(b_2P_n + R_n) - M_nR_n}{R_n^2 + b_1^2(\omega_n^{\pm})^2},\quad V_{sin}^{(n,\pm)} = \frac{\omega_n^{\pm}(P_nR_n + Q_nb_2 + b_1(\omega_n^{\pm})^2)}{R_n^2 + b_1^2(\omega_n^{\pm})^2}. \tag{15}$$

It is easy to verify the conclusion in Lemma 2. □

Lemma 3. *Support* $(\mathbf{H_1})$ *is satisfied. Then,* $Re(\frac{d\lambda}{d\tau})|_{\tau=\tau_n^{j,+}} > 0$, $Re(\frac{d\lambda}{d\tau})|_{\tau=\tau_n^{j,-}} < 0$ *for* $n \in \mathbb{S}_1 \cup \mathbb{S}_2$ *and* $j \in \mathbb{N}_0$.

Proof. According to (9), we have

$$(\frac{d\lambda}{d\tau})^{-1} = \frac{2\lambda + P_n + b_1e^{-\lambda\tau}}{(R_n + b_1\lambda)\lambda e^{-\lambda\tau}} - \frac{\tau}{\lambda}.$$

Then,

$$\begin{aligned}[\mathrm{Re}(\frac{d\lambda}{d\tau})^{-1}]_{\tau=\tau_n^{j,\pm}} &= \mathrm{Re}[\frac{2\lambda + P_n + b_1e^{-\lambda\tau}}{(R_n + b_1\lambda)\lambda e^{-\lambda\tau}} - \frac{\tau}{\lambda}]_{\tau=\tau_n^{j,\pm}}\\ &= [\frac{1}{R_n^2 + b_1^2\omega^2}(2\omega^2 + P_n^2 - 2Q_n - b_1^2)]_{\tau=\tau_n^{j,\pm}}\\ &= \pm[\frac{1}{R_n^2 + b_1^2\omega^2}\sqrt{(P_n^2 - 2Q_n - b_1^2)^2 - 4(Q_n^2 - R_n^2)}]_{\tau=\tau_n^{j,\pm}}.\end{aligned}$$

Therefore, $\mathrm{Re}(\frac{d\lambda}{d\tau})|_{\tau=\tau_n^{j,+}} > 0$, $\mathrm{Re}(\frac{d\lambda}{d\tau})|_{\tau=\tau_n^{j,-}} < 0$. □

We denote $\tau_* = min\{\tau_n^0|\ n \in \mathbb{S}_1 \cup \mathbb{S}_2\}$.
Naturally, we have the following theorem.

Theorem 1. *Assume that* $(\mathbf{H_1})$ *holds; then, the following statements are true for system* (4).
1. $E_*(u_*, v_*)$ *is locally asymptotically stable for* $\tau > 0$ *when* $\mathbb{S}_1 \cup \mathbb{S}_2 = \varnothing$;
2. $E_*(u_*, v_*)$ *is locally asymptotically stable for* $\tau \in [0, \tau_*)$ *when* $\mathbb{S}_1 \cup \mathbb{S}_2 \neq \varnothing$;
3. $E_*(u_*, v_*)$ *is unstable for* $\tau \in (\tau_*, \tau_* + \varepsilon)$ *for some* $\varepsilon > 0$ *when* $\mathbb{S}_1 \cup \mathbb{S}_2 \neq \varnothing$;
4. *Hopf bifurcation occurs at* (u_*, v_*) *when* $\tau = \tau_n^{j,+}$ $(\tau = \tau_n^{j,-})$, $j \in \mathbb{N}_0$, $n \in \mathbb{S}_1 \cup \mathbb{S}_2$.

Because stability switching is a highly concerned dynamic phenomenon [30–32], we provide the following remark about stability switching.

Remark 1. *According to lemma 3, we know that* $Re(\frac{d\lambda}{d\tau})|_{\tau=\tau_n^{j,+}} > 0$, $Re(\frac{d\lambda}{d\tau})|_{\tau=\tau_n^{j,-}} < 0$. *If* $\mathbb{W}_2 \neq \varnothing$ *and there exist* $\tau_* = \tau_{n_1}^{0,+} < \tau_{n_1}^{0,-}$, $\tau_* = \tau_{n_1}^{0,+} < \tau_{n_2}^{0,+} < \tau_{n_2}^{0,-} < \tau_{n_1}^{0,-}$, $\tau_* = \tau_{n_1}^{0,+} < \tau_{n_2}^{0,+} < \cdots < \tau_{n_j}^{0,+} < \tau_{n_j}^{0,-} < \cdots < \tau_{n_2}^{0,-} < \tau_{n_1}^{0,-}$, *or other alternating forms of* $\tau_n^{j,\pm}$. *Then, stability switching may exist.*

3. Properties of Hopf Bifurcation

From [33,34], we learned how to analyze the properties of Hopf bifurcation. For fixed $j \in \mathbb{N}_0$ and $n \in \mathbb{S}_1 \cup \mathbb{S}_2$, we define $\tilde{\tau} = \tau_n^{j,\pm}$. Let $\bar{u}(x,t) = u(x,\tau t) - u_*$ and $\bar{v}(x,t) = v(x,\tau t) - v_*$. By ignoring the bar, (4) becomes

$$\begin{cases} \dfrac{\partial u}{\partial t} = \tau[d_1\Delta u + (u+u_*)\Big(1 - \dfrac{1}{l\pi}\displaystyle\int_0^{l\pi}(u(y,t)+u_*)dy\Big)(u+u_*-a) - \dfrac{c(v+v_*)}{1+s(v+v_*)}], \\ \dfrac{\partial v}{\partial t} = \tau[d_2\Delta v + \dfrac{r(v+v_*)}{1+s(v+v_*)}\Big(1 - \dfrac{v(t-1)+v_*}{u(t-1)+u_*}\Big)]. \end{cases} \tag{16}$$

Then, we rewrite (16) in the following form:

$$\begin{cases} \dfrac{\partial u}{\partial t} = \tau[d_1\Delta u + a_1 u + a_2 v - \hat{a}\hat{u} + \alpha_1 u^2 + (a-2u_*)u\hat{u} + \alpha_2 uv + \alpha_3 v^2 + \alpha_4 uv^2 + \alpha_5 v^3] + h.o.t., \\ \dfrac{\partial v}{\partial t} = \tau[d_2\Delta v - \eta\sigma v + b_1 u(t-1) - b_1 v(t-1) + \beta_1 u^2(t-1) + \beta_2 u(t-1)v + \beta_3 u(t-1)v(t-1) + \beta_4 vv(t-1) \\ \quad + \beta_5 u^3(t-1) + \beta_6 u^2(t-1)v + \beta_7 u(t-1)v^2 + \beta_8 u^2(t-1)v(t-1)] + h.o.t., \end{cases} \tag{17}$$

where $\alpha_1 = 1 - u_*$, $\alpha_2 = -\frac{c}{(1+su_*)^2}$, $\alpha_3 = \frac{csu_*}{(1+su_*)^3}$, $\alpha_4 = \frac{cs}{(1+su_*)^3}$, $\alpha_5 = -\frac{cs^2u_*}{(1+su_*)^4}$, $\beta_1 = -\frac{r}{u_*(1+su_*)}$, $\beta_2 = \frac{r}{u_*(1+su_*)^2}$, $\beta_3 = \frac{r}{u_*(1+su_*)}$, $\beta_4 = -\frac{r}{u_*(1+su_*)^2}$, $\beta_5 = \frac{r}{u_*^2(1+su_*)}$, $\beta_6 = -\frac{r}{u_*^2(1+su_*)^2}$, $\beta_7 = -\frac{rs}{u_*(1+su_*)^3}$, and $\beta_8 = -\frac{r}{u_*^2(1+su_*)}$.

We define a space, $X := \{(u,v)^T : u,v \in H^2(0,l\pi),\ (u_x,v_x)|_{x=0,l\pi} = 0\}$, which is called real-valued Sobolev. $X_{\mathbb{C}}$ is the complexification of X, which has the form $X_{\mathbb{C}} := X \oplus iX = \{u + iv|\ u,v \in X\}$. Then, we define the inner product: $< \tilde{u},\tilde{v} >:= \int_0^{l\pi}\overline{u_1}v_1 dx + \int_0^{l\pi}\overline{u_2}v_2 dx$, where $\tilde{u} = (u_1,u_2)^T \in X_{\mathbb{C}}$, $\tilde{v} = (v_1,v_2)^T \in X_{\mathbb{C}}$.

We define the phase space, $\mathscr{C} := C([-1,0],X)$, which is with the sup norm. Then, we have $\varphi_t \in \mathscr{C}$, $\varphi_t(\sigma) = \varphi(t+\sigma)$ for $\sigma \in [-1,0]$. To define the subspace of $\mathscr{C}$, we made the following definitions: $\alpha_n^{(1)}(u) = (\gamma_n(u),0)^T$, $\alpha_n^{(2)}(u) = (0,\gamma_n(u))^T$, and $\alpha_n = \{\alpha_n^{(1)}(u), \alpha_n^{(2)}(u)\}$, where $\{\alpha_n^{(i)}(u)\}$ is an orthonormal basis of X. Then, we define the subspace of $\mathscr{C}$ as $\mathbb{B}_n := \text{span}\{< \varphi(\cdot),\alpha_n^{(j)} > \alpha_n^{(j)}|\varphi \in \mathscr{C}, j = 1,2\}$, $n \in \mathbb{N}_0$. For $\theta \in [-1,0]$ and $\varphi \in \mathscr{C}$, the 2×2 matrix function $(\eta^n(\theta,\tilde{\tau}))$ can satisfy the following: $-\tilde{\tau}D\frac{n^2}{l^2}\varphi(0) + \tilde{\tau}L(\varphi) = \int_{-1}^0 d\eta^n(\theta,\tau)\varphi(\theta)$. Then, Equation (18) defines the bilinear form on $\mathscr{C}^* \times \mathscr{C}$ for $\psi \in \mathscr{C}, \phi \in \mathscr{C}^*$.

$$(\phi,\psi) = \phi(0)\psi(0) - \int_{-1}^0\int_{\xi=0}^{\theta}\phi(\xi-\theta)d\eta^n(\theta,\tilde{\tau})\psi(\xi)d\xi, \tag{18}$$

Let $\tau = \tilde{\tau} + \mu$. When $\mu = 0$, the characteristic equation of the system has a pair of purely imaginary roots $(\pm i\omega_{n_0})$, and the system undergoes Hopf bifurcation at $(0,0)$. Assume that A represents the infinitesimal generators of the semigroup, and A^* represents the formal adjoint of A under the bilinear form (18).

We define

$$\delta(n_0) = \begin{cases} 1 & n_0 = 0, \\ 0 & n_0 \in \mathbb{N}. \end{cases} \tag{19}$$

Let $\eta_{n_0}(0,\tilde{\tau}) = \tilde{\tau}[(-n_0^2/l^2)D + L_1 + L_3\delta(n_{n_0})]$, $\eta_{n_0}(-1,\tilde{\tau}) = -\tilde{\tau}L_2$, and $\eta_{n_0}(\sigma,\tilde{\tau}) = 0$ for $\sigma \in [-1,0]$. We define $p(\theta) = p(0)e^{i\omega_{n_0}\tilde{\tau}\theta}$ $(\theta \in [-1,0])$ as the eigenfunction of $A(\tilde{\tau})$ for $i\omega_{n_0}\tilde{\tau}$, and $q(\vartheta) = q(0)e^{-i\omega_{n_0}\tilde{\tau}\vartheta}$ $(\vartheta \in [0,1])$ is the eigenfunction of A^* for $i\omega_{n_0}\tilde{\tau}$. Let

$p(0) = (1, p_1)^T$, $q(0) = M(1, q_2)$, where $p_1 = \frac{1}{a_2}(\mathrm{i}\omega_{n_0} + d_1 n_0^2/l^2 - a_1 - \hat{a}\delta(n_0))$, $q_2 = \frac{a_2}{\mathrm{i}\omega_{n_0} + b_1 \mathrm{e}^{\mathrm{i}\omega_{n_0}} + d_2 n^2/l^2}$, and $M = (1 + p_1 q_2 + \tilde{\tau} q_2 b_1 (1 - p_1) e^{-\mathrm{i}\omega_{n_0}\tilde{\tau}})^{-1}$. Then, (16) becomes

$$\frac{dU(t)}{dt} = (\tilde{\tau} + \mu) D\Delta U(t) + (\tilde{\tau} + \mu)[L_1 U(t) + L_2 U(t-1) + L_3 \hat{U}(t)] + F(\mu, U_t, \hat{U}_t), \quad (20)$$

where

$$F(\phi, \mu) = (\tilde{\tau} + \mu) \begin{pmatrix} \alpha_1 \phi_1(0)^2 - (2u_* - \beta)\phi_1(0)\hat{\phi}_1(0) + \alpha_2 \phi_1(0)\phi_2(0) + \alpha_3 \phi_2(0)^2 + \alpha_4 \phi_1^3(0) \\ + \alpha_5 \phi_1^2(0)\phi_2(0) + \alpha_6 \phi_1(0)\phi_2^2(0) + \alpha_7 \phi_2^3(0) \\ \beta_1 \phi_1^2(-1) + \beta_2 \phi_1(-1)\phi_2(-1) + \beta_3 \phi_2^2(-1) + \beta_4 \phi_1^3(-1) + \beta_4 \phi_1^2(-1)\phi_2(-1) \\ + \beta_6 \phi_1(-1)\phi_2^2(-1) + \beta_7 \phi_2^3(-1) \end{pmatrix} \quad (21)$$

for $\phi = (\phi_1, \phi_2)^T \in \mathscr{C}$ and $\hat{\phi}_1 = \frac{1}{l\pi}\int_0^{l\pi} \phi dx$. Then, we decompose the space $(\mathscr{C})$ as $\mathscr{C} = P \oplus Q$, where $P = \{zp\gamma_{n_0}(x) + \bar{z}\bar{p}\gamma_{n_0}(x) | z \in \mathbb{C}\}$, $Q = \{\phi \in \mathscr{C} | (q\gamma_{n_0}(x), \phi) = 0$, and $(\bar{q}\gamma_{n_0}(x), \phi) = 0\}$. Then, (21) is rewritten as $U_t = z(t)p(\cdot)\gamma_{n_0}(x) + \bar{z}(t)\bar{p}(\cdot)\gamma_{n_0}(x) + \omega(t, \cdot)$, and $\hat{U}_t = \frac{1}{l\pi}\int_0^{l\pi} U_t dx$, where

$$z(t) = (q\gamma_{n_0}(x), U_t), \;\; \omega(t, \theta) = U_t(\theta) - 2\mathrm{Re}\{z(t)p(\theta)\gamma_{n_0}(x)\}. \quad (22)$$

We found that $\dot{z}(t) = \mathrm{i}\omega_{n_0}\tilde{\tau}z(t) + \bar{q}(0) < F(0, U_t), \beta_{n_0} >$. Then, C_0 and ω can have the following form near $(0, 0)$:

$$\omega(t, \theta) = \omega(z(t), \bar{z}(t), \theta) = \omega_{20}(\theta)\frac{z^2}{2} + \omega_{11}(\theta)z\bar{z} + \omega_{02}(\theta)\frac{\bar{z}^2}{2} + \cdots. \quad (23)$$

We restrict the system to C_0 such that $\dot{z}(t) = \mathrm{i}\omega_{n_0}\tilde{\tau}z(t) + g(z, \bar{z})$. Let $g(z, \bar{z}) = g_{20}\frac{z^2}{2} + g_{11}z\bar{z} + g_{02}\frac{\bar{z}^2}{2} + g_{21}\frac{z^2\bar{z}}{2} + \cdots$. By direct computation, we have

$$g_{20} = 2\tilde{\tau}M(\varsigma_1 + q_2\varsigma_2)I_3, \;\; g_{11} = \tilde{\tau}M(\varrho_1 + q_2\varrho_2)I_3, \;\; g_{02} = \bar{g}_{20},$$

$$g_{21} = 2\tilde{\tau}M[(\kappa_{11} + q_2\kappa_{21})I_2 + (\kappa_{12} + q_2\kappa_{22})I_4],$$

where $I_2 = \int_0^{l\pi} \gamma_{n_0}^2(x)dx$, $I_3 = \int_0^{l\pi} \gamma_{n_0}^3(x)dx$, $I_4 = \int_0^{l\pi} \gamma_{n_0}^4(x)dx$, $\varsigma_1 = (a - 2u_*)\delta_{n_0} + (\alpha_1 + p_1(\alpha_2 + \alpha_3 p_1))$, $\varsigma_2 = e^{-2i\tau\omega_n}(\beta_1 + 2\beta_8 + e^{i\tau\omega_n}(\beta_2 + 2\beta_3\beta_4)p_1)$, $\varrho_1 = \frac{1}{4}(2\alpha_1 + 2(a - 2u_*)\delta_{n_0} + 2\alpha_3\bar{p_1}p_1 + \alpha_2(\bar{p_1} + p_1))$, $\varrho_2 = \frac{1}{4}e^{-i\tau\omega_n}(2e^{i\tau\omega_n}(\beta_1 + 2\beta_8) + (\beta_2 + 2\beta_3\beta_4)\bar{p_1} + e^{2i\tau\omega_n}(\beta_2 + 2\beta_3\beta_4)p_1)$, $\kappa_{11} = 2W_{11}^{(1)}(0)(2\alpha_1 + a(1 + \delta_{n_0}) - 2u_*(1 + \delta_{n_0}) + \alpha_2 p_1) + 2\,W_{11}^{(2)}(0)(\alpha_2 + 2\alpha_3 p_1) + W_{20}^{(1)}(0)(2\alpha_1 + a(1 + \delta_{n_0}) - 2u_*(1 + \delta_{n_0}) + \alpha_2\bar{p_1}) + W_{20}^{(2)}(0)(\alpha_2 + 2\alpha_3\bar{p_1})$, $\kappa_{12} = 2e^{-i\tau\omega_n}W_{11}^{(2)}(0)(\beta_2 + 2\beta_3\beta_4) + e^{i\tau\omega_n}W_{20}^{(2)}(0)(\beta_2 + 2\beta_3\beta_4) + 2e^{-i\tau\omega_n}W_{11}^{(1)}(-1)(2\beta_1 + 4\beta_8 + e^{i\tau\omega_n}(\beta_2 + 2\beta_3\beta_4)p_1) + W_{20}^{(1)}(-1)(2e^{i\tau\omega_n}(\beta_1 + 2\beta_8) + (\beta_2 + 2\beta_3\beta_4)\bar{p_1})$, $\kappa_{21} = \frac{1}{2}p_1(3\alpha_5\bar{p_1}p_1 + \alpha_4(2\bar{p_1} + p_1))$, $\kappa_{22} = \frac{1}{2}e^{-2i\tau\omega_n}\,(e^{3i\tau\omega_n}\beta_7 p_1^2 + \bar{p_1}(\beta_6 + 3\beta_3\beta_4 p_1) + e^{i\tau\omega_n}(3\beta_5 + \beta_8\bar{p_1} + 2\beta_8 p_1 + 2\beta_7\bar{p_1}p_1) + e^{2i\tau\omega_n}p_1(2\beta_6 + 3\beta_3\beta_4(\bar{p_1} + p_1)))$.

Next, for $\theta \in [-1, 0]$, we compute W_{20} and W_{11} to obtain g_{21}. According to (22), we have

$$\dot{\omega} = \dot{U}_t - \dot{z}p\gamma_{n_0}(x) - \dot{\bar{z}}\bar{p}\gamma_{n_0}(x) = A\omega + H(z, \bar{z}, \theta), \quad (24)$$

where

$$H(z, \bar{z}, \theta) = H_{20}(\theta)\frac{z^2}{2} + H_{11}(\theta)z\bar{z} + H_{02}(\theta)\frac{\bar{z}^2}{2} + \cdots. \quad (25)$$

By comparing the coefficients of (23) with those of (24), we have

$$(A - 2\mathrm{i}\omega_{n_0}\tilde{\tau}I)\omega_{20} = -H_{20}(\theta), \;\; A\omega_{11}(\theta) = -H_{11}(\theta). \quad (26)$$

Then, we have

$$
\begin{aligned}
\omega_{20}(\theta) &= \frac{-g_{20}}{\mathrm{i}\omega_{n_0}\tilde{\tau}} p(0) e^{\mathrm{i}\omega_{n_0}\tilde{\tau}\theta} - \frac{\bar{g}_{02}}{3\mathrm{i}\omega_{n_0}\tilde{\tau}} \bar{p}(0) e^{-\mathrm{i}\omega_{n_0}\tilde{\tau}\theta} + E_1 e^{2\mathrm{i}\omega_{n_0}\tilde{\tau}\theta}, \\
\omega_{11}(\theta) &= \frac{g_{11}}{\mathrm{i}\omega_{n_0}\tilde{\tau}} p(0) e^{\mathrm{i}\omega_{n_0}\tilde{\tau}\theta} - \frac{\bar{g}_{11}}{\mathrm{i}\omega_{n_0}\tilde{\tau}} \bar{p}(0) e^{-\mathrm{i}\omega_{n_0}\tilde{\tau}\theta} + E_2,
\end{aligned} \tag{27}
$$

where $E_1 = \sum_{n=0}^{\infty} E_1^{(n)}$, $E_2 = \sum_{n=0}^{\infty} E_2^{(n)}$,

$$
\begin{aligned}
E_1^{(n)} &= (2\mathrm{i}\omega_{n_0}\tilde{\tau} I - \int_{-1}^{0} e^{2\mathrm{i}\omega_{n_0}\tilde{\tau}\theta} d\eta_{n_0}(\theta, \tilde{\tau}))^{-1} < \tilde{F}_{20}, \beta_n >, \\
E_2^{(n)} &= -(\int_{-1}^{0} d\eta_{n_0}(\theta, \tilde{\tau}))^{-1} < \tilde{F}_{11}, \beta_n >, \;\; n \in \mathbb{N}_0,
\end{aligned}
$$

$$
< \tilde{F}_{20}, \beta_n >= \begin{cases} \frac{1}{l\pi}\hat{F}_{20}, & n_0 \neq 0, n = 0, \\ \frac{1}{2l\pi}\hat{F}_{20}, & n_0 \neq 0, n = 2n_0, \\ \frac{1}{l\pi}\hat{F}_{20}, & n_0 = 0, n = 0, \\ 0, & other, \end{cases} \qquad < \tilde{F}_{11}, \beta_n >= \begin{cases} \frac{1}{l\pi}\hat{F}_{11}, & n_0 \neq 0, n = 0, \\ \frac{1}{2l\pi}\hat{F}_{11}, & n_0 \neq 0, n = 2n_0, \\ \frac{1}{l\pi}\hat{F}_{11}, & n_0 = 0, n = 0, \\ 0, & other, \end{cases}
$$

and $\hat{F}_{20} = 2(\varsigma_1, \varsigma_2)^T$, $\hat{F}_{11} = 2(\varrho_1, \varrho_2)^T$.

Thus, we can obtain

$$
\begin{aligned}
c_1(0) &= \frac{\mathrm{i}}{2\omega_n\tilde{\tau}}(g_{20}g_{11} - 2|g_{11}|^2 - \frac{|g_{02}|^2}{3}) + \frac{1}{2}g_{21}, \quad \mu_2 = -\frac{\mathrm{Re}(c_1(0))}{\mathrm{Re}(\lambda'(\tilde{\tau}))}, \\
T_2 &= -\frac{1}{\omega_{n_0}\tilde{\tau}}[\mathrm{Im}(c_1(0)) + \mu_2 \mathrm{Im}(\lambda'(\tau_n^j))], \quad \beta_2 = 2\mathrm{Re}(c_1(0)).
\end{aligned} \tag{28}
$$

Theorem 2. *The following results are true for any critical value (τ_n^j ($n \in \mathbb{S}$, $j \in \mathbb{N}_0$)).*

1. *If $\mu_2 > 0$ (or <0), the Hopf bifurcation is forward (or backward);*
2. *If $\beta_2 < 0$ (or >0), the bifurcating periodic solutions on C_0 are orbitally asymptotically stable (or unstable);*
3. *If $T_2 > 0$ (or $T_2 < 0$), the period increases (or decreases).*

4. Numerical Simulations

To analyze the influence of the fear effect parameter (s), the strong Allee effect parameter (a), and gestation delay (τ) on model (4), we performed the following numerical simulations.

We fixed

$$c = 0.1, \;\; r = 0.25, \;\; d_1 = 0.5, \;\; d_2 = 0.1, \;\; l = 1.5.$$

The existence of a positive equilibrium is provided in Figure 1. Obviously, the equilibrium (u_2, v_2) is unstable through the following analysis, so we pay attention to the stability of the equilibrium (u_1, v_1), which is positive. The bifurcation diagrams of model (4) with parameters s and a are provided in Figures 2 and 3, respectively. In Figure 2, we can observe that increasing parameter s can increase the stable region of the equilibrium and eliminate the periodic oscillation. In Figure 3, we find that increasing parameter a can decrease the stable region of the equilibrium and induce periodic oscillation.

If we choose $a = 0.05$ and $s = 0.1$, then model (4) has two coexisting equilibria: $(u_1, v_1) \approx (0.9029, 0.9029)$ and $(u_2, v_2) \approx (0.0559, 0.0559)$. By direct calculation, the hypothesis $(\mathbf{H_1})$ holds for (u_1, v_1) and does not hold for (u_2, v_2). Therefore, we mainly analyze the coexisting equilibrium (u_1, v_1). By direct computation, we have $\mathbb{S}_1 = \{0, 1, 2\}$ and $\mathbb{S}_2 = \mathbb{S}_3 = \emptyset$, as well as $\tau_* = \tau_1^0 \approx 5.9478 < \tau_0^0 \approx 6.1053$. Theorem 1 shows that the coexisting equilibrium (u_1, v_1) is locally asymptotically stable if $\tau \in [0, \tau_*)$ (Figure 4). For model (4), Hopf bifurcation occurs if $\tau = \tau_*$. According to Theorem 2, we have

$$\mu_2 \approx 16.1916 > 0, \;\; \beta_2 \approx -0.6295 < 0, \;\; T_2 \approx 0.5672 > 0.$$

Therefore, when $\tau > \tau_*$, the bifurcating periodic solutions are stably spatially inhomogeneous (Figure 5). When we continue to increase parameter τ, the bifurcating periodic solutions are still stably spatially inhomogeneous (Figure 6).

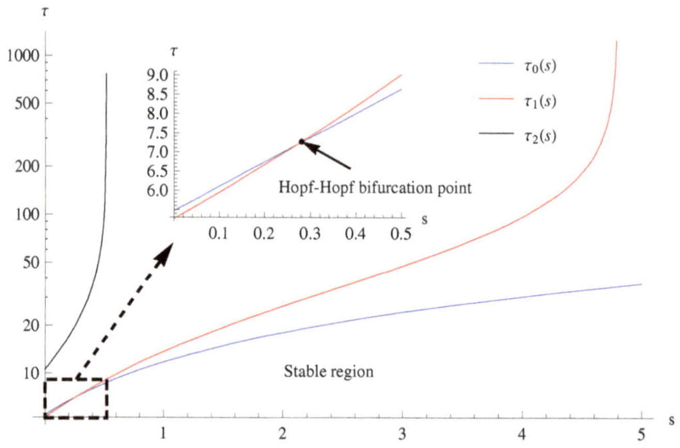

Figure 2. Bifurcation diagram for s and τ with $a = 0.05$ at the coexisting equilibrium (u_1, v_1).

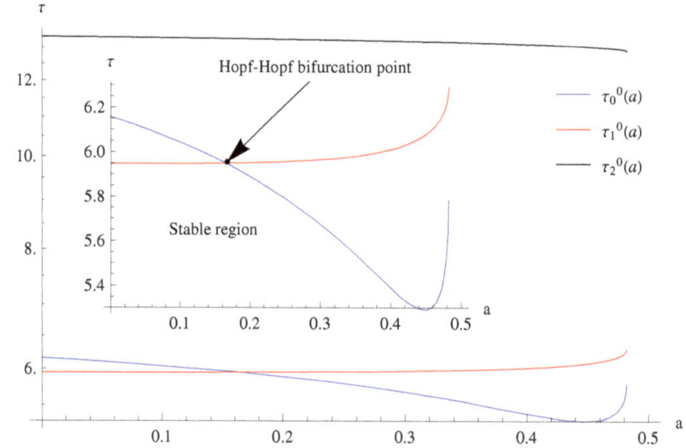

Figure 3. Bifurcation diagram for a and τ with $s = 0.1$ at the coexisting equilibrium (u_1, v_1).

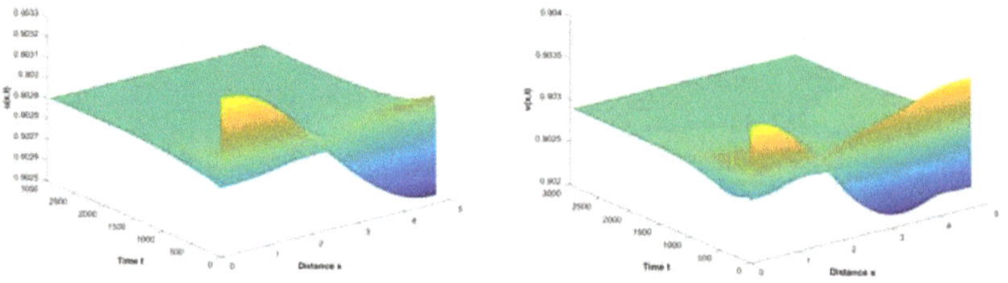

(a) (b)

Figure 4. Numerical simulations for model (4) when $\tau = 5.92 < \tau_1^0$ and for the initial values of $u_0(x) = u_* + 0.001\cos x$, $v_0(x) = v_* - 0.001\cos x$. (**a**) Prey. (**b**) Predator.

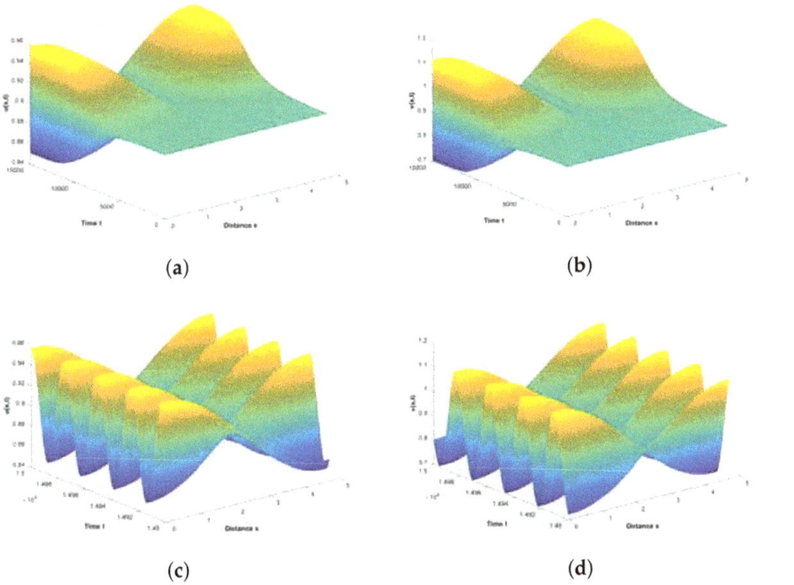

Figure 5. Numerical simulations for model (4) when $\tau = 6.05 \in (\tau_1^0, \tau_0^0)$ and for the initial values of $u_0(x) = u_* + 0.001\cos x$, $v_0(x) = v_* - 0.001\cos x$. (**a**,**c**) Prey. (**b**,**d**) Predator.

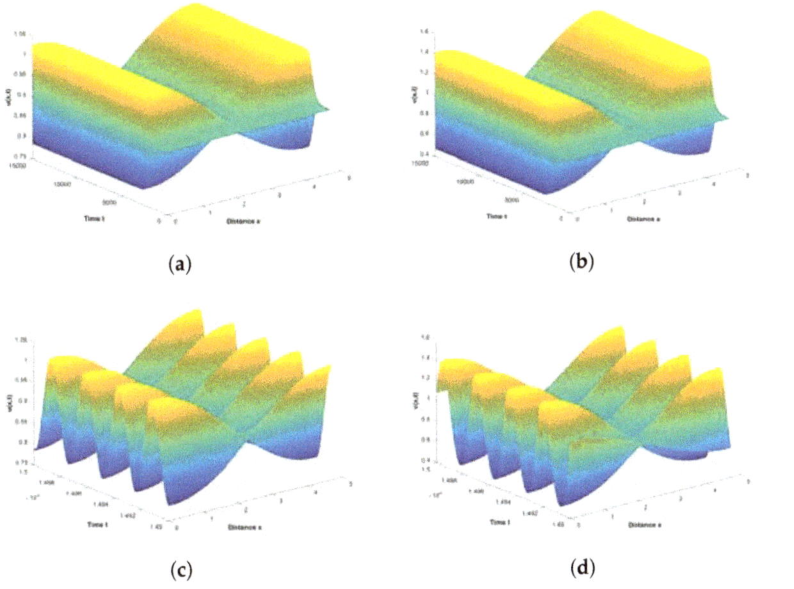

Figure 6. Numerical simulations for model (4) when $\tau = 6.2 > \tau_1^0$ and for the initial values of $u_0(x) = u_* + 0.001\cos x$, $v_0(x) = v_* - 0.001\cos x$. (**a**,**c**) Prey. (**b**,**d**) Predator.

If we choose $a = 0.2$ and $s = 0.1$, then model (4) has two coexisting equilibria: $(u_1, v_1) \approx (0.8811,\ 0.8811)$ and $(u_2, v_2) \approx (0.2290,\ 0.2290)$. By direct calculation, the hypothesis $(\mathbf{H_1})$ holds for (u_1, v_1) and does not hold for (u_2, v_2). Therefore, we mainly analyzed the coexisting equilibrium (u_1, v_1). By direct computation, we have $\mathbb{S}_1 = \{0,\ 1,\ 2\}$

and $\mathbb{S}_2 = \mathbb{S}_3 = \emptyset$, as well as $\tau_* = \tau_0^0 \approx 5.8910 < \tau_0^1 \approx 5.9517$. Theorem 1 shows that the coexisting equilibrium (u_1, v_1) is locally asymptotically stable if $\tau \in [0, \tau_*)$. For model (4), Hopf bifurcation occurs if $\tau = \tau_*$. Theorem 2 shows that

$$\mu_2 \approx 43.8547 > 0, \ \ \beta_2 \approx -1.6464 < 0, \ \ T_2 \approx 10.3338 > 0.$$

Thus, when $\tau > \tau_*$, the bifurcating periodic solutions are stably spatially homogeneous (Figure 7). When we continue to increase parameter τ, the bifurcating periodic solutions are still stably spatially homogeneous (Figure 8).

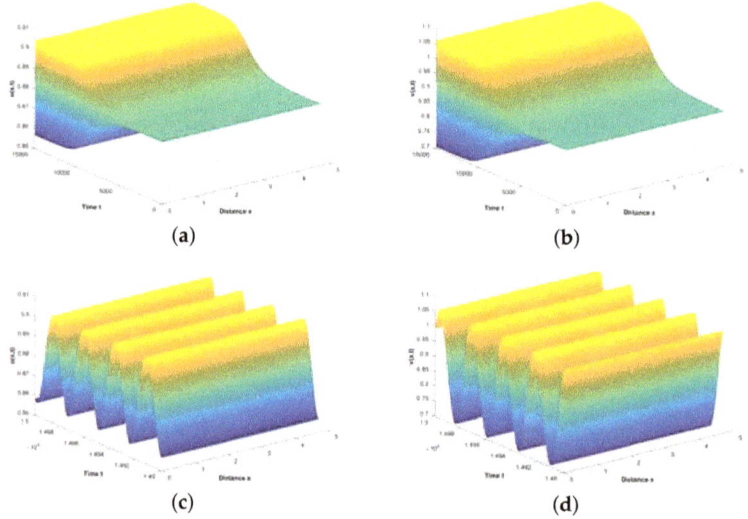

Figure 7. Numerical simulations for model (4) when $\tau = 5.92 \in (\tau_0^0, \tau_1^0)$ and for the initial values of $u_0(x) = u_* + 0.001\cos x$, $v_0(x) = v_* - 0.001\cos x$. (**a**,**c**) Prey. (**b**,**d**) Predator.

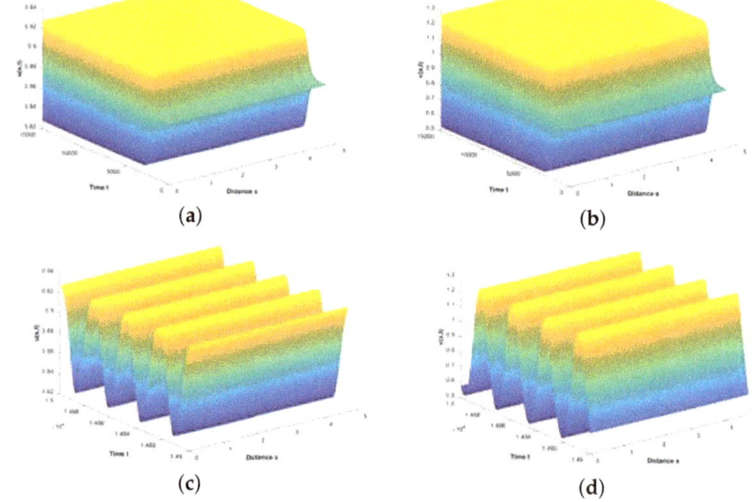

Figure 8. Numerical simulations for model (4) when $\tau = 6.05 > \tau_1^0$ and for the initial values of $u_0(x) = u_* + 0.001\cos x$, $v_0(x) = v_* - 0.001\cos x$. (**a**,**c**) Prey. (**b**,**d**) Predator.

5. Conclusions and Discussion

In this work, we propose a delayed self-diffusive predator–prey model with a strong Allee effect on the prey and a fear effect on the predator. Unlike [17], in this paper, we added a time delay, self-diffusion, and nonlocal competition to the model, which makes the model more consistent with actual situations in nature and leads to homogeneous and inhomogeneous periodic solutions. By analyzing the eigenvalue spectrum, we studied the local stability of the coexisting equilibrium and the existence of Hopf bifurcation. By using the method of the center manifold theorem and the normal form method, we investigated the properties of Hopf bifurcation.

Next, we will discuss the influences of the fear effect and the strong Allee effect. The following conclusions can be drawn. Increasing the fear effect on the predator is beneficial to the uniform distribution of the prey and predator populations in space because the stable region of coexistence increases with the increase in the fear effect, and with the increase in the fear effect, a spatially inhomogeneous periodic solution appears first. However, when the fear effect is greater than a critical value, a spatially homogeneous periodic solution appears. However, increasing the strong Allee effect on the prey is not beneficial to the stability of the coexisting equilibrium because the stable region of coexistence decreases with the increase in the strong Allee effect. Whether the bifurcated periodic solution is spatially homogeneous or inhomogeneous depends on the strong Allee effect and the fear effect because with the increase in the strong Allee effect (or fear effect), a spatially inhomogeneous periodic solution appears first. However, when the strong Allee effect (or fear effect) is greater than a critical value, a spatially homogeneous periodic solution appears.

The main findings show that a strong Allee effect and the fear effect can be used to control the growth of prey and predator populations. For example, we could produce predation risk and affect the reproduction of sparrows by broadcasting their natural enemies' sounds (such as those of magpies, shrikes, sparrow eagles, etc.) during sparrows' entire breeding season. In this way, we can protect sparrows from direct killing and ensure that any effects on reproduction will only be ascribed to fear; this is the direction of our future research. Moreover, we found a Hopf–Hopf bifurcation point in the course of our research, which complicates the dynamic behavior of predator–prey systems and also requires further investigation.

However, questions remains as to whether emulating fear during an entire breeding season of a species is realistic, whether doing so would have other damaging consequences on the behavior of the species, and whether it would result in the species becoming acquainted with such sounds and no longer feeling fear (if the sounds perpetuate without any predation, the prey might consider that there is no danger after a while). This is also worth further research, especially in cooperation with biological experts.

Author Contributions: Y.X., J.Z. and R.Y. contributed to the study's conception and design. Material preparation, data collection, and analysis were performed by Y.X. and R.Y. All authors have read and agreed to the published version of the manuscript.

Funding: This research was supported by the Fundamental Research Funds for the Central Universities (grant No. 2572022DJ05), the Harbin Science and Technology Bureau Manufacturing Innovation Talent Project (CXRC20221110393), the Heilongjiang Science and Technology Department Provincial Key R&D Program Applied Research Project (SC2022ZX06C0025), the Heilongjiang Science and Technology Department Provincial Key R&D Program Guidance Project (GZ20220088), and the Postdoctoral Program of Heilongjiang Province (No.LBHQ21060).

Data Availability Statement: Data sharing is not applicable to this article, as no datasets were generated or analyzed during the current study.

Conflicts of Interest: The authors have no relevant financial or non-financial interest to disclose.

References

1. Faria, T. Stability and Bifurcation for a Delayed Predator-Prey Model and the Effect of Diffusion. *J. Math. Anal. Appl.* **2001**, *254*, 433–463. [CrossRef]
2. Faria, T.; Magalhaes, L.T. Normal Forms for Retarded Functional Differential Equations with Parameters and Applications to Hopf Bifurcation. *J. Differ. Equ.* **1995**, *122*, 181–200. [CrossRef]
3. Faria, T. Normal forms and Hopf bifurcation for partial differential equations with delays. *Trans. Am. Math. Soc.* **2000**, *352*, 2217–2238. [CrossRef]
4. Yi, F.; Wei, J.; Shi, J. Bifurcation and spatiotemporal patterns in a homogeneous diffusive predatoršCprey system. *J. Differ. Equations* **2009**, *246*, 1944–1977. [CrossRef]
5. Song, Y.; Shi, Q. Stability and bifurcation analysis in a diffusive predator-prey model with delay and spatial average. *Math. Methods Appl. Sci.* **2022**, *46*, 5561–5584. [CrossRef]
6. Xiang, C.; Huang, J.; Wang, H. Bifurcations in Holling-Tanner model with generalist predator and prey refuge. *J. Differ. Equ.* **2023**, *343*, 495–529. [CrossRef]
7. Yang, R.; Nie, C.; Jin, D. Spatiotemporal dynamics induced by nonlocal competition in a diffusive predator-prey system with habitat complexity. *Nonlinear Dyn.* **2022**, *110*, 879–900. [CrossRef]
8. Yang, R.; Wang, F.; Jin, D. Spatially inhomogeneous bifurcating periodic solutions induced by nonlocal competition in a predator-prey system with additional food. *Math. Methods Appl. Sci.* **2022**, *45*, 9967–9978. [CrossRef]
9. Allee, W.C. Animal Aggregations. In *A Study in General Sociology*; University of Chicago Press: Chicago, IL, USA, 1931.
10. Stephens, P.A.; Sutherl, W.J. Consequences of the Allee effect for behaviour, ecology and conservation. *Trends Ecol. Evol.* **1999**, *14*, 401–405. [CrossRef] [PubMed]
11. Courchamp, F.; Clutton-Brock, T.; Grenfell, B. Inverse density dependence and the Allee effect. *Trends Ecol. Evol.* **1999**, *14*, 405–410. [CrossRef]
12. Berec, L.; Angulo, E.; Courchamp, F. Multiple Allee effects and population management. *Trends Ecol. Evol.* **2007**, *22*, 185–191. [CrossRef] [PubMed]
13. Bazykin, A. *Nonlinear Dynamics of Inteiveracting Populations*; World Scientifc: Singapore, 1998.
14. Panday, P.; Samanta, S.; Pal, N.; Chattopadhyay, J. Delay induced multiple stability switch and chaos in a predator-prey model with fear effect. *Math. Comput. Simul.* **2019**, *172*, 134–158. [CrossRef]
15. Qi, H.; Meng, X.; Hayat, T.; Hobiny, A. Bifurcation dynamics of a reaction-diffusion predator-prey model with fear effect in a predator-poisoned environment. *Math. Methods Appl. Sci.* **2022**, *45*, 6217–6254. [CrossRef]
16. Liu, T.; Chen, L.; Chen, F.; Li, Z. Dynamics of a Leslie-Gower Model with Weak Allee Effect on Prey and Fear Effect on Predator. *Int. J. Bifurc. Chaos* **2023**, *33*, 2350008. [CrossRef]
17. Liu, T.; Chen, L.; Chen, F.; Li, Z. Stability analysis of a Leslie-Gower model with strong Allee effect on prey and fear effect on predator. *Int. J. Bifurc. Chaos* **2022**, *32*, 2250082. [CrossRef]
18. Song, Y.; Peng, Y.; Zhang, T. The spatially inhomogeneous Hopf bifurcation induced by memory delay in a memory-based diffusion system. *J. Differ. Equ.* **2021**, *300*, 597–624. [CrossRef]
19. Akhmet, M.U.; Beklioglu, M.; Ergenc, T.; Tkachenko, V.I. An impulsive ratio-dependent predator-prey system with diffusion. *Nonlinear Anal. Real World Appl.* **2006**, *7*, 1255–1267. [CrossRef]
20. Liu, Y.; Wei, J. Double Hopf bifurcation of a diffusive predator-prey system with strong Allee effect and two delays. *Nonlinear Anal. Model. Control.* **2021**, *26*, 72–92. [CrossRef]
21. Yang, R.; Jin, D.; Wang, W. A diffusive predator-prey model with generalist predator and time delay. *AIMS Math.* **2022**, *7*, 4574–4591. [CrossRef]
22. Banerjee, M.; Takeuchi, Y. Maturation delay for the predators can enhance stable coexistence for a class of prey-predator models. *J. Theor. Biol.* **2017**, *412*, 154–171. [CrossRef]
23. Meng, X.; Jiao, J.; Chen, L. The dynamics of an age structured predator-prey model with disturbing pulse and time delays. *Nonlinear Anal. Real World Appl.* **2008**, *9*, 547–561. [CrossRef]
24. Britton, N.F. Aggregation and the competitive exclusion principle. *J. Theor. Biol.* **1989**, *136*, 57–66. [CrossRef]
25. Furter, J.; Grinfeld, M. Local vs. non-local interactions in population dynamics. *J. Math. Biol.* **1989**, *27*, 65–80. [CrossRef]
26. Geng, D.; Jiang, W.; Lou, Y.; Wang, H. Spatiotemporal patterns in a diffusive predator-prey system with nonlocal intraspecific prey competition. *Stud. Appl. Math.* **2021**, *48*, 396–432. [CrossRef]
27. Liu, Y.; Duan, D.; Niu, B. Spatiotemporal dynamics in a diffusive predator-prey model with group defense and nonlocal competition. *Appl. Math. Lett.* **2020**, *103*, 106175. [CrossRef]
28. Geng, D.; Wang, H. Normal form formulations of double-Hopf bifurcation for partial functional differential equations with nonlocal effect. *J. Differ. Equ.* **2022**, *2022*, 741–785. [CrossRef]
29. Djilali, S. Pattern formation of a diffusive predator-prey model with herd behavior and nonlocal prey competition. *Math. Methods Appl. Sci.* **2020**, *43*, 2233–2250. [CrossRef]
30. Pati, N.C.; Ghosh, B. Stability scenarios and period-doubling onset of chaos in a population model with delayed harvesting. *Math. Methods Appl. Sci.* **2022**. [CrossRef]
31. Barman, B.; Ghosh, B. Explicit impacts of harvesting in delayed predator-prey models. *Chaos Solitons Fractals* **2019**, *122*, 213–228 [CrossRef]

32. Ghosh, B.; Barman, B.; Saha, M. Multiple dynamics in a delayed predator-prey model with asymmetric functional and numerical responses. *Math. Methods Appl. Sci.* **2023**, *46*, 5187–5207. [CrossRef]
33. Wu, J. *Theory and Applications of Partial Functional Differential Equations*; Springer: Berlin/Heidelberg, Germany, 1996.
34. Hassard, B.D.; Kazarinoff, N.D.; Wan, Y.H. *Theory and Applications of Hopf Bifurcation*; Cambridge University Press: New York, NY, USA, 1981.

MDPI
St. Alban-Anlage 66
4052 Basel
Switzerland
Tel. +41 61 683 77 34
Fax +41 61 302 89 18
www.mdpi.com

Mathematics Editorial Office
E-mail: mathematics@mdpi.com
www.mdpi.com/journal/mathematics

www.ingramcontent.com/pod-product-compliance
Lightning Source LLC
LaVergne TN
LVHW070358100526
838202LV00014B/1338
* 9 7 8 3 0 3 6 5 7 8 8 4 2 *